44th Edition

THE ARMY OFFICER'S GUIDE

Lt. Col. Lawrence P. Crocker, U.S. Army (Ret.)

Stackpole Books

THE ARMY OFFICER'S GUIDE
Copyright © 1988 by
STACKPOLE BOOKS
Cameron and Kelker Streets
P.O. Box 1831
Harrisburg, PA 17105

Continuously published and copyrighted since 1930 as *The Officer's Guide* by The National Service Publishing Co., Washington, D.C. (1930); The Military Service Publishing Co., Harrisburg, Pa. (1936–1958); and The Stackpole Co., Harrisburg, Pa. (1959–

This book is not an official publication of the Department of Defense or Department of the Army, nor does its publication in any way imply its endorsement by these agencies.

Color photographs of medals and badges by Ken Smith.

The Library of Congress has cataloged this serial publication as follows:

The Army officer's guide, 39th–ed.
[Harrisburg, Pa.] Stackpole Books [c1977–

v. ill. 24 cm.

Continues: Officer's guide
ISSN 0148–6799 = The Army officer's guide.

1. United States. Army—Officer's handbooks.
U133.A6O3   355'.00973   77–641374
                                                 MARC–S
Library of Congress   77[8410]

44th Edition

Printed in U.S.A.

Contents

Part Five—THE ARMY

Foreword

As this 44th edition of *The Army Officer's Guide* is used by the members of today's Army, the book is completing its sixth decade of service. Throughout the period, each edition has served as a trustworthy and convenient first place of reference, providing sound advice and guidance for the Army's officers of that time. The publisher and the author are confident that this 44th edition continues that tradition and that *The Army Officer's Guide* continues to merit the trust and confidence of all the Army's officers.

The Army Officer's Guide is not an official publication of the U.S. Army. Both the author and the publisher, however, have a strong interest in the Army, and they are dedicated to the continued excellence of the Army. Moreover, as with previous editions, the contents of this 44th edition reflect the strong support of many Army personnel, without which a publication such as *The Army Officer's Guide* could not exist. These include the various post commanders and service school commandants, together with their protocol and information officers, the major Army commanders, many staff officers at Headquarters, Department of the Army (HQDA), a number of people at the Officer Personnel Management Directorate (OPMD), and other individuals, all of whom have given generously of their time and their thoughts to help assure that the book is timely and represents the very latest official positions. Their advice and guidance are cheerfully given in the interest of making *The Army Officer's Guide* a better publication, and their assistance is gratefully acknowledged.

New to this edition is a special chapter regarding warrant officers, which gathers into one presentation all of the information regarding the history, present status (and probable future) of the Warrant Officer Corps, as well as specific information on professional development, promotions, schooling, and evaluations as these topics apply to warrant officers. The contents of the chapter were prepared by the officers heading the Total Warrant Officer System (TWOS) study for the Department of the Army. Their interest and the results of their efforts are most appreciated.

Also new to this edition are color photographs of the Army's decorations, service medals, and badges, which were obtained with the generous cooperation and assistance of the Institute of Heraldry, and in cooperation with the Army National Guard.

A major objective of the book always has been to provide sound advice to junior officers and to those who are contemplating becoming officers. Part 1 of this 44th edition discusses the selection of the Army as a career, what the young officer may expect of the Army and, more important, what the Army and our nation will expect of the officer. Part 2 attempts to dispel any mystery surrounding Army life, military courtesy, service customs, and the social aspects of life as a member of the world's finest team. Parts 3 and 4 address those aspects of the Army that are of continuing and vital interest during an entire career. Part 5 discusses the Army itself and provides a brief glimpse of the activities and interests of the Army's branches.

The Appendix provides summary advice regarding performance of many of the "extra duties" that confront officers, particularly junior officers. While the emphasis of the book is on the junior officer, it is of value also to more experienced, senior officers who will find it a convenient way to stay abreast of regulation changes and other matters that affect them personally, as well as members of their organizations. Following the Appendix is a list of acronyms used in the book.

A prime goal of *The Army Officer's Guide* always has been to provide up-to-date information and sound advice to the Army's officers. That has remained the objective of this edition, and both the author and the publisher are confident that goal has been met. We take pride in presenting this 44th edition of *The Army Officer's Guide* for the consideration of the Army's officer corps.

Preface

Address by General of the Army Douglas MacArthur

General Westmoreland, General Groves, distinguished guests, and gentlemen of the Corps. *

As I was leaving the hotel this morning, a doorman asked me, "Where are you bound for, General?" and when I replied, "West Point," he remarked, "Beautiful place, have you ever been there before?"

No human being could fail to be deeply moved by such a tribute as this. [Thayer Award] Coming from a profession I have served so long, and a people I have loved so well, it fills me with an emotion I cannot express. But this award is not intended primarily to honor a personality, but to symbolize a great moral code—the code of conduct and chivalry of those who guard this beloved land of culture and ancient descent. That is the meaning of this medallion. For all eyes and for all time, it is an expression of the ethics of the American soldier. That I should be integrated in this way with so noble an ideal arouses a sense of pride and yet of humility which will be with me always.

Duty—Honor—Country. Those three hallowed words reverently dictate what you ought to be, what you can be, what you will be. They are your rallying points: to build courage when courage seems to fail; to regain faith when there seems to be little cause for faith; to create hope when hope becomes forlorn. Unhappily, I possess neither that eloquence of diction, that poetry of imagination, nor that brilliance of metaphor to tell you all that they mean. The unbelievers will say they are but words, but a slogan, but a flamboyant phrase. Every pedant, every demagogue, every cynic, every hypocrite, every troublemaker, and, I am sorry to say, some others of an entirely different character, will try to

---

*To the Members of the Association of Graduates. U.S.M.A., The Corps of Cadets and Distinguished Guests upon his acceptance of THE SYLVANUS THAYER AWARD, United States Military Academy, West Point, New York, 12 May 1962. Published by permission of General MacArthur.

(Photo by U.S. Army)

General of the Army Douglas MacArthur

26 January 1880—5 April 1964

downgrade them even to the extent of mockery and ridicule. But here are some of the things they do. They build your basic character, they mold you for your future roles as the custodians of the nation's defense, they make you strong enough to know when you are weak, and brave enough to face yourself when you are afraid. They teach you to be proud and unbending in honest failure, but humble and gentle in success; not to substitute words for actions, nor to seek the path of comfort, but to face the stress and spur of difficulty and challenge; to learn to stand up in the storm but to have compassion on those who fall; to master yourself before you seek to master others; to have a heart that is clean, a goal that is high; to learn to laugh yet never forget how to weep; to reach into the future yet never neglect the past; to be serious yet never to take yourself too seriously; to be modest so that you will remember the simplicity of true great-ness, the open mind of true wisdom, the meekness of true strength. They give you a temper of the will, a quality of the imagination, a vigor of the emotions, a freshness of the deep springs of life, a temperamental predominance of courage over timidity, an appetite for adventure over love of ease. They create in your heart the sense of wonder, the unfailing hope of what next, and the joy and inspiration of life. They teach you in this way to be an officer and a gentleman.

And what sort of soldiers are those you are to lead? Are they reliable, are they brave, are they capable of victory? Their story is known to all of you; it is the story of the American man-at-arms. My estimate of him was formed on the battlefield many, many years ago, and has never changed. I regarded him then as I regard him now—as one of the world's noblest figures, not only as one of the finest military characters but also as one of the most stainless. His name and fame are the birthright of every American citizen. In his youth and strength, his love and loyalty he gave—all that mortality can give. He needs no eulogy from me or from any other man. He has written his own history and written it in red on his enemy's breast. But when I think of his patience under adversity, of his courage under fire, and of his modesty in victory, I am filled with an emotion of admiration I cannot put into words. He belongs to history as furnishing one of the greatest examples of successful patriotism; he belongs to posterity as the instructor of future generations in the principles of liberty and freedom; he belongs to the present, to us, by his virtues and by his achievements. In twenty campaigns, on a hundred battlefields, around a thousand campfires, I have witnessed that enduring fortitude, that patriotic self-abnegation, and that invincible determination which have carved his statue in the hearts of his people. From one end of the world to the other he has drained deep the chalice of courage.

As I listened to those songs of the glee club, in memory's eye I could see those staggering columns of the First World War, bending under soggy packs, on many a weary march from dripping dusk to drizzling dawn, slogging ankle-deep through the mire of shell-shocked roads, to form grimly for the attack, blue-lipped, covered with sludge and mud, chilled by the wind and rain; driving home to their objective, and, for many, to the judgment seat of God. I do not know the dignity of their birth but I do know the glory of their death. They died unquestioning, uncomplaining, with faith in their hearts and on their lips the hope that we would go on to victory. Always for them—Duty—Honor—Country; always their blood and sweat and tears as we sought the way and the light and the truth.

And twenty years after, on the other side of the globe, again the filth of murky foxholes, the stench of ghostly trenches, the slime of dripping dugouts; those boiling suns of relentless heat, those torrential rains of devastating storms; the loneliness and utter desolation of jungle trails, the bitterness of long separation from those they loved and cherished, the deadly pestilence of tropical disease, the horror of stricken areas of war; their resolute and determined defense, their swift and sure attack, their indomitable purpose, their complete and decisive victory—always victory. Always through the bloody haze of their last reverberating shot, the vision of gaunt, ghastly men reverently following your password of Duty—Honor—Country.

The code which those words perpetuate embraces the highest moral laws and will stand the test of any ethics or philosophies ever promulgated for the uplift of mankind. Its requirements are for the things that are right, and its restraints are from the things that are wrong. The soldier, above all other men, is required to practice the greatest act of religious training—sacrifice. In battle and in the face of danger and death, he discloses those divine attributes which his Maker gave when He created man in His own image. No physical courage and no brute instinct can take the place of the Divine help which alone can sustain him. However horrible the incidents of war may be, the soldier who is called upon to offer and to give his life for his country, is the noblest development of mankind.

You now face a new world—a world of change. The thrust into outer space of the satellite, spheres, and missiles marked the beginning of another epoch in the long story of mankind—the chapter of the space age. In the five or more billions of years the scientists tell us it has taken to form the earth, in the three or more billion years of development of the human race, there has never been a greater, a more abrupt or staggering evolution. We deal now not with things of this world alone, but with the illimitable distances and as yet unfathomed mysteries of the universe. We are reaching out for a new and boundless frontier. We speak in strange terms: of harnessing the cosmic energy; of making winds and tides work for us; of creating unheard synthetic materials to supplement or even replace our old standard basics; of purifying sea water for our drink; of mining ocean floors for new fields of wealth and food; of disease preventatives to expand life into the hundred of years; of controlling the weather for a more equitable distribution of heat and cold, of rain and shine; of space ships to the moon; of the primary target in war, no longer limited to the armed forces of an enemy, but instead to include his civil populations; of ultimate conflict between a united human race and the sinister forces of some other planetary galaxy; of such dreams and fantasies as to make life the most exciting of all time.

And through all this welter of change and development, your mission remains fixed, determined, inviolable—it is to win our wars. Everything else in your professional career is but corollary to this vital dedication. All other public purposes, all other public projects, all other public needs, great or small, will find others for their accomplishment; but you are the ones who are trained to fight; yours is the profession of arms—the will to win, the sure knowledge that in war there is no substitute for victory; that if you lose, the nation will be destroyed; that the very obsession of your public service must be Duty—Honor—Country. Others will debate the controversial issues, national and international, which divide men's minds; but serene, calm, aloof, you stand as the nation's war-guardian, as its lifeguard from the raging tides of international conflict, as its gladiator in the arena of battle. For a century and a half you have defended, guarded, and protected its hallowed traditions of liberty and freedom, of right and justice. Let civilian voices argue the merits or demerits of our processes of government; whether our strength is being sapped by deficit financing, indulged in too long, by federal paternalism grown too mighty, by power groups grown too arrogant, by politics grown too corrupt, by crime grown too rampant, by morals grown too low, by taxes grown too high, by extremists grown too violent; whether our personal liberties are as thorough and complete as they should be. These great national problems are not for your professional participation or military solution. Your guidepost stands out like a ten-fold beacon in the night: Duty—Honor—Country.

You are the leaven which binds together the entire fabric of our national system of defense. From your ranks come the great captains who hold the nation's destiny in their hands the moment the war tocsin sounds. The Long Gray Line has never failed us. Were you to do so, a million ghosts in olive drab, in brown khaki, in blue and gray, would rise from their white crosses thundering those magic words, Duty—Honor—Country.

This does not mean that you are war mongers. On the contrary, the soldier, above all other people, prays for peace, for he must suffer and bear the deepest wounds and scars of war. But always in our ears ring the ominous words of Plato, that wisest of all philosophers, "Only the dead have seen the end of war."

The shadows are lengthening for me. The twilight is here. My days of old have vanished tone and tint; they have gone glimmering through the dreams of things that were. Their memory is one of wondrous beauty, watered by tears, and coaxed and caressed by the smiles of yesterday. I listen vainly for the witching melody of faint bugles blowing reveille, of far drums beating the long roll. In my dreams I hear again the crash of guns, the rattle of musketry, the strange, mournful mutter of the battlefield.

But in the evening of my memory, always I come back to West Point. Always there echoes and re-echoes Duty—Honor—Country.

Today marks my final roll call with you, but I want you to know that when I cross the river my last conscious thoughts will be of The Corps, and The Corps, and The Corps.

I bid you farewell.

Part One • Selection of an Army Career

1

An Army Career

I am convinced that there is no more important vocation or profession than serving in the defense of the nation—not just any nation, but a nation that is prepared to provide the dignity to man that God intended—our nation. All the benefits that our citizens enjoy exist behind the defense barrier that is manned by the members of the military establishment. No greater honor can be given to any man than the privilege of serving the cause of freedom.—Gen. Harold K. Johnson, Fargo, North Dakota, 1967, Chief of Staff, United States Army, 4 July 1964–2 July 1968.

This chapter has been developed as an objective analysis of the current national importance of the professional military officer, with a candid discussion of the favorable and the unfavorable factors of an Army career. Its purpose is to assist the interested individual who is eligible for appointment as an Army officer to make an informed analysis. The subject is of vast importance to our nation. The Army's officers and soldiers are serving on all continents and in more than seventy foreign nations. Their specific duties are infinite in variety. The total mission of our military leaders is a part of the single objective to maintain the security of our country and our people, and, in accordance with policy determined by our nation's elected civil leaders, to help maintain the freedom of friendly nations who need and request our help. The realist understands that the price of peace is firmness with patience, judgment as to what is right and what is wrong, and a constant readiness for future trials that may beset the nation. Thoughtful citizens understand that until universal peace is obtained, our nation with our allies must be ready to parry any threat or win any war that may be thrust upon us.

THE MILITARY PROFESSIONAL

It is the career officer, always the volunteer, who provides the professional foundation and the continuity upon which our military strength is based. While the interest of members of the general public in their military services may fluctuate between wide extremes, as international relations are tensed or relaxed, national security requires at all times a sufficient number of professional military leaders who are men and women of integrity, competence, and determination, prepared and willing to carry the highest responsibilities of military leadership under any conditions, anywhere. In view of the history of this century, citizens should clearly see the need for armed forces under competent leadership.

Throughout our nation's long history, the very core of military leadership has been the professional military officers. In this modern era they are products of varied educational and military background, as should be the case in our democratic America. They are graduates of West Point, or the ROTC; many enter from the Officer Candidate Schools, and others are appointed from civil life to meet Army needs in professional, scientific, or technical fields. Whatever their background at the outset, if they remain as career officers, they continue to demonstrate a sense of mission to serve the national purpose coupled with a commitment—the "soldier's soul," as Professor Huntington, a penetrating writer on military subjects, has described it. It is a commitment that drives them just a little farther when the going is roughest—for that last fifteen minutes in battle when victory is often won, or lost forever; it is a personal sense of duty—a love of country—that maintains an unflagging standard of excellence on the job from day to day. These are the true professionals—the "pros"—who are needed today to a degree that may not be fully understood.

In these harried days, much is made of dissent, a privilege granted under our precious Constitution. The reasons for sharp disagreement with national policy are varied. They may be expressions of idealism or the reaching of conclusions different from government policy after careful consideration of the same set of basic facts. The reasons may also stem from ignorance, weakness, or concealed intent for subversion. Only the dissenter knows his or her own motive. Despite our troubled years, our citizens cling with undiminished determination to our great freedoms. Our proud nation may become stronger as it learns to accept or to cope with these vast turmoils of expression.

What must be clear to thoughtful citizens is the pressing need for maturity of judgment in reaching long-range decisions, followed by the courage of decisive action. Our United States has been thrust into a position of world leadership, a status it did not seek. International catastrophe might be inevitable if this responsibility is terminated. We must continue to reach for the utopia of international peace and tranquility between nations, while we stand ready to thwart threats to our lands or people either from within or from without our national boundaries. The military professionals surely will continue to be the final rampart for the preservation of our form of government against change by force, as well as the security of our people from outside aggression or internal insurrection. They must provide a living reflection of the words DUTY, HONOR, COUNTRY, in their broadest, most meaningful context. The life of our proud nation depends upon it.

The life of the Army officer is rewarding and stimulating for those individuals who are adapted by their convictions and their talents for its requirements. It is an exacting life with its own cherished code, special hazards, and rewards. Not all individuals will find the life either attractive or agreeable, which is a reason for laying the facts on the line in this chapter. The person who wants a sheltered, safe, uneventful life, with work from nine to five, the five-day week, and other niceties of today, is unlikely to be adaptable to the vast variety of missions and worldwide places of assignment of the Army officer. But the future security of our nation requires that a sufficient number of our splendidly qualified young citizens elect this choice of career. For them, it will be a good life. There must be capable hands and minds all along the slender line from lieutenant to general. There is a clear need for young men and women to enter the corps of officers and to progress in grade and responsibility to meet with competence the unknown requirements of our nation in the years ahead.

THE PEOPLE WITH WHOM YOU LIVE AND WORK

In the enjoyment of any career the quality of the people with whom you are associated is of high importance. Your success will be influenced by the manner in which they perform their duties. Among them you will find the personal friends who may enrich your life.

Much of the work of officers is with soldiers who, for the most part, are young people in their formative years, of excellent physique, with fine minds. They have the enthusiasms, the ambitions, and the interests of youth. There are few responsibilities equal in satisfaction to training, developing, and leading young soldiers. In these tasks you will be assisted by older soldiers who are the noncommissioned backbone of our Army and who will become individuals you will respect and treasure.

Army officers are a carefully selected corps, talented and well educated. The larger portion are trained to lead and to command troop units. Included also are physicians and dentists, lawyers, clergymen, engineers, scientists of many kinds, and specialists in many fields of importance today.

During the past few decades, the Army has made a continuing, determined effort to assure that its corps of officers is exceptionally well educated. Educational opportunities, in both military schools and civilian institutions, are detailed in chapter 13, *Army Schools and Career Progress.*

As a result of this emphasis on education, in the Regular Army of today more than 97 percent of the commissioned officers possess at least a bachelor's degree. In addition, approximately 25 percent of all Regular Army commissioned officers also have advanced degrees—master's, PhDs, or professional. Fewer than 2 percent of all Regular Army commissioned officers have had less than two years of college.

The off-duty standards, interests, and activities of officers will be found to be about the same as other successful men and women of better-than-average educational and cultural background. It is a subject worthy of careful consideration in choosing a vocation.

THE APPEALS OF MILITARY DUTY AND ARMY LIFE

After you have evaluated the vocation as to its true worth and considered the characteristics of your potential associates, it is logical to proceed to analyze the broad pattern of its duties and its life, remembering to consider years of peace as well as war or emergency. Will you find stimulating the tasks, missions, or responsibilities that you will be required to complete? Will you be interested by the travel involved in many changes of station as well as duty assignment, within the United States and in other lands? Will you enjoy and cherish the comradeship and friendship of the sort of people who adopt the military life as a vocation?

The person of action who likes to lead, to work with people, to get things done, to express personal views and to stand firmly is quite likely to enjoy the military life. Or he or she may wish to develop in some military technique or professional specialty, such as medicine or the law, or as a chaplain. The scope of Army requirements is very wide. In the paragraphs that follow we attempt an analysis of some of these characteristics.

The Officer's Code of Duty and Conduct. This is a most important consideration. The officer lives under a strong and inspiring code that acts as a guide in the standards of official and personal acts. It assures the officer that he or she will be associated in worthwhile missions with other officers whose loyalty to the nation, personal trustworthiness, and honor are of the highest order. Here will be found the welding of common interests that results in military teamwork, in comradeship, and in friendships with others of all ages and grades. It provides an environment that its members regard with pride and self-respect. It is the sort of life that many good men and women have loved and do love. Life under the code is good for the nation, and for most officers it is a rich and gratifying experience. (See chapter 3, *The Code of the Army Officer.*)

The Officer as a Leader. At the outset of your career you may expect opportunity to command, to train others, to guide and direct, to lead and set the example. As you progress in experience you will be taught more and more of leadership. It pertains to the leadership of tactical units and to units in support; it applies also to tasks of management or administration other than in tactical units. You will be "in charge" of something for which you are responsible. You will have a mission. In the usual case other officers, soldiers, or civilian employees will be assigned to assist you in the discharge of mission. You will be a manager. Initially, you will be a junior executive, progressing with experience to command or executive responsibilities of the greatest scope. This is the part of Army life that has the strongest appeal for many officers because they reach positions of responsibility requiring the use of leadership more swiftly than in other careers. Military leadership is never static; it is continually embracing new conditions. It is growth-leadership, not standstill leadership. Furthermore, the ultimate expectancy as to scope of leadership is far greater than in other vocations. If opportunity to lead is the primary reason for electing the military life, you choose wisely. Responsibility and leadership will be your life.

CONSIDER THE SCOPE OF MILITARY LIFE

The single purpose of service in the Army or its sister services is the nation's security in this divided and troubled world. Although the life has this single purpose, the one certainty of the Army officer is that his or her duty assignments will have infinite variety, with location of duty throughout the United States and in many foreign lands.

As your training proceeds and your capabilities are recognized, you will encounter progressively the full force and flavor of missions of great variety. The work of the Army must be done and its missions achieved. Abroad there are our forces in Europe and Asia, working in close unison with our allies. There are also military aid and assistance groups, military missions, and our Army attaches stationed wherever we have State Department representation. You must expect to live and serve, and to execute ably the assigned mission, wherever you are needed.

Within the United States there is the structure for the total administration and development of the Active Army and the Reserve components. There is the training of individuals and organizations at training centers, at Army and civilian schools, and in tactical units. There is research and development into scientific and other fields to increase our security of the present and future. There is the logistical support of Army units and personnel everywhere, from guns and ammunition to their medical and hospital requirements. There is much more. The mission of the Army officer involves a great variety of individual assignments that will take him or her from one end of our country to the other and to other countries as well.

But let us keep this great variety of mission and location in a reasonable perspective. It is true that there is the widest opportunity for an interesting, useful life, in almost worldwide locations. There is also routine. There is humdrum. All is not top secret and all is not glamorous. It is a life of service with important rewards and many disappointments. As an officer, you may live and work under the highest standards of surroundings or facilities; it is equally true that you may expect to live and work under some conditions that are most difficult indeed. Over the years of a professional career, you may feel that there are too few of the former and too many of the latter. At the end, you may realize that your greatest achievements occurred where the going was hardest and roughest. It is necessary to see deeply into the expectancies in order to choose wisely.

The Chance to Grow in Capability and Knowledge. The Army officer is provided with unique opportunities to increase personal knowledge and to expand personal capabilities. These good things develop from the consecutive assignments, which increase in importance with experience. It is an intentional, planned program, accomplished through the Army's extensive system of service schools and colleges, with the use of civilian institutions of learning. There is opportunity to complete necessary college-level courses to qualify for an academic degree. And there are opportunities to attend a university to attain an advanced degree. The strongly emphasized career planning program of the Army provides guidance and control to the undertaking. The goal is to develop the individual officer so that each may reach his or her own level of maximum capacity. (See chapter 12, *Professional Development,* and chapter 13, *Army Schools and Career Progress.*) For those individuals who have the character, the zeal, and the inherent ability to absorb and apply knowledge and to work effectively with their fellow men, it is opportunity unlimited.

Travel. Over the years an officer may expect to serve at several stations within the United States and in other countries. You will travel extensively. You may acquire considerable knowledge of London, Paris, Rome, and other capitals of Europe, as well as Tokyo, Seoul, and other great cities of the Far East. You will acquire a broad and thorough understanding of our own great country, and you will learn much of other lands and other people. Through this experience you will gain understanding of the crosscurrents of world opinion. Your interests will tend to become national and international, in contrast to local and restricted. Your acquaintanceships will expand to other individuals of many vocations who also have broad interests. It is a constant education.

This is a satisfying phase of military life of primary attractiveness to most officers. The individual who prefers the roots established by life in a single community, with sameness in the place of residence, the daily experiences, and associates, is unlikely to enjoy the military life. It is a point of serious consideration. (See chapter 10, *Army Posts and Stations,* and chapter 11, *Foreign Service.*)

The Courtesies, the Customs, and the Off-duty Life. Military life includes the use of ceremonial procedures that give it dignity and charm. They consist of courtesies paid to the National Anthem and the flag; between senior and junior; between officer and soldier; to the high civilian officials of government or of friendly foreign governments; and to the military dead. (See chapter 6, *Military*

Courtesy.) There are customs of the service as universally observed as the prescribed courtesies that add to the smoothness and enjoyment of official as well as
unofficial and social contacts. They are procedures that are learned quickly and
applied gracefully. They are quite similar to the protocol of the foreign service or
to that applied to faculty members on a university campus or other grouping of men
and women where there is recognition of position. The only thing unique about
the Army's customs and courtesies is that they have been established over many
years and for that reason are less subject to change. (See chapter 7, *Customs of
the Service.*)

For those whose assignments are on military posts, particularly where there are
quarters for family occupancy, the athletic, social, and cultural opportunities are
often outstanding. This is especially true of the large, older stations where there is
a considerable amount of permanent construction of family quarters and facilities.
The officers' club is often the focal point of social and off-duty activities for the
officer and adult members of his or her family. This traditional institution of good
fellowship provides about the same sort of service to its members as the faculty
club at a university, or the country club or city club whose members are the
professional and business leaders of a community. Officers' clubs operate by
means of dues and profits from activities, without expense to the government.
These clubs are a distinct advantage in the military community because of the
opportunity for group activities and the broadening of acquaintanceships. (See
chapter 8, *The Social Side of Army Life.*)

CONSIDER THE TOTAL REMUNERATION

It is entirely fitting that an individual contemplating a career as an officer should
consider with great thoroughness the complete situation as to service pay; allowances; special pay for which he or she may qualify; service rights and benefits;
rights as to retirement; and the benefits after retirement, including veterans' benefits, which are provided by our government. *The Army officer must have the right
to aspire and to achieve at least the same standard of living and security as do
people of similar education and responsibility in other vocations, civil or government. Indeed, since the officer may be required to lay his or her life on the line
in the performance of assigned duties—a hazard excluded from the usual expectancies of other fields of employment—a case can be made that he or she should
receive special consideration.*

Military Pay. Pay is a proper factor for an individual to consider in choice of
career. There are others, of course, as discussed in this chapter. But the dollars-
and-cents item is certainly to be considered in choosing a vocation and in determining one's own willingness to serve our government as an officer. You should
be secure in the conclusion that throughout your years of active service you will
be able to support your family, including educating your children, at an acceptable
standard of living. After retirement, you should be confident that you and your
spouse will live in comfort and dignity. If you should predecease your spouse,
before or after retirement, you should feel secure that his or her essential needs
are assured. This is a broad view of "remuneration."

This discussion does not presume to argue that total armed service pay and total
remuneration are either sufficient or insufficient for the responsibilities, the hazards, and other factors involved. Refer to chapter 20, *Pay and Allowances,* and
to chapter 9, *Financial Planning,* as to service and Social Security benefits available to the officer and his or her dependents. The aggregate should be carefully
evaluated. Is the total sufficient, in comparison with other vocations? It is a determi-

nation to be made by each individual. In candor, however, it should be stated that career officers who have observed reasonably good financial management of their affairs, with reasonably farsighted and prudent planning for their own futures, have been able to provide the financial obligations of parenthood, to lead interesting lives, and then to enjoy rewarding, financially secure, comfortable lives during their retirement years.*

Promotion. Subject to performance of duty in an efficient manner, with the continued observance of required standards of personal honor and conduct, advancement in rank and position is quite certain for the Army officer. Under provisions for promotion currently in effect, the opportunity for promotion on a selective basis is favorable for the outstanding officer who works hard and achieves highly. Merit will take the officer upward.

The officer who enters the service at the normal age of the early or mid twenties may anticipate a career of thirty years or to age sixty. Most will retire in their fifties through the operation of laws. Promotion is selective and above the grade of first lieutenant or CW2 is on the "best qualified" basis. Essential are the retention of good health, maintenance of good physical condition, and the receipt of commendable evaluation reports and ratings. Many officers who continue on active duty will attain the grade of colonel, which is a very high grade indeed. A small portion of officers will become generals, to provide the topmost leadership in the Army. On a percentage basis it is clear that only a few will achieve the grade of general. The stars are there, however, for those of special aptitude or capability. Highly successful officers may be confident of attaining the grade of colonel before retirement, with a few in the grade of general. (See chapter 15, *Promotion.*)

Tenure of Position. The Regular officer has a very important degree of protection as to tenure of position. The Regular cannot be separated from active duty for such administrative reasons as "reduction in force," nor separated at all except by due process of applicable laws. If the officer's work is of acceptable standard, and his or her conduct above serious reproach, and if he or she retains physical and mental health, the officer may expect with confidence to retain a commission with all its rights and benefits until retirement and thereafter in retired status until death.

During the first three years after appointment the Regular Army officer is in probationary status and the appointment subject to administrative termination. Elimination may occur after the probationary period by approved findings of a Board of Officers because of low standards of duty performance, or for character or other weakness. Elimination may occur through failing twice to be selected for promotion to a new permanent grade. Conviction by general court-martial may involve dismissal. Physical disability acquired during the first eight years' service results in severance pay, not retirement, but important VA rights accrue. Beyond service in the eighth year, retirement pay for physical disability depends upon degree of disability and length of service. (See chapter 26, *Resignation and Elimination,* and chapter 27, *Retirement.*)

Annual Leave with Pay. The Army provides thirty days' leave annually with pay, which may accumulate for two years. (See chapter 24, *Authorized Absences.*)

---

*The motivation for choosing a service career has been above a dollars-and-cents evaluation. The nation has been most fortunate in the caliber of people who have been attracted to its service and continued with it—through thick and thin. Officers of the stature of Generals Marshall, Eisenhower, MacArthur, Bradley, Taylor, Wheeler, Johnson, and Westmoreland, and thousands of others of their brother and sister officers of all eras similarly motivated, have placed the nation's security and the privilege of its service as the reason for their choice of career. Their value to the nation is beyond price, and there will always be a need—with ultimate appreciation—for more like them.

Medical Care and Hospitalization. The officer is provided medical care and hospitalization without cost, except for a small subsistence charge when hospitalized. Spouses and children of service members are able to obtain very complete medical and hospital care, in service facilities or in civilian facilities, without regard to the military station of the military member of the family. Especially gratifying is the provision for major help for handicapped or mentally retarded children of service families. This medical coverage continues, under slightly altered rules, after the officer retires.

The provisions for medical care and hospitalization for an officer and his or her family members, while in active service or in retired status, are an important benefit to career service. (See also chapter 9, *Financial Planning.*)

Six Months' Pay as Death Gratuity. Upon the death of a military person on active duty, the beneficiary receives six months' pay, $3,000 maximum, tax exempt, as a gratuity.

Privileges of the Post Exchange and Commissary. The post exchange and the commissary are highly appreciated institutions with histories that reach deep into the past.

In addition to being convenient for on-post residents, they provide many items at savings to all who have the privilege of using them. Their associated facilities of laundry, dry cleaning, shoe repair, barber shop, bowling alleys, snack bars, delicatessen, gas station, and so on provide other opportunities to stretch one's dollars and still lead the good life. Commissaries derive no profits, although a 5 percent surcharge is used to pay for new commissaries, to renovate old ones, and to pay for such things as grocery carts, meat-slicing machines, and paper bags. The small dividends from post exchange sales are given to welfare funds for athletics and recreation.

Retirement. The Regular Army officer has an important factor of security in the retirement laws. (Refer to chapter 27, *Retirement.*) They provide for voluntary retirement upon completing twenty years of service, subject to departmental approval. There is retirement for physical disability for those who have completed eight years of service. Forced retirement becomes operative upon attaining the statutory age limit. Low efficiency, character weakness, or failure twice to be selected for promotion may cause obligatory retirement. (See chapter 15, *Promotion;* and chapter 26, *Resignation and Elimination.*)

Veterans' Benefits and Other Rights and Privileges. Any veteran, including the retired Army officer, has many rights and privileges. The Veterans Administration is the agency of administration.

CONSIDER THE DISADVANTAGES

There are factors concerning the military service that many will consider disadvantages of serious importance. Some of them may be eliminated as time passes, for our officials have made real progress in improving the life and lot of service people of all grades. Some may be added as our elected officials struggle with the problem of balancing the federal budget. Some are inherent to the service itself and depend upon international conditions, the requirements and missions to be met, even the conduct of war. The disadvantages deserve evaluation.

The officer must be prepared to perform an officer's duty in war or in conflict short of war. There are hardships and there are hazards. It is the reason the government granted the commission or warrant.

The Shortage of Family Housing at Posts and Stations. While real progress has been made in recent years in increasing the number of quarters available for assignment to officers at our posts and stations, the shortage continues. It varies between stations, as can be seen quickly by consulting chapter 10, *Army Posts and Stations.* The most enjoyable and the most economical life is obtained by occupying suitable quarters on the post of assignment. Great care is taken to assign the quarters, which are available on a fair and equitable basis. But at many stations there is a wait, and at others the number of officers assigned is so far above the number of sets of quarters available as to make residence off-post the expectancy. The situation improves each year as new funds are provided for quarters. But the shortage persists and must be faced.

Family Separation. The nature and place of duty assignments have caused some necessary separation of families. There have been wars, and combat short of formal war. The Army mission has required some officers and soldiers to be sent into regions so undeveloped or unhealthy that families cannot be accommodated. These regions are short-tour areas where duration is curtailed to eighteen months or less; however, the duty is essential to the national security that officers and their spouses have accepted as an essential national service. The duration of tours unaccompanied by families is indicated in chapter 11, *Foreign Service.*

The American public and our elected officials know that family separation in peacetime is abnormal. It is Army policy established in AR 614–30 that family separations are directed only when there are no accommodations for family members, or when the family's presence would have an adverse effect upon a unit's mission or combat capability. These are facts of life that the officer and his or her spouse must be prepared to face. The occasions are infrequent; such duties are distributed carefully so that individuals do not bear a disproportionate degree of separation. Still, when the international situation becomes tense and uncertain, potential zones of combat are not the place for families. It is a fact to be faced courageously.

Frequent Changes of Station. Station changes occur from causes integral with service opportunities or needs. In times of military quiet, when economy rules with a firmer hand, the officer may wish for more frequent station changes. Take this one in stride.

REACHING CONCLUSIONS

At the beginning of this chapter the purpose was stated of presenting a calm and objective discussion of the vocation of an Army officer, with its advantages as well as its recognized disadvantages. Frequent references are made to other chapters of *The Army Officer's Guide* where detailed information on each important subject may be found. The purpose has been to present facts so that you, as an eligible young man or woman, can decide a little more accurately your own election as to military life.

The security of our great nation requires a sufficient number of able leaders of all grades and ages, from top to bottom, who are eager to serve their country wherever and however such service is needed; they will serve their country because they think the task is worthy, because they like the military life as well as their associations with others of like mind; and they will place their confidence in the appropriate officials of government as to pay and other benefits of future service. For the government has the first interest here and must be relied upon to treat fairly its defenders in uniform. If it should fail to do so, it will cease to attract and hold in willing career service the quality and numbers of individuals needed for the nation's future security. Indeed, a person who has genuine fears as to the fairness of our government officials had best elect another career, for in one sense it is their powers and capacity to govern justly we stand ready to fight to preserve.

Needed by the Army are young men and women of good minds and education, of good physique to stand the rigors of service, who are willing to work, to study, and to learn, so as to be ready for greater responsibilities as they come.

The young persons of today who select an Army career may expect to reach the time of retirement some thirty years in the future. During those years they will undertake tasks not yet envisioned but that we may be certain will be challenging and interesting. When that final day comes it is almost a certainty that these officers will not be persons of wealth from savings from their salaries. But their monthly pay will have enabled them to live lives of fairly adequate financial security. The officers will have endured some bruises and suffered some hardships, for their lives will not have been easy ones. But overshadowing all these matters will be a pride of service in having completed successfully, at home and overseas, many interesting and important assignments. The officers will have helped make history, always more interesting than merely reading of the exploits of others. They will have developed valued comradeships and strong friendships, priceless beyond measure. The officers' interests will center in national and international affairs, and their friends are likely to include many people of similar interests who may be civilian or military. The officers will be familiar and at home in most parts of the United States and in many oversea regions and nations because their duties will have taken them there. They will probably have a genuine love of the service, its responsibilities, its unique life, and its cherished associations. The officers might say, as many other officers are saying as they leave active service in these fascinating days, "If I could live it over, I would choose the Army again. For me it has been best." It is such men and women the nation will need in the challenging years ahead, and it is for such men and women, who may become our future revered leaders, that this chapter has been written.

> I'm glad I'm in the Army, not only for the people who are in it and for the breadth of experience which it offers, but because of the feeling I have of belonging to an outfit which really matters, one which has a mission of tremendous significance.—Gen. Maxwell D. Taylor, Chief of Staff, 1955–1959, Chairman, Joint Chiefs of Staff, 1962–1964, Ambassador to Vietnam, 1964–1965, and Special Assistant to the President of the United States, 1965–1968.

2
The Sources of Army Officers

The Army provides broad opportunities to win appointment as an officer. The Active Army, the Army National Guard, and the Army Reserve must have stable and constant sources of new officers to perform the Army mission of the present and future.

This chapter contains a summary discussion of the separate roads to a commission or warrant, with historical background.

SOURCES AND PREREQUISITES

Sources. The sources for training and selection of Army officers are as follows:

> The United States Military Academy (USMA)
> The Reserve Officers Training Corps (ROTC)
> The Officer Candidate School (OCS)
> Appointment from civil life
> Combat zone appointments
> Warrant officer appointments

Prerequisites. There are prerequisites to appointment that applicants must satisfy. They must be citizens, be within specified age brackets for the component and branch in which they seek appointment, be of good physique as established by a thorough physical examination, and be of high moral character. Relatively few are appointed who have not received an academic degree. Information about the complete requirements for appointment should be sought from the Personnel Officer of any Army post or station.

Numbers of Appointments. Approximately 1,000 second lieutenants are appointed annually from the U.S. Military Academy. The number is limited by the size of the Academy. The annual appointment of officers from the Reserve Officers Training Corps varies according to the needs of the Army and the number of graduates available. Since the total number of officers potentially available to the Army each year from the Military Academy and from the ROTC is relatively constant and not subject to rapid change, the annual input of officers from the OCS program and by direct appointment is varied by the Army to meet its actual yearly needs. Warrant officers are appointed in numbers sufficient to satisfy the Army's requirements for these highly skilled specialists.

METHODS OF APPOINTMENT

Throughout our nation's history there have been different methods by which citizens have obtained appointment as Army officers. In our democracy it is an absolute necessity that the nation's military officers be completely free from even a suspicion that any appointment was made on any basis other than individual merit in meeting established standards. Selection must be from the best qualified individuals. While this has not always been the case, it is noteworthy that the present system of officer selection, training, and appointment has the trust of the nation and of the members of the Army.

THE UNITED STATES MILITARY ACADEMY

The United States Military Academy, West Point, New York, since its establishment by the Congress in 1802, has provided well-educated, highly trained professional Army officers who have served the nation with distinction. Its famed Long Gray Line, which includes the names of Generals Grant, Lee, Pershing, Bradley, MacArthur, and Eisenhower, to name a few where it would be better to name many, has fulfilled its mission through all emergencies and all the wars that have confronted the nation since the founding of the Academy. The Active Army of today has approximately 13,000 graduates.

Appointment to the Academy. A prospective candidate for West Point must first obtain a nomination from an authorized nominating source. Approximately 85 percent of the nominations available each year are from members of Congress for residents of their states or congressional districts. Competitive examinations determine the appointments from several eligible groups.

Forty appointments at any time are available to the children of veterans, either deceased or with 100 percent disability, of any recognized war or conflict including Vietnam. There are 170 appointments awarded annually on a competitive basis to enlisted men and women of the Regular Army and the Army's Reserve components. Sons and daughters of members of the Regular components of the Armed Forces, who are still in service, retired, or who died while serving, and of officers in the Reserve components who have served a minimum of eight years and are still on active duty, are eligible to compete for 100 cadetships reserved annually for Presidential appointment. There is no limit on the number to be accepted from sons and daughters of recipients of the Medal of Honor, our nation's highest award for valor. There are twenty additional appointments provided annually to honor military schools (high school or junior college level); honor military schools are determined annually by Department of the Army (DA) or Navy inspectors.

Regardless of the categories mentioned above, all candidates must be medically qualified and must successfully pass a physical aptitude test and academic examination.

West Point Preparatory School. Noteworthy is the Army's USMA Preparatory School at Fort Monmouth, New Jersey, where successful active-duty enlisted personnel who are applicants for West Point undergo intensive training and instruction. Instruction lasts from mid-August to the end of May.

USMA Course. The four-year course leads to a baccalaureate degree, with military training to orient cadets toward careers as officers of the Regular Army. The scope of the instruction includes the humanities, engineering, history, military training in all branches, physical development, and character building. AR 350-5 and the USMA Catalog of Information provide detailed information; write to Director of Admissions, USMA. West Point, NY 10996.

RESERVE OFFICERS TRAINING CORPS

The Reserve Officers Training Corps (ROTC) was formally established by the National Defense Act of 1916. But the concept of military training in degree-granting institutions of higher learning had its origin at the American Literary, Scientific and Military Academy, in 1820, at Norwich, Vermont. It was founded by Capt. Alden Partridge, a graduate of West Point, and its Superintendent prior to 1820. Subsequently, in 1834, its name was changed to Norwich University. It continues to provide graduates into military as well as civil leadership at its present location at Northfield, in the state of its origin. Virginia Military Institute (alma mater of General of the Army George C. Marshall, World War II Army Chief of Staff), Lexington, Virginia, in 1839, and the Citadel, Charleston, South Carolina, in 1842, were the next degree-granting institutions to adopt the principle of the John Milton (1608–1674) *Tractate on Education: "I call therefore a complete and generous education that which fits a man to perform justly, skillfully and magnanimously all the offices, both private and public, of peace and war."*

President Lincoln saw the need for increased educational facilities, including a requirement for military training. Under his leadership the Morrill Act of 1862, known as the "Land Grant Act," provided for the establishment of state universities, which encouraged the start of many of our great state universities of today.

Many officers of the World War I period received training in the military training programs of the Land Grant colleges and universities. During World War II more than 100,000 ROTC graduates were on active duty from the beginning of the emergency and served in all grades. During the war in Korea more than 120,000 Reserve officers served on active duty, the vast majority from the ROTC. In the Active Army of today, approximately one-fourth of the Army's general officers and over 40 percent of all its officers were appointed as officers from the ROTC.

The Junior Division, ROTC, provides military training in secondary schools. Included are some 650 public and private schools having a total enrollment of about 115,000, including about 35,000 female cadets.

The Senior Division, ROTC, offers military training at college level, providing officers for the Army Reserve and the Regular Army. Enrollment varies from year to year, but it is about 65,000 in nearly 300 colleges and universities and almost a dozen junior colleges. Female enrollment in the Senior ROTC comprises about 20 percent of the total.

Honor graduates from these courses may be appointed into the Regular Army, while the balance of the graduates are appointed into the Army Reserve and may or may not be called to immediate active duty.

The Senior ROTC program includes four- and two-year programs. The four-year program involves a two-year basic course followed by a two-year advanced course with a six-weeks summer training camp normally attended between the junior and senior years. The two-year program was designed for students who were for some reason unable to enroll in the basic course. Transfer students from junior colleges that have no ROTC program are in this category. In lieu of the basic course, they must attend a six-weeks basic summer camp prior to taking the advanced course. The student receives monthly pay plus travel pay at basic summer camp.

Those enrolled in the advanced course receive $100 per month for subsistence. While at advanced summer camps, they receive one-half the base pay of a second lieutenant with less than two years' service. Upon graduation and initial entry on active duty, the officer receives a uniform allowance of $300.

High school graduates who enroll in the four-year program may apply for a four-year scholarship. Applicants for a two-year scholarship apply during their second year of the basic course. Scholarship winners agree to accept a commission and to serve not less than four years on active duty. They must meet certain age requirements. They do receive $100 per month for the duration of the scholarship, plus tuition, textbooks, and laboratory expenses.

OFFICER CANDIDATE SCHOOLS

Officer Candidate Schools are a tradition of the modern Army. They have produced well-trained officers to meet swiftly expanding Army requirements during World Wars I and II, the Korean War, and Vietnam. It is a program to meet emergencies.

The origin of the OCS is attributed to two voluntary camps, held during the summer of 1913, for undergraduate students age seventeen or older. At Gettysburg, Pennsylvania, 159 young men from sixty-three universities and colleges, and at Monterey, California, 85 young men from sixty-three institutions of higher learning, received military training. Expenses for transportation, subsistence, and clothing were paid by the trainees. Subsequently, in 1915, under the inspiration of General Leonard Wood, a military camp of instruction for business leaders and professional men was held at Plattsburgh, New York. With the Declaration of War, May 6, 1917, there followed swiftly the establishment of several *First Officers' Training Camps*. These and others that followed provided the bulk of the Army's officers for World War I.

The program was resumed in 1941, which resulted in the training and appointment from the warrant officers and enlisted men of the Army of more than a quarter million Army officers, exclusive of the similarly large program of the Army Air Corps. Many of these officers were subsequently appointed in the Regular Army.

AR 351-5 details the regulations for volunteering for OCS for enlisted personnel and warrant officers. Enlisted men and women are permitted to return to college for twenty-four months to obtain certain baccalaureate degrees with the Army's financial assistance, after which they attend OCS. College graduates may enlist for the purpose of attending an OCS course, serving two years after appointment. They receive eight weeks' basic training prior to starting the OCS course. Length of the OCS course is fourteen weeks. This selective process and the program of training provide officers splendidly trained and ready for assignment as junior officers of their branch.

The Officer Candidate School is located at Fort Benning, Georgia. Both male and female candidates attend this school.

Following the OCS course, the new officers attend the Basic Officer Course at their branch service school. Selection of candidates is for the most part confined to those who are college graduates or who have had some college training. The number selected each year is established according to the Army's needs to augment the annual officer input from the ROTC and the Military Academy.

Warrant Officer Candidate Courses. Warrant officer candidate courses are con-ducted as needed by the Army to meet requirements for warrant officers. At present only two such courses are in operation, one at the Aviation School at Fort Rucker, Alabama, providing training for entry into the Aviation career field, and one at the Academy of Health Sciences at San Antonio, Texas, which provides training for entry into the Health Services career field.

OFFICERS APPOINTED FROM CIVIL LIFE

Officers may be appointed from civil life, without completing a special course of training in order to qualify for a commission. The Army has a continuing need for officers who have completed their professional or technical training. For exam-ple, physicians and surgeons may be commissioned directly from civil life, or they may be appointed after completion of ROTC training. Other examples are chap-lains, lawyers, and others needed to meet Army requirements.

When the need is great, as in time of war or emergency, members of professions or vocations of civil life may be appointed in an appropriate grade, depending upon their achievements in their profession with a consideration also of their age and background.

The Army does, in practicality, recognize the civilian competition for these essential individuals and that they have devoted additional years toward attaining their education, specialization, and status. Consequently, special inducements are proffered to gain their initial service and to retain them on active duty.

Individuals who wish to obtain information about appointment as an officer in a profession or other specialty are advised to consult a personnel officer of a nearby Army post or the Headquarters of the U.S. Army in the area of their residence.

REGULAR ARMY APPOINTMENTS

An appointment as an officer of the Regular Army may be achieved in several different ways. West Point is an important source but at its present size can supply only a portion of the total requirement. The ROTC provides approximately 40 percent of the number appointed each year through its Distinguished Military Graduate program. Graduates of the U.S. Naval Academy and the U.S. Air Force Academy may apply upon graduation for an Army appointment. Distinguished graduates from the U.S. Army Officer Candidate School may apply for regular appointments. Officers on active duty, and college graduates who, as students, did not have an opportunity to participate in an ROTC program, are eligible to apply. In accordance with the Defense Officer Personnel Management Act of 1981 (DOPMA), each active duty officer must have accepted a Regular Army commis-sion prior to the eleventh year of service. (See chapter 15, *Promotion*.) The broad field of eligibility is noteworthy and in its implementation provides members of the corps of officers from representative backgrounds to add their talents to meet the Army's needs.

The requirements for appointment as a Regular Army officer are substantially the same for all applicants. He or she must be a loyal citizen of the United States, be of good moral character, and be able to meet a high standard of physical fitness as determined by examination. With exceptions, as in the case of appointees from the professions, an applicant for initial appointment in the Regular Army must be at least twenty-one and less than twenty-seven years of age.

APPOINTMENTS IN A COMBAT ZONE

In combat, warrant officers and soldiers who demonstrate a high potential in leadership deserve special recognition and utilization of their full capabilities.

Battlefield (direct) appointment of such individuals was authorized during World War II.

WARRANT OFFICERS

Warrant officers are appointed by warrant by the Secretary of the Army to meet Army requirements for personnel with particular skills and knowledge. The Department of the Army projects vacancies and invites applications from interested personnel who desire to compete for an appointment. Selection for appointment is made on a best-qualified basis by a selection board at Headquarters, Department of the Army. Eligible personnel include enlisted men and women from the Active Army, the Reserve components, and other military services. Qualified civilians also may apply, as may commissioned officers, provided their application is accompanied by a conditional resignation of commission.

Initial appointments are in the U.S. Army Reserve with concurrent call to active duty and an obligated service tour, normally three years. The regulations provide that at the end of the obligated service tour, individuals may apply either for appointment in the Regular Army or for a Voluntary Indefinite status. The applicable regulations are AR 135-100, AR 611-85, AR 611-112, and DA Pam 600-11.

There are distinctions between commissioned officers and warrant officers as regards command status (for which see AR 600–20) and certain other matters. In general, however, and as used in this book, the term *officer* includes both commissioned officers and warrant officers.

Warrant officers have the status and privileges of commissioned officers, as stated in chapter 6, *Military Courtesy.*

Chapter 16 provides a complete discussion of the history, present status, and probable future of the Army's warrant officers.

3

The Code of the Army Officer

Selection of the Army as a career demands that you concurrently adopt the code of the Army officer; this adoption must be done wholeheartedly, without any mental reservations. The code is a standard, a set of principles. It will be the beacon that guides your life. As an Army officer, you will be expected to follow the code in the performance of your official duties and in your relations with other individuals, military and civilian, on duty and off duty. It is not a harsh code but it is demanding. Adherence to the code does not start at reveille and end with the sounding of retreat. It is a twenty-four-hours-a-day, seven-days-a-week code that will guide you throughout your military career and all the years that follow. The code sets the tone for a way of life that many honorable, dedicated men and women have found rewarding—the Army way of life.

But what is this code that is of such importance to the Army officer? It is part official and written, but it is mostly traditional and unwritten. Let us examine it more closely.

OFFICIAL BASIS FOR THE CODE

The Oath of Office. A written basis for the code of the Army officer is provided by the Oath of Office. Note these words carefully:

> I, *(Name),* having been appointed an officer in the Army of the United States . . . in the grade of *(Grade),* do solemnly swear (or affirm) that I will support and defend the Constitution of the United States against all enemies, foreign and domestic; that I will bear true faith and allegiance to the same; that I take this obligation freely, without any mental reservation or purpose of evasion; and that I will well and faithfully discharge the duties of the office upon which I am about to enter; SO HELP ME GOD.

27

The Oath of Office is executed by each officer upon receipt of a commission or warrant. Think deeply about its phrasing. These are not mere ceremonial words. They mean exactly what they say. Having accepted an officer's commission or warrant, you will have become an official of our government, and you will be expected to do your utmost to uphold and defend our way of life. Note also that the words of the Oath of Office are the same for officers of the National Guard and Army Reserve as for officers of the Active Army. Regardless of component, officers bear the same obligation and responsibility.

The Officer's Commission or Warrant. The written basis for the code is expanded by the officer's commission or warrant. Examine the words of these documents and again think deeply about their meaning. In accepting your commission or warrant, you have embarked upon a life of public service to our great nation. Our nation's leaders and its citizens have every right to expect that you will discharge all assigned duties in an exemplary manner and that, by accepting your commission or warrant, you have every intention of doing your utmost to support our way of life.

The Uniform Code of Military Justice; Ethical Codes; Code of Conduct; Regulations. The official, written basis for the code of the Army officer is reinforced by other documents that establish standards and impose requirements on military personnel. The Uniform Code of Military Justice imposes many restrictions upon members of the armed forces, far beyond those that pertain to the ordinary citizen. There also are published official codes of ethical conduct, with procedures to enforce them.

The Code of Conduct establishes standards for military personnel in combat and for prisoners held by an enemy. Army regulations expand upon and more closely define the "do's and don'ts" expected of Army personnel, and as such they also become a part of the code.

The Army does not stand alone with its code, because the Navy, the Air Force, and the Marines have codes of similar strength and meaning. Collectively, these codes establish an ideal of national service, a way of life, essential for the nation's perpetual security and as the final rampart of defense of our people and our Constitution.

SIGNIFICANCE OF THE CODE

Is this code important? Other honored professions have their own codes and precepts. Honorable people in humble or high station in life, or around the world among members of the great religions, follow their own respected standards of ethics. While these are personal standards, for the most part, they nevertheless contribute to the security of a nation or even to the course of history. The extreme importance of the code of the Army officer stems from its significance to the United States. These responsibilities, shared equally with officers of the Navy, the Marine Corps, and the Air Force, involve the security of our nation, the protection of our people, plus the support of our nation's policies in its chosen courses of action in its relations with other countries. These missions, which the officer and all members of the armed forces are obligated to accept, may lead him or her to the distant places of the world and, if combat is encountered, may involve the life or death of subordinates as well as the success or the failure of the nation's mission. The duty may include placing the officer's own life on the line, for in combat all share the certain hazards. These are reasons our armed forces are maintained, and why the code of the Army officer has such vast significance.

When and if our nation's civil leaders decide that war has been forced upon us, as at Pearl Harbor, or decide that the nation's obligations lead into combat short of declaration of war, as in Vietnam, it is the officer who provides the military leadership to restore the peace. In our republic—our democracy, if you prefer—the confidence of all of our people in the integrity and the professional capabilities of members of the corps of commissioned officers is a matter of supreme importance. Weigh this truth carefully. Without high confidence in the nation's military leaders, our citizens would be reluctant to serve in the armed forces, or to entrust their sons, their daughters, or other citizens to the military service of their own country. Further, if this confidence were to become lacking, the President, his advisors, and members of Congress would be hesitant to adopt courses of action that might generate the need for force, no matter how essential such action might be to the nation's basic interests. These are reasons that make the code of the Army officer of such extreme importance to all of our citizens during this century of ferment and conflict.

What is the origin of this code of such national importance? Historically, there can be no truer foundation for the code of the Army officer than the example set by General Washington, with his own high standard of personal honor, of discipline, of personal sacrifice, of leadership, of complete devotion to his mission. Other great men in our history, whose names are household words of respect and trust, have embraced this code while adding to its strength—men like Generals Grant and Lee, General of the Armies Pershing, Generals of the Army Marshall, Eisenhower, MacArthur, Bradley, with their more recent counterparts, Generals Wheeler, Westmoreland, and Abrams. An infinite number of persons in junior as well as senior position, noncommissioned officers and soldiers as well as officers, have helped to build and to sustain the code. Include always those legions who have won the Medal of Honor, the Distinguished Service Cross, and other awards of valor, the Distinguished Service Medal, the Legion of Merit, and other awards of achievement. Our code was developed and followed throughout our Army's history and is supported by members of our great Army of today in the proudest tradition of our military service.

The military code is a standard of action with much depth. It is a firm belief that the preservation of our nation is decidedly worthwhile. It is unswerving confidence in the loyalty of our people and their sons and daughters who wear their country's uniform. It is a solid conviction that the courses followed by our government are sound and just to all people everywhere. It is faith.

We shall adopt as expressing the code a statement made by Abraham Lincoln in his Cooper Union Address, 27 February 1860. *"Let us have faith that right makes might; and in that faith let us to the end, dare to do our duty as we understand it."*

FOUNDATION OF THE CODE

It is an honor to serve in the armed forces of the United States. It also is a duty of our citizens to serve in the armed forces, as volunteers or in accordance with our nation's laws, and to perform the military missions that this service may require. If the day should come when a large portion of our citizens regard this service as less than an honor, and less than an obligation of citizenship, our proud nation will have begun the descent to lie beside other peoples who were unable or unwilling to fight for their principles or for the retention of their freedoms.

The very foundation of the officers' code, the basic principle, is that all members of the Army accept and do their best to act upon all orders and missions directed to them by the President, within his authority under the Constitution. In practice,

THE PRESIDENT OF THE UNITED STATES OF AMERICA

To all who shall see these presents, greeting:

Know ye that, reposing special trust and confidence in the patriotism, valor, fidelity, and abilities of   MARY ANN SMITH   , I do appoint   SECOND LIEUTENANT, REGULAR ARMY   in the

United States Army

to RANK as such from the THIRTIETH day of MAY , nineteen hundred and EIGHTY-EIGHT . This officer will therefore carefully and diligently discharge the duties of the office to which appointed by doing and performing all manner of things thereunto belonging.

And I do strictly charge and require those officers and other personnel of lesser rank to render such obedience as is due an officer of this grade and position. And, this officer is to observe and follow such orders and directions, from time to time, as may be given by the President of the United States of America or other superior officers, acting in accordance with the laws of the United States of America.

This commission is to continue in force during the pleasure of the President of the United States of America, under the provisions of those public laws relating to officers of the **Armed Forces of the United States of America** and the component thereof in which this appointment is made.

Done at the City of Washington, this TWENTY-NINTH day of JULY in the year of our Lord, one thousand nine hundred and EIGHTY-EIGHT and of the Independence of the United States of America, the

By the President:

The Adjutant General.

John O. Marsh, Jr.
Secretary of the Army

THE OFFICER'S COMMISSION.
(sample)

THE

ARMY

OF

THE UNITED STATES OF AMERICA

To all who shall see these presents, greeting:

Know Ye, that reposing special trust and confidence in the patriotism, valor, fidelity and abilities of ———— JOHN FRANCIS DOE ————,

the Secretary of the Army has appointed him *a*

WARRANT OFFICER W-1, REGULAR ARMY

in the United States Army

to rank as such from the TWENTY-NINTH *day of* APRIL *nineteen hundred and* EIGHTY-EIGHT. *This Warrant Officer will therefore carefully and diligently discharge the duties of the office to which appointed by doing and performing all manner of things thereunto belonging. And all subordinate personnel of lesser rank are strictly charged and required to render such obedience as is due a Warrant Officer of this grade and position. And this Warrant Officer is to observe and follow such orders and directions, from time to time, as may be given by Superior Officers and Warrant Officers acting in accordance with the laws of the United States of America.*

Done at the City of Washington, this TWENTY-EIGHTH *day of* JUNE*, in the year of our Lord one thousand nine hundred and* EIGHTY-EIGHT*, and of the Independence of the United States of America the* TWO-HUNDRED AND TWELFTH YEAR*.*

The Adjutant General

WARRANT OFFICER WARRANT.

(sample)

OATH OF OFFICE - MILITARY PERSONNEL

For use of this form, see AR 135-100: the proponent agency is TAGCEN.

INDICATE THE APPOINTMENT FOR WHICH OATH IS BEING EXECUTED BY PLACING AN "X" IN APPROPRIATE BOX. REGULAR ARMY COMMISSIONED OFFICERS WILL ALSO SPECIFY THE BRANCH OF APPOINTMENT WHEN APPOINTED IN A SPECIAL BRANCH.

(See Instructions Below)

COMMISSIONED OFFICERS	WARRANT OFFICERS
[X] REGULAR ARMY ___AGC___	[ ] REGULAR ARMY
(Branch, when so appointed)	
[ ] ARMY OF THE UNITED STATES, WITHOUT COMPONENT	[ ] ARMY OF THE UNITED STATES, WITHOUT COMPONENT
[ ] RESERVE COMMISSIONED OFFICER	[ ] RESERVE WARRANT OFFICER

I, ___JOHN FRANCIS DOE___   ___XXX-XX-XXXX___
(First Name - Middle Name - Last Name)   (Service Number)

having been appointed an officer in the Army of the United States, as indicated above in the grade of ___2LT___

do solemnly swear (or affirm) that I will support and defend the Constitution of the United States against all enemies, foreign and domestic, that I will bear true faith and allegiance to the same; that I take this obligation freely, without any mental reservation or purpose of evasion; and that I will well and faithfully discharge the duties of the office upon which I am about to enter; SO HELP ME GOD.

/s/ John Francis Doe
(Signature - full name as shown above)

SWORN TO AND SUBSCRIBED BEFORE ME AT Military District of Washington, USA, Washington, D.C.

THIS ___29th___ DAY OF ___July___, 19 88

___CPT, RA___   /s/ Thomas Roe
(Grade, component, or office of official administering oath)   (Signature)

INSTRUCTIONS

This form will be executed upon acceptance of appointment as an officer in the Army of the United States as indicated at top of form. Immediately upon receipt of notice of appointment, the appointee will, in case of acceptance of the appointment, return to the agency from which received, the oath of office (on this form) properly filled in, subscribed and attested. In case of non-acceptance, the notice of appointment will be returned to the agency from which received, (by letter) indicating the fact of non-acceptance.

FOR THE EXECUTION OF THE OATH OF OFFICE

1. Whenever any person is elected or appointed to an office of honor or trust under the Government of the United States, he is required before entering upon the duties of his office, to take and subscribe the oath prescribed by Section 1757, Revised Statutes, (5 U.S.C. 16, M.L. 1949, Section 118).

2. 10 U.S.C. 3394 eliminates the necessity of executing oath on promotion of officers.

3. The oath of office may be taken before any commissioned officer of any component of any Armed Force, whether or not on active duty (10 U.S.C. 1031), or before any warrant officer serving on active duty as an adjutant

assistant adjutant, acting adjutant, or personnel adjutant in any of the Armed Forces (See UCMJ, Article 136; 10 U.S.C. 936). A warrant officer administering the oath of office will show his title in the block to the left of his signature.

4. Oath of office may also be taken before any civil officer who is authorized by the laws of the United States or by the local municipal law to administer oaths, and if so administered by a civil official, the oath must bear the official seal of the person administering the oath, or if a seal is not used by the official, the official's capacity to administer oaths must be certified to under seal by a clerk of court or other proper local official.

DA FORM 71 1 AUG 59   PREVIOUS EDITIONS OF THIS FORM ARE OBSOLETE.   ☆U.S. Government Printing Office: 1981—341-646/8552

THE OATH OF OFFICE.
(sample)

this means accepting also all orders and missions assigned by others-lawfully appointed to positions of authority over the Army members. Our national leaders, and our thoughtful citizens, all take for granted—as they have a right to do—that each officer and each soldier will do his or her full part in the national mission assigned, accepting with courage the sacrifices and the hazards this service to our nation involves.

In recent years, strident voices of a vocal minority of our citizens have expressed very strong opposition to national policies. The verbal barrages have been aimed specifically at the military forces and the so-called military-industrial complex. This vocal opposition reached a crescendo during the early 1970s and led to our withdrawal from Vietnam and abandonment of the brave people of that country. The active protestors have included, among others, elected officials of our government, a surprising number of educators and students, members of the clergy, plus the rather open advocacy of opposition to the national policies by some columnists, news broadcasters, and other citizens. Their motives must remain concealed in their own minds, whether idealistic, pacifistic, based upon their analysis of facts or opinions that they accept, or subversive. This is not a new phenomenon in our nation, although during the 1970s it may have attained a broader base than during any period since the Civil War. It is a matter that is being dealt with by the nation's civil leadership.

There is an anomaly here that is rarely acknowledged; it deserves attention. As a citizen, the officer or soldier has the same right to weigh the factors leading to a decision and important action by the President as any individual who has spoken or acted violently in opposition. Indeed, the service member may conclude that a policy established by the President is entirely wrong. Now we reach a point of singular importance within the officer's code, and in such sharp contrast to the open opposition of some public officials and citizens as to justify thought and emphasis: *All officers of the armed forces, and all soldiers too, are bound by their oath to do their utmost to achieve the prompt and successful completion of the mission assigned, even at the risk of their lives when necessity requires, and without regard to their personal views as to the correctness of the national policy or the wisdom of the orders under which they act.* * The elected civil leaders of our nation decide these matters of high policy in international relations that may restore the peace, or result in war, or in combat short of formal declaration of war. *Once national policy has been decided by the constitutional civil leaders of our national government, the officer and the soldier must support it as their orders require. And this support must be with all their skill and all their determination, never divulging that they have doubts or that they have ever had doubts as to its wisdom.* Further, this obligation is identical for all members of the military services, without regard to their source of appointment.

This is the keystone of the code of the Army officer. He or she is an officer of the Executive Branch of our national government. The officer's appointment depends upon taking the Oath of Office. His or her retention anticipates and requires continual compliance with that oath. In the final analysis, the officer's readiness and willingness to lead U.S. troops in campaign or battle, or other mission, anywhere in the world the President may direct, against any kind of threat or enemy, foreign or domestic, is the true measure of the worth of the officer to our government, which entrusted him or her with its commission. In these days, with our military forces deployed around the world and with our national policies and our armed forces under attack at home, the principle needs understanding. It is an important element in the preservation of our government and the security of our people. For all the years that lie ahead, the Army and its sister services will continue to accept and to carry out this basic principle of the officer's code.

"My country. May it always be right, but my country right or wrong."— Stephen Decatur.

---

*Still, experienced military leaders know that officers and soldiers fight more courageously and sacrifice more willingly when they hold a deep conviction as to the worthwhileness and the justice of the cause for which they fight.

TRADITIONAL BASIS OF THE CODE

The Oath of Office, the officer's commission or warrant, and the other published codes and regulations provide the official basis for the code of the Army officer, but these are merely the skeleton for the code. The richness and fullness of the code can be understood only by an examination of the high standards, the devotion, and the dedication with which officers traditionally have approached their duties and their lives.

The basic standard of individual and group performance of military responsibilities is perhaps best expressed by the code of the United States Corps of Cadets, which is Duty, Honor, Country. This concept, which underlies all that is done in the field of character building of cadets at West Point, is equally the standard of the Army officer. This is the platform on which personal conduct and performance of duty are based.

Duty. In the Army, the performance of duty to the best of one's ability is a first requirement. Missions must be accomplished up to standard and on time. In thinking of duty in the Army, always remember that it includes willingness to fight, to enter areas of great personal danger, to accept the hazards of battle death. There is little tolerance of slipshod work or halfway measures. Your reputation depends upon the successful performance of all assigned duties, regardless of their size or their perceived importance.

Most orders are of the mission type, which state the job to be done but leave to the officer the selection of method. As an officer you will be expected to select methods that will accomplish the desired results, at the time required, with due regard for costs.

See work that needs doing and, without transgressing into the responsibilities of others, do it. Within your own sphere of responsibility do not wait to be told.

Stand on your own feet. Your seniors are interested in your past only in so far as it may indicate future capacity. They want to know how well you perform your duty today, so that they may estimate what you will do tomorrow. The reputation that counts most is the one you earn today.

Honor. Honor is the hallmark of officerlike conduct. It is the outgrowth of character. An honorable person has the knowledge to determine right from wrong and the courage to adhere unswervingly to the right. It means that an officer's written or spoken word may be accepted without question. Facts will be identified as facts, and opinions for what they are. Actions will be made on considerations of the good of the unit, the Army, the nation. They are all included in personal integrity.

The meaning of honor, in the sense used here, includes the narrower term *ethics.* As a part of honor in service of country, the officer is expected to lead the decent life.

An officer does not lie, cheat, steal, or violate moral codes. An officer must never stoop to the petty chicaneries of wrongful acts "not specifically illegal," nor shady acts of any sort not mentioned specifically in departmental regulations. That is, he or she does not chisel. The officer is expected to rise and live above the frailties of other people in less exacting professions.

Do all officers follow this exacting code at all times, under all conditions? Of course not. Utopia has not arrived. But it can be said without chance of successful contradiction that the great bulk of officers do so as a matter of course. Those who do not live by its standards earn first the scorn of their associates, and if the offenses are more than trivial, they stand a fine chance of trial for conduct unbecoming an officer and gentleman or lady.

The code requires all officers to live and conduct all their activities so that they may look all persons squarely in the eye knowing that they are honorable individuals associating themselves with other honorable individuals.

Country. The profession of arms in which the officer is appointed a leader is a public, not a private, vocation. The American people maintain military forces for the preservation of their security and the sovereignty of the United States. They have the right to expect the highest standards of personal and official conduct from their officers. The responsibilities of the officer embrace all the people, and his or her Oath of Office prescribes the protection of the Constitution.

The Army officer holds a commission or warrant by choice. Each officer is a volunteer. He or she accepted a commission or warrant, and with it all its hazards and responsibilities as well as its rights and privileges. Each officer is a patriotic citizen who places country above self. Patriotism has this definition: "The willingness to sacrifice and endure discipline for the welfare of the community." From the occasionally maligned Thomas Paine: "Those who expect to reap the blessings of freedom, must, like men, undergo the fatigue of supporting it."

The Army officer and others who serve the United States willingly are patriots. Any citizen of our country may be a patriot. Here is a simple definition worthy of thought: *A patriot is one who exerts himself to promote the wellbeing of his country; one who maintains his country's freedom and rights.* Note in the definition the word *exerts.* A patriot is one who does something, or stands ready to do something, for his or her country's freedom or rights. The test of patriotism lies in the basic beliefs of each individual. Our nation will thrive and remain secure as long as patriots are in the vast majority and while that patriotism remains as an honored and honorable state.

An occasional citizen, even persons of passing importance, scoff at the patriot as a shortsighted person of a passing era. Theirs is the philosophy of Samuel Johnson, 1709–1784, who originated the statement, "Patriotism is the last refuge of a scoundrel." Even then, even now, there are individuals who belittle the patriot and acclaim the greater importance of their own selfish goals or preferences above those of our nation and its government. Patriotism is part of the code of the Army, its sister services, and their members who serve as volunteers or serve willingly, exerting themselves in the interests of the security of the nation.

It is not always true that the general public appreciates the value of its patriots in military service. When the threat of war recedes, there are real tests of fortitude by those who wear the uniform. Such reactions are not limited to our own country and are as old as armies. One of Marlborough's veterans, writing some three centuries ago, saw the same phenomenon and had this to say about it:

> God and the soldier, we adore
> In time of danger, not before;
> The danger passed and all things righted,
> God is forgotten, and the soldier slighted.

The Standard Identical for All. The degree to which observance of the code is expected is the same for all officers, without regard to grade, or branch, or sex, or component, or length of service. Perhaps the meaning may be illustrated by comparison with the observance of the rules of a game, such as golf; the player whose score is rarely below 100 should be as careful to avoid improving the lie of the ball in the rough as the champion.

Now let us temper this principle with reason. Officers of short service require instruction in what is right and what is wrong as to many military requirements, just as they must be instructed in military techniques. Some deviations will be regarded as a subject for instruction or mild rebuke. For example, it is a custom that an officer provide first for the needs of his or her soldiers, before devoting time to personal needs; the officer who fails to do so may expect to be reminded of his or her duties. On the other hand, an offense involving character or honor, or deliberate fraud, will be regarded equally serious if committed by a newly appointed junior as by the oldest and most experienced senior.

It is true that in matters of honor the standard is the same for all. But never to be forgotten is another great truth: The impetus for honor and honorable actions must come from the top. The officer and the senior officer must set the example.

Integrity, the Essential Ingredient. The essential attribute of the Army and its members is integrity. It is the personal honor of the individual; it is the selfless devotion to duty that produces performance integrity in the discharge of individual missions; and it is the integrity of the Army as a whole in providing its share of the security of the nation in war or in peace.

The Army officer has a public vocation as an official of the government. Members of the officer's unit are sworn to obey his or her lawful orders and, in so doing, perform their own public duty. In time of war, the decisions the officer makes, and the orders he or she issues, may be matters of victory or defeat, life or death. The people of our country place their trust in Army officers, and officers of the sister services, so they may sleep peacefully at night, and so they may pursue their chosen vocations with minimum attention to military matters. The United States could not entrust its security to officers about whose integrity there is the slightest doubt.

There is a reward that accrues to the corps of officers, and to the individual officer, because of the wide acceptance of their integrity. Officers hold the trust of most government officials. Their statements of fact are accepted, and their opinions are respected as sincere. Communities extend to officers many privileges unavailable to the general public because of the high standing of officers and their spouses. There is the important fact of acceptance by honorable members of other vocations, *because he or she is an officer and presumed honorable.* It endures until the officer proves to be unworthy. These valued customs are a priceless heritage bequeathed to officers of today by their brother officers of the past. It is the reward of sustained integrity. Officers of the present era must preserve the code for officers of the future, if the nation is to remain secure in their charge. Integrity generates trust.

The present product of the heritage of integrity of Army officers and officers of the other services was reflected in national polls conducted in late 1986 by the respected Gallup and Harris organizations. These national opinion surveys revealed that our citizens have more trust and confidence in the military than they do in Congress; federal, state and local governments; business; the legal profession; organized labor; the news media; the Supreme Court; the medical profession; higher education; and even organized religion. In short, the military is held in higher esteem than any of the other national institutions. This is the product of sustained integrity and adherence to the officer's code.

Ethics. Much has been written in recent years regarding the need for the Army to adopt a code of ethics to guide individuals in their behavior, with particular emphasis on the need for guidelines to prescribe a proper balance between promotion of self-interest and accomplishment of the Army's mission. Development of such a set of guidelines would be difficult and, at best, would be incomplete, for no one could possibly foresee all the special situations where some guidance might be necessary.

It is proper, of course, for the individual to be concerned with his or her self-interest. Other things being equal, it is to be expected that an officer will take that course of action most likely to result in personal success. In most cases, this course of action should coincide precisely with accomplishment of mission. It is only those instances where personal enhancement and accomplishment of mission are in conflict that give cause for concern.

But is a particular set of ethical guidelines necessary? Read again the earlier words on the meaning of Duty, Honor, and Country as setting the basic standard for performance. How much simpler it is to test one's proposed action against this standard. Is what you are proposing an honorable act? After you have taken it, will you be able to look others squarely in the eye knowing that your honor is untarnished? If so, you are on the right track. Now, examine whether your proposed action, if successful, will accomplish your mission. Will a successful outcome meet the intent as well as the letter of your assigned task, and do so within the time and resource constraints without unnecessary risk? If so, proceed. You will be doing your duty. As a final check, consider the outcome in terms of the Army and our nation. Will the results of your proposed action be in their best interest? An affirmative answer to this question, also, means that by all three measures—Duty, Honor, Country—your proposed action is correct. You may proceed with confidence.

In most cases, the correct course of action as verified by the above checks should also coincide with your own best interests, whether or not you perceive that to be the case. In any event, even if it does not, there still is no problem with a decision. Your Oath of Office, your commission, and your adherence to the code of the Army officer demand that you do what is right, regardless of personal outcome.

THE MILITARY TRADITIONS

There are traditions of military service that have guided its members throughout all the years of our national existence and form an important part of the code of the Army officer.

Tradition of Public Service. As an Army officer, you are a public servant. You go where you are ordered and perform the tasks that your duty requires. In peace you prepare yourself and your subordinates for the requirements of war. During war you lead American troops in battle against the nation's enemies. It is neither the officer nor the Army who decides when a state of war exists; that responsibility is borne by the Congress and the President. But the peace having been forfeited, it is the duty of the officer to assist in restoring it. It may cost the officer's life, and sometimes this occurs at an age at which members of other professions have retired to the garden and the front porch. The military life is devoted to the public service, and the officer is a public servant.

Tradition of Achieving the Mission. Accomplishment of mission is recognized as the primary requirement of the military leader and indeed of all members of the service. The "Army way" of undertaking a mission is to display enthusiasm, boldness, and aggressiveness in getting any job done.

This means big things must be done, if properly ordered or required by the mission assigned. In battle, the attack objectives must be taken and the defense objectives held. Training programs must be carried out effectively so that all are prepared for their tasks. Administrative and logistical responsibilities must be completed at the required high standards.

It means doing the little things correctly, too, as a matter of normal routine. The officer or soldier must be at the station directed at the time required and must wear the prescribed uniform with pride in the proper manner. It means following a directed course of action, and extending cooperation to adjoining units as may be required by the situation.

Whether the task is tremendous in its scope and importance or a routine require-ment, the military person is expected as a matter of course to undertake it as required and complete it up to standard, and on time. In these tasks he or she must accept the hazards of the vocation and the frequent hardships of service. This is the important military tradition that the mission must be accomplished.

Tradition of Leadership. The officer is trained to lead. From your earliest days as an officer the tradition will be ground into you. You will become accustomed to receive and execute missions. This will require you to plan work, to assign missions to others, and then to see that their work is done skillfully and in cooperation with others. As you grow older your training and experience will broaden and increase your capacities; this is generally accompanied by greater responsibilities. Thus the tradition of leadership deepens. Just as you are trained to lead others, you will be trained to be led by others. For no military person can rise so high, or attain so great a position, that he or she is not responsible to another. Military leadership requires ability to develop teamwork and at the same time to be a part of the team.

Tradition of Loyalty. Loyalty is demanded of the Army officer. It extends through-out the chain of command to the President, the Commander-in-Chief. It extends to your subordinates to include the newest private. And it extends to your peers. It must be a true loyalty, and there is an essential reason for it. Members of the corps of officers have the common mission of protecting the nation and our people, which requires the coordinated best efforts of each individual. Even the suspicion of disloyalty would destroy the usefulness of any officer, for no one would trust him or her or give the officer responsibility. It must include the chief whom you may dislike; your peers with whom in a sense you are in competition; and each of your subordinates. Think about it deeply. Once trust is forfeited it may never be regained. The loyalty of officers to the nation, to the Commander-in-Chief, to their seniors, their juniors, their peers, has been traditional in the Army since its very beginning.

The Tradition That an Officer's Word Is His or Her Bond. An officer's statement of fact, opinion, or recommendation must conform fully with his or her belief. You must take adequate care that when you make a statement as to facts you can provide the evidence to support it. If you render an opinion or make a recommen-dation, you must have given sufficient thought to the subject to enable you to reach a reasoned conclusion. All this must be true whether the statements are oral, or in writing, or are just your initials extending a concurrence. The added statement "I certify" must not be interpreted as meaning "something extra" as to truth. Your word is your bond.

Tradition of Discipline. In order to develop discipline within an organization, the leader must set the example of discipline. Since the unit you command is only a part of a larger organization, or of the Army, you must execute objectives or missions that reach you as orders from your own superior officers. The United States Army is a disciplined army. And no army that is undisciplined is worth a nickel of the taxpayer's dollar. An undisciplined army would be worse than useless, for it would constitute a public menace in itself. The tradition of discipline is as deeply ingrained into the mind and heart of the successful officer as the tradition of leadership.

Tradition of Readiness. One of the most striking qualities required of the Army officer is that he or she be in a position of readiness to meet whatever tasks arise, including sudden leadership in campaign and combat. In the broad sense this means that, in the event of surprise action by a new enemy, the officer takes troops into the field to fight effectively. There are countless other such examples in warfare. Unless the nation can rely upon its military leaders to shift their thoughts and actions from a state of peace to the immediate requirements of war our people are being deceived.

The principle applies with equal force to the routines of duty and the smaller things. You must be ready for an unexpected change of station, or duty assignment. You must be prepared to accept and execute effectively new requirements of your mission. The tradition of readiness includes flexibility of mind and mental processes; a willingness to reach out for new ideas; an ever-broadening capacity to undertake and do new things.

Your leadership capability and command efficiency are measured by your unit's readiness. Such readiness includes personnel, equipment, and unit training, to which must be added morale and discipline, which are evidenced when the real test—combat—comes.

Tradition of Taking Good Care of Soldiers. A former Chief of Staff, Gen. Maxwell Taylor, said, "Second only to accomplishing his mission, the officer's duty is to improve the moral, physical, and intellectual quality of his men. . . . The Army is the service which, by the nature of its requirements, attaches the greatest importance to human values. It recognizes man as the basic element of military strength. . . . It creates for them an environment of decent, clean living, intolerant of vice, dissipation, or flabbiness."

The officer who has the best record for accomplishment of battle missions with lowest sick and casualty rates is likely to be one who has cared best for his or her soldiers. This means that members of a command must receive thorough training for their duties; have in their possession the individual and organization equipment and supplies according to their authorization and needs; receive as good quartering and mess facilities as is possible under the circumstances, and except under rigorous field conditions this standard should be no less than healthful and comfortable. They must have available splendid medical support under all conditions of service, including battle, and in any area where troops are dispatched in the world. It means many other things, such as religious guidance and activities, athletic and recreation programs, and advice and help on personal problems including legal counsel. It includes a sound discipline, with proper use of awards and punishment. It involves fairness and justice in all things, including spreading the work load and hazards among all eligible individuals; complete absence of favoritism; promotions to be made on merit—all these things and more.

Tradition of Cooperation. Cooperation is the art of working with others to attain a common goal. This is a daily expectancy of service duties, and it is traditional that cooperation be willing and wholehearted.

Neither a commander nor a staff officer, no matter how senior, can "go it alone." An officer must cooperate with others, and others must cooperate with him or her. In any staff or any command the problems for solution are very likely to involve two or more staff agencies, or a reconciliation of views between the unit commanders who execute a plan and those who plan it. It takes coordination and cooperation to accomplish a mission. The officer who neglects to cooperate with others invites failure.

Tradition of Being a Lady or Gentleman. It is a part of the code and traditional that officers are expected to be ladies or gentlemen. This must be manifest in their moral standards, their conduct, appearance, manners and mannerisms, as well as the professional standards they establish in the performance of duty. It must be displayed in the things they avoid doing. They avoid vulgarity. They do not drink to excess. They do not avoid the payment of just bills or tender bad checks.

The general good of the officer corps demands that all individuals display the qualities of ladies or gentlemen. Great prestige attaches to officers because as a group they have been generally accepted as such. They are accepted to membership in civilian clubs and associations often because of their commission. Their credit rating is high. Their word is accepted in and out of service. Their opinions bear weight. As a group they have the confidence and trust of the people. The officers themselves must guard and cherish this standing, and they must realize that the unfit among them reflect upon and damage the standing of all.

Tradition of Avoiding Matters of Politics. It is traditional, and also required by law, that the Army member avoids partisan politics. This is particularly important for the career officer. The career officer serves in support of national policies without regard to the political party in power, and with equal zeal in his or her effective performance. The Oath of Office requires each officer to serve the elected leaders of the nation, without regard to their political party and without regard to the officer's own political beliefs or affiliations.

It could not be otherwise and must never be otherwise. The armed forces are the final bulwark for the preservation of the Constitution and the security of the nation. We could not tolerate "Republican officers" and "Democrat officers," with a vast switch of positions with each change of party in national power. Loyalties go to the nation and to its form of government.

Tradition of Candor in Making Recommendations. It is a normal experience of Army officers of all grades and degrees of experience to be asked by their commanders, or chiefs, for their opinion or recommendation. Such missions are the daily experience of staff officers, for it is always the commander who makes the decision.

The duty reaches its zenith in the recommendations made by the Chief of Staff and senior members of the Army Staff, and the commanders of Joint and Specified Commands, in their relations with the Secretary of the Army, the Secretary of Defense, and the President, and with the committees of the Congress as they consider legislation governing the armed forces. How far should the military leaders go in advancing their considered views? What is their duty if their views should be challenged? What is their duty if the decision goes contrary to their convictions and their recommendations?

Here is a guide. In his first meeting with the Army Staff, Gen. Matthew B. Ridgway, former Chief of Staff of the Army, had this to say about this vital subject:

"The point I wish to make here, and to repeat it for emphasis, is that the professional military man has three primary responsibilities:

"*First,* to give his honest, fearless, objective, professional military opinion of what he needs to do the job the nation gives him.

"*Second,* if what he is given is less than the minimum he regards as essential, to give his superiors an honest, fearless, objective opinion of the consequences.

"Third, and finally, he has the duty whatever the final decision, to do the utmost with whatever is furnished."

It has never been said better.

RELATIONSHIP AMONG OFFICERS

There is a very special relationship among officers that must be understood as a part of the code. They are appointed into the service for the same general purposes, and therefore have much in common. There is trust between them because they are officers and have subscribed to the officer's oath. An understanding of the status of the officer, and the relationship or responsibility of one officer to all others of the corps, are matters of primary importance. We shall examine these matters.

Officer Defined. In the United States Army there are commissioned officers and warrant officers. Together, they constitute the corps of officers.

The term *officer* has this dictionary definition: "A person lawfully invested with military rank and authority by virtue of a commission issued him by or in the name of the sovereign or chief magistrate of a country." In our Army, commissioned officers are appointed by the President, or in the name of the President, with the approval of the Senate. Warrant officers, who rank next below commissioned officers, are appointed by warrant by the Secretary of the Army.

Your Brother/Sister Officers. The officers of the Army are a cross section of the American public, drawn from all states and sections in representative numbers, and from all classes of the social order. A large percentage are graduates either of the Military Academy at West Point, or of the colleges and universities of the nation. Periodic attendance at service schools, postgraduate studies at great universities for some, extensive travel, and the nature of the duties performed further increase their educational background. As a group, they are subject to the same ambitions, the same variations in viewpoint, even the same human frailties as the people whom they serve. Drawn from the whole nation by a selective process they are fairly (no more and no less) representative of that larger group of citizens that furnishes the leaders in business, professional, and public life. The common denominator that binds this heterogeneous group together is interest in the welfare of the nation and in the national defense.

The corps of officers is strengthened by the bonds of comradeship. It is the desire of all that a new officer succeed, and to aid in attaining that objective for others, many will go to great lengths. It will be taken for granted, when an officer joins an organization, that, commensurate with his or her experience, the officer knows the job and has every intention of doing it well. If the officer fails it is likely to be his or her own fault. Competition exists in the Army as in all life, but it is the healthy striving for professional standing and the good will of associates, not alone for bread and meat. One officer's preferment can hardly be gained at the expense of another since the opportunity to compete is open to all. In the main, the best officers flow to the best assignments and there is room for all. The code of Duty well performed, of Honor, and of Country above self is the unspoken guide with which there is no compromise. It is a high standard. The unworthy eliminate themselves. For those who habitually meet the code, the good will, professional recognition, and associations that ripen into friendships accrue to officers of all ranks and of all ages.

THE UNITED STATES ARMY SOLDIER

The incoming enlisted soldier to the Active Army will represent a cross section of American citizens, within a required age group, and less those found to be ineligible for service because of physical or other reasons. The great majority will be self-respecting, patriotic, decent, good citizens willing to serve our country effectively and well. Their level of education is about the same as those who served during the wars and emergencies of previous years. Their understanding of national and international events will be deeper because of the vast increase in recent years of radio and television news coverage. Most will understand why the turmoil and the wars of our century have not faded into the millennium of peace, as all thoughtful people of all nations have hoped so ardently. In today's all-volunteer Army, every soldier serves as a matter of choice, although the degree of individual motivation may vary. The leader has no choice as to the individuals assigned to his or her jurisdiction for training or for employment on important or hazardous unit missions. The leader's personal success will depend upon gaining the maximum possible performance of duty from each soldier.

The military leader must provide the example of national service and the kind of leadership that the great majority of our young people will follow willingly.

THE OFFICER'S RELATIONS WITH ENLISTED PERSONNEL

Every enlisted member wants to feel certain of getting a fair deal from his or her commander. Indeed, each officer wants to feel that he or she, too, will get a square deal from his or her commander and the Army itself. The Army has its faults. But there are mighty few large American organizations that do better, and none that try harder or have more dedicated professional leadership. The Army must discharge its worldwide missions, and at the same time act with the conviction that it is soldiers who do the Army's jobs and that the motives to which soldiers respond best must be protected and observed. Some of the Army's ways and traditions are not always understood by either its critics or its members. This discussion seeks to clarify a few of the principles.

The relationship between a commander and his or her personnel must be developed to stand the strains of campaign and combat, as well as the less demanding conditions at posts and stations in the United States. There is no precise parallel with other vocations as to this total responsibility against which to evaluate the need for unusually high standards of conduct, including abstentions. The relationship must include mutual trust and mutual respect. For our present purposes our subject is the off-duty, unofficial, and social relationships *on an individual basis* of officers and enlisted personnel.

In our Army, it is strong tradition that an officer does not gamble, nor borrow money, nor drink intoxicants, nor participate in ordinary social association with enlisted soldiers on an individual basis. Aggravated violations of the tradition may be handled under the Uniform Code of Military Justice. All are matters of simple common sense. Here is why. The officer must not have favored associates, or "buddies," chosen from enlisted personnel. To do so would first place in question and then weaken the vital belief in the officer's impartiality. Noncommissioned officers and soldiers want no favoritism whatever in the decisions of their seniors. In following the wise course, an officer may observe that one or more of the enlisted personnel may have an equal or greater educational background, or wealth, or civilian achievement, and several may exceed the officer's own length and variety of Army service. No matter. The officer is the responsible person, the one who leads and directs, with standards to uphold.

The officer need not sorrow as to these truths, nor be embarrassed by them. It is a natural preference that most enlisted soldiers prefer to associate socially or off duty with their own military peers. Experienced noncommissioned officers, whose value in our Army is vast, are certain to support this point of view. There are some on-post and many off-post occasions attended by both officers and soldiers, such as athletic, civic, religious, and fraternal, as well as social events. Good judgment should indicate the wise course to follow under all circumstances.

Even the suspicion of favoritism must be avoided. If an officer has social companions, obvious favorites, or "buddies," among his or her soldiers, and then sponsors one or more of them for promotion, a preferred assignment, or exemption from duty of special hardship or hazard, the officer destroys in the all-seeing eyes of others the essential standard of mutual trust and respect. Resentment by the less-favored will be prompt. The officer's usefulness declines. No officer and no soldier will choose to encourage the belief of personal inadequacy or untrustworthiness by his or her comrades. Indeed, determination to stand high in the judgments of comrades of all grades drives many good soldiers on to acts of great achievement and heroism. There must be no favoritism nor justified suspicion of favoritism. The officer cannot be a "jolly good fellow," nor "one of the boys." If he or she is popular in the minds of subordinates it is a by-product of leadership, human fairness, knowledge, and wise decisions.

These are reasons for the Army traditions that an officer does not gamble, nor borrow money, nor drink intoxicants, nor engage in casual social relationships on an individual basis with enlisted members.*

In today's Army, where women make up an increasingly large percentage of both the officer corps and the enlisted ranks, this matter deserves even closer attention. Since we are all human, there are bound to be occasions when officers, be they male or female, are attracted to enlisted members of the opposite sex. No good can come from any relationship resulting from such attraction. Both the officer and the enlisted member would earn the scorn of their peers for establishing such a relationship, and the effectiveness of both members to the Army would be reduced. To any officer who may think of establishing a relationship with an enlisted member, we can offer only one word of advice: DON'T!

ACTION UPON OUTSIDE PRESSURES

The Army officer must expect to face requests or even demands from civilian sources that we call "pressures." Sought will be a change of an Army action regarding the conduct of its affairs. We are a democracy. Our people are interested in the national defense and in the citizens who are members of the armed forces. When a course of action taken by the Army is contrary to their point of view, some are likely to object. Such objections may come from a newspaper editorial, a letter or petition, or a visit by an individual or group having a common purpose. Members of Congress provide many examples. The company commander, the commander of an Army post or of a major command, or a senior official of the Department of the Army may expect to receive many such applications. Needed are a personal code of action and a manner of proper procedure to apply when such occasions arise.

Dismiss at once from consideration the large number of mere requests for information. The Army is close to the people and many matters of its daily operations are of proper interest to citizens. Included are routine requests from members of Congress, or other officials, who ask for proper information that they wish to supply to a constituent. Be certain the disclosure is authorized and, if so, provide with promptness and courtesy the answer requested. It is routine.

---

*For related discussions see chapter 5, *Your First Station,* and its discussion, THE EARLY DUTY DAYS; chapter 4, *The Officer Image,* with its epilogue, AS A SENIOR NCO SEES IT; and chapter 17, *Responsibilities of Command,* and its main heading TAKING CARE OF YOUR SOLDIERS.

But what of those pressures that seek reversal of an Army action or policy? Are they all selfish, wrong in intent, each to be denied? Not at all. Some may be very worthy objections and suggestions. They may be in the highest public interest. A company commander may receive a letter from a distraught parent about his soldier son or daughter. A post commander may receive a letter from an excited mayor. Required is a consideration of the matter as represented by the outside source, balanced against the facts as known by the Army. New and important facts may be introduced from the outside that were unknown when the action under examination was taken. Army actions are made with judgment but are not infallible. *Still, Army decisions, actions, policies, must not be changed lightly, or merely to accommodate an influential person, for to do so would invite endless confusion.* Even so, when the merits of the case are such as to indicate the justice of a change in a matter of some importance, the proper action may be to make the change. Otherwise, deny it. Choose the course of the Army's best interest, and one with which you can live as an officer worthy of trust.

Investigation of other such requests received from persons or groups, even individuals of importance, are quickly seen as unsound, selfish, and advanced for reasons other than those stated.

The apparent motive may be repugnant. Just determine the facts. Analyze the matter objectively. Remember that an Army action is not to be changed lightly. And take just and fair action. Objective action is necessary, and a sound decision must be reached regardless of the motive behind the objection.

A final bit of psychology may be noted. If you decide to say "Yes" to a request, suggestion, even a demand, do so, and do it gracefully. If you decide to say "No," say it clearly, but say it. Never say "No but maybe—," or "No at this time—"; to give a qualified answer invites reopening at an early date with the whole gamut to run again. When the action is negative, avoid disclosing reasons for your action. Just say something like this: "After considering the facts in the situation that you have presented, I must conclude that the action you seek would be contrary to the public interest. Thank you for your interest in bringing it to my attention." Save your reasons for your commanding officer if he or she should inquire about your action.

There is an exceptional situation that deserves illumination. Assume that a negative action has been taken on a subject of importance. Assume further that an appeal to higher military authority is made, urging reversal of the negative action taken. No junior should be reversed except in those rare instances of real importance where failure to do so would injure the national interest or do a real injustice. Perhaps new facts are brought forth. Perhaps the situation was not fully known by the officer. Whatever the reason, assume that the senior officer decides it is necessary to reverse the action of a subordinate. How should it be done? *The officer must inform the junior of the imminent reversal, with reasons, before any other person learns of the action. Humiliation of the junior must be avoided. Perhaps it would be appropriate to extend opportunity for the junior to change his or her own stand, although the senior must stop short of urging or seeming to force a change of viewpoint. Extend opportunity for the junior to make the announcement of the reversal.* Such instances are uncommon. When reversal is considered to be necessary, the procedure must be done with judgment, lest great harm be perpetrated. The Army must be right and just, even when it is embarrassing to correct an error. Do it only when necessary as an act of justice; but do it right.

STANDARDS OF CONDUCT FOR ARMY MEMBERS

The Army has issued its own publication establishing standards of conduct, AR 600-50, based in part upon Executive Order 11222. These are basic rules, requirements, and prohibitions that are applicable to all active duty officers and soldiers and to retired personnel. This Army regulation is of such high importance, and so broad in its scope, that officers are urged to obtain a copy and place it in their personal libraries for reference.

CODE OF CONDUCT FOR MEMBERS OF THE UNITED STATES ARMED FORCES

The President issued an Executive Order in 1955 that establishes a Code of Conduct for members of the armed forces of the United States while in combat or captivity as a prisoner of war. See also AR 350–30, as amended. The order requires that specific training be given to all members liable to capture to better equip them to counter and withstand enemy efforts against them.

1. I am an American fighting man. I serve in the forces which guard my country and our way of life. I am prepared to give my life in their defense.

2. I will never surrender of my own free will. If in command I will never surrender my men while they still have the means to resist.

3. If I am captured I will continue to resist by all means available. I will make every effort to escape and aid others to escape. I will accept neither parole nor special favors from the enemy.

4. If I become a prisoner of war, I will keep faith with my fellow prisoners. I will give no information or take part in any action which might be harmful to my comrades. If I am senior, I will take command. If not I will obey the lawful orders of those appointed over me and will back them up in every way.

5. When questioned, should I become a prisoner of war, I am bound to give only name, rank, service number and date of birth. I will evade answering further questions to the utmost of my ability. I will make no oral or written statements disloyal to my country and its allies or harmful to their cause.

6. I will never forget that I am an American fighting man, responsible for my actions, and dedicated to the principles which made my country free. I will trust in my God and in the United States of America.

CADET PRAYER

It is fitting that this chapter, *The Code of the Army Officer,* end with the Cadet Prayer of the Corps of Cadets, United States Military Academy, for it states best the true code as to character and conduct that guides all men and women who are privileged to wear our country's uniform. The prayer:

O God, our Father, Thou Searcher of men's hearts, help us to draw near to Thee in sincerity and truth. May our religion be filled with gladness and may our worship of Thee be natural.

Strengthen and increase our admiration for honest dealing and clean thinking, and suffer not our hatred of hypocrisy and pretense ever to diminish. Encourage us in our endeavor to live above the common level of life. Make us to choose the harder right instead of the easier wrong, and never to be content with a half truth when the whole can be won. Endow us with courage that is born of loyalty to all that is noble and worthy, that scorns to compromise with vice and injustice and knows no fear when truth and right are in jeopardy. Guard us against flippancy and irreverence in the sacred things of life. Grant us new ties of friendship and new opportunities of service. Kindle our hearts in fellowship with those of a cheerful countenance, and soften our hearts with sympathy for those who sorrow and suffer. Help us to maintain the honor of the Corps untarnished and unsullied and to show forth in our lives the ideals of West Point in doing our duty to Thee and to our Country. All of which we ask in the name of the Great Friend and Master of men.—Amen.

4

The Officer Image

Oh wad some power the giftie gie us
To see oursel's as others see us!
It would frae mony a blunder free us,
And foolish notion.—Robert Burns.

An individual who has selected the Army as a career, and who has made a conscious decision to adopt wholeheartedly and without reservation a life under the Army officer's code, will wonder what actions he or she can take, or avoid taking, to demonstrate that he or she is a worthy member of the Army's corps of officers. This chapter is a thought-provoking stimulant for self-analysis. It has been developed as a study in human relations . . . "to see ourselves as others see us," and to weigh the importance of such impressions formed in the minds of others. Opportunities will abound to apply and to benefit by this concept in all assignments that pertain to an Army career.

The officer is an official of the Army, and hence of our government, and has authority sufficient for the discharge of assigned responsibilities. He or she receives a duty assignment and a mission, or series of missions, and is required to complete these tasks up to standard, on time, with the personnel and the equipment provided for his or her use. The officer's duty may be free from hazard or may involve the gravest hazards from enemy action; it may be routine or of critical importance. It may involve technique, or tactics, or strategy; or the exercise of leadership or management with respect to other tasks. The accomplishment of mission—no matter what obstacles are encountered—is the dominant point to remember about an officer's responsibilities.

On most Army assignments, the officer has subordinates who are responsible for the execution of such of his or her responsibilities as he or she may delegate to them. In turn, the officer is responsible to a superior officer who is also his or her rating officer for the rendition of evaluation reports. There are still higher levels in the chain of command. The officer will also have associates, in the usual case, who have parallel missions to perform for the same chief, or commander, with whom the officer must act in smooth coordination and effective teamwork. The officer's responsibilities include those assigned by his or her immediate commander. There are also staff officers with whom smooth and effective official relations are essential. The conclusions or the impressions—the *image*—formed about an officer in the minds of these other human beings are important, and their shaping is the purpose of this discussion.

It is obvious that an officer's day involves many contacts with other people, on duty or off duty, personal or official, casual or of high importance. Each such contact may influence for better or worse the impression, or image, the officer makes upon others. With the passage of time, and as the observations increase in variety and number, the image deepens and fills out in the minds of others. Each passing day has had its effect, and each new day presents its opportunity.

What is the image we should like to project? Some introspection here may prove quite rewarding. Before we consider means to communicate the image, let us (following the advice of the Apostle Paul) examine ourselves, and where we find a bit of rust or tarnish let us first diligently remove it.

What are the characteristics of this image we would portray in the minds of others? And how may these essential qualities be presented for observers to identify? To change the point of view in the quotation from Robert Burns, how can we be seen by others as we wish to be seen?

INTEGRITY

Personal integrity is the foundation upon which the standing of an officer rests in the minds of subordinates, associates, and superior officers. It is simple, basic, personal honesty. It is the hallmark of the honor code of the United States Corps of Cadets at West Point. See General MacArthur's Preface to this book. In chapter 3, *The Code of the Army Officer,* integrity is shown as the essential ingredient of the Army code; it accounts for the sense of security taken for granted by our citizens whenever the Army is involved.

What is there about a person of integrity that identifies him or her to others? He or she possesses the self-discipline to see clearly the honorable course and to follow it. Such a person obtains and considers all the facts bearing upon a decision, or choice, and as a result his or her acts and orders are fair and just, as a matter of standard practice. Decisions are objective and impartial, free from favoritism or bias, or desire for personal gain. If such a person makes a mistake, he or she takes the rap for it. When credit is due others, they get it. When asked for an opinion, after gathering and evaluating the facts, that person says what he or she thinks, and means it. That person's word is good. His or her signature on a document is sufficient proof of personal belief in its correctness. Such a person of integrity proceeds in good conscience, in full retention of self-respect.

There is *performance integrity,* as well as personal integrity. It is the very best effort in achievement of mission within your capability. Your performance represents you and creates your personal duty image. In the Army, as in other vocations, some duties are more interesting, or more rewarding, or more pleasant, or more hazardous than others. Whatever your preferences, be certain that the record you build is developed by performance. If you seek an image of excellence, you must perform all duties with excellence. In any case, you may as well understand that the Army insists upon standard results on all assignments.

Does this seem to be a goal unattainably or unnecessarily high? Or unrealistic? Think awhile before cutting it back in importance. You are an official of government. You are a leader and you must achieve your mission through leadership of others in such a manner as to command their respect and their wholehearted cooperation. You must get results, and this means next week and next month, as well as today and tomorrow. Under predictable circumstances, you may be obliged to make decisions and direct actions that involve victory or defeat, life or death. As a member of the corps of officers, you may some day find you must make decisions that conceivably could determine the survival of the nation or even the freedom of our people. The personal and the performance integrity of each officer of the corps of officers is an asset beyond price in the life and security of our nation.

How can you convince others of your personal and performance integrity, in word and deed? In such matters, people cannot be deceived for long, if at all. How shall we go about establishing this favorable image?

Let us think for a moment of *good will,* an intangible having a very high dollar value in commerce and industry. Good will has been defined as "the sum of an infinite number of favorable impressions." A pertinent corollary: "The value of a product lies in the hidden ingredient, the *honor* and *integrity* of the manufacturer." Now we may return with clearer insight to the building of the favorable image. It is formed day by day, through innumerable contacts or observations, of large things and small ones, routines and emergencies, off duty and on duty; each one in some degree will influence the building of the image or impression formed about an officer. If on each occasion you are loyal, objective, fair, and unswerving in devotion to duty, the favorable image will grow. (And if, on some occasions you fall short of these goals, the blemish will be retained.) An image is taking form.

PROFESSIONAL COMPETENCE

The importance of integrity as a base or foundation for a proper image of an officer cannot be overemphasized. But standing alone it is not enough. A structure must be built upon it.

The officer must know his or her job. The soldier has a right to expect an officer to be proficient in the military arts of his or her arm or service, and of the organization of which both are members. The soldier expects to receive effective instruction. The professional competence of an officer must be demonstrated in daily contacts with seniors and subordinates in the same manner and for the same reasons that the officer's integrity must be held under continual observation. The image of professional competence of an officer must be earned.

In our Army, the educational system and the professional development programs provide splendid opportunities throughout a long career. Successive, planned assignments are opportunities for increasing experience and capability. In each of our wars and emergencies, our system of officer selection, training, and development has produced in abundance officers of all grades who provided the leadership that met and removed the perils to our nation.

In this year, as in the past, and into the future as far as we may peer, each officer assuming the responsibilities of an assignment will desire to develop in the mind of each subordinate a favorable answer to the question: "Does my commanding officer know his or her job?" Your own commander, chief, or boss will also seek an answer to the same question.

How do you go about securing this favorable image of professional competence, of knowing your job? You must know your mission and the time set for its successful completion. You must know your personnel, their degree of training, their training shortcomings. You must know your equipment and its condition, and if there are shortages in items that can be replaced, you must do so. You must possess the priceless capability of identifying the right thing to do, and then decide the timing to commence as well as to complete the mission.

First, you must take your unit through the training process of individual and small unit training to bring them up to the standard required. Here they learn the fundamentals. You must be an effective teacher, or trainer, for no leader can effectively command until his or her subordinates are trained, disciplined, and ready to act in a determined, coordinated effort with others. "This is what we are to do," you tell them; "This is the way to do it," you show them; then direct them, "Now you do it," and under your guidance or the guidance of your assistants the soldiers undergoing instruction acquire their individual skills. Your image begins to form at the start of these instruction periods. You demonstrate your professional capability as you impart your knowledge in the training process.

Second, upon completion of the training cycle there may follow a period in readiness to respond promptly for whatever emergency action may be directed by our government; or there may be missions concerned with the national security; or there may follow prompt deployment in battle. There is the ever-present need to keep sharp and ready the ability of the unit to function effectively in combat. For this reason, as opportunity offers, there will be a return to training to refresh knowledge, or to correct weaknesses as they are disclosed, or to undertake new or more advanced training. You may be a leader, a commander, a teacher, an administrator, or a staff officer, as your mission requires. Whatever your assignment, you must be competent in your field for your grade and the extent of your training, with display of foresight, and with standards kept high, in whatever situation or mission you face. As observations multiply and experience broadens, the image you will inspire in others becomes more pronounced.

Third is caring for your personnel. This is a part of professional competence that also requires knowledge. A leader must care for subordinates to be successful. Never forget it. This factor is not a popularity contest where, for example, you know you soldiers like beer, so you arrange to expend unit funds to get them beer. Such superficialities have little application. *It means that you know your subordinates:* their abilities, training, integrity; their debts and their family situations; their health, their habits, their weaknesses; and, of course, what you may expect from each of them as to performance of duty. Knowing your subordinates, you are in an improved position to get from each his or her very best performance. *You must train your soldiers;* soldiers who are really trained will be far more successful in achievement of mission, and far less likely to be killed or wounded through the unwise acts of the inexperienced. *You must look after their personal welfare;* this includes many matters that may give concern to soldiers, or relieve their worries, or assist them in helping themselves. There is much good in the timely and proper provision of creature comforts, including on occasion the cold beer, and more essential items. These are things to do all day long, all week long, always.

Can any person know everything about the needs of his or her assignment? Of course not. You must learn as you go, recognize the new problem, and devise ways to meet it. You think, study, confer, and plan, today and tonight, for the missions of tomorrow, or next week, or later. You must be ready with planned action for your responsibilities as they arise.

As illustration of the need to be prepared for entirely new conditions and missions, consider the mission assigned to General Harkins in Vietnam, and the transfer of these responsibilities to General Westmoreland and later to General

Abrams. Decide for yourself whether in all our national history any leader, military or civilian, has received a more unique mission. United States forces were sent there to help—only to help—the people of Vietnam fight to retain their freedom. Our representatives could "advise" or they might "urge," but they could not "require" and they did not "command." The increase of our forces and the acceptance of ground, air, and naval action in combat did not change the status of advisors to the South Vietnamese forces. Its reference here is to illustrate the need of the officer to be ready to meet the unexpected. In the ever-changing conditions of our world, this may indicate a common situation of the future. Who can foretell? The certainty is that other situations and conditions will arise of importance to our nation and our allies, and that officers must be able—and willing—to handle with professional skill whatever threats may develop.

The responsible officer must identify the new opportunities and hazards, grow in professional capacity, and rise to the requirements of his or her mission. The assignment of an important military mission provides a fertile and rewarding field for all of one's wisdom, and all of one's foresight and courage. If the security of our nation, and our allies, seems important to you during these troubled years, look forward to your part in future history with anticipation and with determination. There are rewards as well as trials.

As time passes and these various cycles are completed, impressions about the professional competence of the officer form with clarity in the minds of all observers. The image of the officer has developed swiftly. He or she has been identified as a person of integrity and professional competence.

But there is more.

THE COURAGE TO ACT

You must prepare yourself to take action, often swift, sometimes hazardous, occasionally into the unknown. Your missions are infinite in variety. As a commander in combat, you may be required with your unit to defeat an enemy before the enemy can defeat you. Or to seize a hill, cross a river, hold a position against strong attack. Or to unload a ship, build a road or a bridge, or clear a harbor. There is a need also for courage to act on assignments other than command, in peace as well as in war. Peacetime decisions involve courage, guts, and, in a controversial matter under development or discussion, the need to fight—with hard logic—for your own well-considered point of view. The courage to act when action is needed is an essential requirement for an officer whatever the nature of the mission or assignment.

There are preliminaries to action, of course. They vary as to the time available for development of plan and deployment for execution of plan from many months (as for the plans for the cross-channel invasion of Europe in World War II) to the instantaneous response to opportunity or emergency (as the crossing of the Remagen bridge over the Rhine, or the swift execution of the invasion of Grenada). There must be a consideration of facts and the reaching of a decision—*what is to be done?* There must be planning—*where* and *how* will the action be taken, *when,* and *by whom?* Orders must be issued to subordinate leaders so they will know their own missions, the timing, and the essential coordination with others.

These essential steps—deciding, planning, ordering—are preludes to action. They are essentials in the practice of command, or of being in charge in an administrative assignment. They are as necessary to the officer in the discharge of a mission as gasoline is to an automobile climbing a hill, or sunshine to growing corn. Opportunities to acquire these leadership skills are abundant. They are taught, logically and ably, at service schools and colleges, in maneuvers and training exercises. But without downgrading the importance of these institutions, their instruction is but a preliminary to the action that an Army officer must be prepared to accomplish.

In battle, and even in situations other than battle, there may be a vast difference between the requirements of the military leader in comparison with leaders in other fields. *In all decisions, the military leader must be right!* He or she must be right because there will be no second chance. The fact of being right may bring victory or success, instead of defeat and failure. Indeed, it may make the difference between life and death. It is an essential part of Army philosophy and training that the mission must be achieved. "Being right" must be a part of the code of the Army officer, which requires as a matter of course that you apply to vital responsibilities all of your knowledge and your training, and all of your courage, to reach and direct a sound, workable solution at the instant needed.

We reach a quality, or a strength, that rises above character building and professional knowledge. Not all persons of fine physique, of splendid character, of excellent academic education, and of thorough professional training and patriotic motives will make the best officers. Consider it carefully.

The officer who is a commander must be the one to order: "FOLLOW ME!" or "FIRE!" or "GO!" *He or she must have the courage to act at the very instant action is needed.* The commander will realize the hazards and the potential losses, and will measure the danger of defeat as well as the fruits of victory. There is no room here for a timid soul. Lost would be the brilliant thinker with faint heart who reaches a perfect decision tomorrow on a critical situation or a fleeting opportunity demanding action today. These are the situations that separate the best officers from those not quite up to the highest standards.*

Now we may put into place the keystone of the conclusions that we have sought to develop in the inquisitive, searching, questioning minds of subordinates, associates, and superior officers who are also rating and reviewing officers. Without this final quality there may be defeat instead of victory, failure instead of success, despite an officer's integrity and professional competence. There must be *courage to act decisively* at the most favorable time, as well as in a sound manner. We reach the final conclusion as to what the officer should establish as his or her image: "When things need doing, this officer gets them *done right*—and fast!"

PERSONAL CHARACTERISTICS THAT AFFECT YOUR IMAGE

Your personal integrity and professional competence and your courage to make the right decisions at the right time are the bedrock qualities upon which your image will be built. You cannot succeed as an officer without these, but there is more. The image you form in the minds of others also is the product of many lesser traits and attitudes and mannerisms. Attention to these matters also is important as you seek to convince others of your worthiness to be a member of the corps of officers.

Officers and soldiers of the Army of today have the same human aspirations, likes and dislikes, strengths and frailties, as they had a decade ago or ten decades

---

*In military actions, choices may not be sharply defined. In our Army, there are two ever-present responsibilities of a commander that may seem, at times, to oppose one another:

First, the requirement for accomplishment of mission; second, the safety and preservation of the command.

Quoting General Wolfe before Quebec, in 1759: "Next to valour, the best qualities in a military man are vigilance and caution."

The truth must be understood. Prompt, decisive action—so strongly advocated—is never to be confused with ill-conceived, foolhardy action with needless sacrifice of lives. Aggressiveness, which invites severe, avoidable losses, is not invited by the principle. Wisdom must accompany the swiftest action.

ago. All are responsive to human appeals, and some are prone to succumb to human temptations. Listed below are a number of human characteristics, or qualities, that are especially worthy of consideration. It is people who make the Army, and people who win its victories. Human relationships are important, always.

Guidelines. *Be Strong on Principle.* This lets people know where you stand. It helps create a feeling of confidence among associates.

Be Coolheaded. Learn the facts, establish the truth, then stand up and be heard. Those who do are sought out for preferred assignments.

Be Willing to Adjust. Without compromising mission or basic issues, there is the need to hear and consider the views of others or the interests of others. This often involves negotiation or adjustment in order to gain understanding and agreement.

Be Certain to Preserve Unity. Disrespect and distrust develop disunity, and disunity invites defeat. Recognize and treat with respect members of the sister services. Recognize as fact that branches of the Army other than your own are important and treat their members with the respect that is their due. The good officer builds unity.

Don't Be a Diehard. Be not the last to identify a truth or adopt the new. While a military leader must often follow the hard right instead of the easy wrong, there can be an avoidance of sheer bullheadedness. (A bullheaded person has been defined, we wish we knew by whom, as a person with very determined ideas, many of them unsound, to which he or she clings with more than usual tenacity.)

But Don't Be a Timid Soul. Don't fear to advance your considered views, or to take issue, or to point out a fault, just for fear of causing annoyance. Don't go along with the crowd for fear of expressing a contrary view. Don't hold back to let another grasp the lead. The retiring person on the fringe of discussion, who may have the skill to reason and arrive at sound conclusions but lacks the fortitude to express or defend them, will have little influence on history or the outcome of battles.

Nor a Know-it-all. On a par of ineffectiveness with the timid soul is the know-it-all, or wise guy, who has a glib solution to all problems with or without knowledge of the subject or time for consideration. In a meeting this person is the one to advance an immediate solution without waiting to hear the facts bearing upon the problem. "Off with his head," before hearing the evidence. Or, if a platoon leader, such an individual may direct an unwise action because he or she failed to explain the task and listen to the suggestions of the NCOs. Neither the timid soul nor the wise guy will have much, if any, influence on history, and such influence as the latter does have is likely to be negative. The timid soul will supply nothing, either good or bad; but the wise guy may do much harm until his or her associates learn better. Aggressive advancement of hasty conclusions may sound plausible and be adopted, only to develop bugs at a later time.*

Seek the Loyalty of Subordinates. It is not enough to seek it, this loyalty, you must earn it. Fair treatment and the human touch will help. If there is something good to which your soldiers are entitled and are not getting, go after it and get it. Stand up for your troops or for your employees. While you are not to conceal their transgressions, or let their offenses go unpunished, you can certainly identify and

---

*Attributed to Gen. Freiherr von Hammerstein-Equord of the German Army of pre–World War I, is the following advice about officer classification. *The Army Officer's Guide* is pleased to perpetuate it. "I divide my officers into four classes as follows: The clever, the industrious, the lazy, and the stupid. Each officer always possesses two of these qualities. Those who are clever and industrious I appoint to the General Staff. Use can under certain circumstances be made of those who are stupid and lazy. The man who is clever and lazy qualifies for the highest leadership posts. He has the requisite nerves and the mental clarity for difficult decisions. But whoever is stupid and industrious must be got rid of, for he is too dangerous."

encourage their strengths. Be the first to get the full share of improved facilities for living, for work, or for recreation, if you can, and seek opportunities for your subordinates to advance their own goals. When the "boss" does these things his or her rewards may be abundant. And when he or she fails to do so, the penalties may be severe. When subordinates have thoughtful reason to respect and trust their commander, or chief, the results can become important.

Associate with the "Comers." It is a good idea to identify the officers of an organization who stand high officially, have attained a promising record, and seem destined to go forward rapidly. They are the ones worth knowing. They should be the most interesting associates, too, because of their probable breadth of experience and knowledge. Have a wide acquaintance, of course, and seek to gain the good will, trust, and respect of all. But identify yourself more closely with those whom you consider to be headed for big and interesting things.

Avoid the Political. Be somewhat guarded in your political comments. Officers are entitled to have as firm opinions on matters of politics and national policy as any citizen. They have the same right and duty to vote and record their convictions. But it is unwise for officers to become too outspoken in approval or disapproval of either political party, or of the leading members of either party. Indeed, officers are prohibited from using disrespectful language about government officials, for which see chapter 25, *Rights, Privileges, and Restrictions.* Army officers serve in turn Democrat and Republican administrations. Soldiers must be nonpolitical and serve each with equal zeal. The higher the grade they achieve, the more important becomes this caution.

The "First Name" Problem. There has developed in the Army an excessive use of first names by seniors to juniors, officer to officer, even officer to soldier. The problem deserves consideration.

In the prescribed uses of military courtesy, members of the service are addressed by their proper titles on all official occasions. On social occasions, the practice should be governed by good taste. In athletic sports, or hunting and fishing trips, or other activities wholly unconnected with official relationships, it is merely two or more kindred spirits out for the enjoyment of a hobby. This discussion pertains to the use of first names on official duty.

This is not to advocate the "stuffed shirt" attitude, or the martinet. It states a principle with which you can live. As leaders, officers have stern duties involving discipline, reward and punishment, selections for promotion, selections for favored assignment or hazardous duty. *Officers must never play favorites or by their actions permit the suspicion that they are doing so.* Officers simply cannot be on terms of personal familiarity today, and tomorrow, when duty requires that they admonish an individual, revert to the official title.

There is just one rule to follow on this first-name business in official relationships: *Don't use it.*

Influence of the Officer's Spouse and Family. A spouse's attitude and conduct within the military or civilian community in which the officer performs his or her duties may have a profound bearing upon the officer's effectiveness. If the spouse exerts a wholesome, normal, pleasant influence, he or she will meet the basic standard. There are some assignments involving extensive semiofficial relations with others not in our own service where the role of the spouse is extremely important. A helpful reference is chapter 8, *The Social Side of Army Life.* Objectionable incidents may nullify an officer's otherwise outstanding record.

Conclusion. We seek through the above illustrations of common traits of the good and bad variety to illustrate a principle. Military reputations are not built alone on schools attended, battles fought, or assignments held satisfactorily. There are important personal factors. As the officer goes about building an image in the minds of others, he or she should be mindful of them.

AVOIDING TARNISH ON YOUR IMAGE

It is not sufficient to strive through job performance to construct a good image. You must also strive to avoid any tarnish to the image you have fashioned in the minds of others. About this latter we can be very precise. Officers may be accorded preferment on the intangibles of faith, confidence, and the like. But they are punished, held back, or eliminated in many cases by definite acts of transgression or shortcomings. Stated below is a summary of those shortcomings that can tarnish an image and mar or seriously injure an otherwise exemplary record. Therefore, a guide to the avoidance of tarnish on your image is quite easy to prepare: Conduct yourself in such a manner as to avoid the likelihood of any of the following things appearing on your evaluation reports or in your other military records, or even causing raised eyebrows among your associates.

Shortcomings in Personal Conduct. These shortcomings can be identified and corrected.

Intemperance in the Use of Liquor. Excessive drinking, or the results thereof, probably has ruined the careers of more officers than any other single cause. Drinking to any degree of intoxication while on duty is punishable and can reflect severely upon an officer's record. Similarly, excessive drinking when off duty, particularly when your resultant behavior reflects on the service, or your intemperance lowers your following performance of duty, can result in a marred record. The single beer at noon can develop into a martini. Remember that it is far easier not to start a bad habit than to stop one, and that it is easier to avoid a bad episode than to undo one. Few commanders or seniors of any grade insist upon their officers being teetotalers. Rather, they will expect that there will be about the same percentage of users and abstainers as in our general population. An officer who wishes to remain in the Army and enjoy a successful career, however, must avoid excesses in the use of liquor and avoid permitting its immoderate use to reduce the effectiveness of his or her work or to warrant criticism for personal conduct.

Financial Difficulties. Officers have the same sort of family and personal financial responsibilities and difficulties as other citizens. It is not to be expected that many officers will avoid debt at one time or another or many times in their lives. Debt is credit and a standard practice in our economy. Trouble arises when the officer assumes greater obligations than he or she can discharge within the time limit of the agreement to pay. When debts have not been paid when due, it is a frequent practice for merchants to write to the commander or to The Adjutant General, and ask for assistance in making the collection. The receipt of a number of such letters is very harmful to the reputation of an officer. It indicates a deficiency in conducting personal affairs and implies a weakness in ability to administer affairs of the Army.

Avoid financial difficulties! Live within your income—with some to spare, if possible. Maintain close scrutiny of your spouse's checkbook as well as your own, and avoid writing checks on the assumption that "The money will be in the bank by the time the check clears." Should you for some reason become submerged in debt, make an exact list of the indebtedness, go to your creditors, and seek to arrange a plan of payment that is agreeable to them and within your means. If complaints are likely to be filed, go to your commanding officer and lay the cards on the table. He or she may be able to suggest to you a solution. At least your commander will know that your intentions are honorable.

The Army cannot permit its officers to acquire a general reputation of being poor credit risks, for such a condition would reflect upon all who wear the uniform. Such action uncurbed in a few officers would harm the general credit standing of all. The officer in debt must have a definite understanding with creditors as to when and how much he or she can pay on overdue accounts. Having reached such an agreement, the officer must meet these obligations or negotiate a new understanding. The worst action an officer can take is to permit the creditor to reach a conclusion that the debtor seeks to evade an honest and just debt. More than a few officers over a period of years are considered for elimination because they have failed to observe these simple practices.

Transgressions of Moral Codes. Such transgressions constitute another avenue to acquire tarnish on the image and stand a fine chance of being mentioned on evaluation reports. For the male officer, be honorable in your dealings with all women. Avoid association with prostitutes; such association is crude and indicative of a lack of moral strength befitting an officer. Avoid also entanglements with other men's wives; treat all women as you would like your wife or your sister to be treated. The shadows of AIDS, venereal disease, divorce, contempt of one's fellow officers, and disciplinary action overhang all immoral associations. A similar admonition is appropriate for female officers. Rating officers generally will comment adversely upon officers who have openly and flagrantly violated the codes of conduct, or do so under conditions that bring discredit upon an organization or group of officers.

Closely akin to this situation is gross vulgarity or obscenity in any form. By definition, an officer is a gentleman or a lady and is expected to avoid the use of coarse, crude, or vulgar language. Habitual use of vulgarity indicates first, that the person speaking is too lazy to search for the right descriptive word and second, that the person speaking is no gentleman or lady. Avoid the use of vulgarity yourself and avoid continual association with vulgar persons. Neither can do your reputation, your image, or your evaluation report any good.

Officers are expected to be gentlemen or ladies in their personal as well as their official conduct. Tarnished images and low evaluation ratings inevitably will follow transgression of moral codes.

Violations of Honor. An officer's word, signature, or initials of concurrence must be backed by facts, accuracy, and honor. There must never be a doubt as to the truth of any statement that bears his or her authentication. The officer's oral or written word is his or her bond. If your statements, either written or oral, contain opinions as well as facts, take care to identify the opinions for what they are.

The acceptance of an officer as an honorable individual by all who meet or know him or her is traditional in the Army. Thus it has always been and thus it must always be if the Army is to retain its status as a reliable instrument to implement national policy. It goes without further emphasis that acts of deliberate cheating, lying, or quibbling cannot be condoned. Violations of honor will surely be filed in the minds of others as well as noted on the evaluation report or other records.

Misconduct. Misconduct or misuse of official position are items that surely will affect the evaluation report and tarnish the reputation of an officer; serious frauds, minor acts for personal gain, personal use of government property, abuse of privileges, and rowdy or disorderly conduct are examples of these weaknesses.

RELATIONSHIP WITH THE "BOSS"

The preceding discussion talked about the personal integrity, the professional competence, and the courage to make decisions that must be the foundation upon which your image is built. We have discussed also the lesser traits, attitudes, and mannerisms that can affect that image, as well as selected shortcomings that almost certainly would have an adverse impact on that image. Let us turn briefly now to consideration of your relationship with your commander, the "boss," for it is your image in his or her eyes that determines your evaluation report ratings, upon which all else hinges.

It is a fact that the military leader must be pleased with the work of an officer, and satisfied with that officer's personal standards of conduct, before signing an evaluation report containing numerous flattering entries. There are some very human and commonsense elements to be considered about earning good reports. We shall discuss some important ones. But first, let us be sure one fact is clearly understood: *The "boss" will be pleased only when there has been effective execution of duty throughout the period.* Make no mistake about that. Our subject has nothing to do with laughing at poor jokes, dating an unattractive daughter, performing subservient actions, or making unworthy efforts to avoid the results of poor work.

Much has been written about the way a senior officer should treat junior officers and soldiers. Now we seek to put the shoe on the other foot. Beyond the conventional prescribed actions and attitude, how should the junior treat the senior?

Treat your commander or chief, your "boss," as a man or woman. At the same time do your own part of acting as an adult. You are both mature, trained officials of government. The junior officer is not a child standing in the presence of a stern parent, nor an ignorant tyro facing a person of unique skill. You are a capable officer of one grade, presumably, associated in a joint undertaking with a more experienced officer who holds a higher grade, or higher relative rank. In most cases a senior will be older in years. Treat your chief honorably and respectfully behind his or her back as well as face-to-face. Be businesslike. Stand on your own feet.

Respect the authority of your commander. Understand his or her mission and responsibilities, for your own will be a fraction of the total. Your commander's success depends, in part, upon the results of your work. Teamwork means harmonious effort with all members of the organization—not just with the "boss."

Keep your chief informed. Give him or her the information needed as to your own progress and give it straight, clear, and on time. Don't conceal bad news, or try to slip it past. Don't embellish the good news. Your chief needs essential facts for his or her own planning and for coordination with other subordinates. There are few furies equal to that of a military leader who makes a wrong decision that was based with logic upon incorrect or misleading reports from a subordinate.

Apply standard military courtesies and customs of the service, neither over-drawn nor underdrawn. Know these things and apply them sensibly. Let the chief set the pace in the degree of formality or informality of routine, official contacts. Especially let this be the case as to outside-of-duty relationships. In these latter contacts a chief may call you "Bob," but be certain to address him or her as "Captain." Extending compliments to your chief is in poor taste, and will be so regarded. Don't do it! Knowing how to work for and with your commander is a very important goal, and this brief discussion of commonsense matters of military courtesy deserves careful compliance.

Know your chief's military and personal background. Identify his or her human likes and dislikes. Commanders are human, to the same degree as subordinates. Be attuned, or responsive, to these characteristics of your chief, as you also avoid acts or mannerisms that serve no real purpose and that you learn are upsetting to him or her. An understanding of the person for whom you work is helpful in developing proper teamwork.

Some commanders issue broad, mission-type orders and encourage subordinates to exercise considerable latitude as to the method or procedure for execution. Others give detailed instructions that they wish followed meticulously. Do not take advantage of the one with unnecessary delay, or a bit of laziness; and don't rebel at the latter because you prefer your chief to work with a looser rein. In fact, don't fight this problem at all. Learn what your chief wants and conform to it.

Engrave in your mind: You are a part of your commander's team, not he or she of yours. You are the head of your own team, with your own subordinates. Develop your team wisely.

SUMMARY

So, to return to the question at the beginning of the chapter, what is the image we are attempting to project to others? It is the image of an officer who has great personal integrity, who is professionally competent and is not afraid to make decisions, whose personal traits make him or her a pleasure to be around, who scrupulously avoids acts or situations that could cast a shadow on the image, and who can be depended upon as a loyal member of the team. Strive for these goals and you may be assured that the image you are projecting is of the highest caliber. It is the image you should seek.

THE NATIONAL IMAGE OF THE OFFICER CORPS

The consensus of our citizens as to the integrity and the professional competence of the corps of officers of the armed forces has a vast national importance. While it is our elected civil leaders who make the war-or-peace decisions, it is the officers of the armed forces who provide the military leadership required for such peace-preserving or peace-restoring missions. If trust and confidence in our officers were to be weakened, our civil leaders would face severe handicaps in taking the courageous action that the best interests of our nation may require. Equally serious would be the reluctance of our citizens to serve or to entrust their sons or daughters to the armed forces. The importance of universal trust in the integrity and the professional competence of our military leaders of all grades, and of all services, should be very clear to thoughtful people. These qualities involve the nation's security.

What is not so clear, however, is the manner in which this total image is acquired by most citizens. Individual opinions about all officers are likely to be formed from observation of a small number. No person could observe more than a tiny portion of the total number of officers. A reason for this truth is that officers are seen in uniform, which aids the generalization that this one lieutenant (captain or major, colonel or general) must have a similarity to all others of his or her grade. Hence, each officer has a very important influence upon the beliefs developed about all officers in the minds of observers. The nation's trust in its military leaders is a priceless asset that all officers must protect.

Lest a reader gain the impression that all Army officers must achieve the standards and standing of a Marshall, Eisenhower, or MacArthur, or of any of the renowned leaders of today's great Army, be sure to understand that officers are not expected to become "supermen." But they are required to be individuals of integrity, of unquestioned loyalty to their country, of courage both mental and physical, and of high professional competence. Their acts and their achievements should help to create in the minds of all thoughtful observers the impression that they possess these attributes. This is the "image" of national importance, to which each officer contributes to a degree greater than he or she may realize.

LOOKING FORWARD

Why is the individual and corps image of officers so important? Because a sound image is essential for effective leadership. Good soldiers stay with good leaders, and satisfied soldiers reenlist. Or they return to their civilian vocations with pride in their service. The nation's military missions require an abundance of dedicated, capable, trusted, respected officers, noncommissioned officers and other grades who can surely be relied upon to get the jobs done, wherever they occur and however prolonged or difficult the task.

The Army places its greatest trust and its highest expectations upon the capabilities and the determination of its officers and enlisted personnel. They must have the most effective weapons and equipment, of course. There must be an adequate allowance of time for training and for development of teamwork. When this stage of readiness has been attained, and missions have been assigned in combat or in support of combat objectives, it is the officer who is the leader. In time of combat, missions involve real hazard, for the enemy is as determined to avoid defeat as we are determined to inflict it. Soldiers fight best when they are led best. They will risk most when they have confidence in the integrity, the professional skill, and the wisdom of the orders of their officers. These intangibles are included in the image formed day by day in the minds of noncommissioned officers and soldiers as they observe their officers, and in the minds of junior officers as they observe their seniors. Be sure this truth is understood. Then strive to earn an image of which you may be proud. Battles are won, and peace restored, by officers, noncommissioned officers, and soldiers, working together in the attainment of national objectives. The need for a wholesome national image of the corps of officers should be clear.

As we look into the remainder of the 1980s, and the years that extend beyond, it is wise to glance again upon Robert Burns and evaluate ourselves according to his ageless wisdom—*to see ourselves as others see us*. Weapons will change through these coming years, and techniques will be modified as swiftly as increased knowledge will require. The officers of these coming years must keep pace. They must continue to provide military leadership for the nation's security and the completion of its military missions. The actions that win the approval of soldiers, and the motivations that encourage them to give their finest service, will remain unchanged. The officer who aspires to a high image will observe the importance of the simple virtues of integrity, of loyalty, and of knowing his or her job, and will demonstrate the courage to act. Whether you are in your first or your twentieth assignment, you must give your best. Your image will form progressively as the result of what you are and what you do. There can never be a lessening of the importance of these truths.

This chapter has been developed to assist thoughtful officers to prepare themselves to stand with pride and confidence beside thousands of their fellow officers of the Army and the sister services, from all components and all origins of initial appointment, in dedicated national service. They are to be found in abundant numbers. As long as our nation possesses them, it is secure. They are citizens of character, persons who know their jobs, dependable individuals. They are men and women of action with courage to act swiftly and wisely when action is required. Their image will be lasting and it will be good. It is such officers of the present and the future for whom this chapter has been written. They are the ones who count.

AS A SENIOR NCO SEES IT*

The following is the text of an address by Sgt. Maj. John G. Stepanek to graduates of the Basic Course of the U.S. Army Transportation School, Fort Eustis, Virginia.

---

*Credit is extended to *Army Digest*, August 1967.

While the address was given many years ago, the thoughts expressed have a timeless quality. They succinctly sum up the thrust of this chapter.

I feel a tinge of regret that I am not young enough to be sitting out there as one of you. You have so many years of challenge and adventure to look forward to. So many of these years are behind me.

Soon you will meet your platoon sergeants, your first sergeants, your sergeants major, your other noncommissioned officers and your troops. What do we expect from you as officers, commanders, leaders?

We expect of you unassailable personal integrity and the highest of morals. We expect you to maintain the highest state of personal appearance. We expect you to be fair—to be consistent—to have dignity, but not aloofness—to have compassion and understanding—to treat each soldier as an individual, with individual problems.

And we expect you to have courage—the courage of your convictions—the courage to stand up and be counted—to defend your men when they have followed your orders, even when your orders were in error—to assume the blame when you are wrong.

We expect you to stick out your chin and say, "This man is worthy of promotion, and I want him promoted." And we expect you to have even greater courage and say, "This man is not qualified and he will be promoted over my dead body!" Gentlemen, I implore you, do not promote a man because he is a nice guy, because he has a wife and five kids, because he has money problems, because he has a bar bill. If he is not capable of performing the duties of his grade, do not do him and us the injustice of advancing him in grade. When he leaves you, or you leave him, he becomes someone else's problem!

Gentlemen, we expect you to have courage in the face of danger. Many of you will soon be in Vietnam where there are no safe rear echelons. During your tour, opportunities will arise for you to display personal courage and leadership. Opportunities could arise from which you may emerge as heroes. A hero is an individual who is faced with an undesirable situation and employs whatever means are at his disposal to make the situation tenable or to nullify or negate it.

Do not display recklessness and expose yourself and your men to unnecessary risks that will reduce their normal chance of survival. This will only shake their confidence in your judgment.

Now gentlemen, you know what we expect from you. What can you expect from us?

From a few of us, you can expect antagonism, a "Prove yourself" attitude.

From a few of us who had the opportunity to be officers, and didn't have the guts and motivation to accept the challenge, you can expect resentment.

From a few of us old timers, you can expect tolerance.

But from most of us you can expect loyalty to your position, devotion to our cause, admiration for your honest effort—courage to match your courage, guts to match your guts—endurance to match your endurance—motivation to match your motivation—esprit to match your esprit—a desire for achievement to match your desire for achievement.

You can expect a love of God, a love of country, and a love of duty to match your love of God, your love of country, and your love of duty.

We won't mind the heat if you sweat with us. We won't mind the cold if you shiver with us. And when our cigarettes are gone, we won't mind quitting smoking after your cigarettes are gone.

And if the mission requires, we will storm the very gates of hell, right behind you!

Gentlemen, you don't accept us; we were here first. We accept you, and when we do, you'll know. We won't beat drums, or carry you off the drill field on our shoulders. But, maybe at a company party, we'll raise a canteen cup of beer and say, "Lieutenant, you're O.K." Just like that.

Remember one thing. Very few noncommissioned officers were awarded stripes without showing somebody something, sometime, somewhere. If your platoon sergeant is mediocre, if he is slow to assume responsibility, if he shies away from you, maybe sometime not too long ago someone refused to trust him, someone failed to support his decisions, someone shot him down when he was right. Internal wounds heal slowly; internal scars fade more slowly.

Your orders appointing you as officers in the United States Army appointed you to command. No orders, no letters, no insignia of rank can appoint you as leaders. Leadership is an intangible thing; leaders are made, they are not born. Leadership is developed within yourselves.

You do not wear leadership on your sleeves, on your shoulders, on your caps or on your calling cards. Be you lieutenants or generals, we're the guys you've got to convince and we'll meet you more than halfway.

You are leaders in an Army in which we have served for so many years, and you will help us defend the country we have loved for so many years.

I wish you happiness, luck and success in the exciting and challenging years that lie ahead.

May God bless you all!

Part Two • Your Life and Family

5

Your First Station

You have selected the Army as a career or have at least determined to sample Army life by a tour of active duty. You understand you will be ordered to report for duty at an Army post. Beyond that, all is hazy and perhaps somewhat mysterious or unsettling. What is an Army post like? What will happen to you when you arrive? How do you know how to get started?

This chapter is aimed at removing some of the unknowns and perplexities encountered by newly appointed officers in reporting for duty at their first Army station. At the same time, there is discussion of several matters of interest concerning the process of becoming established in the military environment. As will be made clear, it is neither complex nor difficult.

INITIAL ASSIGNMENT EXPECTANCY

The initial assignments of newly appointed officers are dependent upon their source of commissioning and their branch of assignment. Following is the current expectancy, included as a general guide.

Graduates of the United States Military Academy. The initial assignment of USMA graduates will be to their basic course of sixteen to twenty-four weeks' duration, which includes both general and branch-oriented training prior to reporting to a unit. Or, depending upon quotas, physical fitness, and volunteering, they may first attend either the nine-week Ranger Course or the three-week Airborne Course, or both. Ranger training is limited to combat arms, signal officers, and officers going to Ranger units. There is no set sequence.

Graduates of the ROTC Program. ROTC graduates also attend a basic course of sixteen to twenty-four weeks, depending upon branch assignment, upon entry to active duty. They may volunteer for further training in courses like the Airborne Course and flight training.

Distinguished Military Graduates. Distinguished military graduates who accept a regular commission are trained similarly to USMA graduates. They have a priority for early attendance at their basic course.

Graduates of the OCS Program. OCS commissioned officers upon graduation attend the basic officer course of their commissioning branch prior to reporting to their first duty station.

Doctors and Lawyers. Doctors and lawyers when called for active duty will usually receive training involving orientation, specialization, or bringing the officer up to date (refresher), depending upon their experience and professional background.

Warrant Officers. All candidates for appointment as warrant officer are required to attend a Warrant Officer Entry Course (WOEC) of six weeks' duration conducted at Fort Sill, Fort Rucker, or Aberdeen Proving Ground. This is an OCS-type leadership and ethics course. Following completion of this course, students attend technical functional training at a proponent service school. Aviators are promoted to warrant officer upon successful completion of their flight training program at Fort Rucker, Alabama. Physician's Assistant warrant officers are promoted to that grade upon successful completion of their training at the Health Services Command at Fort Sam Houston, Texas.

Suggestions When the Initial Assignment Is on Temporary Duty (TDY). Newly appointed officers may expect to be sent to attend a basic course, or other initial instruction, on temporary duty (TDY). (See chapter 10, *Army Posts and Stations.*)

Under normal conditions, sufficient time is allowed between delivery of orders for assignment and the date of reporting for duty to adjust personal affairs and prepare for Army service.

For TDY assignments there is a travel allowance for the officer. There is no provision for the travel of family members, nor are government quarters provided for a spouse who accompanies the officer at personal expense. Officers attending a basic course are usually assigned bachelor officers' quarters (BOQ). A prescribed maximum weight of personal property may be shipped to the TDY station at government expense. (Consult chapter 21, *Travel Allowances.*)

Suggestions When the Assignment Is Under Permanent Change of Station (PCS) Orders. Orders for permanent change of station may be the first orders received upon coming to active duty, or they may follow completion of the first TDY assignment.

Under orders for PCS the officer collects an allowance for personal travel; there is an allowance for the travel of specified family members including spouse and children; the shipment of household goods and personal property within a prescribed weight limit is at government expense.

Chapter 10, *Army Posts and Stations,* will be very helpful. Many station commanders send to officers under orders to their command a booklet of information more complete than contained in this chapter. If this information is not received, or there are questions not answered in chapter 10, it is customary to write a letter to the station adjutant and request the information desired. Include the number and date of your assignment order and the date you are to report for duty. The letter should include the information the adjutant will need to answer your questions.

The Initial Purchase of Uniforms. Prior to reporting to your first duty station, you should procure at least a minimum supply of uniforms. (And at the same time abandon any idea you may have had of making a saving from the uniform allowance for other purposes.)

Information about the officer's uniform, including procurement, is contained in chapter 22, *Uniforms of the Army.* The uniform allowance is stated in chapter 20, *Pay and Allowances.* Uniforms may be purchased at any Army post having a clothing sales store or post exchange; as an officer under orders to active service, you will be permitted to purchase from these establishments by identifying yourself and showing a copy of your orders.

After reporting, and learning the expected conditions of service and duty, the total requirements may be added as found necessary.

However limited your initial supply of uniforms, see to it that what you wear is clean and neatly pressed, with insignia clean and placed accurately, shoes clean and neatly shined. For the time being, let care make up the shortages that you will soon correct.

WHAT YOU MAY EXPECT UPON ARRIVAL

You may expect to be received at your new station with matter-of-fact courtesy and efficiency. The reception of individuals into a unit or station complement, whether newly appointed as an officer, warrant officer, noncommissioned officer, or soldier, or as an experienced old-timer, is regarded as an important duty by commanders. It is carefully planned and required to be carried out with courtesy, understanding, and efficiency. The unit commander will often appoint a sponsoring officer to write to you in advance and to assist you upon arrival. The commander knows the importance of your first impression.

If your first station is on a TDY assignment to attend your branch service school, as is most likely to be the case, you may expect to be one of many officers arriving on the same day at about the same time. There normally will be signs directing you to where you should report, but in case of doubt don't hesitate to ask for directions. You will find a reception center, designed and staffed to process all incoming student officers as rapidly and efficiently as possible.

The needs of newcomers are usually anticipated and prompt information is provided; uncertainties will be removed by prompt answers to questions. There will be no hazing or embarrassments for the mere fact of your newness. Newness is not a novelty in the Army of today. Enter with confidence and you will be made welcome, for your service is needed. If you should encounter an individual of the reception detail who is thoughtless and seems uninstructed, do not let the episode influence your conclusions about the Army or its programs. He or she will be the exception. Read your instructions carefully and complete them promptly. If there is something unclear, just inquire. People expect to help you, and they will help you. Perhaps they were the new ones a few weeks earlier. Later, when you are helping to receive newcomers, do your part to be helpful and understanding.

GETTING ESTABLISHED

You now know what your initial duty assignment is likely to be, and you have some feel for what you may expect by way of reception at your new station. But how do you go about actually reporting for duty and getting established? It is not complicated, but there are certain matters that must be promptly attended to so that you will be able to devote your time and your attention to your new duties.

How to Report for Duty. Orders assigning an officer to a station for duty include a date of reporting. You are complying with the order if you reach the station and report to the proper official prior to midnight of the date prescribed. But you should arrive during the hours of the ordinary business day, if at all practicable. Try to arrive before noon and as early as 0900 if you can. This will allow you to complete many important official and personal arrangements on the day of reporting. Try to report not later than 1600. If the date of reporting lies within your discretion, you should avoid arrival at a new station on Saturday, Sunday, or an official holiday.

Should an officer report in uniform? Or is it acceptable practice to report in civilian clothing? Mindful of the usual long automobile drive and the difficulty of appearing neat, freshly pressed, and with everything in top condition, the choice needs discussion. The correct garb is the uniform, clean, neat, well pressed, like the book says. *Suggestion:* Consider arriving in the area on the afternoon before you are due for reporting, stay at a convenient motel, and make the necessary preparations. A good start is important. Reporting in civilian clothing is not unknown in this day and age, but a good start is as important today as any time in the past.

Carry with you several copies of your orders. At least two copies will be needed for your travel pay voucher, and other copies will be needed for administrative purposes at the new station. Ten should be sufficient. A copy should be placed in your personal records file.

Proceed to the post or station headquarters to report for duty.

In those cases where a large number of officers report within a short period, as at a training center, port of embarkation, or other large troop concentration, the reception of arriving officers may be handled by a receiving committee. In such a case the formality of reporting consists only of presenting yourself at the proper office (which is usually indicated by signs), presenting your orders, signing the register, and receiving instructions. A member of this committee usually handles quartering and messing arrangements and provides, often in a mimeographed order, the information the newcomer requires. At a later time a meeting may be held at which the commanding officer or a representative addresses the group for purposes of organization or orientation. When this procedure is followed be certain that you have received all of the instructions that should be in your possession and that you understand them thoroughly.

At other times the arrival of a single officer or a small group of officers is but an incident in the day's work, and no such elaborate machinery will be set up. Proceed to the post headquarters and the office of the adjutant. Remove your cap, knock, enter, and, if the adjutant is senior in grade to yourself, salute and report: "Sir, Lieutenant —————— reports for duty"; at the same time extend a copy of your orders. If the adjutant is the junior in grade, as an Army custom it is proper to state: "I am Major —————— reporting for duty." It is likely that the adjutant will welcome you to the garrison and give you the information you will need. He or she will arrange a time for you to call upon the commanding officer and arrange for you to meet your subordinate commander. The adjutant will tell you your quarters assignment or whom to see to obtain this information. It is probable that he or she will arrange for the delivery of your baggage to your quarters. Request a copy of the local garrison regulations, a map of the reservation, and any other information normally supplied to new arrivals. When you leave the adjutant there should be no doubt in your mind as to what you are to do initially and when and where you are to do it. Your first task, more than likely, will be to establish yourself in your quarters and prepare yourself for the duties to come.

Getting Established in Quarters. After reporting for duty, immediately get yourself established. If the assignment is for TDY, this may mean only the location of the BOQ and moving into your assigned room. If you arrive on PCS orders, and you have family members, getting established will involve the assignment and occupancy of government quarters, or the rental or purchase of other housing.

Most Army posts operate guest houses, which are available for short periods to newly assigned personnel until they can find permanent housing. Rates are nominal. Space is usually reserved, when available, by application in advance of need to the Billeting Officer.

Subject to some limitation, like the unit going on maneuvers, the officer is normally given a reasonable period of time to arrange for personal affairs. (See *Permissive TDY,* under OTHER ABSENCES, in chapter 24, *Authorized Absences.*) Your unit sponsor may have made some arrangements for you. In the case of reporting to a major post for a school or for further assignment to a unit, it is best that you arrive a few days earlier than required. A major post will have persons to assist you, like the Billeting Officer, and will have an Army Community Service Center, at which you can get a wealth of current information, an issue of cots, blankets, and so on, to help your family, and many other kinds of assistance.

Collection of Travel and Transportation Allowances. Soon after arrival at the new station, you will wish to submit vouchers for collection of cash allowances such as those for your personal travel, family travel if such travel has been made, dislocation, per diem, or any other allowance, such as the uniform allowance, to which you may be entitled. Inquire of the Personnel Officer for the procedure and request assistance as needed. Copies of travel orders will be required.

Identification (ID) Card. The officer and family members are required to possess an identification (ID) card, and to show it upon request, in order to patronize the post exchange, the commissary, or the post motion picture theater. In addition, a special card is required for family members to obtain out-patient care or hospitalization at station medical facilities. The Personnel Officer will provide assistance in obtaining them.

Garrison Regulations. Make a careful study of the local garrison regulations. They usually contain much useful information on local conditions, facilities, and conveniences, as well as requirements that will assist you in making adjustments to the new environment. Comply with them fully.

The Post Exchange. A visit should be paid to the post exchange soon after arrival. It is a community store operated under the supervision of the Army and Air Force Exchange Service. At most stations the exchange consists of a general store, a tailor shop, shoe repair shop, cafeteria, and barber shop. It supplies other services for the benefit of the officers and enlisted personnel of the garrison. It is noteworthy that profits resulting from the operation of the exchange revert to the organization for expenditure as provided by regulations primarily for the benefit of the troops through the Central Welfare Fund.

The Commissary. Nearly every Army post has a commissary; certainly the post of your first assignment will have one. Operated by the U.S. Army Troop Support Agency, commissaries are very similar to commercial supermarkets. If your first assignment is on TDY, you may not feel the need to use the commissary. If you have your spouse and family with you, however, you certainly will want to do the bulk of your grocery shopping at the commissary. Foodstuffs and other household items may be purchased at the commissary at significant savings.

Post Transportation Officer. The post Transportation Officer will assist you with problems associated with the movement of your personal and household property and any claims occasioned by loss or damage.

Learn Your Way Around. Study a map of the post and locate the important buildings, roads, training areas, and recreational facilities.

Reporting Time for Starting to Work. Instructions from the adjutant or your immediate commander will indicate the time allowed you to become established.

THE EARLY DUTY DAYS

Arrival at a first station and assignment to duty with a unit provides an exceptional, interesting challenge. We shall examine it in detail to provide some light for guidance.

Start with this initial conviction of personal confidence: The Army selects its officers most carefully and trains them so they will succeed. The education and the training programs at West Point, at Reserve Officer Training Corps units at our colleges and universities, at Officer Candidate Schools, and at the branch service schools where most new officers go for initial active duty training are all most carefully conducted. Although all newly appointed officers will have more to learn, a state that continues throughout the careers of all officers, each officer should start with confidence in his or her preparation.

Commanders of companies and battalions are fully aware of the problems encountered by newly appointed, incoming officers. They know the additional instruction each will require. Do understand that the success in command responsibility sought by your new commander, or chief, depends in part upon your own success. *Let this sink in—real deep:* Everyone gains when the incoming officer adjusts quickly and identifies with new associates as a trustworthy, capable addition to the command. Further, all stand to lose if the newcomer should fail. It is fully understood that no officer could possibly know everything upon arrival. For this reason the newcomer will certainly receive detailed information, probably some material for study, and time to complete his or her preparation. The procedure is based upon infinite experience, free from mystery. Always—if you don't know—inquire, and don't hesitate to ask officers of your own rank and your subordinates.

The next essential step is up to you, and no one can do much to help, except to provide the needed time and opportunity. At once, start getting acquainted with your people, whether officers, enlisted members, or civilians. If you are to command the unit, start with the senior who will become your number one assistant. Learn his or her name and use it. Learn his or her background, special training, service experience, and aspirations. Invite his or her cooperation and his or her suggestions, which you will need. Never belittle yourself in doing these things, nor seem to boast, but explain your background, too, so he or she can judge wisely how best to advise you. Similarly, meet and talk with your other officers and noncommissioned officers, learn and *use* their names, and learn their service training and background. As time is available, talk with each soldier in the same manner. These interviews should be informal, objective, and impersonal, but keep in your mind that you are inquiring, searching, learning, and starting to build a new team with you as chief. A basic principle of leadership is to know your personnel, and the step described is essential at the very start.

When you start your new responsibilities, be very sure to understand the mission of today and tomorrow, next week, even next month. Your commander, or chief, will inform you. Go over the mission with your senior subordinate. You may find it wise to hold a discussion meeting with your noncommissioned officers, hearing their suggestions or special problems. This procedure starts the development of mutual understanding and teamwork and is one good way of avoiding initial mistakes. It should not be long before you are prepared to say something like this, with confidence: "This is our job for tomorrow ——————. This is the way (and place and time) we will do it. Sergeant Jones, your mission is ——————. Sergeant Smith, you have the special mission of ——————." And so on with clarity, organization of work, and teamwork. Finally, "Any questions? Make your own preparations and I will meet you here ready to go at 0700." Without cautious delay, take the baton of command in your own hand, and develop quickly the correct attributes of a leader.

Finally, and it is important, there is learning and adjusting to the "Army Way." It is a good way and need be neither confusing nor frustrating. Meet and become acquainted with your fellow officers in your quarters or theirs, at the open mess, at work, at battalion meetings, official or social. Although there may be some good-natured jesting, there is no period of hazing nor of probation. Each has been new. They will take for granted that you know your job and that you are determined to do it well. They hope you will succeed, for your success will help them.

All of the above guidance is essential. It works. The Army knows how to welcome and to prepare the new officer. If you have completed the training process, you can do the job. Never doubt it. Give it your best thought and your best effort. You will find help and guidance as it may be needed. But do make good. You are serving the nation.

OFFICIAL CALLS

The adjutant or other qualified officer will inform you of the local policy about official and social calls. Don't be apprehensive about them. They serve useful purposes in the military community because of swift changes of personnel.

Refer to chapter 6, *Military Courtesy,* as to required calls. Refer also to chapter 8, *The Social Side of Army Life,* for information about calling cards and social calls. Unless you have calling cards, delay their purchase until after reporting to learn the local custom.

ADJUSTMENT TO SERVICE LIFE

After the hurried experiences of reporting for duty, getting established, meeting new people, and starting to work, there arrives a time to take stock. There are things to learn and things to do by the bachelor officer as well as the officer arriving with a family. The new Army spouse will share in these opportunities. It is a good time to review other chapters in this book: chapter 3, *The Code of the Army Officer;* chapter 4, *The Officer Image;* and the established service standbys, chapter 6, *Military Courtesy;* chapter 7, *Customs of the Service;* and chapter 8, *The Social Side of Army Life.*

There are basic differences between the life and experiences of the Army officer and those of a person of similar education and background in civilian employment. An officer does not hold an "office hours" job; your responsibilities will continue around the clock although on many assignments you will follow established hours. You are expected to observe and to uphold officerlike standards at all times. You do not shed your responsibilities at 5:00 P.M., as you leave for the day, and you devote the hours to the duties that your responsibilities require.

Adjustment to Post Life. A sincere desire on your part to contribute your efforts and talents to appropriate post activities wherever they are desired or needed is a sound philosophy to adopt from the start. As a member of a garrison you will find some of your greatest pleasures in participation in the community, athletic, and social events that are provided, as well as in the performance of your duties.

Early Membership in the Officers' Open Mess and Club. At most stations all officers are members of the officers' open mess and club, and in many instances membership for new arrivals is automatic. A modest monthly fee is charged. Early contact should be made at the club office to learn of local facilities, membership policies, and costs. For further information refer to chapter 7, *Customs of the Service.*

The "Good" Station and the "Poor" Station. Some Army stations are ideal. Some are less desirable than others from the standpoints of climate, locations near or away from cities, geography, size, and other matters. But within the meaning of this discussion, the descriptions *good* or *bad* are to be found in the mind of the individual.

Resolve to take each station in stride, getting the most from each in professional progress and personal satisfaction. You will soon develop the mixed emotions of experienced officers—always hating to leave a pleasant station but eager for the challenges and experiences of a new one.

Scorn the Habitual Critic. You will harm your personal standing in the eyes of worthy fellow officers by associating more than casually with the continual complainer and critic. Most organizations have one or more of this type. Such individuals are almost certainly of small capacity and mediocre record and deserve the low esteem in which they are held. Correct them if they work for you. Avoid them if they don't.

Personal Records File. The day of arrival is not too soon to start a permanent file of personal papers and records. Start with Department of the Army orders covering your initial assignment. Add to it all official documents that pertain to you as an individual. Notes may be added of important matters that may require later reference. Add to this file photographs of environmental things that you may find of interest in later years, not forgetting pictures and notes concerning other officers who have interested you particularly. Twenty years hence when the stirring events of today have retreated into the background, you will appreciate the opportunity of refreshing your memory on the numerous friendships and interesting events experienced during your career. Keep a record of the names, grades, and permanent addresses of your several commanding officers and the dates of your service with them. Such a file will serve many useful purposes.

REASSIGNMENT

As an Army officer, you must expect periodic changes in station assignment and in duty assignment. The nature of the Army mission and Army service makes it inevitable. Each officer will attend one or several service school courses. Oversea service is by roster and rotation so there is a reasonable sharing of this duty. Some assignments have a standard or a maximum duration. Always the work of the Army must be done, and its mission is under continual change. For these reasons among others, you should be prepared for unexpected change of station and duty assignment.

These periodic changes provide advantages to you as an officer. Your experience is broadened. Your acquaintances are multiplied. You will have the opportunity to see and enjoy different sections of our country, as well as nations on other continents. Each change extends an opportunity to make a new start and earn a better record.

Action upon Receipt of Orders for Change of Station. The officer on duty confronted with reassignment must take prompt steps for relief from present responsibilities as well as arranging personal affairs prior to departure. A clean break must be made from all responsibilities.

There are few shortcomings more injurious to an officer's standing than leaving a residue of unfinished official business to annoy and confuse the officer's successor and his or her commander. Since an evaluation report will be prepared on your departure it is doubly important that you make arrangements for relief from current responsibilities completely and efficiently. Clearance must be obtained for all property and fund responsibilities. All unfinished transactions such as disposition of unserviceable or lost property, vouchers for fund expenditures, and the like, must be set forth clearly and fully, for responsibility will not be finally terminated until these matters are completed. Individual and organizational records that require action by the responsible officer must be brought up to date before departure, or be completed by mail after departure. A clear picture of the mission and responsibilities must be passed on to your successor so that he or she may start with essential information.

Personal bills and obligations must be satisfied and clearance from the post obtained. It is especially important that obligations to civilian merchants be paid before departure, or that, prior to that time, definite arrangements acceptable to the merchant be made for deferring payment.

Farewell calls should be made upon the next two senior commanders, upon other Army associates as is considered appropriate, and upon civilian friends who have extended their welcome. Drop around at the various offices where you have had frequent official transactions and say a pleasant farewell to all.

On the day of departure, check-out must be made with the organization to which assigned and with post headquarters.

6

Military Courtesy

Life is not so short but that there is always time enough for courtesy.—Ralph Waldo Emerson.

Courtesy is essential in human relationships. It stimulates harmonious association of individuals, smooths the conduct of affairs, and adds a welcome note to all manner of human contacts, civilian as well as military. It pertains to wholesome relationships between juniors and seniors, between young and old—with all persons. The importance of favorable impressions of others is discussed in chapter 4, *The Officer Image.* Courtesy includes as an essential element a full and proper appreciation of the rights of others. Military courtesy includes special acts and ceremonial procedures, which are prescribed in official regulations.

Our subject is far more inclusive than the newcomer or the poorly informed person might consider to be the case. It includes the respects paid to the national flag and the National Anthem; the courtesies appropriate for a soldier to extend to an officer or a junior officer to extend to a senior officer, as well as the answering courtesies paid as a matter of course by the senior; the honors extended to high military or civilian dignitaries; and finally, the honors and respectful procedures extended to the military dead. There are many things to learn about military courtesy; by learning them you will replace the embarrassments of ignorance with the confidence of knowledge.

The official sources from which the subjects discussed in the chapter are extracted are the following documents:

FM 22–5	AR 840–10
AR 600–25	DA Pam 600–5.

The courtesies enjoyed within the service include as a matter of course all those common acts of civility, good breeding, and thoughtfulness observed by ladies and gentlemen of the American scene. There are related subjects discussed in this volume of special interest to the officer and the officer's family. Reference is made to chapter 7, *Customs of the Service;* and to chapter 8, *The Social Side of Army Life.* To add depth to understanding give thoughtful consideration to chapter 3, *The Code of the Army Officer.* When you understand those chapters, you should see more clearly that there is nothing wrong with being military or with military courtesy; you will understand that the prescribed courtesies are a part of the ceremonial procedures that contribute color and dignity to our lives; they are a part of the discipline needed for the attack to succeed and the defense to hold; and they are a part of the comradeship that binds together service members of all grades and ages who share the common responsibility of the nation's security.

An officer is expected to be a lady or a gentleman, and ladies and gentlemen have been defined as persons who are never intentionally rude.

THE CORRECT USE OF TITLES

Each member of the Army has a military grade, private to general, and this grade becomes his or her military title by force of regulation and custom. In official documents a member's grade, or title, always accompanies his or her name. In conversation it is also used, and below are listed several illustrations. Through custom and usage, military titles are used between civilians and the military just as custom has established the usage of "Doctor," or "Professor," or "Governor."

A person who has attained a military title carries it permanently, if so choosing, including into retirement.

Titles of Commissioned Officers. Lieutenants are addressed officially as "Lieutenant." The adjectives "First" and "Second" are not used except in written communications.

The same principle also holds for other ranks. In conversation and in nonofficial correspondence (other than in the address itself), brigadier generals, major generals, and lieutenant generals are usually referred to and addressed as "General." Lieutenant colonels, under the same conditions, are addressed as "Colonel."

Senior officers frequently address juniors as "Smith" or "Jones," but this does not give the junior the privilege of addressing the senior in any way other than by the senior's proper title.

"Ma'am" may be used in addressing a female officer under circumstances when the use of "sir" would be appropriate in the case of a male officer.

All chaplains are officially addressed as "Chaplain" regardless of their military grade or professional title.

Warrant Officers. The warrant officer formally ranks below second lieutenant and above cadet. He or she is extended the same privileges and respect as a commissioned officer and differs only in that there are certain regulated restrictions on command functions. The warrant officer is the Army's top-grade specialist and is addressed as "Mister" or "Miss (Mrs.)," as appropriate. Under less formal situations, warrant officers are often addressed as "Chief."

Titles of Cadets. Cadets of the United States Military Academy are addressed as "Cadet" officially and in written communications. Under less formal situations, they are addressed as "Mister" or "Miss."

Noncommissioned Officers. Sergeants major are addressed as "Sergeant Major." A first sergeant is addressed as "First Sergeant." Other sergeants, regardless of grade, are addressed simply as "Sergeant," while a corporal is addressed as "Corporal." Officers generally address privates as "Jones" or "Smith." The full titles of the enlisted members are used in official communications.

Use of Titles by Retired Personnel. Individuals retired from the armed services not on active duty are authorized to use their titles socially, and in connection with commercial enterprises, subject to prescribed limitations. Official signatures will include the designated retired status after the grade, thus: "USA Retired" will be used by members on the U.S. Army Retired List (Regulars); "AUS Retired" will be used by those borne on the Army of the United States List, and nonregulars on the Temporary Disability Retired List. (DA Pam 600–5, *Retired Army Personnel Handbook.*)

THE SEVERAL MILITARY SALUTES

History of the Military Salute. Men of arms have used some form of the military salute as an exchange of greeting since the earliest times. It has been preserved and its use continued in all modern armies that inherit their military traditions from the Age of Chivalry. The method of rendering the salute has varied through the ages, as it still varies in form among the armies of today. Whatever the form it has taken, it has always pertained to military personnel, and its use has been definitely restricted to those in good standing.

In the Age of Chivalry the knights were all mounted and wore steel armor that covered the body completely, including the head and face. When two friendly knights met it was the custom for each to raise the visor and expose his face to the view of the other. This was always done with the right hand, the left being used to hold the reins. It was a significant gesture of friendship and confidence, since it exposed the features and also removed the right hand—the sword hand—from the vicinity of the weapon. Also, in ancient times the freemen (soldiers) of Europe were allowed to carry arms; when two freemen met, each would raise his right hand to show that he held no weapons in it and that the meeting was a friendly one. Slaves were not allowed to carry arms, and they passed freemen without the exchange of a greeting. In the Middle Ages gentlemen often went about clothed in heavy capes under which swords were carried; upon meeting a friend, the cloak was thrown back by raising the right arm, thus disclosing that the right hand was not on the sword hilt. The civilian counterpart of the salute is manifested in various ways such as raising the hand when greeting a friend, tipping the hat when meeting a lady, and using a sign of recognition between lodge members. This sign is always one of greeting between friends and is given willingly. The military salute is given in the same manner—that of pride in giving recognition to a comrade in the honorable profession of arms. The knightly gesture of raising the hand to the visor came to be recognized as the proper greeting between soldiers, and was continued even after modern firearms had made steel armor a thing of the past. The military salute is today, as it seems always to have been, a unique form of exchange of greeting between military personnel.

The Different Forms of the Salute. There are several forms in which the prescribed salutes are rendered. The officer normally uses the hand salute; however, when under arms he or she uses the salute prescribed for the weapon with which armed. Under certain circumstances, when in civilian clothes, the member salutes by placing the right hand over the heart (see the accompanying illustration); if a male officer is wearing a headdress, he salutes by first removing the headdress and holding it in his right hand such that the hand is over the heart while the headdress is over the left shoulder.

In this chapter, unless stated otherwise, the hand salute is intended.

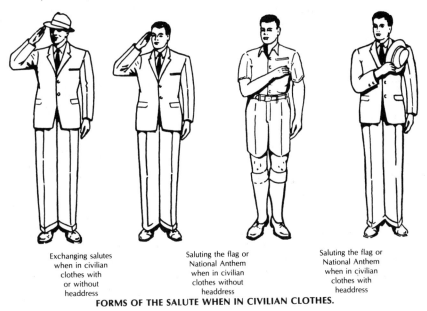

Exchanging salutes
when in civilian
clothes with
or without
headdress

Saluting the flag or
National Anthem
when in civilian
clothes without
headdress

Saluting the flag or
National Anthem
when in civilian
clothes with
headdress

FORMS OF THE SALUTE WHEN IN CIVILIAN CLOTHES.

When to Use the Hand Salute and the Salute with Arms (AR 600-25). All Army personnel in uniform are required to salute at all times when they meet and recognize persons entitled to the salute, except in public conveyances such as trains and buses or in public places such as theaters, or when a salute would be manifestly inappropriate or impractical.

Salutes will be exchanged between officers (commissioned and warrant) and between officers and enlisted personnel. Salutes will be exchanged with personnel of the United States Army, the Navy, the Air Force, the Marine Corps, and the Coast Guard entitled to the salute. It is customary to salute officers of friendly foreign nations when recognized as such. Civilians may be saluted by persons in uniform when appropriate, but the uniform hat or cap will not be raised as a form of salutation.

Military personnel under arms will render the salute prescribed for the weapon with which they are armed, whether or not that weapon ordinarily is prescribed as part of their equipment.

If the exchange of salutes is otherwise appropriate, it is customary, although optional, for military members in civilian clothing to exchange salutes upon recognition. Civilian personnel, including civilian guards, do not render the hand salute to military personnel or to other civilian personnel.

Except in formation, when a salute is prescribed the individual either faces toward the person or colors saluted or turns the head so as to observe the person or colors saluted.

Covered or uncovered, salutes are exchanged in the same manner.

If running, a person comes to a walk before saluting.

The smartness with which the officer or soldier gives the salute is held to indicate the degree of pride the member has in his or her military responsibilities. A careless or half-hearted salute is discourteous.

Methods of Saluting Used by Officers. The hand salute is the usual method. While in most instances it is rendered while standing or marching at attention, it may be rendered while seated, e.g., an officer seated at a desk who acknowledges the salute of an officer or soldier who is making a report.

The salute by placing the right hand over the heart is used under three conditions. At a military funeral all military personnel dressed in civilian clothes use this form of salute in rendering courtesies to the deceased. Male members of the services in civilian clothes and *uncovered* (without headdress) and female members in civilian clothes, *uncovered* or *covered* (with headdress), salute this way during the National Anthem, *To the Color,* or *Hail to the Chief.* While in the same dress, this salute is used in paying homage to the national flag or color. Males in civilian clothing who are *covered* stand at attention, holding the hand over the heart with the headdress held in the right hand over the left shoulder as a courtesy to the National Anthem or to the national flag or color.

Execution of the Hand Salute. Do you *really* wish to salute correctly; to demonstrate to others that you are an officer; to show that this sign of recognition and greeting between military members means something to you? You may read the technical details below, but set about it in this manner. Before the instant arrives to render the salute, stand or walk erectly with head up, chin in, and stomach muscles pulled in. Look squarely and frankly at the person to be saluted. If you are returning the salute of a soldier, execute the movements of the salute in the cadence of marching, *ONE, TWO.* If you are saluting a superior officer, execute the first movement and HOLD the position until the salute is acknowledged, and then complete your salute by dropping the hand smartly to your side. Do these things correctly and you will derive many rewards. Your soldiers will be quick to notice it and will vie with you in efforts to outdo their officer—a particularly healthy reaction. Thus you may set the example, which may then be extended to other matters.

To execute the hand salute correctly, raise the right hand smartly until the tip of the forefinger touches the lower part of the headdress or forehead above and slightly to the right of the right eye, thumb and fingers extended and joined, palm to the left, upper arm horizontal, forearm inclined at 45°, hand and wrist straight; at the same time turn the head toward the person saluted. To complete the salute, drop the arm to its normal position by the side in one motion, at the same time turning the head and eyes to the front.

The junior member executes the first movement, holds the position until it is returned by the senior, and then executes the second movement.

Accompanying the hand salute with an appropriate greeting, such as "Good morning, Sir," and its reply "Good morning, Sergeant," is encouraged.

The salute is rendered within saluting distance, which is defined as the distance within which recognition is easy. It usually does not exceed thirty paces. The salute is begun when about six paces from the person or color saluted or, in case the approach is outside that distance, six paces from the point of nearest approach.

Some of the more frequently observed errors in saluting are these: Failing to hold the position of the salute until it is returned by the officer saluted; failure to look at the person or color saluted; failure to assume the position of attention while saluting; failure to have the thumb and fingers extended and joined, a protruding thumb being especially objectionable; a bent wrist (the hand and wrist should be in the same plane); failure to have the upper arm horizontal. Gross errors include saluting with a cigarette in the right hand or in the mouth or saluting with the left hand in a pocket or returning a salute in a casual or perfunctory manner.

Uncovering. Officers and enlisted personnel under arms as a general rule do not uncover except when:

Seated as a member of or in attendance on a court or board. (Sentinels over prisoners do not uncover.)

Entering places of divine worship.

Indoors when not on duty and it is desired to remain informal.

In attendance at an official reception.

Interpretations of "Indoors" and "Outdoors." The term *outdoors* includes such buildings as drill halls, gymnasiums, and other roofed enclosures used for drill or exercise of troops. Theater marquees, covered walks, and other shelters open to the sides where a hat may be worn are also considered outdoors.

When the word *indoors* is used, it is construed to mean offices, hallways, mess halls, kitchens, orderly rooms, amusement rooms, bathrooms, libraries, dwellings, or other places of abode.

Meaning of the Term "Under Arms." The expression *under arms* will be understood to mean with arms in hand or having attached to the person a hand arm or the equipment pertaining directly to the arm, such as cartridge belt, pistol holster, or automatic rifle belt.

Cannon Salute. In addition to the salutes rendered by individuals, the regulations (AR 600-25) prescribe the occasions and the procedures for rendering cannon salutes.

A salute with cannon (towed, self-propelled, or tank mounted) will be fired with a commissioned officer present and directing the firing. Salutes will not be fired between retreat and reveille, on Sundays, or on national holidays (excluding Memorial and Independence Days) unless, in the discretion of the officer directing the honors, international courtesy or the occasion requires the exception. They will be rendered at the first available opportunity thereafter, if still appropriate. The interval between rounds is normally three seconds.

The salute to the Union consists of firing one gun for each state. It is fired at 1200 hours, Independence Day, at all Army installations provided with necessary equipment.

The national salute consists of twenty-one guns. It is fired at 1200 hours on Memorial Day. The national flag, displayed at half-staff from reveille until noon on this day, is then hoisted to the top of the staff and so remains until retreat. In conjunction with the playing of appropriate music, this is a tribute to honored dead.

Cannon salutes are rendered on the occasion of the death and funeral of the President or the Vice President of the United States, and other high civil and military dignitaries, as prescribed in AR 600-25.

The number of guns and the accompanying honors to be rendered to high dignitaries are shown in a chart later in this chapter.

The flag of the United States, national color, or national standard, is always displayed at the time of firing a salute except when firing a salute to the Union on the day of the funeral of a President, ex-President, or President-elect. On these occasions, the salute will be fired at five-second intervals immediately following lowering of the flag at retreat. Personnel will not salute.

COURTESIES RENDERED BY JUNIORS TO SENIORS

Application of Saluting Rules. The general rules for exchange of salutes are stated in an earlier paragraph.

Covered or uncovered, salutes are exchanged in the same manner.

The salute is rendered but once if the senior remains in the immediate vicinity and no conversation takes place.

A group of enlisted personnel or officers within the confines of military posts, camps, or stations, and not in formation, on the approach of a more senior officer, is called to attention by the first person noticing the senior officer; if in formation, by the one in charge. If out of doors and not in formation, they all salute; in formation, the salute is rendered by the person in charge. If indoors, not under arms, they uncover.

Drivers of vehicles salute only when the vehicle is halted. Gate guards salute recognized officers in all vehicles. Salutes otherwise are not required by or to personnel in vehicles. Members in civilian attire need not exchange salutes. Also, military headgear need not be worn while in other than official vehicles.

Organization and detachment commanders (commissioned and noncommissioned) salute officers of higher grades by bringing the organization to attention before saluting, except when in the field.

In making reports at formations, the person making the report salutes first regardless of rank. An example of this is the case of a battalion commander rendering a report to the adjutant at a ceremony.

Members of the Army are urged to be meticulous in rendering salutes to and in returning salutes from fellow Army members and personnel of the sister services. Such soldierly attitudes enhance the feeling of respect that all should feel toward comrades in arms. *The salute must never be given in a casual or perfunctory manner.*

When NOT to Salute. Salutes are NOT rendered by individuals in the following cases:

An enlisted member in ranks and not at attention comes to attention when addressed by an officer.

Details (and individuals) at work do not salute. The officer or noncommissioned officer in charge, if not actively engaged at the time, salutes or acknowledges salutes for the entire detail.

When actively engaged in games such as baseball, tennis, or golf, one does not salute.

While crossing a thoroughfare, not on a military reservation, when traffic requires undivided attention.

In churches, theaters, or places of public assemblage, or in a public conveyance, salutes are not exchanged.

When carrying articles with both hands, or when otherwise so occupied as to make saluting impractical.

When on the march in combat, or under simulated combat conditions.

No salute is rendered to persons by a member of the guard who is engaged in the performance of a specific duty, the proper execution of which would prevent saluting.

A sentinel armed with a pistol does not salute after challenging. He or she stands at *Raise pistol* until the challenged party has passed.

The driver of a vehicle in motion is not required to salute.

Indoors, salutes are not exchanged except when reporting to a senior.

Reporting to a Superior Officer in His or Her Office. When reporting to a superior officer in his or her office, the junior (unless under arms) removes any headdress, knocks, and enters when told to do so. Upon entering, the junior marches up to within about two paces of the officer's desk, halts, salutes, and reports in this manner, for example: "Sir, Private Jones reports to Captain Smith" or "Sir, Lieutenant Brown reports to the Battalion Commander." After the report, conversation is carried on in the first or second person. When the business is completed, the junior salutes, executes about face, and withdraws. A junior uncovers (unless under arms) on entering a room where a senior officer is present.

Courtesies Exchanged When an Officer Addresses a Soldier. In general, when a conversation takes place between an officer and a soldier the following procedure is correct: Salutes are exchanged; the conversation is completed; salutes are again exchanged. *Exceptions:* An enlisted person in ranks comes to attention and does not salute. Indoors, salutes are not exchanged except when reporting to an officer.

Procedure When an Officer Enters a Messroom or Mess Tent. When an officer enters the messroom or mess tent, enlisted personnel seated at meals remain seated at ease and continue eating unless the officer directs otherwise. An individual addressed by the officer ceases eating and sits at attention until completion of the conversation. In an officers' mess, although other courtesies are observed through custom, the formalities prescribed for enlisted men and women are not in effect.

Procedure When an Officer Enters a Squad Room or Tent. In a squad room or tent, individuals rise, uncover (if unarmed), and stand at attention when an officer enters. If more than one person is present, the first to perceive the officer calls, "Attention."* In officers' quarters, such courtesies are not observed.

Entering Automobiles and Small Boats. Military persons enter automobiles and small boats in inverse order of rank; that is, the senior enters an automobile or boat last and leaves first. Juniors, although entering the automobile first, take their appropriate seat in the car. The senior is always on the right.

OFFICIAL CALLS

Official calls are those prescribed by AR 600-25. They are in contrast to social calls, which are discussed in chapter 8, *The Social Side of Army Life.*

We quote the official regulation:

GENERAL. The exchange of visits of courtesy is the primary basis for the establishment of those social contacts among officers of the Army essential to the development of that mutual understanding, respect, confidence, and teamwork which together with professional competence and physical ability ensures adequate military leadership at all echelons. The present size and complexity of the Army may preclude the exchange of courtesy calls in accordance with traditional concepts. However, the established customs of the service in this respect should be adhered to by all concerned to the extent practicable. Failure to follow these customs of official and polite society may be prejudicial to the best interests of the service. Commanders will adhere as closely as possible to the principles outlined in this regulation but may exercise individual discretion as to the extent to which these principles can be observed in a given situation. Individual officers will obtain guidance as to the commander's wishes from the organization or installation adjutant, the commander's aide, or the executive officer of their agency, as applicable.

Visits of courtesy will be paid promptly and should be of approximately fifteen minutes' duration. They should be made at a time presumably convenient to the officer being visited.

Visits of courtesy other than those made by departing officers should be returned in person within ten days except in the following instances:

In cases where the numbers are so great that this is not possible, a general officer occupying the position of a major general or higher may designate a staff officer to return the courtesy visit of an officer below general officer grade.

In case of sickness or other unavoidable circumstances, such visits may be omitted. In such

---

*On suitable occasions the officer commands "Rest" or "At Ease" when expecting to remain in the room and not desiring them to remain at Attention.

cases the officer should send his visiting card and a brief note expressing his regrets and the cause of his failure to pay the visit.

Calls may be returned by senior officers through a mass social function.

Courtesy visits are not required in connection with short absence on leave or temporary duty away from a home station.

MEANING OF TERMS. The terms "commander" and "commanding officer" as used in this regulation include chiefs of staff sections, installation commanders, division commanders, and heads of branches, offices, and agencies of comparable size.

VISITING CARDS. Visiting cards are used during calls as an individual optional courtesy. The grade of rank indicated on visiting cards will be the grade of rank in which the officer is serving and the service designated as United States Army. The visiting cards of chaplains will not designate grade of rank. Indication of branch is optional and component will not be shown. Size and type are optional; however, the most commonly accepted size is 3 1/4 by 1 1/2 inches, with shaded Roman engraving.

BY NEWLY ARRIVED OFFICERS. A newly arrived officer who will remain at an installation for over 24 hours will pay a visit of courtesy to his immediate superior and that officer's immediate superior. For example, a lieutenant assigned to an infantry battalion would call upon his company commander and his battalion commander. If the arriving officer is of higher rank than the ranking commander of the installation, the latter will pay the first visit. Official calls should be made at the offices of those called upon, within 48 hours after the officer's arrival. Courtesy visits to commanders will be repeated at their quarters as soon as practicable after arrival, at proper calling hours; the newly arrived officer's spouse should accompany him, unless, by reason of duty assignment, distances to be traveled make such visit impractical. Officers should inquire of the adjutant of the organization or installation, or the executive officer, as to normal calling hours.

BY DEPARTING OFFICERS. Officers who are about to depart permanently from an installation or unit will inquire of the adjutant thereof as to the visits of courtesy which should be made.

TO NEWLY ARRIVED OFFICERS. Each officer assigned or attached for duty to a company or battery; battalion, group, or comparable headquarters; division of a staff section of a corps, army or comparable headquarters; or branch of a staff section of a higher headquarters, except the commanders referred to above will pay a welcoming courtesy visit to each officer who has more recently arrived under permanent assignment to duty in the same organizational element.

ON NEW YEAR'S DAY. It is customary for all officers of a unit, organization or installation to call upon the commanding officer on New Year's Day. Usually the commander will designate a convenient hour and place for receiving such visits.

COURTESIES TO THE NATIONAL FLAG AND NATIONAL ANTHEM

The Flag of the United States. There are four names in use for the flag of the United States: *flag, color, standard, ensign.*

The *national color,* carried by dismounted units, measures 3 feet hoist by 4 feet fly and is trimmed on three sides with golden yellow fringe 2 1/2 inches in width. The *standard,* identical to the *color,* is the name traditionally used by mounted, motorized, or mechanized units. The *ensign* is the naval term for the national flag (or flag indicating nationality) of any size flown from ships, small boats, and aircraft. When we speak of flags we do not mean colors, standards, or ensigns.

There are four common sizes of our national flag. The *garrison flag* is displayed on holidays and special occasions. It is 20 feet by 38 feet. The *post flag,* 10 feet by 19 feet, is for general use. The *storm flag,* 5 feet by 9 feet 6 inches is displayed during stormy weather. The *grave decorating flag* is 7 inches hoist by 11 inches fly.

Organization Colors. Regiments and separate battalions, whose organization is fixed by Tables of Organization, are authorized to have organization colors symbolic of their branch and past history. Such units are "color-bearing organizations." The size is the same as the *national color.* The word *color*, when used alone, means the national color; the term *colors* means the national color and the organization or individual color.

Individual Colors. Individual colors, 4 feet 4 inches hoist by 5 feet 6 inches fly, are authorized the President, Vice President, cabinet members and their assistants, the Chairman of the Joint Chiefs of Staff, the Chief of Staff, and the Vice Chief of Staff, United States Army.

Pledge to the Flag. According to Congressional Resolution, 22 December 1942, the following pledge of allegiance should be rendered while standing, with the right hand over the heart:

> *I pledge allegiance to the flag of the United States of America and to the republic for which it stands, one nation under God, indivisible, with liberty and justice for all.*

Reveille and Retreat. The daily ceremonies of reveille and retreat constitute a dignified homage to the national flag at the beginning of the day, when it is raised, and at the end of the day, when it is lowered. Installation commanders direct the time of sounding reveille and retreat.

At every installation garrisoned by troops other than caretaking detachments, the flag will be hoisted at the sound of the first note of reveille. At the last note of retreat, a gun will be fired if the ceremony is on a military reservation, at which time the band or field music will play the National Anthem or sound *To the Color* and the flag will start to be lowered. The lowering of the flag will be regulated so as to be completed at the last note of the music. The same respect will be observed by all military personnel whether the National Anthem is played or *To the Color* is sounded.

The Flag at Half-Staff. The national flag is displayed at half-staff on Memorial Day until noon as a salute to the honored dead, and upon the death and funeral of military personnel and high civilian dignitaries (AR 600-25).

When the flag is displayed at half-staff it is first hoisted to the top of the staff and then lowered to the half-staff position. Before lowering the flag it is again raised to the top of the staff. For an unguyed flagstaff of one piece, the middle point of the hoist of the flag should be midway between the top and the bottom of the staff.

Memorial Day. On Memorial Day (the last Monday in May) the national flag will be displayed at half-staff from reveille until noon at all Army installations. Immediately before noon the band will play an appropriate air, and at 1200 hours the national salute of twenty-one guns will be fired at all installations provided with the necessary equipment for firing salutes. At the conclusion of the salute, the flag will be hoisted to the top of the staff and will remain so until retreat. When hoisted to the top of the staff, the flag will be saluted by playing appropriate patriotic music by a band or a bugler or from a recording, depending upon availability. In this manner, tribute is rendered the honored dead.

Independence Day. On Independence Day (4 July), a fifty-gun salute to the Union commemorative of the Declaration of Independence will be fired at 1200 hours at all Army installations provided with the necessary equipment for firing salutes.

When Independence Day occurs on a Sunday, the salute will be fired the following day.

Flag Day. Flag Day is celebrated on the fourteenth of June, upon proclamation by the President, which calls upon officials of the government to display the flag on all government buildings and urges the people to observe the day as the adoption on 14 June, 1777, by the Continental Congress, of the Stars and Stripes as the official flag of the United States of America.

Salute to the President's Flag. When the President of the United States, aboard any vessel or craft flying the President's flag, passes an Army installation that is equipped to fire salutes, the installation commander will cause the national salute to be fired. (See exceptions stated earlier under the discussion of Cannon Salutes, which would exclude firing this particular salute between retreat and reveille.)

Salute to Passing Colors. When passing or being passed by the uncased national color, military personnel render honors by executing a salute appropriate to their dress and formation as indicated previously. If indoors and not in formation, personnel assume the position of attention but do not salute. If the colors are cased, honors are not required.

Reception of an Officer on Board a Naval Vessel. The salutes to be exchanged upon boarding a naval vessel and leaving a naval vessel are prescribed in the following paragraph of United States Navy Regulations, to which all members of the Army visiting a naval vessel will conform (AR 600-25):

2108. Salutes to the National Ensign.

1. Each person in the naval service, upon coming on board a ship of the Navy, shall salute the national ensign if it is flying. He shall stop on reaching the upper platform of the accommodation ladder, or the shipboard end of the brow, face the national ensign, and render the salute, after which he shall salute the officer of the deck. On leaving the ship, he shall render the salutes in inverse order. The officer of the deck shall return both salutes in each case.

2. When passed by or passing the national ensign being carried, uncased, in a military formation, all persons in the naval service shall salute. Persons in vehicles or boats shall follow the procedure prescribed for such persons during colors.

3. The salutes prescribed in this article shall also be rendered to foreign national ensigns and aboard foreign men-of-war.

For further information as to Navy courtesies and customs see *Navy Customs Army Officers Should Know,* chapter 7.

Courtesies to the National Anthem. *Outdoors.* Whenever and wherever the National Anthem, *To the Color,* or *Hail to the Chief* is played:

At the first note all dismounted personnel in uniform and not in formation, within saluting distance of the flag, will face the flag, or the music if the flag is not in view, salute, and maintain the salute until the last note of the music is sounded. Men not in uniform will remove the headdress with the right hand and hold it at the left shoulder with the hand over the heart. If no headdress is involved, stand at attention holding the right hand over the heart. Men in athletic uniform should stand at attention, removing headdress if any. Women not in uniform should salute by placing the right hand over the heart.

Vehicles in motion will be brought to a halt. Persons riding in a passenger car or on a motorcycle will dismount and salute. Occupants of other types of military vehicles and buses remain seated at attention in the vehicle, the individual in charge of each vehicle dismounting and rendering the hand salute. Tank and armored car commanders salute from the vehicle.

The above marks of respect are shown the national anthem of any friendly country when it is played at official occasions.

Indoors. When the National Anthem is played indoors, officers and enlisted personnel stand at attention and face the music, or the flag if one is present. They do not salute unless under arms.

Reveille. At reveille the procedures outlined above will be followed.

The method and personnel required for raising and lowering the flag on a flagstaff are prescribed in FM 26-5, *Interior Guard Duty.*

Dipping the Flag or Colors. The flag of the United States, national color, and national standard are never dipped by way of salute or compliment except by naval vessels. The organizational color or standard will be dipped in salute in all military ceremonies while the United States National Anthem, *To the Color,* or a foreign national anthem is being played, and when rendering honors to the organizational commander or an individual of higher grade to include foreign dignitaries of higher grade, but in no other case.

The United States Army flag is considered to be an organizational color and as such is also dipped while the United States National Anthem, *To the Color,* or a foreign national anthem is being played, and when rendering honors to the Chief of Staff of the United States Army, his direct representative, or individual of higher grade to include a foreign dignitary of equivalent or higher grade, but in no other case.

The authorized unit color salutes in all military ceremonies while the National Anthem or *To the Color* is being played and when rendering honors to the organizational commander or an individual of higher rank, but in no other case.

Display and Use of the Flag. International usage forbids the display of the flag of one nation above another nation's in time of peace. When the flags of two or more nations are to be displayed, they should be flown from separate staffs, or from separate halyards, of equal size and on the same level.

The national flag, when not flown from a staff or mast, should always be hung flat, whether indoors or out. It should not be festooned over doorways or arches, or tied in a bowknot, or fashioned into a rosette. When used on a rostrum, it should be displayed above and behind the speaker's desk. It should never be used to cover the speaker's desk or to drape over the front of the platform. For this latter purpose, as well as for decoration in general, bunting of the national colors should be used and the colors should be arranged with the blue above, the white in the middle, and the red below. Under no circumstances should the flag be draped over chairs or benches, nor should any object or emblem of any kind be placed above or upon it, nor should it be hung where it can be easily contaminated or soiled. When carried with other flags the national flag should always be on the right (as color bearers are facing) or in front. The flag of the United States of America should be at the center and at the highest point of the group when a number of flags of states or localities or pennants of societies are grouped and displayed from staffs.

When flown at a military post, or when carried by troops, the national flag is never dipped by way of salute or compliment. The authorized unit color is dipped as a salute when the reviewing officer has the rank of a general officer. This is done by lowering the pike (as the staff of a color is called) to the front so that it makes an angle of about 45 degrees with the ground. The national flag is used to cover the casket at the military funeral of present or former members of the military service. It is placed lengthwise on the casket with the union at the head and over the left shoulder of the deceased. The flag is not lowered into the grave and is not allowed to touch the ground.

The display and use of the flag by civilians or civilian groups is contained in Public Law 829—77th Congress as amended by Public Law 344—94th Congress.

HOW TO DISPLAY THE FLAG.

1. When displayed over the middle of the street, the flag should be suspended vertically with the union to the north in an east and west street, or to the east in a north and south street.

2. When displayed with another flag from crossed staffs, the US flag should be on the right (the flag's own right) and its staff should be in front of the staff of the other flag.

3. When flown at half-mast, the flag should be hoisted to the peak, then lowered to the half-mast position; but before lowering the flag for the day it should again be raised to the peak.

4. When the flags of states or cities or pennants of societies are flown on the same halyard with the US flag, the latter should always be at the peak.

5. When the flag is suspended over a sidewalk from a rope extending from house to pole at the edge of the sidewalk, the flag should be hoisted out from the building, toward the pole, union first.

6. When the flag is displayed from a staff projecting horizontally or at any angle from the window sill, balcony, or front of a building, the union of the flag should go to peak of the staff (unless the flag is to be displayed at half-mast).

7. When the flag is used to cover a casket, it should be so placed that the union is at the head and over the left shoulder. The flag should not be lowered into the grave or allowed to touch the ground.

8. When the flag is displayed other than by being flown from a staff, it should be displayed flat whether indoors or out. When displayed either horizontally or vertically against a wall, the union should be uppermost and to the flag's own right, that is, to the observer's left. When displayed in a window it should be displayed in the same way, that is, with the union or blue field to the left of the observer in the street.

9. When carried in a procession with another flag or flags, the US flag should be either on the marching right, or when there is a line of other flags, in front of the center of that line.

10. When a number of flags of states or cities or pennants of societies are grouped and displayed from staffs with our national flag, the latter should be at the center or at the highest point of the group.

11. When the flags of two or more nations are displayed they should be flown from separate staffs of the same height and the flags should be of approximately equal size. International usage forbids the display of the flag of one nation above that of another nation in time of peace.

DISPLAY OF UNITED NATIONS FLAG

There are no United States laws or policies adopted by the United Nations that cause conflict in the display of the United States flag in conjunction with the United Nations flag.

When the two flags are displayed together the United States flag is on the right, best identified as "the marching right." This is in accordance with United States law. The United Nations flag code states it can be on either side of a national flag without being subordinate to that flag. Both flags should be of the same size and displayed at the same height.

It should be noted that the United Nations flag may be displayed at military installations of the United States or carried by United States troops only on very specific occasions such as the visit of high dignitaries of the United Nations, when the United Nations or high dignitaries thereof are to be honored, or as authorized by the President (AR 840-10).

PRECEDENCE OF MILITARY ORGANIZATIONS IN FORMATION

Whenever two or more organizations of different components of the armed forces appear in the same formation, they take precedence among themselves in order as listed below. This means from right to left in line, the senior organization on the right; and from head to tail of a column, the senior organization at the head (AR 600-25).

Cadets, United States Military Academy
Midshipmen, United States Naval Academy
Cadets, United States Air Force Academy
Cadets, United States Coast Guard Academy
Midshipmen, United States Merchant Marine Academy
United States Army
United States Marine Corps
United States Navy
United States Air Force
United States Coast Guard
Army National Guard of the United States

Army Reserve
Marine Corps Reserve
Naval Reserve
Air National Guard of the United States
Air Force Reserve
Coast Guard Reserve
Other training organizations of
    the Army, Marine Corps, Navy, Air
    Force, and Coast Guard in order,
    respectively

During any period when the United States Coast Guard operates as a part of the United States Navy the cadets, U.S. Coast Guard Academy, the U.S. Coast Guard, and the Coast Guard Reserve will take precedence, respectively, next after the midshipmen, U.S. Naval Academy, the U.S. Navy, and the Naval Reserve.

PERSONAL SALUTES AND HONORS TO DISTINGUISHED MILITARY AND CIVIL OFFICIALS

Certain military and civil officials in high position, including foreign officials, are accorded personal honors consisting of cannon salutes, ruffles and flourishes played by field music, and the National Anthem of our country or of the foreign country, the General's March, or march played by the band. These honors are extended upon presentation of the escort and as part of the parade or review of troops. The accompanying chart (from AR 600-25) states the specific honors of all persons who may be accorded such honors. A military escort is supplied during their rendition.

Ruffles and Flourishes. Ruffles are played on drums, flourishes on bugles. They are sounded together, once for each star of the general officer being honored and according to the accompanying table of honors for other dignitaries. Ruffles and flourishes are followed by music as prescribed in the table.

Action of the Person Receiving the Honors. It is the usual custom for the person receiving the honors to inspect the escort. The appropriate time to do this is at the conclusion of the honors rendered by the escort upon his or her reception.

Entitlement to Honors— Grade, Title, or Office	Number of Guns Arrival	Departure	Ruffles and Flourishes	Music*
President............................	21	21	4	National Anthem or "Hail to the Chief," as appropriate.
Ex-President or President-elect	21	21	4	National Anthem.
Sovereign or Chief of State of a foreign country or member of a reigning royal family	21	21	4	National Anthem of foreign country.
Vice President........................	19	..	4	"Hail Columbia"
Speaker of the House of Representatives	19	..	4	March.
American or foreign ambassador, or high commissioner while in country to which accredited	19	..	4	National Anthem of United States or official's country.
Premier or prime minister	19	..	4	National Anthem of United States or official's country.
Secretary of Defense	19	19	4	March.
Cabinet member, President protempore of Senate, governor of a state, or Chief Justice of the United States........................	19	..	4	March.
Deputy Secretary of Defense.............	19	19	4	March.
Secretary of the Army	19	19	4	March.
Secretary of the Navy or Air Force........	19	19	4	March.
Director of Defense Research and Engineering	19	19	4	March.
Chairman, Joint Chiefs of Staff............	19	19	4	General's or Admiral's march, as appropriate.
Chief of Staff, United States Army; Chief of Naval Operations; Chief of Staff, United States Air Force; or Commandant of the Marine Corps..........................	19	19	4	General's or Admiral's march, as appropriate.
General of the Army, Fleet Admiral, or General of the Air Force	19	19	4	General's or Admiral's march, as appropriate.
Assistant Secretaries of Defense and General Counsel of the Department of Defense....	17	17	4	March.
General or admiral....................	17	17	4	General's or Admiral's march, as appropriate.
Governor of a territory or foreign possession within the limits of his jurisdiction........	17	..	4	March.
Chairman of a Committee of Congress......	17	..	4	March.
Under Secretary of the Army	17	17	4	March.
Under Secretary of the Navy or Air Force ...	17	17	4	March.
Assistant Secretaries of the Army	17	17	4	March.
Assistant Secretaries of the Navy or Air Force	17	17	4	March.
American envoys or ministers and foreign envoys or ministers accredited to the United States.............................	15	..	3	March.
Lieutenant general or vice admiral	15	..	3	General's or Admiral's march.
Major general or rear admiral (upper half) ...	13	..	2	General's or Admiral's march, as appropriate.
American ministers resident and ministers resident accredited to the United States......	13	..	2	March.
American charges d'affaires and charges d'affaires accredited to the United States	11	..	1	March.
Brigadier general or rear admiral (lower half)	11	..	1	General's or Admiral's march.
Consuls general accredited to the United States...............................	11	..	..	March.

*The music indicated in the table will follow the ruffles and flourishes without pause. Unless otherwise directed, civilian officials of the Department of Defense and military departments receive the thirty-two-bar medley in the trio of "The Stars and Stripes Forever."

Foreign military persons holding positions equivalent to those of Department of Defense and military department officials, both military and civilian listed above, will be rendered the honors to which the equivalent United States official is entitled, regardless of actual military rank. All other military persons will receive the honors due their actual rank or its United States Army equivalent.

A designated representative of an official entitled to honors will be afforded honors based on the representative's rank. (AR 600-25.)

During the playing of the ruffles and flourishes and music, as indicated in the chart, the person honored and those accompanying him, if members of the armed forces, salute at the first note of the ruffles and flourishes and remain at the salute until the last note of the music. Persons in civilian clothes salute by uncovering.

Action of Persons Witnessing the Honors. Members of the armed forces who witness the salutes and honors render the hand salute, conforming to the action of the official party. Individuals in civilian clothing uncover.

MILITARY FUNERALS

Officers should be thoroughly familiar with the prescribed courtesies to the military dead.* This involves a knowledge of the ceremonies incident to the conduct of a military funeral including correct procedure on the following occasions:

Officer in charge of a funeral.
Honorary pallbearer.
Command of a funeral escort.
Attendance as a mourner.
Essential references: AR 600-25, FM 22-5.

Courtesies at a Military Funeral. At a military funeral, all persons in the military service in uniform attending in their individual capacity will face the casket and execute the hand salute at any time when the casket is being moved, while the casket is being lowered into the grave, during the firing of the volley, and while *Taps* are being sounded. Honorary pallbearers in uniform will conform to these instructions when not in motion. Male personnel in civilian clothes, in the above cases and during the service at the grave will stand at attention, uncovered, and hold the headdress over the left breast, or if no headdress is worn the right hand will be held over the heart. Female personnel in civilian clothes will hold the right hand over the heart. During religious graveside service, all personnel will bow their heads at the words, "Let us pray." All personnel except the active pallbearers will follow the example of the officiating chaplain. If he uncovers, they will uncover; if he remains covered, they will remain covered. When the officiating chaplain wears a biretta (clerical headpiece) during the graveside service all personnel as indicated above will uncover. When the officiating chaplain wears a yarmulke (skull cap, Jewish) all personnel will remain covered.

The active pallbearers will remain covered and will not salute while carrying the casket and while holding the flag over the casket during the service at the grave.

Female military personnel will remain covered during military funerals.

Badge of Military Mourning. The badge of military mourning is a straight band of black crepe or plain black cloth four inches wide, worn around the left sleeve of the outer garment above the elbow. But no badge of military mourning is worn with the uniform, except when prescribed by the commanding officer for funerals, or when specially ordered by the Department of the Army. As family mourning, officers are authorized to wear the sleeve band described above while at the funeral, or enroute thereto or therefrom. (AR 670-5)

Elements of Military Funeral Ceremony. The military funeral ceremony that has been developed to demonstrate the nation's recognition of the debt it owes to the services and sacrifices of soldiers is based on a few simple customs and traditions. The casket of the soldier is covered with the American flag. It is usually transported

---

*For burial rights of military personnel see chapter 9, *Financial Planning.*

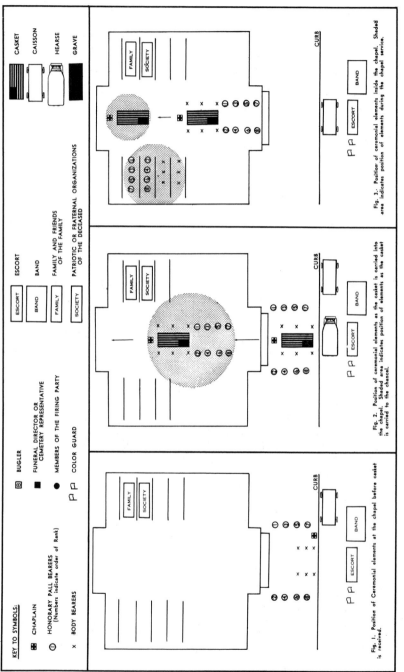

KEY TO SYMBOLS:

⊞ CHAPLAIN	⊞ BUGLER
⊖ HONORARY PALL BEARERS (Numbers indicate order of Rank)	■ FUNERAL DIRECTOR OR CEMETERY REPRESENTATIVE
× BODY BEARERS	● MEMBERS OF THE FIRING PARTY
	⊓⊓ COLOR GUARD

ESCORT	■ CASKET
BAND	CAISSON
FAMILY	HEARSE
SOCIETY	■ GRAVE

ESCORT

BAND

FAMILY AND FRIENDS OF THE FAMILY

PATRIOTIC OR FRATERNAL ORGANIZATIONS OF THE DECEASED

Fig. 1. Position of Ceremonial elements at the chapel before casket is received.

Fig. 2. Position of ceremonial elements as the casket is carried into the chapel. Shaded area indicates position of elements as the casket is carried to the chancel.

Fig. 3. Position of ceremonial elements inside the chapel. Shaded area indicates position of elements during the chapel service.

MILITARY FUNERALS, ARMY.

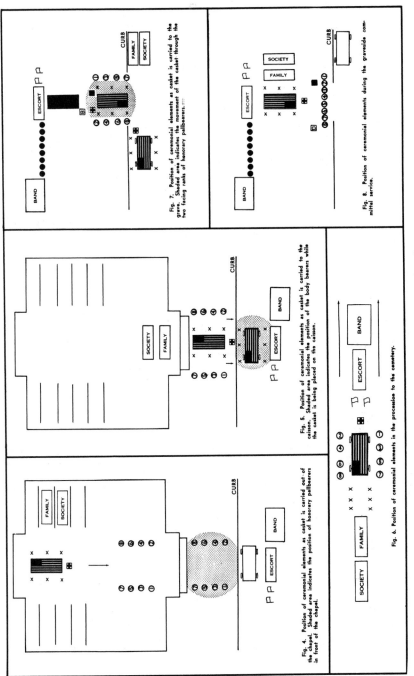

Fig. 7. Position of ceremonial elements as casket is carried to the grave. Shaded area indicates the movement of the casket through the two facing ranks of honorary pallbearers.

Fig. 8. Position of ceremonial elements during the graveside committal service.

Fig. 5. Position of ceremonial elements as casket is carried to the caisson. Shaded area indicates the position of the body bearers while the casket is being placed on the caisson.

Fig. 6. Position of ceremonial elements in the procession to the cemetery.

Fig. 4. Position of ceremonial elements as casket is carried out of the chapel. Shaded area indicates the position of honorary pallbearers in front of the chapel.

MILITARY FUNERALS, ARMY—Continued.

to the cemetery on a caisson.* It is carried from the caisson to the grave by six military body bearers. In addition to the body bearers, honorary pallbearers are usually designated who march to the cemetery alongside the caisson. At the cemetery, the casket is placed over the grave and the body bearers hold the flag-pall waist high over the casket. After the committal service is read by the chaplain, a firing party fires three volleys. A bugler stationed at the head of the grave sounds *Taps* over the casket and the military funeral is completed. The body bearers then fold the flag and it is presented to the next of kin. These basic elements are the foundation of all military funerals, whether last rites are being conducted over a private's casket or final honors are being paid at the grave of a general.

Honorary Pallbearers. The honorary pallbearers arrive at the chapel before the hearse arrives. They take positions in front of the entrance to the chapel in two facing ranks, as indicated in the accompanying illustration.

Upon arrival of the hearse and when the body bearers remove the casket from the hearse, honorary pallbearers execute the hand salute.

When the casket is carried between the two ranks that they have formed, they come to the order, execute the appropriate facing movement, fall in behind the casket, and enter the chapel, the senior preceding the junior and marching to the right.

In the chapel, they take places in the front pews to the left of the chapel as indicated in the illustration.

After the chapel service, the honorary pallbearers precede the casket in column of twos as the two active pallbearers push the church truck to the chapel entrance. The honorary pallbearers again form an aisle from the chapel entrance to the caisson or hearse and uncover or salute as prescribed. When the casket has been placed on the caisson or in the hearse, they enter their conveyances or march. When marching, the honorary pallbearers form columns of files on each side of the caisson or hearse, the leading member of each column opposite the front wheels of the caisson or hearse.

When the entrance to the burial lot is reached, the honorary pallbearers take positions on either side of the entrance. As the body bearers lift the casket from the caisson, the honorary pallbearers execute the hand salute.

When the casket has been carried past them, they come to the order and fall in behind the casket, marching to the grave site in correct precedence of rank, senior to the right and to the front.

At the grave site they stand in line behind the chaplain at the head of the grave; the senior stands to the right and the junior to the left. They execute the hand salute during the firing of volleys, the sounding of *Taps,* and the lowering of the casket into the grave.

After the ceremony is over they march off in two files behind the colors.

Family. The family arrives at the chapel before the casket is received and is seated in pews in right front of the chapel.

When chapel service is over, family members follow the casket down the aisle until they reach the vestibule of the chapel, where they wait until the casket is carried outside and secured to the caisson.

When the procession is ready to form, members of the family take their places in the procession immediately behind the body bearers.

When the procession arrives at the graveside, the members of the family wait

---

*Since caissons are no longer used in the Army, the vehicle carrying the casket is generally a civilian hearse or sometimes a light, open Army truck or an ambulance adapted for the purpose. This will be understood wherever the word *caisson* is employed in this description.

until the band, escort, and colors have taken their positions at the grave, and the casket is carried between the double rows of honorary pallbearers.

The members of the family take their positions at the side of the grave opposite earth mound side for the funeral service.

When the graveside ceremony is finished, a member of the family receives the interment flag from the chaplain, cemetery representative, the officer in charge of the funeral, or the individual military escort.*

The family then leaves the cemetery.

Significance of Military Funeral. The ceremonial customs that comprise the elements of all military funerals are rooted in ancient military usage. In many cases, these traditions are based on expedients used long ago on the battlefield in time of war. The use of a caisson as a hearse, for example, was an obvious combat improvisation. In a similar manner, the custom of covering the casket with a flag probably originated on the battlefield where caskets were not available and the flag, wrapped around the dead serviceman, served as a makeshift pall in which he could be buried. Later, these customs assumed a deeper significance than that of mere expediency. The fact that an American flag is used to cover the casket, for example, now symbolizes the fact that the soldier served in the Armed Forces of the United States and that this country assumes the responsibility of burying the soldier as a solemn and sacred obligation.

Finally, the sounding of *Taps* over the grave has an obvious origin in military custom. Since *Taps* is the last bugle call the soldier hears at night, it is particularly appropriate that it be played over his grave to mark the beginning of his last, long sleep and to express hope and confidence in an ultimate reveille to come.

---

*Upon this ending of the service it has become customary for close friends to express regrets to the bereaved at the graveside.

7

Customs of
the Service

Nothing is stronger than custom.—Ovid.

A custom is an established usage. Customs include positive actions—things to do—and taboos—things to avoid doing. Like life itself, the customs that mankind observes are subject to a constant but slow process of change. Many practices that were habitual a generation or two ago have passed through a period of declining observance, and then into limbo. New customs arise to supplant the old. The resurrection of those that have become outmoded would first be thought amusing, then peculiar. Others live on and on without apparent change. Humans are eager to rely upon established practice, upon precedent or custom, to an astounding degree. The realization that the action they are taking coincides with that which has been followed by others in similar circumstances bolsters their confidence, thus encouraging them to adhere to their course. Customs change with need; during a war period this process is greatly accelerated. But, whether old or new, the influence of custom is profound. It is man's attempt to apply to the solution of his immediate problems the lessons of the past. It is itself a custom. Army customs conform to the code of the Army officer, as they also conform to the established rules of military courtesy.*

Army Customs and Their Importance. As long as harmonious human relations continue to be important, which will be a very long time indeed, the observance of useful, gracious, thoughtful customs will be important in the lives of the Army's officers and their families.

*Commended for interesting reading is *Military Customs and Traditions,* Major Mark M. Boatner III, David McKay Company, Inc., New York.

The established customs have come into general use by evolution and represent the preferences of officers and their spouses. The community of interests of officers on the same assignments, or at the same locations, with the singleness of purpose of the national security, provides opportunity as well as need for the recognition of customs. Customs enrich our life of national service. The newcomers are made welcome, given prompt opportunity to become known and to know others, to feel welcome and to "belong." There are ceremonial ways that add to the color of military life. There are things to do and things to avoid doing. Those who are departing receive a pleasant farewell. The sum of these customs adds appreciably to the interests, the pleasures, and the graciousness of Army life.

Life in the Army can be colorful, interesting, and rich with friends and experiences. The customs and the courtesies help to establish these patterns. The commanding officer, or officer in charge of an activity, who overlooks an opportunity for building camaraderie is injuring his or her own cause and image. Leadership in observing worthy customs will help. Such observance smooths the way for harmonious official and personal relationships. They are the lubricants for developing teamwork and service pride. Have you questioned these views? If so, some earnest thinking is suggested. Army customs change with times and circumstances, but they have been developing through the years. They have stood the tests of many difficult periods, and they have not been tossed into limbo.

Did you know that the costs of many official or semiofficial social occasions, or social get-togethers, are borne by your general or colonel, major, or captain? Only when foreign dignitaries are present, and then only in small amounts, is there an official allowance. These costs have been accepted by many senior commanders, when within their means, as a part of their responsibility. They know the importance of officers and their wives or husbands meeting and becoming acquainted with one another, with their general and colonel; and for all to know and recognize the general's spouse and the colonel's spouse. It is a step in developing pride in military service and of stimulating acquaintances and interests, as well as in generating smooth and understanding official as well as community relationships.

This analysis should invite conclusions as to the potential rewards and pleasures of service life. There is the welcome extended to all—come out, become known, know others! Participate in the activities of your military community. Contribute your talents for worthwhile activities. Be more than a typed name on the official rolls. The glory of the Army is its fine people and the rewarding associations that may flow in abundance from its work and its life. It is a good life, a wholesome, interesting, rewarding life, if you learn its ways and grasp the opportunities extended. It can never be more to you than you, yourself, make it.

This chapter has been included in order to explain and to help perpetuate customs that have enriched many, many lives for many, many years. Your effort will soon be rewarded with enjoyable experiences and new friendships formed, all strengthening the purposeful service the mission requires.

Many customs originating in antiquity are observed in our Army.* They are forms of military pageantry most of which are followed in one way or another in many armies. While most professional military people are convinced that their life has greater interest and stimulation than other vocations it is a fact that it has its drab aspects. These old customs add color, pageantry and ceremony to daily life and deserve careful perpetuation. For the most part they consist of acts honoring

---

*The student of military customs of antiquity and of the older armies will find enlightening *Military Customs,* Edwards and Kipling, Aldershot, Gale and Polden Ltd., Aldershot, Hampshire, England, 1961. It should be available in station libraries.

the nation's flag or the military dead, or of paying respects to comrades in arms. Each heightens the concept of purposeful men and women serving their country in an honorable profession.

The Salute. An interesting history of the military salute, one of the most ancient and universal military customs, is contained in chapter 6, *Military Courtesy.*

The Evening Gun. The evening gun, fired at the time of the Retreat ceremony, signifies the end of the normal military day at which time in our service the flag is lowered. It is an extremely old custom of armies with one legend indicating that in the beginning the gun was fired at evening to drive away evil spirits. Whatever the facts may be as to its true origin it is particularly appropriate to signal the arrival of Retreat throughout a military reservation. In any event its precedent extends over centuries.

The Retreat Ceremony. The Retreat ceremony honors the nation's flag at the end of day. In our service it is known to have been in use during the American Revolution at which time it was sounded with drums. The Retreat parade in which a ceremonial parade is combined with the Retreat ceremony including the sounding of the evening gun is one of the most inspiring Army ceremonies. It is appropriate for all members of a garrison out of doors at the time to pause for a moment in salute to the nation's flag and the National Anthem.

The "Sound Off" and the Three Cheers. During a ceremonial parade the adjutant commands "SOUND OFF." The band, in place, plays the *Sound Off* of three chords. It then moves forward, and changing direction while playing a stirring march, troops the line or marches past the troops in formation, then returns to its post. Upon halting it sounds the Three Cheers.

This custom is believed by some students to have originated at the time of the Crusades. The legend appears to have substance. At that time when detachments were sent away on those faraway campaigns it was the custom to assemble the garrison in formation with the departing troops in the place of honor on the right. The band of the period marched past troops being honored much as is now done during Sound Off. Three cheers for their departing comrades were then given by the troops remaining behind. The simple notes of the three cheers as they are used today could very well have this symbolic meaning. In any event it is a pretty legend with logic as to its authenticity.

The Three Volleys Over Graves. A special ceremonial at graveside honoring a military deceased is an ancient custom in itself, the details of which are fully explained and pictured in chapter 6, *Military Courtesy.*

After the committal service is read by the chaplain, a firing party fires three volleys with rifles. This ceremony is followed by a bugler sounding *Taps* from a position at the head of the casket over the grave. This completes the military funeral.

The use of this custom by military people is said by students to have been in use during the seventeenth century. In concept it traces to the Romans who honored their dead by casting earth three times upon the grave, calling the name of the dead, and saying "Farewell" three times. It is also likened to the intent of saying an honorable farewell by the Three Cheers as used during the Crusades, discussed above.

The Raising of the Right Hand in Taking Oath. From the earliest days the taking of an oath as to the truth of statements or testimony has been a solemn and serious matter accompanied by ceremony. In essence it has always meant that the taker of the oath called upon his God to bear witness that the truth would be told. Ancient men bared their heads and raised their arms in appeal to their deity as a symbol of truth and honesty. A cynic might surmise that an ancient judge required the act as a means of increasing the probity of the testimony he was obliged to hear. Certainly this custom is as old as mankind, adding dignity and ceremony to a serious occasion.

The Wearing of Decorations. The rewarding of individuals who have performed acts of military valor is very old in armies of history. An interesting sketch of the development is contained in chapter 23, *Decorations, Service Medals, and Badges.*

The Wearing of Unit Badges or Emblems. This custom originated as to our service during the American Civil War. An account of the occasion for its adoption may be found in a footnote, chapter 22, *Uniforms of the Army.*

THE STRONGEST TRADITION: COMRADESHIP

The comradeship of military associates is the strongest and most enduring of Army customs. It is a reserved status. It is enjoyed by comrades in arms who have served together in some vast experience, such as a great campaign, where individual as well as group pride has developed. Age and grade are submerged here. It is an abiding trust and confidence in one's fellows that may develop swiftly in the hard crucibles of military service.

Men and women who are true comrades in arms have faith that when the chips are down each may depend fully upon his or her fellows. Ordinary soldiers will often choose the course of great hazard in the accomplishment of mission in preference to revealing themselves as weak in the eyes of their comrades. It is the ultimate in a feeling of belonging.

It is a powerful tradition. Here is the hidden ingredient that binds those who serve the nation with pride and competence as dependable associates, comrades in arms.

The Stand-To! A special form of unit officer comradeship that has developed is the *stand-to.* Expect to hear the directive, "All officers Stand-To at 1730." This means to join the unit officers at their local club for a beer and conversation. Usually held on Fridays, the custom calls for light-hearted jesting about the events of the week, or airing a minor gripe, and blowing off a little steam. The point to understand is the totally informal atmosphere in which the commander and the unit officers—and occasionally their spouses—stand together celebrating the week's passing with that good feeling of mission accomplished.

Battalion Parties and Command Performances. Battalion parties and command performance parties are also a periodic custom, especially in areas where officers and their families live off post. Their purpose is to increase and strengthen acquaintances and to weld the interest of all members in their unit. They are held on the occasion of arrivals, departures, promotions, or just for the fun of it. Don't miss them even if you prefer the entertainment elsewhere. These occasions serve many purposes of building unit cohesiveness and esprit. Command performances are similar to battalion parties, but there is a clear inference to be drawn that your presence is expected. If they cost more than your current resources permit, or if you have sufficient reason to be elsewhere, tell your commander and request permission to be absent. He or she will accept your statement as reasonable and will not assume you to be antisocial, unfriendly, or unresponsive to the commander's implied desires. But it is better to attend and help make the affair successful. Put on a happy face—and go!

Dining-in. The *dining-in* is a formal dinner function for members of a military organization or unit. The practice of dining-in is believed to have originated in the monasteries and early universities in England. The British military adopted the custom for use in the officers' mess. From there, it was picked up by the U.S. military forces during World Wars I and II and was an integral part of the old regimental mess. The practice of dining-in declined in popularity after World War II, but it is again becoming more prevalent, and perhaps will become even more popular with the advent of the the Army's new regimental system.

The dining-in provides an occasion for the officers of a unit to meet socially. It may be used as an opportunity to welcome new officers, to bid farewell to departing officers, to honor distinguished visitors, or merely as a chance for the officers of a unit to get together socially as a means of building unit esprit. The dining-in should be viewed as an opportunity to enjoy the comradeship of one's fellow officers rather than as a mandatory function.

Careful, detailed planning is required to ensure that the occasion proceeds smoothly and enjoyably. The details of the dining-in vary according to its purpose, but those details must be thought through in advance. Formal invitations generally are in order, extended far enough in advance to elicit formal responses so that firm planning can proceed. The dinner menu may consist of from three to seven courses. Toasts are considered a mandatory part of the dining-in. Activities generally are divided into a predinner social period with cocktails, the formal dinner, and an informal period following the formal activities.

The formal portion of the dining-in includes the posting of the colors, an invocation if desired, appropriate toasts, introductory remarks by the presiding officer and introduction of guests, a toast to the guests, dinner service, conduct of the events of the evening, concluding remarks by the presiding officer, retirement of the colors, and adjournment to the informal period.

The Protocol Office of the United States Military Academy at West Point produces an informative pamphlet on the conduct of a dining-in, which should be of considerable assistance to anyone planning such a function.

RANK HAS ITS PRIVILEGES (RHIP)

General. Rank does indeed have its privileges, but there are important points for all officers to consider. Although certain courtesies, customs, and privileges are traditional and, indeed, historical, they were established and are honored for impersonal reasons. It may be difficult for a younger officer of lower rank to accept this; it is a little easier to understand as one gets more experience. Some privileges may be difficult to rationalize as being a matter solely of rank. For instance, getting quarters on a post involves rank, date of arrival, the number of quarters for your grade, the size of your family, and even the physical condition of members of your family. The lieutenant may not like the influence of rank on quarters assignment but the same can be said for the sergeant as he or she views the lieutenant's opportunities.

A second point to reflect on is that rank has no influence on many military matters. Enemy artillery shells do not seek out the captains alone; in combat all are vulnerable. To a well-trained sniper, rank may be a special distinction resulting in a dubious privilege. The thousands of officers of all ranks who have been in replacement systems would have great difficulty in identifying any privileges granted because of their rank since all were equally and impartially processed with no special treatment according to rank.

A third point to consider is that privileges are dividends and rewards for faithful service and achievements and for having more responsibility than those of lower rank. All of us are human and require recognition beyond salaries. If officers believe their achievements are recognized and their service appreciated by the evidence of intangibles, such as the privileges of rank, the Army is going to gain and retain better officers. These intangibles cannot be weighed or counted but they do greatly affect one's attitude, devotion, and, ultimately, one's capability.

It is useful to observe that all society is organized and all organizations have a structure of ranks. This structure of ranks with resulting degrees of privilege is obviously not unique to the military. Churches, colleges, corporations, government organizations, and many other professional groupings observe rank, status, and privileges. The junior officer does not have to apologize for entitled privileges to the noncommissioned officer or accept the more senior officer's privileges with bitterness and rancor. Such privileges are an entitlement, occasioned by rank, that each officer receives and each officer observes without compromise of any personal principles.

The Privilege of Being First to Choose. Whenever a choice is to be made, such as selection of billets or quarters, electing means of transportation, or numerous other examples, the option of selection follows rank, the senior first.

"I Wish" and "I Desire." When the commanding officer states, "I wish," or "I desire," rather than "I order that you do so-and-so," this wish or desire has all the force of a direct order.

The Place of Honor. The place of honor is on the right. Accordingly, when a junior walks, rides, or sits with a senior, the junior takes position abreast and to the left of the senior. The deference that a young officer should pay to his or her elders pertains to this relationship. The junior should walk in step with the senior, step back and allow the senior to be the first to enter a door, and render similar acts of consideration and courtesy.

Use of the Word "Sir." The word *Sir* is used in military conversation by the junior officer in addressing a senior, and by all soldiers in addressing officers. It precedes a report and a query; it follows the answer of a question. For example: "Sir, do you wish to see Sergeant Brown?" "Sir, I report as Old Officer of the Day." "Private Brown, Sir." "Thank you, Sir."

Departing Before the Commanding Officer. Officers should remain at a reception or social gathering until the commanding officer has departed.

New Year's Call on the Commanding Officer. It is Army tradition that officers and their spouses make a formal call upon the commanding officer during the afternoon of New Year's Day. The pressures of the current Army mission, the desires of the commanding officer, and local or major unit custom bear upon the holding of the event as well as the way it is done.

As a general guide, when the commanding officer elects to hold the event, timely information is provided as to the time and place, and the uniform to be worn. Branch blazers may be authorized. At large stations, the event usually is held at the officers' open mess as a reception with a receiving line; it may include a dance with light refreshments. If the senior commander does not hold the event, commanders of component units such as the brigade or battalion, may choose to do so. Official funds are not provided to defray the costs. Officers whose duties of the day permit are expected to attend. In any case, think of it as a pleasant, ceremonial social function, adding color to the military scene, starting the New Year in a spirit of general comradeship.

How to Obtain an Appointment with the Commanding Officer. It is the custom to ask the adjutant, the executive officer, or an aide, as may be appropriate, for an appointment with the commander or other senior officer. There is no special formality about it. Just inquire, "May I see the commanding officer?" Often it will be appropriate to state the reason. Take your minor administrative problems to an appropriate staff officer of your own headquarters and avoid consuming the time of your commanding officer. Save your personal requests to him or her for a major matter that others cannot resolve in your behalf, or resolve as well.

Permission of the First Sergeant. It is the custom that enlisted personnel secure permission from the first sergeant before speaking to the company commander. It is essential to discipline that each soldier knows that he or she has the right to appeal directly to the captain for redress of wrongs.

The Open-door Policy. The soldier's right to speak to the company commander is echoed by each commander at a higher level. It is the "open-door" policy that permits each person in the Army, regardless of rank, to appeal to the next higher commander. Indeed, this right is checked and enforced by The Inspector General. It is not uncommon for a private soldier to talk to the battalion commander, since many administrative matters are performed by the battalion staff. The officer needs to expect this and not be arbitrary about barring his or her door to soldiers. Usually, if there is disagreement between a soldier and an officer, or a soldier believes he or she has a real grievance, the soldier has the right to speak to the next senior commander and to have the matter resolved.

Payment for Personal Services. In the past, some soldiers in addition to their regular duties could also work, if willing to do so, as personal servants to officers and their families. In the Army the custom has always been that such work was entirely voluntary, with the officer compensating the soldier for his work. Historically, these men were known as orderlies or strikers. Some soldiers desired such jobs to supplement their service pay, just as some soldiers of this period take off-duty jobs, called "moonlighting." By custom and official restrictions the use of soldiers as servants of officers and their families in garrison assignments has terminated except for some senior officers and for special reasons in each case. However, for units in the field, in training or combat, an officer may be assigned a soldier orderly for personal services so the officer can devote maximum time to the responsibilities of command. Many times it is the driver of the vehicle assigned to the officer who performs such personal services.

Whenever officers utilize soldiers for personal services, always with the soldier's consent, compensation at some established or otherwise stipulated rate is required.

THE NEWCOMER SHALL BE WELL RECEIVED

Reception of a Newly Joined Officer. It is a custom that newly joined officers shall be cordially received and many acts of courtesy extended to the officer and his or her family to make their arrival more pleasant and convenient. It is taken for granted that a newly joined officer knows his or her professional duties and has every intention of performing them ably.

Whenever conditions permit such niceties, the adjutant sends a letter of welcome to an officer under orders to join, with information on local conditions that may be important or interesting for the officer to know before arrival. If the arrival is by train or plane, transportation may be arranged to be at the station or airport to meet the new arrival.

Most stations and most units welcome incoming families through the sponsor system under which a designated military member and his or her family on the scene act as hosts and advisers to the new arrivals. Many officers believe that this one custom has been responsible for making more enduring friendships than any other. Certainly the warm welcome and thoughtful courtesies extended to newly arrived members of a unit go a long way to gain the good start.

The adjutant usually introduces the newly joined officer to the commanding officer and at the first assembly to the other officers of the unit. The adjutant should also inform the newcomer as to local regulations and customs that will be needed at once. A copy of the garrison regulations and a map of the post are especially useful to the stranger.

The officer and adult members of the family are usually accorded the courtesy of being in the receiving line at the first appropriate function after their arrival. As newcomers, they may also be welcomed at a battalion party, as described above. If you are the newcomers, make the most of the opportunity to meet and start acquaintanceships; if you are the old-timers, do your full share of making the occasion useful and pleasant.

Receiving Officers of Sister Services. The officers of the host service accord a high degree of cordiality and hospitality to visiting officers from other services. This may include provisions for quarters, invitation to use an officers' mess, extension of club privileges, social invitations, introduction of the visitor to appropriate officers, and the like. But it includes above all else the hand of fellowship and comradeship to a brother or sister officer to stimulate a feeling of being welcomed among friends.

Military Weddings. Military weddings follow the same procedures as any other except for additional customs that add to their color and tone. Consult your chaplain for details and arrangements that will be suitable in making wedding plans.

At military weddings all officers should wear an appropriate dress uniform. Medals, or merely ribbons, may be worn with propriety. Badges may also be worn.

Frequently the national and unit colors are crossed just above and behind the position of the chaplain.

The saber? In all likelihood enough sabers to form the ceremonial arch of older days cannot be found. Perhaps if one is found it may be used for the first cut of the wedding cake as a polite bow to old tradition.

Reception of a Spouse. Under conditions of today, bride and groom are usually placed in the receiving line at an appropriate social function and introduced to the officers and their spouses of the organization in that way. Customs vary with conditions and with regard to official missions and times.

Birth of a Child. When a child is born to the family of an officer the unit commander may send a personal letter of congratulation to the parents on behalf of the organization. The wives of the unit officers may purchase a silver cup from their club funds with appropriate engraving. The unit commander sends a letter of congratulations to an enlisted man and his wife, or to the enlisted woman and her husband.

Upon request of parents it is usual that the organization color is made available for christenings so that the child may receive the ceremony under the colors of the member's organization. For the ceremony of baptism both the national and organization color may be made available.

CUSTOMS IN CONNECTION WITH SICKNESS AND DEATH

Visiting the Sick. An officer who is sick in hospital is visited by the officers of the unit in such numbers as may be permitted by the surgeon. An officer or soldier of the officer's unit visits the sick officer daily in order that his or her comfort or desires may receive attention.

An officer's spouse who is sick in hospital receives flowers sent in the name of the officers of the unit and their wives or husbands.

Death of an Officer or Family Member. When an officer dies another officer is immediately designated by the commanding officer to render every possible assistance to the bereaved family. A similar courtesy may be tendered, if desired, in the case of a death of a member of an officer's family.

A letter of condolence is written by the unit commander on behalf of the brigade, regiment, group, or similar unit. Flowers are sent in the name of the officers of the unit and their spouses.

Death of an Enlisted Person. When an enlisted person dies a letter of condolence is written to the nearest relative by the immediate commander of the deceased soldier.

Flowers are sent in the name of the members of the decedent's unit for the funeral.

The funeral is attended by all officers and soldiers of the deceased soldier's unit who so desire and whose duties permit.

SUPPORT OF POST AND ORGANIZATION ACTIVITIES

General. An officer is expected to support the activities of the unit, such as a brigade or battalion, to which he or she is assigned, as well as the activities of the entire garrison. The unit to which you are assigned consists of a closely knit group around which are entwined official duties, and athletic, social, and cultural activities for the benefit of all. You are a member of an official family. Your assignment must mean more than the place where your required and official duties are performed, important as they may be. You are expected to support and assist, at least by your presence, many events that form a part of military life. Proper interest and pride in all activities of your unit and garrison are factors in stimulating morale. Each officer should be a good military citizen, sharing with other good citizens responsibility for the unofficial life and activities of the garrison.

The Officers' Club and Mess. The open mess, or officers' club, is the nucleus around which revolves much of the off-duty social and recreational life of officers and their spouses. At a large station there may be branches to serve the needs of separate organizations, or of distant areas, and there are also at all stations similar establishments for noncommissioned officers. The open mess is an integral part of the Army establishment, subject to the control of the station commander. Its activities are conducted in accordance with AR 230-60 and its funds are controlled and audited under AR 230-7.

Membership is voluntary and has three classifications:

Active. Such members may vote and hold office. The right of active membership is extended to all officers of all services on duty at the installation.

Associate. Such members neither vote nor hold office but may enjoy all of the club's services and facilities. Associate membership is extended to officers at the installation who are on temporary duty, detached service, attached unassigned, or in a transient status.

Honorary. Extends the same privileges as the associate membership, usually on a non-dues-paying basis.

Attendance at Unit and Organization Parties Sponsored by Enlisted Members. It is customary for officers and their spouses, when invited, to attend special social events sponsored by enlisted members of a unit or organization. Conditions vary so widely throughout the Service that no general customs as to details of attendance can be identified. The best source of guidance is the commanding officer.

These principles would have general agreement. Officers, or officers and their spouses, would be invited only on special occasions. When invited, officers attend in their official capacity as officers to assist in enhancing pride of service, morale, and esprit. In conduct they will be mindful of the normal social amenities and be guided by the example set by the senior officer present. If the unit or organization is authorized to serve intoxicants, it is accepted practice for the officer to drink in marked moderation; the nondrinker should ask for a soft drink, without excuse. Excessive drinking, exhibitionist dancing, and other ungentlemanly or unladylike behavior would harm the purpose of attendance and be frowned upon. At an appropriate time and after the customary amenities, officers depart with or immediately after the senior officer attending, leaving the party for the enjoyment of its enlisted members.

Attendance at Athletic Events Is Desirable. As a matter of policy to demonstrate an interest in organization affairs, as well as for personal enjoyment, officers should attend athletic events in which their unit teams participate.

Ceremonies at Holiday Dinners. On Thanksgiving, Christmas, and New Year's Day many organizations have a tradition that the officers will visit the companies during the meal or prior to the serving of the meal. The method varies rather widely. As an example only, the brigade, battalion or similar commander, his or her staff, and field officers visit each mess hall just prior to the serving of the dinner. Officers of the company, their families, and families of married enlisted men of the company may dine with the companies on these holidays.

Farewell Tendered a Departing Officer. Prior to the departure of an officer from his or her organization or station on change of assignment, a reception, or other suitable function, is usually given in honor of the departing officer and family. Often one of the unit social functions is used for the purpose.

TABOOS

Uniform Must Not Be Defamed. The officer's uniform and official or social position must not be defamed. Conduct unbecoming an officer is punishable under Article 133, Uniform Code of Military Justice. The confidence of the nation in the integrity and high standards of conduct of the officers of the Army is an asset that no individual may be permitted to lower.

Never Slink under Cover to Avoid Retreat. As a good military person, always be proud and willing to pay homage and respect to the national flag and the National Anthem. Now and then thoughtless people in uniform are observed ducking inside a building or under other cover just to avoid a Retreat ceremony and the moment of respect it includes. Or do they merely convict themselves of ignorance as to the purpose of the ceremony and their own actions as it proceeds? See chapter 6 for honors paid at Retreat. Never slink away from an opportunity to pay respect to our flag and our anthem.

Spouses and children of Army families will wish to stand at attention and face the colors, too, if the ceremony is explained to them.

Proffer No Excuses. Never volunteer excuses or explain a shortcoming unless an explanation is required. The Army demands results. More damage than good is done by proffering unsought excuses.

Abstentions by Officers, Relations with Enlisted Members. It is strong Army tradition that an officer does not associate with enlisted soldiers as individuals in ordinary social affairs, nor gamble, nor borrow money, nor drink intoxicants with them. See the discussion in chapter 3, *The Code of the Army Officer,* under the main heading, THE OFFICER'S RELATIONS WITH ENLISTED PERSONNEL. Refer also to the several discussions, above, under SUPPORT OF POST AND ORGANIZATION ACTIVITIES.

Use of Third Person by Officers in Poor Taste. It is in poor taste for officers to use the third person in conversation with their seniors. For example, do not say, "Sir, does the Colonel desire . . .?" Instead, say "Sir, is it your desire . . .?" Most senior officers frown upon the use of the third person under any condition as it is regarded as a form of address implying servility.

Servility Is Scorned. Servility, "bootlicking," and deliberate courting of favor are beneath the standard of conduct expected of officers, and any who openly practice such things earn the scorn of their associates.

Avoid Praising Your Commander to His or Her Face. Paying compliments directly to your commander or chief is in poor taste. However genuine may be your high regard for your chief, to so express it suggests apple polishing or flattery and thus is capable of misinterpretation.

If you particularly admire your boss you can show it by extending the standard military courtesies—and meticulously carrying out his or her policies and doing all in your power to make the organization more effective.

With respect to subordinates, on the other hand, recognition of good work on their part is an inherent part of the exercise of command; do not hesitate to commend a subordinate whose actions are praiseworthy.

"Old Man" to Be Spoken with Care. The commanding officer acquires the accolade, "the Old Man," by virtue of his position and without regard whatever to his age. When the term is used it is more often in affection and admiration than otherwise. However, it is never used in the presence of the commanding officer, and if used would be considered disrespectful.

Avoid "Going over an Officer's Head." The jumping of an echelon of command is called *going over an officer's head* (for example, a company commander making a request of the brigade commander concerning a matter that should first have been presented to the commander of his or her battalion). The act is contrary to military procedure and decidedly disrespectful.

Harsh Remarks Are to Be Avoided. The conveying of gossip, slander, harsh criticism, and fault finding are unofficerlike practices. In casual conversation, if you can find nothing good to say about a person, it is wiser to say nothing about that individual.

Avoid Vulgarity and Profanity. Foul and vulgar language larded with profanity is repulsive to most self-respecting men and women. Its use by officers is reprehensible. An officer is expected to be a lady or a gentleman and, however the traditional terms are defined, certainly they exclude the use of vulgarity and profanity in one's conversation.

Never Lean on a Senior Officer's Desk. Avoid leaning or lolling against a senior officer's desk. It is resented by most officers and is unmilitary. Stand erect unless invited to be seated. Don't lean!

Never Keep Anyone Waiting. Report at once when notified to do so. Never keep anyone waiting unnecessarily. On the drill field when called by a senior officer, go on the double.

Avoid Having People Guess Your Name. Do not assume that an officer whom you have not seen or heard from for a considerable period will know your name when a contact is renewed. Tell him or her at once who you are, and then renew the acquaintance. If this act of courtesy is unnecessary, it will be received only as an act of thoughtfulness, while if it happens to be necessary it will save embarrassment. At official receptions always announce your name to the aide.

Carrying an Umbrella in Uniform. There is a longstanding Army taboo against a male officer in uniform carrying an umbrella. However. it is both authorized and proper for women in the Army to do so when not in formation.

Smoking. The Army officially discourages smoking, both for reasons of personal health and in deference to the rights of nonsmokers. In public buildings, smoking is permitted only in specially designated areas. Smoking by spectators during outdoor ceremonies, such as parades, also is considered objectionable. Indoors, in quarters or other areas where smoking may be permitted, the considerate officer who does smoke still should be sensitive to the rights of others.

Noncommissioned Officers Not to Work on Fatigue. A custom said to be as old as the Army is that which exempts noncommissioned officers from performing manual labor while in charge of a fatigue detail or while on fatigue.

THE ARMY'S BUGLE CALLS

Bugle calls by phonograph recordings, colorless and scarcely recognized, serve as reminders of past eras when the calls of the bugler regulated the military day, and served as an essential means of communication in battle. Remaining is *Taps*, the last sound of the bugle, as a soldier is laid to rest.

Historically, the beats of the drum and the calls of the bugle go far into past centuries. The calls in current use date back to the very beginning of our Army and reflect the influence of the British and French armies. It is noteworthy that before the Civil War, each branch had its own calls, with the Infantry using the beats of the drum. But this created confusion when several units were involved in battle. In 1867, Gen. Emory Upton prepared a document embodying changes made necessary by the Civil War, and requested Maj. Truman Seymour (later General) to prepare a new system of calls for all arms and branches of the Army. They have been continued in use. The history of a few selected calls follows.

First Call. Similar to the French cavalry call, "Le Garde à Vous."

Reveille. Same as the French call, this dates from the Crusades. (The armies of the Crusaders were amazed and frightened at the military music of the Saracens, and their instruments were captured and copied. Thereafter, the European armies used music to greater advantage in both battle and ceremony.)

Assembly. The old cavalry assembly call, in use from about 1835, was replaced in 1867 by the present more martial-sounding call.

Mess Call. Similar to the French call "Le Rappel."

Retreat. French cavalry call dating from the Crusades.

To the Color. The old cavalry call "To The Standard," in use from about 1835, was replaced in 1867 by the present more military-sounding call.

THE BUGLER, MOUNTED, POST–CIVIL WAR PERIOD.

Tattoo. Originated during the Thirty Years War and called the *Zapfenstreich.* At 9:00 P.M., when the call was sounded, all bungs (*Zapfen*) had to be replaced in their barrels, signifying the end of the nightly drinking bout. A chalk line (*Streich*) was then drawn across the bung by the guard so that it could not be opened without evidence of tampering. "Tap-to" thus became "Tattoo." (See "Taps.")

In the United States Army, "Tattoo" is the longest call, consisting of twenty-eight measures, but is still far short of the elaborate ceremony used in the British and German services. The first section of eight measures is the same as the French call "Extinction des Feux," (Lights Out) and was at one time used for *Taps* in our Army. This French call was composed for the Army of Napoleon, and was the Emperor's favorite. The last section of twenty measures of our "Tattoo" is taken from the British "First Post," and comes originally from an old Neapolitan cavalry call, "Il Silencio."

Prior to the adoption of the present "Tattoo" in 1867, two other versions were in use, the first during 1835–1861, and the second during the Civil War.

Attention. Taken from the British call "Alarm," at which time the troops turn out under arms.

Church Call. Same as the French "Church Call," this was one of those retained in the revision of 1867. It was taken from the "Sonneries de Chasseurs d' Orleans," promulgated in 1845.

Taps. General Daniel Butterfield of the Army of the Potomac composed the call in July 1862, for use in his own brigade, supposedly to replace the three volleys fired at military funerals so the Confederates would not know a burial was taking place. Soon thereafter, it replaced "Tattoo" as the last call of the day. Its use became popular throughout the Union Army.

When Major Seymour prepared the present set of bugle calls in 1867, he apparently did not know of General Butterfield's version, since the music was not changed to its present notation until 1874, when it first appeared in the Infantry drill regulations.

Reference to the word *Taps* has been found as early as 1861 and is variously explained, one version being that it originally was soldier slang for "Tap-To," as "Tattoo" was first spelled, and "Tap-To" in the Infantry was sounded on a drum— thus *Taps*. (See "Tattoo.")

The earliest official reference to the mandatory use of *Taps* at military funeral ceremonies is in the *U.S. Army Drill Regulations of 1891*. Its unofficial use as a finale to the firing salute had been customary since its inception in 1862. (In the British Army, "Last Post" has been sounded over soldier's graves after interment since 1885, being prescribed in Standing Orders since that year.)

Fire Call. Similar to certain British and French calls.

First Sergeant's Call. This call is first mentioned in *Martial Music of Camp Dupont*, 1816, when it was a drum call sounded when the adjutant wished to summon the first sergeant. The present bugle call, used to notify all first sergeants to report to the adjutant or sergeant major, comes from the German Army.

NAVY CUSTOMS ARMY OFFICERS SHOULD KNOW

Courtesies. There are Navy customs applicable to shore duty and to the special situations of life aboard a naval vessel. The courtesies pertaining to a naval vessel are provided as of noteworthy interest to officers of the Army on any occasion when they visit or serve aboard a unit of our fleet.

On appropriate occasions when visiting naval vessels, officers of the armed services, except when in civilian clothes, are attended by sailors known as side boys when they come aboard and when they depart. This courtesy is also extended to commissioned officers of the armed services of foreign nations. Officers of the rank of lieutenant to major inclusive are given two side boys, from lieutenant colonel to colonel four side boys, from brigadier to major general six side boys, and lieutenant general and above eight side boys. Full guard and band are given to general officers, and for a colonel, the guard of the day, but no music.

During the hours of darkness or low visibility an approaching boat is usually hailed "Boat ahoy?" which corresponds to the sentry's challenge, "Who is there?" Some of the answers are as follows:

Answer	*Meaning:* Senior in boat is:
"Aye aye"	Commissioned officer
"No no"	Warrant officer
"Hello"	Enlisted
"Enterprise"	CO of Enterprise
"Seventh Fleet"	Admiral commanding Seventh Fleet

Similarly if the Commanding General of the 1st Infantry Division is embarked or the Commanding General of Fort Monroe, the answers would be "1st Infantry Division" or "Fort Monroe."

On arrival, at the order, "Tend the side" the side boys fall in fore and aft of the approach to the gangway, facing each other. The boatswain's mate-of-the-watch takes station forward of them and faces aft. When the boat comes alongside, the boatswain's mate pipes and again when the visiting officer's head reaches the level of the deck. At this latter instant the side boys salute.

On departure, the ceremony is repeated in reverse; the bos'n's mate begins to pipe and side boys to salute as soon as the departing officer steps toward the gangway between the side boys. As the boat casts off the bos'n's mate pipes again. (Shore boats and automobiles are not piped.)

You uncover when entering a space where men are at mess and in sick bay (quarters) if sick men are present. You uncover in the wardroom at all times except when under arms and passing through. All hands except when under arms uncover in the captain's cabin and country.

You should not overtake a senior except in emergency. In the latter case slow, salute, and say, "By your leave, Sir." Admirals, commanding officers, and chiefs of staff when in uniform fly colors astern when embarked in boats. When officials visit they also display their personal flags (pennants for commanding officers) in the bow. Flag officers' barges are distinguished by the appropriate number of stars on each side of the barge's hull. Captains' gigs are distinguished by the name or abbreviation of their ships surcharged by an arrow.

Use of Navy Titles. In the Navy it is customary to address officers in the grade of lieutenant commander and below, *socially,* as "mister" or "miss," and officers in the grade of commander and above by their titles. *Officially,* officers in both staff and line are addressed by their ranks.

Title of Commanding Officer of a Ship. Any officer in command of a ship, regardless of size or class, while exercising command is addressed as "Captain."

Visiting. Where accommodation ladders are rigged on both sides, the starboard ladder is reserved for officers and the port ladder for enlisted personnel. At the discretion of the officer of the deck (OOD), either ladder may be made available to both officers and enlisted personnel. See chapter 6 for a quotation of Navy Regulations on courtesy to the Ensign.

Seniors come on board ship first. When reaching the deck you face toward the colors (or aft if no colors are hoisted) and salute the colors (quarterdeck). Immediately thereafter you salute the OOD and request permission to come aboard. The usual form is, "Request permission to come aboard, Sir." The OOD is required to return both salutes.

On leaving the ship the inverse order is observed. You salute the OOD and request permission to leave the ship. The OOD will indicate when the boat is ready (if a boat is used). Each person, juniors first, salutes the OOD; then faces toward the colors (quarterdeck), salutes, and debarks.

The OOD on board ship represents the captain and as such has unquestioned authority. Only the executive and commanding officer may order him or her relieved. The authority of the OOD extends to the accommodation ladders or gangways. The OOD has the right to order any approaching boat to "lie off" and keep clear until the boat can be safely received alongside.

The OOD normally conveys orders to the embarked troops via the troop commander but in emergencies may issue orders direct to you or any person on board.

The *bridge* is the "command post" of the ship when underway, as the quarterdeck is at anchor. The officer of the deck is in charge of the ship as the representative of the captain. Admittance to the bridge when underway should be at the captain's invitation or with his or her permission. You may usually obtain permission through the executive officer.

The *quarterdeck* is the seat of authority; as such it is respected. The starboard side of the quarterdeck is reserved for the captain (and admiral if a flagship). No person trespasses upon it except when necessary in the course of work or official business. All persons salute the quarterdeck when entering upon it. When pacing the deck with another officer the place of honor is outboard, and when reversing direction each turns toward the other. The port side of the quarterdeck is reserved for commissioned officers, and the crew has all the rest of the weather decks of the ship. However, every part of the deck (and the ship) is assigned to a particular division so that the crew has ample space. Not unnaturally every division considers it has a prior though unwritten right to its own part of the ship. For gatherings such as smokers and movies, all divisions have equal privileges at the scene of assemblage. Space and chairs are reserved for officers and for CPOs, where available, and mess benches are brought up for the enlisted personnel. The seniors have the place of honor. When the captain (and admiral) arrives those present are called to attention. The captain customarily gives "carry on" at once through the executive officer or master-at-arms.

Messes. If you take passage on board a naval vessel you will be assigned to one of several messes on board ship, the wardroom or junior officers' mess. In off-hours, particularly in the evenings, you can foregather there for cards, yarns, or reading. A pot of coffee generally is available.

The executive officer is ex-officio the president of the wardroom mess. The wardroom officers are the division officers and the heads of departments. All officers await the arrival of the executive officer before being seated at lunch and dinner. If it is necessary for you to leave early ask the head at your table permission to be excused as you would at home. The seating arrangement in the messes is by order of seniority.

Calls. Passenger officers should call on the captain of the ship. If there are many of you, you should choose a calling committee and consult the executive officer as to a convenient time to call. The latter will make arrangements with the captain.

Ceremonies. Gun salutes in the Navy are the same as in the Army except that flag officers below the rank of fleet admiral or general of the Army, are, by Navy regulations, given a gun salute upon departure only.

Saluting. By custom, Navy personnel do not salute when uncovered, although it is customary for Navy officers to return the salute of Army and Air Force personnel whether covered or not. Aboard ship, seniors are saluted only during the first greeting in the morning. The commanding officer (or any flag or general officer) is saluted whenever met.

AIR FORCE CUSTOMS ARMY OFFICERS SHOULD KNOW

Courtesies*. The rules governing saluting, whether saluting other individuals or paying honor to the color or National Anthem, are the same for the Air Force as the Army. Because the most frequent contact between the Air Force and the other services is probably as a result of riding in military aircraft, a special section is devoted to passengers in military aircraft.

Visiting. It is assumed that the majority of officers visiting an Air Force base are there in conjunction with air travel to or from the base. In addition to the Base Operations Officer, who is the commander's staff officer with jurisdiction over all air traffic, the Airdrome Officer is charged with meeting all transient aircraft,

---

*See *The Air Force Officer's Guide*, Stackpole Books, Harrisburg, Pennsylvania.

determining the transportation requirements of transient personnel, and directing them to the various base facilities. General officers and admirals usually are met by the base commander, if practicable. RON (remain over-night) messages may be transmitted through base operations.

Passengers from other services who desire to remain overnight at an Air Force base should make the necessary arrangements with the Airdrome Officer, and not attach themselves to the pilot who will be busy with his or her own responsibilities. By the same token, passengers of other services who have had a special flight arranged for them should make every effort to see that the pilot and crew are offered the same accommodations that they themselves are using, unless that base has adequate transient accommodations.

Passenger vehicles are never allowed on the ramp or flight lines unless special arrangements have been made with the Base Operations Officer; this permission will only be granted under the most unusual circumstances.

Travel in Military Aircraft. The assigned first pilot, or the airplane commander, is the final authority on the operation of any military aircraft. Passengers, regardless of rank, seniority, or service, are subject to the orders of the airplane commander, who is solely responsible for their adherence to regulations governing conduct in and around the aircraft. In the event it is impracticable for the airplane commander to leave his or her position, orders may be transmitted through the co-pilot, engineer, or crew chief, and have the same authority as if given personally by the pilot.

The order of boarding and alighting from military aircraft—excluding the crew—will vary somewhat with the nature of the mission. If a special flight is arranged for the transportation of very important persons (VIPs), official inspecting parties, or other high-ranking officers of any service, the senior member will exit first, and the other members of the party will follow either in order of rank, or in order of seating, those nearest the hatch alighting first.

In routine transportation flights, officers will normally be loaded in order of rank without regard for precedence, except that VIPs will be on- and off-loaded first. In alighting, officers seated near the hatch generally debark first, and so on to those who are farthest away. In the event dependents are being carried, they together with their sponsor generally are loaded and unloaded after any VIPs and before the officers.

Aircraft carrying general or flag officers will usually be marked with a detachable metal plate carrying stars appropriate to the highest rank aboard, and will be greeted on arrival by the Air Force base commander, if the destination is an Air Force base. Other aircraft are usually met by the Airdrome Officer, who is appointed for one day only, and acts as the base commander's representative.

Since aerial flights are somewhat dependent on weather, especially when carrying passengers, the decision of the pilot to fly or not to fly or to alter the flight plan en route will not be questioned by the passengers of whatever rank or service. Regulations governing the use of safety belts; against smoking during take-off, landing, and fuel transfer, or in the vicinity of the aircraft on the ground; and in wearing parachutes are binding on all classes of passengers.

A FINAL WORD OF CAUTION

There is a tendency, sometimes, to confuse customs, traditions, and social obligations. Customs of the Service that have been treated in this chapter are those that are more universally observed throughout the Army.

Traditions, on the other hand, are considered much less formal than the recognized customs of the Service. There are many more traditions than could be covered here. Many are confined to a particular unit, organization, station, or branch of Service, and one is most likely to become acquainted with them quickly upon reporting for a new assignment. Such traditions may catch on and become widespread because of the mobile nature of Army life, especially so for those that have a more positive influence on one's personal living.

There is a danger, however, in the expectancy that others will quickly accept a particular tradition once you are again outside the area where it has been observed. For example: Many inquiries have been received as to why previous editions of *The Army Officer's Guide* offered no counsel about how an officer recognizes his or her promotion in relation to fellow officers and civilian co-workers, if any. Research into this question reveals that, officially, there is no custom of the Service to provide guidance, nor is there any well-entrenched tradition anywhere. In such an instance as this, inasmuch as promotion is a personal thing, and as such has differing degrees of meaning at various times and places, the officer may choose to do something or nothing, the former on any scale that befits his or her mood, position, or pocketbook at the time.

You are cautioned, therefore, to get acquainted with local traditions and customs and to be sure that you are not a party to unjustified criticism of anyone when there is no tangible understanding in the local military community about what one does upon any particular occasion.

8

The Social Side
of Army Life

At any military station there is a feeling of "oneness" or "belonging" that is a natural outcome of the singleness of purpose of the military mission on which all are engaged. It is enhanced by the fact that the problems, the hopes and expectancies, and even the fears within one military home are similar to those in other military homes. This community of interest is a noteworthy contrast to the experience of newcomers in the usual civilian community where neighbors may not know neighbors and may live in quite different social worlds. Officers and their families are accepted as immediate, full-fledged members of the military community upon their arrival at a station.

This chapter is provided as an extension of the preceding chapter, *Customs of the Service.* Related also to our subject is chapter 6, *Military Courtesy.* The reader should understand that the subjects presented assist in creating an atmosphere and an environment that can provide a pleasant, gracious, and rewarding life. This is important for life in the armed services because of the unusual circumstances of the official missions that are assigned, the frequent changes of station, and occasional difficulties related to living conditions. More rewarding lives can be experienced by a sensible application of service courtesies, customs, and social expectancies.

Officers and their spouses support activities and follow social customs in about the same manner as educated persons in other professions. As they are drawn from all states and regions of our country, they tend to adopt activities that have been enjoyed elsewhere. Army families have the great advantage of being bound together with the common interest of the Army mission and association in joint undertakings. For these reasons, community interests are likely to be extensive and participation quite general. As in social and civic life elsewhere, including church, fraternal, and similar activities, each individual receives in benefit and enjoyment about the same as he or she contributes.

Army Social Customs. Most social practices observed in Army circles today are similar to those in the sister services or in civil life. Indeed, a large portion of the officer corps may be assigned to duties where they are obliged to live within a civilian community, perhaps remote from a military station. During a span of years the officer will have the social experience of the Army station as well as the civilian community. The newcomer may proceed with confidence that the social practices that are in good taste and general observance in our civilian communities have similar application within the service community. It is true that there is a heritage of Army social customs, just as there are special customs observed within other closely knit groups of people. In what other walk of life will there be the arrival of families returning from Europe, the Pacific, Alaska, or other distant lands? Or families departing for these assignments? These situations account for some of the differences. There are infrequent formal dinners and receptions that are held for necessary purposes, such as to honor visiting senior officers or for the reception of a high official of our government. Take them all in stride. This chapter has been prepared to be helpful. Army social life consists of pleasant human relationships, adding to the enjoyment of service associations, and should be approached with anticipation.

This is an officer's book, written especially for officers and their families. Because not discussed herein, let no person assume that on Army stations the unmarried or married enlisted soldier draws a blank in social or cultural activities, for such is not the case. There are noncommissioned officers' and enlisted clubs, the service club, libraries, hobby shops, a broad athletic program, and other activities sponsored generally by Recreation Services.

A Special Message for Newcomers. The newly arriving officer, or officer and family, will find a sincere welcome from the members of the military community. You can set aside any concern you may have had about "newness." Unlike civilian communities, where residents may reside for years and years, the assignment of officers to a station or duty may continue for no more than three or four years at the most, and where it is a command assignment the tenure may be even less. So as a matter of plain fact, all members of an Army garrison, from the most senior to the most junior, are "new" in the sense of length of residence.

No person entering an Army community for the first time need be disturbed about the customs or the social practices. In the first place, Army people are understanding of the special problems of the newcomer, and if given the opportunity will be pleasantly helpful. The social practices are substantially the same as found in any large group of well-educated, professional people. If one is accustomed to the social life of a country club, or a university campus, the activities at an officers' club or open mess will be entirely similar. If you have apprehensions, lay them aside. Enter with confidence this new life, which can offer many rewarding experiences and friendships. Let people know who you are and that you are pleased to be among them. Seek acquaintances with individuals of your special interests, or backgrounds, or activities. You need not be the life of the party or the best dressed person in attendance. Just be a pleasant person, among other pleasant people, and do as you would at a similar social function anywhere.

You will not be expected to do more than normal entertaining, which initially would mean the return of obligations, in due time, and in a manner entirely appropriate to your means. Participate in dutch treat gatherings, informal picnics, swim parties, and such pleasant events as come your way. Later, as you learn your way around and have developed acquaintances, you may even organize inexpensive share-the-cost gatherings. Who knows—you may soon be able to help some newcomer newer than yourself off to a pleasant start. But manage your personal financial affairs, capably and firmly. You know your pay and allowances, as well as the obligations that you have assumed. You may be relieved to learn that most young officers, single or married, also face the "shortage of dollars" problem. Face it and adjust to it. But do a top-notch official job for the Army, and then have such good times with pleasant associates as circumstances permit.

The Officers' Club and Mess. The officers' club and mess, known as the open mess, is the center for social activities for officers and their families. Here there are facilities for dining and for holding private dinner parties, plus a program of dances, card parties, and other forms of group entertainment desired by the members. (See also chapter 7 for operation of the open mess.)

You may wish to attend the dances and other social events sponsored by the officers' club that the payment of dues entitles you to attend. However, it is more likely that you will wish to participate in those activities at the club or elsewhere that are sponsored by the unit to which you are assigned.

An officer with permanent station at a post having a club should become a member at once. To fail to do so will cause the officer and the adult members of his or her family to miss much of the available social life of the post.

Cultural Opportunities. The cultural opportunities available at an established military station equal or exceed those of civilian communities of like size. They provide opportunity for the enjoyment of acquired interests and the development of new ones.

Many such activities are given strong sponsorship by the officers' wives' clubs. In addition to the general meetings there may be groups with special interests in music, literature, the study of antiques, language study, and any other worthy purpose the members desire.

Station libraries are well equipped in nearly all instances, and new books and magazines are received regularly. Libraries are under direction of a professional librarian who may be relied upon to render assistance to serious groups or individuals.

Opportunities for Community Service. Military stations and adjoining civilian communities provide opportunities for community service in many worthy causes. Members of Army families may find rewarding activities that pertain to problems of the garrison or join with civilian organizations in work beneficial to the complete community.

There are a variety of organizations found on every post to which one can volunteer. The Red Cross sponsors Grey Ladies and Nurses' Aides. The United Services Organization (USO) has need for workers and hostesses. Chaplains (and off-post ministers) need teachers and helpers. Schools are supported by the Parent-Teachers Association. Scouting and sports activities, such as Little League baseball, need the support of parents.

Social and Recreational Opportunities for Young People. An Army station is a healthy and interesting environment for young people because of the many very active organizations that in most cases are to be found in thriving condition. There is the same need for social and recreational opportunities for boys and girls living on or near an Army post as in civilian communities.

Little League teams and Boy Scout, Girl Scout, Cub Scout, and Brownie troops are established at most Army stations where families are present. Many stations provide a Teen-Age Club for boys and girls of high school age where there are dances, picnics, and other forms of entertainment attractive to healthy and active young people.

The chaplain sponsors religious activities for young people.

Needed always are adults who will serve as leaders in these splendid activities, and those who do find the experience rewarding and interesting. The corollary, of course, is that officers and their spouses should plan to be active at least in those activities where their children participate.

Building Social Good Will. The building of social good will is the development of respect and esteem. In gist, it is the sum of an infinite number of favorable impressions. Almost certainly it will have an effect upon an officer's career. In any event the giving of social offense must do harm. This discussion deals with its fundamentals.

Strive to be on good terms with all. A member of a military family will have likes and preferences in developing friendships and friendly associations just as any other person. However, it is wise to avoid cliques. Avoid open expressions of criticism or dislike, which develop hard feelings. Do not always restrict your dinner guests, golfing companions, and other social associates to the same individuals. Mix them up. Broaden your acquaintances. By so doing you will reap the reward of building more friendships and finding more people of interest.

Upon receiving a social invitation express appreciation at being included. Accept at once if that is your wish. Decline at once if unable to accept and again extend a courteous word of appreciation. If there is uncertainty about being able to accept state the reason for uncertainty. It is better to accompany uncertainty with a declination so the hostess, if she wishes to do so, may invite others. If invited to accept or decline at a later time give the answer at the earliest possible moment. Do not keep the hostess dangling in uncertainty longer than necessary. Remember in expressing appreciation that it is the hostess or host who is extending the courtesy—not the guest by accepting.

Pay particular attention to written invitations. On many, if not most, you will see the initials *R.S.V.P.* or the words *Regrets Only* in the lower left corner. The former is an abbreviation of the French words *répondez s'il vous plaît,* meaning "please reply," asking that you acknowledge the invitation by either accepting or declining so that your host or hostess will be able to make firm plans regarding the number of attendees. Regrets Only asks for a response only if you cannot attend. Do your host or hostess the courtesy of responding so there will be no doubt as to your intentions.

Have a social calendar and write in the occasion, date, and hour—and then keep track of your commitments!

Arrival for a dinner engagement should be promptly at the hour stated by the hostess. There are problems of timing that apply with equal force to the simple home dinner and the formal dinner for a large gathering. It is rude to arrive late at a dinner unless the tardiness is indeed unavoidable; even then the hostess should be informed by telephone if at all possible. Prompt arrival is also essential at other social events, such as a card party, or gathering for other specific purpose where the presence of all invited guests at a stated time is clearly desirable. Where the invitation is for a stated period, as "6–8," the situation and custom differs. The invited guests may arrive after 6, and depart before 8, but they do not customarily remain more than briefly after the hour stated because it may interfere with other plans of the host and hostess.

PRACTICAL TIPS

The Right Clothes. In these days of informality, selection of the proper clothes to wear on various occasions can be a problem. The first point to consider is whether the the occasion is essentially a military function or a private affair. For military functions, the proper uniform may be specified, thus settling the problem immediately. However, if the proper uniform is not stated, the following are suggested:

Parades and retreats	Service uniform
Official call or informal dinner	Service uniform, with coat
Formal dinner or official reception	Evening dress uniform or mess uniform

For informal private dinners or cocktail parties, a business suit for males or a cocktail dress, simple dinner dress, or dressy business suit for females should be adequate. Casual dress would imply sport shirts for the men and perhaps slack suits for the women. Your host or hostess may thoughtfully suggest appropriate attire for the occasion. When in doubt, it is better to overdress than to underdress for the occasion, but if in real doubt, inquire. And remember that the appropriate attire for your spouse is just as important as it is for you.

If you are proceeding from a cocktail party to a more formal function, it is proper to wear to the cocktail party attire appropriate for the more formal affair.

The Right Words. At any social gathering guests should strive to make the occasion pleasant for all. Conversation is important. Visit with all or many of the other guests. It is better to be a good listener than a good talker. But a good listener needs to be adept at starting subjects of conversation. What are the mutual interests? Who are mutual but absent friends? Has the other guest just returned from an interesting trip? Think of a subject above the commonplace and start the conversation. Then listen. *Avoid controversial subjects.* Let the host and hostess set the pace. Avoid being a wet blanket. Do not take over the party. Be agreeable. Don't be one of the few who are adept at making enemies and antagonizing people. Use the opportunity of your host's hospitality to broaden your acquaintance and strengthen friendships.

Social gatherings of military people will include in many cases officers of a wide span of grade and age. Most senior officers enjoy association with younger officers and their wives or husbands. Make a point of offering a pleasant greeting and having at least a brief conversation with the senior officers present and their spouses. The older or senior guests will do their part in making the younger ones feel at ease. Make a special point of greeting your company, battalion, and higher unit commander and general officers of your station, and their wives or husbands. Meet them as social equals, for such is your status as an officer or officer's spouse. Be polite and respectful but never subservient.

Is there a guest of honor or house guest? If so, make special effort soon after arrival to be sociable with them by conversation that indicates your true interest in them and their visit.

How long to stay as a guest after a dinner or other evening invitation depends upon the program of the hostess. Unless a reason exists to the contrary, a good rule to observe is to depart no more than an hour after the service of dinner is completed. In these busy days within military circles, the custom is for early departure. When the commanding officer is present as a guest, especially at a formal event, he or she is first to depart and has the special obligation of departing at the appropriate time. For purposes of general illustration assuming dinner guests arriving at 8, goodnights are often appropriate by 10:30. At informal affairs of any kind another good guidepost is to depart before host and hostess can possibly begin to wonder as to the departure intentions of their guest.

In making a departure, do not dawdle. There are few things more irritating than the guest who prepares to depart, then stands on and on in hall or doorway, narrating little nothings while hosts stand patiently by. Arise, express your pleasure for the occasion, obtain outer wraps, say your gracious farewells, and leave.

Social Calls. The matter of social calls presents a special problem for consideration. In the years before World War II, social calling was an established Army custom. Social calls were useful to welcome newcomers, to broaden acquaintances, and to bid pleasant farewells prior to departure. The custom was largely set aside during the busy days of the war years and it never really has been revived.

When the custom was followed, social calls were made generally on Sunday afternoons and involved only brief visits of about fifteen minutes duration at the visited officer's quarters. Officers of a unit and their wives, other than the commanding officer, generally made first calls upon newcomers to the unit. These welcoming calls were then returned by the newcomers as soon as practicable. This rather stylized procedure afforded an opportunity for all concerned to become acquainted with one another. Calls also were made during one's tenure at a station as a way of broadening acquaintances. Going away calls were made by departing officers and their wives to bid a pleasant farewell to friends they had made while assigned to the station.

In more recent years, the practice of social calling has been largely replaced by periodic unit or station receptions at which newcomers are welcomed by and introduced to unit or station personnel, often by being included in the receiving line. Similar affairs are often used as a means of bidding farewell to departing officers and their spouses.

Still, the regulation of interest, AR 600–25, states the importance of the exchange of visits of courtesy as the primary basis for the establishment of those social contacts among officers of the Army. These contacts are essential to the development of mutual understanding, respect, confidence, and teamwork. The regulation recognizes that the size and complexity of the Army of today may preclude the exchange of courtesy visits in accordance with the traditional concepts. However, it charges all officers to adhere to the established customs to the extent practicable. Commanders are specifically charged to adhere to the principles for courtesy visits outlined in the regulation but are granted discretion in application of the principles in any given situation.

What is your proper course of action in this matter? First, read again the words from the regulation that are quoted in the section on Official Calls in chapter 6. Then check with the adjutant or executive officer to determine the local custom. Follow the local custom, of course, since it reflects the desires of your commander. Later on, when you are the commander, you may wish to adhere more closely to the traditional concepts than has been the case in the recent past.

Calling Cards. With the passage of the custom of social calling, the use of calling cards also has largely faded into memory. When paying social calls, calling cards were left in prescribed numbers by both the officer and his wife for adult members of the visited officer's family. The use of calling cards was helpful in the difficult problem of names, and a case might be made for their continued use today.

Calling cards still are useful on certain occasions, but use of calling cards is entirely at your option. They generally may be obtained from service school book stores, large department stores, engravers, and many jewelers. When obtained, the cards should be engraved with simple, clear lettering. The cards should indicate your present rank and the service should be designated as United States Army. Indication of branch is optional, but component should not be shown. The cards of chaplains do not indicate rank. The cards shown in the accompanying illustrations are substantially correct in size, shape, and format.

There is no official military counterpart to the civilian business card. Still, in recent years, more and more senior officers have found it convenient to have and use such cards in their contacts with civilian officials and private business concerns.

Introductions. Adeptness must be developed in the art of making introductions. Here are the simple guides:

Introducing your wife to any man (except chiefs of state and very high church dignitaries): "Mary, this is Colonel Brown."

Introducing your husband to another man: "Colonel Brown, may I present my husband, Jack," or "Jack, this is Lieutenant Black." The correct order is to introduce the junior to the senior or the younger to the older, as noted below.

Introducing one lady to another: "Mrs. Jones, may I present Mrs. Green," or "Mary, this is Mrs. Green."

Introducing one officer to another: "Major Smith, this is Captain Brown."

Introducing yourself to an officer senior to you: "Sir, may I introduce myself? I am Captain Jones." (Wait for the other to extend his hand.)

Introducing yourself to an officer of equal or lesser rank: "I'm Captain Jack Jones." (Extend your hand.)

Introducing children or teenagers to adults: "Lieutenant Jones, this is Jane Smith."

Responding to an introduction: "How do you do, Colonel Green."

Thanking host and hostess on departing a social function: "Thank you for a delightful evening."

If you *must* leave a function noticeably early: "Mrs. (Hostess), I'm so sorry I must leave early." (Then give your reason and make it good.)

Using titles with names—

Major General Black: "General Black."

Brigadier General White: "General White."

Colonel Smith: "Colonel Smith."

Lt. Colonel Jones: "Colonel Jones."

First Lieutenant Brown: "Lieutenant Brown."

Second Lieutenant Green: "Lieutenant Green."

Gentlemen are introduced or presented to ladies, not the reverse. This holds even though the gentleman may be very distinguished and the lady very young. *Exceptions:* The President of the United States, a royal personage, a church dignitary.

The most common way to make introductions, always in good taste, is to state the names in proper sequence, the lady, the senior, or more distinguished, or more elderly first. "General Smith—Captain Jones." "Miss Youthful—Colonel Adams." "Mrs. Elderly Lady—General Cole." Use a rising inflection for the first name pronounced. The more formal method: "General Smith, may I present Captain Jones?"

Acknowledgment of an introduction by saying "How do you do?" is always appropriate.

When men are introduced they shake hands, standing, without reaching across

HAROLD LOUIS NEATE

LIEUTENANT
UNITED STATES ARMY

CAPTAIN NOAH MATTHEW JACKSON
AIDE-DE-CAMP TO MAJOR GENERAL SECREST

UNITED STATES ARMY

LIEUTENANT COLONEL AND MRS. NATHAN MENZO NEELY

Edna Trude Shope

Colonel
United States Army

EXAMPLES OF CALLING CARDS.

another person, if possible. They may say nothing, just look pleasant or smile, or say a courteous, "It is nice to meet you," or "How do you do?"

When women are introduced to each other, with one sitting, one standing, the seated one rises to greet her hostess, or a very distinguished lady, as an act of respect. This would apply, for example, to the wife of a very senior officer. In the usual case, the seated lady does not rise. The reply to an introduction may be a simple, "How do you do?"

When a man is introduced to a lady he does not offer his hand unless the lady proffers hers. In Europe, men are taught to take the initiative in hand shaking. A lady does not refuse a proffered hand.

A lady or man, introducing husband or wife to another, may say, "This is my husband," or "May I introduce my wife?"

At a social occasion, host and hostess should shake hands with guests in greeting, and upon their departure.

Memory of Names. Military people meet officially or socially such a large number of people that remembering names is a difficult problem. Still, it is a very important attribute. To remember at all you must first understand the name clearly. Therefore, at time of introduction, be sure to hear and understand the name correctly. Repeat it aloud to assure correctness and to aid your memory; your interest will please and flatter many. During the occasion strive to use the name in conversation, and fix the name to the face of the person. Be very careful in making introductions to state names correctly and distinctly.

Upon arrival at your first station, you should start a notebook in which you record the names of people you should remember. List their complete names and middle initials. List names of husband and wife. For family friends list names of children and birthdays if known. After the passage of months or years such a record may be of much interest and assistance.

A Glance at Social Precedence and Protocol. An understanding of basic principles of social precedence and protocol is essential to officers as well as to officials of many other professional groups who have a recognized or official title. *Examples:* Educators; ministers and high church officials; elected or appointed officials of the national, state, or local government; foreign military, government, or professional dignitaries; others. Protocol in simple definition is "the code of international politeness."

Precedence becomes a factor for host and hostess to consider in deciding who sits where at a dinner, or in deciding places at a speaker's table, or positions in a receiving line, or other formal occasion. It is important at universities whenever the faculty is assembled formally, as at a graduation ceremony. Legislators in state or national capital must make use of it.

The place of honor is on the right or in the lead: *Examples:* The senior walks on the right of the junior. Juniors step aside for the senior to be first to enter a door. The senior is last to enter an automobile but is first to leave, and the right rear seat is reserved for him or her. The senior returns the salute of the junior. An officer of lesser rank is presented to the senior. Age is a very decided consideration in social precedence, especially in a mixed group as to profession and vocation.

The form of address is a related subject. It is "Mr. President," "Mr. Chief Justice," "Mr. Secretary," or "Mr. Secretary of the Army." In Massachusetts and some other states the governor has the official right to the title "Excellency"; thus by custom in all or most states it is "His Excellency, the Governor," or "Excellency"; it can be "Governor Jones," but it is incorrect merely to use the address "Governor."

Formal Receptions and Receiving Lines. For understandable reasons, the formal reception is probably used more within military stations than by other professional groups. This is likely to be true because of the frequency of official visits by military and civilian dignitaries. They are convenient for other special events such as a wedding reception, honoring a newly married bride and groom, or the introduction at a social occasion of a group of newly arrived officers and spouses.

Invitations to official receptions are accepted as first priority unless duty prevents.

An officer will wear the Army blue, other blue or white dress uniform, or service semidress, as prescribed or as local custom makes appropriate. Spouses dress appropriately to the occasion. In the evening a formal evening dress would be customary. In the afternoon a cocktail dress would be in good taste. But let this be emphasized: In these days of swift changes and high prices, a lady dressed neatly in a nice street dress would cause no lifted eyebrows at a social event on an Army post.

Strict protocol is observed at formal receptions. At an official function the host ranks first, then the hostess, and then the honorees. For example, the commanding officer of the unit holding the reception is on the right of the receiving line, his wife on his left; next is the ranking honored guest, with his lady on his left; other officers and their wives extend the line in the same manner. If civilians are members of the receiving line their place is indicated by the host; he will be guided by his own good judgment.

It is customary upon arrival at a reception for the guests to go down a receiving line. An aide or protocol officer is often used to announce the names of the guests to the host. Except at the White House or a diplomatic reception, the lady precedes the gentleman through a receiving line. At the White House the gentleman precedes and is presented to the President of the United States, then the officer presents his wife to the President. Each person in a receiving line usually introduces the guests to the person next on his or her left. A simple, cordial greeting, using correct names, is in order.

The ladies remove gloves for gentle but firm handclasps; it is both awkward and rude to have cigarettes or drinks in your hands when you proceed through the reception line.

Some occasion, dinner, dance, cocktails, and so on, will follow, after which make appropriate farewells to the hosts and the guests of honor.

Order of Seating and Service at Dinner. At a seated dinner with guests the lady of honor sits at the right of the host, the second lady on his left. The gentleman to be honored is seated on the right of the hostess and the second gentleman on her left. (See the accompanying illustrations.)

Where the guests are all from military families the arrangement is a simple one, for all officers have an official standing. Wives are seated in the same order as their husbands. In a mixed military and civilian group some thought must be given to a precedence list to avoid embarrassment. This is true especially when the guests include officials of government, university, church, or other high professional status. It is customary for experienced Army hostesses to accord the first positions to the senior officer present and his or her spouse, unless there is an overriding reason to do otherwise. If the matter seems to be especially important consult Mrs. Commanding Officer, who is almost certain to be an experienced hostess and willing to advise. Then make up the lists, lay out the place cards if used, and go ahead with confidence, making no excuses whatever, and look to the goal, which is a pleasant occasion for all. A skilled hostess having considered seniority and other protocol factors will arrange the seating so that compatible partners result—ones who can entertain each other with mutual sociability and stimulating conversation.

For formal dinners, the correct order of service is as follows: The untouched dish with unused serving utensils is presented to the lady seated at the right of the host. The dish then passes around the table to the right, the hostess being served in turn, and the host last. A second untouched dish may be presented to the second lady as a mark of respect with service thereafter passing to the left. At a luncheon for ladies with a guest of honor seated at the right of the hostess, service is started with the guest of honor and proceeds as stated above. There is only one occasion when the hostess is served first: at a table when the hostess is the only lady present, such as the entertainment of a group of bachelor officers by a captain and his wife.

For wine service a small amount is poured into the host's glass. He tastes it and, if he thinks it a worthy wine, service starts; the host's glass is last to be filled.

A dinner at home, prepared by the hostess and served by the host and hostess, is more the norm these days than is a formal dinner. However, the same rules generally apply as to seating and service. If wine is served, it probably is poured before the hostess calls the guests to dinner. In cramped quarters, use of a buffet table where each guest can serve himself or herself before being seated is perfectly acceptable. As in all matters, common courtesy and graciousness should rule. For these there are no substitutes and they are never incorrect.

Seating Arrangement at a Speaker's Table. At a luncheon, dinner, or banquet where there is a head table or speaker's table, the same principles apply in determining the order of seating. The chairman or other individual presiding at the gathering sits in the center. The most distinguished gentleman, who is usually the speaker, sits at his right. The next most distinguished is on his left, and so on alternately across the head table. If ladies are seated at the table a lady speaker would be seated at the right of the presiding official. If not the speaker, then the most distinguished lady is seated on his left. Thereafter alternate ladies and gentlemen, which places the younger or more junior people at the extremities.

Return of Hospitality Accepted. It is a good and sensible rule that hospitality accepted should be returned. Those who accept all invitations that come their way and never return the hospitality earn deservedly much ill will.

There is another good and sensible rule. No person or family should entertain socially beyond their means. In the service there is no occasion or precedent for "keeping up with the Joneses." Most officers are dependent upon service pay. They have nothing to gain by trying to maintain a social standard beyond their bank accounts, and if they do so they will receive more disapproval than favor. Still, hospitality accepted must be returned.

The saving grace is that hospitality accepted need not be returned on the same standard, or even by the same means. Let us work with an example. Colonel Oldtimer is in command of a brigade and has with him Mrs. Oldtimer, a gracious lady who has a well-equipped and fairly large home of which she is quite proud. Three new officers with their families join the command. Soon all three with their wives or husbands are invited to dinner. The Oldtimers go to some trouble to entertain them well, with their best china, linen, and silver, food and drinks. They have done this with no thought of impressing the newcomers, nor to emphasize their more senior position (and higher pay checks); they wish to show the newcomers that they are welcome and respected as valuable members of the organization. Also, being old-timers, they have accumulated nice things that they enjoy using.

How may such hospitality be returned in good grace? By all manner of means.

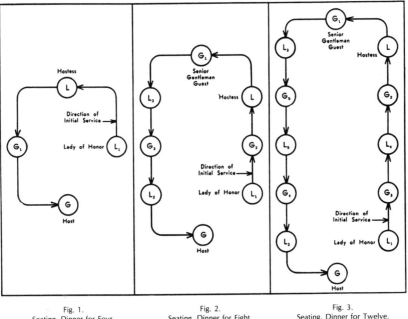

Fig. 1.
Seating, Dinner for Four.

Fig. 2.
Seating, Dinner for Eight.

Fig. 3.
Seating, Dinner for Twelve.

SEATING AND SERVING GUESTS AT DINNER.

By a simple home dinner served by the hostess, aided by the host. By a buffet supper with an inexpensive and simple menu. By an outdoor picnic. By a dinner at the officers' club. Further to reduce expenses, two or more officers may go together as joint hosts and hostesses.

No excuses need be offered and to do so would express poor taste. All officers have gone over about the same financial hurdles. They know the costs of raising a family and the expenses of frequent changes of station. They have about the same unfavorable views of those who elect to live beyond their means. Don't do it.

Bachelor officers should follow the same course. While bachelors may not have quarters suitable for entertaining, there are a number of solutions. A dinner or cocktail party at the officers' club, or a picnic, are examples.

Here is a social program that will meet the requirements and lie within the financial capabilities of nearly all officers. Belong to the officers' mess (club) and attend its social events if desired. Participate in functions arranged by your unit to the extent practicable. Attend all official receptions because you are expected to attend them, if invited, and in general they establish no obligation. Accept invitations from your commanding officers, staff officers, and close official associates, and from those other families whom you know and like, or whose friendship you wish to cultivate. With graciousness and politeness, decline the others.

The Art of Being a Good House Guest. Much has been written about the art of being a good host. But all too little has been written about being a good house guest, and it needs doing. Thoughtlessness or ignorance sometimes plays havoc with cherished friendships. Thoughtfulness will cement and strengthen them. As in all other human relationships, social manners are the result of a proper regard for the rights of others.

The host and hostess should be informed as nearly as practicable of the exact hour of planned arrival and departure. This will enable them to plan your visit and to resume their normal contacts and activities when you have left. Particularly annoying is the invited guest who accepts an invitation and states only that he will arrive "during the day." The hostess is left in the dark. Will arrival be morning, afternoon, or evening? Should she remain at home cancelling other things she has planned in order to be certain to receive the guest upon arrival? Shall she plan the evening meal for the guest's presence? Equally troublesome is the guest who neglects to announce a definite time as to departure. The hostess will wish to extend all possible consideration to the guest but upon departure will wish to resume the threads of other activities. She may wish to keep or cancel important appointments or obligations, or she may need to complete necessary shopping and errands. Uncertainty in these routine arrangements is displeasing. Of course the guest who arrives to stay for a few days and fails to inform the hosts even as to the day of planned departure until descending with packed bags to say farewells passes entirely beyond the pale. Some ways to inform your hosts are by letter, telegram, or telephone call, which might state: "Thanks for your kind invitation. We accept with pleasure. We plan to arrive at your home soon after four Friday afternoon and must start our return before nine on Monday morning." The house guest who accepts a weekend or other invitation of more than short duration without making known these simple things that are usually left to the desires of the guest has taken a firm and certain step that often will prevent him or her from receiving further invitations. Having established these days and dates, bend heaven and earth to keep them.

A guest must adjust to the conditions of the household. A man should keep his things picked up and his room tidy. The bathroom should be left in the same condition as he found it. A lady should take complete care of her room and be similarly thoughtful of the bath. On the day of departure, the bed should be stripped and the used bed linens folded and stacked at the foot of the bed. A guest in a servantless home should share in the household work to the extent that is welcome or acceptable. In this way hosts and guests have more uncrowded hours in which to enjoy one another and the hostess is spared excessive strains.

If plans have been made or suggested, the guest must show pleasure in sharing them. Adaptability is the password.

Both host and hostess will require some time to be by themselves in order to take care of personal responsibilities. Make it easy for them to do so. Take a walk, write a letter, read a book. This will permit the hostess and the host to maintain the normal routine of their household by giving them time to attend to their essential responsibilities.

An invitation by a guest to take the family of the host out to dinner is often a welcomed courtesy but it must not be pressed if once proffered and declined.

Prior to departure be certain no personal belongings are left behind for the host to package and mail. A remembrance to the hosts in the form of flowers, candy, or a book, given either before or after departure, is appropriate and generally most appreciated. A thank-you letter written a day or two after departure is a necessary but often overlooked courtesy.

The guest who fails to do these things and others that will suggest themselves will make true the old saying about "making the hosts twice glad—glad when the guest arrives, and glad when the guest departs." Doing them may result in future invitations. The essence is regard for others.

MORAL STANDARDS

It is natural for the newcomer to the military community to wonder about moral standards to be encountered. Will a person of high standards of morality and conduct be obliged to accept the repugnant from official or social associates? Will a person, man or woman, be helped or harmed by membership in the military garrison?

Officers and their spouses are drawn into the Army from our civilian population. For the most part they are men and women of better than average education and civilian background because of the definite requirements that must be satisfied to become an officer. They bring into the service the customs, standards, and expectancies that are common in the communities in which they have lived. Now they enter a society that is concerned in a common cause. The officer is subject to military discipline and to the Code of Military Justice. He or she may be punished, even dismissed for "conduct unbecoming an officer." Transgressors from moral and conduct codes tend to eliminate themselves. In such a closely knit community it is natural that each person should wish to deserve the goodwill of associates, not their scorn. For these reasons it is a fact that the moral and conduct standards to be encountered in the military service are at least as high, and almost certainly a little higher, than are encountered elsewhere.

Are all the brothers courageous, and all the sisters virtuous? Well, not quite all. Officers and their wives or husbands are people. Among them will be those whose frailties show. There will always be the few in any group who drink too much, or gamble too much. All of the problems of men and women have not been solved by the military.

We will attempt a word of advice: *Put your best foot forward and keep it there.* Think of the effect of your conduct upon others, newcomers and your juniors especially, and give little thought or none to the effect of their conduct upon you. Your morals will continue to be what you make them.

PROBLEMS IN LIVING OFF POST

It must remain true that a very large portion of Army families seek off-post quarters for the inescapable reason that there are too few sets of family quarters to meet the need. Many officers will have a duty assignment within a post or station but reside with their families in a civilian community. This condition presents problems that must be faced and solved as well as opportunities to be embraced.

The usual officer and family will wish to enjoy congenial relations with the residents of the new area. They may wish to participate in some community educational, religious, fraternal, or recreational facilities. Generally these facilities are made available to newcomers upon application, or upon an invitation extended. A little tact is called for. Make judicious inquiries. Remember that the good things enjoyed by a community were obtained by the vision and work of the residents, and paid for by taxes, dues, or donated funds. It is likely that the residents will be entirely willing to share many of these things with the transient military family, but they will do it more willingly when it is appreciated.

There are some negative considerations. If you think your own home town or city, or your last station, or your next one, are to be preferred to the present location—keep it carefully to yourself. If you think a particular merchant or landlord is overcharging, don't denounce all local merchants and landlords as cheats and gougers; just take your patronage elsewhere. Keep quiet about the more favorable prices at post exchange or commissary; local merchants cannot meet all of these prices. Avoid doing or saying the things that irritate and annoy. They may determine whether you receive the hand of fellowship or the cold shoulder.

It is a wise course to meet and make yourself known to the businessmen and others with whom you will wish to have contacts. This means the banker, the grocer, the mechanic servicing your car, the minister of your church, the principal at your child's school. If you will need credit arrangements, make them in a businesslike manner. Establish yourself as a new and desirable member of the community.

You will have the same privileges regarding facilities and activities on post as you would have if living in post quarters. That is to say, you will have full privileges of the officers' open mess and post organizations and facilities of all sorts. Judicious choice must be made between the activities in town and those of the military station. The primary interest may properly lie on post. Divide your activities between post and town on the basis of convenience and use both as desired.

As time passes associations may ripen into friendships, and life itself may be enriched by these local contacts.

ENCOURAGEMENT FOR THE SHORT-TIMER

The officer and spouse who are on a short active-duty tour want to profit by it, yet they have a special problem of understanding and action. Both will wish to receive maximum enjoyment from their service experiences and to enrich their lives as may be possible from service associations and travel. But many short-timers sit back, assume they are neither especially wanted nor really welcome, and drift into the fringes and shadows of the military community. What a pity! This discussion is intended as a start into a more rewarding result.

Good advice to any service family, including especially those of short expectancy of service, is to participate fully in the various recreational and social activities of the military community. No one will care whether you are to become a "long-timer" or "short-timer." You are there today and that is all most people will wish to know about. Attend the official, social, athletic, and other events as time permits. Know your general, your colonel, major, and captain, and their spouses, at the same time making sure as best you can that they know you. At social occasions be sure to introduce yourself to the senior officers, their spouses, and their guests; in departing, to the extent appropriate, express your farewells. You will soon become known. Accept membership on appropriate committees or activities that lie within your interests. Soon your reward will be a widened circle of acquaintances, some of whom will become lasting friends. Point and reason will replace the mysteries of service customs. Indeed, you should find interest and appeal in a life that before might have seemed somewhat dull. The dullness resulted from your timid approach. You will get from the life about what you put into it.

ARMY DISTAFF HALL

The Army Distaff Hall provides a pleasant and congenial home for Army widows age sixty-two or older, and in addition the mother, daughter, sister, or mother-in-law of a Regular Army officer, or of a Reserve officer with twenty years' active service. Eligible also are retired female officers.

It is a beautiful residence placed in beautiful grounds overlooking Rock Creek Park at 6200 Oregon Ave., NW, Washington, DC 20015. It is a four-story multi-winged building designed with professional skill to meet the special needs of the residents. Army families are justified in taking pride in the achievement. A portion of the construction and equipment funds were raised by contributions from Army people and by funds raised at Army stations, as well as gifts from civilian sources.

Sustained financial support from individuals, and the important periodic contributions by officers' wives' clubs, is needed for the financial progress of the Foundation and for the essential assistance of some residents of the Hall.

Inquiries are welcomed about eligibility, vacancies, or other matters of interest. For information, write to the Army Distaff Foundation, at the address above.

CONCLUSION

The social side of Army life may now be understood as opportunity to participate actively in a wide variety of interesting and essential activities. Life will be interesting or dull, stimulating or empty—as *you* make it. There are dances, receptions, and dinners, of course. There are activities of general appeal at the officers' club. There are opportunities for athletics. But beyond the realm of the purely social and entertainment features are the many essential activities of life at an Army station, from assisting at work of the PTA or Red Cross, to acting as Den Mother of Cub Scouts, to coaching a team of the Little League, and many, many others. The garrison of an Army station, including off-post members as well as those who have quarters on post, resembles any other American community, plus the added factor of the military mission that binds all together in common purpose.

9

Financial Planning

Forewarned, forearmed, to be prepared is half the victory. —Cervantes

A prudent officer will have a financial plan to assure personal security. Bachelor officers should plan for security in later life and for the reasonable possibility of leaving the ranks of the unwed. Married officers face the greatest challenge, for their plans must include security for their families. The foundation for the officer's financial planning is what the government provides in return for faithful and often hazardous service. Government benefits are a solid base. Objective, realistic foresight should identify the basic requirements of each person, while timely action will start the mission. As the years pass, the initial program must be adjusted as changing circumstances make necessary. The right start at the right time is important.*

The Army officer accepts definite hazards. Short tours of foreign service may require separation from your family. Each decade beginning with the 1940s has found our country involved in a war or combat short of war, with intervening threats to the nation's security. Many officers of the Army of today have been in combat in Vietnam. In planning for the future, you should include the possibility that part of your future active service may be in combat, or combat support. It is a harsh reality that combat may result in death or disability, but you should recognize the possibility. Further, the very nature of the Army mission requires that you engage in activities that are hazardous, or that you work with hazardous equipment, either of which also pose definite risks. You should identify as accurately as possible your future responsibilities and goals, and decide what action is necessary to attain them.

---

*Suggested supplemental reading: *Armed Forces Guide to Personal Financial Planning*—Stackpole Books, Harrisburg, Pennsylvania. A comprehensive guide regarding personal financial management.

This chapter is provided to help all officers in their financial planning for personal and family security. Other sources of study and reference are cited for detailed guidance. The chapter's goal is to provide a concise, informative introduction to the subject. Thought and foresight are needed. Since the Army wife or husband may need to manage these affairs during the absence of the service member, many officers see the wisdom of sharing the entire process of deciding and acting in program development.

If the task or the responsibility seems heavy, be encouraged by the truth that most career officers find it possible to lead interesting, rewarding lives and at the same time provide for the uncertainties and potential requirements of their future years.

WARPROOF YOUR PERSONAL AFFAIRS

FINANCIAL SECURITY

Financial security is a continuous requirement while one is on active service and after one is retired. A security program thus provides for both emergencies and planned events. An Army husband and wife team must identify their family goals through retirement by planning, budgeting, saving, and otherwise providing for such events as college education, buying a home, paying a major dental bill, and going on a retirement tour. Even without the hazards of combat, parents must face with realism the untimely death of either husband or wife. Having foreseen their obligations and responsibilities, they must previously have taken the security actions that are reasonable, prudent, and adequate for their situation.

Even during cold war service, about 30 percent of the Army is overseas; consequently, you can expect an oversea assignment early in your career. Family separation usually results, sometimes for as long as the complete tour. Hazardous duty, with conflict imminent, calls for the same security measures that combat does. You must do all the things that could be helpful to your spouse before departing, so that he or she can be a good manager of family affairs during the period of separation. Taking careful stock now and placing security affairs in order are joint actions for you and your spouse in honest and sincere recognition of your mutual responsibilities.

The above motivation serves to introduce the need for financial planning and to urge you to implement a planned security program and to review its adequacy and currency at such critical stages as going overseas, the imminent birth of a child, a promotion, retirement, and others. A partial review is in order each year when you compute income taxes. Such planning and reviewing calls for the following steps, which will be detailed in subsequent sections:

Learn the elements of security planning;
Review your current family and financial status;
Choose your short- and long-range goals;
Identify your service benefits;
Establish a reasonable insurance program;
Supplement your estate with investments;
Be aware of the many assistance societies; and
Take care of vital personal administration.

FUNDAMENTALS OF SECURITY PLANNING

Security planning consists of evaluating your financial situation, comparing it to your requirements and goals, and deciding what must be done to have a program that meets today's needs while providing security for the future. "Estate analysis" is a similar term usually employed by insurance salesmen who are oriented on security through insurance programs. As used here, *security planning* involves your total financial program, including salaries, property, savings, insurance program, governmental benefits, investments, and other monetary assets. It involves the integration of these finances into a formal plan. Finally, it takes into consideration today's and the immediate future's needs as well as those of the far future after retirement. Overcommitment of your salary to security programs can deny you and your family the opportunities of building a living estate of wonderful, memorable, and educational recollections of vacations, entertainment, hobbies, and all those other events and circumstances that might not constitute absolute necessities. A term often encountered is *insurance poor* for one who buys too much insurance, but the term applies equally to other types of estate building. Thus, security planning is a management science to some extent, yet it also could be classified as an art because of its intimate relation to personal philosophies.

Reference Material. There are many useful sources of information to assist you in estate planning, such as:

Armed Forces Guide to Personal Financial Planning, Stackpole Books, Harrisburg, Pennsylvania.

Estate Planning for Military Personnel, published by Dyke F. Meyer, C.L.U., Col., USAF Ret., San Antonio, Texas.

Your [Year] Financial Planning Guide, by Dyke F. Meyer, C.L.U., and Walter A. Yohey, Jr., published by the Armed Forces Relief and Benefit Association.

AR 40-121, *Uniformed Services Health Benefits Programs.*

DA PAM 600-5, *Handbook on Retirement Services for Army Personnel and Their Families.*

You do not need to obtain all these since some are special purpose while some duplicate information in the others. There are other references that include more current information in newspapers and magazines, which you can study and save. With a broad understanding of what you are trying to do, and with your references available, you are ready to begin your estate planning.

STATUS, GOALS, AND REQUIREMENTS

The next steps of security planning involve determining your financial situation, establishing your goals, and deciding on the actions required to meet these goals. The first two, status and goals, are to be discussed in this section along with the broad plan of action for establishing security. Detailed sections will then follow on how to implement the broad plan of action.

Your Financial Status. Your financial status is based upon your salary and any other income. To analyze your situation further it is necessary for you to consider your service benefits, insurance programs, savings, investments, Social Security credits, real estate equities, and any other assets. This is the point where you realize what you are worth financially should you live, be incapacitated, or die. It is generally useful to study and review other personal affairs records at this time along with your financial data.

Your Financial Goals. Next, you have to determine personal and family goals. Officers who are fulfilling an obligation for a few years and those who are contemplating careers of twenty to thirty years will have different goals. However, since this is an officer's guide, an officer's career is assumed to be the planning base. Conservative financial planning could be based upon achieving the grade of lieutenant colonel and retiring after twenty-eight years' service. The length of service is most influential on security planning. For example, an officer who is involuntarily separated with more than five but less than twenty years of service is entitled to a separation payment equal to 10 percent of annual base pay times years of service, up to a maximum of $30,000. Officers may retire voluntarily with twenty years of service, and only a few will be allowed to serve more than thirty years before retirement. The amount of retired pay you can expect to receive is a function of your final base pay, or the average of the three years of highest base pay, your total years of service, and the date you entered the Army. Three different retirement systems are now provided by law, depending upon when you entered the Army. See chapter 27, *Retirement,* for details of the retirement system that applies to you.

Next comes your personal plans as to married life. One of the reasons marriage is often called a partnership is the financial relationship of the spouse. The spouse's attitudes, philosophies, financial responsibility, monetary assets, age, health, and other characteristics all influence to some degree an officer's planning. Then there are the children. How many? College education? Establish in business? What is the influence of their personality, intelligence, hopes, educational plans, and other factors that affect the family's way of life and long-range program? These general and philosophical planning components serve to assist in the identification of financial goals and requirements so that subsequent planning to meet them can be realistic, practical, and more logically derived. Once an officer-spouse team has considered all these matters with objectivity, the decisions are made clearer and the courses of action are more readily discerned.

You may be assisted by considering your future lives as comprising a few main periods, and then estimate the conditions that are to be expected within each one, such as the following examples:

- The period of active duty, which should continue until ——— (year) at the earliest, or until ——— (year) at the latest.
- The years in which children are growing up, receiving education, and becoming self-supporting, now foreseen until ——— (year).
- Family wishes for the period immediately following military retirement and reestablishment in a civilian community of their choice.
- The years between military retirement date and eligibility to receive Social Security old-age payments in ———(year).

Also, consider the situation and requirements that would follow the death of either husband or wife during each of the above periods of family planning.

A wise start requires candid and searching answers to personal questions, such as those that follow.

The Spouse and Children to Be Protected. "*What would happen if———?*" The reasonable person recognizes that the duration of life is uncertain. He or she proceeds without undue morbidity or overemphasis to face facts. Proceed as you would in making a military estimate. Is your spouse qualified to be self-supporting if suddenly faced with the necessity to do so? Or would he or she need training to resume a former vocation or to undertake a new one? Consider your spouse's present age, health, potentials, wishes, and inclinations. At what age should it be considered that he or she would be unable to provide a part of the required income, or would not wish to do so? When there are children, at what year will each be prepared for life and be self-supporting? Are there physical or mental frailties to be considered and provided for? How much income per month will be needed, and for how many years, for the support and education of the children? Be realistic and inclusive. Later in your estimate you will balance potential outgo against potential income to see whether there is a gap to bridge. Right now, just determine the facts.

What Is Your Present Life Insurance Program? The family insurance program stands beside family net worth as a sound foundation to family security.

It is true that military service establishes important benefits for family protection far above those of most vocations. But it is equally true that the hazards are greater, and the possibilities of estate accrual are more difficult. The termination of some benefits upon retirement, with the reduction or uncertainties of others, requires careful identification for each family situation. There are gaps to be filled in service benefits during your active career. There are more and wider ones to face upon retirement. Life insurance of the appropriate type, in carefully determined amount, is one proven way of providing at once for the potential needs of the future. There are other ways, of course. Identify the gaps, and fill them prudently.

Do You Have an Investment Program? Many military families have entered upon such a program with farsighted wisdom. They may have bought a home and are increasing their equity through rental. Others are buying securities such as government bonds, mutual funds, and common stock, or have opened an Individual Retirement Account.

Do You Have Reasonable Expectancy of an Inheritance? If so, include it as a possibility. But don't place extensive reliance upon it; old age, ill health and many other hazards, plus taxes, can reduce an estate. Just weigh the possibilities and go ahead.

To What Extent Do Present Military Survivor Benefits Meet the Total Needs? Basic information is contained in this chapter to be studied as a start in this investigation of potential resources. You will wish to make a detailed study of departmental publications and consult experts about some phases of the subject.

You will see at once that for all officers the benefits are valuable. The officer on active duty and the officer's family are better protected than ever before. Upon your retirement there are important benefits but there are also potential gaps in protection that must be identified. Study is needed to apply these laws to your situation and the requirements of your family.

What Sort of Program for the Future Can You and Your Spouse Afford Today? This chapter provides much information about future security, so let us seek for a moment to establish a balance. Each family has its own way of life, with its daily needs and its own dreams of the future. It is true that a family's immediate and continuing happiness—such as children growing up with proper food, clothes, books, family outings, dinners at the club—is important, too. Prudence is needed for family security, of course, and its importance must not be minimized; but prudence is also required in avoiding overcommitting the family income for estate building. Once an officer-spouse team has considered all these matters with objectivity and realism, the best decisions are usually clear. For most families, expenditures of today can be controlled so that some part of income can be diverted to the family program of the future.

Should Your Family Have a Budget? Officers and their spouses usually manage their finances with either a formal budget or a working budget. With a formal budget, a detailed system of planned expenses and records serves to guide the expenditures for the various parts of the living and the security programs. In the working budget, the officer-spouse team establishes habits that allow them to accomplish the basic parts of their programs while not exceeding their income or depleting their cash reserve. A cash reserve is maintained in both cases for emergencies and for planned spending on major events (or things) in the near future. A two months' salary cash reserve is recommended. Savings beyond this should be invested if the other elements of the security program are met. Advised is an interest-bearing checking account for day-to-day use, and a money market mutual fund with check-writing privileges that you can use to accumulate funds for larger expenses such as a new appliance, a trip, clothes for college, and so on. Those who maintain a formal budget usually will do better at managing their finances, but some people do not enjoy the detailed accounting that is required. Having a program, meeting it, and staying within one's income is also a practical way to security without detailed budgeting. The choice is yours.

In this matter of budgeting, the use of credit is deserving of your special attention. In our society of today the use of credit is a normal occurrence. Credit is readily available in the form of charge cards such as VISA, MasterCard, and many others. Using these credit cards can be a handy way to do your shopping, including shopping at the post exchange, without the necessity of carrying large amounts of cash or writing checks for the purchases. The card-issuing companies accumulate the charges over a monthly period and present you with a consolidated bill at the end of the month. Problems can arise when the size of the monthly bill exceeds your ability to pay, since any unpaid amounts are then carried forward to the next month's bill at interest rates that are generally in the range of 1.5 percent or more per month. Without careful attention on your part, it is easy to accumulate large charge card balances on which you are paying high interest rates. What this means is that over a period of time you can wind up paying 20 percent more for your purchases than would have been the case had you used cash. It also indicates that you are living beyond your means; that is, your outgo exceeds your income. It is a path that can lead ultimately to severe financial problems.

If you do use charge cards, it is far better to schedule your purchases so that you can pay the bills in full each month. This may even be better than using cash, since you have the advantage of a "float" of your funds during the month. That is, you use the card-issuing company's funds during the month, while your funds may be drawing interest at the bank until the time you must write a check covering the month's accumulated bills. Do not assume, however, that it will be any easier to pay your bills next month than it is now. You will find that each month has its own special needs that you had not forecasted, and that this month's unpaid bills will be at least 1.5 percent greater next month. If you find yourself falling behind in this matter of credit purchases, it is suggested that you put the credit cards aside and return to using cash for your purchases. Even in today's economy, merchants still accept cash. In any event, do not fall into the trap of accumulating large, unpaid credit card balances.

Your Financial Plan. Having faced the basic questions of financial status and goals, estate planners say that now you are ready to make your basic financial plan. Here is what you must do:
- Establish a solvent financial situation;
- Build a cash reserve;
- Establish a sound insurance program; and
- Invest your remaining income.

You, however, are an officer and cannot complete your security planning until you first consider the benefits of being in the service and a citizen of the United States.

BENEFITS ACQUIRED THROUGH MILITARY SERVICE

There are many benefits acquired through military service. They are provided by the government in recognition of the hazards of military service as well as to supplement your pay and to provide an added inducement for you to select military service as a career. You should be aware, however, that benefits provided by law can also be altered or withdrawn by changes to the law. Over a period of years, the Congress and successive administrations do change the benefits. In general, such changes as are made are aimed at improving the benefit provided, but in some instances benefits previously counted upon have been withdrawn or curtailed. This section attempts to clarify your earned benefits, but you are cautioned to study the regulations, to stay up-to-date with the latest changes as reported in the various service journals, and to seek the advice of experts in the field to help you with your plans.

UNIFORMED SERVICES HEALTH CARE PROGRAM

A detailed description of this program is presented in AR 40-121, *Medical Service, Uniformed Services Health Benefits Program.* However, you can obtain fact sheets and details regarding the program that are perhaps more understandable from the Health Benefits Advisor at any of the Uniformed Services hospitals. Uniformed Services medical facilities include those of the Army, Navy, Air Force, Marines, Coast Guard, and the Public Health Service.

It is important that you know your medical benefits and, for your security and that of your family, to understand where gaps could occur that must be covered by other measures. This section summarizes the more important provisions. However, you may have to consult the regulations for details as to your particular situation. In case of any doubt, consult the nearest Health Benefits Advisor.

The Uniformed Services medical facilities constitute the primary source of health care for you and your family members. Should care at a military facility not be available, it may be obtained, with some restrictions, at a civilian facility under the provisions of the Civilian Health and Medical Program of the Uniformed Services (CHAMPUS). In general, you personally will receive complete medical care at a military medical facility until your retirement. Thereafter, you may use military facilities on a space-available basis, or you may seek civilian medical care under the provisions of CHAMPUS. Your dependent family members may use military facilities on a space-available basis, both during your period of active service and after you retire, but they may also use civilian medical facilities, with certain restrictions, under the provisions of CHAMPUS. At age sixty-five, retirees and their dependents who become eligible for the Social Security Medicare Program must use this program instead of CHAMPUS for civilian medical care, although they are still eligible for space-available treatment at a military facility. Before examining medical care provisions for an officer's dependents, it is important that "dependents" be defined.

Who Is a Dependent? Dependent means any person who bears to a member or retired member of a uniformed service, or to a person who died while a member of a uniformed service, any of the following relationships:

1. The lawful wife.
2. The unremarried widow.
3. The lawful husband.
4. The unremarried widower.
5. An unmarried legitimate child, including an adopted child or stepchild, who either—

Has not passed his or her twenty-first birthday, regardless of whether or not the child is dependent on the active duty or retired member; or

Has passed his or her twenty-first birthday but is incapable of self-support because of a mental or physical incapacity that existed before the twenty-first birthday and is, or was at the time of death of the active duty or retired member, dependent on the member for over one-half of his or her support; or ed his or her twenty-third birthday and is enrolled in a full-time course of study in an institution of higher learning approved by the Secretary of Defense or the Secretary of Health and Human Services, as the case may be, and was at the time of death of the active duty or retired member, dependent on the member for over one-half of his or her support.

b. A parent or parent-in-law, who either—

(1) Is dependent on the active duty or retired member for over one-half of his or her support and is residing in a dwelling place provided or maintained by the member; or

(2) Was, at the time of death of the member dependent on him or her for over one-half of his or her support and was residing in a dwelling place provided or maintained by the member.

In addition, CHAMPUS benefits are extended to divorced spouses of active, retired, or deceased service members under certain conditions. The coverage is dependent upon the date of divorce or annulment, the length of the marriage and active duty service, and the divorced spouse's status and coverage under a sponsored health care plan. See the regulations for details.

Eligibility for Medical Care. When applying for any kind of medical care at a military or civilian facility, military personnel, active and retired, and their dependents, are required to provide evidence of their eligibility by means of the Uniformed Services Identification and Privilege Card (DD Form 2A or DD Form 1173). If a person uses, or allows another to use, this card to obtain medical care to which he or she is not entitled, a fine of up to $10,000 and imprisonment for up to five years may result.

To minimize the possibility of fraudulent use of military health benefits by unauthorized persons, as well as to improve the control of military health care services, the Defense Enrollment Eligibility Reporting System (DEERS) was established. Using DEERS, a military health care facility can quickly check a person's eligibility to use the facility. You are automatically enrolled in DEERS, but you must take special action to enroll your dependents. See your personnel officer. Enrollment of family members is necessary for them to obtain health care either at a military facility or at a civilian facility under the provisions of CHAMPUS. You also should be aware that DEERS ultimately is to be used to check eligibility for other benefits such as access to the post exchange and commissary by linking DEERS to the service identification card.

Election of Facilities. The following beneficiaries may elect to obtain authorized health benefits in Uniformed Services facilities or from civilian sources: retired members and their spouses and children, spouses and children of deceased members, and spouses and children of active duty members who are residing apart from their sponsor. Spouses and children of active duty members who are residing with their sponsor may elect to obtain authorized *outpatient* care and drugs from Uniformed Services or civilian facilities. They are *required,* however, to obtain *inpatient* care in Uniformed Service facilities when such facilities are within reasonable distance of their residence and capable of providing the needed care, except in an emergency, when the residing "apart" changes to residing "with," when already hospitalized or obtaining maternity care, or while on a trip away from the sponsor's household. (See p. 11, AR 40–121). DD Form 1251, *Nonavailability Statement—Dependents Medical Care Program,* will be furnished to spouses and children residing with their sponsors who must use civilian facilities. The nonavailability statement *must* be obtained prior to use of civilian facilities for nonemergency care.

The civilian physician or facility must be participating with the government in the CHAMPUS program for your subsequent reimbursement. You should be sure that the physician or hospital does participate in the CHAMPUS program before you receive treatment if it is possible. After receiving medical care, in particular emergency and costly care, be certain to save *all* receipts for doctor care, hospitalization, medicines, and related services. Costs themselves are explained below. Note that dependent parents or parents-in-law are authorized to seek medical care only in Uniformed Services facilities. They are not entitled to civilian medical care under the provisions of CHAMPUS.

The Army has opened three PRIMUS clinics in the Northern Virginia area and one in Savannah, Georgia. Six more clinics are scheduled to open in fiscal year 1988, two serving Fort Ord, two serving Fort Hood, one near Fort Benning, and one near Fort Bragg. These clinics are available to all active duty and retired personnel and their dependents at no cost. The clinics provide primary care on a walk-in basis, handling minor medical problems such as sprains, colds, flu, and so on. Serious or chronic medical problems are referred to a local military hospital. The PRIMUS clinics are operated by civilians under contract to the Army and are designed to relieve overcrowding of the Army facilities. The other services also are considering PRIMUS-type clinics. All are available to personnel from all military services.

Costs. In military facilities, officers, active and retired, pay a daily subsistence charge of $3.60. The per diem (day) charge is $7.30 for dependents for inpatient service, with usually no charge for outpatient service. However, the law does permit charges if they are considered advisable, and the Administration has announced its intent to experiment with a nominal charge for each dependent outpatient visit.

For outpatient service in civilian facilities, spouses and children of active duty personnel are charged $50 per year per person (but not to exceed $100 per family) and 20 percent of the remaining allowable costs. For retirees and their dependents, the costs are $50 per year per person (but not to exceed $100 per family) and 25 percent of the remaining allowable costs. The total bill for a family unit for twelve months must exceed $100 in both cases for reimbursement of the remaining part by the government. Costs are computed on a fiscal year basis. The fiscal year runs 1 October through 30 September.

Hospitalization costs in civilian facilities for retirees and their dependents and the dependents of deceased personnel are paid at a rate of 25 percent by the person with 75 percent reimbursement by the government. Dependents of active duty personnel pay either $25, or $7.30 per day, whichever is more.

For long-term care of mentally retarded and physically handicapped spouses or children of active duty members, a sliding scale of reimbursement is provided up to a total monthly bill of $1,000.

Cautions. The maximum allowable costs for medical procedures are fixed by law. If you should select a civilian physician or hospital that charges more than allowed, you must pay for the excess costs.

Costs of routine physical examinations and immunizations at *civilian facilities* are not paid for by the government except when the dependents are preparing to go overseas. Note that these are given at military facilities with no charge. Costs of the care of newborn children and, later, their well-baby care at civilian facilities will not be paid by the government. The same applies to eye examinations; however, again, all of these are available, usually by appointment, at military facilities. Drug and medicine costs provided in connection with outpatient care may be reimbursed only in the case of written prescriptions of a licensed physician or dentist. An exception is insulin; an inclusion is oral contraceptives. If you require any drugs or medicines over a long period, you should carefully consult the regulations and authorities to save these costly expenses.

In general, the medical care programs for all service personnel and their dependents are now adequate. As in all matters of government life, the regulations are complex to ensure that the benefits are given to those who earn them.

Dental Care. Full dental care for active duty members is provided by military dental facilities. However, CHAMPUS does not cover costs for dental care, and only limited care for dependents of active duty members in military facilities has been available on a space-available basis in certain overseas locations. Military dental care for retirees and their dependents has been essentially unavailable. This lack of dental coverage underwent substantial change in 1987. A new dental plan for dependents of active duty members became effective on 1 August 1987. In return for a monthly payroll deduction of $3.93 for one dependent or $7.86 for two or more dependents, family members of active duty personnel may now obtain from participating dentists free oral examinations, tooth cleaning and polishing, fluoride treatment, routine dental X-rays, laboratory examinations, and minor emergency treatment. Patients will be required to pay 20 percent of the costs for fillings and other restorative care. The plan does not cover more extensive dental procedures such as braces, tooth extractions, root canals, crowns, dentures, or any procedures for cosmetic purposes.

While the new dental insurance plan is not the final answer to all dental problems, and does nothing to assist retirees and their dependents, it does assure that the families of younger active duty members will have access to the essential dental care generally needed at costs the members can afford. See the nearest Health Benefits Advisor for details regarding the dental insurance plan and a list of participating dentists in your area.

DEPENDENCY AND INDEMNITY COMPENSATION

The Survivors Dependency and Indemnity Compensation Act of 1974 provides for compensation to survivors for the loss of an officer or soldier whose death is attributable to military service. All *service-connected deaths* that occur in peace or wartime in the line of duty qualify the eligible survivors for the Dependency and Indemnity Compensation (DIC). Retired officers' survivors may qualify also providing the Veterans Administration rules the death to have been from service-connected causes. As amended in 1986, the Act now provides monthly payments to an unremarried widowed spouse ranging from $630 for the spouse of a W-1 and an O-1 to $1,274 for the spouse of an O-10. Thus, the higher the pay grade of the deceased member, the higher the compensation payable to the member's survivors. Once established, however, the DIC rate is fixed. Rate increases are only by separate Congressional action. DIC payments are not authorized to the survivors of a retired officer whose death is not service-connected. (A small pension may be paid to the widow or widower, as discussed later, provided her or his income is below a stated minimum.) This gap must receive consideration in developing a total family security plan.

Compensations may be increased for widows and widowers with children under eighteen or with a child over eighteen who is incapable of self-support. An additional sum may be awarded for each child between eighteen and twenty-three who attends a Veterans Administration–approved school. All such compensations are income tax-free. The officer's surviving children will receive compensations should the spouse die. Dependent parents likewise qualify for compensations. Your finance officer or any Veterans Administration office can assist you in computing the various possible compensations and pensions for your particular family situation.

PAY AND SIX-MONTHS' DEATH GRATUITY

At the time of a service member's death, there will be pay due for a month or a fractional part of a month. The spouse receives this arrears in pay upon claim to the nearest finance center, or by writing to the U.S. Army Finance and Accounting Center, Indianapolis, IN 46249.

In addition to the arrears in pay, a death gratuity is payable to the survivors of a service member who dies while on active duty, active duty for training, or inactive duty training (weekly drills), and of a retired service member who dies of a service-connected disability within 120 days after separation from the Active List. The amount of this gratuity is six months' basic pay, with a minimum of $800 and a maximum of $3,000. In practice, military pay rates have increased so much since these limits were established that the six months' gratuity is now $3,000 for all members. Legislation has been introduced in Congress to raise the $3,000 limit.

These payments should be included in the determination of assets and benefits in an individual's estate security plan.

SURVIVOR BENEFIT PLAN (SBP)

The Survivor Benefit Plan (SBP) became effective in September 1972. It allows members of the uniformed services to elect to receive a reduced retirement pay in order to provide annuities for their survivors, for another person with an insurable interest in the service member, or, under certain conditions, for an ex-spouse. Under SBP, the federal government pays a substantial portion of the overall cost. Participation in the SBP is open to all future retirees, including members of the Reserve Forces when they attain age sixty and become entitled to retired or retainer pay. Present retirees have previously been afforded the opportunity to participate.

Under SBP, future retirees may elect to leave up to 55 percent of their retired pay to their selected annuitants. Participation in SBP is automatic at the 55 percent rate for those still on active duty who have a spouse or children. Prior to retirement, the member may fill out an election form, DD Form 1883, electing a reduced coverage, or the member may decline to participate. However, the spouse must concur in the election of reduced or no coverage. The minimum base amount of retired pay upon which SBP is based was initially set at $300 per month; however, beginning in October 1985, the minimum base amount is raised by the same percentage factor as any increase in active duty pay. Effective with the 1 January 1988 pay raise, the minimum base amount for SBP is $324.

Costs for spouse-only coverage under SBP are 2.5 percent of the minimum base amount, plus 10 percent of the remainder. Thus, a member entitled to $1,000 per month in retired pay, who desires to leave 55 percent ($550) to his or her spouse, pays $76.15 per month ($7.95 for the first $318 and $68.20 for the remaining $682). Note that the cost is based upon the total retired pay used to compute the SBP annuity and not upon the amount of the annuity. Extension of the coverage for a child or children costs about one-half of 1 percent of the annuity amount per month. In the above example, this extended coverage would cost the member approximately $2.75 per month.

There are a number of points about the SBP that deserve careful consideration. Most decisions are irrevocable. However, deductions under the plan cease during any month in which there is no eligible beneficiary. Further, the coverage may be switched to a new spouse if the retiree remarries. An important advantage of SBP is that the amount of coverage is tied to the Consumer Price Index (CPI). Whenever retired pay is adjusted on the basis of the CPI, the amount selected by the retiree as an annuity base, the deduction from retired pay covering the adjusted base, and the annuity payable to selected beneficiaries will be adjusted accordingly. The plan thus provides for automatic cost of living adjustments. The plan also contains a provision that when the beneficiary becomes eligible for Social Security survivor benefits, the SBP payments will be permanently reduced by the amount to which the beneficiary is entitled from Social Security, based solely upon the member's military pay, up to a maximum of 40 percent of the SBP payment. However, there is no offset if the surviving spouse is working and has earnings that are too high for Social Security payments to be paid. Neither is there an offset if the spouse is receiving Social Security payments based upon his or her own earnings rather than a widow's or widower's benefit based upon the military member's earnings. In 1985, the law was changed to eliminate the Social Security offset and replace it with a two-tiered system in which the survivor receives 55 percent of the base amount of retired pay until age sixty-two, at which time the amount drops to 35 percent of the base amount of retired pay, which continues for the life of the survivor. Retirees after 1 October 1985 are enrolled in the two-tiered system. The annuity of the survivor of a member who retired prior to 1 October 1985 will be recomputed when the survivor reaches age sixty-two. After that time, the annuity will be either that computed under the older offset system or the newer two-tiered system, whichever is greater.

. The plan also provides that if a retiree dies of a service-connected cause, as a result of which his or her survivors are entitled to DIC payments (see Dependency and Indemnity Compensation earlier in this chapter), the SBP payment will be reduced so that the total of the two payments—DIC and SBP—will be equal to the full amount otherwise payable under SBP. Thus, the total income to the survivors from SBP, DIC, and Social Security can equal or be slightly higher than the SBP income alone, depending upon the extent of the offset for Social Security. On the other hand, since SBP (as well as Social Security) is tied to the Consumer Price Index, the retired member also is assured that the spending power he or she has provided through SBP will remain relatively constant regardless of the effect of inflation.

It is apparent that participation in SBP has definite advantages and, perhaps, disadvantages that call for study, obtaining advice, and care in deciding if coverage is desired and in selecting the amount. SBP is not necessarily a panacea for all military retirees, but it deserves careful consideration as a benefit accruing to you as a result of military service, which is available for use in planning your estate.

SOCIAL SECURITY

Military personnel accrue Social Security benefits for active service as an important element of their overall security program. Participation is mandatory. Under the Social Security program, your base pay is taxed at a prescribed rate. The maximum taxable earnings are increased as average wage levels rise. At the same time, the benefits payable also increase. The amount of the benefit received from Social Security will depend upon the Average Monthly Earnings (AME) and the number of years of credit that have been accrued. The benefit of most general interest is the monthly income that an officer and eligible members of the officer's family attain when the officer reaches age sixty-five. (Reduced benefits may be selected for ages sixty-two, sixty-three and sixty-four, as well.) Payments are provided for disabled officers and for their spouses and children. Monthly income is provided for an officer's widow or widower with children under eighteen years of age, or for children alone, or for the widow or widower at age sixty, or for dependent parents. These important benefits, then, supplement other insurance-type security programs. Application for benefits may be made at any Social Security office.

Note: It is important that you ensure that the Social Security Administration has credited you with the correct contributions. This may be accomplished by requesting the status of your account at approximately three-year intervals. Postcard-type forms are available at any Social Security office to use for this request.

SCHOLARSHIPS AND EDUCATION LOANS

College education costs for children are of growing concern with the increased costs of tuition and board. In planning one's estate, settlement options of life insurance and educational endowment insurance are often selected or purchased as coverage. Some provide this security by purchasing bonds and participating in other savings and investment programs. Should this be insufficient, there are a number of scholarships that can be won through good grades and successful competition through examinations. A current listing of these is contained in DA Pam 352-2, *Educational Assistance and Opportunities—Information for Army Family Members.* Many of the states have statutes and educational programs that provide scholarships and financial aid to dependents of disabled and deceased veterans. These are listed in the cited pamphlet.

The Junior G.I. Bill or War Orphan's Educational Assistance Act of 1964 provides benefits to sons and daughters of service personnel who die or become disabled as a result of a wartime or extra-hazardous peacetime disease or injury. Up to $376 per month for forty-five months may be received. One cannot predict one's disease or disabling injury, but this benefit should be known to the service member.

The National Defense Education Acts of 1958 and 1965 provide low-cost loans to college-age dependents of service personnel. This too cannot be specifically included in an estate plan, but it is comforting to know it is there to assist peacetime veterans and their dependents.

The young married officer will be encouraged by some insurance salesmen to provide for college education of the children through insurance contracts. Such endowment insurance for education is expensive and may not be the best method for you. Competing with insurance for this purpose are the above programs, savings programs such as government bonds, and long-range investment programs.

BURIAL RIGHTS AND BENEFITS

The government provides burial and funeral allowances in the event of the death of active duty, retired, or honorably discharged officers. The allowances vary from complete for an active duty officer's death to a plot allowance for an honorably discharged officer. These allowances should be considered in your security program. You should acquaint your spouse or other responsible dependent with your desires and with an understanding of what services and allowances are available. The government respects its departed service member and desires that interment be proper and at as little expense to the member's survivors as possible.

Officers on Active Duty, Active Duty for Training, or Inactive Duty Training. The government will take charge of most of the arrangements if the surviving kin so desire. The standards of the services provide every proper consideration; it is usually best to leave arrangements to the military authorities at the place of death. The services and allowances provided include:

1. Services of preparation at the place of death (pickup, embalming and preser-

vation, casket, and hearse service to the cemetery or shipping terminal) and funeral director's services.

2. Cremation and a suitable urn for the ashes (if requested in writing by an authorized survivor).

3. A flag for the casket.

4. Transportation of remains with a military escort.

5. An allowance for interment: $1,750 maximum for burial in a private cemetery; $1,180 maximum, when remains are consigned to a funeral director and are interred in a national or post cemetery; or $75 maximum, when remains are consigned directly to the national or post cemetery officials. (The allowances are meant to defray the costs of such items as the coach, flowers, vault, church services, obituary notices, car for the family, services of the funeral director, opening and closing of the grave, and use of cemetery equipment.)

Retired and Honorably Discharged Officers. The Veterans Administration will pay an allowance of $300 as reimbursement for funeral expenses and, if burial is in a private cemetery, an additional plot allowance, not to exceed $150. Honorably discharged (not retired) officers are entitled only to the $150 plot allowance unless they were in receipt of Veterans Administration pensions at time of death. If the retiree died from service-connected causes, an allowance not to exceed $1,100 is authorized in lieu of any other burial benefit.

Social Security Death Benefit. In addition to any allowance or reimbursement received from the Veterans Administration or military service, survivors of retired officers also are entitled to a lump-sum death benefit payment of $255 upon application to the nearest Social Security office.

Dependents. When a dependent dies while the member is on active duty (other than for training) transportation may be furnished for the remains at Army expense. Certain privileges related to national and post burial sites are authorized and discussed below.

Control of Cemeteries. The control of all national cemeteries except Arlington and those operated by the service academies and the Soldier's and Airmen's and the Naval Homes was transferred to the Veterans Administration by PL 93-43. Post cemeteries remain under control of the Army.

Burial in a National or Post Cemetery. The deceased active duty officer may be buried in any national cemetery in which grave space is available. The surviving spouse, minor children, and in certain instances, unmarried adult children, are also eligible for burial in the same cemetery. Only one grave site is authorized per family unit. Burial at a post cemetery is subject to determination and approval of the post commanding officer and in keeping with Army regulations. At post cemeteries, immediate members of the family beyond those authorized at national cemeteries may be buried on post approval. Certain posts will accept grave site reservations in writing for surviving spouses. Retired and honorably discharged service members are, likewise, entitled to burial in a national cemetery, if space is available. Detailed additional information on these matters may be secured from a superintendent of a National Cemetery or from the Office of Support Services, DA, Washington, DC 20315. Local veterans organizations will also provide much assistance and information.

Honors and Headstones. Military honors will be provided by the Army when requested for interment at a national or post cemetery. At certain national and at civilian cemeteries, these honors are rendered by a local Reserve unit or a veterans organization upon request. Chapter 6, on *Military Courtesy,* provides further detail on the ceremony.

Headstones and markers that are proper, appropriate, and otherwise suitable are provided in memory and honor of the service member at little or no cost. Such provision is made by the service, the Veterans Administration, and/or the state. No service member's grave will be unmarked because of lack of funds. At national and post cemeteries, this honor is virtually automatic with no action, other than consent, required by the kin.

In summary, your government is grateful and proud of your service; in the grim instance of death, it is desired that your burial be in keeping with your dedication. Consequently, most of the expenses of burial are paid by or shared by the government as your deserved and earned benefit.

VETERANS' BENEFITS

There are a number of important benefits provided by the government for veterans of service to their country during times of strife. These programs along with the foregoing survivors' benefits are administered primarily by the Veterans Administration with assistance from other federal agencies. Veterans of "cold war" conflict or peacetime service are now included in certain veterans' acts. The basic benefits are the educational assistance, the VA Home Loan, the VA compensation, and the VA pension, which assist active duty, discharged, and disabled veterans and provide financial help to survivors.

Educational Assistance. There are several educational assistance programs now in existence for active duty personnel. Eligibility is determined by dates of service.

Veterans of Vietnam Era. Needed to qualify for benefits are at least 181 consecutive days of active service, any part of which was during the period 1 February 1955 through 31 December 1976. The benefits provide up to forty-five months of full-time education or training, or equivalent part-time. The monthly rates are $376 for a veteran without a dependent, $448 with one dependent, $510 for two dependents, and $32 for each additional dependent. Scaled amounts are provided for part-time schooling. Personnel on active duty may use this benefit. A veteran has ten years from the date of last discharge or release from service after 1 June 1966 to use this benefit. The benefit expires after 31 December 1989.

Post-Vietnam Era. The Veterans Education and Employment Assistance Act of 1976 (PL 94-502) established a contributory system for persons entering military service on or after 1 January 1977. Participants could contribute from $25 to $100 monthly from their pay up to $2,700. The government matches the contributions on a two-for-one basis. Enrollment in the plan is prohibited for persons entering the military after 1 July 1985. (See *New G.I. Bill,* below.) Eligibility to use the benefits begins after completion of six years of active duty. The amount of the fund, up to $8,100 maximum, is divided by the number of months of entitlement to determine the monthly payment to cover educational expenses. This benefit must be used within ten years of leaving the service. Unused contributions by the *individual* will be refunded.

New G.I. Bill. The Veterans Educational Assistance Act of 1984 (VEAP) established a new program for individuals entering the military service after 1 July 1985. The program originally was to operate during a three-year trial period, but it proved so popular it was made permanent in 1987. The permanent legislation was renamed the Montgomery G.I. Bill Act in recognition of the preeminent role played by Representative G. V. (Sonny) Montgomery of Mississippi in helping the legislation achieve permanent status. Participation is automatic with a $100 per month contribution from basic pay each month for the first twelve months of service, unless participation is specifically declined. Participation in the program is closed to graduates of one of the service academies or a senior ROTC program. Three years of active service or two years of active duty plus four years in the Selected Reserve or National Guard will entitle an individual to a post-service benefit of $300 per month for thirty-six months. The benefit is $250 per month for thirty-six months for a two-year active duty enlistment. Supplemental benefits also are available to those who extend their active duty service or fill critical shortage specialties. The current limit on supplemental benefits is $400 per month, although with the right combination of years of service and duty in critical skills areas, a soldier could qualify for a total benefit of $1,300 per month for the thirty-six-month period. For Reservists, no contribution is required. Those who enlist for six years can receive $140 per month for thirty-six months without having to wait until their obligation is completed.

VA Home Loan. The home loan under the Veterans Administration provides the opportunity of buying a home with low down payment. (FHA in-service home loans are also available to the active duty officer and should be investigated by the home-buying officer.) Virtually all veterans who have served on active duty since 16 September 1940, as well as present active duty personnel who have served at least 181 days of continuous duty, qualify for the VA Home Loan program.

VA Compensation. Compensation is payable by the Veterans Administration to an officer who becomes disabled while on active duty or active duty for training provided the disability was incurred in line of duty. The amount of the compensation is based upon the extent of the disability, from 10 percent to 100 percent, which is a legal assessment by the Veterans Administration in consideration of the officer's future capability to earn a living. The compensation goes to the officer. The amounts vary with the percentage and kind of disability, when the disability occurred, and the number of dependents. If the officer dies of service-related disabilities either while on active duty or after leaving the service, compensation for survivors is payable under the Dependency and Indemnity Compensation, discussed earlier.

Disabled service members with less than eight years active duty may or may not receive service disability retirement or severance pay depending on the circumstances. They could receive the VA disability compensation. Officers who are involuntarily separated with more than five but less than twenty years of service are entitled to a separation payment equal to 10 percent of annual base pay times years of service, up to a maximum of $30,000. These matters should be clarified before you leave the hospital and are separated.

VA Pension. Rates stipulated by law and tied to the dependents' other income are payable by the Veterans Administration to the surviving spouse or children of a veteran or retired individual whose separation from the service was not as a result of disability or whose death was not service-connected. The amounts payable are based upon financial need and are at minimal levels. Entitlement ceases if the surviving spouse remarries, unless the remarriage is terminated by death or is voided or annulled. Application for consideration for this benefit may be made at any convenient office of the Veterans Administration.

While this benefit is available, do not count upon it as part of your financial security plan. Your survivors would have to be essentially destitute to qualify.

INSURANCE PROGRAMS

All estate planners advise that the first step to security after having a sound financial base is to establish an insurance program. But how much insurance is enough? There are two solutions to the problem. One is the "needs approach"; the other is to follow the advice of insurance counselors and recommended litera- ture. The "needs approach" calls for an analysis of how much the survivors will require should the breadwinner die. This includes living expenses, housing, and education of children, among many other things. Consider your spouse's earning capability. Remarriage is a difficult planning factor, to say the least, but it should be considered. If in doubt, seek the advice of a reputable insurance salesman or insurance estate planner, and match the advice received against that of the litera- ture referenced at the beginning of this chapter.

One rule of thumb is that you should be covered by insurance in an amount up to five times your annual income. If your family depends also on income from your spouse, she or he should have similar coverage.

The need for expert counsel becomes more apparent when one recognizes there are seven basic types of life insurance: reducing term, level term, ordinary (whole) life, limited pay life (twenty- or thirty-year pay), endowment, annuity (retirement income), and variable insurance. There is no less expensive way to provide for security; however, as more options are selected the costs increase. Other options are found within the basic kinds: war risk, aviation coverage, suicide, disability waivers, dividend options, double indemnity, settlements, endowments for educa- tion, surrender cash values, and loan values. These should be carefully checked in your contract; at least you should understand for what you are paying. Many benefit and mutual associations offer packaged family insurance programs that provide coverage for the entire family at moderate rates. As in other financial programs, if you do not pay very much, you do not accrue much cash or loan value. In insurance programs you do have security, however, not provided by other investment-type programs.

Servicemen's Group Life Insurance (SGLI). This government-sponsored insur- ance program provides $50,000 of life insurance coverage for active duty mem- bers and for drilling members of the National Guard and Reserve at a premium of $4 per month. It also is available to members of the Retired Reserve under age sixty at slightly increased rates, depending upon age. Upon separation from active duty, the coverage is continuable as low-cost term insurance for five years under the Veterans' Group Life Insurance (VGLI), after which you are guaranteed the right to convert to a permanent insurance program whatever the status of your health may be. Since this conversion to permanent insurance would be at rates applicable to your attained age, it could be expensive. You should consider this as a bonus program and definitely not drop or forgo other insurance coverage.

Survivor Benefit Plan (SBP). The SBP has been discussed in an earlier section as a qualified benefit. Actuarial studies indicate that the cost of coverage under SBP is significantly less than the cost for the same coverage by a commercial insurance company. Actual comparison, of course, is dependent upon the age of both the retiree and his or her spouse as well as the amount of coverage selected. Nonethe- less, participation in SBP offers the military member a means of extending impor- tant protection for loved ones into the retirement years. Coverage by SBP should be considered in planning your estate in conjunction with other insurance and investments. Seek counsel related to your personal situation.

Other Kinds of Insurance. In addition to life insurance, other kinds of insurance are necessary for security. These include fire insurance on a home, insurance against loss or theft of personal property, personal liability, and automobile insur- ance. Some later-referenced associations package these kinds of insurance at lower costs to service personnel; your consideration and study of their programs are in order. Each will provide literature, advice, and cost and coverage quotations for your particular situation. As in the case of life insurance, studying referenced literature and seeking the advice of experienced officers and professional counselors can save you significant funds.

INVESTMENT PROGRAMS

By carefully budgeting your salary and after establishing the other discussed priority components of a financial estate, you can arrive at the opportunity for savings and investing. Actually, your retirement income is an annuity that the government is saving for you. The impact of retirement pay as an annuity was previously mentioned; another way to consider its value is to determine how much you would have to invest to receive retirement pay for a certain number of years. Assume you retire on a monthly retired pay of $1,000 and you have a life expectancy of twenty-five years. During your retirement, you would collect $300,000 in retired pay. To receive the same amount from an annuity, you would have had to invest $161,000 at a 5.5 percent interest rate. Should you live for thirty years after retirement, the amount that would have had to be invested at the same interest rate is nearly $175,000. Thus, retirement, like Social Security income, could be included in the percentages of funds considered invested. Further, both Social Security and retirement income provide relatively fixed purchasing power, as opposed to fixed income, since both now are adjusted to offset cost of living increases. You may not have realized that you (with the government's assistance) began two investment programs upon entering the service.

An investment program may consist of fixed dollar investments and variable dollar investments. Fixed dollar investments are those that have a fixed value and return a certain yield, such as bonds and savings accounts. Variable dollar securities grow or decline in value at the risk of the investor. These include common stocks and investment in real estate. There is increased risk in such purchases since there is no guarantee of eventual sale at a stipulated price. The purchase of carefully selected common stocks, or carefully chosen real estate, is made with the goal of increasing values, combined with dividend or rental return. Many investment advisory companies recommend a suitable mix between fixed dollar investments and variable dollar investments—highly rated bonds with highly rated common stocks, as examples.

There are mutual funds that have investments wholly in common stocks, or wholly in bonds, with the major portion having a judicious mix of their own selections of each type of security.

Each service member also is entitled to establish an Individual Retirement Account (IRA) to which he or she can contribute up to $2,000 per year. The amount contributed each year is wholly deductible from your annual income for tax purposes if your taxable pay is less than $25,000, or $40,000 if you are married. If your pay is between $25,000 and $35,000 ($40,000 and $50,000 if married) your IRA contribution is partly deductible. In any case, the earnings in the IRA accumulate tax-free. However, the funds in the IRA cannot be used until age fifty-nine and one half without incurring a penalty. When used, the proceeds from the account are taxed as ordinary income.

When considering investment programs, do not overlook your checking account. Many banks, savings and loan associations, and credit unions pay interest on checking accounts, provided a minimum balance is maintained in the account. While the interest rates on these accounts may be relatively low, it is far better to be earning interest than to maintain a small balance in an account where you quite likely will be required to pay a monthly service charge, or a charge for each check written, or both. The difference between earning interest and paying service charges can add up to significant savings.

How should you enter this interesting and potentially rewarding field? First, you should enter into investment planning as early in your career as possible. *The less you have to invest the more important your study and investigation.* There are good books on investment planning. There are good magazines devoted to business, finance, and investment. There are investment advisory services. There are investment counselors. There are brokers who can provide study material and detailed information, and many will assist in financial planning. As an initial step, go to your local libraries. See what they have available for your reading and study. When you have some investment money—make your start.

ASSISTANCE FACILITIES AND ASSOCIATIONS

Servicemen and women have many assistance and advisory associations that will help them and their dependents in solving problems related to personal affairs and security. There are also many mutual insurance associations that provide all types of insurance at very reasonable rates while also assisting in associated administrative matters. Knowing about them can affect your security planning. They also can and will assist your dependents while you are away or should you die. You should determine your eligibility and study what each association can provide.

Army Community Service (ACS). The Army has consolidated a number of services to personnel and their families with the missions of providing information, assistance, and guidance in meeting personal and family problems beyond the scope of their own resources. The functions of Army Emergency Relief, Army Personnel Affairs, Survivors Assistance Officer, and Retired Affairs are integrated with ACS as local conditions permit. Information is provided on financial assistance, availability of housing, transportation, relocation, medical and dental care, legal assistance, orientation of new arrivals, care of handicapped children, recreation, and many other community matters. The theme is "Self-Help, Service, and Stability." It is particularly devoted to the assistance of dependents whose sponsors are away for whatever purpose. If you or your dependents have a problem, the local ACS on post is a place to begin for information and assistance.

The Veterans Administration. The many services, rights, and benefits of veterans are administered by officials of the Veterans Administration assisted by members of the American Legion and Veterans of Foreign Wars in many cases. Most cities and county seats have offices where you can get assistance.

The American Red Cross. There is a broad program of directed and voluntary aid to military personnel by officials and volunteers of the American Red Cross. Their assistance in hospitals is well known. There will be a director at each post to assist in emergency notifications, investigations, provision of financial aid, child welfare, and other related matters of emergency.

Army Emergency Relief. Although primarily an association to give financial loans and grants to enlisted personnel, the Army Emergency Relief officer at every post can also assist an officer or the officer's family if the situation warrants. Each case is determined on merit and need, usually in association with American Red Cross officials and those of the ACS program.

Social Security Field Offices. The many complex rules and administrative matters of the Social Security program can be clarified at their field offices located in most cities. They will determine eligibility and assist in obtaining the many benefits that this increasing welfare program provides.

Army Distaff Hall. Army widows age sixty-two or older and the mother, daughter, sister, or mother-in-law of a Regular Army commissioned or warrant officer, or of a Reserve officer with twenty years service, are eligible to apply for residence at the Army Distaff Hall. Retired female officers also are eligible. Inquiries should be mailed to 6200 Oregon Avenue, NW, Washington, DC 20015.

Army and Air Force Mutual Aid Association. This mutual insurance association began in 1879. It offers low-cost life insurance to Regular Army and Air Force officers, warrant officers and those Reserve officers and warrant officers in the indefinite category who have completed three years of continuous active service. The Association offices are at Fort Myer, Arlington, VA 22211. They provide gratuitous services for survivors in preparing pension and other claims on the government. They will also store your valuable papers in their vault. All officers are urged to investigate the Association programs.

The Armed Forces Relief and Benefit Association. This worthwhile mutual association has similar eligibility rules as that of the Army and Air Force Mutual Aid Association and provides low-cost group life insurance. It is at 1156 15th Street NW, Washington, DC 20005.

The Association of the U.S. Army. Officers who have joined the Association of the U.S. Army are eligible for group life insurance at very low cost. Generally no physical examinations are required and there are no exclusions. All risk protection and disability waiver of premium payments are included. You can get more information by writing AUSA Members Life Insurance Plan, 1529 18th Street NW, Washington, DC 20036.

United Services Automobile Association. This association provides low-cost automobile insurance for most active and retired officers. The policies are tailored to each officer's need and location. Dividends serve to lower the costs. The Association also provides homeowners, personal liability, boat-owners, household goods and personal effects, and life insurance. It offers no-load mutual funds and a brokerage service for investments. Officers are invited to write to USAA Building, 4119 Broadway, San Antonio, TX 78215.

Armed Forces Insurance. This association, formerly the Armed Forces Cooperative Insuring Association, offers very low cost insurance of personal and household effects in the case of fire, theft, and other like losses without regard to station or duty and at actual cost to members. Eligibility is like that for the Army and Air Force Mutual Aid Association. Members do the promoting and most of the assessing. The association's promptness and payment of reasonable claims without argument are well known throughout the service. It also provides fire insurance on a house and personal liability, and can insure for theft and pilferage losses. Officers are urged to write to Armed Forces Insurance, Fort Leavenworth, KS 66027, for complete information.

Other Associations. There are other associations that insure and assist military personnel. Only a few of the best known and longest established societies have been mentioned. There are, in particular, a number of mutual life insurance associations that offer low-cost protection. Their names are excluded in the interests of brevity but exclusion does not infer that such associations are more expensive, untrustworthy, or unreliable. The ones recommended can save you considerable sums of money should you insure with them or like organizations. Your support of the mentioned societies is not suggested from other than the aspect of their proved assistance to officers throughout the past.

PERSONAL ADMINISTRATION RELATED TO SECURITY PROGRAMMING

No security program review is complete without a study and inspection of one's personal administration. Such matters as records, state and federal taxes, estate and death taxes, wills, trusts, powers of attorney, and joint ownership of property are discussed below. You should review these records each year (at income tax time, for instance) and, in particular, prior to going overseas with or without your spouse. All matters should be clearly explained to your spouse and the places where your records are stored clearly identified.

Records. You should know where all personal records are and their status. The important ones should be filed in a safe deposit box, a safe, or a fireproof vault (the Army and Air Force Mutual Aid Association stores life insurance policies and wills, for example), or some other secure location. Photostatic or otherwise certified copies of the original may then be kept at home as your working file. A partial list of important records would be: birth certificates, marriage certificates, wills, powers of attorney, trusts, deeds, mortgages, active duty and retirement orders, automobile ownership certificate, life insurance policies, bonds and stocks, baptism and confirmation papers, and other valuables and valuable papers. Less important records could be filed at home with a personal file of military records. Such a file would include financial records, promotion records, personal property record, bank and savings account records, other kinds of insurance policies, and so on; the more important ones can and should be filed in a strong, relatively fireproof, portable box.

State and Federal Taxes. All officers must file a federal and (in most cases) a state income tax report each year and pay these taxes as required. Your finance officer withholds federal pay for this purpose and advises you of the amounts withheld each year by means of the W-2 form. Under provisions of the Soldiers' and Sailors' Civil Relief Act of 1940, you are excluded from paying state income and personal property taxes to a state where you temporarily reside because of military duty, provided you can prove to that state you are domiciled—legally reside—in another. You must pay federal income tax on your basic pay, dislocation allowances, and per diem pay in excess of needs, and all other sources of taxable income. All units and posts have personnel advisors who can assist you in most uncomplicated filing matters. Your spouse is not excluded from state income and property taxes, if he or she earns an income and possesses property in that state. It is wise to establish a legal residence in a single state and pay your taxes there accordingly; however, there are states that have no income taxes, and some officers will establish a legal residence in them in the interests of lower overall taxes. Such establishment should be done carefully having in mind the future and not a saving of a few dollars through legal loopholes. Since the career family moves often, this problem will recur. Facing it with honesty, foresight, and advice from experts is in order.

Estate and Death Taxes. The federal government may tax your estate in the event of your death if the adjusted gross estate is sufficiently large. State death taxes take the form of inheritance or an estate tax. Each state has a different system of such taxation; therefore, consult with a nearby legal officer. Your will (and estate) must be examined, appropriately implemented, and taxed by a state official. The process known as probate is accomplished prior to execution of the will or disbursement of the estate. Bank officers will record the contents of safe deposit boxes and may not allow the papers therein to be taken or assumed until after the probate. It is possible to compute your potential estate tax while you are alive. The matter of estate taxes is complicated, however, and the advice of a specialist in estate planning is recommended. Total income including insurance benefits is the basis in many states for the inheritance tax. The issue for you is one of awareness that such taxes do exist so that they can be considered and expected.

Wills. Without exception all references and counselors advise an Army officer to execute a will and to keep it current. Your spouse should also have a will. If you die without one, the state will, in effect, make one for you. Unfortunately, regardless of how little you have, the state cannot make such a will and distribute your estate as well as you could have done by a will. On a draft write what you believe you desire in a will, then go to the legal assistance officer for expert help.

There are many dos and don'ts for will making, a few of which follow: Don't do it by yourself; don't change it by pen and ink unless legally supervised; don't delay doing it; don't fail to reexamine it upon records review and especially when changing legal residence; don't specify amounts (in general use percentages); don't sign more than one copy; do choose an executor with business sense; and do keep the original signed copy in a secure place. Specify names and property or assets only if you have to; many a family has had temporary or permanently strained relationships develop out of contests for estate assets. Use relations and terms like "to the children, share and share alike." The important advice is reemphasized: make a will with legal help and keep it current!

Power of Attorney. A power of attorney is a legal instrument whereby one person may designate another person to act in his or her behalf in legal or personal matters. This authority may be granted by a husband to his wife or any other person of legal age and capacity. It can be made very general and unlimited in scope, or it can be restricted to specific functions, as desired by the grantor. Do not fail to understand that when a power of attorney is given to another person, that person has the legal right to act under it; and if the powers granted include the right to buy or sell, or give away the grantor's property, such acts are binding. *It has been called "the most potentially dangerous document that man has ever devised."* Therefore prudence demands that you entrust such powers only to an individual in whom you have complete trust and confidence.

The document has particular value to officers. Many officers provide their spouses with power of attorney. Thereafter, when the officer is performing extended travel, or is assigned overseas with the family remaining behind, essential business or legal matters may be performed without the officer's presence or signature.

The authority given in a power of attorney, unlike that of a will, becomes invalid upon death of the grantor.

By all means, consult a legal assistance officer or attorney in the preparation of this document. Explain carefully the purpose in mind. It may be true that a restricted rather than a broad form may be best. Again, as with a will, there are variations between state laws. A special form must be used to authorize cashing of government checks. A power of attorney must be acknowledged before a notary public.

The use of a form to give to another these powers is discouraged. Consult a legal assistance officer, or an attorney, and have it done correctly and thoughtfully.

Trusts. A trust is an agreement whereby an individual gives property to a second party, the trustee, for the benefit of a third party, the beneficiary or beneficiaries. Individuals, trust companies, or banks act as trustees. Trusts are special legal contracts. Trusts may be specified while you are alive, as testaments for financial income to specified individuals after your death, as revocable, and as irrevocable. As contracts, they require legal and business advice and should be entered only with knowledge and care.

Joint Ownership by Husband and Wife. For many years, this Guide presented a discussion advocating for husband and wife a joint bank account, and joint ownership with right of survivorship of other property such as real estate, stocks and bonds, and the family automobile. In view of sudden orders for TDY, foreign service unaccompanied tours, and other temporary family separations, the method has definite advantages. The wife or husband staying behind to manage the family and its affairs has fewer strictures. On the death of one of the joint owners, the property passes immediately to the other. It is not subject to the cumbersome processes of the probate courts and there is the avoidance of potentially heavy legal fees. These are important advantages.

As the years have passed, experience has proven that the method has weaknesses. Some states do not recognize joint ownership with right of survivorship. Others are community property states in which wives are presumed to own half the estate accumulated by the husband during marriage. Difficulties arise when the joint owners are divorced or one becomes incompetent. In the absence of a will, difficult problems arise if the co-owners die in a common disaster. There are estate and inheritance taxes, federal as well as state, and if the estate becomes sizable joint ownership presents additional problems. There are gift taxes that may need to be paid in the transfer of title to a spouse. These are all matters for expert guidance, including the special situation of the state in which assigned to Army duty.

Consult the legal assistance officer. Or consult a civilian attorney. State all the facts with candor. Joint ownership is not condemned. Under the conditions of Army service for most officers, it may be the preferred method of ownership. Get legal advice so your decision can be made with prudence and wisdom.

Personal and Property Record. Your complete security program can be detailed on a form and changed with each review if necessary. Many associations provide such forms, and it is in your interest to secure them and to fill them in. You will find as the years go by that such a record requires several pages which can be conveniently bound in a folder or a notebook. Property records are similarly inclined to grow and can be included in your folder. The need to keep the file up-to-date, in a relatively secure location where your spouse can find and review it is obvious but worthy of noting.

SUMMARY

Security or estate planning calls for step-by-step analysis of one's situation, goals, and benefits, and supplementing these with savings, insurance, and investments. The plan must be reviewed and altered as each change in your personal and financial situation occurs but, in particular, prior to departure for overseas and combat. There is no simple plan or checklist for you to follow because of the numerous financial programs and the personal variables introduced by each officer and his or her dependents. This chapter should have provided you with a base for such planning; by following its sections in order and checking off each point as it applies to you, you will be able to draw up your own plan. Then, by reading the references and seeking counsel, you will be able to assure yourself of security for you and your dependents.

Advice for the Widow or Widower. Although the primary purpose of this chapter is to enable officers and their spouses to understand their rights and benefits, and plan for all eventualities in their future lives together, it also contains a great store of information for those who have already become widows or widowers.

The Army and Air Force Mutual Aid Association will provide upon request a booklet, *Notes for a New Widow.* Like a similar one entitled *Help Your Widow While She's Still Your Wife!* provided by the Retired Officers Association, it has blanks to be filled in to constitute a summary of vital information and guidance for the new widow. The guidance is equally applicable to widowers. A thoughtful officer will, of course, keep the information up to date as financial plans and estates are altered.

The Army takes thoughtful, effective, and thorough care of the families of its deceased members. This extends to funeral arrangements and wise counsel as to the settlement of all residual affairs.

The Installation Retirement Services Offices, throughout CONUS, are available to provide information and assistance. The local ACS agency also can provide help. Veterans' organizations are eager to help all service widows or widowers with the complexity of administration of affairs. Contact all of these plus the Social Security field office, your banker, and all insurance companies. Finally, make all contracts and sign all papers with care and counsel. Your spouse would want you to grieve, but be sensible with your emotions when it comes to your and the family's security. All administrative matters of long-range importance can be settled within reasonable periods of time and do not require your immediate attention while you are in mourning. You are urged to read elsewhere in this guide about the social side of Army life for widows and widowers because the Army and its people desire you to retain your ties with the service and your friends.

10

Army Posts and Stations

'Tis a good and safe rule to sojourn in many places, as if you meant to spend your life there; never omitting an opportunity to doing a kindness, or speaking a true word, or making a friend.—John Ruskin.

This chapter contains information of special interest to officers and their families about Army posts and stations in the United States. It has been developed as a dependable "first place to look" after receipt of orders for change of station. The information was obtained through the generous cooperation of post commanders and their information officers and billeting officers. It purposely has been made general in nature, designed to provide only a brief introduction to a particular post or station.

Shortly after receipt of assignment orders, you may expect to receive from your new unit or your new post commander a welcoming letter containing detailed information about the post. Many station commanders send a descriptive pamphlet about their station to officers who receive assignment orders. If this information is not received, it is standard practice for an officer to write to the station adjutant and inquire about matters of prearrival interest. When writing, be sure to include information about your family status, including number, ages, and sex of children so that the adjutant can furnish information specifically applicable to your needs. Be assured that the Army values its members and their dependents, and each commander recognizes the importance of their morale, including the importance of first impressions. Each commander will be anxious that you are fully and accurately informed as to what you may expect at your new post. Any questions you may have will be answered as quickly and as completely as possible.

An assignment to a new post or station should be approached with the feeling that here is a real opportunity not readily available to other persons of our society. It provides the opportunity to see perhaps a new and different area of the country from any you have seen before, with the difference to be measured not only in terms of topography, scenery, climate, or historic sites, but in terms of people and their customs. The new assignment will provide also the opportunity to meet new Army members, many of whom you may never meet again, but others who will become lifelong friends with whom you will serve again on other future assignments. The total opportunity of a new assignment is limited only by your ability to learn, to understand, to meet others and to be met by them, to participate in the activities of the station, and to pursue actively the off-duty recreational activities that will be available. Your own attitude will be the major determinant in making the new assignment a rewarding and pleasant experience.

There is another facet to each new assignment that should not be overlooked. Referred to here is the post itself. Each post came into being as a result of a definite Army need. Examples are Fort Wadsworth and Fort Totten, which originally were Coast Artillery forts helping to protect the approaches to New York harbor from possible attack from the sea. Another example is Fort Riley, Kansas, which served as the base for the operations of Custer's 7th Cavalry Regiment during the days our western states were being settled. Or Fort Sheridan, Illinois, which was established in 1887 in order to have troops near the city of Chicago during the period of labor unrest in that area, of which the Haymarket Riot of 1886 was a part.

As the years have passed, Army needs have changed, resulting in changed or changing missions for the various posts and stations. Some, like Fort Totten, have become housekeeping and support facilities serving Army members and members of the Army's sister services stationed in the area, while others, like Fort Riley, still play an active role in the training and support of Army units, but with a mission changed considerably from that originally assigned.

Study of the origins and historical activities of any post is both interesting and professionally rewarding. Such study does much to increase one's knowledge of the Army's heritage and serves as well as a fine base for more thorough knowledge and understanding of the local area. It is recommended as a subject of early priority upon assignment to a new post.

The typical, established Army post is a pleasant place to live. Where there are quarters for families, the activities will be substantially the same as in civilian communities. The ties of neighborliness and breadth of friendships are especially noteworthy because all are engaged in the common mission of the nation's security. The vast majority of Army members are young and active. The provision of extensive off-duty athletic, cultural, recreational, and social activities recognizes the needs and expectancies of young officers, noncommissioned officers, and soldiers, and their spouses and children. Opportunities for an interesting life are abundant for all individuals who participate actively in the life of the post.

There is a wide variation in the living and recreational facilities of Army stations. Some posts have been in use for decades and have been progressively developed so that the resulting environment is highly pleasing with excellent athletic, cultural, social, and recreational facilities. Others were established during World War II or later and are less extensively developed. The variation in number and adequacy of family quarters is wide; inadequate housing is considered by some officers to be the most serious objection to an Army career. This chapter does not seek to minimize it. But the Army's leaders have fought hard for action to improve it; there has been considerable construction and improvement in the situation during past years. The progress must continue until all of our truly permanent posts and stations are provided with adequate housing that is up to the standards of professional people in other walks of life. The complete environment must be a good place for Army members and their spouses and children to live.

Attention is invited to chapter 8, *The Social Side of Army Life,* and chapter 11, *Foreign Service.*

The facilities described below are common to Army posts.

Commissaries. Most installations are authorized to have a commissary where groceries and household supplies, similar to those sold in commercial supermarkets, may be purchased.

These nonprofit facilities contribute immeasurably to the quality of life of retired and active duty soldiers and their families and other personnel authorized to shop in them. The commissary benefit is the second most important form of nonpay compensation for soldiers and family members.

An identification card is required for entrance, and personal checks may be cashed for purchases. Merchandise is sold at cost, and a 5 percent surcharge is added to the total bill at the check-out counter. Surcharge funds are used for building new commissaries and renovating old ones and to pay for such things as grocery carts, meat-slicing machines, and paper bags.

By shopping in the commissary, customers save an average of 27.46 percent when compared to commercial supermarket prices. Additional savings can be recognized by taking advantage of special promotional sales and using coupons.

Post Exchanges. Excellent post exchanges are provided at Army stations. The Army and Air Force Exchange Service (AAFES) prescribes the items and services that may be sold. Profits generated by exchanges are used for the support of athletic and recreational programs, including provisions for athletic fields and other facilities. Post exchanges add to the convenience of post life and provide economies for all active and retired personnel who use them. An ID card is required for entrance and purchase of merchandise. Checks up to a usual limit of $150 or for the cost of the merchandise may be cashed.

Motion Picture Theaters. All stations in CONUS and overseas are provided motion picture service, and many stations have excellent motion picture theaters. Through the cooperation of the motion picture industry, and the good work of the Army and Air Force Exchange Service, the best and most recently released films are shown. Like the post exchange, the profits are returned as dividends to be expended for athletic, recreational, and other programs for the general improvement of post life.

Athletic Facilities. Athletic programs and essential indoor and outdoor recreational facilities are provided at most stations. At permanent installations the facilities are outstanding. They include playing fields; bleachers and dressing rooms for baseball and football; swimming pools; bowling alleys; tennis courts, many of which are illuminated for night use; and field houses for basketball and other indoor sports; and many posts have excellent golf courses. The climate and recreational potential of the region has a bearing on the activities of maximum popularity. The Army goal is to provide a normal, interesting off-duty life for its members.

Religious Activities. Most Army stations are provided with religious facilities and programs. The services of chaplains of the Protestant, Catholic, and Jewish faiths are almost universally available to military members. Religious programs are conducted in much the same manner as in civilian communities. Chaplains are appreciated and valuable members of the unit or station.

Library Service. Nearly all stations have a good station library and in most instances the services of a professional librarian. New books, newspapers, and magazines are provided regularly. Individuals interested in study may receive important assistance from the librarian and the library facilities.

Officers' Open Messes. All permanent and semipermanent Army stations, and many units, have an officers' open mess, or club, the facilities of which are available to officers and mature members of their families. Dues are charged, which defray the operating expenses. The social life of club members normally centers about the programs and facilities of the open mess. Regular dining facilities are standard. Dances, social gatherings, and athletic activities are examples of recreational opportunities that are usually available. Officers joining a station or unit having an open mess should join it at once, as a matter of course.

Schools. All Army stations at which dependents are authorized are provided as a matter of course with school facilities for children of Army members. In general, the attempt is made to provide on-post schools for children through the sixth grade, with the junior and senior high school students attending local schools near the post. There are exceptions, of course. Many posts have kindergarten facilities. In all cases where any distance is involved, bus transportation is provided free of charge. Parochial or other private schools are available near many posts and may be utilized if desired. Consult the local authorities.

Medical Facilities. Most large Army posts have a station hospital, while smaller posts may be equipped only with a clinic or dispensary, relying upon a nearby military hospital for more extensive medical services. In any case, splendid medical care is available to Army personnel and family members, including those residing in off-post housing. See chapter 9, *Financial Planning*, for a complete description of medical care available and the procedures for obtaining this care.

Family Quarters. As mentioned earlier, the problem of providing adequate quarters for Army members and their families is a serious one. The actual housing situation varies not only from post to post, but also with time at any particular post, depending upon the numbers of arriving and departing personnel. A post with an adequate number of family quarters today could find itself woefully short of quarters tomorrow when a major new unit is assigned.

In general, it should be assumed that upon assignment to any post there will be a waiting period before on-post quarters may be obtained. This necessitates a rental or lease, prior to moving on post, or perhaps purchase of local housing in the nearby civilian community. The actual waiting period may vary from a few days to many months, and in some cases, such as for most personnel assigned to the Washington, D.C., area, there is no post housing available at all. Take this in stride. It is a recognized disadvantage of Army life, but it should be viewed in total context along with the many advantages available to Army members.

In all cases, be realistic and businesslike in your approach to providing housing for your family. It ALWAYS is advisable to obtain the very latest quarters information from the housing officer at your new post. If this information is not received within a few weeks after you receive assignment orders to a post, be sure to write for it. While advice is always welcome from those who have previously been stationed at your new post, remember that their information regarding quarters availability almost surely is out of date. Get the correct, up-to-date information about both on-post and off-post housing from the post housing officer and then make your personal plans accordingly.

One note of caution: When arriving at a new post, be sure to check with the housing office prior to making any commitments for lease or purchase of off-post quarters. While policies vary, in most cases you must have the permission of the housing officer to reside off-post.

Most stations have guest houses or other temporary-type accommodations, which may be utilized for short periods of time (five to ten days usually) while a family is making arrangements for permanent quarters. These facilities generally are limited in number, and reservations are in order well in advance of intended use. Write the post housing officer.

Activities for Spouses and Children. Most Army stations have organizations such as the officers' wives' club, Parent-Teacher Association, and youth activities of many kinds such as Boy Scouts, Girl Scouts, Teen-Age Clubs, and others. Active participation in the undertakings of these organizations is encouraged. It is a way for the newcomer to become acquainted and to add his or her talents to the life of the post.

ARMED FORCES HOSTESS ASSOCIATION

The Armed Forces Hostess Association, Room 1A–736, The Pentagon, Washington, DC 20310, provides a unique service for all newcomers in the Washington metropolitan area. Local files include information on animal care, camps, entertainment, furniture repair, schools, vacation, touring, and other helpful items. Files are also maintained on all CONUS posts. Information on either your CONUS or Washington assignment will be provided on request.

ABERDEEN PROVING GROUND, MARYLAND 21005 AND 21010
Autovon: 298–1110; Commercial: (301) 278–5201 (Aberdeen)
Autovon: 584–1110; Commercial: (301) 671–2011 (Edgewood)

Aberdeen Proving Ground, established in 1917, consists of 72,500 acres on two post areas. The main post is located twenty-five miles northeast of Baltimore, on Chesapeake Bay, adjacent to Aberdeen, Maryland. It is reached via I-95, U.S. 40, or via Bel Air U.S. 1. Edgewood Arsenal merged with the Aberdeen Proving Ground in 1971. The two post areas are separated by the Bush River.

Major Activities. At the Aberdeen area of the post, ZIP 21005, are located the U.S. Army Ordnance Center and School; Hq, Army Test and Evaluation Command; Ballistics Research Laboratory; Human Engineering Laboratory; Material Systems Analysis Activity; and the Army Combat Systems Test Activity. At the Edgewood area, ZIP 21010, are located the Chemical Research, Development and Engineering Center; Army Environmental Hygiene Agency; Army Toxic and Hazardous Materials Agency; and the Army Medical Research Institute for Chemical Defense.

Quarters. There are about 220 units of family housing for officers, about equally divided between the Aberdeen and Edgewood areas. There are about 300 BOQ units at Aberdeen and 70 at the Edgewood area. There is one 37-room guest house at Aberdeen. Nearby off-post housing is limited.

ANNISTON ARMY DEPOT, ALABAMA 36201
Autovon: 571–1110; Commercial: (205) 235–7501

Anniston Army Depot, established in 1941, is a heavily industrialized operation located on 15,000 acres adjacent to Fort McClellan, ten miles west of Anniston, Alabama.

Major Activities. Repair and retrofit of combat tracked vehicles, artillery, missiles, and small arms; receipt and storage of general supplies, ammunition, missiles, small arms, and strategic materials.

Quarters. There are five sets of family quarters for officers. Very limited BOQ space is available. No guest house is provided.

FORT A. P. HILL, VIRGINIA 22427
Autovon: 934–8110; Commercial: (804) 633–5041

Fort A. P. Hill is a subinstallation of Fort Meade. It is located three miles east of the small town of Bowling Green, Virginia, some thirty-six miles north of Richmond and about seventy-two miles south of the nation's capital. The post was opened in 1942 and consists of 76,000 acres. U.S. 301 intersects the post, with a large range complex on the south side of the highway and the post headquarters, training areas, and campsites on the north side.

Major Activity. The post's mission is to support training of active Army and Reserve components as well as training and/or testing by the Navy, Marines, Air Force, and other government agencies. The post has numerous training areas and campsites, some of which use tentage for troops in the field, primarily during the annual training period, which usually runs from May to September.

Quarters. A ten-space trailer court and a MSA Recreational trailer court are available. Limited family quarters are available to A. P. Hill personnel at the Naval Surface Weapons Center at Dahlgren, thirty miles distant. Limited off-post housing is available in Bowling Green and more is available in Fredericksburg, twenty miles away, and in Richmond.

ARLINGTON HALL STATION, VIRGINIA 22212
Autovon: 222–5145; Commercial: (202) 692–5145

Opened in 1942, Arlington Hall Station is located on eighty-seven acres in Arlington, Virginia, two miles west of Fort Myer off Route 50 (Arlington Boulevard).

Major Activity. Home of the Army Intelligence and Security Command.

Quarters. Two units are available for officers. No temporary officer quarters are available. Off-post housing is available, but expensive.

ARMED FORCES STAFF COLLEGE, VIRGINIA 23511
Autovon: 564-5252; Commercial: (804) 444–5252

The Armed Forces Staff College is located off Hampton Boulevard, two miles south of the main gate, Norfolk Naval Base, Virginia.

Major Activity. Under the direction of the Joint Chiefs of Staff and as part of the National Defense University, educates mid-career U.S. military officers, selected civilians, and allies in three separate courses: Joint Planning (twenty-two weeks), Command, Control, and Communication (six weeks), and Electronic Warfare (two weeks). (See also chapter 13, *Army Schools and Career Progress.*)

Quarters. Quarters are sufficient to accommodate most married officers on the faculty and staff. Family quarters are not furnished for students, but BOQs are available. Off-post housing is available.

ARMY MATERIALS TECHNOLOGY LABORATORY
(formerly Army Materials & Mechanics Research Center)
WATERTOWN, MASSACHUSETTS 02172
Autovon: 955-5357; Commercial: (617) 923-5357

Established in 1816 as the Watertown Arsenal. Located on thirty-seven acres at Watertown, Massachusetts, six miles west of Boston, on the north bank of the Charles River.

Major Activity. MTL is the Army's lead laboratory in structural integrity testing, corrosion prevention and control, advanced materials, materials testing technology, solid mechanics, lightweight armor, and manufacturing testing technology.

Quarters. Two sets of family housing are available for officers. No BOQs or guest house facilities are available.

FORT BELVOIR, VIRGINIA 22060
Autovon: 354–6071; Commercial: (703) 664–6071

Fort Belvoir, established in 1912, occupies 8,656 acres located astride U.S. 1, eleven miles southwest of Alexandria, Virginia, and about sixteen miles southwest of Washington, D.C.

Major Activities. U.S. Army Engineer Center and School; Information Systems Engineering Command; Defense Systems Management College; Defense Mapping Agency; Belvoir Research, Development and Engineering Center; 29th Infantry Division (Light) (National Guard); 310th Theater Army Area Command (TAACOM) (USAR); Information Systems Command; Davison Army Airfield; DeWitt Army Community Hospital.

Quarters. There are nearly 500 sets of family quarters for married officers. BOQs are available for both permanent party and TDY personnel. Limited guest house facilities are provided. Off-post housing is available, but expensive.

FORT BENJAMIN HARRISON, INDIANA 46216
Autovon: 699–1110; Commercial: (317) 546–9211

Fort Benjamin Harrison is located on 2,500 acres two blocks off State Highway 67 (Pendleton Pike) and just off I-465, 11 miles northeast of downtown Indianapolis, Indiana. The post was established in 1903.

Major Activities. U.S. Army Soldier Support Institute consisting of the Adjutant General School, Finance School, Soldier Physical Fitness School, Computer Science School, and the Recruiting and Retention School; U.S. Army Finance and Accounting Center; Defense Information School; and the Enlisted Records and Evaluation Center.

Quarters. The post has 431 sets of quarters for married officers, 391 Visiting Officer Quarters, and 17 BOQ units. Sixteen guest house units are available. Off-post housing is available for sale or rent in nearby areas.

FORT BENNING, GEORGIA 31905
Autovon: 784–0110; Commercial: (404) 545–5216

Fort Benning was established in 1918. The post occupies 181,535 acres with the main gate located nine miles south of Columbus, Georgia, off U.S. 27.

Major Activities. U.S. Army Infantry Center and School; U.S. Army Infantry Training Center; 197th Infantry Brigade; 75th Infantry Regiment (Rangers); 36th

Engineer Group; Infantry Board; U.S. Army School of the Americas; 34th Medical Battalion; Martin Army Hospital.

Quarters. There are about 900 sets of quarters for married officers, plus 200 rental units available to all ranks. BOQs are available for 1,140 visiting officers and 48 permanent party officers, and 34 all-ranks guest house units are available. Rental units are available in Columbus, with many types of apartments and houses available.

FORT BLISS, TEXAS 79916
Autovon: 978–0831; Commercial: (915) 568–2121

Fort Bliss was established in 1854. It occupies 125,000 acres adjacent to the city of El Paso, with the main gate located off I-10 or Highway 54, about seven miles from downtown El Paso, Texas.

Major Activities. U.S. Army Air Defense Artillery Center and School; Air Defense Artillery Board; 11th Air Defense Artillery Group; 3rd Armored Cavalry Regiment; U.S. Army Sergeants Major Academy; German Air Force Training Command USA; German Air Force Defense School; NATO Nike Training Center. (See also William Beaumont Army Medical Center.)

Quarters. There are 513 sets of family quarters provided for officers. Ample BOQs are normally available, many with kitchens. Guest house facilities are available. Off-post housing is plentiful, both for purchase and rental.

FORT BRAGG, NORTH CAROLINA 28307
Autovon: 236–0311; Commercial: (919) 396–0011

Fort Bragg was established in 1918. The main gate is located ten miles northwest of Fayetteville, North Carolina, adjacent to Highway 24. The post is 148,609 acres in size, split by the All-American Freeway.

Major Activities. Headquarters, XVIII Airborne Corps; 82nd Airborne Division; 1st Special Operations Command; John F. Kennedy Special Warfare Center and School; 1st Corps Support Command; 16th MP Brigade; 18th Field Artillery Brigade; 20th Engineer Brigade; 35th Signal Brigade; Corps Finance Group; Dragon Brigade; 5th Special Forces Group (Airborne); 7th Special Forces Group (Airborne); 4th Psychological Operations Group; 525th Military Intelligence Group; Hq, First ROTC Region; Readiness Group–Bragg; U.S. Army Airborne and Special Operations Test Board; Womack Army Hospital.

Quarters. There are 990 sets of family quarters available for officers; about 25 percent of the married officers live on post. BOQs and guest house facilities are available. Off-post housing is available at moderate cost.

CAMERON STATION, VIRGINIA 22304
Autovon: 284–6506; Commercial: (202) 274–6506

Cameron Station occupies 168 acres in the city of Alexandria, Virginia, just off I-95 at the Van Dorn Street exit. The station opened in 1942.

Major Activities. Headquarters, Defense Logistics Agency; Joint Personal Property Shipping Office; Army Institute of Heraldry. Provides commissary services for military personnel in the Washington area.

Quarters. None. Off-post housing is available, but expensive.

FORT CAMPBELL, KENTUCKY 42223
Autovon: 635–1110; Commercial: (502) 798–2151

Fort Campbell opened in 1942. The post is 105,000 acres in size, split by the Kentucky-Tennessee state boundary. The main gate is located off Highway 41A, sixteen miles south of Hopkinsville, Kentucky, and five miles north of Clarksville, Tennessee.

Major Activities. 101st Airborne Division (Air Assault); Eagle Support Brigade; 5th Special Forces Group (Airborne) (being transferred from Fort Bragg); Air Assault School; Campbell Army Airfield.

Quarters. There are 755 sets of family quarters available for officers. Several housing projects near Clarksville and Hopkinsville are available at reasonable rentals. Transient quarters are available on post. The post also has a modern motel-type guest house.

CARLISLE BARRACKS, PENNSYLVANIA 17013
Autovon: 242–4141; Commercial: (717) 245–3131

Carlisle Barracks was established in 1757. The post is 400 acres in size adjacent to the eastern edge of the city of Carlisle, on U.S. Highway 11, eighteen miles west of Harrisburg, Pennsylvania.

Major Activities. U.S. Army War College; Strategic Studies Institute; U.S. Army Garrison; U.S. Army Information Systems Command, Operations Group; Omar N. Bradley Museum; Military History Institute; Dunham Army Health Clinic.

Quarters. There are 243 sets of quarters available for married officers, sufficient to house about 80 percent of the staff, faculty, and students. BOQs are available. There is a guest house for limited stays. Civilian housing in the immediate area of Carlisle Barracks is scarce and expensive, although there are many convenient motels and hotels.

FORT CARSON, COLORADO 80913
Autovon: 691–5811; Commercial: (303) 579–5811

Fort Carson, established in 1945, is 137,000 acres in size. The main gate is located four miles south of the city limits of Colorado Springs, Colorado, off Colorado 115 and I-25.

Major Activity. 4th Infantry Division (Mech.).

Quarters. There are 228 sets of family quarters available for officers. BOQs and guest house facilities are provided. Off-post housing is available in Colorado Springs and other nearby communities.

FORT CHAFFEE, ARKANSAS 72905
Autovon: 962–2111; Commercial: (501) 484–2141

Fort Chaffee was established in 1941. The post is a 71,000-acre installation located eight miles southeast of Ft. Smith and about 111 miles northwest of Little Rock, Arkansas.

Major Activity. Support of active Army and Reserve component training.

Quarters. There are no family quarters. BOQs are available.

COLD REGIONS RESEARCH LABORATORY, NEW HAMPSHIRE 03755
Autovon: 684–4100; Commercial: (603) 646–4100

The Cold Regions Research Laboratory is located on a 20-acre site in Hanover, New Hampshire. It opened in 1961.

Major Activity. The laboratory is a field operating agency of the Corps of Engineers. It conducts cold weather research and testing.

Quarters. None.

CORPUS CHRISTI ARMY DEPOT, TEXAS 78419
Autovon: 861–3626; Commercial: (512) 888–3626

The Corpus Christi Army Depot opened in 1961. It occupies 190 acres leased from the Corpus Christi Naval Air Station and is located twelve miles southeast of the city of Corpus Christi, Texas.

Major Activity: Performs overhaul, repair, modification, retrofit, and modernization of Army aircraft.

Quarters. Available at the Naval Air Station.

FORT DETRICK, MARYLAND 21701
Autovon: 343–1110; Commercial: (301) 663–8000

Fort Detrick, established in 1943, occupies 1,100 acres just off U.S. 15 in Frederick, Maryland. It is approximately fifty miles from both Baltimore and Washington, D.C.

Major Activities. The garrison provides services and support for twenty-one tenant activities, representing the Departments of Defense, Justice, Treasury, Agriculture, and Health and Human Services. The Hq, U.S. Army Medical Research and Development Command is located here, along with two of the Command's major laboratories and two separate support agencies. The Defense Medical Standardization Board staff offices are here, along with the managers for the Army and Air Force medical logistics worldwide. Also at Fort Detrick are the USAISC East Coast Telecommunications Center, the National Cancer Institute's Frederick Cancer Research Facility, and the Department of Agriculture's Frederick location, which performs research on plant disease and weed control.

Quarters. There are thirty-two sets of quarters available for officers' families. BOQs are limited. Adequate rental apartments are available in the surrounding community, along with adequate hotels and motels.

DETROIT ARSENAL, MICHIGAN 48397
Autovon: 786–5000; Commercial: (313) 574–5000

Established in 1940, the Detroit Arsenal occupies 341 acres at Warren, Michigan, three miles north of Detroit.

Major Activity. Headquarters, Tank-Automotive Command.

Quarters. Quarters are available at Selfridge ANG Base.

FORT DEVENS, MASSACHUSETTS 01433
Autovon: 256–3911; Commercial: (617) 796–3911

Fort Devens was established in 1917. It is located on 9,338 acres adjacent to the town of Ayer, Massachusetts, off State Route 2, about thirty-five miles northwest of Boston and twelve miles south of the New Hampshire border. A 2,300-acre training annex is located in nearby Sudbury.

Major Activities. First U.S. Army (Forward); U.S. Army Intelligence School, Devens; 10th Special Forces Group (Airborne); 39th Engineer Battalion (Combat); 36th Medical Battalion; Combat Support Battalion (PROV); 46th Combat Support Hospital; 187th Infantry Brigade (USAR); Readiness Group, Devens; Cutler Army Community Hospital.

Quarters. There are 323 sets of family quarters available for married officers. BOQs are provided for 38 single officers. Guest housing is available on a limited basis. Off-post rentals in surrounding communities are scarce and the prices are moderate to high.

FORT DIX, NEW JERSEY 08640
Autovon: 944–1110; Commercial: (609) 562–1011

Fort Dix was established in 1917. It is a 31,000-acre post located off Exit 7, New Jersey Turnpike, near Wrightstown, New Jersey, on State Highway 68, seventeen miles south of Trenton. It is colocated with McGuire Air Force Base.

Major Activities. U.S. Army Training Center; Walson Army Community Hospital.

Quarters. Approximately 430 sets of family quarters are available for married officers. BOQs and a modern guest house are available.

FORT DOUGLAS, UTAH 84113
Autovon: 924–4097; Commercial: (801) 524–4097

Established in 1862, Fort Douglas occupies 119 acres in Salt Lake City. It is a subinstallation of Fort Carson.

Major Activities. Hq Fort Douglas; Hq 96th Army Reserve Command; US Army Readiness Group; US Army Recruiting Battalion Salt Lake; US Navy Recruiting Processing Station; US Air Force Recruiting Squadron; Military Entrance Processing Station; 62nd Ordnance Detachment; 6th Army Reserve Pay Center.

Quarters. There are sixty-one sets of family quarters available to assigned personnel. BOQs, guest housing, or transient quarters are not available.

FORT DRUM, NEW YORK 13602-5000
Autovon: 341-6895; Commercial: (315) 772-6900

Fort Drum was established in 1908. It consists of 107,000 acres and is located nine miles west of Watertown, New York, off I-81 at Exit 48. It is approximately seventy miles north of Syracuse and twenty-five miles south of the Canadian border.

Major Activities. Fort Drum is building an entirely new post to accommodate the 10th Mountain Division (Light Infantry), which should be fully in place by 1990. The post continues its role as a major training center in the northeastern United States; cold weather training site for active Army, Marines, and Canadian forces; supports Reserve and National Guard forces; New York and New Jersey Army National Guard equipment concentration sites; Wheeler-Sack Army Airfield.

Quarters. There currently are 323 sets of family quarters on post, with an additional 1,500 sets under construction with completion scheduled for 1989. In addition, 1,400 sets of 801 housing (private contractor built–Army leased) are under construction in eight communities surrounding Fort Drum, slated for completion in 1988. Transient family quarters and BOQs are in short supply. Off-post rentals are scarce due to the division buildup and the large numbers of construction workers in the area.

DUGWAY PROVING GROUND, UTAH 84022
Autovon: 789–1110; Commercial: (801) 522–2151

Dugway Proving Ground was established in 1942. It occupies 802,000 acres in west-central Utah, about 75 miles southwest of Salt Lake City, Utah. It may be reached via I-80 and unnumbered County Road, or via State Routes 36 and 199 from Tooele, Utah.

Major Activities. Performs test and evaluation of chemical and biological material. HHC, Dugway Proving Ground; 65th MP Platoon; 6501 Range Squadron, USAF; Technical Escort Detachment; Management Evaluation Team; 6515 Test Squadron, USAF; Army Information Systems Command Detachment.

Quarters. There are quarters for all assigned officers with families with no waiting period. Limited transient quarters are available for temporary occupancy. BOQs are provided for single officers.

FORT EUSTIS, VIRGINIA 23604-5000
Autovon: 927–1110; Commercial: (804) 878–5251

Fort Eustis was established in 1918. This 8,200-acre post is located in southern Virginia between Williamsburg and Newport News, Virginia. It may be reached via State Route 60 and is just off I-64.

Major Activities. U.S. Army Transportation Center and School; Aviation Logistics School; TRADOC Training Support Center; 8th Transportation Brigade; Applied Technology Laboratory; 7th Transportation Group.

Quarters. Approximately 360 sets of family quarters are available for officers. Off-post housing is available at reasonable rates. Transient family quarters and BOQs are provided.

FITZSIMONS ARMY MEDICAL CENTER, COLORADO 80045-5000
Autovon: 943–1101; Commercial: (303) 361–8241

Established in 1918, Fitzsimons Army Medical Center is located on 570 acres at Aurora, Colorado, off East Colfax Avenue, about nine miles east of Denver.

Major Activities. Fitzsimons Army Medical Center is a 500-bed teaching hospital; Office for Civilian Health and Medical Program for Uniformed Services; U.S. Army Medical Equipment and Optical School; U.S. Army Dental Activity; U.S. Army Optical Fabrication Laboratory; Edgar L. McWethy, Jr., USAR Center.

Quarters. Approximately 288 sets of family quarters are available, which is insufficient to accommodate assigned officers. Off-post housing is available, but expensive. A guest house of limited capacity is available.

FORT GILLEM, GEORGIA 30050
Autovon: 797–1001; Commercial: (404) 363–5000

Fort Gillem opened in 1941. It is a subinstallation of Fort McPherson, occupying 1,500 acres at Forest Park, southeast of Atlanta, Georgia.

Major Activities. Headquarters, Second U.S. Army; Forces Command headquarters activities; Hq 2nd Recruiting Brigade; 3rd Region CID Command; Hq, 818th Hospital Center (USAR).

Quarters. Ten sets of family quarters are available, along with eight sets of temporary quarters. Off-post housing for rent or purchase is adequate.

FORT GORDON, GEORGIA 30905-5283
Autovon: 780-1110; Commercial: (404) 791–0110

Established in 1941, Fort Gordon occupies 56,000 acres about nine miles southwest of Augusta, Georgia, between U.S. Highways 1 and 78.

Major Activities. U.S. Army Signal Center and School; Dwight David Eisenhower Army Medical Center.

Quarters. Approximately 160 sets of family quarters are available for officers. Off-post housing is available in the moderate to high price range. BOQs and a modern guest house are available.

FORT GREELY, ALASKA (No ZIP)
APO SEATTLE, WASHINGTON 98733-5000
Autovon: 317–872–1113; Commercial: (907) 872–1113

Fort Greely was established in 1942. The post is located about 106 miles southeast of Fairbanks, Alaska, and is 677,000 acres in size. (See also chapter 11, *Foreign Service.*)

Major Activities. Special Troops, Fort Greely; Army Northern Warfare Training Center; Army Cold Regions Test Center.

Quarters. There are fifty-six sets of quarters available for families of married officers. BOQs are available. Off-post housing is extremely limited and expensive.

FORT HAMILTON, NEW YORK 11252-5185
Autovon: 232–1110; Commercial: (718) 630–4101

Fort Hamilton, established in 1825, occupies 170 acres in the Bay Ridge section of Brooklyn, New York, near the Verrazano-Narrows Bridge. Reach it from Exit 13, New Jersey Turnpike, via the Staten Island Expressway (I-278) and the Verrazano Bridge. Take the exit for 92nd St.–Bay Ridge, make two consecutive left turns, and follow the Fort Hamilton Parkway to the main gate.

Major Activities. Headquarters, New York Area Command & Fort Hamilton, which includes also the subposts of Fort Totten, Fort Wadsworth, and the Bellemore Direct/General Support Maintenance Activity on Long Island. Provides administrative and logistical support for Army and Defense activities in the New York metropolitan area. Hq, 8th Medical Brigade (USAR).

Quarters. Approximately 900 units of family housing are available within the command. BOQs and a guest house are available.

HARRY DIAMOND LABORATORIES, MARYLAND 20783-1197
Autovon: 290–2515; Commercial: (202) 394–2515

Established in 1952, the Harry Diamond Laboratories occupy a total of 570 acres (including a site at Woodbridge, Virginia) at Adelphi, Maryland, just outside the District of Columbia.

Major Activity. Headquarters for the U.S. Army Laboratory Command.

Quarters. None. Off-post housing is available, but expensive.

FORT HOOD, TEXAS 76544-5000
Autovon: 737–2131; Commercial: (817) 287–2131

Fort Hood was established in 1942. It occupies 217,000 acres about sixty miles north of Austin and fifty miles south of Waco, with the main gate adjacent to Kileen. U.S. highway 190 provides four-lane controlled access to the post from I-35, the main north-south route through central Texas.

Major Activities. Fort Hood is the largest armored post in the free world. Located here are: Hq, III Corps; 1st Cavalry Division; 2nd Armored Division; 6th Cavalry Brigade (Air Combat); 3rd Signal Brigade; 89th Military Police Brigade; 504th Military Intelligence Group; TRADOC Combined Arms Testing Activity.

Quarters. There are approximately 895 sets of family quarters available for officers. Off-post rental housing is somewhat expensive, but readily available. There are 172 BOQs, 110 VOQs and 9 DVQs available. There are also a 75-room guest house and 8 cottages.

FORT HUACHUCA, ARIZONA 85613-6000
Autovon: 879–0110; Commercial: (602) 538–7111

Fort Huachuca (Wah-CHOO-Kah) is in Cochise County, seventy miles southwest of Tucson, Arizona, on State Highway 90, twenty-eight miles south of I-10, near the Benson exit. The main gate is adjacent to the city of Sierra Vista. The post was established in 1877 and comprises 73,000 acres.

Major Activities. U.S. Army Intelligence Center and School; Hq, Army Information Systems Command; U.S. Army Electronic Proving Ground; Joint Test Element, Joint Tactical Command, Control and Communications Agency; Libby Army Airfield; Raymond W. Bliss Army Community Hospital.

Quarters. There are 407 permanent-type housing units available for officers' families and 128 units of housing are available for permanent party single officers. Off-post housing is available in the communities of Sierra Vista and Huachuca City.

HUNTER ARMY AIRFIELD, GEORGIA 31409
Autovon: 870–1110; Commercial: (912) 767–1110

Hunter Army Airfield is adjacent to Savannah, Georgia. It is a subinstallation of Fort Stewart, which is forty miles away.

Major Activities. 1st Battalion (Ranger), 75th Infantry; Victory Brigade; 24th Aviation Brigade. Support of Ranger training and Reserve Component summer training.

Quarters. More than sixty sets of family quarters for officers are available on post. Guest house facilities and BOQs are provided. Rental housing is available in Savannah.

FORT HUNTER LIGGETT, CALIFORNIA 93928
Autovon: 949–2291; Commercial: (408) 385–5911

Fort Hunter Liggett was established in 1941. It is a subinstallation of Fort Ord, 165,000 acres in size, located about twenty-three miles south of King City, California, at Jolon.

Major Activities. Army Garrison; Combat Developments and Experimentation Activity.

Quarters. There is one adequate set of officer family quarters. Eight substandard houses are available for officers and senior NCOs. There are three BOQs, fifty-six VOQs, and one DVQ available. There also are sixty-eight house trailer rentals available through a contractor. There is an eight-unit guest house. Rental housing is scarce in the local area.

FORT INDIANTOWN GAP, PENNSYLVANIA 17003-5011
Autovon: 235–1110; Commercial: (717) 865–5444

Fort Indiantown Gap opened in 1940 and is 18,000 acres in size. It is located about ten miles northwest of Lebanon, Pennsylvania.

Major Activity. Support of active Army and Reserve Component training.

Quarters. Six sets of family quarters are available for officers. There is no guest house, but transient quarters are available for families assigned to PCS to the station.

FORT IRWIN, CALIFORNIA 93941
Autovon: 470–0111; Commercial: (619) 386–1111

Fort Irwin, established in 1940, is a 642,000-acre post located about thirty-seven miles northeast of Barstow, halfway between Las Vegas, Nevada, and Los Angeles, California.

Major Activity. U.S. Army National Training Center; also NASA's Goldstone Deep Space Tracking System.

Quarters. There are 174 sets of family quarters for officers, including 47 new units, and 109 BOQs are available. Nine 3-bedroom mobile homes are available for newly assigned or transient families. Off-post housing is available in Barstow.

FORT JACKSON, SOUTH CAROLINA 29207-5240
Autovon: 734–1110; Commercial: (803) 751–7511

Fort Jackson was established in 1917. It is a 52,000-acre post located six miles from downtown Columbia, South Carolina, between I-20, U.S. 1, and U.S. 76.

Major Activities. U.S. Army Training Center; U.S. Army Reception Battllion; U.S. Army Drill Sergeant School; TRADOC Pre-Command Course; 120th Army Reserve Command; Moncrief Army Community Hospital.

Quarters. There are approximately 160 sets of adequate family quarters available for officers. BOQs and guest house facilities are available. Numerous apartment complexes located within a three-mile radius of the installation offer a wide variety of styles and accommodations at varying rates.

JEFFERSON PROVING GROUND, INDIANA 47250-5100
Autovon: 480–1110; Commercial: (812) 273–7211

Established in 1941, Jefferson Proving Ground occupies 55,000 acres six miles north of Madison, Indiana, and about fifty miles northeast of Louisville, Kentucky.

Major Activity. Performs testing of ammunition and components.

Quarters. A total of thirteen sets of family quarters are available for assignment to officers or NCOs. There are no BOQs. No guest house is available.

FORT KNOX, KENTUCKY 40121-5000
Autovon: 464–0111; Commercial: (502) 624–1181

Fort Knox was established in 1918. It is a 110,000-acre post located about thirty-five miles south of Louisville, Kentucky.

Major Activities. U.S. Army Armor Center and School; U.S. Army Training Center; 194th Armored Brigade; Hq, Second ROTC Region; U.S. Armor and Engineer Board; Ireland Army Hospital. The U.S. Bullion Depository is located at Fort Knox.

Quarters. Approximately 945 family housing units are available for assignment to married officers. Guest house facilities and BOQs are provided. Nearby off-post housing is limited.

FORT LEAVENWORTH, KANSAS 66027-5000
Autovon: 552–1101; Commercial: (913) 684–4021

Established in 1827, Fort Leavenworth occupies 5,634 acres just north of the city of Leavenworth, Kansas, about thirty-five miles northwest of Kansas City, Missouri.

Major Activities. U.S. Army Combined Arms Center; Command and General Staff College; Combined Arms Combat Developments Activity; Combined Arms Training Activity; TRADOC Analysis Command (TRAC); United States Disciplinary Barracks; 35th Infantry Division (MECH) (NG).

Quarters. There are 1,590 sets of family quarters available for assignment to PCS personnel. The city of Leavenworth is directly adjacent to the post, with the city of Lansing just to the south of Leavenworth. Most military personnel not occupying post quarters live in these two cities. There are sixteen guest house units. BOQs are extremely limited.

FORT LEE, VIRGINIA 23801-5200
Autovon: 687–0111; Commercial: (804) 734–1011

Fort Lee, which opened in 1941, is a 5,575-acre post located three miles east of Petersburg, Virginia, off State Highway 36.

Major Activities. U.S. Army Quartermaster Center/School; AMC Logistics Management Center; TRADOC Logistics Center; Troop Support Agency.

Quarters. There are 357 sets of quarters available for officers' families. Guest house facilities and BOQ spaces are available. Off-post housing is available.

FORT LEONARD WOOD, MISSOURI 65473
Autovon: 581–0110; Commercial: (314) 368–0131

Fort Leonard Wood was established in 1941. This 68,000-acre post is located near Waynesville, Missouri, some 29 miles southwest of Rolla and 135 miles southwest of St. Louis off I-44.

Major Activity. U.S. Army Training Center (Engineer).

Quarters. There are more than 600 family housing units for officers on post, which generally are adequate to accommodate assigned married officers. Excellent BOQs are available, and guest house facilities are provided.

LETTERKENNY ARMY DEPOT, PENNSYLVANIA 17201-4150
Autovon: 570–1110; Commercial: (717) 267–8111

Established in 1941, Letterkenny Army Depot occupies a site of 19,500 acres two miles north of Chambersburg and forty miles south of Harrisburg, Pennsylvania.

Major Activity. Storage, issue, rebuilding, testing, overhauling, and demilitarization of general supplies.

Quarters. There are fifteen units of family housing for officers. A three-unit guest house is available. There are no BOQs.

FORT LEWIS, WASHINGTON 98433-5000
Autovon: 357–1110; Commercial: (206) 967–5151

Fort Lewis was established in 1917. The post is 86,000 acres in size and is located next to Puget Sound some fifty miles south of Seattle, about midway between Olympia and Tacoma, Washington, off I-5.

Major Activities. Hq, I Corps; 9th Infantry Division (Motorized); 1st Special Forces Group (Airborne); Hq, Fourth ROTC Region. Yakima Firing Center is a subpost. Madigan Army Medical Center and McChord Air Force Base are nearby.

Quarters. There are about 755 sets of family quarters for officers at Fort Lewis. BOQs are provided for single officers. Temporary lodging is available at the Fort Lewis Lodge. Excellent motel and hotel accommodations are available within a few miles. Off-post housing is available within a reasonable distance from the post.

LEXINGTON-BLUEGRASS ARMY DEPOT, KENTUCKY 40511-5007
Autovon: 745–1110
Commercial: (606) 293–3011 (Lexington)
(606) 623–7600 (Richmond)

The Lexington-Bluegrass Army Depot opened in 1942. It is located on a total of 15,280 acres (780 at Lexington and 14,500 at Richmond). The headquarters (Lexington) is located thirteen miles east of Lexington, Kentucky. The Bluegrass facility is about forty miles distant, near Richmond, Kentucky.

Major Activity. Performs general supply and maintenance functions on communications security and electronics equipment and ammunition storage.

Quarters. There are fifteen sets of family quarters at Lexington, two of which are for designated officers. The remainder are available to either officers or enlisted personnel. Two sets of family quarters at Richmond (Bluegrass) are reserved for designated officers. A one-unit guest house is located at Lexington. There are no BOQs at either location.

MADIGAN ARMY MEDICAL CENTER, WASHINGTON 98433
Autovon: 357–6432; Commercial: (206) 967–6432

Madigan Army Medical Center is located near Fort Lewis, some fifty miles south of Seattle, about midway between Olympia and Tacoma, Washington, off I-5.

Major Activity. In- and out-patient medical services.

Quarters. There are no family quarters. Married officers are eligible for housing at nearby Fort Lewis. A twenty-four-unit BOQ is available and a guest house is provided.

FORT MCCLELLAN, ALABAMA 36205-5000
Autovon: 865–1110; Commercial: (205) 238–4611

Fort McClellan was established in 1917. The post comprises 45,000 acres and is located three miles north of Anniston, Alabama, off State Highway 21, near U.S. Highways 78 and 431. Anniston is centrally located between Birmingham, Alabama, and Atlanta, Georgia, off I-20.

Major Activities. U.S. Army Military Police School; U.S. Army Chemical School; U.S. Army Training Center; U.S. Army NCO Academy; Training Brigade; DOD Polygraph Institute; Noble Army Hospital.

Quarters. There are 113 sets of family housing units available for married officers. BOQs and guest house facilities are provided. Adequate off-post rental housing is available.

FORT MCCOY, WISCONSIN 54656-5000
Autovon: 280–1110; Commercial: (608) 388–2222

Fort McCoy was established in 1909. It occupies 60,000 acres in west-central Wisconsin, midway between the cities of Sparta and Tomah, off State Highway 21.

Major Activities. Army Reserve Readiness Training Center; 4th U.S. Army Readiness Training Center and Readiness Group; Light Leaders Academy; Regional Maintenance Center; Defense Reutilization and Marketing Office; 88th EOD; Equipment Concentration Site. Fort McCoy is the Army's largest mobilization station and training center for Reserve Component units.

Quarters. There are 16 sets of family quarters with an additional 110 sets scheduled for completion by 1989. Off-post housing is available nearby at low to average rates. Five completely furnished mobile homes are available as temporary housing for new arrivals. Limited guest quarters are available.

FORT MCNAIR, WASHINGTON, D.C. 20319
Autovon: 335–0866; Commercial: (202) 475–0866

Fort McNair was established in 1791. It occupies eighty-nine acres along the Potomac River in southwest Washington, D.C., at 4th and P Streets, SW.

Major Activities. Headquarters, Military District of Washington (MDW); National Defense University, including the National War College and the Industrial College of the Armed Forces; Inter-American Defense College; Company A, 1st Battalion (Reinf), 3rd Infantry (The Old Guard).

Quarters. The limited number of on-post quarters are reserved for key officers. Off-post housing is available.

FORT MCPHERSON, GEORGIA 30330
Autovon: 572–1110; Commercial: (404) 752–3133

Fort McPherson was established in 1885. Fort Gillem in Forest Park, Georgia, and Fort Buchanan, Puerto Rico, are subposts. Fort McPherson's 500 acres are located in southwest Atlanta, Georgia, on U.S. Highway 29 and State Highway 166.

Major Activities. Headquarters, Forces Command; Headquarters, Third U.S. Army.

Quarters. There are sixty-three sets of family quarters available for married officers. Most married officers live off-post. Limited BOQ space is available. Temporary quarters are available on a limited basis.

FORT MEADE, MARYLAND 20755-5025
Autovon: 923–1110; Commercial: (301) 677–6261

Fort Meade was established in 1917. Post size is 13,500 acres. The post is centered in the triangle formed by Baltimore, Maryland, Washington, D.C., and Annapolis, Maryland, about twenty miles from each city. The main gate is about two miles south of the Baltimore-Washington Parkway, with the exit to the post at Route 175 at Jessup or Route 198 at Laurel.

Major Activities. Headquarters, First U.S. Army; National Security Agency; 76th Engineer Battalion; 85th Medical Battalion; Headquarters, 97th Army Reserve Command.

Quarters. Approximately 620 units of family housing are available for married officers. BOQs and guest house facilities are provided.

MILITARY OCEAN TERMINAL, BAYONNE, NEW JERSEY 07002
Autovon: 247–5111; Commercial: (201) 823–5111

The Eastern Area, Military Traffic Management Command has its headquarters at the Military Ocean Terminal, Bayonne, New Jersey. Established in 1964, the terminal occupies 670 acres along New York harbor.

Major Activities. The EAMTMC has jurisdiction over terminal units and activities in the twenty-eight-state eastern and midwestern portion of the United States and in Panama and the Azores overseas. The terminal processes for shipment Department of Defense sponsored cargo and equipment primarily with ocean-going vessels.

Quarters. Approximately 125 units of family housing and a few BOQ facilities are available. Off-post housing is available, but rather expensive.

MILITARY OCEAN TERMINAL, SUNNY POINT
SOUTHPORT, NORTH CAROLINA 28461-5000
Autovon: 488-8011; Commercial: (919)457-8000

Established in 1955, the terminal is sited on 16,000 acres at Southport, North Carolina.

Major Activity. Receives and trans-ships ammunition, explosives, and other hazardous cargo.

Quarters. Five sets of family quarters are available.

FORT MONMOUTH, NEW JERSEY 07703
Autovon: 992–1110; Commercial: (201) 532–9000

Fort Monmouth was established in 1917. It occupies 630 acres about fifty miles south of New York City. It is located between Red Bank and Eatontown, New Jersey, on State Highway 35. When traveling north on the New Jersey Turnpike, exit at Interchange 8, take Route 33 to Freehold and 537 to Eatontown; traveling south, exit at 11 and follow Route 35 to the post. From the Garden State Parkway, exit at 105 and follow the signs.

Major Activities. U.S. Army Chaplain Center and School; Headquarters, Communications-Electronics Command; USAIS Management Activity; Army Satellite Communications Agency; Joint Tactical Command, Control and Communications Agency; Army Avionics R&D Activity; 513th Military Intelligence Group; U.S. Military Academy Preparatory School; Patterson Army Hospital.

Quarters. There are approximately 350 sets of quarters available for officers' families. BOQs and guest house facilities are provided. Off-post housing is available in nearby communities, but may be difficult to obtain during the summer vacation period.

FORT MONROE, VIRGINIA 23651-6000
Autovon: 680–1110; Commercial: (804) 727–2111

Fort Monroe was established in 1823. It occupies 1,000 acres adjacent to Hampton, Virginia, on the waters of Hampton Roads, Chesapeake Bay, and Mill Creek. It is reached via I-64 and U.S. Highways 60 and 258.

Major Activity. Headquarters, U.S. Army Training and Doctrine Command (TRADOC).

Quarters. Approximately 110 units of family quarters are available on post. Off-post housing, while available, may be difficult to obtain during the summer season and is quite expensive. BOQs are available. Guest house facilities are limited, but the Hotel Chamberlain, on the post, offers special rates for personnel under official orders.

FORT MYER, VIRGINIA 22211-5050
Autovon: 226–3249; Commercial: (202) 696–3249

Fort Myer was established in 1862. It occupies 250 acres in Arlington, Virginia, adjacent to Arlington National Cemetery. It is reached via I-395 (the Shirley Highway), and via U.S. 50, Arlington Boulevard, just across the Memorial Bridge from Washington, D.C.

Major Activities. First Battalion, 3rd Infantry (The Old Guard); The U.S. Army Band, "Pershing's Own"; U.S. Army Garrison.

Quarters. On-post family housing is limited in quantity and is largely reserved for assignment to senior officers on the Department of the Army staff. BOQs are limited. Limited guest facilities are available. Off-post housing is abundant, but expensive.

NATICK RESEARCH, DEVELOPMENT AND ENGINEERING CENTER, MASSACHUSETTS 01760
Autovon: 256–4000; Commercial: (617) 651–4000

Established in 1953, the Center is located on seventy-eight acres at Natick, twenty miles west of Boston, Massachusetts.

Major Activity. Responsible for R&D, test and evaluation of textiles, clothing, body armor, food, and personal equipment.

Quarters. There are forty sets of quarters for officers' families. Limited guest house facilities are available. There are no BOQs.

NEW CUMBERLAND ARMY DEPOT, PENNSYLVANIA 17070
Autovon: 977–1110; Commercial: (717) 770–6011

The New Cumberland Army Depot was established in 1918. It is situated on 850 acres about five miles south of Harrisburg, Pennsylvania, off I-83 and Route 114.

Major Activity. Performs general supply mission, including receipt, storage, and distribution of general supplies for CONUS and OCONUS (primarily Europe) destinations; operates Consolidation and Containerization Point, Unit Materiel Fielding Point, and European Redistribution Facilities.

Quarters. There are fifty units of family housing available for officers. About twenty-five BOQs are provided. There is no guest house.

OAKLAND ARMY BASE, CALIFORNIA 94626
Autovon: 859–0111; Commercial: (415) 466–9111

Oakland Army Base was established in 1941. It is located on 560 acres in West Oakland, California, adjacent to the San Francisco Bay Bridge.

Major Activity. The Western Area, Military Traffic Management Command has its headquarters at Oakland Army Base. The Command is responsible for movement of military cargo to oversea destinations.

Quarters. There are about thirty sets of quarters for families of married officers. Limited space is available for visitors. Off-post government leased housing is available and off-post housing in general is plentiful.

FORT ORD, CALIFORNIA 93941
Autovon: 929–1110; Commercial: (408) 242–2211

Established in 1917, Fort Ord is located on 28,000 acres on Monterey Bay, off State Highway 1, about seven miles north of the city of Monterey, California.

Major Activities. Headquarters, 7th Infantry Division (Light); Combat Developments Experimentation Center; Organizational Effectiveness Training Center; Silas B. Hayes Army Community Hospital. Fort Hunter Liggett and the Presidio of Monterey are subposts.

Quarters. There are approximately 730 sets of family quarters for married officers. A limited number of guest units is available for officers and families in transit. Off-post housing is both scarce and expensive.

PICATINNY ARSENAL, NEW JERSEY 07806-5000
Autovon: 880–1110; Commercial: (201) 724–4021

Picatinny Arsenal was established in 1879. It is sited on 6,400 acres at Dover, New Jersey, about forty miles west of New York City.

Major Activity. Headquarters, Army Armament Research, Development and Engineering Center.

Quarters. About seventy sets of family quarters are available for assignment to married officers. There are twenty BOQs provided. There is no guest house available.

FORT PICKETT, VIRGINIA 23824
Autovon: 687–0111; Commercial: (804) 292–7231

Established in 1941, Fort Pickett occupies 45,000 acres. It is a subinstallation of Fort Bragg. It is located off State Highway 40 and U.S. 460, about two miles east of Blackstone, Virginia, and approximately forty miles southwest of Petersburg, Virginia.

Major Activity. Support of active Army and Reserve component training. No units permanently stationed on post.

Quarters. On-post and off-post family housing is extremely limited, both in quantity and quality. A post trailer park is available. Twelve guest cottages are available. Pegram Camp Site has water, sewer, and electric hook-ups.

PINE BLUFF ARSENAL, ARKANSAS 71602-4500
Autovon: 966–3000; Commercial: (501) 543–3000

Established in 1941, Pine Bluff Arsenal is sited on 15,000 acres about eight miles northwest of the city of Pine Bluff, Arkansas.

Major Activity. Manufacture, storage, and demilitarization of chemical munitions.

Quarters. About twenty-three sets of family housing are available for officers. BOQs and VOQs are available. There is no guest house.

FORT POLK, LOUISIANA 71549-5000
Autovon: 863–1110; Commercial: (318) 535–2911

Fort Polk was established in 1941. The post is 198,000 acres in size, located in western central Louisiana some nine miles south of Leesville and about fifty miles west of Alexandria. It may be reached via U.S. 171, which connects with I-20 at Shreveport, about 120 miles to the north, and with I-10 at Lake Charles, about seventy miles to the south.

Major Activities. Headquarters, 5th Infantry Division (Mech); Bayne-Jones Army Community Hospital.

Quarters. There are approximately 300 units of family housing available for officers. About 400 trailer spaces also are available on the post. The post housing office handles assignments of an additional 600 family units that are privately owned and located in New Llano, about eight miles from the post. BOQS are available, most in newly constructed facilities.

PRESIDIO OF MONTEREY, CALIFORNIA 93940
Autovon: 929–1110; Commercial: (408) 242–2211

The Presidio of Monterey, established as an American fort in 1847, occupies 392 acres in the city of Monterey, California, on the site of the original Spanish fort established in 1770. It is a subinstallation of Fort Ord.

Major Activities. Defense Language Institute (Foreign Language Center); Army Research Institute.

Quarters. There are 45 pre–World War Two housing units available for assignment to officers, plus 100 BOQ units. Limited guest house facilities are provided. Off-post housing is expensive.

PRESIDIO OF SAN FRANCISCO, CALIFORNIA 94129
Autovon: 586–1110; Commercial: (415) 561–2211

The Presidio of San Francisco was established in 1850. It occupies 1,700 acres in San Francisco, California, at the foot of the Golden Gate Bridge. The main gate is at Lombard and Lyons Streets, two blocks west of U.S. 101, near the south approach to the bridge.

Major Activities. Headquarters, Sixth U.S. Army; Letterman Army Medical Center; Western Region Recruiting Command.

Quarters. There are 502 sets of family quarters for officers and 43 BOQ units. Temporary accommodations are limited. Off-post rentals are available, but expensive.

PUEBLO DEPOT ACTIVITY, COLORADO 81001
Autovon: 877–4101; Commercial: (303) 549–4111

Established in 1941, the Pueblo Depot Activity occupies 22,000 acres at Pueblo, Colorado. It is a subinstallation of the Tooele Army Depot.

Major Activity. Stores and ships general supplies, maintains missile systems and bridging equipment, and demilitarizes ammunition.

Quarters. There are twenty sets of family housing available for married personnel. No BOQs are provided, and no transient quarters are available.

RED RIVER ARMY DEPOT, TEXAS 75507-5000
Autovon: 829–4110; Commercial: (214) 838–2141

Established in 1941, the Red River Army Depot occupies 19,000 acres some eighteen miles west of Texarkana, about seventy miles north of Shreveport, Louisiana.

Major Activity. Receives, stores, and issues general supplies and ammunition. Maintains light combat vehicles.

Quarters. About fourteen units of family housing are available for active duty personnel. Limited BOQs are available. No VOQs or guest house is provided except for one set of VIP transient quarters.

REDSTONE ARSENAL, ALABAMA 35898-5020
Autovon: 746–2151; Commercial: (205) 876–2151

Redstone Arsenal was established in 1941. It is located on a 38,000-acre site adjacent to the southwest limits of the city of Huntsville, Alabama.

Major Activities. U.S. Army Missile and Munitions Center and School; Hq, Army Missile Command; 6th Infantry Division (Light); Division Support Command; 6th Signal Battalion; Aviation Brigade.

Quarters. There are approximately 390 units of family housing available for married officers. BOQs and a 22-unit guest house are available. Rental housing is available in the immediate area.

FORT RICHARDSON, ALASKA 99505-5320
Autovon: 317–864–0113; Commercial: (907) 864–0113

Fort Richardson was established in 1940. It occupies 62,500 acres adjacent to Anchorage, Alaska. (See also chapter 11, *Foreign Service.*)

Major Activities. 6th Infantry Division (Light); Division Support Command; 6th Signal Battalion; Aviation Brigade.

Quarters. There are 244 units of family housing available for married officers and 48 BOQ units. Temporary VOQ facilities are available. Off-post rental housing is available, but expensive.

FORT RILEY, KANSAS 66442-5000
Autovon: 856–1110; Commercial: (913) 239–3911

Fort Riley was established in 1853. This 100,000-acre post has its main gate located just four miles east of Junction City, Kansas, off State Highway 18. I-70 and U.S. 40 connect with Fort Riley.

Major Activities. 1st Infantry Division (Mech); Hq, Third ROTC Region; 937th Engineer Group (Combat); U.S. Army Correctional Activity; U.S. Army Criminal Investigation District, Sixth Region; Marshall Army Airfield; Irwin Army Community Hospital.

Quarters. More than 530 family housing units are provided for married officers. More than 130 BOQs are available. There is one guest house that provides temporary accommodations. Nearby communities of Junction City and Manhattan as well as smaller communities offer homes for purchase or rental.

FORT RITCHIE, MARYLAND 21719
Autovon: 988–1300; Commercial: (301) 733–7100

Fort Ritchie was established in 1926. The post is 630 acres in size, and is located near Cascade, Maryland, in the Catoctin Mountains, about thirty miles north of Frederick. It is just south of the Pennsylvania border. Nearby Interstate Highways 81, 70, and 270 provide easy access to Harrisburg, Pennsylvania, Baltimore, Maryland, and Washington, D.C., all of which are about seventy-five miles from the post.

Major Activities. Headquarters, 7th Signal Command CONUS Communications Support Activity; Hq, U.S. Army Information Systems Engineering Command (CONUS).

Quarters. There are thirty-eight sets of family quarters available for married officers. A recently remodeled guest house has nine units with kitchenettes. BOQs and VOQs are available.

ROCK ISLAND ARSENAL, ILLINOIS 61299-5000
Autovon: 793–1110; Commercial: (309) 794–6001

Established in 1862, the Arsenal occupies a 946-acre island in the Mississippi River between Moline, Illinois, and Davenport, Iowa.

Major Activity. Hq, US Army Armament, Munitions and Chemical Command.

Quarters. There are fifty-eight sets of family quarters available for assignment to officers. BOQ facilities are provided. A guest house is available.

ROCKY MOUNTAIN ARSENAL, COLORADO 80022
Autovon: 556–2143; Commercial: (303) 289–0143

Established in 1942, the 17,000-acre Arsenal is located at Commerce City, Colorado, about one mile northeast of Denver.

Major Activity. Provides support for AMC installations, Program Manager for Cleanup, and DOD and other agencies. Support approved contamination control, installation restoration programs, and arsenal cleanup.

Quarters. None. Transient quarters are sometimes available at the Fitzsimons Army Medical Center.

FORT RUCKER, ALABAMA 36362
Autovon: 558–3100; Commercial: (205) 255–6181

Fort Rucker was established in 1942. This 57,855-acre post is located northwest of Dothan, Alabama.

Major Activities. U.S. Army Aviation Center; Aviation School; Army Safety Center; Army Aeromedical Center; Army Aviation Development Test Activity; Army Research Institute Field Unit; Army Aeromedical Research Laboratory; USAISC Fort Rucker; Army Aviation Museum.

Quarters. There are approximately 651 sets of family quarters for officers. Student officers on PCS are eligible for these quarters. Motel-type BOQs will accommodate about 540 officers.

SACRAMENTO ARMY DEPOT, CALIFORNIA 95813-5012
Autovon: 839–1110; Commercial: (916) 388–2211

The Sacramento Army Depot was established in 1942. It occupies 485 acres in southeast Sacramento, about seven miles from the city center.

Major Activity. Primary facility for repair, rebuild, and fabrication of communications–electronics items. Major tenants include the Communications Systems Test Activity and the Television-Audio Support Activity.

Quarters. Two sets of family quarters are available. There are no BOQs and no transient facilities.

ST. LOUIS AREA SUPPORT CENTER, ILLINOIS 62040-1801
Autovon: 892–4212; Commercial: (618) 452–4212

The Support Center was established in 1971 upon inactivation of the Granite City Army Depot. It occupies 895 acres at Granite City, Illinois, across the Mississippi River from St. Louis, Missouri.

Major Activity. Provides administrative and logistical services to Army and other federal government elements in the St. Louis area.

Quarters. There are twenty-six units of housing available for officers' families. Limited BOQ spaces are provided. A seven-unit guest facility is available for families.

FORT SAM HOUSTON, TEXAS 78234-5000
Autovon: 471–1110; Commercial: (512) 221–1211

Fort Sam Houston was established in 1876. Its 2,900 acres lie within the city limits of San Antonio, Texas. However, another 27,000 acres are located at its sub-installation, Camp Bullis, twenty-four miles to the northwest.

Major Activities. Headquarters, Fifth U.S. Army; U.S. Army Health Services Command; Brooke Army Medical Center; Academy of Health Sciences; U.S. Army 5th Recruiting Brigade (SW).

Quarters. There are 390 family housing units available for officers, which is sufficient for only about 35 percent of the eligible officers. Off-post rental apartments and houses are adequate. BOQs are available. The Housing Office maintains listings and assists families in finding off-post housing. Adequate motel, hotel, and trailer accommodations are available near the post. Guest house facilities are available.

SAVANNA ARMY DEPOT ACTIVITY, ILLINOIS 61074-9636
Autovon: 585–1110; Commercial: (815) 273–8000

Established in 1917, the Depot occupies 13,000 acres at Savanna, Illinois, about 150 miles west of Chicago.

Major Activity. Munition storage. U.S. Army Defense Ammunition Center and School.

Quarters. There are thirteen units of family housing available for officers. BOQs and guest facilities are not provided.

SCHOFIELD BARRACKS, HAWAII 96857
Autovon: 455–4815; Commercial: (808) 622–1773

Schofield Barracks, established in 1908, is situated on 14,000 acres about seventeen miles northwest of Honolulu, Hawaii. (See also chapter 11, *Foreign Service.*)

Major Activities. 25th Infantry Division; 45th Support Group.

Quarters. There are 800 units of housing available for married officers. Guest house facilities are available.

SENECA ARMY DEPOT, NEW YORK 14541
Autovon: 489–5110; Commercial: (607) 869–1110

Seneca Army Depot, established in 1941, is located on 11,000 acres at Romulus, about fifty miles southwest of Syracuse, New York.

Major Activity. Receipt, storage, maintenance and issue of munitions, and rehabilitation of industrial plant equipment.

Quarters. About fifty sets of family quarters are available for officers. There is no guest house, but an Army Travel Camp with fourteen mobile homes is available for transient use.

FORT SHAFTER, HAWAII 96858
Autovon: 438–9375; Commercial: (808) 471–7411

Fort Shafter, established in 1905, is located on 1,300 acres near Honolulu, Hawaii, off H1 Freeway. (See also chapter 11, *Foreign Service.*)

Major Activities. Headquarters, United States Army Pacific (USARPAC); Western Command; Army Support Command, Hawaii; USAISC Western Command.

Quarters. Assigned personnel may be assigned to any available Army housing units throughout Oahu, most of which are located at Schofield Barracks.

SHARPE ARMY DEPOT, CALIFORNIA 95331-5122
Autovon: 462–2011; Commercial: (209) 982–2011

Established in 1942, Sharpe Army Depot occupies 724 acres at Lathrop, California, about 60 miles east of Oakland.

Major Activity. One of three Army area-oriented depots, Sharpe provides extensive storage and distribution operations for supplies destined to Hawaii, Alaska, eight western states, and the Pacific area.

Quarters. There are thirty units of family housing available for officers. BOQs and guest facilities are not provided.

FORT SHERIDAN, ILLINOIS 60037-5000
Autovon: 459–1101; Commercial: (312) 926–4111

Fort Sheridan was established in 1887. The fort is on 695 acres on the shore of Lake Michigan, adjacent to the communities of Highland Park, Highwood and Lake Forest, Illinois, about twenty-eight miles north of downtown Chicago. It is accessible from U.S. 41, 1½ miles east from the Old Elm Road exit, or by taking I-294 and exiting at Illinois Route 22 (Half Day Road), east about four miles to Route 41, then north two miles to the Old Elm Road exit.

Major Activities. Headquarters, Fourth U.S. Army; Headquarters, U.S. Army Recruiting Command; Hq, 30th Hospital Center (USAR); Hq, 425th Transportation Brigade (USAR). Fort Sheridan is the primary administrative, logistical and maintenance center for active and Reserve units in the upper midwest.

Quarters. About 40 percent of the 496 family quarters are designated for officer occupancy. On a limited basis, BOQs are also available, as are guest house suites for temporary accommodations.

SIERRA ARMY DEPOT, CALIFORNIA 96113
Autovon: 830–9910; Commercial: (916) 827–2111

Sierra Army Depot was established in 1942. It is situated on 36,000 acres at Herlong, California, about sixty miles south-southwest of Reno, Nevada.

Major Activity. Storage of munitions, missiles and war reserves.

Quarters. There are twenty-five sets of family quarters for officers, five of which are held for designated personnel. There are twelve BOQs and thirteen VOQs. Transient quarters are available.

FORT SILL, OKLAHOMA 73503-5100
Autovon: 639–7090; Commercial: (405) 351–1103

Fort Sill was established in 1869. The post is 128,000 acres in size. The main gate is about three miles north of Lawton, Oklahoma, off Route 36.

Major Activities. U.S. Army Field Artillery Center and School; III Corps Artillery; 75th Field Artillery Brigade; 212th Field Artillery Brigade; 214th Field Artillery Brigade; U.S. Army Training Center; Henry Post Army Airfield; Field Artillery Board; Reynolds Army Hospital.

Quarters. Approximately 440 sets of family quarters are provided for married officers. About 25 percent of these are reserved for student officers attending the Advanced Course. BOQs are plentiful. Guest house facilities are available. Off-post housing is available in nearby Lawton.

FORT STEWART, GEORGIA 31314
Autovon: 870–1110; Commercial: (912) 767–1110

Established in 1940, the Fort Stewart reservation consists of 284,000 acres near Hinesville, about forty miles southwest of Savannah. State routes 63, 67,

119, 129, and 144 pass through the reservation. (Hunter Army Airfield is a subinstallation.)

Major Activities. Headquarters, 24th Infantry Division. The post is used in the summer for National Guard and Reserve training.

Quarters. More than 170 sets of family quarters are available for married officers. Guest house facilities and BOQs are provided. Rental housing is limited in Hinesville and the surrounding area.

FORT STORY, VIRGINIA 23459-5000
Autovon: 438–7305; Commercial: (804) 422–7305

Fort Story was established in 1914. It occupies 1,451 acres at the mouth of Chesapeake Bay, adjacent to Virginia Beach.

Major Activity. Amphibious training site for active Army and Reserve components, and the Army's Logistics-over-the-Shore testing and training site.

Quarters. Approximately 160 sets of family housing are available for assignment to officers and senior NCOs. A 12-unit visitors quarters is provided.

TOBYHANNA ARMY DEPOT, PENNSYLVANIA 18466-5042
Autovon: 795–7110; Commercial: (717) 894–7000

Established in 1953, the Depot occupies 1,293 acres at Tobyhanna, about twenty-five miles southeast of Scranton, Pennsylvania.

Major Activities. Stores general supplies; repairs and modifies communication-electronics equipment. U.S. Army Calibration and Repair Center; U.S. Army Medical Maintenance Materiel Agency; Defense Reutilization and Marketing Office.

Quarters. There are forty-two sets of family quarters for officers and senior NCOs. BOQs and VOQs are available. Two guest houses are provided.

TOOELE ARMY DEPOT, UTAH 84074
Autovon: 790–1110; Commercial: (801) 833–3211

Established in 1943, Tooele Army Depot (pronounced TOO-illa) is situated on 24,000 acres about thirty-five miles southwest of Salt Lake City, Utah.

Major Activity. Performs overhaul of tactical wheeled vehicles.

Quarters. Four sets of family quarters are available for designated officers. A fifty-one-unit Wherry Housing project, privately owned, is available for rentals, but is little used by assigned military personnel. Off-post rental housing is available. There are no BOQs and no guest house. Four VOQ units are provided.

TRIPLER ARMY MEDICAL CENTER, HAWAII 96859-5000
Autovon: 315–6661; Commercial: (808) 433–6661

Established in 1920, the Tripler Army Medical Center is sited on 360 acres adjacent to Fort Shafter, about five miles northwest of Honolulu, Hawaii, off H1 Freeway. (See also chapter 11, *Foreign Service*.)

Major Activity. In- and out-patient medical services.

Quarters. Approximately seventy sets of family housing are provided for married officers. BOQs and guest house facilities are available.

UMATILLA DEPOT ACTIVITY, OREGON 97838-9544
Autovon: 790–1110; Commercial: (503) 567–6421

Umatilla Depot was established in 1940. A subinstallation of Tooele Army Depot, it is located on 19,727 acres about ten miles west of Hermiston, Oregon.

Major Activity. Receives, stores, ships, renovates, and demilitarizes conventional and chemical munitions; stores general supply commodities.

Quarters. There are seven sets of family housing available for officers or senior NCOs. Two of the units are reserved for designated personnel. One BOQ unit is available.

VINT HILL FARMS STATION, VIRGINIA 22186-5010
Autovon: 249–0111; Commercial: (703) 347–6000

Vint Hill Farms Station was established in 1942. It is located on a 700-acre site near Warrenton, Virginia, about forty-five miles southwest of Washington, D.C.

Major Activities. Center for Signals Warfare; Electronic Material Readiness Activity; 166th Military Intelligence Company.

Quarters. There are 244 sets of family quarters for all grades. There is a guest house consisting of 9 rooms and 2 trailers. Limited BOQs are available.

FORT WAINWRIGHT, ALASKA 99703
Autovon: 317–353–9113; Commercial: (907) 353–7500

Fort Wainwright is sited on 656,000 acres about one mile east of Fairbanks, Alaska. Originally established as an Army Air Field in 1940, and later designated as Ladd Air Force Base, Fort Wainwright was so named in 1961 when the Army assumed command of the post. (See also chapter 11, *Foreign Service.*)

Major Activities. 2nd Brigade, 6th Inf Div; Combat Aviation Brigade.

Quarters. Approximately 314 units of family housing are available for officers, plus 300 units of 801 housing on post. Guest house units and BOQs are available.

WALTER REED ARMY MEDICAL CENTER, WASHINGTON, D.C. 20012
Autovon: 291–3501; Commercial: (202) 576–3501

Walter Reed Army Medical Center was established in 1909. Including the Forest Glen and Glenhaven areas, it occupies 215 acres in Washington, D.C. Walter Reed is located off 16th St., NW, near Silver Spring, Maryland.

Major Activities. Walter Reed Army Medical Center; Walter Reed Institute of Research and Army Institute of Dental Research; Armed Forces Institute of Pathology; Army Medical Biochemical Research Laboratory. At the Forest Glen section is the Army Physical Disability Agency.

Quarters. There are several sets of quarters for key officers whose presence is needed on post. Apartments are plentiful in the Washington and Maryland suburbs, with rates ranging from moderate to expensive.

WATERVLIET ARSENAL, NEW YORK 12189-4050
Autovon: 974–1110; Commercial: (518) 266–5111

Watervliet Arsenal was established in 1813. It is sited on 140 acres at Watervliet, about six miles north of Albany, New York. It is the oldest continuously operating manufacturing arsenal in the United States.

Major Activity. Watervliet Arsenal is the nation's only cannon-manufacturing facility. It has the national mission for quality assurance and procurement of cannon/tank guns. Manufactures thick- and thin-walled cannon.

Quarters. There are about twenty family housing units available for officers. Two BOQs are provided. There is no guest house.

WEST POINT, NEW YORK 10996
Autovon: 688–1110; Commercial: (914) 938–4011

West Point was established in 1802. The reservation includes 15,900 acres on the west bank of the Hudson River, about fifty miles north of New York City and twelve miles south of Newburgh, New York, on U.S. 9W. From New York City, cross the George Washington Bridge, turn right onto the Palisades Parkway (north). Proceed to the end of that highway to the Bear Mountain circle, thence north on U.S. 9W approximately three miles.

Major Activity. The United States Military Academy.

Quarters. There are approximately 900 sets of quarters for officers' families. BOQs and guest house facilities are also available. (These facilities are located on both West Point proper and at Stewart Army Subpost near Newburgh, New York.) The Hotel Thayer, on the reservation, provides temporary accommodations at reasonable rates.

WHITE SANDS MISSILE RANGE, NEW MEXICO 88002-5047
Autovon: 258–2211; Commercial: (505) 678–2121

Established in 1945, the White Sands Missile Range occupies 1,874,666 acres with the main facilities located about twenty-seven miles northeast of Las Cruces on Route 70.

Major Activities. The Army's main missile test site. TRADOC Operations and Research Activity; TRADOC Systems Analysis Activity.

Quarters. There are approximately 195 sets of quarters for married officers. Limited BOQ and guest facilities are available.

WILLIAM BEAUMONT ARMY MEDICAL CENTER, TEXAS 79920
Autovon: 979–2121; Commercial: (915) 569–2121

This Army Medical Center is in El Paso, Texas, adjacent to Fort Bliss.

Major Activity. U.S. Army Medical Center with teaching, outpatient and specialized treatment facilities.

Quarters. There are approximately seventy sets of family quarters for married officers. Off-post housing is available in El Paso. Guest house facilities are provided.

FORT WINGATE DEPOT ACTIVITY, NEW MEXICO 87301-9503
Autovon: 790–6300; Commercial: (505) 488–5411

The Fort Wingate Depot Activity, established in 1860, is a subinstallation of the Tooele Army Depot. It is located on 22,000 acres about ten miles east of Gallup, New Mexico.

Major Activities. Stores, renovates, and ships conventional ammunition. Active support of Reserve components.

Quarters. Six sets of family quarters and limited BOQ facilities.

YAKIMA FIRING CENTER, WASHINGTON 98901-5000
Autovon: 355–8205; Commercial: (509) 454–8250

The Yakima Firing Center was established in 1941. It is a subinstallation of Fort Lewis, occupying 263,000 acres in eastern Washington, with the main gate about seven miles northeast of the city of Yakima. It is the Army's primary training area in the Pacific Northwest.

Major Activity. Provides ranges and maneuver areas to all branches of the active and Reserve components of the U.S. military and allied military forces.

Quarters. There are no family quarters and 253 inadequate BOQ spaces.

YUMA PROVING GROUND, ARIZONA 85365
Autovon: 899–1110; Commercial: (602) 328–2151

Established in 1943, the Yuma Proving Ground occupies 1,000,000 acres, with the main facilities located about thirty-one miles northeast of Yuma, Arizona.

Major Activity. Home of the Atmospherics Science Laboratory. Performs desert testing for all types of materiel.

Quarters. There are about seventy-five units of family quarters for officers. Limited BOQ space is provided. A guest house is available.

MAJOR RESERVE COMPONENT
TRAINING SITES

In addition to the posts and installations previously listed, there are a number of nonactive installations capable of handling maneuver training for units of brigade size or larger. Most are federally owned and operated by the state, but some are entirely state owned. Others are leased from other federal or state agencies. These installations are shown below:

ATTERBURY TRAINING AREA	Edinburgh, Indiana 46124 Autovon: 699–3917; Commercial: (812) 526–9711
CAMP BLANDING	Starke, Florida 32091 Autovon: 860–3420; Commercial: (904) 533–2268
CAMP EDWARDS	Bourne, Massachusetts 02532 Autovon: 881–1644; Commercial: (617) 563–9037
GOWEN FIELD	Boise, Idaho 83707 Autovon: 941–5261; Commercial: (208) 385–5261
CAMP GRAYLING	Grayling, Michigan 49738 Autovon: 722–8200; Commercial: (517) 348–7621
CAMP GRUBER	Muskogee, Oklahoma 74423 Autovon: None; Commercial: (918) 487–5647
CAMP GUERNSEY	Guernsey, Wyoming 82214 Autovon: 943–6273; Commercial: (307) 836–2197
POHAKULOA TRAINING AREA	Hilo, Hawaii 96720 Autovon: None; Commercial: (808) 737–8550

CAMP RILEA	Astoria, Oregon 97103 Autovon: 355–3903; Commercial: (503) 861–3835
CAMP RIPLEY	Little Falls, Minnesota 56345 Autovon: 825–4675; Commercial: (612) 632–6631
CAMP ROBERTS	San Miguel, California 93451 Autovon: 629–1624; Commercial: (805) 238–5559
CAMP JOSEPH T. ROBINSON	North Little Rock, Arkansas 72118 Autovon: 731–8213; Commercial: (501) 758–4053
CAMP SANTIAGO	Salinas, Puerto Rico 00751 Autovon: 860–9165; Commercial: (809) 824–4955
CAMP SHELBY	Hattiesburg, Mississippi 39407 Autovon: 731–9375; Commercial: (601) 545–2871
CAMP SWIFT	Austin, Texas 78621 Autovon: 954–5071; Commercial: (512) 321–2497
CAMP W. G. WILLIAMS	Salt Lake City, Utah 84065 Autovon: 924–4065; Commercial: (801) 524–3732

TRAVEL AND RECREATION

Military posts or facilities, either of the Army or its sister services, are located in each of the fifty states and around the world where there are concentrations of U.S. military personnel. As a general rule, each of these facilities has some provision to accommodate visitors, although the quality of the accommodations may vary from austere to modern, motel-like structures. In addition, many of the military bases operate recreation areas, either on the station or close to nearby attractions. As with the guest quarters on the bases, the facilities at the recreation areas vary widely. Some are equipped only for daytime use, while others have accommodations ranging from camp sites to dormitory rooms, to individual cottages.

All of these temporary quarters and recreation areas have one thing in common. They are available for the use of any military personnel, active or retired, and their families. Proper identification is required. In some cases there are priorities for occupancy, and there generally are limits on how long the post guest facilities or recreation facilities may be used. However, by making proper inquiry and planning ahead, it is possible for a military family to travel around the country and to vacation in the mountains or at the seashore, and at many attractive spots in between, all at prices substantially below the cost of commercial facilities. It is an important benefit that accrues to all military personnel.

A good source of information on Space-A military air travel, temporary military lodging, and "R&R" (see chapter 24, *Authorized Absences*) is Military Living Publications. This company publishes a travel newsletter, the *R&R Report;* a Washington, D.C., area magazine, *Military Living;* and travel books. Military Living books include *Military Space-A Air Opportunities Around the World; U.S. Forces Travel Guide U.S.A. & Caribbean Areas; Assignment Washington: A Guide to Washington Area Military Installations; Temporary Military Lodging Around the World;* and *Military RV, Camping & Rec Areas Around the World.* The *R&R*

Report contains current information on temporary military lodging; space-available travel on U.S. military aircraft; military recreation areas; and more. The $-Saver section of the *Report* provides information on discounts available to military I.D. card holders in the civilian travel sector to include hotels, motels, transportation, food, and entertainment. The *R&R Report* serves as a clearinghouse for information provided by military readers sharing their travel experiences around the world. (Sample issues are available for $2.)

To receive information on any of these publications, write: Military Living Publications, P.O. Box 2347, Falls Church, VA 22042; or call (703)237-0203. Phone orders are accepted with major credit cards. Military Living will send a free welcome kit to anyone on orders to the Washington, D.C., area.

For a thorough discussion of installations in the continental United States and overseas, consult *The Guide to Military Installations.* It is published by Stackpole Books, P.O. Box 1831, Harrisburg, PA 17105.

11

Foreign Service

Where a man can live, there he can also live well.—Marcus Aurelius

This chapter is provided as a source of "first information" for Army families under orders for oversea assignment. It includes information extracted from official publications, gathered from the experiences of Army members who have provided suggestions, and supplied by oversea commands. There are informative official pamphlets on most oversea commands, which are supplied to officers after they receive orders for change of station. The oversea commands also mail informative pamphlets that they have prepared for incoming personnel. These pamphlets are especially important since they include recent developments that may be of great interest.

The following travel documents are of special importance: AR 55-46, *Travel of Dependents* and PAM 608-1, *Dependent Travel Information.*

ARMED FORCES HOSTESS ASSOCIATION

An information service of unique value is provided by the Armed Forces Hostess Association, Room 1A736, The Pentagon, Washington, DC 20310. Telephone (202) 697–3180.

This is a volunteer association of officers' wives from all Services who will provide you upon request considerable information on your oversea post, including climate, appliances, schools, clothes, travel, shipment of pets, and other helpful tips. Be sure to give the exact location (APO if possible) and expected date of departure.

THE OPPORTUNITY AND THE RESPONSIBILITY

During the span of a normal Army career, you may expect several oversea assignments. Today, with approximately one-third of the

181

Army serving overseas, it is typical that an officer can expect to spend about one-third of his or her tours in oversea assignments. Tour duration will generally be three years or less.

Here is opportunity unlimited to observe and to learn the history, the culture, the language, the economics, the religions, and the ways of life of other nations. Army people, including Army children, enjoy a unique opportunity to broaden their knowledge of the people and problems of these nations.

You and your family will have many opportunities to enrich your interest and your understanding about the flood of events that shape our world.

Army officers and their families who have served the conventional oversea assignments have become travel sophisticates who know their way about our nation and our world, what to do, how to do it, and also what not to do, and why. Most have taken advantage of their travel opportunities. They have taken the pains to learn enough of the history and culture of the countries visited to be well informed. Some have learned the language of the host nation. Most have made lasting friendships, with memories to be cherished. These well-traveled, well-informed people are a national asset, and they have earned a wider recognition as to this truth than has been extended. They have done well and deserve credit for it.

International Emergencies and Family Travel. There is one phase of family life in the services that had best be faced with candor and fact. Members of the Army must be sent into international trouble spots in order to discharge the nation's responsibilities. In addition, there are regions of the world where facilities for families are so scant, or so primitive, as to make the presence of Army families inadvisable. Assignment to these primitive or troubled areas is indeed a hardship, but the Army is careful to distribute such hardship tours to make family separations as few and as equitable as possible. But in a troubled world, with the vast responsibilities faced by our nation, the situation must be understood. Army families must look to the administration in control of our government, and to departmental officials, to keep family separations at a minimum.

FOREIGN SERVICE TOURS

The policies regarding foreign service for officers are stated in AR 614-30 and are summarized below.

The Broad Policy Selection. The paramount consideration in selecting an officer for service outside CONUS is the existence of a valid requirement coupled with the officer's military qualifications to perform the duties required. To the maximum extent practicable, oversea tours will be alternated between long and short tour areas, and attempts will be made to achieve geographic and climatic variety. CONUS and Hawaii are the sustaining bases for all oversea assignments, and officers can normally expect a minimum of twelve months in CONUS or Hawaii after completion of an oversea tour. However, the requirements of the Army dictate the length of a tour in CONUS prior to return overseas. The policy is that each officer will receive a proportionate share of foreign service. The oversea commands have the option to fill vacancies either with qualified individuals already in their commands or through requisition upon the continental United States. As to an assignment in the continental United States, some are of fixed duration from which an officer may not be released prior to its completion, even for an oversea assignment. So it goes. In principle, the officer with the right grade and the right qualifications with the least credit for oversea service will generally be the next to fill a requisition from an oversea command.

Officer Volunteers. Officers may volunteer for oversea assignment ahead of their normal expectancy for such duty. They may state a preference for a specific oversea command or for several commands in order of preference. Officers who volunteer are considered to be available when HQDA approves their applications and they have been assigned in CONUS at least twelve months. However, officers serving in stabilized positions will not be voluntarily reassigned until they have completed their stabilized tours.

Temporary Deferment of Oversea Assignment. Where the oversea movement of an officer would cause serious hardship, it is possible to secure temporary deferment for compassionate reasons. Officers who find it necessary to seek deferment are advised to study DA Pam 600–8–10 before making request.

Length of Foreign Service Tour. Normal tours of foreign service for all Army personnel are shown in AR 614-30. For purposes of departmental records, foreign service tours commence on the day an individual departs from an ocean or air terminal in the United States and terminate on the date of return to such a U.S. terminal. The day of return is counted as a day of foreign service.

Personnel who are accompanied or joined by their dependents will serve the tour prescribed for those "With Dependents" or twelve months after arrival of dependents, whichever is longer. The tour prescribed for "All Others" will be served by personnel who elect to serve overseas without their dependents; are serving in an area where movement of dependents is restricted; are not authorized movement of their dependents at government expense; or who do not have dependents. There are special rules and provisions for Army members married to each other. In specified European countries, and in Japan and Canada, careerist bachelor officer and enlisted personnel, male and female, will serve the "With Dependents" tour.

Tours normally are uniform for personnel of all services at the same station. The service having primary interest (the most personnel) will develop, in coordination with the other affected services, a mutually satisfactory tour length applicable to all military personnel in the locality.

Personnel who have dependents entitled to be present at the oversea station, but who elect to serve unaccompanied, must complete the prescribed "All Others" tour.

There are provisions for reassignment between oversea commands without intervening tours in CONUS. The rules for computing tour lengths in this case are complex and can easily be misunderstood. The first delineation involves voluntary versus involuntary reassignment. Officers are advised to consult their personnel officers and AR 614-30 for details. An officer who is voluntarily reassigned will serve the complete prescribed tour in both areas. An officer who is involuntarily reassigned between oversea commands or between areas within an oversea command will serve a prorated tour in the new command in accordance with the formula in AR 614–30. The tour in the new area will be adjusted to give credit for that portion of the normal tour in the new area corresponding to the portion of the normal tour already served in the area from which reassigned. For example, an officer who completed one-third of some other tour would be credited with having served four months of the normal twelve-month tour in Korea.

Geographic Areas and Tour Lengths. Consistent with Army requirements, oversea assignments are made so as to provide a variety in the geographic areas to which assigned. Thus, an officer who has spent a tour in Europe should fully expect the next oversea tour to be in a different geographic area, such as Korea. Similarly, the Army attempts to equalize the burden of family separations. In the above example, if the European tour had been a thirty-six-month "With Dependents" tour, the officer should not be surprised if the subsequent Korean tour were a twelve-month, unaccompanied tour, as prescribed for "All Others."

AR 614–30 provides a complete list of oversea assignment areas and tour lengths. You should consult the regulation for specific details regarding an oversea assignment. However, in general, the "With Dependents" tour in European countries and other modern areas is thirty-six months, decreasing to twenty-four months in less-desirable locations, while the corresponding "All Others" tour lengths range from twenty-four months to a minimum of twelve months.

PREPARATION FOR OVERSEA TRAVEL

Action Before Departure. Official orders of the Department of the Army assigning you to an oversea command prescribe the timing, method of transportation, and other essential information about the journey. At the outset you should receive, or should have prepared, about fifty copies of your orders, needed on many occasions incident to the movement. For example, six copies are required with each shipment of personal property. Orders will also be required for pay, travel allowances, and other matters en route and after arrival.

Upon receipt of orders, you should immediately report to the personnel officer, finance officer, quartermaster, transportation officer, and surgeon to obtain detailed instructions regarding the pending move. Be certain to understand these instructions and follow them to the letter. You must set your official and personal house in order so that no dangling, unfinished business will arise the last minute before departure or, worse, after departure. All personal bills or obligations must be paid, or definite arrangements made for future payment. See chapter 9, *Financial Planning,* on wills, insurance, and check-up suggestions for personal affairs.

Concurrent Travel of Families. Families may accompany you to an oversea station (concurrent travel), or they may be obliged to join you after a period of delay when it has been determined that there will be quarters available upon their arrival. The regulation of general information is AR 55–46, which should be consulted upon receipt of orders for oversea movement.

Shipment of Household Goods. The amount of household goods that may be shipped overseas on permanent change of station is stated in chapter 21, *Travel Allowances.* Area restrictions or other temporary reductions in allowances may ,occur. Consult the transportation officer. For duty at those oversea stations where furniture and equipment are supplied to a military family, the authorized allowances for shipment of personal belongings are sharply reduced.

With careful planning, and consideration of the advice you have received, you should be able to ship all of the necessities plus a few "nice-to-have" items within the weight limit prescribed. The special items may not be essential but may add to satisfaction with the new environment; these items could include a favorite painting, a choice piece of furniture, a popular family game, a few cherished books, or any of many other items that could add to family enjoyment.

Shipment of Automobile. In most oversea assignments the use of a privately owned automobile is essential. Consider at once the suitability of the car owned. Service for the car including spare parts is the thing to consider.

If shipment of a car is desired, the best advice you can possibly get is to consult the transportation officer at once. He or she will give you the detailed information that may assist in having your car arrive at the oversea destination in much less time than would be the case if one essential step is missed along the line. It is also recommended that you review AR 55–71, *Transportation of Personal Property and Related Services.*

See to it that your orders permit travel to the port in your own car, if such travel is your desire. Be sure to deliver the car at the port no later than the time prescribed. Further, since cars may be loaded in order of arrival, it may be wise to get there a day early. The same advice applies to shipment of a trailer. Have ready several copies of your travel orders, a Certificate of Title to the car, or a statement that the vehicle is free from any legal encumbrance that would preclude its shipment.

Ask your transportation officer about buying marine insurance, which generally is regarded as desirable but is not required.

It is not unusual for a car to arrive overseas as much as a month behind the owner. Careful attention to the requirements that may permit it to be shipped on an earlier transport may save lots of walking.

Shipment of Pets. If you own pets, you need to ascertain definite information as to the regulations governing the shipment of pets to the oversea destination, and also the laws or regulations governing their re-entry into the United States upon termination of tour.

The shipment of pets must be planned with the same care as the travel of the rest of the family to avoid a family crisis. Pets must be vaccinated, placed in crates on some occasions, fitted with muzzles as required, be fed, exercised, and for some destinations, be shipped separately.

Passports. You should ascertain at your home station whether passports will be required either for yourself or for your family. AR 600–290 governs the procedures to obtain passports. See also par. 18, AR 55–46. Consult chapter 21, *Travel Allowances.* If passports are required, take action early to obtain them, since considerable time is often required.

Mode of Travel. The standard mode of travel for Army members and their dependents to, from, and between oversea commands is by air. Sea travel is authorized only as an exception when the Service member or the member's dependents, for medical reasons, cannot travel by air. Still in the military vocabulary, however, are many terms left over from the days of sea transport, such as hand baggage, hold baggage, and port of embarkation. These terms generally are applied to air transport just as they were in the past to sea transport.

Hand Baggage and Hold Baggage. Hand baggage is that baggage accompanying the passenger on board the aircraft, either in the flight cabin or checked for stowage in the cargo compartment. For travel outside the continental United States, hand baggage normally is limited to sixty-five pounds per person.

Hold baggage is that additional baggage authorized to be shipped with the traveler, as contrasted to household goods, which generally follow later. Hold baggage is limited to 600 pounds per person and generally is packed and shipped prior to the date of departure so as to be available at the destination at about the time the traveler arrives.

Judicious use of the weight allowances for the hand and hold baggage will enable you and your family to have on hand at the oversea destination those clothes and other essentials you will need during the month or more you may have to wait before arrival of your household goods.

Action at Port of Embarkation (POE). The orders for oversea movement will prescribe the point of departure and the date and hour arrival at the POE is required.

Be certain to arrive on time. Report to the prescribed headquarters or to the office charged with processing transient personnel. Receive from them detailed and complete instructions and study them carefully. Quarters will be provided while awaiting departure, including quarters for families. It is considered more satisfactory to utilize quarters furnished than to choose to await departure at a hotel or the homes of friends. Sometimes you must go to a local hotel because the terminal facilities are crowded; if you arrive early enough in the day the chances for space assignment are increased. The more children and pets you have, the more time you must allow the terminal personnel to help you. While the government quarters furnished you may not be luxurious, they will certainly be comfortable, clean, and adequate for the short stay required. Terminal commanders take pride in these facilities as well as the smoothness of their operation; recreation facilities are provided; you and your family may be reached promptly for medical or other processing requirements; and costs are low.

Travel Aboard Aircraft. The Military Airlift Command (MAC) provides oversea transport service for personnel including family members, and freight, serving equally all military services. As noted earlier, except as may be authorized for medical reasons, all personnel movement now is by aircraft.

Travel aboard airplanes of the MAC is substantially the same as aboard commercial airlines—in fact, MAC uses many aircraft chartered from the commercial airlines. Stewardesses or stewards are provided. Special diets for babies and young children must be taken aboard by the sponsor.

While MSTS transport may be involved with troop transport to areas of conflict, it can be expected that air transport will be the standard mode. MAC has a proud tradition of service and will provide outstanding transportation to those who follow its advice and regulations. If you plan and think through your air travel and follow instructions you and your family should have a delightful, but short, travel experience and arrive overseas in the best condition.

TIPS FOR FAMILY TRAVEL

High standards of personal conduct, including that of the children, with due regard for the rights of others, are a necessity. While it is true that the journey by air is of much shorter duration than was the case when travel was by ship, it also is true that the quarters are more cramped. Thoughtfulness and consideration by all fellow travelers will do much to make the trip a pleasant experience for all.

A large, all-purpose bag or handbag will be handy for carrying aboard the aircraft the personal items that will be needed during the journey. Do not overlook a few books, toys, or small games that can help the children pass the hours.

You will be informed by or for the terminal commander as to the time your presence is required for processing prior to boarding the aircraft. For the long oversea flights, this normally is two hours prior to flight time, to enable complete processing of passengers and their baggage. Transportation from your temporary quarters to the terminal will be provided. It is necessary only that you be at the starting point on time, with hand baggage, official orders, passports (if required), immunization records, and any other pertinent papers, ready to board the aircraft.

After the short delay for check-in, which is necessary to assure that all personnel are present who are scheduled for that particular flight, and that they have the required official papers, as well as for processing baggage, you will board the aircraft. Families normally board first so that they may arrange seating by family groups, followed by any VIPs who may be on the flight, followed by other military members traveling alone.

As an aside to our readers who may be traveling without dependents, it is often the case that you will note at the air terminal a mother with perhaps several small children, proceeding overseas to join her husband. She will be encumbered with bags, and more often than not the processing procedures will be strange to her. It is perfectly proper to offer your services to help her wrestle bags or children, or both, and to help make their journey a more pleasant one. Such a practice will pay rich dividends, not only in terms of the gratitude of the mother involved, but in terms of the day when your family may be traveling overseas to join you and a stranger offers a helping hand. Such acts of courtesy and thoughtfulness are in keeping with service customs and the officer's code.

Special for Families with Children. Each service family generally comes equipped with several children. Thus, it is quite possible for the number of children aboard an aircraft to exceed the number of other passengers. A journey overseas provides a unique test of the way parents have reared their children. Within a few hours in the air, all passengers will have ample opportunity to judge the results of your efforts in this regard.

No one expects children to be other than children, but sometimes even this can be fearsome when the quarters are cramped. Try to plan your trip to have on hand those items that will entertain and satisfy the needs of your children. Such forethought will go a long way toward earning for you, as for most other service families, the accolades of fellow passengers for a job well done.

Words of Caution. Except when there are unusual circumstances of health, the care of your family at air terminals (POEs), on MAC aircraft, and at the port of debarkation overseas will present no great problems if you and your family think out your plans well in advance and you follow instructions carefully. If you understand the requirements well, if facilities are adequate, and if you follow carefully the standing operating procedures as to events, time, and place, everything will proceed smoothly and pleasantly. Personnel operating the POEs and aircraft have been confronted by nearly all possible problems and generally have a solution ready to apply promptly and with good grace. But if there are unusual circumstances, such as medical supplies for a child, or special foods, or other unusual matters, you should make all necessary plans and arrangements in advance and in person.

Foresight at the home station before departure will pay rich dividends. What to take and what to leave behind in storage is an important matter. Considerations of the climate to be encountered will answer many questions. Within limitations of baggage and freight allowances, in case of doubt it is wiser to take questionable articles of personal property than to leave them behind. Fragile or valuable nonessentials are best left behind in storage; even under the assumption that packing and crating will be done perfectly, which is an overly generous assumption, these shipments are subject to much handling, which involves considerable hazard of damage and pilferage. However, do not relegate your best things to storage just because they are your best. Remember that you will probably be spending 10 percent or more of your service career at the oversea station and you will want to have and to use your best things there as well as at stations within the continental United States.

SATISFACTION OF FAMILY NEEDS IN OVERSEA COMMANDS

The Army is keenly concerned about physical facilities to serve the needs of its officers and enlisted personnel and their families overseas. This concern has been necessary because provision for at least a reasonable minimum of the necessities of Army families is essential to the peace of mind of its members, which in turn permits them to devote their full energies to their duties.

Grade school and high school facilities are provided in all established commands. Standards are closely supervised. Considering the intangible values to be derived from travel and life in an oversea land for a span of a few years, most parents consider that their children have benefited by the experience. In the unusual case where children's schools are not provided under military control, such as when on attache duty, parents should inform themselves of facilities used by American citizens resident in the area, or ascertain the possibilities for instruction by mail with home tutoring. Unless there are very unusual circumstances indeed, there is no strong reason for Army families to be separated merely because of the school situation of their children, because educational facilities for our children have been provided in a manner that is acceptable to most parents.

Post exchanges in most oversea commands are not so sharply restricted as to what can be sold as is the situation in the United States where civilian retail facilities are available. Although unusual needs must be anticipated, and arrangements made for their satisfaction, the ordinary wants and necessities, with some items of luxury, may be obtained from that source. If you know you will have special needs, it is wise to arrange with a U.S. merchant before departure so that special requirements can be shipped upon receipt of an order from you. All oversea exchanges have working arrangements with large U.S. mail-order houses so that merchandise not stocked in the exchange may be obtained.

Officers' clubs and recreational facilities are provided at nearly all stations.

Movies are provided by the Army and Air Force Exchange Service on a standard comparable to that in CONUS, and the pictures shown are the latest produced by the industry.

Commissaries are provided at which the usual commissary items may be purchased as at posts in the United States.

LIFE IN OVERSEA COMMANDS

The following information about living conditions in oversea areas where U.S. Army personnel are stationed, accompanied or joined by their families, is presented as a helpful "first reference" for officers receiving foreign service orders. The discussions have been extracted from official publications, with up-to-date references from the headquarters of our commands.

In all cases, official information is sent to officers receiving assignment orders to reach them as early as practicable.

ALASKA

The U.S. Army in Alaska has its headquarters at Fort Richardson, near Anchorage, with mail zip code number 99505. Other Army installations are at Fort Wainwright (ZIP 99703) near Fairbanks, and Fort Greely (APO 98733 Seattle), 106 miles southeast of Fairbanks.

An Army family whose sponsor receives orders to duty in Alaska may look forward to the experience. Quarters, schools for children, and shopping facilities are available, and recreational, cultural, and sporting facilities and opportunities are abundant.

Excellent documents about service in Alaska are supplied to officers soon after they receive their assignment orders. The pamphlets are current, well illustrated, and informative. The following documents were consulted in choosing the extracts herein, as initial information of immediate interest to officers and their families: *Unofficial Newcomer's Guides to: Fort Richardson, Fort Wainwright, Fort Greely.*

Concurrent Travel. Officers should request concurrent travel to Alaska, for which see AR 55–46. If approved, apply to the nearest transportation officer for shipment of household goods. A sponsor's program assists incoming officers and their families and direct communication with the sponsor is encouraged.

Shipment of Automobile. Privately owned automobiles (one per service member), after authorization, are shipped from the port of Seattle at government expense. Consult the transportation officer. Recommended is that cars be put in the best possible mechanical condition, as cost of repairs and maintenance is high; and that cars be winterized to $-40°$ for the Anchorage area and $-75°$ for the Fairbanks area. Recommended items include an engine block heater or a battery blanket.

Travel by Alaska Highway and Ferry. Travel via the Alaska Highway or Alaska Marine Highway (ferry) may be authorized provided certain conditions are met. Requests for permission for such travel should be sent to Headquarters, 6th Infantry Division (Light), ATTN: G-1, Fort Richardson. Consult your finance officer for authorized reimbursement for travel via the ferry or highway.

Family Quarters. Government quarters are generally apartment-style, frame two-story, or single and duplex style with a full basement. Basements are concrete, warm and dry, with outlets for appliances. These quarters are available at Fort Richardson, Fort Wainwright, and Fort Greely.

All personnel electing to serve an accompanied tour are authorized a full household goods weight allowance. Single officers may request shipment of full household goods weight allowance but should be aware that government storage for excess household goods is not available. Officers should plan to bring (or plan to purchase) all household goods (draperies, lamps, and so on) and furniture that will be needed for a two- or three-year stay. Quarters on post are equipped with a washer, dryer, refrigerator, and electric stove. Shipment of duplicate items is discouraged due to limited storage. Temporary issue of basic household goods can be arranged, if needed, and some furniture items may be available on a permanent basis. The ACS loan closets can supply temporary cooking utensils, silverware, and cribs.

Off-post housing of the one- and two-bedroom apartment-type units are more readily available than larger units. Rental rates and utility costs are higher than in most CONUS locations. There is an additional quarters allowance for individuals authorized to occupy off-post housing.

Clothing Suggestions. Winter clothing may be purchased from local stores at slightly higher prices than normal, and from exchanges that supply practically any item normally available in CONUS. Mail-order service is satisfactory and utilized extensively. There are national chain-type department stores in Anchorage and Fairbanks.

Quartermaster laundry and dry cleaning facilities are available.

Schools for Children. On-post schools provide adequate educational opportunity for children. Smaller children, below the age of five, may attend preschool at Forts Richardson, Wainwright, and Greely. The minimum age for entrance to Alaska schools is five years, and this age must be reached by 1 November of the school year. A birth certificate is required for kindergarten and evidence of promotion for all other grades. Immunization records for DPT, DT, or TD; polio; measles; and rubella (or a signed physician's waiver) are required for entry to any grade.

On-post school facilities include: Fort Richardson, kindergarten through 6th grade; Fort Wainwright, kindergarten through 6th grade; and Fort Greely; kindergarten through 8th grade.

Family members at Fort Wainwright (7th through 12th grades), Fort Greely (9th through 12th grades), and Fort Richardson (7th through 12th grades) attend schools in the local community with bus transportation furnished by civilian authorities.

Your Leisure. Posts in Alaska have much the same opportunities for recreation as those in CONUS.

Officers' and noncommissioned officers' clubs and service clubs are found at each post. Craft, woodworking, and ceramics shops are provided. There are snow-machine, flying, parachute, and youth swim clubs, as well as drama and arts groups.

Individual sports include swimming, golf, tennis, bowling, skiing, skating, sled dog racing, and more.

Camping and hiking are popular activities and you can hunt and fish to your heart's content at small expense.

HAWAII

The state of Hawaii, Paradise of the Pacific, is "foreign service" only in the sense that it is outside the continental limits of the United States. Its climate resembles Southern California and Southern Florida. It is one of the few areas where local claims as to climate and scenery are justified by experience. See DA Pam 608-14.

The Army's stations are Fort Shafter, Tripler Army Medical Center, and Schofield Barracks.

Major Activities. The U.S. Army Pacific (USARPAC) is headquartered at Fort Shafter and is one of the two major Army commands in the Asia-Pacific area. (The other is the U.S. Eighth Army located in Korea.) Designated in 1987, USARPAC is the Army component of the Joint U.S. Pacific Command. USARPAC's area of operation covers 100 million square miles and includes 2.5 billion people in fifty different countries.

Major subordinate units under USARPAC include: U.S. Army Japan/IX Corps; Hq, IX Corps (Reinforcement); 25th Infantry Division; U.S. Army Support Command, Hawaii; 45th Support Group; and U.S. Army Chemical Activity, Johnston Island.

U.S. Army Japan/IX Corps is a dual-hatted command. USARJ has the primary mission of commanding all assigned and attached U.S. Army units and developing and maintaining mutual cooperation and understanding between the U.S. Army and the Japan Ground Self-Defense Force in the pursuit of common goals.

IX Corps plans and conducts bilateral training activities and exercises with the Japan Ground Self-Defense Forces.

USARJ/IX Corps has two subordinate commands: the 9th Area Support Group (Prov), headquartered at Camp Zama on the island of Honshu; and the 10th Area Support Group (Prov), headquartered at Torii Station in Okinawa.

Headquarters, IX Corps (Reinforcement) is a U.S. Army Reserve element of IX Corps. Based in Hawaii, it can combine with the USARJ personnel to form a tactical headquarters capable of commanding up to five divisions with supporting forces.

The 25th Infantry Division (Light), located at Schofield Barracks in Hawaii, is designed as a rapid strike force of nearly 11,000 soldiers with the specific mission as the Pacific Command's ground combat reserve force.

The U.S. Army Support Command, Hawaii, operates all Army installations in Hawaii, providing installation management service and logistical support for more than 69,000 Army military and civilian personnel in eighty-four tenant units located at twenty-nine subinstallations in Hawaii, Guam, American Samoa, the Northern Marianas, and Johnston Island.

The 45th Support Group, headquartered at Schofield Barracks, provides combat support and combat service support to USARPAC to include engineering, transportation, maintenance, ordnance, mapping, medical, and financial support.

The U.S. Army Chemical Activity on Johnston Island, 825 miles southwest of Hawaii, provides integrated command and management of all U.S. Army activities on the island, and oversight for operations maintenance of the Johnston Atoll Chemical Agent Disposal System. This system will dispose of obsolete and unserviceable chemical munitions under stringent security and safety standards.

Tripler Army Medical Center is a large hospital facility serving all military forces and their dependents on the islands.

Family Quarters. Station and civilian facilities are at least equal to their mainland counterparts.

Under normal conditions as to size of the Army strength, the number of family-type housing units is short of the number needed for married families. Studio and one-bedroom apartments are in good supply. Civilian housing for families of more than four members is scarce. Rents are high. The Oahu Consolidated Family Housing Office at Fort Shafter will assist in securing temporary as well as permanent-type accommodations.

Temporary Lodging Allowance. Costs for temporary housing can be extremely high. There is a housing allowance, separate from the basic allowance for quarters, which may be obtained to defray excess housing costs pending assignment of government quarters or obtaining permanent civilian housing. See AR 37-104 and the Joint Travel Regulations for the amounts, which are variable. As a maximum, this allowance can last no more than thirty days. *Caution:* Within one working day after arrival, application for government quarters should be made to qualify for payment of *Temporary Lodging Allowance* and establish priority for obtaining government quarters based on date of departing CONUS.

Schools for Children. Adequate school facilities are available throughout the command. There are several outstanding private schools.

Automobile. A privately owned automobile is quite essential. Consult the transportation officer as to authorization for shipment.

Pets. Pets can be taken to Hawaii and returned to the mainland. Dogs and cats must undergo mandatory quarantine in Hawaii for 120 days at the State Quarantine Station.

Recreation Facilities. Service in Hawaii provides for unusually varied and enjoyable recreation facilities. There are extensive facilities for team sports, golf, tennis, and water sports of all kinds, with outstanding programs for participation. There are active organizations to sponsor interesting activities for young people, and officers' clubs and open messes function in Hawaii as elsewhere.

The Armed Forces Recreation Center, Fort DeRussy, in the heart of Waikiki, is especially cherished as a service benefit. Individuals and families can secure accommodations for a day or several days, and enjoy at small cost all the pleasures of the tourist paradise at Waikiki. DeRussy has a fine beach for swimming, picnic area, a good restaurant, and a club with entertainment. In addition, a post office, liquor store, post exchange with car rental, laundry, flower shop, and outdoor ice dispenser. A high-rise hotel, the Hale Koa, provides comfortable, modern temporary quarters. It can be contacted via a toll-free telephone number — (800) 367-6027.

In addition to the Hale Koa on Waikiki Beach, the Army has two other fine recreation sites on Oahu. The Waianae Army Recreation Center on the west coast offers beautiful beaches, cabins, and dining facilities, in addition to the rental of almost anything you need to make your "getaway" more enjoyable. The Army's beach on the famed north shore at Mokuleia features a secluded swimming, sunbathing, and picnic area for those who don't enjoy the crowded beaches on the southern end of the island.

On the island of Hawaii is the Kilauea Military Camp, a recreation facility adjacent to the Hawaii National Park. Military families go there at minimal expense for a stay of several days duration. The camp is at an elevation of 4,000 feet, which provides a climate change—and a temporary need for warmer clothing than is worn on Oahu. Tours by bus are scheduled to points of beauty and interest. The accommodations are adequate and include a restaurant.

GERMANY AND BELGIUM

Service with the U.S. Army, Europe (USAREUR), provides an opportunity for service of importance to the nation and, in addition, an unusual opportunity for travel and acquiring an understanding of the people, the cultures, and the problems of the nations of Europe allied with the United States. See DA Pam 608-12, DA Pam 360-419, and USAREUR Pam 360-8.

Major Army Installations in Germany. The main Army installations in Germany are located in or near the following cities:

Ansbach	Giessen	Neu Ulm
Augsburg	Goeppingen	Pirmasens
Bad Kreuznach	Hanau	Schwaebisch Gmuend
Baumholder	Heidelburg	Schwaebisch Hall
Berlin	Kaiserslautern	Stuttgart
Bremerhaven	Karlsruhe	Wiesbaden
Darmstadt	Mainz	Worms
Frankfurt	Mannheim	Wurzburg
Fulda	Munich	Zweibruecken
Garlstedt	Nuernberg	

Preparation for Travel to Germany. *Passports.* Each member of your family will need a passport. For many assignments, passports are not needed by military personnel; however, passports are required to take leave in certain oversea countries. Ask your installation passport agent for assistance. Failure to perform this task in a timely fashion could cause unnecessary delays in travel of family members.

Immunizations. No immunizations are required for travel to the European theater; however, you should check with your local immunization clinic. Animal immunizations before departure for Europe are required. Check with local veterinary clinics for information.

Hand Baggage and Hold Baggage. Plan these choices most carefully. An earlier discussion in this chapter supplies details as to allowances. It is recommended that there be included in hold baggage a small supply of bed linens, bath linens, and cooking utensils for use prior to the arrival of household goods.

Travel Conditions En Route to Germany. Travel to Germany will be via aircraft of the Military Airlift Command (MAC), in commercial aircraft chartered by MAC, or in commercial aircraft when MAC flights and MAC charter aircraft are unavailable. The accommodations are equivalent to commercial tourist class. The prescribed uniform for travel is any authorized combination of the Army Green uniform. Officers arriving in Frankfurt process through the 21st Replacement Battalion, which serves as the interim sponsor for all arriving military and DA civilian personnel. The battalion receives, processes, feeds, and transports personnel to the gaining unit of assignment via commercial contract bus, with an escort provided by the battalion. Your designated sponsor will meet you at your destination rather than traveling to Frankfurt.

Climate in Germany. The climate is mild. German summers are delightful with warm days and cool nights. There are very few thunderstorms, but considerable gentle rain. Winters are less severe than in our northern and central states; they compare with those of Maryland or Virginia. There is some snow, but except in the mountains it does not remain long. In the mountainous areas winters are much colder and the snow deeper, and winter sports are popular.

Housing Situation. Government family housing continues to be in short supply at most locations in USAREUR, but the situation is improving. More quarters are being added annually. Plans are to have enough housing on hand, or under construction, by fiscal year 1990 to provide government housing within sixty days after arrival. The present waiting periods vary from a few weeks to several months, depending upon your grade, bedroom requirements, and location. On the other hand, barring unusual circumstances, private rental housing generally can be obtained within one to eight weeks. Rental rates for private rental housing are generally high, and most landlords require a security deposit equal to a minimum of one month's rent. Soldiers who reside in private rental housing approved by the Housing Referral Office (HRO) are paid an Overseas Housing Allowance (OHA). The allowance paid is the difference between actual rental cost and the Basic Allowance for Quarters (BAQ). Annual cost surveys are required to authorize the payment and to adjust the allowance.

Family Housing. Upon arrival in Germany, all personnel with present or future requirements for family housing must report to the local housing office. You will be advised of the local housing conditions and waiting periods for economy and government housing, and will be assisted in applying for and locating housing. If your dependents did not accompany you, the housing office will assist you in sending for them after you have located housing. You will also be advised of your entitlements, including Temporary Lodging Allowance (TLA). While at the housing office, you may place your name on waiting lists for temporary government quarters, permanent government quarters, and rentals on the economy. If you move into economy housing, you can still remain on the list for permanent government quarters and later move at government expense to the permanent quarters; however, USAREUR policy is that you must live in private rental housing for a minimum of one year before moving into government quarters.

Government quarters consist of both on-post housing and off-post government-leased housing. The on-post housing is primarily two-, three-, and four-bedroom units in multifamily apartment buildings. Laundry and drying rooms, complete with washers and dryers, are located in each building. The government-leased quarters are of varying sizes and styles. They may be small two- to six-family units, row houses, or apartments. There are even a few single houses. These leased quarters are all within commuting distance of your duty station and are assigned on the same basis as on-post quarters. Almost all quarters, government and economy, are supplied with 220-volt, 50-cycle electrical current.

Unaccompanied Officer Quarters. The same basic rules apply as stateside. Single (unaccompanied) officers, commissioned and warrant, are authorized to reside off post regardless of the availability of quarters except for reasons of military necessity or when serving in a dependent-restricted area unless adequate govern-ment-controlled quarters are not available. Bachelor quarters vary in size and some include community kitchens. Availability of private rental housing and waiting periods for government housing are similar to those for married personnel.

Private Rental Housing. Over 62,000 military and civilian personnel reside in private rental housing in Germany. More than half are military families who are eligible for government housing. Private rental housing is owned by German land-lords who lease to American soldiers and civilians. Army policy requires that all personnel, soldiers and civilians alike, register with the local Housing Referral Office (HRO) before entering into a lease agreement. Do not sign a lease until it has been checked by your HRO representative! This is for your benefit and protec-tion, as well as being a requirement. In addition to approving private rentals, HROs maintain lists of available apartments and houses, assist in locating suitable housing, provide interpreter assistance, provide transportation to view apartments, and provide a multitude of other services to you as you search for and then occupy private rental housing. You also can go to a rental agent; however, the fees usually amount to one or two months' rent and the Army will not reimburse you for the expense. While rents vary according to the size and location of the apartment or house, it is fair to say that rents are higher than for comparable housing in the United States. With deposits and initial start-up costs, it is not at all uncommon to face an initial cash outlay of $1,500 or more to get set up in private rental housing.

Persons who have experienced living on the German economy can tell you that there are significant differences between renting housing in Germany and renting in the states. The first thing one notices about German housing is that when they say unfurnished, they mean it. You may find no light fixtures, no stove, no kitchen cabinets, and no refrigerator, and it is a rare German apartment that has closets. Appliances such as refrigerators, stoves, and hot water heaters, when provided, are much smaller than American appliances. This is not a scheme to cheat the Ameri-can, but a reflection of the German way of life.

You may not be able to get American TV, which is broadcast in color by the Armed Forces Network-TV, unless you are very near an Army installation. On the brighter side, watching German TV is an excellent way to begin to understand the language and learn the German customs.

Living on the economy in rental housing can be a wonderful experience and, if you enjoy your privacy when you get off work, you most likely will find it living in a German neighborhood.

Helpful Hints. Your HRO will assist you with these matters, but here are a few things of which you should be aware:

- Payment of rent is in German currency (deutsch marks).
- Under German law, a verbal agreement is a valid contract.
- The German rule requires three months' written notice to terminate a lease. It is strongly recommended that you use the approved bilingual rental contract available at the HRO. This will allow a military tenant to terminate a rental contract with thirty days' written notice, or fifteen days if required.
- German law has provisions for the protection of tenants. If you receive a notice to vacate, or a rent increase, consult your HRO.
- It may be advisable for you to obtain insurance in case you are sued for apartment damage or your pet bites someone. Check with your legal assist-ance office. For your protection and the protection of your own furniture, you will probably want to obtain relatively inexpensive insurance, which can be combined with rental insurance coverage for your household goods.
- Germans are conservative and respect private and public property; they will expect you to do the same.

- Landlord house rules may limit your social activities, and late-night entertaining is usually not permitted. Loud playing of radios, TV, or stereo or other excessive noise is prohibited by law, particularly from 1300 to 1500 hours and after 2200 hours.

Furniture and Household Equipment. The type of family housing, furniture, and household equipment support provided to you in Europe depends largely on your eligibility and the location of your duty station. If you are assigned to a duty station in the United Kingdom, the Netherlands, Belgium, or Italy, you usually are authorized to ship your full Joint Federal Travel Regulation (JFTR) weight allowance. (See chapter 21, *Travel Allowances.*) If you are assigned to a duty station in Germany you normally will be authorized shipment of only a reduced weight allowance, referred to as the Administrative Weight Limitation (AWL). If your orders indicate that you are authorized to ship your full JFTR weight allowance, you can plan on receiving a refrigerator, range, washer, dryer, and dishwasher for your entire tour. You also can plan on using a loaner set of essential furniture items for a period of up to ninety days inbound and sixty days outbound, pending the arrival or after the shipment of your own household goods. You also will receive curtains, wardrobes, kitchen cabinets, and light fixtures if not built in or otherwise provided by your landlord. If your orders indicate that you are authorized only the AWL shipment, you will receive full government furnishings support in accordance with the Common Table of Allowance (CTA). This will include furniture for a complete kitchen, dining, and living room, and for the number of bedrooms you are authorized for your family. If you reside in private rental housing, this support will include light fixtures, wardrobes, and kitchen cabinets (if not provided by your landlord). In instances where an authorized item is not in stock, an additional weight allowance will be added to your orders to cover shipment of identical privately owned items. Be sure to include them in your household goods.

If you plan to live in private rental housing, you should bring anything you can use for storage space, such as small closets, kitchen cabinets, portable shelves, and hutches. Private rentals are usually not as well equipped for storage space as in CONUS.

Most Army Community Service Centers in Europe can lend you such items as cookware, kitchen utensils, flatware and chinaware, irons, ironing board, high chairs, baby cribs, and transformers until your own household goods arrive.

One bit of advice. If you haven't been to Europe before, contact someone who has for advice and assistance in making your shipping arrangements. Be sure to contact your sponsor. Since government furniture stock varies from community to community, your sponsor can advise you about furniture availability at your new station. Your sponsor also should be able to assist with information regarding typical apartment size and configuration, floor plans of standard government quarters, and advice about household goods you should ship or leave behind.

Electrical Appliances. Electrical power in Europe is 220-volt, 50-cycle, instead of the 110-volt, 60-cycle power we have in the United States. Because of this difference, caution must be exercised in the use of U.S. electrical appliances. You will need a transformer to step down the 220-volt power to operate 110-volt appliances. However, the transformer adjusts only the voltage, not the frequency. Thus, motor-driven appliances designed for use in the United States will operate at only five-sixths normal speed in Europe. Some appliances such as vacuum cleaners, electric razors, mixers, and blenders will operate satisfactorily at this reduced speed but not at peak efficiency. Others will not work at all. For example, an electric clock designed for use in the United States would lose ten minutes every hour when operating on European electric current. Most appliances with heating elements, such as toasters and irons, operate satisfactorily with a transformer. However, transformers are inconvenient, particularly in the larger sizes. Therefore, it is easier to leave at home those appliances that require a large transformer, such as coffeemakers, toasters, hair dryers, or irons, and purchase 220-volt appliances in Europe. These items are sold at military exchanges, thrift shops, and European retailers.

Following are a few general guidelines for the use of lamps and small appliances.

Lamps. Floor, desk, and table lamps that use incandescent bulbs can be used by changing to a 220-volt bulb and adding an inexpensive adapter plug to match the electrical outlet. (Bulbs and adapters are available at the PX.)

Televisions. American models must be modified by an electrician to receive European stations. This service is available at the PX. However, a modified color TV will receive European programs only in black and white. Some government housing areas receive American TV programs that are broadcast by the Armed Forces Network (AFN). Ask your sponsor about AFN reception. Dual voltage TV sets, which can receive color broadcasts from both European and American stations, may be purchased at the PX.

Video Recorders. Videos can record AFN TV broadcasts, but the clock timer will not operate properly. American movies are available through video clubs and Army stores. Only specially designed video recorders are equipped to record German TV signals.

Home Computers. These will operate with a transformer.

Radios, Stereos, Turntables, and Tape Decks. Radios and stereos work satisfactorily with transformers and receive both AFN and European stations. Turntables and tape decks can be modified to run at the proper speed.

Microwave Ovens. As a general rule, microwave ovens for use with 60-cycle power cannot be used at 50 cycles and will not operate properly with a transformer. A 60-cycle microwave oven may be damaged when used on 50-cycle power. Special microwave ovens that can be used in Europe and converted for use in the United States are available at the exchanges.

Clothing. You will need the same uniforms as would be required for duty in the United States. Uniforms may be purchased in Germany. The standard uniform for the large majority of soldiers in Europe is the battle dress uniform.

Civilian clothing is authorized for wear by all military personnel in Germany. It may be purchased at post exchanges or at German stores. Many excellent tailors are to be found. English textiles can readily be obtained.

Dependents are advised to take with them a complete wardrobe. Evening clothing is worn on occasion by both men and women.

Also advised is establishment of a mail-order account with a stateside department store. Mail-order service is also utilized in Germany through Sears Roebuck and Montgomery Ward. Mailing costs, owing to the APO system, are low.

Civilian clothing for men, women-and children is available at post exchanges.

The Currency Exchange Rate. For many years following World War II, American personnel in West Germany benefited from a very favorable, fixed exchange rate between the dollar and the deutsch mark. The effect was that items purchased on the local economy were very inexpensive in terms of dollars. In the late 1960s the fixed rate was abandoned and the dollar was allowed to "float" with market conditions. It slumped to about half its previous value, resulting in considerable hardship to military personnel and their families stationed in Germany. Although the dollar has recovered several times, current market conditions are again unfavorable. However, some entitlements have been established to minimize hardships due to the declining value of the dollar. A Cost of Living Allowance (COLA) is paid to all soldiers (except those in Greece and Turkey). The COLA, which is determined by base pay, number of command-sponsored dependents, and duty location, is paid to give soldiers the same spending power as CONUS-based soldiers of comparable grade, years of service, and number of dependents. An Overseas Housing Allowance (OHA) is paid to assist in renting/leasing private rental quarters. The amount is based on the actual rent paid, up to a ceiling determined by grade and duty location. Both allowances are reviewed twice-monthly by the DOD Per Diem Committee. If the currency rate of exchange changes by 3 percent or more, the OHA and COLA are adjusted accordingly.

Army and Air Force Exchange Service (AAFES). The Army and Air Force Exchange Service, Europe, operates an extensive chain of retail stores plus automotive, food, and personal services stores. Concessionaire-operated specialty shops featuring fine European crystal and china, furniture, gift items, and a host of other merchandise augment the main retail stores. Personal services include laundry and dry cleaning; barber, beauty, optical, floral, and tailor shops; car and equipment rentals; and much more. Overall, authorized AAFES customers are offered a wider selection of merchandise and services than their stateside counterparts because fewer congressional constraints apply to oversea exchanges.

The Privately Owned Automobile. An automobile for a family in Germany is a "must." It may be shipped from the United States for pickup at Bremerhaven or bought second hand from another American; you may purchase one of the many excellent English or European cars; or you may purchase certain American models through AAFES. Most service people recommend against shipping an American car. Maintenance and repairs are very expensive. A foreign car may be imported to the United States for personal use without paying an import tax. The individual, however, must pay transportation charges.

AAFES-Europe operates fifty-seven gasoline stations throughout the Federal Republic and West Berlin, including three stations on West Germany's autobahns. All stations dispense regular and premium gasoline; however, only a few offer diesel fuel. Payment at AAFES stations may be made in U.S. dollars or with coupons purchased through AAFES. The coupons may also be redeemed at BP, Fanal, and ESSO autobahn locations, and at most ESSO stations off the autobahn throughout Germany.

The operator is required to have the official USAREUR operator's license and meet the requirements as to physical condition, knowledge, and driving ability. Vehicles must meet safety standards and be registered. No vehicle may be registered unless covered by recognized liability insurance; in this connection, one of the several authorized companies is our own (mutual) United Services Automobile Association. (See chapter 9, *Financial Planning.*) The International Insurance Certificate ("Green Card") will be required if you plan to travel in countries other than West Germany. An international driver's license may also be required.

Germany provides good driving conditions on the autobahn, which is comparable to our best interstate highways, and on secondary roads, most of which are asphalt. Operators must learn the international road signs. AAFES operates repair shops and lubrication facilities and arranges for spare parts. However, AAFES cannot maintain a complete stock of repair parts for all cars.

Elementary and Secondary Schools. Education in kindergarten through grade twelve is provided for eligible dependents. Students from outlying areas are transported daily or live in dormitories. Quality of instruction and accreditation meet the standards of the North Central Association of Colleges and Secondary Schools. There are approximately 5,000 carefully selected American teachers.

College-Level Education. Opportunities abound for officers stationed in West Germany to continue their personal and professional development. College-level courses are offered at Army Education Centers at most USAREUR installations. Courses are offered by eight colleges and universities and include programs for certificates as well as associate, baccalaureate, and advanced degrees. There are opportunities to take vocational, academic, and technical courses. Credit hours acquired may be applied to degrees to be received overseas or used as transfer credit to colleges and universities in the United States.

Medical and Dental Facilities. Medical facilities comparable to those in the United States are available to military personnel and family members. It is advised that dental treatment be completed before travel to Germany. Dental care is provided; however, it is on a space-available basis for family members. All family members of USAREUR military personnel, including those family members who are not command-sponsored, are entitled to free medical care. Civilian medical care reimbursable under CHAMPUS (see chapter 9) is available for family members under certain circumstances.

Recreation and Club Activities. A tour in Germany provides an exciting opportunity to encounter different people and cultures; visit some of the world's most historic and scenic places; attend colorful folk festivals; sample delicious food and drink; or ski and mountain climb in the Alps. In addition to these unique aspects of overseas life, military personnel and their families can participate in most of the recreation and club activities available back home. There is a full range of on-base leisure activities, including team sports, theater, libraries, rod and gun clubs, multi-crafts, and so on. The U.S. Forces also operate vacation centers in Garmisch, Berchtesgaden, and Chiemsee, where the cost of staying in world-famous resorts is significantly reduced.

Family Support Program. In Germany there are a number of programs designed to cater to the special needs of Army family members. Army Community Service, the community's social service agency, helps individuals and families in everyday living situations, as well as during times of special need. Among its many programs are relocation assistance, consumer affairs, financial counseling, family member employment assistance, foster care, outreach programs, spouse and child abuse prevention, and so on. Other family support programs include Child Development Service and Youth Activities. Child Development Services are aimed at providing quality child development care at affordable, standardized prices in centers or in certified homes. The Youth Activities Program offers recreation activities to meet the interests and needs of school-age American youth in Germany.

Belgium (Supreme Headquarters Allied Powers Europe and the NATO/SHAPE Support Group). Much of the information concerning Germany applies also to these two organizations in Belgium. The NATO/SHAPE Support Group (80ASG) supports the U.S. military community in Belgium. The NSSG headquarters is located at Caserne Daumerie, about ten miles from SHAPE. Other NSSG offices are located at Chievres Air Base, at SHAPE, and in Brussels. Chievres Air Base has a base exchange and commissary. There are about 600 sets of family quarters on base at SHAPE Village for both officers and enlisted personnel. Housing at SHAPE Village is for all nationalities represented at SHAPE. About 2,500 units of housing are being rented by SHAPE members on the local economy. SHAPE International

School has an American elementary and secondary section. SHAPE has a nursery school and childcare center.

JAPAN

Most U.S. Army installations and troop units on mainland Japan are in the area southwest of Tokyo, convenient to both Yokohama and Tokyo. The climate is very similar to Washington, D.C. Substantial snowfalls are rare; June and September are rainy; and the summers are hot and humid. The climate in Okinawa is more tropical. See DA Pam 608-10 and USARJ Pam 360-1.

Concurrent Travel. Except for officers in grades 0-6 and above, who are automatically authorized concurrent travel, approval of dependent travel at government expense is based on availability of government housing or approved private rental housing.

Family Quarters. With the exception of Akizuki Ammunition Depot, all government quarters in Japan are on or near the installations. Single and unaccompanied officers are housed in BOQs. Officers are required to occupy government housing when it is available. Family quarters are attractive and comfortable, although slightly smaller than the average American home. There are large, well-equipped play areas for children; chapels; theaters; clubs; and post exchange, recreational, and hobby facilities. As of this update, every Army location within Japan has, as a minimum, a commissary annex. The Armed Forces Radio and Television Service provides radio and television broadcasts.

Mainland Japan is a weight-restricted area; you will be allowed to ship 25 percent of your weight allowance. (See chapter 21, *Travel Allowances.*) Standard furniture items, stove and refrigerator, washers and dryers, and air conditioners are government-furnished.

Infant furniture is not furnished by the government but is available from ACS on a temporary loan basis.

The electrical current is 50 cycles, 120 volts. Many electrical appliances can be adjusted or are set by the manufacturer for 50/60 cycles, and will run fine. Some 60-cycle items that do not operate correctly are clocks, some record or tape players, and some appliances with heating elements.

Side-by-side refrigerator/freezers are available for large families. If you own a freezer, there is no restriction against bringing it, but remember that your quarters may not be as large as your present home, and you may wish to use your allowable weight for other items. Microwave ovens that can be converted from 60 to 50 cycles are readily available through the post exchange. If your microwave is not convertible, you may want to consider storing it during your tour.

DODDS. Your children will attend Department of Defense Dependent Schools (DODDS), either on your installation or on a neighboring (perhaps sister-service) installation.

Child-Care Facilities. Almost every Army installation in Japan has, or has access to, a certified child-care facility. Many of the facilities are brand-new or recently renovated. The Army has also recently started a program certifying in-home caregivers. See ACS upon your arrival.

Private Automobiles. Japan has an embargo against foreign vehicles. Non-Japanese cars built after March 1976 are not allowed to enter the country. Used Japanese cars are readily available and are normally inexpensive. Driving in Japan is on the left side of the road, and it is much easier to learn to drive on the left with a car designed for that purpose. All privately owned vehicles must be registered with the Japanese government and with the Provost Marshal. Liability insurance is mandatory in amounts of $5,000/$10,000/$15,000. A Japanese compulsory insurance law requires vehicle owners to purchase Japanese insurance in addition to liability coverage.

Any driver's license you may possess is invalid on U.S. installations in Japan; however, it makes you eligible to receive a U.S. Forces Operator's Permit after passing a written test on local traffic laws and regulations. Family members below the age of eighteen may not drive off post.

Currency and Banking. The U.S. dollar is the authorized currency on all U.S. installations in Japan. The local currency (yen) can be purchased at each installation for transactions on the economy.

Military banking facilities furnish all expected services, although you may wish to retain your stateside account. Credit unions also are available.

Adult Education. U.S. installations in Japan offer educational opportunities at all levels. Students may complete their GED or pursue an associate's/bachelor's/advanced degree through American colleges that offer classes overseas. The Education Center will answer all your questions and assist you in setting up an individual program.

Medical/Dental Care. Military health-care facilities are comparable to those found in the United States. In addition to military personnel and their family members, health care is available to Department of the Army civilians and their families on a pay basis.

Pets. Pets must be shipped by commercial carrier at the owner's expense. The pet may accompany the owner or be shipped at a later time. Although there is no quarantine period, there are specific immunization and health certificate requirements that must be met. Coordination with your sponsor is important to ensure proper information on the requirements. Also, pets accompanying the owners must in most instances be boarded, due to restrictions while in temporary government housing.

Domestic Help. Domestic help is available. Costs depend on the yen-dollar exchange rate.

Passport. A passport is required by each dependent family member.

Civilian Clothing. Military personnel are authorized to wear civilian clothing after duty hours and as regulations permit.

Recreation and Culture. USARJ offers a wealth of activities. Facilities include fitness centers, lighted athletic fields, tennis courts, handball/racquetball courts, swimming pools, bowling alleys, skeet ranges, golf courses, and driving ranges. There are many associations and clubs, arts and crafts facilities, organized youth activities, and scouting. Travel offices are available to arrange trips in Japan and the Far East.

Family Member Employment. There are opportunities throughout USARJ for family member employment. Recent regulatory changes ensure that family members are given priority consideration in filling many vacancies. While certain occupational specialties have few openings, volunteer positions exist that allow skills to be maintained while overseas.

Sponsorship Program. USARJ has a very active sponsorship program. Shortly after receiving your orders, you will be receiving a letter and welcome packet from your sponsor. Make the program work for you—write your sponsor immediately to acknowledge the letter and to ask for any further information you may need.

KOREA

In most of metropolitan Korea, living approaches a near-western style. The climate is four-seasonal and similar to that of the eastern seaboard of the United States. DA Pam 608-15, *Helpful Hints for Personnel Ordered to the Eighth U.S. Army, Korea,* contains information that most service members have found useful. Another excellent source of information is a booklet published by the Public Affairs Office, U.S. Forces, Korea, entitled *KOREA—Your new assignment.* This booklet, along with other orientation material, is included in the official Army Community Services welcome packet.

Military Activities. There are four major military commands headquartered in Korea. The United Nations Command monitors the Military Armistice that ended the Korean conflict in 1953. Subordinate to that, the Combined Forces Command (ROK/US) combines Korean and American military units in defense of the Republic of Korea. The U.S. component of Combined Forces Command is the U.S. Forces Korea, which includes U.S. Army, Air Force, Navy, and Marine units. Eighth U.S. Army units comprise the ground forces element of USFK. ROK Army enlisted personnel are assigned duty with Eighth Army under the Korean Augmentation to the U.S. Army (or KATUSA) program.

The major subordinate Army commands include the U.S. element of the Combined Field Army, 2nd Infantry Division, and 19th Support Command. Other supporting elements include 1st Signal Brigade, the 501st MI Brigade, JUSMAG-K, and the USA Support Group, Joint Security Area.

Many staff and troop duties involve close coordination with members of the ROK military.

Command Sponsorship. Of the approximately 40,000 military positions in Korea, only about 3,000 are "command-sponsored" two-year tours, which permit service members to bring their families at government expense and allow the full range of government benefits for them during the tour. Living on a military base in a command-sponsored status is very similar to living in a military community in the states.

Bringing family members on unaccompanied tours is officially discouraged and may cause extreme financial hardship and stress on all concerned.

Noncommand-sponsored personnel who bring their family members to Korea do so at their own expense and are not eligible for transportation reimbursement or additional housing allowances. Depending on location, noncommand-sponsored family members may only receive medical and dental care on a "space-available" or "emergency care" basis. Only command-sponsored personnel are authorized ration control privileges, which control access to the PX and commissary, as well as the purchase of alcohol, cigarettes, baby items, and gasoline. If the family members are not command-sponsored, the sponsor's ration control spending limits are limited to approximately $300 per month in the commissary and exchange combined. All other shopping must be done on the economy.

Housing. Government family quarters are limited and are available only in Yongsan, Taegu, Osan, Pusan, and Chinhae, and only to command-sponsored families in those locations. Waiting lists are kept for each grade category and are subdivided into bedroom categories. Travel of command-sponsored family members to Korea will generally be deferred until adequate housing will be available within ten days of arrival.

Many command-sponsored families live comfortably in off-post Korean communities. Western-style economy housing is scarce and expensive. Rents of up to $800 per month and security deposits of up to $3,500 are common; however, command-sponsored families may receive increased housing allowances to help offset the additional cost. Also, the Finance Office will loan money for the security deposit, which must be repaid prior to departure. Contact the housing office at your gaining unit for more detailed information.

Education. There are fifteen education centers serving U.S. Army personnel in Korea. The centers offer a variety of high school, vocational, and military programs. Undergraduate and graduate degree programs are available through on-post offices of the Universities of Maryland, Southern California, Oklahoma, and Texas for service members of all ranks and their family members.

Command-sponsored children in grades kindergarten through twelfth are guaranteed tuition-free schooling provided by the Department of Defense Dependent School System in on-post schools. DoD schools are similar to the better public schools throughout the United States. Teachers are fully certified and all DoD schools are fully accredited.

Noncommand-sponsored dependent children of DoD personnel assigned to Taegu, Pusan, and Chinhae may enroll in DoD schools on a space-available basis. There are three private schools available in the Seoul area. Annual tuition costs for these private schools range from $2,500 to $5,000.

Preschools are available in Taegu and Yongsan.

Banking and Currency. The dollar is used in all U.S. military facilities, while the Korean "won" must be used for all transactions off-post.

The American Express Bank provides full banking services on many military installations, and mobile banking vans provide service in other locations. The United Services of America Federal Credit Union also has branches on many installations. Check-cashing services are available at these two institutions and at the PX and military clubs throughout the Republic.

Recreational and Cultural Activities. The Community, Family, and Soldier Support Command Korea (CFS) provides a wide range of activities for soldiers and their families throughout the Republic of Korea. CFS conducts an extensive program at both remote and large sites, providing entertainment, physical fitness, athletic competition, tour and travel, library services, recreation centers, arts and crafts centers, and all other quality-of-life programs.

The extensive athletic competition for adults includes company-, post-, and service-level competition in a year-round sports program. In Seoul, Pusan, and Taegu, CFS also conducts an extensive youth activities and sports program.

Tour and travel centers throughout the peninsula offer low-cost package tours to both in-country and out-of-country locations. The extensive Army club system offers social and leisure activities, good food at reasonable prices, and both local and stateside entertainment.

Korea is a country that truly welcomes Americans and provides many opportunities for cultural exchange, understanding, and friendship. These include subsidized tours around Korea, cultural shows, outdoor activities, visits to the homes of Korean families, and a Reunion in Korea program that allows family members to visit service members stationed in Korea.

Americans have access to up-to-the-minute news and entertainment through American Forces Korea Network radio and TV and *Pacific Stars and Stripes* daily newspaper. Most military units also publish a newspaper to keep their audience informed of on-post activities and military news.

Part Three • Building Your Career

12

Professional Development

The Army provides for its officers of all grades exceptional opportunities for development of their own potentials which may lead with relative certainty into rewarding assignments of importance to the nation. The programs for professional development have been improved progressively by the best talent in this complex field. You are certain to benefit if you study the total program as presented briefly in this chapter and strive to take maximum advantage of your opportunity. The prime purpose of this chapter is to assist you as a junior officer in the beginning and early years of your service in advancing your career progress.

The official documents DA Pam 600-3, *Commissioned Officer Professional Development and Utilization* or DA Pam 600-11, *Warrant Officer Professional Development,* should be obtained from your unit personnel officer, studied, and believed, and pertinent material should be extracted for your personal file. Copies of these important documents are updated regularly and published in the *Officer Ranks Personnel Update.*

There are differences in the professional development programs for commissioned officers and warrant officers, arising principally from differences in their utilization. The commissioned officer is expected to be a leader first but with particular areas of expertise in which these leadership qualities may be employed. The warrant officer is expected to be highly skilled in a particular technical area or areas and to serve repetitive assignments in positions utilizing these skills. In view of these differences, as well as differences in the accession path, in schooling, in promotion, and in other areas, information pertaining specifically to warrant officers is gathered in chapter 16, *Special for Warrant Officers.*

There are related subjects in this program of professional development. The chapters listed here relate directly to the subject, and their study along with this chapter is urged. These are matters of extreme importance in gaining total understanding of the surest and quickest way to achieve a successful Army career.

Chapter 3: *The Code of the Army Officer.* This is your foundation.

Chapter 4: *The Officer Image.* You must earn a good one.

Chapter 13: *Army Schools and Career Progress.* Opportunity is abundant.

Chapter 14: *Evaluation Reports.* Strive to deserve the best.

Chapter 15: *Promotion.* Above lieutenant and CW2, it is for the "best qualified."

Chapter 26: *Resignation and Elimination.* There are ways out.

RESPONSIBILITIES FOR PROFESSIONAL DEVELOPMENT

Officer professional development is the result of the combined efforts of (1) the individual officer, (2) the officer's commander, (3) the career field proponent, and (4) the Officer Personnel Management Directorate (OPMD) at the Total Army Personnel Agency (TAPA).* Each of these plays an important part in helping the individual officer develop his or her full potential so as to achieve the maximum in satisfaction from an Army career and to make the maximum contribution toward accomplishing the Army's mission.

In order to take full advantage of the opportunities that are available for your professional development, you must understand the role and functions of OPMD and of the proponent for your career field. It is essential that you understand the responsibilities placed upon your immediate commander. But most of all, you must understand what you are expected to do about your own career development and how you should go about it. With an understanding of these four areas of responsibility, of which your own is the base, you can proceed into your Army service with knowledge of how your career may be developed.

Let us briefly examine these four supporting elements for officer professional development to understand how they interact to achieve the goals of the program. Later we will examine each in more detail.

The Department of the Army, through its Officer Personnel Management Directorate (OPMD) at the Total Army Personnel Agency (TAPA), provides the overall framework within which officers' careers are managed. Assignment managers and professional development officers at OPMD are available to provide valuable and realistic assistance to individual officers regarding their careers. You may obtain counseling from OPMD regarding your overall performance and a subjective evaluation of how you stand relative to your peers. You may obtain guidance on what actions you should take to better qualify yourself for desired future assignments. You are encouraged to contact your assignment manager at OPMD by telephone, in writing, or by a personal visit.

Each of the officer career fields, as described later in this chapter, has a proponent assigned in accordance with AR 600-3. For the branch career fields, the proponent generally is the branch service school. The proponents establish professional development guidelines for their respective career fields. They determine which career fields are required for particular duties and the minimum training requirements for each career field. The proponents communicate routinely with

---

*In October 1987, the Total Army Personnel Agency (TAPA) was formed as a major field agency operating under the direction of the Deputy Chief of Staff for Personnel at the Department of the Army. TAPA was formed from, and replaces, the Military Personnel Center (MILPERCEN), but it has expanded functions. The Officer Personnel Management Directorate (OPMD) of what was MILPERCEN is now the OPMD of TAPA.

their constituents, and they forecast the professional development needs of their career fields for the future.

Your commanding officer plays a vital role in your professional development. Your commander normally is your rater (see chapter 14, *Evaluation Reports*) and is charged with evaluating your performance of duty. Armed with knowledge of the requirements of your chosen career field, your duty performance, and your potential for future assignments, your commander can advise you about actions you should take regarding future assignments and schools. He or she may be able to reassign you to different duties within the unit so that you may obtain needed experience. Counseling sessions with your commander should help reveal any weak areas in your performance or professional capabilities that require special attention on your part. You should actively seek the advice and counsel of your commander.

The Army, through the OPMD at TAPA, provides the means for your professional development; the proponent establishes the guidelines for the overall development pattern you should follow in your chosen career field; and your commander can provide counseling and advice regarding your performance and your career needs. But all of this will be of little benefit unless you take a personal interest and an active role in your professional development. You are the one who must establish goals for yourself, and you are the one who must do the studying and seek the training and assignments desired to allow you to attain those goals.

REACH FOR THE TOP

In this matter of goal setting, you should be aware of two important facts. First, a considerable portion of the Army's career officers can legitimately aspire to attain positions of responsibility for very large and very important enterprises that require the highest levels of leadership and managerial skills. Except for the Army's sister services, there is no other large professional group in our society that has such extensive opportunities to undertake tasks of maximum importance. As you begin your Army career, there is no reason you should not aspire to reach these high levels. You will be afforded ample opportunity to develop your capabilities, so that when the time comes you will be able to discharge these important duties in an exemplary manner.

Second, you must recognize that our Army is competitive. While there is room at the top for a large number of officers, there is not room for all who begin an Army career. Above the grade of lieutenant, promotion is by central selection. (See chapter 15, *Promotion.*) Students attending the senior service colleges are chosen from among the best qualified. The more important assignments to command and staff or to managerial or other major missions are made on a "best-qualified" basis after a thorough comparison of the records and capabilities of the available officers. Selection by qualification is utilized far more often than selection by seniority. Thus, as your Army career develops, you will be in competition with your brother and sister officers for the more desirable assignments. If you are to be selected for such assignments, your Official Military Personnel File (OMPF) will have to indicate that you are among the best qualified of your peers.

Regarding this matter of competition with your peers, as used here the term does not mean that you have to win or to beat someone. It means that you *will* have to make the most of the opportunities that will be offered so you develop both a record and a reputation as a highly qualified, competent officer. Remember that any assignment you undertake will be with other officers, noncommissioned officers, soldiers, and civilians. To be successful, you will have to develop teamwork with your own commander and his or her staff, within your own unit, with your peers in adjacent units, and with your subordinate units or individuals. The good will of subordinates, seniors, and associates is a vital ingredient in any person's program for success. Choose your own goals, qualify early for the prerequisite steps, and compete strongly, but very fairly.

OFFICER PERSONNEL MANAGEMENT SYSTEM (OPMS)

Beginning during World War II and in all the years that have followed, the Army has been in the midst of a continually accelerating technological revolution. One has only to review the changes that have taken place in aviation, or in communications, or in the development and use of the computer to understand how great these changes have been. These changes have had an impact on the Army and its sister services at least as great as, and perhaps greater than, the impact on our country's business and industrial community.

Technological changes have had a profound impact upon the Army's officer corps. With each new development, each advanced capability, the Army has needed officers who were specially trained and able to understand the new capabilities and to use them correctly and efficiently. This need has not been confined to the technical fields and advances in weaponry. There have been corollary requirements for improved logistics management, intelligence functions, and communications as well. The warrant officers with their special skills have filled much of the need for specialists, as evidenced by the fact that about 14 percent of the active duty officers in today's Army are warrant officers.

However, there also has been a need for commissioned officer specialists, and during the quarter century following World War II the Army encouraged qualified commissioned officers to participate in various specialist programs such as logistics, research and development, atomic energy, or aviation. During this period, officer assignments were controlled by the officer's basic branch, and each commissioned officer was expected to maintain proficiency in his basic branch. That is, the officer was expected to remain "branch-qualified." This included serving tours of duty in the type assignments followed by other members of his branch, including serving the requisite tours in command of troops.

As the years passed and the need for specialists expanded, it became increasingly apparent that a commissioned officer really could not be expected to be a specialist in one particular area of Army need while still maintaining complete branch proficiency. During tours spent in a specialty assignment, the individual officer tended to lose touch with what his branch was doing, while during tours with his branch to maintain proficiency in that area, he tended to lose touch with advances in his specialty area. The result was that many fine officers found themselves in positions where they not only were behind in their specialty but also were not really equipped to perform all of the duties that may have been required of officers of their grade and branch. The situation was further compounded by a promotion system that failed to recognize that officers in specialty assignments had little opportunity for troop command assignments.

In an effort to correct this problem, in 1970, under the direction of the Deputy Chief of Staff for Personnel, a study of the officer corps was undertaken. The study results indicated that in an era of decreasing size of the Army, a skill imbalance in the officer corps was developing. There were continually increasing needs for officer specialists of various types, and there were decreasing opportunities for commissioned officers to command the fewer Army units. At the same time, however, the promotion system still encouraged generalization and emphasized command duty.

A need for change was identified both to improve the professionalism and at the same time enhance the career satisfaction of the Army's officers. The result was a basic change in the way the Army managed its officer corps, through adoption of the Officer Personnel Management System (OPMS) in April 1972. After a several-year transition period, OPMS became fully implemented in 1975.

The Officer Personnel Management System encompasses all policies and procedures by which commissioned officers are procured, trained, assigned, developed, evaluated, promoted, and separated from active duty. It is the Army's reaction to the rapidly changing technological environment with its attendant demands for increasing expertise; to changing attitudes toward specialization and job satisfaction among younger career officers; to the need to assure equitable opportunity for advancement among officers serving in diverse career fields; and last, to the increased challenges of troop command, coupled with more limited command opportunities in a smaller Army.

As instituted in 1975, the heart of OPMS was dual specialty professional development. Each commissioned officer, upon entry to active duty, was assigned an initial entry, or accession specialty. Then, by about the eighth year of service, each officer was also assigned an additional specialty. The intent was that officers would maintain proficiency in each of the specialties and could be assigned to duties requiring either. Branch affiliation was of secondary importance.

Over time, this led to a situation where certain officers, particularly those in the technical specialties, were having difficulty because of competing demands of schooling and assignment requirements. In addition, the dual specialty program had weakened the officer's ties with his or her branch. Indeed, many officers were assigned to specialties monitored by two different branches. A major review of the program was undertaken in 1983, and the results of the study were approved in 1984. The approved changes are now being implemented; they are evolutionary in nature and are scheduled to be fully implemented by 1989.

Under the revised OPMS, officers will be affiliated with only one branch. Most officers will remain assigned to their entry branch, although transfers are permitted. Indeed, since relatively fewer combat arms officers are needed in the higher grades as compared to the need for senior officers in the combat support and combat service support branches, combat arms officers may be required to transfer branches unless there are an adequate number of volunteers for such transfer.

The term *functional areas* now describes what previously were classed as non-accession additional specialties. Functional areas are not related to any specific branch. The terms relating to specialties have been eliminated. Officers are now classified according to Branch, Functional Area, and Skill, and with Areas of Concentration within branches and functional areas. These terms are defined and described on the accompanying chart.

The new system provides for two types of career patterns. Some officers may now follow a single-track pattern in which they serve repetitive assignments in their branch. Most will follow a dual-track pattern where they serve in assignments in both their branch and their functional area. During the early years of service, professional development and development of skills associated with the officer's branch are emphasized. Later, a functional area is assigned. All officers will have had an opportunity to select a career pattern and to indicate a preference for functional area designation by the end of their seventh year of service.

Some officers may elect to single-track in their functional area. This normally would occur after the seventh year of service but could occur earlier depending upon the officer's qualifications and special training. The revised OPMS incorporates the concept of *primacy,* which acknowledges that during an officer's early career, qualification in his or her branch is the primary development objective. It

OPMS—DEFINITIONS, DESCRIPTIONS, AND CRITERIA

Branch	Functional Area	Skill
• Group of officers by arm or service	• Group of officers by career field other than arm or service	• Can be related to more than one branch or functional area
• Means of accessing	• Not a means of accessing	
• Interrelated grouping of tasks and skills	• Interrelated grouping of tasks and skills	• Specialized skill required to perform duties of specific position
• Requires significant education, training and experience	• Usually requires significant education, training and experience	• May require significant education, training and experience
• Repetitive tours	• Repetitive tours	• Repetitive tours not required
• Permits progressive assignments from LT to COL	• Permits progressive assignments from LT/CPT/MAJ to COL	• Progressive assignments from LT to COL not required
• Identifies principal position designator and officer possessing those skills	• Identifies principal position designator and officer possessing those skills	• Identifies specialized skill required to perform duties of specific position, or an officer possessing that skill
• An officer will serve only in one branch	• An officer may be assigned only one functional area	• An officer may have more than one skill
(Example: IN, MI, QM)	(Example: R&D, FAO, Procurement)	(Example: Airborne, Recruiter, Language)

Area of Concentration
• Area of expertise within a branch or functional area
• Identifies officer possessing requisite expertise
• An officer may serve in more than one area of concentration
  (Example: MECH IN, STRATEGIC INTELL, PETROLEUM MGT)

also recognizes that later in a career, primacy may have to shift from the branch to the functional area.

The revision to OPMS also recognizes that many positions in the Army require officers possessing only general military qualifications; that is, no special skills or expertise are needed to fill those positions other than the general qualifications of an officer. These positions are now coded as Branch Immaterial and may be filled by any officer. Positions requiring a general knowledge of the combat arms are coded as Combat Arms Immaterial and may be filled by any Infantry, Armor, Field Artillery, Air Defense Artillery, Aviation, or Engineer officer. Similarly, positions requiring a general knowledge of logistics are coded as Logistics Immaterial and may be filled by officers from the Ordnance Corps, Transportation Corps, or Quartermaster Corps; while positions requiring a general knowledge of personnel are coded Personnel Immaterial and may be filled by officers from the Adjutant General Corps or those whose functional area is Personnel Management.

Conversely, the revised OPMS also recognizes that some positions require special expertise. Therefore, TOE (Tables of Organization and Equipment) battalion staff positions are coded to require officers from the branch of the battalion for the S1, S3, and S4 positions, and a Military Intelligence officer for the S2 position. The battalion C-E (communications-electronics) officer will be a Signal Corps officer, and the battalion chemical officer will be from the Chemical Corps.

The purpose of OPMS is to enhance the effectiveness and professionalism of the officer corps. Within limits of the Army's needs, it also provides the mechanism to take advantage of the wide diversity of aptitudes and interests of the individual officers. OPMS applies to all of the Army's officers except those in the Judge

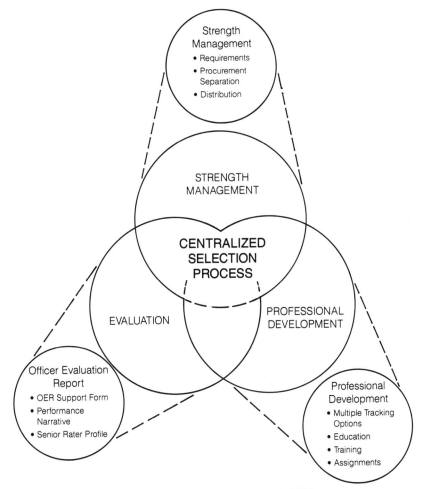

OFFICER PERSONNEL MANAGEMENT SYSTEM.

Advocate General Corps and the Chaplain Corps. Each of these branches has its own professional development program.

The Officer Personnel Management Directorate (OPMD), which is responsible for the implementation of OPMS, has four primary objectives:

1. To access officers in the right numbers and right skills to meet Army requirements.

2. To develop the professional capabilities of officers through planned schooling and progressive assignments.

3. To assign officers to meet Army requirements.

4. To separate officers to meet individual and Army needs.

Interrelated with these objectives are the three major subsystems of OPMS shown on the accompanying chart. These include everything that is done from the time an officer is brought on active duty until he or she separates from the service.

These subsystems are interactive, and a major change in one subsystem may result in a reaction within another subsystem. The centralized selection process plays a major role in OPMS and is closely interrelated with these three subsystems.

Branches and Functional Areas. Within OPMS, a male officer may be assigned to any one of sixteen branches when he enters the Army. (Note that Special Forces is a non-accession branch.) After completion of initial branch training and development of branch skills, the officer may then request one of thirteen functional areas for further development. Together, these branches and functional areas, as shown on the accompanying chart, comprise the career fields that are available to the Army's officers. An officer may be assigned to only one branch and to only one functional area, although a request for branch or functional area transfer may be made in accordance with AR 614-100. Female officers are eligible for assignment to all functional areas and to all branches except Infantry, Armor, and Special Forces. They also are prohibited from serving in positions whose incumbents may be involved in close combat and in certain battalion-size units. Except for these restrictions, female officers have the same professional education and assignment opportunities as male officers.

COMMISSIONED OFFICER CAREER FIELDS

Code	Branches	Code	Functional Areas
11	Infantry	41	Personnel Programs Management Staff
12	Armor		
13	Field Artillery	45	Comptroller
14	Air Defense Artillery	46	Public Affairs
15	Aviation	47	USMA Permanent Faculty
18	Special Forces*	48	Foreign Area Officer
21	Corps of Engineers	49	Operations Research/Systems Analysis
25	Signal Corps	50	Force Development
31	Military Police Corps	51	Research and Development
35	Military Intelligence Corps	52	Nuclear Weapons
38	Civil Affairs (RC only)	53	Systems Automation Officer
42	Adjutant General Corps		
44	Finance Corps	54	Operations, Plans, and Training
74	Chemical Corps		
91	Ordnance Corps	97	Contracting and Industrial Management
92	Quartermaster Corps		
95	Transportation Corps	99	Combat Procurement

*Non-Accession Branch

PROFESSIONAL DEVELOPMENT PLANNING AT THE DEPARTMENT OF THE ARMY

The Officer Personnel Management System is administered by the Department of the Army through the Total Army Personnel Agency (TAPA), which functions under the Army Staff supervision of the Deputy Chief of Staff for Personnel. The internal organization of TAPA includes an Officer Personnel Management Directorate (OPMD) and an Enlisted Personnel Management Directorate. An organization chart of the OPMD accompanies this discussion.

The OPMD has nine divisions, seven of which are directly concerned with officer development and assignments, and two of which, plus an Administrative Support Office and a Special Actions and Information Management Office, are in a general support role for the Directorate. The Directorate handles the monitoring and assignment of all of the Army's officers except for those assigned to the Judge

Advocate General Corps and the Chaplain Corps. Officers of these branches are controlled by their own branch.

The *Combat Arms Division* of OPMD has six branches. The Infantry Branch, Armor Branch, Aviation Branch, Field Artillery Branch, Air Defense Artillery Branch, and Special Forces Branch each monitor officers of all grades, from lieutenant through lieutenant colonel, who are assigned to that branch. Similarly, the *Combat Support Arms Division* monitors officers assigned to the Combat Support Arms branches of that division, and the branches of the *Combat Service Support Division* monitor officers assigned to those branches. From the time an officer is selected for promotion to colonel, monitoring responsibility is passed to the *Colonels Division,* which monitors the assignment of all colonels, regardless of branch assignment. The *Functional Area Management and Development Division* (FAMDD) monitors the assignment and development of officers in their designated functional areas. The *Health Services Division* monitors all officers, regardless of grade, who are assigned to one of the six corps of the Army Medical Department. The *Warrant Officers Division* is responsible for monitoring the development and assignment of all of the Army's warrant officers controlled by OPMD.

At times, the four objectives of OPMD (mentioned earlier), with due regard for the expressed desires of the individual, will seem in conflict with one another. The worldwide missions and duties assigned to the Army must be performed, and this requires the assignment of qualified individuals in numbers sufficient to do the job. Despite conflicting requirements and new missions requiring officers, the assignment officers of OPMD strive for a high degree of officer satisfaction by carefully weighing every consideration in making each assignment. The need for an equitable means of ensuring that one group of officers is not exposed to undue hardship, in comparison with others, is a daily concern. In these troubled years, we must face the inescapable fact of occasional conflicts in Army requirements, career management planning, and officer desires. The work of the Army must be done. But the desires and needs of the individual are considered, if disclosed to the OPMD by statement of preference, and where circumstances permit, they are observed.

Capable people are assigned to perform these selective tasks, and officers may feel complete confidence that assignment selections are made objectively, wholly on their merits, with the best interests of the individual and the Army thoroughly considered.

Professional Development Phases. There are five phases of professional development that are managed by OPMD. Related to grade levels, each phase contains assignment, training, and education opportunities aimed at certain broad objectives, including qualifying for promotion to the next higher grade. Necessarily, the phases are somewhat flexible, depending on Army requirements and each officer's capabilities and demonstrated performance. In addition, there are variations depending upon the branch or functional area of assignment. DA Pam 600-3, *Officer Professional Development and Utilization,* contains typical assignment patterns for each of the branch and functional area career fields.

Lieutenant Phase. This phase starts upon entry to active duty and lasts until promotion to captain at about three and a half years of service. It includes attendance at the branch officer basic course, which provides instruction related to the overall mission and function of the officer's branch, along with technical instruction that equips each officer with the detailed knowledge and required skills associated with the branch. Some officers may receive additional training such as Ranger or Airborne or both during this phase. Initial assignments should allow the officer to apply branch school training and to develop leadership skills. Each officer

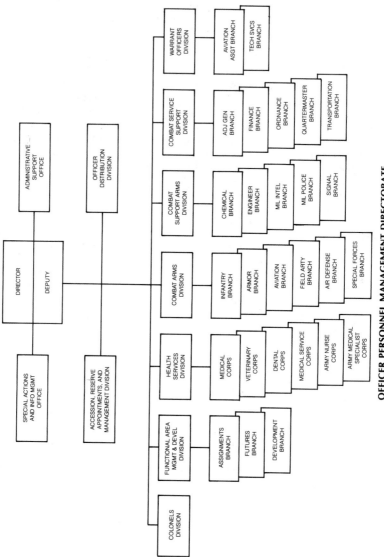

OFFICER PERSONNEL MANAGEMENT DIRECTORATE.

should seek duty in troop units as a means of acquiring an understanding of Army operations and military life that will provide the foundation for future service. During the basic course, officers are counseled by representatives of their branch regarding professional development goals and personal factors that should be considered when requesting future assignments and schooling.

Captain Phase. This phase runs from about three and a half years to ten years of commissioned service. The objectives of this phase are to continue development in the officer's branch and perhaps in a functional area, while continuing to grow in practical leadership experience and professional knowledge. Attendance at the advanced course for their branch is the normal expectancy for most officers, although some may attend the advanced course of another branch. Prior to completion of the seventh year of service, officers will be queried regarding their preferences for a career pattern and functional area. Assignment of a functional area is based upon the officer's desires and qualifications, consistent with the Army's needs.

Following attendance at an advanced course, each officer also will complete the Combined Arms and Services Staff School (CAS³) while in the grade of captain. This includes a nonresident course of instruction followed by a resident phase at Fort Leavenworth on TDY status prior to the tenth year of commissioned service. Each officer should strive to serve as a company commander during this phase, or in a similar position of authority commensurate with the officer's branch. Some officers may be assigned to immaterial assignments during this phase, but generally only after they have completed their branch qualification.

Major Phase. The major phase runs from about the tenth year to the sixteenth year of service. The objective of this phase is for the officer to continue development in his or her branch and to be utilized in his or her functional area, if designated. Assignments will be to positions of increasing responsibility where previously developed skills can be applied. Officers should seek assignments in new environments that will require the application of the abilities they have developed.

Approximately 50 percent of each year group of officers will attend the Command and General Staff College (CGSC) at Fort Leavenworth during this phase, or a comparable Command and Staff College of another service. Other officers may complete the CGSC course by nonresident instruction. Some of the resident students at Fort Leavenworth may remain for a second year to continue their military studies through the Advanced Military Studies Program. Completion of these courses will prepare officers to serve as commanders and staff officers and for promotion to lieutenant colonel.

Lieutenant Colonel Phase. This phase starts at about the sixteenth year of service and runs until about the twenty-second year of service. The objectives during this phase are to continue to advance in attainment of the professional objectives of the officer's branch and functional area, and to demonstrate potential for assuming positions of greater responsibility. Assignments during this phase will be to progressively more responsible and challenging positions commensurate with demonstrated performance, ability, and potential. About 30 percent of the eligible officers will attend the Army War College (AWC) or another Senior Service College during this phase. Some officers may be selected to complete the AWC studies by correspondence course. The purpose of these studies is to prepare officers for highest level command and staff duties. Education during this phase stresses the development of managerial skills and techniques.

Colonel Phase. This phase starts at about the twenty-second year of service and lasts for the remainder of the officer's career unless he or she attains general officer rank. The objective of this phase is maximum utilization of each officer's technical abilities, managerial skills, and executive talents in positions of high responsibility and leadership in his or her designated career field or career fields. There are additional opportunities for special training or additional schooling during this phase, as explained in chapter 13, *Army Schools and Career Progress.*

Professional Development Opportunities. The accompanying chart presents the overall professional development opportunities available to officers. It is necessarily general in nature. Typical assignment patterns that might be followed by an officer assigned to a specific branch or functional area are contained in DA Pam 600-3.

These assignment patterns provide guidance in officer assignments. They show each officer the program appropriate in his or her case and indicate the type assignments to seek to advance personal progress. They are also a guide to field commanders and supervisors, as well as to officers of the OPMD in Washington, in the assignment of officers.

The goal is so easily overlooked in our interest in details, we shall look at it again: The purpose of the Army is the nation's security. If war should come, the Army's purpose is the restoration of peace with the defeat of our enemies. All our people of the armed forces, our weapons, and our equipment are provided by our government so our citizens may practice in safety the arts of peace.

PROPONENT RESPONSIBILITIES

Within the guidelines established by the Department of the Army through its OPMS for overall professional development and utilization of officers, proponent agencies are tasked with developing specific guidelines for development and assignment of officers in specific career fields. Personnel proponents are assigned their responsibilities by AR 600-3. For the seventeen branch career fields, the proponent agencies are the appropriate branch schools, except that the Office of the Quartermaster General is the assigned proponent for the Quartermaster career field and the JFK Special Warfare Center is the assigned proponent for the Special Forces and Civil Affairs career fields. Proponents for the functional areas are logically selected, with the Signal Center charged with proponency of the Systems Automation Officer (FA:53); and the AG School with proponency for Personnel Programs Management Staff (FA:41). The Comptroller of the Army, the Office of the Chief of Public Affairs, and the U.S. Military Academy are proponents for the Comptroller (FA:45), Public Affairs (FA:46), and USMA Permanent Faculty (FA:47), respectively. The Combined Arms Center at Fort Leavenworth is the proponent for Operations Research/Systems Analysis (FA:49), Force Development (FA:50), Nuclear Weapons (FA:52), Operations, Plans, and Training (FA:53), and Combat Development (FA:99). Proponency for Research and Development (FA:51) and Contracting and Industrial Management (FA:97) is the responsibility of the U.S. Army Materiel Command.

Each of the proponents has developed a typical education and assignment pattern to be used as a guide by officers in that particular branch or career field. These patterns are displayed in DA Pam 600-3. In general, the patterns follow the chart presented with this discussion, but they are tailored to the specific needs of officers in the particular career fields. The proponents forecast the professional development needs of their constituent officers, and they communicate regularly with these officers during the branch basic and advanced courses and through branch and professional magazines.

The proponents fill a vital role in the professional development of officers, since

Years of Service: 0 1 2 3 4 5 6 7 8 9 10 11 12 13 14 15 16 17 18 19 20 21 22 23 24 25 26 27 28 29 30

DOPMA Promotion Objectives: 02 (~1), 03 (~3), 04 (~10), 05 (~16), 06 (~22)

Military Schooling:
- O B C
- CAS3*
- Officer Advanced CRS
- CMD & Staff College
- Senior Service College
- AWCCSC
- Additional Skill Producing Schools
- Functional Schools in Preparation for a Specific Duty Position
- Pre-Command Courses

Civilian Schooling:
- Completion of OBV
- Schooling at Civilian Institutions

Career Field Experience:
- Development in Branch Code
- Functional Area Development Branch or Immaterial Assignment
- Utilization in Branch and/or Functional Area

Staff Experience:
- Battalion Squadron
- Brigade Group MACOM FOA's Installation
- Division-Corps MACOM ARSTAFF FOA's Installation
- MACOM/ARSTAFF Joint Combined/DOD

*After completion of OAC

COMMISSIONED OFFICER PROFESSIONAL DEVELOPMENT OPPORTUNITIES.

they are in the best position to know the education and skill requirements that are required of officers in their particular career fields.

THE COMMANDER'S RESPONSIBILITIES

An officer's immediate commanding officer, or chief, has important responsibilities for that officer's professional development. Higher commanders in the chain of command are also responsible. Indeed, the success of the program requires the effective completion of the commander's missions.

The commander should consult the typical career pattern of the officer and check the progress made in completing essential assignments, in comparison with the officer's length of service. What has the officer completed and what are the lacks? A commander may be able to rotate an officer within the unit to provide the experience that is contemplated in the career pattern. The officer may command a platoon or company and then be rotated to a position on the battalion staff. A battalion or a brigade has different types of units as to weapons or mission, and breadth of experience may be advanced by rotation through two or more such assignments. If the needed duty is not available within a command, the commander may report the need to a higher commander with a recommendation.

All this is extremely important if officers are to gain in minimum time the breadth of experience they need. However, let another part of this picture be considered. The efficiency and perhaps the combat readiness of the unit must be the first consideration. Rotation of officers can be accomplished, but there must also be recognition of mission.

Commanders are instructors and in this capacity they use their experience to advise their subordinates. No military unit can ever be "commanded" in the true sense of the word until each member is instructed and proficient in individual duties. "This is what we are to do," the commander will direct; "This is the way we shall do it," and he or she announces specific missions for subordinate units and key individuals; then, at the proper time, "Let's go." If officers or soldiers do something that is incorrect, or in a manner of reduced efficiency, tell them or show them how to do it right. The commander uses his or her greater experience to increase the knowledge of members of the command. Teaching may not always be understood as part of professional development, or career planning—but it is.

A commander, or chief, who has officers under his or her command or jurisdiction has the responsibility for rendering evaluation reports on them. This is the most important series of reports that accumulate about each officer's achievements, personality traits, and value to the service. These records are consulted within the Department of the Army and evaluated, and from their study, officers are chosen for all assignments, including duties that are most sought by those working hard to reach maximum goals. The officer who prepares the evaluation report on another officer accepts a very important responsibility.

The commander's counseling of officers for whom he or she will prepare evaluation reports is an especially important responsibility. Counseling may start on the day an officer reports for duty, as the need to do so occurs, and continues as an important command responsibility throughout an officer's assignment. Effective counseling helps the officer to improve performance of duty and the progress of his or her career.

The OER Support Form, DA Form 67-8-1 (see chapter 14, *Evaluation Reports*) requires that, at the beginning of each rating period, the rating officer, who normally is the immediate commander or chief, discuss with the rated officer the duties and the performance objectives that he or she will be expected to accomplish during the rating period. These duties and responsibilities should also be reviewed with the rated officer as necessary during the rating period. Each of these discussion sessions should be used by the rating officer as an opportunity for counseling the rated officer.

What does counseling really mean? Just as the confidence of officers is enhanced and reinforced by recognition of their special capabilities, talents, and strengths, officers must be informed early in their careers of their weaknesses and their deficiencies, and positive means for improvement suggested. Subsequent consultation periods should be arranged in order that favorable results can be accomplished prior to the date an evaluation report must be prepared. In the great majority of instances where wise, objective counseling is done at the appropriate time, the results will be favorable. Further, a priceless feeling of mutual trust and respect may follow a good job of counseling because officers aspire to succeed and appreciate guidance that will help them forward. The commander may benefit more than he or she could possibly have anticipated; by making a study of the officer, and the officer's work, aspirations, and career pattern, the commander is likely to discover individuals who have unused talents he or she had not identified. It works both ways. The worth of any military unit is the sum of the capabilities, the determination, and the developed teamwork of its subordinate units and all of its individual members.

THE OFFICER'S RESPONSIBILITY FOR CAREER PROGRESS

The commanders and personnel managers from units and commands up to the Department of the Army really try to provide individual professional development and management. However, officers are responsible in large part for their own development and progress toward the top.

The Officer's Initial Choice. At the very beginning of a service career the commissioned officer exercises individual choice, or preference, for a branch assignment. It is an important decision. Unless the officer later transfers to another branch, which may be done, most subsequent assignments during the first ten years of service will pertain to that branch; service school training will be at that branch service school; and a branch manager, in conjunction with the professional development officer in OPMD, will monitor successive assignments, evaluate the officer's capabilities, and make many decisions or recommendations that determine the officer's assignments and progress.

By the end of the seventh year of service, a functional area will be assigned to most officers. Assignment is based upon the officer's stated desires, any special training or qualifications possessed by the officer, the officer's demonstrated performance and potential, and the Army's needs. From that point through the major and lieutenant colonel phases of development, successive assignments will be monitored by the officer's branch manager in conjunction with the functional area manager. The officer may expect assignments in either the branch or functional area, designed to develop and maintain his or her skills and abilities. Colonels may expect assignments in either branch or functional area, or in immaterial assignments, as dictated by Army requirements.

How does an officer determine at the start of a military life the sort of Army activities of his or her greatest interest or aptitudes? For many officers the choice is clear. When the individual has been trained as a physician, dentist, lawyer, clergyman, or engineer, he or she will enter the appropriate branch as indicated by the professional training. For others, the field of their college training may indicate the choice that may also be acceptable to the Army. The field of one's college training may not suit the individual as a career preference, or fit the requirements of the Army as to utilization of the knowledge. But for the majority of individuals, college training is an important factor in choosing the branch assignment and later a functional area of interest.

Where do your innermost interests lie? What sort of work gives you the greatest thrill or satisfaction? What are your best attributes as to education? These are a number of the considerations that should guide you in initial planning of your military life. Does this illuminate the problem? Do you begin to see the influences you are expected to have upon your own career?

One of the greatest needs of the Army, and for many persons its most attractive opportunity, is the requirement for leaders to command its units. Do you enjoy working with people, and especially young people? Do you enjoy training them, organizing and inspiring them, leading them into interesting achievements? Or would you like to learn how? You will be welcome indeed, for leaders must be identified and trained to fill command assignments all along the slender line from lieutenant to general. Infantry, Armor, Aviation, Field Artillery, or Air Defense Artillery may be your choice of branch. It is in this field of command that the Army may hold forth its greatest inducements, because officers attain rewarding assignments earlier in their careers than in other vocations. In time of war, skilled military field leaders are the priceless ones; it is their names that are perpetuated in honor in our national history.

The Army needs the very best battalion and brigade commanders. While nearly every officer will have an opportunity during his or her early years to command a platoon or company level unit, only those officers who are selected by a DA Selection Board will be given command of OPMS-designated battalions or brigades. The key elements of the selection procedure of officers to fill battalion- and brigade-level command positions are as follows:

Separate DA selection boards are convened for combat arms, combat support arms, and combat service support.

Selection boards designate officers best qualified for troop command and prepare a rank order list by command category.

Assignments are made by DA based on command position vacancies, an officer's standing on the selection board's rank order list, the qualifications desired by the field commander, and the officer's qualifications.

Later Choices That Influence a Career. As an Army career lengthens, other options or opportunities arrive that may influence a career. New developments are introduced; international conditions change; all manner of changing conditions serve to provide new opportunities to consider, adopt, or reject. It is important to understand this condition, and it is essential that it be utilized. The one certainty of an Army career is change, and the alert officer must be ready for it.

The Importance of the Officer's Evaluation Record. The officer who aspires to ultimate selection for the higher schools and colleges and the more important assignments must deserve and receive a commendable series of evaluation reports. These assignments are selective on the "best-qualified" basis, which is the best system for the individual as well as the Army. This need not be a cause for alarm. Rating officers are required to prepare the reports objectively, thoughtfully, in accordance with Army regulations for the subject. It is not required that an officer be in the upper 1 percent, or 10 or 20 percent. But it is necessary to have a sustained record of successful performance of duty with an accompanying favorable personal record of integrity and conduct. This is more important than percentage placement. Do a good job and you will fare well.

Individual Records of Importance. There are official records of special importance to each officer. Be sure yours are in order. When changes occur in your status, your qualifications, your desires, or special matters pertaining to your family that should be considered in future assignments, be sure to have them promptly recorded. These records are: *Professional Development Planning Worksheet,* DA Form 4190-R; *Officer Assignment Preference Statement,* DA Form 483; *Officer Record Brief* (ORB); and *Official Military Personnel File* (OMPF).

Professional Development Planning Worksheet, DA Form 4190-R. This worksheet provides the officer, the commander, and the personnel manager with a general sense of direction desired by the officer, and it highlights career objectives. It should be prepared soon after entry on active duty and filed with the officer's branch assignment manager in OPMD. It is a living document that may be updated at any time. It should be updated and the revised copy filed with OPMD upon selection for promotion and prior to completion of the advanced course and attendance at Command and Staff College.

Officer Assignment Preference Statement, DA Form 483. This form enables an officer to state preferences for CONUS or overseas duty, including several preferences for CONUS and oversea tour locations, as well as preferences for type of duty. Space is provided on the form to indicate whether the type of duty or the location is of primary importance to the officer. The form also has space for indication of the officer's desires regarding additional schooling, whether the officer is married to another service member, and whether there are special family problems or other considerations that should be taken into account when assignments are made.

The DA Form 483 is designed to be machine-readable, and information from the form is used to update the Official Military Personnel File (OMPF). The latest preference information submitted by an officer is readily available at the desktop computer terminal of the officer's career manager at OPMD when assignments to school or new duty positions are made. Each officer must ensure that his or her preferences are correctly stated to OPMD if these preferences are to be factored into the assignment process.

There are five occasions when you should submit an updated preference statement: (1) about twelve months before completing an oversea tour; (2) upon arriving in a short-tour area; (3) about twelve months after reporting to a CONUS station; (4) within sixty days after enrolling in a civilian school or a military training course that requires a permanent change of station move; and (5) when family considerations change. The back of the form provides instructions for properly filling out the form together with instructions on how and where to submit the form.

Officer Record Brief (ORB). The Officer Record Brief is produced automatically, upon demand, from the information stored in the Official Military Personnel File, a computerized collection of data pertaining to each officer. The ORB contains all pertinent data on each officer necessary for the officer's consideration for assignments, school selection, promotion, and other decisions affecting his or her career. Maintaining up-to-date data on the ORB is thus of extreme importance and is the responsibility of the individual officer. You will have the opportunity annually to audit your ORB to assure that it is correct.

Official Military Personnel File (OMPF). The OMPF is the computerized source of data from which the ORB is produced when desired. It is maintained up-to-date by the annual audits of the ORB conducted by the officer concerned and by data fed to the file by the unit personnel officer. Each officer should be sure that the

OFFICER ASSIGNMENT PREFERENCE STATEMENT.

OMPF reflects important changes affecting his or her career, such as service school courses completed, changes as to civilian education, credit for oversea tour, changes in numbers of dependents, and so forth. The file should contain a relatively recent photograph of the officer. You should review your OMPF file periodically, at about three-year intervals if possible, to assure completeness and accuracy.

FINDING OUT HOW YOU STAND

If you aspire to the maximum development of your capabilities in the shortest span of years, you need to find out from time to time exactly how you stand, and you are encouraged to do so. This discussion is provided as a summary of well-known procedures, often considered separately, which are really a single, continuing need. In any case, here are definite steps for your consideration.

It is essential that you study your own professional development plan before consulting other officers. You should consider your present and past assignments, including school courses, and decide for yourself whether you are falling behind. When you have a pleasant assignment in a location you enjoy, a commander you admire, or a set of quarters especially pleasing, it is easy to succumb to the attempt to keep things as they are. This is one way to fall behind. Check your own accomplishments against the typical assignment pattern for your career field and see. Another measure that should be verified before consulting others is that your expression of desires is stated fully and accurately on your *Officer Assignment Preference Statement,* which is on file with the Officer Personnel Management Directorate in Washington.

Gaining Your Commander's Conclusions and Advice. The first source of information is your immediate commanding officer, or chief, for he or she is the one charged with an important part of your professional development and the one who prepares your evaluation reports on which so much depends. You may request an interview with your commander for a personal discussion. Prior to each such session, review your professional development plan to see how you stand, making note of the items of particular interest about which you will seek your commander's advice. Decide before the discussion session the precise information you wish to learn, and then, during the discussion, be sure to bring up these subjects of special interest about which your commander can provide advice based upon his or her greater experience or knowledge.

Such questions as the following might be appropriate: You are in your sixth year of service and have no staff experience as depicted by your assignment pattern. Inquire about what can be done to fill this gap. You have not attended the Advanced Course. Can the commander suggest action that will help secure the assignment? Mindful that evaluation reports are based upon performance of duty and the image that is in continual formation by observation, it is appropriate to ask these pointed, personal questions: Can the commander suggest ways to improve your standard of work? which is a polite way of inquiring—"If you believe my work can be improved, please tell me specifically what to do about it." Be sure you are prepared to hear the truth, for if you ask candid questions you are almost certain to receive candid answers—the only ones worthy of adoption. You may ask, "Can you suggest ways to improve my personal mannerisms to get better results?"

There will be other questions, of course. Ask them, being sure from start to finish that your commander is certain to understand that you are seeking guidance in order to do a better job and become a better officer. Never offer alibis or become argumentative. Can such an inquiry do harm to an officer's standing? Will such questions offend the commander or rating officer? No, certainly not, if the questions are asked objectively, and if the answers are received without argument or objection. Indeed, most commanders welcome such discussions with their subordinates.

Visits to OPMD. When you are in the Washington area, you are encouraged to visit OPMD to inspect your Official Military Personnel File and to discuss your particular situation with your assignment manager. OPMD is located in the Hoffman II Building in Alexandria, Virginia, near the junction of Interstate 95 and Telegraph Road. It may be reached by taking the Huntington Avenue metro (Yellow Line) from the Pentagon to the Eisenhower Avenue metro station. It is wise to call ahead for an appointment.

Or, you may request a written copy of your OMPF by writing to the Commander, OPMD, ATTN: DAPC-OP-(appropriate career branch), 200 Stovall Street, Alexandria, VA 22332-0400. By waiting for several months after submission of your latest Officer Evaluation Report (OER), your OMPF should contain that report plus the Senior Rater Profile of your rating officer. (See chapter 14, *Evaluation Reports.*)

You may also contact your assignment manager by telephone, although a personal visit with a face-to-face discussion is bound to be more productive and satisfactory. The Autovon prefix for OPMD is 221; the commercial prefix is (202)-325. An initial call to extension 8141, 8142, or 8143 should elicit the correct extension for your career branch.

How often should you inspect your Official Military Personnel File? Certainly you should do so when you are passing through Washington if you have not inspected the file recently. You will have an opportunity to inspect your Officer Record Brief each year, and it is produced from the information in the OMPF. However, inspection of the complete OMPF every few years would be in order to assure that it presents a complete and accurate description of your performance, your assignment history, and your accomplishments.

Forecasting the future of any individual is difficult and uncertain in any vocation. The Army provides this exceptional opportunity for personal participation for the excellent reason that it strives hard to help each officer attain maximum capability as early in the officer's career as his or her talents and hard work may justify. The officer who knows the goal sought may learn by these visits whether he or she is following the right road at the right speed, and the hurdles, if any, which must be cleared.

THE FINAL POINT

In this discussion there has been frequent reference to selection of the "best qualified" officers for assignments of the highest importance. It is entirely true that there is competition for the choice positions. It is one of several reasons our nation has such a splendid Army today, and such a fine corps of officers. But this competition has some points about it that need understanding. *First,* there is no favoritism, or influence or pull; an uninformed person may attempt such pressures but they will be negative as to results. For one important reason, these choices go through many hands for evaluation and recommendation, or for concurrence in a recommended choice. *Second,* the Army is fortunate in having a wealth of talent so that the selection of the "best qualified" is made from a number of officers who are "fully qualified." *Third,* the Army is large enough, and its mission broad enough, that positions requiring the highest talents are abundant and all officers may expect to be placed in assignments that utilize their full talents, always remembering the work of the Army must be done. *Finally,* each officer has a personal responsibility in the development of his or her career. This chapter has been written to help each officer understand the importance of this point.

13

Army Schools
and Career Progress

The program for training and developing the Army's leaders is the very foundation of the nation's security. Missions and weapons change. Times and requirements change. Administrations change and bring new viewpoints. Officers must be replaced continually through termination of active duty, retirement, death, or other causes. The Army faces limitless tasks during peace, in war, or the gray in-between of the cold war. It is the Army's educational system that produces the leaders with the essentials of character, knowledge, and professional skill, as well as the essential capability for growth.

ARMY EDUCATIONAL OPPORTUNITIES

This chapter is provided to disclose the scope of the total program, and to provide information to help the individual officer choose his or her own goals for military and civil school training. It is an essential part of career development.

It is helpful to think of the Army military and civil school programs as having three purposes: (1) Selection and training of highly qualified young men and women to become officers; (2) development of officers to proficiency in their branches and functional areas; and (3) training and development of officers who have the highest potential for the most important responsibilities of command, staff, and special fields.

Suggestion is made that this chapter be considered with chapter 12, *Professional Development,* and chapter 14, *Evaluation Reports.* Information about the United States Military Academy, the ROTC Program, and the Officer Candidate Schools has been placed in chapter 2, *The Sources of Army Officers.*

THE ARMY SCHOOL SYSTEM

Army officers receive their initial branch training, following appointment as officers, at the basic course. The advanced course is to be

completed prior to completing 9 years' service. Between advanced course graduation and the end of the ninth year of active commissioned service, the officer must
complete the Combined Arms and Services Staff School (CAS³). Thereafter, if
selected as "best qualified," the officer may attend one of the intermediate and
senior level courses conducted at the Army's colleges, at the colleges conducted
under the supervision of the Joint Chiefs of Staff, or at the Air Force, Navy, or
Marine colleges. The British Staff College, Camberly, and the School of the Americas are also available at the intermediate level, as are the Canadian Defence
College, the Italian Center for Higher Defense Studies, the Italian National Defense
College, and the Japanese Institute of Defense Studies at the senior level.

It is a progressive system, resembling extended postgraduate education, to prepare the required number of officers for the assignments of peace or war of greatest
importance to the Army and to the nation. These courses are interspersed with
assignment to duty with troops, staff, administrative, instructor, specialist, and
other responsibilities.

Attention is invited to the diagram accompanying this discussion: *Commissioned
Officer Professional Education System.*

Basic Course. This is a course to prepare newly appointed commissioned officers
for their first duty assignments. The emphasis is on fundamentals required at
company, battery, or troop level.

Advanced Course. Commissioned officers will attend an advanced course between the time of selection/promotion to captain and prior to commanding at the
grade of captain. This instruction prepares them fully for assignments pertaining to
the heavier responsibilities of command, to include company command, and for
duty as staff officers at the battalion and brigade level. Completion of this course
is a prerequisite for consideration for the Combined Arms and Services Staff
School, and later for the Command and General Staff College.

Combined Arms and Services Staff School (CAS³). A mandatory course of
instruction for all officers specifically designed to teach staff skills. Attendance will
be prior to completion of the ninth year of active federal commissioned service.
The course duration is nine weeks. CAS³ requires a nonresident instruction phase
and successful completion of a comprehensive examination as a prerequisite for
resident attendance.

Command and General Staff College. This instruction deals with command and
staff responsibilities for large units of the combined arms and with many other vital
matters of major commands and staffs. It prepares officers for duty as commanders
of battalions, brigades, and equivalent-size units. It is a prerequisite for consideration for attendance at a senior service college. Selected Army commissioned
officers may attend the Air Command and Staff College, the Naval College of
Command and Staff, the Marine Command and Staff College, the School of the
Americas, or the British Staff College, Camberly, in lieu of attendance at the Army's
Command and General Staff College.

Armed Forces Staff College. This is a joint service school with students chosen
from each of the services. It prepares commissioned officers for staff and command
duty in joint and combined operations. The Army has a quota of about 200
commissioned officers who receive a military education equal to the Command
and General Staff Course.

Senior Service Colleges. The Army War College, the National War College, the
Industrial College of the Armed Forces, the Naval War College, the Air War

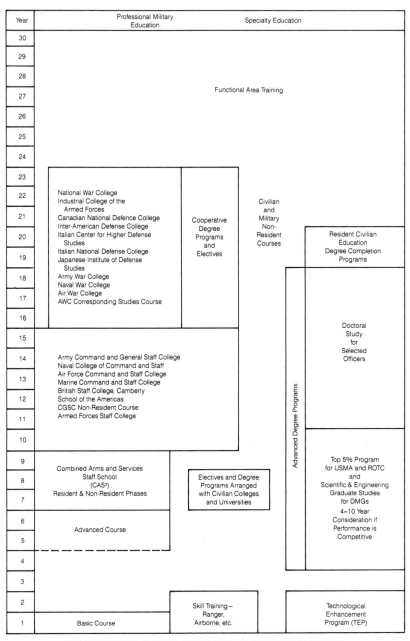

Year	Professional Military Education	Specialty Education			
30					
29					
28		Functional Area Training			
27					
26					
25					
24					
23	National War College		Civilian and Military Non-Resident Courses		
22	Industrial College of the Armed Forces				
21	Canadian National Defence College	Cooperative Degree Programs and Electives			
20	Inter-American Defense College / Italian Center for Higher Defense Studies			Resident Civilian Education Degree Completion Programs	
19	Italian National Defense College / Japanese Institute of Defense Studies				
18	Army War College				
17	Naval War College / Air War College / AWC Corresponding Studies Course				
16					
15				Doctoral Study for Selected Officers	
14	Army Command and General Staff College				
13	Naval College of Command and Staff / Air Force Command and Staff College				
12	Marine Command and Staff College / British Staff College, Camberly				
11	School of the Americas / CGSC Non-Resident Course / Armed Forces Staff College				
10					
9	Combined Arms and Services		Advanced Degree Programs	Top 5% Program for USMA and ROTC and Scientific & Engineering Graduate Studies for DMGs	
8	Staff School (CAS³)	Electives and Degree Programs Arranged with Civilian Colleges and Universities			
7	Resident & Non-Resident Phases				
6	Advanced Course			4–10 Year Consideration if Performance is Competitive	
5					
4					
3					
2		Skill Training— Ranger, Airborne, etc.		Technological Enhancement Program (TEP)	
1	Basic Course				

COMMISSIONED OFFICER PROFESSIONAL EDUCATION SYSTEM.

College, the Inter-American Defense College, the Canadian National Defence College, the Italian Center for Higher Defense Studies, the Italian National Defense College, and the Japanese Institute for Defense Studies are considered senior service colleges of the same military educational level. A total of approximately 300 commissioned officers are selected to attend these colleges each year. No Army commissioned officer may attend more than one of these colleges.

Schools of Other Military Services. In order to promote better interservice understanding, to provide the Army viewpoint and insights, and to acquire skills and specialties not taught in Army schools, selected commissioned officers are sent to various schools of the Navy, the Marine Corps, and the Air Force.

Schools of Foreign Nations. Selected commissioned officers pursue courses of instruction at schools of foreign nations. The purpose of such attendance is to afford these officers the opportunity to broaden their knowledge and experience by close relationship with the language, techniques, and staff procedures of other armies. These assignments are voluntary and in most cases are tied to a subsequent in-country assignment.

Schools of Federal Civilian Agencies. Commissioned officers are regularly trained in the schools maintained by many civilian agencies, such as the Department of State, the Department of Labor, the Treasury Department, and the U.S. Civil Service Commission. This training is conducted under the Interagency Training Programs.

The Army Civil School Program. The Army makes extensive use of civilian colleges and universities in its program of officer training. Civilian schools augment the courses provided at Army and armed forces schools and colleges.

The general educational development of officers is conducted through off-duty academic instruction. In addition, there is a Degree Completion Program under which officers may apply to attend a civilian educational institution on permissive temporary duty (TDY) for periods up to twenty weeks, or on PCS for periods of from twenty weeks to eighteen months, to satisfy degree requirements. Selections are made by the career branches.

Where a definite military requirement exists in a civilian field, selected officers are sent to civilian universities to receive the needed training. In all cases this includes a course leading to a master's or doctor's degree, followed by an assignment to utilize the knowledge for the benefit of the Army. The expenses are borne by the Army.

Officers, both commissioned and warrant, selected for this education are required to remain on active duty for three years for each year of schooling or fraction thereof, with a maximum obligation of six years.

Language Training. Army officers are performing assignments in more than seventy foreign countries. Language fluency is essential for the effective accomplishment of many of these missions, and will be helpful in all of them. Career officers are encouraged to attain and to maintain proficiency in at least one foreign language. This instruction may be obtained by extension courses, on-duty study, and other means. The Department of Defense provides very extensive language study courses at the Defense Language Institute, Presidio of Monterey, California.

On-the-Job Training. Saved until last, perhaps the most important of all educational opportunities is on-the-job training. Here the individual officer comes to grips with a specific mission, officers and enlisted personnel with whom to work, and a series of actual problems that must be solved in infinite variety and scope. This is the testing ground.

Completion of service school courses helps greatly, of course. But in many instances the requirements of an assignment have not been covered in a school course, or its responsibilities may attain heights beyond the scope of their instructional mission. Such tasks must be learned while performing the tasks, often with little or no opportunity to prepare at all. On the highest level, consider the self-training that General Eisenhower had to complete to enable him to do his job as Supreme Commander. Or the new responsibilities thrust upon him by assuming the task of organizing the Supreme Headquarters, Allied Powers Europe. A further example was the discharge by General MacArthur of his occupation tasks in Japan. Or the ways of accomplishing his mission that had to be developed by General Bradley as first Chairman of the Joint Chiefs of Staff.

But it is not alone in these assignments of tremendous responsibility that on-the-job training is applicable. It is valuable and common all down the scale of military responsibilities. The young officer will prepare today and tonight for the tasks of tomorrow and next week; will consult noncommissioned officers who may be expert in some activity in which aid is needed; and will read, and study, and think.

There is no educational opportunity more important than that of holding a responsibility, and bending heaven and earth to do it well. This is on-the-job training, the most important of all.

Summary. The Army's system of progressive education of its officers is very extensive and very thorough. With selective assignments interspersed with service college courses, the pathway to careers of important national service is well established. This is a competitive Army, in the proper meaning of the term. Selection to attend the service colleges, and the key assignments that flow to their graduates, is on the solid basis of the "best qualified." Opportunity is abundant, but it must be won. The Army has the finest corps of officers in its history. The program of military education through the branch service schools and the service colleges deserves a fair share of the credit for this national asset.

The information for this chapter has been extracted from the official sources listed below and from discussions with knowledgeable officers:

AR 351-1, *Individual Military Education and Training.*

AR 10-41, *United States Army Training and Doctrine Command.*

AR 350-101, *Joint Colleges.*

AR 621-1, *Training of Military Personnel at Civilian Institutions.*

AR 621-7, *Acceptance of Fellowships, Scholarships or Grants.*

DA Pam 600-3, *Commissioned Officer Professional Development and Utilization.*

THE U.S. ARMY BRANCH SERVICE SCHOOLS

Each branch of the Army conducts its own service school to prepare officers for branch assignments. There are also other Army service schools that are attended by officers without regard to their branch assignments, such as the Airborne School, Military Assistance School, and others. For information about the several courses conducted at each school, their duration and dates of beginning, consult a unit training officer who will have available the Army Formal Schools Catalog with its latest changes.

Name and Location

U.S. Army Adjutant Generals School, Fort Benjamin Harrison, Indiana.

U.S. Army Air Defense School, Fort Bliss, Texas.

U.S. Army Armor School, Fort Knox, Kentucky.

U.S. Army Aviation School, Fort Rucker, Alabama.

U.S. Army Aviation Logistics School, Fort Eustis, Virginia.

U.S. Army Chaplain School, Fort Monmouth, New Jersey.
U.S. Army Chemical School, Fort McClellan, Alabama.
U.S. Army Engineer School, Fort Belvoir, Virginia.
U.S. Army Field Artillery School, Fort Sill, Oklahoma.
U.S. Army Finance School, Fort Benjamin Harrison, Indiana.
U.S. Army Infantry School, Fort Benning, Georgia.
U.S. Army Institute/JFK Center for Military Assistance, Fort Bragg, North Carolina.
U.S. Army Intelligence School, Fort Huachuca, Arizona.
U.S. Army Judge Advocate General's School, University of Virginia, Charlottesville, Virginia.
U.S. Army Medical Field Service School, Fort Sam Houston, Texas.
U.S. Army Military Police School, Fort McClellan, Alabama.
U.S. Army Ordnance Missile and Munitions School, Redstone Arsenal, Alabama.
U.S. Army Ordnance School, Aberdeen Proving Ground, Maryland.
U.S. Army Organizational Effectiveness Training Center, Fort Ord, California.
U.S. Army Quartermaster School, Fort Lee, Virginia.
U.S. Army Signal School, Fort Gordon, Georgia.
U.S. Army Soldier Support Institute, Fort Benjamin Harrison, Indiana.
U.S. Army Transportation School, Fort Eustis, Virginia.

Branch School Courses. The branch schools of the Army, such as the Infantry School, conduct commissioned officer basic courses and advanced courses. The *Officer Basic Course* is to prepare newly commissioned officers for their first duty assignments with emphasis on leadership and on the fundamentals, weapons, equipment, and techniques required at company/battery/troop level. Basic courses last from nine to nineteen weeks with most of the officers being on temporary duty (TDY) and billeted in BOQs.

The *Officer Advanced Course* is for career officers who normally will attend while in the grade of captain. This course is to prepare commissioned officers for command and staff at battalion and company level. Emphasis is primarily on command with understanding of command functions, branch responsibilities of command support, and development of managerial skills. Nonactive duty Reserve officers attend an advanced course. Duration of these courses requires a permanent change of station (PCS) with a variety of billeting and on- and off-post housing situations.

Army Extension Courses. Army Extension Courses provide a progressive nonresident course of instruction for personnel of all components of the Army. Courses are available from branch training level through the U.S. Army Command and General Staff College level to that of U.S. Army War College where the education includes all Services. Reserve officers are able to gain point credits for retirement and to meet certain promotion requirements.

STAFF COLLEGES OF THE ARMY AND THE ARMED FORCES

Combined Arms and Services Staff School (CAS³). All commissioned officers are required to attend a CAS³ course of nine weeks' duration prior to completion of their ninth year of active federal commissioned service. This course is specifically designed to teach staff skills at brigade and higher level.

Officers selected for promotion to major, majors, and lieutenant colonels through their thirteenth year of active federal commissioned service, who are advanced course graduates, are automatically considered for attendance at an intermediate service college designed to prepare them to assume command and staff positions at battalion and higher level.

The U.S. Army Command and General Staff College. The C&GSC, Fort Leavenworth, Kansas, conducts the following courses:

The Command and General Staff Officer Course

The Command and General Staff Officer Course (Reserve Component)

The Command and General Staff Officer Course (Nonresident)

The Command and General Staff Officer Refresher—Division Support Command (RC)

The Command and General Staff Officer Refresher—Combat Division (RC)

The Command and General Staff Officer Refresher—Separate BDE/ACR (RC)

Battalion Command Group Refresher Course (RC)

U.S. Army Reserve Instructor Orientation Course (RC)

Allied Officer Preparatory Course

Pre-Command Course (Phase III/IV)

The purpose of the Command and General Staff Officer Course is to prepare selected commissioned officers for duty as battalion and brigade commanders and as principal general staff officers with the Army and at all levels of the defense establishment; to provide these officers with an understanding of the functions of the Army General Staff and of major Army, joint, and combined commands; and to develop their intellectual depth and analytical ability.

The Navy, the Marine Corps, and the Air Force also operate colleges equivalent to the C&GSC. Several Army commissioned officers normally are selected to attend these colleges each year.

The Armed Forces Staff College. The Armed Forces Staff College under control of the National Defense University is located at Norfolk, Virginia. The Chief of Naval Operations is charged with the responsibility for the operation and maintenance of required facilities.

Its mission is to conduct a course of study in joint and combined operations, planning and operations, and in related aspects of national and international security. It prepares selected Army, Navy, and Air Force commissioned officers for duty in all echelons of joint and combined command.

There are two courses per year, each of five months' duration, beginning about the first week of January and the first week of August. Each class numbers about 270 officers, drawn from each of the three services.

SENIOR SERVICE COLLEGES OF THE ARMY AND THE ARMED FORCES

The Army and its sister services operate five coequal senior service colleges (SSCs) designed to prepare commissioned officers for command and staff duties ranging up to the highest levels within our military establishment. Attendance at one of these SSCs is on a "best-qualified" basis, although 50 percent of available seats are filled based upon the Army's needs for individuals in particular specialties. Only a portion of the Army's officers can expect to attend one of these SSCs, although all should aspire to do so, since credit for attendance is required for many high-level assignments and is given due consideration by promotion boards. It is from among graduates of the SSCs that the Army's top leaders are selected.

Three of the SSCs are the Army War College, the Naval War College, and the Air War College, under control of their respective services. The Joint Chiefs of Staff control the National War College and the Industrial College of the Armed Forces, both subordinate elements of the National Defense University. In addition, the Canadian National Defence College, the Italian Center for Higher Defense Studies, the Italian National Defense College, the Japanese Institute for Defense Studies, and the Inter-American Defense College are considered equivalent to an SSC. Selected

Fellowships are also considered equivalent. An Army commissioned officer may attend only one of these colleges.

Attendance at any of the ten SSC-level colleges is upon recommendation by a DA selection board and approval by the Secretary of the Army. To be eligible for attendance, an Army commissioned officer must have completed not more than twenty-three years of promotion list service as of October 1 of the year the course begins; must be in the grade of lieutenant colonel as of the date the selection board convenes; must be a graduate of, or have credit for attendance at a service college of the command and general staff level; and must not have attended, nor declined to attend, any of the ten SSC-level colleges.

The U.S. Army War College. The Army War College (AWC), Carlisle Barracks, Pennsylvania, is the senior college under Army control. It prepares selected senior commissioned officers for command and high-level staff duty with emphasis on Army doctrine and operations, and it advances interdepartmental and interservice understanding.

The length of the course is forty-two weeks, one course annually, starting in August. Each class consists of Army, Navy, Marine, Coast Guard, and Air Force commissioned officers, plus a few civilians from various federal departments, and international Fellows.

The National Defense University. The National Defense University was created by the Department of Defense in 1975. The National War College (NWC) and the Industrial College of the Armed Forces (ICAF), co-located at Fort McNair, Washington, D.C., are subordinate elements of the NDU, each maintaining its own mission and unique identity. The mission of the NDU is to ensure excellence in professional military education in the essential elements of national security and their interrelationships, to enhance the preparation of selected personnel of the Department of Defense, Department of State, and other governmental agencies for the exercise of senior policy, command and staff functions, the planning of national strategy, and the management of resources for national security. The mission is achieved primarily through the educational programs of the National War College and the Industrial College of the Armed Forces. The National Defense University also controls the Armed Forces Staff College (AFSC) at Norfolk, Virginia, and the Inter-American Defense College (IADC).

The National War College. The National War College, a component of the National Defense University, is a unique military educational institution. The NWC mission is to conduct a senior-level course of study and associated research in national security policy, with emphasis on its formulation and future directions, in order to enhance the preparation of selected personnel of the Armed Forces, the Department of State, and other U.S. government departments and agencies for the exercise of joint and combined high-level policy, command, and staff functions in the planning and implementation of national strategy.

One class is conducted each year, usually commencing in the latter half of August and lasting about ten months. A class normally consists of 140 students, three-fourths military and one-fourth civilian. Students are selected for assignment to the National War College by their parent organization on the basis of superior past professional performance and outstanding future potential. They are colonels or lieutenant colonels or equivalent naval ranks or civilian grades.

The Industrial College of the Armed Forces. The Industrial College of the Armed Forces is an equally unique component of the National Defense University. It is the only senior service college dedicated to the study of management of resources for national security. ICAF's mission is to conduct senior-level courses of study and associated research in the management of resources in the interest of national security in order to enhance the preparation of selected military commissioned officers and senior career civilian officials for positions of high trust in the federal government.

A class normally consists of about 180 students: Army, Navy, Marine, Air Force, and various governmental departments and agencies. The student composition and class size vary from year to year depending on the personnel requirements of the individual services. As with the National War College, students are selected to attend the Industrial College of the Armed Forces by their parent organization based on superior performance and future potential to hold positions of increased responsibility and high trust in the federal government. They are colonels or lieutenant colonels or equivalent naval ranks or civilian grades.

Both NWC and ICAF also have a research program, e.g., Army Research Associates Program (ARAP). For approximately six–ten students of each course, ARAP deals with independent research on topics decided upon between school officials and the individual students.

OPPORTUNITIES FOR ACADEMIC EDUCATION

While the completion of courses at Army schools or schools under control of the Joint Chiefs of Staff constitutes the main source of officer training, there are other important opportunities that should be understood. Officers who desire to be considered for this training as it applies to specific programs should consult the appropriate regulations and apply. Assistance may be obtained from the training or personnel sections of any army or unit staff.

Degree Status, Commissioned Officers of the Active Army. As pointed out in chapter 1, *An Army Career,* the Army has made a determined effort to assure that its officers are highly educated. In the case of the Regular Army, this policy has resulted in more than 97 percent of all Regular commissioned officers possessing at least a bachelor's degree. Approximately 28 percent of all career commissioned officers also have master's degrees. The actual percentage figures may be less for the active Army since it consists also of officers receiving commissions through the Officer Candidate Schools, who may not have had an opportunity to attend college. For those commissioned officers without degrees who remain on active duty, this is a situation that can be, and generally is, remedied.

The desired goal for commissioned officers is a bachelor's (baccalaureate) degree and for warrant officers the goal is an associate degree. Those officers who do not meet these goals are strongly urged to pursue on- and off-duty courses to supplement their education. Such educational activity along with enrollment in extension courses often occasions a favorable evaluation report comment concerning self-improvement, thereby influencing selection for promotion, desirable assignments, and attendance at service schools and colleges.

Courses at Colleges and Universities. The Army provides exceptional opportunities for higher education in civilian colleges and universities.

Commissioned officers appointed into the Regular Army in recent years have been selected from individuals having academic degrees. There has also been a sharp increase in the number of commissioned officers holding advanced degrees, with a continuing program for commissioned officers to pursue courses leading to the higher degrees. This is accomplished under the Advanced Degree Program wherein officers on PCS status can pursue a graduate degree for up to two full years (although normally limited to eighteen months) while on full pay and allowances and with tuition and an allowance for books paid by the Army.

The Degree Completion Program provides an opportunity for officers to attend a civilian college or university to complete studies for a baccalaureate degree, with temporary duty up to twenty weeks, or on PCS for periods of from twenty weeks to eighteen months. In some cases, part of the costs will be borne by the government through veterans' educational assistance programs. The Army encourages officers who are near completion of a degree to complete their studies. Funding limitations and the requirements for assignment on required missions are limiting factors for the number who can participate in the program at one time.

Attendance at civilian colleges or universities to take studies to satisfy Army requirements, culminating in a master's or doctor's degree, are assignments highly sought by officers of the highest professional standing and attainments. Assignments are on the "best-qualified" basis.

Officers selected for this education are required to remain on active duty for three years for each year of schooling or fraction thereof, with a maximum obligation of four years. Normally, the officer is assigned directly to a utilization tour of duty applicable to this education.

Officers who are interested in any phase of the civil school program are urged to consult their unit personnel officer and their assignment officer in Washington, and are referred to DA Pam 600-3, *Commissioned Officer Professional Development and Utilization,* and the Army Regulations cited below.

The general publication of reference, which includes administrative matters, is AR 621-1, *Training of Military Personnel at Civilian Institutions.*

Training with Industry in industrial procedures and practices and advanced management training programs are available to Army officers. Training with Industry (TWI) normally is accomplished over a one-year period.

The Advanced Management Program (AMP) is for colonels and is conducted at several universities throughout the world. Course duration varies from one to six weeks.

Officers of the several corps of the Army Medical Service have exceptional opportunities for further professional training in Army schools as well as civilian professional medical schools. Reference: AR 350-219, *Professional Training of Army Medical Department Personnel.*

Unit or station personnel officers and training officers should be consulted as to opportunities available at any particular time.

Advanced Degrees, Top 5 Percent of West Point and ROTC Graduates. AR 621-1 provides that cadets from both West Point and the ROTC entering the Regular Army who graduate in the top 5 percent of their classes have priority over other civilian schooling applicants and will be able to attend graduate school during their fourth through tenth years of commissioned service providing their manner of performance on active duty is equal to or better than those of officers being selected for fully funded advanced civil schooling. The graduate schooling is authorized only in those disciplines for which the Army has a valid requirement. A maximum period of eighteen months is allowed to complete the requirements for the advanced degree.

Advanced Degrees, ROTC Graduates. Graduates of the ROTC entering the Regular Army may delay entry on active duty for up to two years in order to obtain an advanced degree (AR 145-1).

Scholarships, Fellowships, and Grants. Regular Army officers and Reserve officers in a Voluntary Indefinite category are authorized to compete for certain scholarships, fellowships, and grants. Regular officers must not have more than nineteen years of promotion list service and Reserve officers not more than fifteen years of federal active service at the time of commencement of the education. The academic study or grant research tours normally will not exceed twenty-four consecutive months, although exceptions may be authorized. See AR 621-7 for details.

Advanced Degree Program for ROTC Instructor Duty. This program is designed to increase the overall academic qualifications of all commissioned officers assigned to ROTC instructor duty, by allowing the officers to pursue advanced degrees prior to serving as ROTC instructors. Officers without a master's degree may apply. Applicants will be permitted to attend advanced civil schooling for up to fifteen months to obtain their degree. Following schooling, officers are assigned as ROTC instructors for a three-year stabilized tour. All direct schooling costs are borne by the officer, although eligible officers may use VA benefits to help defray expenses. See AR 621-1 for details.

Extension Courses Leading to College Credits. Officers are eligible to participate in the program of Extension Courses leading to college credits, sponsored by the Armed Forces Information and Education Program.

Off-Campus Study Programs. Those officers fortunate to be near universities and colleges that have continuing education programs can attend off-duty courses. These courses, like extension courses, can be taken to receive credits toward degrees but, unlike extension courses, are taught by professors accredited by or from the college. The local service (Army, Navy, Air Force) education office can provide information. Tuition funds are available that partially defray education costs and that incur service obligations. The Veterans Administration also provides in-service schooling benefits. (See chapter 9, *Financial Planning.*) A veterans' counselor will assist you at most colleges.

14

Evaluation
Reports

The system of evaluation ratings and periodic reports on the performance of duty of each officer of the Army is of the highest importance
to the Army as to its personnel management and administration, and
to each officer as to his or her own career development. It is a program
for increasing human effectiveness. It provides better careers for Army
officers, and it produces higher standards throughout the corps of
officers.*

All officers aspire to a favorable record, or series of evaluation
ratings, and to reach their maximum capability as their experience
increases. This chapter has been developed to explain the important
parts of the system. See chapter 4, *The Officer Image*, for suggestions
on how to increase the probability of receiving good reports.

The main subjects discussed in this chapter are the following—
The Evaluation Report and Career Planning.
Features of the Officer Evaluation Report, DA Form 67-8, 1979.
Evaluation Report Appeals.
Academic Evaluation Reports.
Efficiency Report, 1813 Model.

The subject of evaluation ratings has such a strong, abiding, and
determinative influence upon the career of each officer, starting at his
or her first assignment, that it is a wise plan to study the related
subjects that are discussed in the following chapters: 1, *An Army*

---

*The Army pioneered the evaluating and rating of officers. The requirement for submitting an annual efficiency report
(now, evaluation report) began early in this century, with less formal letter reports in earlier periods, as illustrated at chapter
end with the 1813 example. A standard rating scale was used successfully during World War I. DA Form 67-8, effective
from 15 September 1979, is a direct descendant of the "Form 67," adopted soon after World War I. The form reproduced
in this chapter is the eighth major revision since World War II. Each edition of *The Army Officer's Guide,* starting with
the third edition, 1939, contains copies of the successive forms with helpful information to readers of the period covered.

Career; 3, *The Code of the Army Officer;* 4, *The Officer Image;* 12, *Professional Development;* 13, *Army Schools and Career Progress;* and 15, *Promotion.*

This chapter seeks to explain important features of the report and the accompanying regulation. It contains additional information based on experience.

It is emphasized that this chapter is not a substitute for nor a condensation of AR 623-105. Consulted also in the preparation of the chapter: DA Pam 600-3, *Commissioned Officer Professional Development and Utilization.* For the preparation and submission of evaluation reports, see the official regulations, always.

THE EVALUATION REPORT AND CAREER PLANNING*

The most important periodic contribution to the officer's record is the official rating and description provided by the evaluation report. This report is used in all personnel actions at Headquarters, Department of the Army, including the following important matters for each officer:

Promotions	Regular Army integration
Assignment	Elimination
Selections for schools	Others

Unless the officer's capabilities and deficiencies are reflected accurately in evaluation reports, intelligent assignment and evaluation cannot be accomplished. Each evaluation report must contain a comprehensive, objective appraisal of an officer's abilities and capabilities. Positive recommendations for the correction of weaknesses and deficiencies, together with results of counseling by the rating officials, serve to provide a basis for comparison of future reports concerning these deficiencies.

The evaluation report requires careful consideration and thorough preparation by the rating officer and senior rater who must prepare it. Evaluation reports that are lacking in completeness, accuracy, and objectivity deprive commanders and personnel action agencies of any firm basis for evaluating progressive development and may injure the individual officer.

FEATURES OF THE OFFICER EVALUATION REPORT, DA FORM 67-8, 1979

The evaluation procedure now used by the Army first became effective on 15 September 1979. It builds upon the best features of its predecessors, but it represents a significant change from earlier evaluation forms and procedures. The aim of the current procedure is to dampen the inflated ratings that occurred with the earlier evaluation reports, provide improved performance counseling to the rated officer, increase communications within the chain of command, and provide a better evaluation of performance and potential. A major objective of the present procedure is to increase the role of senior officers in the evaluation process.

In the past it was sometimes difficult to identify the best officers within a group of superior, highly rated individuals. Selections for the most important assignments of command, staff, and technology, for the senior service colleges, and for university training to attain a master's or doctor's degree, are on the basis of choosing the best qualified. Promotion to commissioned grades above lieutenant is highly competitive and also on the basis of the best qualified. Records that facilitate wise selections are clearly essential in the interests of the officers considered, and of the Army itself.

---

*This is the substance of DA Pam 600-3, *Commissioned Officer Professional Development and Utilization,* as it pertains to the importance of evaluation reports.

OFFICER EVALUATION REPORT SUPPORT FORM

For use of this form, see AR 623-105; the proponent agency is DCSPER.

Read Privacy Act Statement on Reverse before Completing this form

PART I — RATED OFFICER IDENTIFICATION

NAME OF RATED OFFICER (Last, First, MI)	GRADE	ORGANIZATION

PART II — RATING CHAIN — YOUR RATING CHAIN FOR THE EVALUATION PERIOD IS:

	NAME	GRADE	POSITION
RATER			
INTERMEDIATE RATER	NAME	GRADE	POSITION
SENIOR RATER	NAME	GRADE	POSITION

PART III — VERIFICATION OF INITIAL FACE-TO-FACE DISCUSSION

AN INITIAL FACE-TO-FACE DISCUSSION OF DUTIES, RESPONSIBILITIES, AND PERFORMANCE OBJECTIVES FOR THE CURRENT

RATING PERIOD TOOK PLACE ON _____ _____

RATED OFFICER'S INITIALS _____ RATER'S INITIALS _____

PART IV — RATED OFFICER *(Complete a, b, and c below for this rating period)*

a. STATE YOUR SIGNIFICANT DUTIES AND RESPONSIBILITIES

DUTY TITLE IS _____ , THE POSITION CODE IS _____ .

b. INDICATE YOUR MAJOR PERFORMANCE OBJECTIVES

DA FORM 67-8-1 FEB 85   EDITION OF SEP 79 IS OBSOLETE.

OFFICER EVALUATION REPORT SUPPORT FORM, DA FORM 67-8-1.

The current evaluation procedure uses three forms. DA Form 67-8 is the Officer Evaluation Report (OER) form. An OER is prepared on each officer in the Army at least annually, or more often as prescribed by the regulations (AR 623-105). The completed OER is forwarded to the Department of the Army where it becomes a permanent portion of the rated officer's personnel records. The new procedure also uses a Support Form, DA Form 67-8-1, which is designed to involve the rated officer in a meaningful way in the evaluation process and to improve counseling.

The third form, DA Form 67-8-2, is designed for the use by Headquarters, Department of the Army. This form is titled Senior Rater Profile Report and is provided to maintain a rating history of each senior rater. This form tracks the rating history and makes it available to both the senior rater and Headquarters, Department of the Army.

The current procedure uses a rater and a senior rater for the evaluation of a rated officer. In those cases where there is an intermediate level of supervision between the rater and the senior rater, provision is made for an intermediate rater in the evaluation process. The rater normally is the immediate supervisor of the rated officer. The senior rater must be senior to the rater and (if any) to the intermediate rater, must have a grade of at least major, and must be at least two grades higher than the rated officer if the rated officer is a warrant officer or a commissioned officer through the grade of major. For the rating of officers in the grades of lieutenant colonel and colonel, the senior rater should be two grades higher, but circumstances may arise where a senior rater only one grade higher may be authorized. Brigadier generals and major generals must have a senior rater who is at least senior in date of rank to the rated officer, the rater, and the intermediate rater (if any). Provisions are made for civilian raters and senior raters in the regulations. If the senior rater is a civilian, then the first Army officer in the chain of command above the senior rater will provide an additional review of the completed OER, using an addendum to the report.

Rated Officer. Under the present procedure, the rated officer has two formal requirements associated with the rating process. (See the copy of the Support Form, DA Form 67-8-1, accompanying this discussion.)

As the rated officer, you are required to have a face-to-face discussion with your rating officer within the first thirty days of the rating period. This discussion is designed to encourage communication with and counseling by the rating officer. It is intended to result in development of your duties, responsibilities, and performance objectives in concert with and with the approval of your rating officer. These duties, responsibilities, and performance objectives are entered in Part IV of the initial working copy of the Support Form. You and the rating officer then indicate in Part III of the form the date of this discussion, and both of you initial the form. The results of this discussion and counseling will serve as a guide for your performance, but they are not necessarily all-inclusive. You are also responsible for all that is normally expected of an officer of your grade and duty position.

In those instances where this face-to-face discussion cannot take place within the first thirty days of the rating period because of geographic separation between you and the rating officer, correspondence and telephone conversations may be used as alternatives. However, these alternatives must be followed by a face-to-face discussion at the earliest opportunity. The Chief of Staff of the Army has stressed the importance of this face-to-face discussion with and counseling by your rating officer. Its accomplishment is a matter of interest to The Inspector General.

Following this face-to-face discussion and partial filling out of the initial working copy of the Support Form, you are then required to maintain the form during the remainder of the rating period. You should review the agreed-upon duties, responsibilities, and performance objectives periodically during the rating period. If necessary, you should request additional meetings with your rating officer to adjust the entries on the form to assure that it reflects any changes in missions or emphasis.

At the end of the rating period, you will be expected to fill out completely a final copy of the Support Form, including your significant accomplishments and contributions in Part IVc of the form. Also in Part IVc, you must include the results of your Army Physical Fitness Test (APFT) and your height and weight. You will then sign the form in Part IVc. At the same time, you will receive a copy of your Evaluation Report, DA Form 67-8, with appropriate information entered in Parts I and II. (See the copy of DA Form 67-8 accompanying this discussion.) You will be responsible for verifying the correctness of this information entered on the form. You then forward both the Evaluation Report and the completed Support Form to your rating officer.

Rater. The rater is required to counsel the rated officer within thirty days of the start of the rating period as to the rated officer's major duties and responsibilities and the performance objectives for the period, and to indicate by his or her initials in Part III of the Support Form the date that this counseling took place. At the end of the rating period, the rater then evaluates the rated officer as to his or her performance of these duties and the rated officer's potential for promotion.

As a rater, you have considerable latitude in developing the rated officer's duties and objectives. You may develop them yourself, you may develop them during your discussion with the rated officer, or you may task the rated officer to develop them. Remember, however, that the Support Form is only a guide. The rated officer is still responsible for, and should be evaluated on, all that is normally expected of an officer of that grade serving in that duty position. During the rating period, you should assure that the duty description and major performance objectives of the rated officer are kept current. This periodic review affords you an excellent opportunity to coach or counsel the rated officer and to provide him or her with the benefit of your knowledge and experience.

At the end of the rating period, you will receive the completed Support Form and the partially completed OER from the rated officer. The information on the Support Form should enable you to write a more accurate and complete OER. You should review the Support Form and sign it on the back. If the information on the form is inadequate or inaccurate, it is appropriate to discuss this with the rated officer and to suggest changes. However, you may not require the rated officer to change the information on the Support Form. You then fill out Parts III, IV, and V of the OER.

Take heed that the success of the officer evaluation system depends upon the complete and accurate use of the report and the regulations governing its preparation. You must understand that the success or failure of the evaluation system depends in part upon your ability to report accurately and objectively. You should also be mindful as the report is prepared that you are helping to make a selection of the future leaders of the Army. It is a heavy responsibility of leadership. You must apply the same painstaking care in the completion of reports rendered on subordinates as you would expect in the preparation of your own reports. The rated officer is to be evaluated fairly, as an individual, based upon current grade, experience, and military schooling, in comparison with officers of similar grade.

Note that Part V of the OER is to be used to comment on the specifics of the rated officer's performance. What did the officer do and how well did he or she do it? Gimmicks such as underlining or excessive capitalization are not permitted, and generalizations that are unsupported are of no value. This is the place to "tell it like it is." When you have completed your evaluation of the rated officer, you forward both the Support Form and the OER to the senior rater (or to the intermediate rater, if any).

Intermediate Rater. In most cases, there will be no intermediate rater. For those instances where an intermediate rater is designated, the intermediate rater will use

Part VI of the OER form to comment on the rated officer's performance and potential. If there is no intermediate rater, Part VI of the form is left blank.

Senior Rater. The senior rater is responsible for both the final rating chain review of the OER and for a critical evaluation of the rated officer's potential. Part VII of the OER is reserved for the use of the senior rater.

As senior rater, you are expected to provide an objective evaluation of the performance and potential of the rated officer, based upon your additional experience, a broad organizational perspective, and your focus on organizational requirements and actual performance results. You are required to compare the potential of the rated officer against a hypothetical average population of 100 officers of the same grade. Your evaluation should recognize that across the entire officer corps, there is a normal distribution in terms of quality and potential. It is highly unlikely that all or most of the officers for whom you act as senior rater are in the top few percent of the officer corps. Your evaluation should be accurate and fair, both to the rated officer and to the Army. As with the rater, you must "tell it like it is."

You accomplish your evaluation by placing an X in the appropriate box in the column marked SR, and your comments in block b. Your comments generally should address the potential of the rated officer, but they may also address performance, administrative review, or the evaluations of the rater and the intermediate rater (if any). You then return the Support Form to the rated officer and forward the completed OER to the servicing Military Personnel Service Center (PSC) or the appropriate administrative office.

At Headquarters, DA, your evaluation of the rated officer will be combined with your ratings of other officers of similar grade to produce an updated profile of your rating tendency. This profile, for officers of that grade or grade grouping, will be entered in Part VII of the OER by DA, providing a graphic indication of your general rating tendency and how you rated this particular officer compared to all other officers of his or her grade that you have previously rated.

The box(es) checked most frequently by the senior rater create a "center of mass" in the profile that may be compared to the box checked for the rated officer in order to determine if that officer is in, above, or below the "center of mass" of the senior rater's profile. This "center of mass" concept is the best method for interpreting the senior rater profile and is how DA Selection Boards interpret the evaluation.

Your Senior Rater Profile, DA Form 67-8-2, will be produced annually by DA, based upon the cumulative total by grade or grade grouping of all of your senior rater evaluations. One copy of this Senior Rater Profile is retained by DA in your personnel records and one copy is forwarded to you. The form is designed to track your general rating tendency and to make this information available both to you and to DA, where it may be used by various selection boards in their consideration of how you have performed your duty. Use of the Senior Rater Profile is intended to emphasize your responsibility to provide credible evaluative information to DA. This responsibility is considered to be one of your most important, since it affects the selection of the Army's future leaders and it has a critical impact on the way the Army accomplishes its missions.

Form 67-8, 1979, has space for the rater, the intermediate rater and the senior rater to provide narrative comments on matters not specifically covered elsewhere or to amplify other parts of the report. It is expected that the narrative will be completed within the space provided. Careful wording is required to permit cogent but full evaluation of the officer, while avoiding less meaningful but lengthier narratives. It should be clear that brevity is an objective but more important are

SEE PRIVACY ACT STATEMENT
ON DA FORM 67-8-1

For use of this form, see AR 623-105; proponent
agency is US Army Military Personnel Center.

PART I – ADMINISTRATIVE DATA

| a. LAST NAME · FIRST NAME · MIDDLE INITIAL | b. SSN | c. GRADE | d. DATE OF RANK | e. BR | f. DESIGNATED SPECIALTIES | g. PMOS (WO) | h. STA CODE |
| | | | Year | Month | Day | | | | |

i. UNIT, ORGANIZATION, STATION, ZIP CODE OR APO, MAJOR COMMAND | j. REASON FOR SUBMISSION | k. COMD CODE

l. PERIOD COVERED						m. NO. OF MONTHS	n. MILPO CODE	o. RATED OFFICER COPY *(Check one and date)*	p. FORWARDING ADDRESS
FROM			THRU						
Year	Month	Day	Year	Month	Day			1. GIVEN TO OFFICER	
								2. FORWARDED TO OFFICER	

q. EXPLANATION OF NONRATED PERIODS

PART II – AUTHENTICATION *(Rated officer signature verifies PART I data and RATING OFFICIALS ONLY)*

| a. NAME OF RATER *(Last, First, MI)* | SSN | SIGNATURE |
| GRADE, BRANCH, ORGANIZATION, DUTY ASSIGNMENT | | DATE |

| b. NAME OF INTERMEDIATE RATER *(Last, First, MI)* | SSN | SIGNATURE |
| GRADE, BRANCH, ORGANIZATION, DUTY ASSIGNMENT | | DATE |

| c. NAME OF SENIOR RATER *(Last, First, MI)* | SSN | SIGNATURE |
| GRADE, BRANCH, ORGANIZATION, DUTY ASSIGNMENT | | DATE |

| d. SIGNATURE OF RATED OFFICER | DATE | e. DATE ENTERED ON DA FORM 2-1 | f. RATED OFFICER MPO INITIALS | g. SR MPO INITIALS | h. NO. OF INCL |

PART III – DUTY DESCRIPTION *(Rater)*

a. PRINCIPAL DUTY TITLE   b. SSI/MOS

c. REFER TO PART IIIa, DA FORM 67-8-1

PART IV – PERFORMANCE EVALUATION – PROFESSIONALISM *(Rater)*

a. PROFESSIONAL COMPETENCE *(In Items 1 through 14 below, indicate the degree of agreement with the following statements as being descriptive of the rated officer. Any comments will be reflected in b below.)*

| | HIGH DEGREE | | | LOW DEGREE | |
| | 1 | 2 | 3 | 4 | 5 |

1. Possesses capacity to acquire knowledge/grasp concepts	8. Displays sound judgment
2. Demonstrates appropriate knowledge and expertise in assigned tasks	9. Seeks self-improvement
3. Maintains appropriate level of physical fitness	10. Is adaptable to changing situations
4. Motivates, challenges and develops subordinates	11. Sets and enforces high standards
5. Performs under physical and mental stress	12. Possesses military bearing and appearance ,
6. Encourages candor and frankness in subordinates	13. Supports EO/EEO
7. Clear and concise in written communication	14. Clear and concise in oral communication

b. PROFESSIONAL ETHICS *(Comment on any area where the rated officer is particularly outstanding or needs improvement)*

1. DEDICATION
2. RESPONSIBILITY
3. LOYALTY
4. DISCIPLINE
5. INTEGRITY
6. MORAL COURAGE
7. SELFLESSNESS
8. MORAL STAND-
   ARDS

DA FORM 67-8
1 SEP 79

REPLACES DA FORM 67-7, 1 JAN 73, WHICH IS OBSOLETE, 1 NOV 79.

US ARMY OFFICER EVALUATION REPORT

OFFICER EVALUATION REPORT, DA FORM 67-8 (FRONT).

accuracy, objectivity, fairness, and amplification or explanation of other parts of
the report.

EVALUATION REPORT APPEALS

An officer may discover upon reviewing the evaluation report file that some
administrative or substantive error was made. In such a case, the officer may file
an appeal in the form of a military letter, in duplicate, addressed to HQDA,

PERIOD COVERED

PART V – PERFORMANCE AND POTENTIAL EVALUATION (Rater)

a. RATED OFFICER'S NAME

SSN

RATED OFFICER IS ASSIGNED IN ONE OF HIS/HER DESIGNATED SPECIALTIES/MOS ☐ YES ☐ NO

b. PERFORMANCE DURING THIS RATING PERIOD. REFER TO PART III, DA FORM 67–8 AND PART III a, b, AND c, DA FORM 67–8–1

☐ ALWAYS EXCEEDED REQUIREMENTS   ☐ USUALLY EXCEEDED REQUIREMENTS   ☐ MET REQUIREMENTS   ☐ OFTEN FAILED REQUIREMENTS   ☐ USUALLY FAILED REQUIREMENTS

c. COMMENT ON SPECIFIC ASPECTS OF THE PERFORMANCE. REFER TO PART III, DA FORM 67–8 AND PART III a, b, AND c, DA FORM 67–8–1. DO NOT USE FOR COMMENTS ON POTENTIAL!

d. THIS OFFICER'S POTENTIAL FOR PROMOTION TO THE NEXT HIGHER GRADE IS

☐ PROMOTE AHEAD OF CONTEMPORARIES   ☐ PROMOTE WITH CONTEMPORARIES   ☐ DO NOT PROMOTE   ☐ OTHER (Explain below)

e. COMMENT ON POTENTIAL

PART VI – INTERMEDIATE RATER

a. COMMENTS

PART VII – SENIOR RATER

a. POTENTIAL EVALUATION (See Chapter 4, AR 623-105)

b. COMMENTS

SR | DA USE ONLY

HI

LO

A COMPLETED DA FORM 67-8-1 WAS RECEIVED WITH THIS REPORT AND CONSIDERED IN MY EVALUATION AND REVIEW   ☐ YES   ☐ NO (Explain in b)

OFFICER EVALUATION REPORT, DA FORM 67–8 (BACK).

(DAPC-MSE-A), Alexandria, VA 22332. This is OPMD, located at 200 Stovall Street in Alexandria. If the appeal concerns the substance of the report, it must be accompanied by substantial evidence in support of the appeal. This substantial evidence can be in the form of documentary evidence from official sources and/or sworn statements by third parties who were in official positions that enabled them to observe directly the manner of performance of duties during the rated period by the officer concerned.

Appeals are screened by, and those based on a claim of administrative error are resolved by, OPMD. Other appeals are forwarded through the officer's career managers to the Department of the Army Special Review Board. The Board determines if the claim has foundation and decides what corrective action, if any, is warranted. The Board may instruct OPMD to leave the report in the officer's file or amend it or delete it as deemed appropriate. OPMD will notify the officer of the decision on the appeal. All appeals should be submitted within five years of the "thru" date reflected on the DA Form 67-8 concerned.

ACADEMIC EVALUATION REPORTS

Academic Evaluation Reports are rendered on service members to explain the accomplishments, potential, and limitations of individuals while attending courses of instruction or training. DA Form 1059, Service School Academic Evaluation Report, is used to report the performance of students attending Army service schools, USAR schools, NCO academies, and schools sponsored by the other services. The Civilian Institution Academic Evaluation Report, DA Form 1059-1, is used to report the performance of students attending courses at civilian educational, medical, or industrial institutions. DA Form 1059-2, senior service college Academic Evaluation Report, is used to report the performance of students attending Senior Service College level courses. The same care and attention must be exercised in preparing these reports as is exercised in preparing Officer Evaluation Reports.

EFFICIENCY REPORT, 1813 MODEL

This 1813 example of an Army efficiency report is authentic. It was printed in *The Adjutant General's Bulletin, 1942,* and has been reproduced in many editions of *The Army Officer's Guide.* Although it is an amusing throwback to our early years, it separates the good ones from the bad ones, and the very good ones from the merely acceptable. This rating officer described his officers with accuracy, precision, candor. It is an example of accurate, colorful observation worthy of retention and consideration.

Sir: "Lower Seneca Town, August 15th, 1813.

I forward a list of the officers of the —th Regt. of Infty. arranged agreeable to rank. Annexed thereto you will find all the observations I deem necessary to make.

Respectfully, I am, Sir,

Yo. Obt. Sevt.,

Lewis Cass"

—th Regt. Infantry

Alexander Brown—Lt. Col., Comdg.—A good natured man.
Clark Crowell—first Major—A good man, but no officer.
Jess B. Wordsworth—2nd Major—An excellent officer.
Captain Shaw—A man of whom all unite in speaking ill—A knave despised by all.
Captain Thomas Lord—Indifferent, but promises well.
Captain Rockwell—An officer of capacity, but imprudent and a man of violent passions.

Captain Dan I. Ware   Strangers but little known in the regiment.
Captain Parker

1st Lt. Jas. Kearns   Merely good—nothing promising.
1st Lt. Thomas Dearfoot

1st Lt. Wm. Herring   Low, vulgar men, with the exception of Herring. From the
1st Lt. Danl. Land   meanest walks of life—possessing nothing of the char-
1st Lt. Jas. I. Bryan   acter of officers and gentlemen.
1st Lt. Robert McKewell

1st Lt. Robert Cross—Willing enough—has much to learn—with small capacity.
2nd Lt. Nicholas Farmer—A good officer, but drinks hard and disgraces himself and the Service.
2nd Lt. Stewart Berry—An ignorant unoffending fellow.
2nd Lt. Darrow—Just joined the Regiment—of fine appearance.

2nd Lt. Pierce 2nd Lt. Thos. G. Slicer 2nd Lt. Oliver Warren	Raised from the ranks, but all behave well and promise to make excellent officers.
2nd Lt. Royal Gore 2nd Lt. Means 2nd Lt. Clew 2nd Lt. McLear	All promoted from the ranks, low, vulgar men, without one qualification to recommend them—more fit to carry the hod than the epaulette.
2nd Lt. John G. Sheaffer 2nd Lt. Francis T. Whelan	Promoted from the ranks. Behave well and will make good officers.

Ensign Behan—The very dregs of the earth. Unfit for anything under heaven. God only knows how the poor thing got an appointment.

Ensign John Breen Ensign Byor	Promoted from the ranks—men of no manner and no promise.

Ensign North—From the ranks. A good young man who does well.

CONCLUSION

A fitting conclusion for this chapter, which succinctly states the case for striving to receive a series of commendable evaluation reports, is the following quotation from *The Rubaiyat* of Omar Khayyam.

The Moving Finger writes; and, having writ
Moves on: nor all thy Piety nor Wit
Shall lure it back to cancel half a Line,
Nor all thy tears wash out a word of it.
—The Rubaiyat.

15

Promotion

Few men have the natural strength to honor a friend's success without envy. —Aeschylus

The Army uses a very sound promotion system. Officers who meet the standards, and most do so, are justified in believing that their future promotions will be spaced to provide a rewarding career. At the same time, the work of the Army must be done, and its promotion system must and does provide the flow of trained and ready officers to move into higher and higher responsibilities. These future leaders must be identified, trained, and finally provided with the degree of authority which each will need to discharge greater responsibility. Training of good officers through schools and successive selected assignments is the justification for promotion so that good men and women will be ready when needed.

The Army promotion system for commissioned officers operates in accordance with the provisions of the Defense Officer Personnel Management Act (DOPMA), which became effective on 15 September 1981. DOPMA applies equally to all the military services and assures that the promotion systems of all the services operate under a common set of guidelines. An Army officer can expect to be advanced at about the same rate as his or her counterpart in the Navy or the Air Force. DOPMA applies only to commissioned officers.

For the Army, DOPMA established a single promotion system for all active duty commissioned officers, be they Regular or Reserve, and it eliminated any distinctions, real or perceived, that may have existed previously between male and female officers as regards promotion. All of the active Army's commissioned officers are treated equally under DOPMA.

The intent of DOPMA is to encourage a career commissioned officer corps of Regulars. Toward this goal, the DOPMA law increased the authorized size of the Army's corps of Regular officers to 63,000, and authorized the Army to establish an all-Regular commissioned officer force beyond the eleventh year of service.

This chapter explains the system of promotion as an aid to the officer who seeks the full attainment of the rewarding service the Army provides its members. The chapter is based upon AR 624-100.

GOALS OF A SOUND PROMOTION SYSTEM

The system of selection for promotion in use by the Army is of the highest importance. Unless it causes the best officers to reach the positions of importance and highest responsibility, the mission of the Army as well as the security of the nation is endangered. Unless officers are satisfied that hard work and achievement will place them in line for promotion, and that a reasonable career expectancy as to promotion may be anticipated, they cannot be satisfied fully with their choice of vocation. The present system of promotion is considered to be an equitable program, fair to the government and fair to individual officers. Only wartime promotion actions should change such a system, and then only to hasten decision through decentralization or to include other promotion authorizations made advisable by circumstances.

These are its goals:

To provide career incentives so as to draw men and women of high potential into the corps of officers of the Army.

To retain the officers of high potential, in willing, career-duration service, including those who possess special training for new or swiftly developing programs.

To advance to the higher grades during the peak years of their effectiveness the best qualified officers according to their achievement records.

To give promotion opportunity to officers of all branches and functional areas.

To provide equality of promotion opportunity among officers of the Active Army.

To eliminate the ineffective officers, as they show themselves to be below standard, as early as such a determination may be justly made.

PROMOTION AND CAREER PLANNING

The Army's promotion system is an essential part of its broad program of career planning. A commendable series of evaluation reports is a prerequisite to promotion on the "best-qualified" basis, and is also a decisive factor in career planning. It is urged that officers study the promotion system, in this chapter and its official references, with chapter 12, *Professional Development,* and Chapter 14, *Evaluation Reports.*

A sound promotion system is recognized as an important motivating factor in choosing a career as an Army officer. Officers wish to be assured that if they earn good evaluation ratings, their periodic promotions will coincide with their increasing capabilities for heavier responsibilities. Commissioned officers wish to feel confident that they will reach field grade, and the senior field grades, at an age sufficiently young to constitute a true reward for their finest efforts. They wish to reach eligibility for selection to the grade of colonel, and to general officer, at an age that, if they are selected, will allow adequate length of service in those grades.

THE GRADE STRUCTURE OF THE ARMY

The grade structure of the Army is controlled by The *Defense Officer Personnel Management Act.* The table below lists the grade authorizations for various officer strengths of the Active Army.

When total officer strength is:	Colonel	This distribution is allowed as a maximum: Lt. Colonel	Major
70,000	3,447	8,718	12,963
75,000	3,631	9,107	13,654
80,000	3,814	9,495	14,346
85,000	3,997	9,884	15,037
90,000	4,496	10,532	16,060

It should be noted that the officer strength varies in accordance with the overall strength of the Active Army. When the total number of Army members is increased, as during World War II or the Korean War or the years in Southeast Asia, the number of officers on active duty must be increased to provide the necessary, excellent leadership to which our soldiers are both entitled and accustomed. Conversely, when the crisis is past and the total Army strength is reduced, the number of officers on active duty also is reduced.

The actual number of officers on active duty with the Army at any time approximates 10 percent of the total Army active duty strength. Warrant officers on active duty comprise approximately 14 percent of the officer corps, depending upon the Army's needs for these highly skilled specialists.

Promotions Depend Upon Vacancies. When the authorized grade strengths are attained, future promotions depend upon vacancies. Vacancies occur from many causes including death, retirement, termination of active duty, resignation, and others. A promotion requires a corresponding vacancy.

PROMOTION PROCEDURES

There are a number of terms and concepts that need to be understood in order to understand the promotion system.

Promotion Selection Boards. The Army makes use of selection boards to recommend which officers should be promoted. Board members must be senior in grade to the officers they are to consider for promotion. Each member arrives at an independent conclusion as to the selection of each officer. The entire record of each officer considered is available for examination and is used in making individual determinations. A majority vote is required from board members to select an officer for promotion.

After the boards have acted and submitted their recommendations, and after the recommendations have been approved, promotions are made as vacancies occur. Approval of selection board recommendations is by the President, although the Secretary of the Army normally approves promotions for grades through colonel; by the President for brigadier generals and major generals; and by the President, subject to confirmation by the Senate, for lieutenant generals and generals.

Promotion Consideration. Consideration for promotion is on a year group basis. That is, all officers with dates of rank in a given year group will be considered for promotion with that year group. The system is arranged so that all officers, regardless of year group size, have the same cumulative opportunity for promotion. Officers whose records are good, and without conduct or character blemish, may approach the time of selection with confidence; the probabilities for their selection are strong. However, attention is invited to the earlier table showing numbers of officers authorized at the various grade levels. There are only about two-thirds as many lieutenant colonels authorized as there are majors, and only slightly more than one-third as many colonels as there are lieutenant colonels. Selection for promotion to the higher grades is highly competitive with a smaller portion of eligible officers attaining promotion as the grade levels increase.

The groups of officers considered by a selection board for promotion come from three zones.

Primary Zone. That year group of officers who are under primary consideration for promotion by a particular selection board are in the primary zone. The majority of selection board recommendations are from this year group.

Secondary Zone. Officers in the year group following the year group under primary consideration are in the secondary zone of consideration. For colonel selection boards, two year groups comprise the secondary zone. An officer in the secondary zone who has an outstanding record has an opportunity to be selected for promotion ahead of his or her contemporaries. The maximum selection rate of secondary zone officers is established at 10 percent of the list for any grade. This rate may be raised to 15 percent by the Secretary of the Army. However, the current maximum below-the-zone, or secondary zone, selection rates are set at 5 percent for promotion to major and 10 percent for promotion to lieutenant colonel and colonel.

Previously Considered. Officers who were previously considered for promotion, but who were not selected, i.e. "passed over," have an opportunity to be selected on a subsequent promotion list. As can be seen from the charts following, the odds of a previously considered, but passed over, officer being subsequently selected for promotion, at least to the grades of major and lieutenant colonel, are quite good. A pass-over does not signal the end of an Army career. It does, however, signal to the officer concerned that he or she should take immediate and effective steps to improve the manner of performance so that the next selection board might look upon him or her more favorably. Nonselection from a secondary zone list does not constitute a pass-over.

Fully Qualified for Promotion. This term applies to officers considered by a promotion board as qualified professionally and morally, and capable of performing the duties and assuming the responsibilities of the next higher grade. This method of promotion is utilized for all officers being considered for promotion to first lieutenant. The several promotion lists are named in a separate paragraph, below.

Best Qualified for Promotion. Under this method the selection boards recommend officers whom they consider the best qualified of the fully qualified in the zone of consideration.

The promotion board bases its recommendations on an impartial consideration of all officers in the zone of consideration. The factors considered include, but are not limited to, ability, efficiency, seniority, and age, together with those special instructions received in the Letter of Instructions to the board. The actions of the board are advisory in nature. That is, they recommend to the President or to the Secretary of the Army. The composition of the board and the Letter of Instructions to the board may be changed until such time as the recommendations of the board have been finally approved.

The board recommendation categorizes the officers considered as follows:

Recommended—Those officers the board recommends for promotion, listed in
    order of seniority.

Not Recommended—Those officers not recommended for promotion. This
    recommendation by the board is not subject to appeal for reconsideration
    except in cases where there was a material error in the records of an officer
    in the primary zone.

Selection Rates. The established selection rates for promotion to major, lieutenant colonel, and colonel are shown on the following table:

	SELECTION RATES		
	Major	*Lt. Colonel*	*Colonel*
Previously Considered	19%	13%	4%
Primary Zone	76%	64%	47%
Secondary Zone	5%	10%	10%
Cumulative Promotion Opportunity	80%	70%	50%

Each year group has the same cumulative opportunity for promotion, regardless of the size of the group. A large year group results in a large selection list, while a smaller year group results in a smaller selection list. Since the number of officers that can be promoted is dependent upon the vacancies that occur in the grade to which they are to be promoted, how fast a selection list is exhausted depends both upon the size of the list and the number of vacancies that occur. Note that while about eight of ten captains may anticipate promotion to major, only about one of two lieutenant colonels can expect promotion to colonel. It is a fact to be faced in planning your career. Not everyone can reach the top. However, if you do a fine job and acquire a series of commendable evaluation reports, with no major blemishes on your record, you should have little concern about promotions. They will come.

Selection for promotion to first lieutenant is made on a fully qualified basis. All such officers who are deemed to be fully qualified will be promoted at the appropriate time. See the later section on *Promotion through Colonel*.

Promotion Lists. There are twelve Army Promotion Lists, and promotions are made separately from each of these lists.

Separate promotion lists are maintained for:

Army	Judge Advocate General
Army Medical Specialist Corps	Medical Corps
Army Nurse Corps	Medical Service Corps
Chaplains	Professors, USMA
Dental Corps	Veterinary Corps
General Officers Seniority List	Warrant Officers

The Army Promotion List includes all of the combat arms, combat support arms, and combat service support arms, except the Chaplain Corps, the Judge Advocate General Corps, and the six corps of the Army Medical Department. Unless otherwise stated, the information throughout this chapter pertains to the Army Promotion List as modifications are provided in the other lists.

Effect of DOPMA on Active Duty Officers. Under DOPMA the Army has adopted an all-Regular force concept. By the eleventh year of service, all active duty officers must integrate into the Regular Army. DOPMA authorized an increase in Regular Army strength to 63,000 officers to accommodate the all-Regular force concept.

Company grade Reserve officers on active duty are encouraged to integrate into the Regular Army during their early years. Those who have not become Regular Army officers by the time they are selected for promotion to major, or by their eleventh year of service, are required to integrate into the Regular Army at that time or be separated from the service without being promoted.

Under DOPMA, a single active duty list is maintained for all commissioned officers. Promotion consideration is by year group from this active duty list.

CAREER EXPECTATIONS

Under the provisions of DOPMA, it is possible to plan your career, depending upon the assumptions you make regarding your relative standing among other officers of your grade and service.

Promotion through Colonel. Under the single promotion system established by DOPMA, there are minimum time-in-grade requirements established for "due course" officers. A "due course" officer is one who is selected for promotion along with his or her contemporaries, neither at an advanced rate by virtue of being promoted from a secondary zone nor delayed for promotion by being passed over by one promotion board and then later selected for promotion from among the group of previously considered officers. These minimum time-in-grade requirements are shown in the following table. Exceptions are made to allow for early secondary zone promotions.

Promotion to:	Minimum Time-In-Grade
First Lieutenant	18 months
Captain	2 years
Major	3 years
Lieutenant Colonel	3 years
Colonel	3 years

As noted earlier, actual promotions are dependent upon vacancies since there are maximum numbers of officers authorized by law at each grade level. A promotion cannot occur without a corresponding vacancy. The time in service (TIS) promotion opportunity for officers is expected to be about as follows:

Promotion to:	TIS	Cumulative Opportunity
First Lieutenant	18 months	Fully Qualified
Captain	4 ± 1 years	90%
Major	10 ± 1 years	80%
Lieutenant Colonel	16 ± 1 years	70%
Colonel	22 ± 1 years	50%

Maximum Career Expectation. A commissioned officer who enters the active Army today, either as a Regular Army officer or as a Reserve officer who later integrates into the Regular Army, and who achieves the grade of colonel, may expect to serve a full career of thirty years. If the top grade attained is lieutenant colonel, the maximum career expectancy is twenty-eight years.

A major who twice fails to be selected for promotion to lieutenant colonel may be separated from the service. Based upon the expected promotion expectancy, this would occur at about the seventeenth year of service. However, DOPMA provides for selective continuation on active duty of some majors who fill specialty needs. If the major in question were to be selected for continuation, he or she could serve to a maximum of twenty-four years, at which time the officer would be eligible to retire in the grade of major.

Similarly, a captain who twice fails to be selected for promotion to major may be separated from the service. The second pass-over would be expected to occur at about the eleventh year of service. However, captains also can be selectively continued to fill Army specialty needs. A captain who is selectively continued can remain on active duty to a maximum of twenty years, and thereafter be eligible for retirement.

Lieutenants, captains, and majors who receive two pass-overs and who are not selected to be continued on active duty in grade (captains and majors only) must be separated from the active Army.

Separation Pay. Officers who are separated from the Active Army involuntarily because of nonselection for promotion prior to completion of twenty years of service are not entitled to draw retired pay based on length of service. Nonetheless, these officers have performed valuable service to the Army. The DOPMA law contains provisions for such officers to receive a one-time separation payment equal to 10 percent of their latest annual base pay times their years of service, up to a maximum payment of $30,000. The separation payment rewards the officer for service to the nation and provides funds to tide the officer over until a new career is selected.

Promotion of General Officers. A single promotion system is established for promotion to the general officer grades as a continuation of the system used for lower ranking officers. Under the law, colonels and brigadier generals must serve at least one year in grade before they are eligible for promotion.

Promotion to brigadier general confers tenure for up to thirty years of service or five years in grade, whichever occurs later. Promotion to major general, lieutenant general, or general confers tenure to thirty-five years of service or five years in grade, whichever occurs later. Promotion to lieutenant general and general is subject to confirmation by the Senate, as are the subsequent assignments and reassignments of these officers.

Under the law, the President may vacate or cancel a promotion to brigadier general before the officer has served eighteen months in grade. The law also contains provisions for selective early retirement of brigadier generals and major generals who have reached the four-year time-in-grade point. The President also may extend the service of major generals, lieutenant generals, and generals beyond their mandatory retirement dates.

POLICIES FOR PROMOTION SELECTION BOARD

It is essential that officers have confidence in the objectivity and impartiality of the system used by the Army for the selective promotion of officers, both in decentralized field promotions and by the decisions reached by promotion boards in the Department of the Army. There is obvious need for general belief that it is done fairly, studiously, and objectively, and that selections are made by officers senior to those being considered and who hence cannot benefit personally. These goals are attained by the Army.

Whenever lists are published, and individuals note the names omitted as well as those fortunate enough to have been selected, there is natural wonder as to the good fortune of one and the misfortune of another. No informed person would deny the chance of human error because choices must be made following study and analysis of official records that were prepared by human beings in the discharge of their duties. Indeed, when we consider the extremely high quality of the corps of officers as to education and military training and dedication to the performance of their service, and the importance to the nation of a high proportion of current assignments, it should be understood that the borderline between those selected and those to be left in grade is often very slender. But officers who have performed duty as board members, and others who have observed them, know for sure that they are determined to make the choices accurately, wisely, and objectively in the interests of the Army and the individuals considered.

The Letter of Instructions provides information that guides board members in the matters to be considered in their selections. The evaluation reports accumulated during an officer's service are the principal records, but there are other records that are also made available as appropriate to enable wise decisions to be reached. Officers who wish to develop detailed knowledge of the complete system are urged to study the regulation.

NAMES OMITTED FROM PROMOTION ANNOUNCEMENTS

There are severe disappointments endured by those officers who read the lists of those who are selected for promotion and search in vain for their own names. It may extend from disappointment, through chagrin, with acute apprehension about termination of military career. Nonetheless, it is a necessary policy that provides for the nation the best possible corps of officers and better careers for the officers who serve the expected standard length of service. There are very important human problems involved.

Missing Names, Secondary Zone of Consideration. Selections of officers from the secondary zone of consideration are on the order of one in ten, or one in twenty of those promoted from both zones. These few officers gain a considerable advantage over their contemporaries. Competition among those who have the very highest evaluation ratings is very keen, and the selections are very close. The officers chosen will certainly have all the prerequisites of outstanding achievements, and a "something extra" that was convincing to members of the promotion board. Even so, there is widespread chagrin among those who were considered but not selected for swift promotion. Take this one in stride! Be the first to congratulate the fortunate ones. There are ample opportunities ahead.

Officers Categorized "Not Recommended." These officers receive an official pass-over. There may be a slender chance for their subsequent selection for promotion because elimination requires negative action by two promotion boards. Surely their chances for selection are not great, but neither are the odds insurmountable.

What to do? Perhaps the officer knows a great deal about his or her total record from contacts with OPMD, from knowledge of personal evaluation reports, or from counseling sessions conducted by the rating officer. Whatever course the officer elects to follow, he or she must make the final choice between staying on active duty as long as the law permits, and thereby qualifying for separation pay (see the earlier discussion) if ultimately separated involuntarily as a result of a second pass-over, or resigning. Those officers who choose to strive for favorable future board action as to their promotion will receive fair and even kindly consideration, but they should realize that the odds are against them.

THOUGHTS FOR ALL OFFICERS

At times in the Army, one might hear that "they" (whomever "they" are) say that some individual was selected for promotion based upon political pull or because he or she was in special favor for some reason. Dispel this notion from your mind. Promotion boards are composed of human beings, all subject to human frailties, but each member of each promotion board is an honorable member of the corps of officers, and each is equally determined to do the best he or she can to assure selection of the most highly qualified individuals for advancement. Political pressures are without value in gaining special consideration for any individual by a promotion board; any in-service pressure that may be applied is equally sterile. Let there be no doubt, the Army's promotion system is impartial, thorough, and fair.

PROMOTION OF OFFICERS IN THE RESERVE COMPONENTS

The policies and procedures for promoting commissioned officers of the Reserve Components of the Army below the grade of brigadier general are published in AR 135-155.

USAR promotions of Army Reserve officers are effected by the area commander within whose geographical area the officer's records are maintained. There are three exceptions: (1) USAR officers on active duty, except for second lieutenants under the jurisdiction of the area commander for Reserve matters, will be considered for promotion at Headquarters, Department of the Army. (2) An Army Reserve second lieutenant on six months' active duty for training (ACDUTRA) will be considered for promotion by the area commander under whom the officer is serving the ACDUTRA, provided he or she is otherwise qualified. (3) Army National Guard of the United States (ARNGUS) promotions for all ARNGUS officers will be made at Headquarters, Department of the Army.

In 1986, the Defense Department submitted proposed legislation to Congress to bring Reserve and National Guard officers not on active duty under a management system similar to that for active duty officers. The proposed Reserve Officer Personnel Management Act (ROPMA) would change many of the appointment, promotion, separation, and retirement laws now incorporated in Title 10, U.S. Code. The new act would establish a promotion system for all nonactive duty reserve officers based on a "best-qualified," quota-based, competitive selection method, with zones of consideration, including secondary zones, that would be adjusted annually to meet the Army's actual or anticipated needs.

A single Reserve Active Status List (RASL) would list all Reservists and Guardsmen on active status. Maintained by rank and competitive category, the RASL would be used to determine promotion eligibility, and for continuation and separation considerations. The law would set a minimum and maximum time in grade (TIG) for promotion and eliminate the existing criteria regarding total commissioned service (TCS). Zones of consideration for promotion would be set each year within the minimum and maximum TIG limitations of the law. The unit vacancy promotion system would be changed to a position vacancy system. To be eligible for promotion, an officer would have to meet the minimum TIG requirements, be fully qualified for promotion, be available (geographically) to serve in a designated position, and be recommended by a position vacancy promotion board. Proposed TIG requirements are as follows:

	Minimum	Maximum
First Lieutenant	18 months	—
Captain	2 years	5 years
Major	4 years	7 years
Lieutenant Colonel	3 years	7 years
Colonel	1 year	—
Brigadier General	1 year	—

The proposed law would provide for selective continuation of officers who had not been promoted. Captains could be selectively retained until completion of twenty years' service, majors through twenty-four years' service, lieutenant colonels through thirty-three years, and colonels until thirty-five years. If not selectively continued, captains who had been twice passed over would be separated. Twice-passed-over majors would be separated after twenty years' service, lieutenant colonels after twenty-eight years, and colonels after thirty years.

16

Special for
Warrant Officers

Previous editions of *The Army Officer's Guide* have had special considerations for warrant officers scattered throughout the book in those places where the regulations or policies pertaining to warrant officers differ from those governing commissioned officers. While the book as a whole is applicable to all officers, commissioned and warrant, there are differences, especially as regards professional development, schooling, evaluation reports, and promotion.

For this edition, thanks to the efforts of the officers heading the study that resulted in the Total Warrant Officer System (TWOS), all of the special information pertaining to warrant officers, such as the history of the Warrant Officer Corps, promotion policies, professional development opportunities, schooling, and special considerations for evaluation reports has been gathered in this chapter. It is presented in the pages following, together with an informed outlook on what the future likely holds in store for the Army's warrant officers.

HISTORY OF THE WARRANT OFFICER CORPS

The warrant officer designation has long been recognized by various navies of the world. In the navy, the warrant officer traditionally has been a technical specialist whose skills and knowledge were essential for proper operation of the ships. The warrant officer grade in one form or another has been in continuous use in the U.S. Navy since that service was established. In the U.S. Army, the warrant officer lineage can be traced back to the Headquarters Clerks of 1896, later designated Army Field Clerks. However, the recognized birth date of the Army's Warrant Officer Corps is 7 July 1918.

On that date, an Act of Congress established the Army Mine Planter Service as part of the Coast Artillery Corps and appointed in it warrant officers to serve as masters, mates, chief engineers, and assistant engineers of each vessel. An act of 1920 expanded the use of warrant officers, authorizing their appointment in clerical, administrative, and band-leading activities. In effect, the act of 1920 designated the warrant officer grade as a reward for enlisted personnel of long service and as a haven for former commissioned officers of World War I who lacked either the education or other eligibility requirements to retain their commissions after that war.

Between 1922 and 1935, no warrant officer appointments were made except for a few band leaders and Army Mine Planter Service personnel. In 1936, competitive examinations were held to replenish lists of eligible personnel, and some appointments began being made again. Warrant officers who were qualified pilots were declared eligible for appointment as lieutenants in the Air Corps in 1939. By 1940, warrant officer appointments began to occur in significant numbers for the first time since 1922, although the total strength of the Warrant Officer Corps decreased until 1942 because of the large numbers of warrant officers who were being transferred to commissioned status during that period.

The second truly important piece of legislation affecting Army warrant officers was passed in 1941. An act of August 1941, amplified by an Executive Order in November of that year, provided that warrant officers could be assigned duties as prescribed by the Secretary of the Army and that when such duties necessarily included those normally performed by a commissioned officer, the warrant officer would be vested with all the powers usually exercised by commissioned officers in the performance of such duties. The act of 1941 also established two warrant officer grades, Chief Warrant Officer and Warrant Officer Junior Grade, and authorized flight pay for those whose duties involved aerial flight.

Warrant officer appointments were made by major commanders during World War II, and warrant officers served in some forty occupational areas during that war. In January of 1944, the appointment of women as warrant officers was authorized, and by the end of the war there were forty-two female warrant officers on active duty.

After World War II, the concept of using the warrant rank as an incentive rather than a reward was instituted. It was to be a capstone rank into which enlisted personnel could advance. This use of the warrant officer grade, combined with the earlier concept of using the grade as a reward for long and faithful service, resulted in mixed utilization so that, in practice, warrant officers became largely interchangeable with junior commissioned officers or senior enlisted personnel.

The Career Compensation Act of 1949 provided two new pay rates for warrant officers. The designations of Warrant Officer Junior Grade and Chief Warrant Officer were retained, but the grade of Chief Warrant Officer was provided with pay rates W2, W3 and W4. In the Warrant Officer Personnel Act of 1954, these three pay rates became grades and the Warrant Officer Junior Grade became Warrant Officer, providing the four warrant officer grades we have today.

Warrant officers were used extensively during the Korean War, but by 1953 it had become apparent that use of the warrant officer grade as either a reward or an incentive was inadequate. Needed as a basis for continuation of the Warrant Officer Corps was a new concept consistent with functional Army requirements. From 1953 until 1957, the Department of the Army conducted an analysis to determine whether or not the warrant officer program should be continued and, if so, in what form and for what purpose.

In January of 1957, as a result of the Department of the Army study, a new warrant officer concept was announced that affirmed the need for the warrant officer and the continuation of the Warrant Officer Corps. It stipulated that the warrant officer grade would not be considered as either a reward or an incentive for enlisted men or former commissioned officers, and it defined a warrant officer as "a highly skilled technician who is provided to fill those positions above the enlisted level that are too specialized in scope to permit the effective development and continued utilization of broadly trained, branch-qualified, commissioned officers."

In 1966, as part of a continuing effort to improve operation of the new concept, a study group was formed at DA with a mission to develop a formal warrant officer career program that would be responsive to future Army requirements while offering enough career opportunities to attract high-quality personnel. The study group examined all aspects of the Warrant Officer Corps and made a number of recommendations in areas such as pay, promotion, utilization, and education. Provisions for below the zone selection for promotion to grades CW3 and CW4 were implemented in 1967. The Regular Army program was reopened to warrant officer applicants in 1968 after having been closed for twenty years, and subsequent changes reduced service eligibility criteria and simplified application procedures. Since 1968 the military education available to warrant officers has been expanded. Before then, there was no formal progressive military schooling program for warrant officers. By the end of 1972 a tri-level education system had been established that provided formal training at the basic or entry level for warrant officers in fifty-nine occupational specialties, at the intermediate or midcareer level for fifty-three specialties, and at the advanced level for twenty-seven specialties. In 1973 the three levels of training were redesignated from "basic," "intermediate," and "advanced" to "entry," "advanced," and "senior," respectively. Simultaneously, as the result of successful testing of the concept, the Warrant Officer Senior Course (WOSC) was established to provide all warrant officers with access to the highest level of professional education.

In 1973, DA began to implement a plan to close the gaps in the warrant officer military education system by directing the expansion or modification of existing advanced (formerly intermediate) courses to accommodate all warrant officer specialties. Civil schooling opportunities were also increased during this period. The educational goal for warrant officers was upgraded from two-year college equivalency to attainment of an associate degree, and warrant officers, for the first time, were authorized entry into fully funded civil school programs. As a means of aiding progression toward goal achievement, cooperative degree programs were established in colleges and universities near the installations conducting the warrant officer career courses. These programs were implemented to provide students in the military establishment the opportunity to complete requirements for MOS-related associate degrees while in attendance at their career courses.

In consonance with increased educational opportunities, duty positions requiring warrant officers with bachelor's or master's degrees were validated for the first time by the Army Education Requirements Board (AERB). By the close of 1975, the Army's capability for professionally developing the Warrant Officer Corps had been significantly expanded, and warrant officers in the modern program were being offered developmental opportunities that their predecessors never had available.

To satisfy the recognized need for qualified, highly trained individuals available to expand the active Warrant Officer Corps rapidly in time of emergency and to meet other Army requirements, Reserve Component warrant officers not on active duty and National Guard warrant officers are integrated into the Army's professional development program. Reserve Component warrant officers are provided a balanced mix of training, experience, and career opportunities through periodic rotation at predetermined points in their careers between the Selected Reserve Troop Program Units (TPU) and the Individual Ready Reserve (IRR), attendance at requisite military schools, and short periods of counterpart training with active component organizations.

The years following inception of the Warrant Officer Career Program saw increasing warrant officer participation in the development of policies and programs. Increasingly, the warrant officer viewpoint was sought in the development of plans that had an effect upon the Warrant Officer Corps. Since 1973 warrant officers have been authorized as voting members on various HQDA Selection Boards that consider warrant officers. Warrant officer positions were established in the Offices of the Deputy Chiefs of Staff for Personnel (DCSPER), Operations and Plans (DCSOPS), and Logistics (DCSLOG) to provide warrant officer perspective at the highest level of the Army.

THE TOTAL WARRANT OFFICER SYSTEM (TWOS)

A new era for warrant officers began when the Department of the Army Total Warrant Officer Study Group was chartered by the Chief of Staff, Army (CSA), in September 1984. This was the first Department of the Army-level comprehensive study of warrant officer management (preappointment through retirement) across the Total Army. Essentially, the study was required to answer the following questions: "What are warrant officers doing now?" "What should warrant officers be doing in the future?" and "What is the definition of a warrant officer?" The study group developed this mission statement: "Examine the role and utilization, professional development, management, compensation programs, policies and procedures, and recommended changes where the effect would enhance combat readiness for the Total Army."

The study group accomplished this mission by reviewing current systems; program analysis; surveying warrant officers and commissioned officers; proponent workshops; warrant officer steering groups; and general officer advisory groups. The study group briefed its findings and recommendations to the CSA on 24 June 1985.

The approved recommendations of the Total Warrant Officer Study resulted in the Total Warrant Officer System (TWOS), a new personnel management system for warrant officers of the Total Army (Active and Reserve components). TWOS is a disciplined, requirements-based, life-cycle management system designed to meet Army requirements for warrant officers, from initial recruitment and appointment through retirement or separation.

As shown on the accompanying chart, the decisions of the Army Chief of Staff are influencing today's warrant officer in four key areas:
- Rank and job classification
- Training
- Revised career management
- Legislation

Redefining the Role of the Warrant Officer. The definition of a warrant officer, as developed by the study group, is: "An *officer* appointed by warrant by the Secretary of the Army based on a *sound level* of *technical and tactical competence*. The warrant officer is the highly specialized expert and *trainer* who, by gaining *progressive levels* of expertise and *leadership,* operates, maintains, administers, and manages the Army's equipment, support activities, or technical systems for an *entire career.*"

The new warrant officer definition is the cornerstone of TWOS. While previous

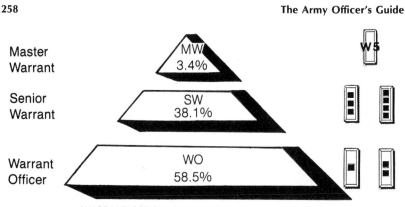

WARRANT OFFICER REQUIREMENTS BY RANK GROUP.

definitions focused exclusively on the need for technical competency, the new definition stresses the importance of both technical and tactical proficiency.

The warrant officer's traditional role as a technical expert and trainer on complex systems remains unchanged. He or she can expect to start with a sound level of proven competence and to serve in challenging jobs at progressive levels of increasing responsibility commensurate with grade and experience.

Consideration of the tactical dimension ensures that the warrant officer is prepared to lead subordinates under modern battlefield conditions (pockets of resistance and 360-degree battle orientation) where the warrant officer's tactical skill may spell the difference between victory or defeat.

Warrant Officer Requirements Classified by Rank Group. Previously, the system for identifying warrant officer requirements for a given unit or installation did not specify the degree of skill or experience required to do a given job. When making an assignment, a personnel manager referred to authorization documents that simply reflected the code "WO," signifying that a warrant officer was needed to fill a position. This meant that any warrant officer, WO1 through CW4, could have been selected to fill any position authorized for his or her military occupational specialty at any point in his or her career.

Under TWOS, warrant officer positions will be coded to reflect one of three rank groups: warrant officer (W1/W2), senior warrant (W3/W4), or master warrant (W5). (Until legislation is passed establishing the grade of W5, senior W4s will be selected by DA boards, trained, certified, and used as master warrant officers.) This change will enable assignment managers to fill each job with a warrant officer possessing the appropriate skills, training, experience, and grade required to meet a commander's needs.

Document coding for the active component has been completed, and OPMD began assigning individuals to jobs by rank groups in early 1988, with initial report dates in October 1988. The accompanying chart shows the warrant officer requirements by rank group.

Recruiting. In the past the Army depended on self-initiated applications from members of the enlisted force to meet the Army's need for warrant officers. The results of this procurement program were mixed at best, resulting in shortages in several warrant officer MOS (Military Occupational Specialty). Under TWOS, a proactive requirements-based recruiting system was developed. The U.S. Army Recruiting Command (USAREC) was given the mission to implement the new

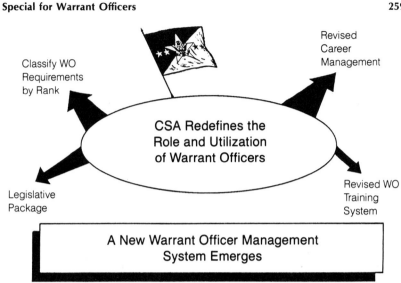

Classify WO
Requirements
by Rank

Revised
Career
Management

CSA Redefines the
Role and Utilization
of Warrant Officers

Legislative
Package

Revised WO
Training
System

A New Warrant Officer Management
System Emerges

warrant officer recruiting system. USAREC assumed this mission on 1 January 1987, and initial results have been encouraging.

Revised Warrant Officer Training System. A progressive training system based upon the skills needed to fill Army warrant officer requirements is being developed by Training and Doctrine Command. Training will precede utilization in each of the three distinct career phases. Warrant officers will be certified at each training level to ensure that technical and tactical standards are attained and maintained.

Under the revised training system, warrant officer candidates will receive officership and technical training (warrant officer training) prior to their appointment and utilization in jobs coded for W1/W2. After gaining on-the-job experience and selection for promotion to CW3, warrant officers will attend senior warrant officer training to prepare them for jobs at the W3/W4 level. Finally, the warrant officer senior course has been terminated. A master warrant officer training course has been developed for warrants selected for MW/W5 assignments. This training system is illustrated on the accompanying chart.

Warrant officers will complete MOS functional training as required to support assignment requirements.

Civil Schooling. The TWOS civil education goal is for each warrant officer to possess at least an associate degree in an MOS-related discipline by the end of his or her seventh year of warrant officer service. The fully funded associate degree program is often used by warrant officers to attain the civil education goal. The officer attends school full time while drawing full pay and allowances. The Army pays school costs. A period of up to eighteen months is authorized for the warrant officer to complete the requirements for an associate degree. A limited number of warrant officers may also be authorized baccalaureate or graduate level training to fill positions validated by the Army Education Requirements Board. Warrant officers who are interested in any phase of the civil school programs can contact their post/installation education officer or their Department of the Army career

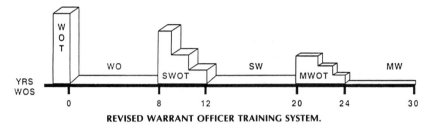

REVISED WARRANT OFFICER TRAINING SYSTEM.

manager. Useful information is also found in DA Pam 600-11, *WO Professional Development*, and AR 621-1, *Training of Military Personnel at Civilian Institutions*.

Total Warrant Officer System Career Plan. Changes can be expected in the personnel management policies affecting warrant officer schooling, promotions, assignments, and retirement under TWOS.

Warrant officers will be managed by years of Warrant Officer Service (WOS) rather than by years of Active Federal Service (AFS). This means the personnel management "clock" will be reset to zero when an enlisted soldier is appointed as a warrant officer. This will enable each individual to retain seniority for purposes of pay and retirement, while affording him or her the *opportunity* to serve a full thirty years as a warrant officer, or until the mandatory retirement age of sixty-two (whichever comes first).

Once TWOS is fully implemented, warrant officers will be required to integrate into the Regular Army upon promotion to CW3. Warrant officers promoted to CW4 could serve at least twenty-four years of WOS under proposed changes. Warrants selected for training and utilization as master warrants would have the opportunity to serve a full thirty-year warrant officer career. This career plan is illustrated on the chart accompanying this discussion. Note, however, that the promotion opportunities depicted on the chart are estimates based on computer modeling and may vary due to changing Army requirements by grade and MOS.

Legislative Initiatives. Some features of TWOS require changes in law. A legislative package has been prepared that requests changes in law to authorize:
- Creation of the new grade of rank of CW5.
- Establishment of a single promotion system to replace the current dual (temporary and permanent) promotion system.
- Personnel management procedures permitting selective retirement when needed to control the size of the retirement-eligible force.
- Regular Army (RA) warrant officers to sit on warrant officer selection boards.
- Equivalent time to mandatory separation for both commissioned and warrant officers after two-time nonselection for RA promotion (currently two months for warrant officers, six months for commissioned officers).

The Army proposal must be staffed with the other military services and receive budget support from DoD and the Office of Management and Budget. With the switch to a two-year defense budget cycle, it is unlikely the legislative proposals will be considered by Congress before fiscal year 1990.

Summary. The primary tenets of TWOS can be summarized as follows:

Obtain Earlier. The TWOS philosophy calls for accessing a warrant officer based on the applicant's possession of a sound level of technical/tactical competence in

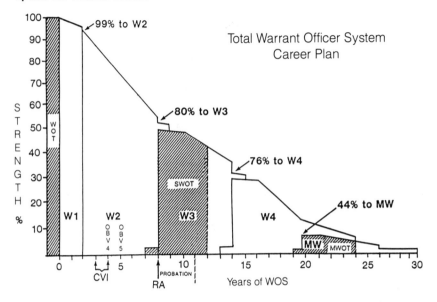

his/her MOS. This sound (minimum) level of required expertise is determined by each MOS proponent; varies by MOS; and is not, in all cases, measured by the applicant's enlisted rank. In some MOS, training received in the former enlisted or civilian status can be substituted for grade or time in service. The TWOS career plan is designed for individuals accessed early enough in their military career to allow them to serve for thirty years as a warrant officer prior to reaching age sixty-two.

Train Better. Under TWOS, all warrant officer training courses are requirement-based and have been developed under the systems approach to training. Warrant officer positions have been surveyed to determine the skills and tasks required in each job. Based on these data, training courses have been revised to teach the students the skills, jobs, and tasks associated with their MOS, position, and grade. Additionally, all career training courses will be progressive in nature, with course content designed to build upon previously conducted instruction.

Retain Longer. Under TWOS, attainment of warrant officer status is not a capstone or reward for long and meritorious enlisted service. The TWOS creates the environment and provides a method to encourage a service member to serve a full career as a warrant officer. Progressive training, coupled with progressive utilization, will enhance warrant officer retention, thus saving training dollars.

PROMOTION OF WARRANT OFFICERS

Warrant officers are not included under the provisions of the Defense Officer Personnel Management Act (DOPMA) of 1981, which instituted a single active duty list promotion system for officers with rank of second lieutenant and above. Until the TWOS legislative initiative (which calls for a single promotion system for active duty warrant officers) is enacted, warrant officers will continue to be considered for promotion under existing laws, which provide for both temporary and permanent grades.

Temporary (AUS) Promotions. The total Active Army force is known as the Army of the United States (AUS). This force includes both Regular Army (RA) and other than RA (OTRA) warrant officers. When the AUS exceeds the Regular Army in size, Active Army grade vacancies are usually filled by temporary (AUS) promotions. It is the individual's temporary grade that normally determines pay, assignments, and authorized insignia.

Some other features of the temporary promotion system:

1. Temporary promotions are administered at HQDA with the exception of promotion to CW2, for which authority has been delegated to field commanders. Under this authority, warrant officers considered fully qualified may be promoted to CW2 (AUS) after completing twenty-four months in grade W1.

2. Temporary promotion to CW3 and CW4 does not occur at fixed points of service. Changes in Army authorizations and varying attrition rates create fluctuations in AUS grade vacancies, which in turn cause variations in the time-in-grade that personnel in grades CW2 (AUS) and CW3 (AUS) must serve before coming into the zone for their next higher AUS promotion.

3. Below-the-zone AUS promotions to grades CW3 and CW4 permit the accelerated promotion of those warrant officers whose demonstrated performance and indicated potential are superior to their peers.

4. An OTRA officer nonselected for temporary (AUS) promotion to CW2 will be released from active duty within ninety days of approval of the recommendation that the officer not be promoted. In the case of OTRA warrant officers in grade CW2 (AUS) and CW3 (AUS), release from active duty is required after twice failing to be selected for the next higher AUS grade.

Permanent Promotions. Permanent promotions fall into two categories—Regular Army (RA) and United States Army Reserve (USAR). Permanent (RA) promotions occur at fixed points of service. Upon completion of three years' service, fully qualified W1s are promoted to CW2. For advancement to CW3 and CW4, HQDA convenes a promotion board to select the best qualified personnel in the zone of consideration for promotion. Selected individuals are promoted upon completion of six years' time-in-grade. Unlike the temporary promotion system wherein both time-in-grade and selection rates may vary widely depending on fluctuations in AUS vacancies, the RA promotion system operates by law at fixed promotion intervals and at the minimum selection rate of 80 percent of those being considered for the first time required by law.

Permanent promotions of Reserve warrant officers serving on full-time active duty will not result in board action if already serving in the next higher AUS grade. If the requisite time for permanent promotion is served and the individual (USAR) has still not been selected for temporary (AUS) promotion to the next higher grade, the individual must continue serving in the lower temporary (AUS) grade if remaining on active duty. Nonactive duty USAR and National Guard warrant officers only receive permanent promotions, which will occur automatically at prescribed points. Active duty warrant officers who are twice nonselected for permanent promotion (if RA) or temporary promotion (if USAR) will be separated from active duty unless they are within two years of being retirement eligible, in which case they will normally be retained to twenty years of service.

Service obligations. Warrant officers of any component who accept either a temporary or a permanent promotion that causes an active duty grade change to W3 or W4 incur a service obligation of two years from date of promotion.

The TWOS legislative proposal will replace the dual system with a single promotion system for active duty warrants. All promotions will be permanent and will occur at varying points of service based on Army requirements, very similar to the current temporary promotion points.

WARRANT OFFICER RETIREMENT

Warrant officers are eligible to retire after serving twenty years of active federal service. Current policy requires all Reserve Component warrant officers to be mandatorily released from active duty when they complete twenty years of active federal service (AFS), unless they are selected for retention by HQDA or they incur a promotion lock-in period. Warrant officers to be released may apply for voluntary retirement under the provisions of AR 635-100, chapter 4, to be effective no later than their scheduled release date. Regular warrant officers are required by law to retire upon completion of thirty years of AFS. However, warrant officers can be retained to age sixty-two with approval of the Secretary of the Army.

After passage of TWOS legislation, mandatory retirement of Regular Army CW4s will occur upon completion of twenty-four years' warrant officer service (WOS), or thirty years' WOS for RA CW5. In neither case shall the warrant officer be permitted to serve beyond age sixty-two.

COMMISSIONING OF WARRANT OFFICERS

Title 10 of the United States Code was changed by the ninety-ninth Congress to provide for the commissioning of warrant officers. The primary purpose of the legislation was to standardize the procedures used by the military services to appoint warrant officers.

Regular Army warrant officers will be commissioned by the President upon promotion to Chief Warrant Officer. An other-than-regular Army warrant officer will be commissioned as permanent Chief Warrant Officer by the Secretary of the Army. Temporary promotions under the Army of the United States system have no effect on commissioning. Warrant officers in grade WO1 will continue to be appointed, not commissioned, by the Secretary of the Army. There is no legal distinction between Presidential and Secretarial appointments. New policy provisions pertaining to commissioned warrant officers were approved in May 1987 by the Deputy Chief of Staff for Personnel. Under the new policy, commissioning has little practical effect on assignments, but could have some effect on utilization. Warrant officers will continue to be assigned to warrant officer positions in their primary or additional military occupational specialties. Under unusual circumstances, a warrant officer may be assigned outside his or her MOS or in a commissioned officer position only upon his or her commander's recommendation and with DA concurrence.

The main effect of commissioning is on the powers of a commissioned warrant officer. The commissioned warrant officer is authorized to:

- Order enlisted soldiers into arrest or confinement.
- Administer an oath of enlistment or reenlistment.
- Administer various oaths in performance of duties when acting as an adjutant, assigned as a military personnel officer, or specifically designated by other Army regulations.
- Sit on courts of inquiry or be detailed as a general staff officer or inspector general.
- In the grade of CW3 or higher, when appointed by a general court-martial convening authority, act as a summary court-martial officer to try criminal offenses, conduct inquests, or dispose of personal effects.

- In the grade of CW4, when appointed by a general court-martial convening authority (except a warrant officer possessing MOS 713A), act as an investigating officer under the provisions of Article 32, UCMJ.

These and other powers of the warrant officer are defined in AR 611-112, *Manual of Warrant Officer Military Occupational Specialties.*

WARRANT OFFICER EVALUATIONS

Since the warrant officer is a distinct category of officer, the rating chain must recognize the basic differences between warrant and commissioned officers when evaluating performance and potential. Both commissioned and warrant officers are authorized to perform similar functions (i.e., command a station, unit, or detachment; certify vouchers; administer oaths; disburse funds; and impose discipline). Both categories of officer personnel must be technically and tactically competent. Despite their mutual functions, the professional development, use, and evaluation of warrant officers differ from those of commissioned officers. These differences must be considered when evaluating warrant officers.

Warrant officers are appointed to serve in technical military occupational specialities (MOS). Thus, their professional development is aimed at increasing competence in their specialties. Because of their technical orientation, warrant officers are qualified to supervise personnel serving in technical occupations similar to their own. Warrant officers are technical operators, managers, administrators, or maintainers throughout their careers. Because of these differences, warrant officers should be evaluated on their potential for continued service in the technical positions for which they are trained and qualified. They should not be evaluated on their potential to fill positions of responsibility outside their specialties.

In addition to the requirement to maintain technical and tactical competence in their MOS, warrant officers must demonstrate performance and potential as Army officers. They must display leadership qualities, managerial talents, and technical and tactical competence in both their principal duty and in special emphasis areas involving other missions, tasks, and objectives that support the primary organizational mission. That is, in addition to MOS qualifications, warrant officers are expected to:

- Communicate (brief their supervisors and counsel their subordinates).
- Deal sensitively with people.
- Mix a variety of tasks efficiently (special emphasis areas as well as principal duties).
- Make, execute, and supervise plans.

When evaluating the warrant officer's performance of special emphasis areas, his or her training and experience must be considered; it must not be assumed that he or she is able to do all types of special emphasis area work. If a warrant officer performs duty in special emphasis areas outside his or her technical specialty, he or she should be evaluated on willingness to assume responsibility, innovation, organizational ability, supervisory talents, thoroughness, and so on.

Individuals who must evaluate warrant officers should study AR 623-105, *Officer Evaluation Reporting System,* and DA Pam 600-11, *Warrant Officer Professional Development,* before preparing evaluation reports.

17

Responsibilities of Command

Command of an Army unit of any size is a rewarding and satisfying assignment. In the command of the platoon or company, even the battalion, the commander and other officers assigned have the rich experience of personal contact where they know their troops, and troops know their officers. Teamwork flows from working together, and with healthy teamwork comes confidence in the personnel who form the unit. An officer assigned in any capacity to duty with troops is privileged and should enter upon responsibilities with determination to succeed.

Duty with a troop unit involves a wide variety of different responsibilities. There is the mission, or a series of missions; the training of members of the command or training of incoming replacements; supply, care, and maintenance of equipment; provision for a mess and its continual supervision; unit transport; unit administration; the overall requirement for good management; finally, all of the infinite variety of human problems in being responsible for men and women. The total requirement is leadership combined with professional competence.

All officers assigned to troop units need an understanding of Army command policy, and they need to know and apply sound methods of management. The service schools provide excellent instruction in the subjects an officer requires with a unit of his or her arm or service. But there is a distinct difference between a thorough "knowing about," in the academic sense, and the "knowing how," which is gained by on-the-job experience. The capability of knowing how is the goal to seek.

The subjects discussed in this chapter are common to Army units of each arm and service. They are included for the officer made responsible for one or more of these missions, often effective at once, who has the need for immediate reference information, suggestions, guidance. What is stated here represents the experience of many officers and is provided as sound counsel. The brief discussions are to help you make a confident start. You will need to study the official manuals, of course, just as you must learn at once the standing orders in effect for your unit. These discussions are important for reference by officers on troop duty, and the sooner experience is gained in these essential duties the better.

Army Command Policy	Unit Administration
Management Principles	Leadership and Article 15
Training of Junior Leaders	Taking Care of Your Soldiers
Food Service	Off-duty Activities
Unit Status	Special Problems
Training of Personnel	Conclusion

Readers are referred to the Appendix for a brief discussion, with references to the pertinent regulations, of many of the more common additional duties to which officers may be assigned. It is a first place to look for the officer with a newly assigned additional duty who wants to start off on the right foot.

ARMY COMMAND POLICY (EXTRACTS AND DEFINITIONS)

Army Command Policy and Procedure, AR 600-20, is of such importance that officers are urged to add a copy to their personal library for reference in routine as well as emergency situations.

Right to Command. Command is exercised by virtue of office and the special assignment of members of the armed forces holding military rank who are eligible by law to exercise command.

Assignment and Command. Members of the Army are assigned to stations or commands where their services are required, and are there assigned to appropriate duties by the commanding officer.

Warrant Officers. Warrant officers may be assigned duties as station, unit, or detachment commander, and, when so assigned, they are vested with all powers normally exercised by a commissioned officer except as indicated in AR 611-112. Warrant officers are now commissioned upon promotion to chief warrant officer (CW2, CW3, or CW4). As such they are vested with the same powers as other commissioned officers.

Military Rank. Military rank is the relative position or degree of precedence bestowed on military persons. It marks their station and confers eligibility to exercise command or authority in the military service within the limits prescribed by law.

Conferring honorary titles of military rank upon civilians is prohibited.

Chain of Command. The chain of command is the most fundamental and important organizational technique used by the Army. It is the succession of commanders, superior to subordinate, through which command is exercised. It extends from the President, as Commander-in-Chief, down through the various grades of rank to the enlisted persons leading the smallest Army elements and to their subordinates. Staff officers and administrative noncommissioned officers are not in the chain of command. A simple and direct command channel facilitates transmittal of orders from the highest to the lowest levels in a minimum of time and with the least chance of confusion.

No distinction is made between the terms *commander* and *leader.*

The command channel extends upward in the same manner for matters requiring official communication from subordinate to superior.

Each individual in the chain of command is delegated sufficient authority to accomplish assigned tasks and responsibilities.

Every commander has two basic responsibilities in the following priority: *Accomplishment of mission and the care of personnel and property.* (Italics supplied.)

A superior in the chain of command holds subordinate commanders responsible for everything their command does, or fails to do. Thus, in relation to his or her superior, a commander cannot delegate any responsibilities. However, in relation to subordinates, an officer does subdivide assigned responsibility and authority and assigns portions of them to various commanders and staff members. In this way an appropriate degree of responsibility and authority becomes inherent in each command echelon. The necessity for a commander or staff officer observing proper channels in issuing instructions or orders to subordinates must be recognized. Constant and continuous utilization of the chain of command is vital to the combat effectiveness of any Army unit.

Temporary Command. In the event of the death, disability, or temporary absence of the commander of any element of the Army, the next senior regularly assigned commissioned officer, warrant officer, cadet, noncommissioned officer, specialist, or private present for duty and not ineligible for command will assume command until relieved by proper authority. A member in temporary command will not, except in urgent cases, alter or annul the standing orders of the permanent commander without authority of the next higher commander.

Emergency Command. In the event of emergency, the senior commissioned officer, warrant officer, cadet, noncommissioned officer, specialist, or private among troops at the scene of the emergency will exercise control or command of the military personnel present. These provisions are also applicable to troops separated from their parent units under battlefield conditions or in prisoner of war status. *(Caution by* The Army Officer's Guide: *This is a matter that officers should understand and be prompt to apply when emergencies occur. A natural catastrophe, such as a fire, tornado, railroad wreck, or a riot, or other unexpected, potentially dangerous situation requires the senior present to take charge of all troops present, and to take prompt action as the situation demands.)*

Obedience to Orders. All persons in the military service are required to obey strictly and to execute promptly the lawful orders of their superiors.

MANAGEMENT PRINCIPLES

Management in Leadership. Expert execution of command responsibility is never an accident. It is always the result of clear purpose, earnest effort, intelligent direction, and skillful execution. It is thoughtfully directed hard work. The recurring problems of command are not complex. Quoting Mr. C. F. Kettering, a great industrial leader, "Any problem thoroughly understood is fairly simple."

Good management is an essential tool of the commander in the discharge of responsibilities. It is the judicious use of the available means to accomplish a mission.

Management often includes improvisation to make the best use of what you have to get what you want. Here "what you have" includes your available resources in personnel, equipment, funds, and time. In the military it will be rare that you have all you want of anything; you must strive to succeed with what you have.

These steps have broad application to the approach of any problem.

First, Understand the Mission, Objective, or Job. Know exactly what is to be done.

The mission may be a continuing command responsibility, such as we discuss in this chapter. Or it may be a precise, detailed order. Or it may be a mission-type order that requires the officer to determine intermediate objectives.

Objectives of a commander are wisely regarded as of two categories. First, the long-range objective, which is to be attained in six months or a year, and which may involve accumulation of funds, or construction, or special training. Second, the short range objectives, which can be undertaken at once and completed quickly.

Second, Develop a Detailed Plan. Now comes programming or scheduling, which is a part of planning. After a decision of what is to be done there must follow how it will be done and who will do it. A part of this step is the issuance of orders or instructions, with whatever incidental training, discussion, or explanation is advisable or necessary.

Subordinate leaders and technicians must know their own responsibilities as they must also know the soldiers and equipment available to them for the work directed. This requires also the decentralization to subordinates of a stated degree of authority and responsibility. When this is done subordinates need not stumble about in uncertainty because they can go ahead with confidence, as most people wish to do, and give their boss exactly what is wanted.

Third, Announce a Definite Time for Completion of Mission. Timing is essential to coordination. It is especially true when two or more commands or groups must mesh together in teamwork. There are some variants. "Task to be completed by 1500 hours today." Or, "Not later than 3 November." Or, "Without delay." The latter means to get at it at once and bring it to successful completion with effectiveness and dispatch. Time scheduling provides for coordination and more nearly ensures completing the task at a projected time.

Let us now consider two necessary cautions. A good and necessary reason for time scheduling is to keep appropriate pressure upon subordinates. But this use may be abused and results harmed. Some officers demand speed to the point of absurdity. Unless an officer is willing to accept the half-done and slipshod, he or she must allow sufficient time for the capable, willing worker to do the job well. A Pentagon expression that applies to this situation is, "If you want it bad, you get it bad." Avoid becoming an officer who demands regularly that tasks be completed "yesterday."

But there is another caution, almost in conflict. Think of it well. In this military life there are rare occasions when the leader must ask the almost impossible in life-or-death, victory-or-defeat requirements. We differ from the humdrum vocations. Under some of these circumstances brave soldiers will try, even at the risk of death, and sometimes the finest among them will win. Here are the winners of the Medal of Honor; those who landed first in Normandy and pushed forward; those who drove on to the Yalu; the brave, superbly trained soldiers who executed "search and destroy" missions through the torrid, steamy jungles of Vietnam. In other days they were the soldiers who stuck it out at Valley Forge, and one such officer carried the Message to Garcia.

Complete Work—Clean as You Go. The phrase "clean as you go" means that jobs started are finished. It means order and thoroughness as a matter of course. It means policing of an area to keep it clean and tidy, in contrast to a periodic, hurried clean-up to make it momentarily fit to be seen. It means each soldier on top of his or her job, all the time, and proud of it. It means confidence and pride in doing a worthwhile job well. Beyond all this it means pride in organization, and pride in military service itself, not a grudging minimum of unwelcomed service. The wise commander will make it a command practice and advance the principle: *Go clean as you go.*

Give Generously of Command Interest and Control. Issue of orders is the prelude. But management is not just planning; it is carefully supervising the execution phase to assure compliance with instructions and to adjust plans, if necessary. This includes minor on-the-spot adjustments, a word of praise or encouragement here, some prodding there. The commander must leave behind an improved and strengthened clarity of purpose and renewed determination to get on with the task and do it well.

Many a well-planned mission has failed because of the commander's failure to see that the execution phase was properly supervised.

Sizing Up the Task. The very first step for the officer is to evaluate or size up the assigned task as to the status of the organization and of the individuals who are its members. Is it an old unit partially or wholly trained? Or is it newly activated with an experienced cadre and untrained members?

Suppose It Is a New Unit. You must inform yourself as to the total mission; the time available to complete it; the capabilities of the officers, noncommissioned officers, and technicians available to assist you; the physical facilities available. Now you must gain knowledge about each member you are to train. Study the records to determine the education, civilian vocation or training, physical condition, aptitudes, age, and former military training of each. Interview each member; talk about these things; learn individual interests and aspirations; seek the personal understanding of the task and the cooperation to attain it from each. (Reference: the later paragraph, *Exploiting Acquired Skills.*) How much better is this approach to the task than the too-common assumption that all soldiers to be trained are without usable knowledge, equally able to absorb knowledge, and equally interested in doing well? From this first contact you must be seeking the exceptional individual who can be raised quickly to become a leader or highly skilled technician; you must also identify the personnel who learn slowly or who may require patient handling and additional instruction to keep them abreast of the bulk of unit members; along with these slow learners are others who join late, or have missed instruction because of sickness, or who have been absent from a period of instruction. This is a summary of the way the good leader learns about subordinates and guides their individual and collective progress to attain the necessary results.

Suppose It Is an Old Unit. You must of course know the mission, and the time, personnel, and facilities available as for any other task. But you must determine quickly such things as the following: Is it a fine, well-trained unit of high esprit? Or is it below standard in some specific way? Is it weak in discipline? Is it behind identical units in training or below their standards of training accomplishments? Has it failed in battle? Why? These are a few of the special situations that may face an officer in command of an established unit.

Once these matters have been identified and evaluated, the course to follow is really quite similar to that described above. Study the records; study the individuals; plan a course that fits them and fits the goal. But in the case of the old unit, find the best way to remove the cause of the unit's difficulties. Perhaps that way is the replacement of ineffective officers or noncommissioned officers. It may include improvement in things that have caused discontent, such as poor food service, poor sanitation, or poor policies regarding leaves and passes. These are only examples. You must determine all the reasons the organization has been considered substandard and then apply all measures within your control and power to correct them.

Exploiting Acquired Skills. The most important asset of any unit is the degree of usable skill possessed by each member of the command. This knowledge may have been acquired prior to entry into the Army, in school or college, or as a result of former employment and on-the-job training. The Army has an excellent classification system that identifies and records the special skills or knowledge of new personnel. After this initial classification, men and women are assigned to units or to training centers where opportunities will occur to utilize this experience. When the skill possessed by an individual is one for which the Army has a need, the classification and assignment procedure operates smoothly. Personnel are placed where they can do the best work for the Army and the nation.

But there are some factors that need understanding. Civilian life has no specific counterpart for the infantryman or the artilleryman, as examples, and soldiers trained to meet these needs must be produced in very large numbers. More personnel may arrive with training in a civilian vocation than the Army needs on such duties; the surplus will be assigned to other duties. There are other civilian vocations for which there is no Army requirement whatever. These readily understood truths are stated because of the frequent charge of misuse of civilian talents, usually objecting to assignment to the Infantry. They need understanding.

Acquired knowledge and acquired skills must be identified quickly and, to the extent such individuals are needed, they must be properly and promptly assigned. The Tables of Organization list most of the skills needed, each of which is identified as a Military Occupational Specialty (MOS). You must obtain explicit information as to the unit's needs for trained personnel. You must then consult the individual records to ascertain the resources in personnel trained in the missions required. Then by interview and testing, as well as by observation, you decide what you have and balance it against your known needs.

One way of evaluating the Army training requirement is the filling of the gap between the skills brought into the Army, or possessed by its members, and the training needed to meet the complete mission of the unit. If truck drivers are needed, the first place to search is the training and experience of your troops to determine whether you have them but they are on other duties. The examples can be infinite. The training load is magnified enormously unless the classification and assignment procedure is effective and properly used. Take for granted that every member desires to perform service of the maximum value to the Army and the nation. The Army leaders are determined to make the best possible use of each individual. Make your job easier, and your achievements greater, by making the best possible use of each individual, whether officer or soldier.

Our classification and assignment procedures are good. Observe and understand them. But in so doing, remember that assignment of individuals to specific duties is a command responsibility, and do your part as a responsible officer in placing your personnel wisely to meet Army needs.

Summary. This is an indication of the way you must apply your knowledge of leadership. You must size up your task and learn all about any special situation that confronts you. You must learn as much as possible about each assistant and each subordinate to be trained. Then with your feet planted firmly on the ground, and a feeling of confidence in your mind, go ahead and from day to day apply the fundamentals of sound leadership to your specific task.

TRAINING OF JUNIOR LEADERS

One of the most important duties of a commander is the training of junior leaders, officer and noncommissioned officer alike. It is a duty deferred or ignored by some commanders who convince themselves it is easier and quicker to do it themselves; or who resort continually to precise, detailed instructions to be followed by rote. There is work in preparing a well-planned, well-conducted instructional program to develop self-reliant, confident junior leaders who can proceed effectively under mission-type orders. Hesitant commanders may rationalize that it is better for their subordinates to do a job right, that is, the way the senior would do it, than to chance a blunder. Such a course may seem to solve the requirements of the moment, but in the long run the performance of the entire unit will suffer. There must come a day when the commander is absent and an emergency arises; at that instant the lack of trained junior leaders to step in and do the job with confidence and skill will be painfully apparent. If you really aspire to rise to positions of great responsibility in our Army, demonstrate it by good training of junior leaders.

Training includes more than studying and learning the contents of the applicable field manuals, regulations, and other publications. It must include also a chance to practice what has been learned from the books. This opportunity to practice is voided if you tell your subordinates not only what to do, but also how to do it.

It is natural that the senior officer often feels that he or she knows precisely how to tackle a particular problem so it will be solved in the minimum amount of time, with the minimum of effort, and with the minimum expenditure of materials. That you do know the correct procedure is one of the reasons you are the senior officer. However, when you impart this knowledge to subordinates in the form of step-by-step instructions, you rob them of a chance to use their own initiative, to think a problem through, to try their hand at arriving at the correct procedure. In so doing, you will have ignored a vital requirement of the training process.

In the performance of your leadership duties, see to it that you do not rob your subordinates of a chance to display their own initiative and capabilities. Issue mission-type orders—that is, define precisely what is to be accomplished and furnish information as to the equipment and materials available, the time by which the assignment is to be completed, and any other pertinent information that may help define the limiting boundaries of the problem. But then let your subordinates make their own plans as to the step-by-step accomplishment of the mission. They will make mistakes. Expect them—and be ready to deal with them. However, as time passes, the mistakes will be fewer and your own job will be made easier, for you truly will have trained your junior leaders. And who knows, in the process you may even learn better ways to accomplish a job for which you once knew the "right" procedure.

Special Note Regarding Noncommissioned Officers (NCOs). The NCOs have been called "the backbone of the Army." This is no idle phrase. Good NCOs are tremendously important to the Army; with them, a unit functions like a smooth-running machine; without them, the best of unit officers will lead a hectic existence and probably will see poor unit performance besides. The NCO is a vital link in the chain of command.

In addition to being in the formal chain of command, noncommissioned officers also function in a noncommissioned officer support channel that parallels the chain of command. The support channel begins with the command sergeant major and extends through subordinate unit command sergeants major to unit first sergeants and then to other noncommissioned officers and enlisted personnel of the units. This NCO support channel supplements the chain of command. Through it, the senior noncommissioned officers maintain a watchful oversight of many matters that affect performance of the command. Matters properly within the purview of this support channel include development of NCOs, setting and maintaining performance standards for NCOs, supervision of unit operations within established guidelines, care of individual soldiers and their families, proper wearing of the uniform, appearance and courtesy of enlisted personnel, care of arms and equipment, care of living quarters, area maintenance tasks, and operation of recreational and other facilities. The list could go on and on. Operating within this support channel, however, in addition to the chain of command, the NCOs assure the smooth functioning of the unit and lighten the load of the commander.

Good NCOs are made in much the same way that good commissioned officers are made. The preceding paragraphs apply equally to both commissioned and noncommissioned officers. But there is more.

An NCO is truly an officer in a unit. That the NCO holds his or her position without a commission is indicative only of relative rank and perhaps also background and training. Each NCO should have specific duties and responsibilities assigned and should be delegated sufficient authority to enable accomplishment of these assigned tasks. NCOs spend most of their time among the troops in a unit. They are the ones who actually supervise the details involved in the accomplishment of the mission, but to do their jobs properly, they must have the respect of the troops. It is here that the attitudes of their seniors are very important. *In order to accomplish their duties properly, NCOs must have the respect and support of their seniors.*

Accord your NCOs the same respect that you feel your superior officers should give you. Support your NCOs as you would expect to be supported by your company commander or your battalion commander. Ensure that your NCOs are properly trained, and include opportunities for them to exercise their own initiative and judgment. Expect and require that they carry their share of the inherent and assigned load of the unit. Do all these things, while not neglecting your own responsibilities regarding supervision and inspection, and you will be pleasantly surprised at how smoothly your unit functions. Your assigned tasks will be made lighter. You will have trained a true backbone for the unit—good NCOs.

FOOD SERVICE

It is true that the consolidation of many support activities has lifted much of the responsibility for food service out of the company and battery level, and with it the routine appointment of a company food service officer to act for the commander in dining facility supervision. Even so, there remains a definite command responsibility whether in garrison or in campaign conditions, because what soldiers are provided for food influences their morale, their willingness to serve, and their efficiency far beyond the power of any printed words. Officers assigned to duty with troops must be everlastingly mindful of the proper food service of their soldiers. The serving of a well-chosen menu, with well-prepared food items, in attractive surroundings, are all matters of the first magnitude.

Commanders operating an appropriated-fund dining facility, whether consolidated or not, must pay particular attention to the daily operations to ensure that the Army Food Program is being carried out properly. The Army Food Program covers the personnel, procedures, and resources involved in feeding troops worldwide. The program has been developed by experts of the highest standing and experience, and it is directed by the U.S. Army Troop Support Agency. Everything is included, from research and development of a food item through the cooking and serving process. The purpose of the program is to provide the best-tasting, most nutritious, and most wholesome meals possible within the basic daily food allowance (BDFA).

Menus. *Master Menu.* A monthly publication. It is a standard menu for each meal for one month, with items required.

Revised Menu. This is a revision of the master menu, which is prepared and published locally under direction of the food service supervisor. It takes into consideration local supplies and conditions. This is the menu to be followed by the food service sergeant unless there are very compelling reasons to depart from it.

The Dining Facility. In garrison, with a consolidated dining facility, what should a company commander or a company officer supervise? Local policies will establish the actual responsibility of unit officers. But in any case, a considerable interest by unit officers should be displayed in the quality of the food service. You must assure yourself that your troops are satisfied, or that you make appropriate recommendations to the responsible officials. You should know about the choice of menu components; the quality of food preparation; the attractiveness of the food service and the surroundings; the orderliness of the kitchen and personnel; and the entire area as to sanitation.

In the field, or in active combat conditions, circumstances may arise where food service responsibility is placed entirely under the control of the company or equivalent commander. Each company will have its TOE (Tables of Organization and Equipment) kitchen equipment to maintain in garrison, including the passing of unit readiness tests and command inspections; in the field, this equipment is mounted in the back of a truck according to locally prescribed methods. The ingenuity of company officers in organizing the field kitchen truck and preparing for its actual use is a challenge.

But the real challenge is the effective operation of a satisfactory food service under combat or field conditions, when called upon to do so. The food may be prepared in the area of the battalion trains. Or the members of units in campaign or combat may dine on combat rations under the control of company officers. Clearly, there are important responsibilities for the company commander and his or her officers that require knowledge and leadership.

There are a number of important considerations that should receive your attention both before going to the field and in the actual operation of a field kitchen. Be certain that your unit has its authorized TOE field cooking equipment, that it is all in good working order, and that your food service personnel know how to operate it properly and safely. Provide training time for practice in setting up and taking down kitchen tents and in setting up and preparing the kitchen equipment for movement. Your unit may also be involved in the use of Kitchen Company Level Field Feeding (KCLFF) equipment used for preparing T-rations. If so, training time on this equipment should be included.

Ensure that your food service personnel know and practice field food service sanitation principles. And don't neglect basics such as map reading and camouflage techniques. Meals may have to be delivered to points designated by map coordinates, while the kitchen may have to be concealed from enemy observation. Finally, ensure that the needs of your food service personnel are properly accounted for in your unit loading plan. Provisions must be made for the field equipment and food, of course, but be certain that provisions also are made for a water trailer, water cans, gas cans, and any other support items that may be required.

In the field, ensure that the kitchen is set up in an area with good drainage and easy access, and preferably with built-in concealment. Be certain that adequate waste disposal facilities are provided and that trash and garbage are properly disposed of. Do not neglect camouflage if necessary, and precautions against nuclear, biological, and chemical (NBC) contamination. By all means, keep your food service sergeant informed of your plans so meals may be properly prepared at the right times and delivered to the correct sites, if necessary. If you have done your job well while in garrison, you can rely on your food service sergeant and the other food service personnel to run the field kitchen without your detailed attention.

Suggested Points for Check and Correction. Under the assumption that a company or equivalent unit has a food service responsibility under field or combat conditions, the following items are listed to assist an officer who may be assigned the responsibility.

Check the Food Service Personnel and Be Certain of Their Qualifications. Go another step, and assure yourself of a workable division of duties and responsibilities as to working procedures. If the unit is to have good meals, served at the right place, at the right time, under suitable conditions of sanitation considering all the circumstances, it will require good personnel, hard work, and effective leadership.

Check the Food Supplies and the Storage. Be certain the food supply is adequate, stored properly to prevent spoilage, and secure from pilferage.

Check Your Kitchen Equipment. Assure yourself that the food service personnel have the needed or authorized tools and equipment and that these are serviceable.

Recognize the Importance of the Kitchen Police (KP). Never to be overlooked is the importance of the kitchen police. Few soldiers, if any, enjoy the task. But an appreciative word of instruction by an officer about the importance of the duty may help. It is better to regard KP as a military duty and rotate the duty by roster; most experienced officers have learned that it is wrong to use the duty as punishment. Besides, it is a good way to identify personnel who have an interest in cooking who may later be trained as cooks for the food service mission.

Field Inspections. In campaign or field conditions careful inspection of the food service is especially important. It is harder for the staff to maintain a high standard of cleanliness and to operate at the needed high standard. Whenever a unit operates its own food service under field conditions, it becomes a first responsibility.

You must be certain of adequate food supplies.

Kitchen equipment must be checked frequently to be certain the required items are on hand and serviceable. In the field, an item broken or lost through carelessness or pilferage may cause real difficulties.

Sanitation is extremely important. It requires continual observation. Clean dishes used by the troops, or in food preparation, must be *free from grease.* Make a spot check, as extensive as circumstances may require; feel the dish surface, don't just look at it. If any grease is found, the item is unclean and may result in serious illness. Have you ever been sick from food poisoning? It isn't pleasant, at all. You must make this check when it lies within your responsibility, and be certain that adequate facilities are available to obtain cleanliness, which includes a generous supply of very hot water and soap or detergents.

Check the disposal of garbage and wastes. This can become a frightful nuisance and a threat to health. An ever-watchful eye is needed.

Food Service Checklist. There are official checklists, and good ones. This one has been used by thousands of officers until an official list is obtained or prescribed. It is included as an aid. Select the items that pertain to your situation, and add others as you need them.

1. *Bulletin board:* Check the food handlers' certificates.
2. *Food service accounts:* Check arithmetic of the forms used.

3. *Menu:*
   Posted near cook.
   Foods listed being served?
   Time of preparation—meals ready on time? Cooking completed too early?
4. *Serving of meals:*
   Hot foods hot; cold foods cold.
   Serving system carried out?
5. *Uniform and cleanliness of food service personnel.*
6. *Kitchen equipment and special points to observe:*
   a. Cooking ranges
   b. Baking ovens
   c. Fryolator; any grease on inside?
   d. Steam cookers; any food stains on inside?
   e. Coffee percolators; any coffee stains on inside?
   f. Mixer; any food particles on inside or on attachments?
   g. Meat block
   h. Pots and pans; examine edges and corners carefully
   i. Utensils; examine handles carefully and test cutting edges
   j. Refrigerator room; temperature (40°–50° F.)
   k. Ice-cube freezer
   l. Storeroom and bread box
   m. GI cans for bulk foods; lids should fit tightly
   n. Sinks and dish washers
   o. Potato peeler; any potato fragments on inside?
7. *Dining room equipment:*
   a. Steam table; examine corners and shelves carefully
   b. Dishes and cafeteria trays; any grease film?
   c. Glasses; hold to light to observe any spots
   d. Tables; any water streaks on top?
   e. Silverware; any food particles or food stains?
8. *Floors:* Any grease spots?
9. *Garbage stand:*
   Lids should fit tightly; exteriors must be clean.
   Any refuse on cans, stand, or ground in vicinity of stand?
10. *Weekly schedule of cleaning:*
    On Saturdays make complete inspection; on other days make list of items you will inspect, always including inspection of food service accounts.

UNIT STATUS

The Army's combat readiness objective is to provide units capable of performing their assigned missions in support of operational requirements. To conserve resources, only those units required early in support of contingency plans are normally maintained at the highest level of readiness (resource level). Other units are maintained at lower resource levels. By resources, we mean personnel, equipment, funds, and time and facilities for training and maintaining equipment. Each unit commander is responsible for maintaining the highest levels of unit training proficiency and equipment serviceability within the limitations of the resources provided. The unit commander is responsible for assuring that unit status ratings reflect actual unit conditions and that available resources are applied as necessary to prevent or correct degradation of unit readiness. Higher-level commanders are charged with reviewing the status reports of subordinate units and taking such action as is within their capabilities to improve the readiness condition of these subordinate units.

The desired readiness condition of a unit is described by an Authorized Level of Organization (ALO). The ALO is the authorized level of manpower and equipment against which a unit may requisition personnel and equipment. The ALO may be expressed either numerically or by letter designations which represent percentages of full TOE/MTOE authorizations. For example, ALO 1 is 100 percent, ALO 2 is approximately 90 percent, ALO 3 is approximately 80 percent, and ALO 4 is approximately 70 percent. Units may be authorized different levels of personnel and equipment, in which case the lower of the two levels is considered to be the unit ALO.

Unit status reports, which are submitted both monthly and when a change of overall unit rating occurs, are designed to assist higher commanders in the allocation of resources and to assist in the assessment of total force readiness. Unit ratings for personnel, training, and equipment are computed in accordance with the detailed instructions provided in AR 220-1. In addition, the unit commander determines an overall unit rating that he or she feels best describes the unit's ability to accomplish its mission. Ratings are computed against full wartime requirements and are indicated as numerical levels. A rating of C1 indicates the unit is combat ready with no deficiencies. A rating of C2 indicates the unit is combat ready, but with minor deficiencies, while a C3 indicates combat readiness, but with major deficiencies. A rating of C4 indicates that the unit is not combat ready. A C5 rating applies to units that are not combat ready by virtue of HQDA action or programs, such as units undergoing reorganization or major equipment conversion, or units placed in a cadre status. The overall unit rating may differ from the resource area ratings (except for C5), but it must be explained by the unit commander.

No unit is expected to achieve a status rating higher than the ALO for the unit. That is, if the unit is authorized to have on hand only 80 percent of its TOE personnel and equipment (ALO 3), it is not expected to have a unit status rating higher than C3. The goal is to achieve a status rating equal to the authorized ALO and to train to the highest level of proficiency possible with the resources provided to the unit. Since the reports are designed to inform higher levels of command, all the way up to Headquarters, Department of the Army, of the actual status of the unit, the reports must be accurate. Commanders at levels higher than the reporting unit are forbidden to change the rating provided by the subordinate unit commander.

Each level of command from Headquarters, Department of the Army, to the unit is responsible for achieving the greatest capability within the available resources and for accurately assessing and reporting the actual unit status regardless of the resources allocated. Unit status is essentially the end product of a total command effort at all levels of the Army. Therefore the status of a unit should not be attributed solely to the leadership and managerial efforts of the reporting unit commander. To attempt to do so would ignore the limitations that exist within the system. The unit status report is designed to indicate the actual status of unit readiness within these limitations and to serve as a management tool so that higher levels of command can determine where personnel and equipment resources can best be applied to achieve an optimum readiness level for all Army units. *The report is not designed to provide an evaluation of unit commanders.*

TRAINING OF PERSONNEL

As a unit commander, your first responsibility is to assign and use your assigned personnel in accordance with their prescribed military occupational specialty,

MOS. Second, you should seek opportunity for your subordinates to attend service schools that provide training or advanced training in their specialties. Third, you must train them on the job, using the already trained and experienced personnel in your unit. Finally, you must be watchful that personnel trained for a definite position, or MOS, are not erroneously or carelessly assigned to duties of lesser importance. Correct assignment of personnel is a command responsibility and is an essential element in training.

"Train and Maintain." When a unit is not in combat, the mission is to "train and maintain." Follow the training schedules with precision, using all available lesson plans, field manuals, and training aids. Inject realism. Use and test your equipment. Conduct the training with vigor and enthusiasm and it will rub off on your soldiers.

Equipment. The unit must have its authorized equipment on hand (including spares and repair parts). It should be stored in equipment store rooms or on the proper vehicles as prescribed, ready for inspection or for movement. The junior officer has a major responsibility for the maintenance of unit equipment. Maintenance procedures are prescribed in technical manuals and bulletins. The end-of-day maintenance periods should be organized and performed with the same seriousness as the training periods earlier in the day. Operational maintenance must be supervised by the officer and the NCOs; never leave the unit area until the equipment is combat-ready and until, as the responsible officer, you are certain of it.

The Reward of Thoroughness. The Army's splendid units of this period have proven the value of the procedures over and over again. Many Army units have passed from training situations directly into combat without delay or confusion, confident of their own "combat readiness." The junior officer in a unit has a heavy responsibility. He or she must learn the standards of unit readiness and "adhere to the book." The "book" is the accumulation of experience. Lean upon the knowledge and the experience of the old hands. Be a tough inspector, fair and thorough, but never chicken. Require your soldiers to prove their own capabilities and the readiness of their equipment. These painstaking steps can mean the difference between combat success and combat failure, and for some of your soldiers the difference between life and death. The reward of thoroughness is confidence—and a clear conscience.

UNIT ADMINISTRATION

The company, battery, and troop are administrative units in the sense that their commanders are required to prepare and forward to battalion or similar headquarters prescribed records and essential data. Supervision of these administrative, or paperwork tasks, is a continual responsibility of the commander. He or she may delegate to others the daily tasks of preparing reports, checking accounts, and records, verifying inventories, and submission of whatever data is required. But it is the commander's responsibility.

There is great importance to this constant problem. Unless data are correctly supplied as to each individual's records, all manner of complications follow with respect to pay accounts, later claims for disability under veterans' benefits, and the like. Strength reports originating in the company form the basis for all personnel accounting, and if they are incorrect all is wrong. Individual and unit property records must be accurate. Strive for the *Zero Error* objective of all administrative managers.

Some officers have a serious misconception of this matter. As they abhor paperwork, they shun the responsibility, or content themselves with slipshod results.

There are other officers who devote so much of their own time to the task, instead of a proper decentralization with supervision, that they have inadequate time for other responsibilities, such as training. Both concepts are wrong. Here are some tests: Are there complaints about reports being submitted after the date or hour due? Do they "bounce" because of inaccuracies? Have outside checks of mess records, supply records, individual records shown an abnormally high number of errors? Is it necessary for the commander to personally prepare detailed reports that should be done by others? Or in nearly all cases is it necessary only that he or she sign the reports? The point is this: Unit administration requires a sound leadership, just as there must be leadership in training, in food service management, in supply management, and in other responsibilities of command. The officer who neglects administrative tasks is riding for a hard fall as is the officer who devotes so much time to the task that other responsibilities are neglected.

Leadership in Administration. Unless you are a capable administrator you are unlikely to succeed as a commander. The first requirement is to learn, as to each responsibility within the organization, the records and reports that are required to be prepared; exactly what they include; how they are kept; and when recorded or submitted.

The next step in management is to assign to appropriate personnel the specific missions of preparation and maintenance of records. This should be precise and include the what, how, when, and who.

As in all other tasks, there is an important element of training. Very likely in the processes of personnel assignment there are precious few individuals with clerical, typing, bookkeeping, and such skills, who reach the small units. Most of these trained individuals are screened out and assigned elsewhere.

More than likely, the company or battery commander must find and train soldiers to perform these tasks.

This is not so difficult. The records to be kept are not complex. It is only that there are many of them, and each must be correct. Select individuals for the tasks who are intelligent, thorough, reliable, and who have some aptitude for such work. See that they have correct reference sources, or models, on which to base their work. Require the supervisory leaders to make careful checks, point out mistakes, conduct training periods, and report progress. As records must be legible, hold fast to the requirement for easily read, neat writing. Hammer on accuracy, completeness, and timeliness.

It is a certainty that a small unit must train its own typists. Provide a standard typing manual and encourage or require practice. Insist upon correct form from the start, however slowly it is executed. An alert person can develop into a fair typist in a short time, though perhaps establishing no speed records. Avoid selecting the mentally sluggish who are all thumbs, for they cannot progress.

Once the separate administrative tasks are identified and allotted to specific individuals for execution, with a supervisory system for checking plus time for developing individual proficiency, the situation should be in hand. Thereafter the commander should be able in most instances to read a proposed paper or report, accept as facts the statements therein made as facts, and sign, if he or she agrees, with minimum consumption of time. It is another form of leadership.

Military Correspondence. AR 340-15, *Preparing Correspondence,* provides detailed explanations and sample formats for nearly any kind of letter, memorandum, note, or endorsement that might be required. This regulation provides the detailed guidance that should remove all doubt in the minds of officers and their clerks as to the correct forms of correspondence.

Special Note. All officers should be aware that the Army has now officially changed the spelling of a number of words that have caused some difficulty in the past. Specifically, the revised spelling should be:

> *endorse* instead of *indorse*
> *endorsement* instead of *indorsement*
> *enclosure* instead of *inclosure*
> *ensure* instead of *insure*

AR 340-15 also provides some commonsense rules to be applied to all correspondence to assure that it is short, simple, strong, and sincere. You are urged to study these guidelines carefully and then to restudy them periodically before you sign your name to a letter or report that has strayed from the objective of clear, simple writing.

Official Signature. An official signature consists of the name, grade, branch of the Army, organization, and title.

RICHARD D. AMES
Major General, USA
Commanding

K. K. KELLY
Major, IN
Transportation Officer

A signature that pertains to the signer personally, includes his or her Social Security account number (SSAN).

RODGER D. HILL
512-34-0849
MAJ, Inf
3d Inf Regt

MARY L. SMITH
363-28-6675
CPT, QMC

The signed name will be written plainly and legibly and will be identical with the typewritten, stamped, or printed name when used. Use only black or blue-black ink.

> IMPORTANT CAUTION: *An officer's signature on an official document means that he or she vouches for the accuracy of the facts stated, and that each recommendation represents his or her carefully considered, professional view. A false official statement, whether oral or written, is a grave offense. Your word, or your signature, is your bond. Be very certain of the correctness of the official papers you sign.*

LEADERSHIP AND ARTICLE 15

The relationship between a commander's leadership responsibility, the standard of discipline maintained within the unit, and the commander's use of the authority to punish under Article 15, are subjects so closely tied together as to constitute in some respects a single function of command. Certainly it is informative to analyze and consider them together.

We have always claimed that "the Army builds men," and it is true. But we have never been very convincing as to how it is accomplished. Perhaps it includes with other things the wise application of leadership, the right sort of discipline and encouragement, and the use of punishment as a corrective rather than a punitive measure. The subject is worthy of contemplation.

What Is Leadership? Consider these definitions: *"A leader is a person fitted by force of ideas, character, or genius, or by strength of will or administrative ability to arouse, incite, and direct men in conduct and achievement." "Leadership is* *the art of imposing one's will upon others in such a manner as to command their respect, their confidence, and their whole-hearted cooperation."*

Many thoughtful observers who have enjoyed prolonged opportunity to study military leaders in the routine conduct of their duties have reached a similar conclusion: "Officers who are proficient in leadership have a high standard of discipline in their units, and in their day-to-day experience they encounter few disciplinary problems; also, their need to invoke or to use their power to punish under Article 15, or other powers stated in the *Manual for Courts-Martial,* is used with less frequency than in units with less-capable leaders." Continuing this same line of thought, under similar conditions in combat, the quality of leadership and the standard of discipline in a unit has a direct and predictable bearing upon accomplishment of mission and the number of casualties. When there is good leadership and good discipline, achievement of mission with minimum casualties is a standard expectancy.

It is instructive to consider discipline and punishment as major parts of the duties and responsibilities of Army leaders.

The Importance of Discipline. One difference between a fine military unit and a mere rabble is the degree of obedience to the will of the leader. The combat value of units is determined by their training, experience, morale, and "will to fight." It may be explanatory to approach the subject through a negative: *"I say to this man GO, and he goeth,"* is not a proof or even a test of discipline; he may start briskly at the word GO, and later turn off into a green or alluring pasture, instead of plunging onward through the morass of jungle and marsh beyond which lies his mission. A continual responsibility of military leaders, especially of those officers in direct command of soldiers such as company and platoon commanders, is intelligent, willing, and cheerful achievement of assigned missions or compliance with orders. This is discipline. Fine discipline is the cement or cohesive force of a good organization. Where discipline is weak, leadership is faulty.

The way to obtain a disciplined command, as a habit of individual and group conduct, is to make certain of two things: (1) the leader must be careful that orders are militarily correct and capable of execution by subordinates; and (2) the leader must ensure by observation that orders are meticulously complied with by each individual. Don't be fooled by superficialities. Discipline goes deep and is the result of many mission achievements, of complete tasks, of compliance with orders, and of attaining little objectives as well as great ones.

Apply the reasoning to the continuing responsibilities, such as the kitchen staff to serve good meals, on time, under high conditions of sanitation; leaders charged with training to proceed from day to day bringing along their soldiers to meet the desired high standard; the maintenance of high standards of individual neatness of dress and personal appearance; the regular observance of military courtesies; always being at the prescribed place at the stated time. Apply your doctrine of good discipline also to the new and specific tasks that occur daily, even in combat: In the attack, to seize an area starting from a prescribed place, at a definite time, following a planned route; to go on patrol to accomplish a definite mission; to repair a truck, or to do any other necessary job. The habit of obedience, or achievement of mission, is the proof of discipline. The leader obtains it by example in meeting the goals established by his or her own commander, and by requiring compliance with orders or mission.

The officer has strong powers to exact obedience. But their use should be graduated from mere statement of the shortcoming to show that it was observed, mild admonition, rebuke, denial of privilege, official reprimand, withdrawal of rating, and as last resort or for genuinely serious offenses, trial by court-martial. Consider always the soldier and his or her past record, the intent, and the gravity of the offense or failure. Act objectively and calmly. Choose always the lesser punishment until convinced it will be ineffective. Never resort to scorn or ridicule. Get all the facts before action of any kind. Assume, as an example, failure of a group under an NCO to arrive at a distant point at the time prescribed. Quietly get from the NCO a statement of the reason. Assume these answers: "The bridge was out at Blankville and we were obliged to make a thirty-mile detour." The lateness may be dropped. "I took a wrong road and lost the way." A check of the NCO's map reading ability, or instruction, or caution, or mild admonition should be the action because it was simple carelessness or ignorance. "The truck driver let the gas tank run dry and we had to send back ten miles for gasoline." This is buck passing and unacceptable; the NCO must be instructed firmly as to his or her responsibilities. "I spent the night in town and no one told the troops to be ready to move out." This is lack of appreciation of an NCO's responsibilities and, if indicative of habit or unreliability generally, consideration should be given to extensive training, or reduction. The point is, the leader must detect transgressions, determine the cause, and apply sound corrective action. If the leader habitually overlooks transgressions, or lightly passes them by, he or she is lost; when the big test comes, the unit will fail to take the hill and soldiers will die who should have lived.

This, we submit, is true discipline and how to attain it.

How Should a Leader Use the Power to Punish under Article 15? Discussed very briefly above is the importance of good military leadership and its proven influence upon achievement of mission with the minimum of casualties; discussed also is the true meaning of discipline with the observation many individuals have noted that when leadership is of a high order few disciplinary problems are presented. Soldiers strive to please the leader they trust and admire, with avoidance of acts that would lower their personal standing in his or her eyes.

Even so, as long as most soldiers are young, and as long as people are people, which will be a very long period indeed, there will continue to be human transgressions that require the application of the military leader's power to punish. The leader is authorized to use a carefully regulated power to enforce obedience and discipline, according to the severity of the offense and the past record of the offender. Most such acts are taken in small units, such as the platoon, company, or battalion, under the provisions of Article 15, concerning which extensive instruction is provided at courses in service schools and in unit instruction. It is discussed below only as to its close relation to sound discipline and to good leadership.

There are three possible actions that a commander may take when an offense has been committed: *First,* a soldier may be given extra attention and certain prescribed duties without resort to a recorded action. This applies especially to trivial or minor offenses, and to first offenders. Most young soldiers intend to do the right things. *Second,* a soldier or officer may be punished under Article 15. This punishment is minor, nonjudicial, and may be administered by a company commander or a battalion commander for which procedure the reader should consult the Manual for Courts-Martial. After each such disciplinary action the individual should be counseled; not scolded, not threatened, but advised, counseled. Sometimes it is best to transfer the soldier to a different leader, or into different work. When a soldier leaves the unit his or her record of punishment under Article 15 is destroyed. (Not so as to the officer; for the officer, Article 15 action becomes a part of his or her permanent record.) *Third,* repeated offenders under Article 15, and those guilty of serious offenses, may be tried by a court-martial.

Leadership, Discipline, and Punishment as Part of the Truth, "The Army Builds Men and Women." Most soldiers are young men and women in their late teens or their twenties. As to their habits of obedience, behavior, diligence at work, ambition for advancement, and understanding of the obligations of the citizen to perform military service, they are individuals who have been produced by our family life, our schools, our churches, and our national environment. Don't sell them short, or be deceived by the critic who belittles our modern young citizens; they will be equal to any test, as their predecessors have proven, and the great majority of them will have all that it takes, and more, to provide for the national security. In any case, you, as the commander, must take those assigned to your unit and work out your destiny with them. You must resolve to lift each soldier entrusted to your care to that individual's highest level of capability. You must provide a high standard of leadership and sound discipline, and when necessary you must resort to a proper measure of punishment.

We are talking of building men and women. Good leaders are careful to issue clear instructions and to make certain they are understood. They avoid trivial, irritating restrictions. They never show favoritism, or threaten, or belittle. They are careful to note good work by a soldier and comment about it. "Good work, Soldier" (but know and use his or her name), heads off many little disobediences. When a soldier does something wrong, skilled leaders tell or show the person how to do it right, and follow up to see that the lesson is learned. When necessary, they caution, or admonish, in private. When punishment is performed it is to be done impersonally, objectively, without rancor. The goal is to convince transgressors that they have everything to gain by doing their duty and being good soldiers.

Occasionally a soldier is encountered who is so determined to avoid military service and to obtain a discharge that he or she chooses a most damaging course of action. The individual may deliberately commit a series of offenses in order to receive punishment under Article 15, or by court-martial, hoping to be separated from the service administratively under AR 635-206, for misconduct, or under AR 635-200 for incompatibility with service life or discipline. Here is a severe challenge to leadership. The temptation may be strong to "throw the book" at the offender. Such separations are a serious and permanent blot on an individual's life as well as his or her military record. The individual is thereafter considered to be unfit for further service and could not serve our country during war. There should be a sincere attempt at instruction and rehabilitation of the offender before permitting completion of such a disastrous course of action. As long as the leader feels there is something good in an offender that can be brought out and developed, the officer should be loathe to accept failure by having the soldier discharged.

Experienced officers know that many thousands of soldiers who have started off with the wrong concepts of military service, or sour on service in war or peace, have been brought into healthful understanding and have gone on to build commendable records of honorable service. Of course, there are others who cannot be influenced constructively and whose discharge is necessary. But first a sincere effort for rehabilitation should be made.

Finally, to emphasize an axiom stated at the outset of this discussion, it is a fact that anyone may verify by observation that few of our more effective Army commanders—starting at platoon level—encounter serious problems of discipline or of offenses requiring severe punishment. Such extremes occur, but they are rare. Most soldiers choose to serve their country with honor and with pride.

TAKING CARE OF YOUR SOLDIERS

Let us peer into the old truism that "a commander must take care of his or her soldiers," seeking to determine why he or she does this and precisely what is done to accomplish this goal.

Why has there always been such heavy emphasis upon the duty of commanding officers to take the best care of their soldiers? The commander provides as best he or she can for the physical, mental, and recreational welfare of the unit's personnel to make more certain that they are receptive to training, able and willing to perform their individual missions capably, proud of their own unit, and willing to perform military service in accordance with their enlistment contract.

The commander is provided with very strong authority, under federal law, by virtue of his or her commission and specific assignment to command a particular unit. Authority is power. The commander has far broader power than is extended to a civilian chief. Obedience to the commander's orders in battle may result in forfeiture of life under conditions where refusal to obey a proper order could result in trial with sentence of death. This is power, indeed. But with this great power goes at the same time a heavy responsibility. The unit personnel are responsible to the commander who, in turn, is responsible for them and all that they do in the performance of their duty. Authority and responsibility must go together.

The commander must train his or her soldiers, and this is a part of the job of taking care of them. Unless they are thoroughly and properly trained the chance is increased that the unit will fall short of its mission. Individuals who are improperly or inadequately trained are far more likely than others to become battle casualties.

As an illustration, here are some of the things that are done as routine by a captain commanding a company upon completion of a long march before withdrawing to his or her own tent or quarters: assigns unit bivouac areas or quarters; designates locations for kitchen, vehicle park, latrines; checks that arrangements are made at once for sick call or the medical attention of any soldiers who are injured or sick; provides for foot inspection; makes certain that arrangements are made for emergency issue of equipment. You must not look to your own personal comfort first, or permit yourself to be entangled with some single facet of the task of getting the company settled. You must see to the whole job. Necessarily you must see that the subordinate leaders follow the same course. When these tasks are finished, with others that circumstances require, you may go to your own quarters. The needs of your troops come first. "Take care of your soldiers and they will take care of you," is an old Army axiom to remember and to apply, for it is as true today as in earlier times.

The leader of a company or smaller unit must know a great deal about each individual. He or she must learn their names quickly, call them by name, and learn their specialties, their strengths, and their weaknesses. This creates a personal bond between the individual and the commander. "My captain knows me," the soldier will think, "and he knows of my hopes. He also knows the things I do wrong. My captain is a fair man and I am glad to serve in his company." The captain may think, "Jones is a lazy cuss. But if I am in a tight spot where I need someone I can depend on I would want him with me." A bond of mutual understanding born of knowing the soldier and the soldier knowing his or her officers is essential to success in a command. Soldiers cannot be fooled. They will not mistake a poor commander for a good one. The relationship is one of daily contacts and is too continuous, too varied, and too close to allow for this kind of deception. If they are satisfied that their commander is taking good care of them, there is no question that they will do their best to accomplish an assigned mission, however they may regard it, and look out for the commander's interests in doing it.

The Officer's Relationship with His or Her Troops. Command is a very personal relationship. The smaller the unit the more personal it becomes. How then should the officer conduct himself or herself with and before the unit personnel?

Some officers are always official, rather stern, unbending. Not arrogant, not heartless, not unjust. But official, stern, unbending. Others have a warm and friendly relationship to a point but are careful to maintain a dignity or reserve. They smile, make light of hardships, take hard things in stride. Still others carry this trait to extreme, seem to strive to shed responsibility, to be "one of the boys." Which is correct? Certainly not the latter example, for this is the path of weakness and failure. But of the first two, we can say only this: Each officer must follow the course which seems most natural and which gives the best results. For that officer, that way is best. Be yourself. Be natural.

This too can be said:* No officer can be on terms of personal intimacy with a few soldiers while holding others at a distance, without developing the conviction among the less favored that he or she is playing favorites. You must be objective, fair, and impersonal, and do as to each soldier what duty requires. You are the commander. You cannot, and do your duty, display partiality, or favoritism, or preference.

Never use ridicule. The worst violation of commonsense and human decency a commander can adopt is to pour scorn or ridicule upon a soldier, or permit others to do so. Never refer to a soldier as an "8-ball," or a poor marksman on the range as a "bolo." To do so is to encourage others in the organization to use the same terms and apply them broadly. Pride is destroyed. Hatred may arise instead of tolerance.

Never talk down to your troops, as it will be resented even by the ones who are slow to learn. American young people have a high level of education, and it will often be true that the enlisted ranks of a unit contain individuals of superior educational achievements. Such individuals are our greatest hope for leadership development and for technical assignments; talking down will occasion first resentment and then amusement among them. Never seem to be patronizing or "Big I and little you."

In any group of men or women there are variations in individual intelligence, mechanical aptitude, educational background, character, and all other human attributes. The military leader must take the individuals assigned to his or her unit, determine their potentials, assign them, and train them for the most appropriate place in the organization, and do the best possible with them. The leader must get the most from each individual assigned to the unit, however far up or down the scale that "most" may be placed. Ridicule and scorn will reduce or destroy the capacity of any individual. Let it be clear that you recognize and value highly the talents of your soldiers, and that you expect each one to achieve highly.

Health and Physical Welfare. The line commander has a very definite responsibility for the health and physical welfare of his or her troops. Our splendid medical service will care for individuals who are sick, wounded, or injured; through checks, surveys, and examinations of all kinds our medical service will avoid or reduce all practicable hazards to the health of the command; they will inspect and advise commanders as to their health and sanitation situation. It is a joint job for the medical service and the organization commander.

---

*See also chapter 3, *The Code of the Army Officer,* and its discussion, THE OFFICER'S RELATIONS WITH ENLISTED PERSONNEL, and chapter 4, *The Officer Image.*

What are some of the definite responsibilities if you are a line commander? You avoid unhealthy conditions in camp or in the field as conditions allow. You insist upon organization cleanliness through adequate clean-up and police measures. You insist upon individual cleanliness as to person and clothing; this will often require that you provide measures for bathing, individual washing of clothes, or provisions to get clothing to a laundry and back again for use. In the organization dining facility you must provide at all times for adequate refrigeration and a high standard of sanitation, including facilities for washing cooking utensils and dishes, with cleanliness of all food handlers. There must be adequate lavatory and latrine facilities maintained in a sanitary, orderly condition. These are daily responsibilities of the line commander, which have for their purpose the maintenance of health. They are illness-preventive measures in the eyes of the doctor.

There are the safety measures to avoid accidents. The military arts are especially hazardous. Great care must be used in the handling of weapons and explosives. Power equipment in the hands of the poorly trained individual or the novice may be lethal. Accidents in the driving of motor vehicles of all kinds are a continual threat.

Receiving the New Soldier. The way a new soldier is received into an organization has a profound effect upon his or her immediate impressions. It may have lasting effect. Combat organizations of the Army have the ever-present problem of assimilating replacements (a poor word that some wise person should improve, and let it never be forgotten that the replacement of today is the veteran of tomorrow!). There is a place at once for the replacement's energy and skill, zeal in the cause, and the new soldier's determination to win.

Then we should take those steps that will enhance the new soldier's immediate value, and avoid those things that will delay or destroy it.

As the very first step, take care at once of the new soldier's creature necessities and comforts, while at the same time letting him or her know that all in the organization are glad he or she has arrived. See that the new arrival is fed, given a place to stow personal gear, and a place to sleep, and made to feel a member of an up-and-coming organization that knows how to care for its members and intends to do it.

At the very first opportunity, the unit commander should meet and interview the new arrival. Who is he or she? Learn about the person's training, service, age, home community, education, family, and service aspirations. Let the new arrival know that the commander wants to know his or her soldiers, is interested in them, and means to use them wisely.

Repeat the process by interviews held by junior officers and appropriate non-commissioned officers. Decide promptly upon the individual's squad assignment. Introduce the soldier to members of the squad who must be encouraged to extend the hand of comradeship.

If these measures are taken thoughtfully, newness will wear off very promptly; shyness, wishful thinking of former comrades, and other deterrents will disappear to be replaced by satisfaction of assignment, a feeling of belonging, and determination to get on with the job whatever it may be.

A Look at Coddling. Coddling is overlooking things soldiers do that are wrong. Avoiding night training, or long marches, or training in rain or cold to spare physical discomfort are examples. It is to fail to send out a patrol when there is grave need for information because it is a dangerous mission, only to have many soldiers killed by surprise action of the enemy that might have been detected. Now is a good time to return to a definition of leadership in an earlier edition that starts, "The art of imposing one's will . . ." The leader must be a determined person, in matters concerning his or her duty and mission, holding subordinates squarely to the mark, but at the same time providing in every way for the training, feeding and supply, administration, medical attention, recreation, and the human touch of welfare as it is needed. Coddling is weak and wrong. But full provision for the contentment of unit personnel is eternally right.

OFF-DUTY ACTIVITIES

While the training day or working day of a military organization is long, the commander has not discharged his or her responsibilities because recall has sounded. The average age of soldiers of a company may be under twenty-five, or even under twenty. Many will be single or will not have their families nearby. Because they are young most of them will have abundant energy to be employed when the official day has ended. Again the responsibilities of the military leader carry far beyond those of a civilian chief. This void in time must be filled by worthy opportunities, or soldiers through boredom may fill it otherwise.

It is Army policy to make the off-duty life of posts and stations so attractive and interesting that all personnel will find some one or more activities that will consume their time and interest. People vary as to their interests. Most but not all like to take part in athletics; a portion will wish to read or study; the service club with its dances and activities will attract many. Others will prefer to remain in barracks with the activities immediately at hand. The point is this: There must be opportunities on a large scale for off-duty enjoyment, and there must be wide diversification in the things under way.

A sound off-duty program is a three-pronged affair. *First,* and possibly of highest importance, are the facilities at the barracks such as a suitable day room, and facilities for informal athletics. This is the primary responsibility of the company commander. *Second,* an extensive program for the garrison as a whole. Here we have the activities of Recreation Services in off-duty recreation; a broad athletic program; the religious program of the chaplain; theaters; the educational programs of Information and Education. These are responsibilities of the station commander assisted by staff members. *Third* are activities in adjacent civilian communities provided for personnel in uniform, such as those provided by USO, civilian and civic organizations, churches, lodges, and the like. When the soldier leaves the post these facilities provide a place to go and things to do. These are responsibilities of the station commander, aided by his or her staff, in coordination with civilian leaders.

Recreational Program of a Company. Leadership is needed within a company if it is to have an attractive off-duty recreational program. Many commanders assign an officer or noncommissioned officer to supervise this program in addition to other duties.

Two programs have direct application to the company in barracks. They are the day room, or recreation room, and the organization athletic program; this may consist of informal athletics of many kinds for wide participation, or the forming of company teams for scheduled games in a battalion, brigade, or station league.

The leader of the activity may proceed on this line of action. Make a careful check of facilities, both as to items issued and those purchased from unit funds. Visit a number of organizations to see the general standard, and observe for especially popular ideas. Fix upon a standard of facilities and activities and go after it.

Apply first attention to the day room, or recreation room. Here is the place soldiers will assemble when off duty, in fair weather or foul, more regularly than elsewhere. A proper day room is equipped to be interesting, well lighted, clean, and attractive in appearance. The equipment should include a number of comfortable lounge chairs; a larger number of straight chairs because they require less space; a large table; small tables as appropriate; floor or wall lamps. All must be strongly built. As to things to do, all or most of the following should be provided: basic supply of newspapers and magazines, remembering that the soldier has available the station library; radio; record player; television; pool table; and table tennis.

Strive to arrange facilities so as to provide reading (and studying) and hobby rooms away from the vociferous day room activity. Many soldiers are taking study courses for various goals and should be assisted by access to a quiet area while off duty.

Part of the day room furnishings may be obtained by issue through the morale support officer of the station. The remainder may be purchased from the unit fund, with the approval of the company commander.

A good company athletic program is a matter of facilities, equipment, and guidance. The goal here is for everyone to participate—"athletics for all." Again, the officer in charge of company off-duty activities should survey what equipment is on hand and what is unserviceable and can be repaired. By conference with NCOs he or she can determine what is wanted. Some athletic equipment may be obtained from the station morale support officer by issue. Anything additional must be provided by purchase from organization nonappropriated funds. A desired equipment list, with detailed costs, must be presented to the company commander for approval or amendment.

The Morale Support Officer. The morale support officer of posts and stations, and of large units, heads all recreational services including voluntary athletics. The closest coordination and support should be developed between commanders, especially small unit commanders, and the morale support officer.

The Chaplain. Religious freedom is one of the basic foundations of the American form of government. Military chaplains are provided in the U.S. Army to ensure availability of a free choice in the exercise of religion. Ordained clergy perform as an extension of their denomination in conducting worship services, administering rites and sacraments, and providing an active religious education program. The chaplain is a technical expert serving on the personal staff of the commander and assists the commander in fulfilling command responsibility concerning matters of religion, morals, and morale as affected by religion.

The religious and spiritual welfare of the members of a command is an important factor in the development of individual pride, morale, and self-respect, essentials in a military organization. While Kipling may have over-emphasized the sordid side of the life led by some soldiers in saying that men in barracks do not grow into plaster saints, it is a fact the environment in some instances leaves a little to be desired. We are a religious people and our soldiers are subject to a wholesome, religious influence. There is a relation between morals and morale just as there is a relation between fair and just treatment and morale, or cleanliness and morale. The organization commander who is mindful of the religious and spiritual environment of his or her soldiers will be able to make a strong appeal to the better instincts of all, which may be impossible to attain for those who neglect it.

Unit Nonappropriated Funds. The earnings resulting from the operation of exchanges and motion picture theaters are paid monthly into unit nonappropriated funds. Each company receives a distribution of funds, as does the central post fund, for an entire station, and the major command fund, such as an army in the CONUS. Expenditures from the funds are authorized for the good of an entire organization for things not supplied by the government, as stated in detail in AR 215-1. As to company funds, expenditures and accounts are a personal responsibility of the commander that may not be delegated to another officer.

AR 215-5 provides further regulations on fund management and the commander's responsibility. It is wise to consult with an experienced auditor, often the battalion executive officer, on the details and techniques of keeping the book, obtaining vouchers, and administering unit fund property. A council within the unit of officers and NCOs will advise the commander, but the management of the fund is still his or her responsibility. Like all savings, they are hard to accumulate and easy to spend; but, unlike personal savings, the regulations are very specific on what can be purchased. (See the Appendix for duties of the unit fund council members.)

The United Service Organization, USO. The facilities provided by the USO for off-post recreation are of high value and deserve strong support from commanders. The Army itself has made notable progress in improving the recreation and athletic facilities within military stations through its strongly supported Morale Support program. The USO provides its assistance in nearby civilian communities through club and service facilities. A clean and attractive gathering place in cities visited by large numbers of service men and women is essential. Their activities of many kinds provide needed recreation. The USO also sends shows to overseas commands to entertain our service members.

Funds for support of the USO are raised through the annual Community Chest and United Givers Fund drives, all by volunteer giving.

Unit commanders can assist the USO program by knowing where the USO facilities are established, close acquaintance with the local leaders, cooperation by informing their personnel about USO, and a regular announcement of current activities. A frequent visit to the facilities by commanders of all grades is helpful to demonstrate a sustained interest in the work of the organization. They can assist in the fund-raising program by telling civilian leaders of the need for USO in cities and towns near Army stations.

SPECIAL PROBLEMS

There are special problems the leader will encounter in all categories of units. Several of these recurring problems, with suggestions as to their handling, are discussed below. There are others, of course, and some may have a "newness" that will startle the commander. In each such case, the officer must find the way to proceed quietly and objectively to determine the facts, weigh them, and decide what action, if any at all, should be taken for the benefit of either the individual concerned or the unit, or the broader good of the Army and the nation. The officer's commission is a public trust; he or she is expected to choose a wise course of action and have the courage to follow it.

Absence without Leave. Commanders of companies will certainly be faced with the problem of absence without leave. It is the military example of "cutting classes," or staying away from work, which the civilian chief calls "absenteeism." But in a military command it is far more serious. Skulking in battle is an aggravated form of AWOL. Like other problems it can be reduced greatly, if not entirely eliminated, by a sound approach.

Many times soldiers are absent without leave when by asking they could as easily have received permission to be away. The first essential is that all personnel understand clearly how and when they may obtain passes for short absences and leaves for longer ones. As duty permits there should be readiness to grant this authority within the scope of regulations. Then when duty requires all to be on duty continuously, individuals will be better prepared mentally to accept the situation.

Instruction will constitute the preventive for a large portion of the unit. Good soldiers cherish their standing in the eyes of their superiors and of their fellows. They must understand that such an absence is prejudicial to promotion or assignment to a responsible position. They should be made aware of the standing of the organization itself in this matter because senior commanders watch carefully the comparative standings of their units in AWOL and other transgressions. They must understand about loss of pay for the offense. The fact that essential instruction is missed will influence some soldiers. The problem is reduced by being certain that sound, positive instruction is given about the gravity of the offense as to its individual effects, although it may not be eliminated by this method.

After an individual returns from an unauthorized absence there must be an interview with the commander. What was the true reason for the absence? Did the soldier understand the policy for leave or pass? Was he or she denied authority for absence? Was the absence an important one as to personal affairs, or trivial, or an example of character weakness? The commander must strive to learn the cause and having done so to apply such corrective action as is indicated.

A series of such interviews is almost certain to disclose that soldiers most prone to offend in this matter are those of lowest intelligence, education, or ambition, or weakest in character. Patience in instruction of such individuals may be necessary.

Strong action must be taken as to repeated offenders who continue the practice despite instruction, sound appeals to pride, and milder punishments. Here will be found those most prone to skulking on the battlefield or to self-inflicted wounds. They are the ones most likely to be asleep when they should be alert to detect enemy action or to turn back from a patrol. In such cases the only remaining action may be to let trials by court-martial run their course.

The commander must face this problem with wisdom and sound action.

Debt and the Commander's Responsibility. Debt beyond immediate capacity to pay is not a new problem of a soldier (or officer). "All men are good soldiers— when they are broke," is ancient, but it has a vestige of truth.

There are merchants within the United States and abroad who go to extremes to get a soldier or an officer to place his or her name on an installment contract. It is one of our less admirable national traits that we want to have at once all the enjoyments of our contemporaries. It is the "travel now—pay later" philosophy extended. The legal assistance counselors, who see the seamy and greedy side of it, say "Keep your pen in your pocket!"

What is the responsibility of the commander? He or she has a duty to instruct because some soldiers, even senior NCOs and officers, contract obligations beyond their capacity to pay. The commander can be certain that the majority of temptations are disclosed, such as car, appliance, china, travel, book, insurance, clothing, on and on. He or she can also prevent salesmen encroaching upon training time, or even the unit premises unless the salesman has an authorization in hand from appropriate authority.

When the damage is done, the commander may assist the person in financial difficulty to make a consolidated loan, save interest, and have repayment placed on an attainable basis. In some instances such loans may be obtained from the Red

Cross, or Army Emergency Relief. This procedure includes opportunity to instruct in order to develop the "never again" attitude.

An associated administrative problem is the barrage of letters from creditors demanding collection assistance. There is a regulation that requires commanders to assist bona fide creditors in collecting amounts properly payable to them; and there is the accompanying duty of a commander to protect his or her soldiers against fraudulent or incorrect claims. Some creditors resort to threats against the commander as well as the debtor. What course should a commander follow? He or she should require the creditor to provide a copy of the contract, or a written agreement or record to substantiate the claim, with a statement of all payments to date; consult the soldier (or the officer) to determine whether there is an agreement between creditor and debtor; and determine the soldier's version of the indebtedness. Some cases may require guidance from the legal assistance officer. When the commander is satisfied that there is an indebtedness, and payment is in arrears, it becomes his or her duty to require or try to arrange a suitable method of payment. A soldier (or officer) may be punished for failure to pay just debts.

This is an unpleasant duty that falls to commanders of companies and even to battalion commanders. Expect to encounter the problem and regard it as a challenge to leadership.

About Those Who "Hate the Army." Regrettably, there are some soldiers and even some officers quite brazen in saying, "I don't like . . ." or "I hate the Army." Some few are so loud and insistent about it, and seemingly so proud of it, as to cause wonder about their loyalty to the nation that favors them with citizenship. For too many years we have overlooked such occurrences with a good-natured tolerance, but the situation deserves consideration. What is the real meaning behind such assertions? What can be done to change the view of those who are antagonistic to the nation's defense forces? How can we change these individuals from poor and unreliable members into useful ones? Not by ignoring them, surely.

What these individuals are voicing, perhaps without intent, is their hatred of the United States, their rejection of the duties of a citizen, or their fervent unwillingness to do anything whatever to protect their individual freedoms and opportunities, which they take for granted. Our country can endure a small portion of such individuals; but if the time should ever come that the majority of our people choose this philosophy, our nation will go the way of ancient Rome and other vanished nations of the modern as well as the ancient eras. The correction of shallow beliefs and unpatriotic actions is worth a strong effort.

Some who do it are intentionally subversive, and let us not delude ourselves about it. Anything such individuals can do to weaken the determination of others to give their best in military service, or to destroy confidence in the nation, its defense forces, or its military or civil leadership is beneficial to the secret cause of the subversive person.

It is entirely true that in the great majority of cases the service member or exmember who makes hateful or derogatory remarks about the Army (or the Air Force or Navy as well) does so without intentional subversive intent. He or she is merely exercising an inalienable right to "blow off steam." Such persons may be stupid, uneducated, lazy or indifferent to the national needs in a troubled world. Also, they may be highly intelligent, well-educated persons, and it is a tragedy for the Army to fail to gain the understanding support of its potentially most capable members. We can spare the stupid and lazy, for their contributions will be of small value, at best. But we must seek to obtain the active support and best efforts of the true intellectuals, for otherwise there is heavy damage to the cause of free people everywhere.

What can a commander do about it? How can this waste of potential high capability be saved and applied to constructive uses? Wisdom is needed here. If it is merely getting rid of a gripe, ignore it, certainly. Is the offender momentarily enraged because of one or more occurrences, or with one or more individuals? Has the soldier been the recipient of an action that he or she believes unfair or unjust? Or is the offender lazy, stupid, indifferent to national needs? Finally, does the individual really have a deep-seated "hate the Army" complex?

There are also the protestors, objectors, and racists, who are signs of our times and who present a special problem to be handled wisely. They require a patient, thoughtful leader whose emotions are circumscribed by commonsense and the official regulations. The first step is to study the published regulations and ascertain the command policy. Important references are AR 600-50, *Standards of Conduct for Department of the Army Personnel;* AR 600-20, *Army Command Policy and Procedure;* and the Uniform Code of Military Justice (UCMJ). For specific situations the unit commander may also expect to receive local directives. Discussions with such individuals will be enhanced by a patient, thoughtful, well-informed leader who has the firm intention of making useful, willing, capable soldiers who are assigned under his or her jurisdiction out of persons who might otherwise become severe, undependable drags. Pitch the discussions to the intelligence and education level of the individual or individuals involved. A serious effort to reach minds with logic and reason is worth a major effort. Our nation needs citizens who are loyal and willing to perform the arduous duties of citizenship.

Not all will change their stated beliefs, or reveal their inner purposes. They must be apprised of their rights and limits in the presence of immediate commanders, officers, and NCOs. It is wise to do this openly, calmly, and objectively, in low key. This is not a new problem, and in our democracy it may never be old. Even so, the wisdom of Tom Paine continues to apply: *"Those who expect to reap the blessings of liberty, must, like men, undergo the fatigue of supporting it."*

The Curbing of Vulgar and Profane Language. It is Army policy that profanity and vulgarity are not condoned in the conduct of instruction or in official conversation. As ladies and gentlemen, officers should be scrupulous in avoiding foul, offensive language and should never permit its use in their presence.

The Venereal Problem. A curse of mankind, including armies, is venereal infection resulting from unwise or foolish sexual contacts. The more recent appearance of AIDS is even worse, since there is no known cure for this disease. It is a command responsibility to instruct soldiers on the broad subject of morality and clean living as well as on measures to avoid infection.

The Complaint Problem. The commander must be accessible to members of the unit who wish to state a complaint. Some of the complaints will be petty. Others may be deliberate attempts to injure the reputation of another with a charge that is without foundation. There are other occasions, however, even in the best organizations, where genuine cause for dissatisfaction may occur. This is information that the commander must obtain lest the morale of the unit be seriously impaired. Members must know that they may state a cause for complaint to their commander with the knowledge that he or she will give them a hearing and correct the grievance if convinced of its truth. The Army has an open door policy that calls for easy access to the commander through appropriate subordinate commanders unable to resolve the complaint. Good soldiers will seek to avoid making a complaint. But when ideas, or suggestions, or reports are stated to the commander that affect the welfare, the efficiency, or the morale of the unit, or any individual therein, they must be heard sympathetically. If the condition reported can be corrected, or deserves correction, the action should be taken at once. (See *Redress of Wrong,* in 25, *Rights, Privileges, and Restrictions.*)

Delivery of Mail. Homesickness may well be said to be the "occupational disease" of the American soldier. Next in importance to food, the student of soldier psychology might place the prompt delivery of mail. Indeed, for the soldier with a wife or husband, a son or daughter, a sweetheart or a beloved father or mother, mail may be of far greater lasting importance than food. Commanders of units must pay particular attention to this necessary task. They must see to it that mail reaches the soldier quickly and safely. They must make very certain that none is lost and that chance of malicious opening and violation of privacy is reduced to the vanishing point. A letter from home is of the highest importance to the soldier, as it serves to unite him or her for a moment with loved ones. For the most part, letters will quiet the soldier's apprehensions and dispel the worries that beset those who are far removed from their homes. Knowledge that all is well at home secures a peace of mind so strong that it justifies every effort a good mail service requires.

The commander is urged to check the method of receiving, guarding, and distributing the mail as it reaches the organization. Are the individuals charged with handling it completely trustworthy? Or are there unsolved complaints of rifled or stolen letters? Is the mail guarded scrupulously from the time of receipt until it is handed to the soldier? Or is it allowed to lie about, subject to scrutiny and mishandling? Is it tossed promiscuously into a milling throng with small regard to its actual delivery? Or is it handed to the individual to whom addressed? Is it held for long hours after receipt to be distributed at the whim of some individual? Or is the mail delivered as promptly as circumstances permit after receipt? Are registered and special delivery pieces handled with due regard to postal regulations? Are your receipts for these classes of mail maintained exactly as prescribed? The soldier treasures packages from home. Are packages zealously guarded so that petty pilfering is surely prevented? These are all matters that are very important in the daily life of the soldier.

Personal Problems of Soldiers. All soldiers have left interests, or roots, or problems behind them that may require their attention or action while in the military service. At home the soldier would turn for advice to a parent, a friend, a lawyer, a minister or priest, or other person in whom he or she has trust and confidence. In the Army, the soldier will usually turn to the company commander.

These occasions provide a fine opportunity for the commander to show a deep interest in the welfare of his or her soldiers. The commander should adopt an impersonal and kindly attitude in hearing these problems. If the matter is confidential it must never be divulged improperly. When it is proper to do so, the commander should give the counsel he or she knows to be correct, or obtain the necessary information, or direct the soldier to an authority who can supply the information.

In many cases, after hearing the soldier's problems, the officer will need to refer the soldier to another authority. The legal assistance officer for legal matters; the American Red Cross field director for investigation and action about family conditions at home; the chaplain on many matters of religion, marriage, and human relationships; the surgeon if the problem is one of worry about health.

A good leader must have a genuine understanding of human relations. His or her tools are men and women, and therefore the leader must be able to deal with people. The necessary warmth of military leadership may be demonstrated when soldiers carry their baffling personal problems to their commander for advice or solution.

Importance of Letters to Parents. In a number of organizations, commanders make it a practice to write letters to parents of their soldiers when important personal events have occurred in which they may take pride. The people of the United States are tremendously and vitally concerned about the progress of the Army to which they have given the services of their sons and daughters. Their impressions are formed by the reports they receive from their children and their neighbors and friends. No amount of big-name announcements as to Army morale and conditions will offset the local effect of an unfavorable report from a personal acquaintance. The interest and satisfaction that can be developed by contact, even by letters, with the folks at home are worth the effort required.

Many company, battery, or platoon leaders write these letters. "Dear Mrs. Brown," they may write, "I am pleased to tell you that I have recommended your son for promotion to the grade of corporal. He has worked hard here and his record is splendid. He is a good soldier." Or this: "As you know, your daughter has been confined to the station hospital. I have visited her several times and have had frequent reports about her condition from her medical officer, the chaplain, and others. I can tell you now that she is well on the road to recovery, and her return to her organization will occur very soon. She is performing a service to her nation of which you and she, too, will always be proud." The American soldier is a young man or woman who is usually away from home for the first time. The soldier's parents are anxious that he or she perform creditably.

Have you been present when a letter is received from a young soldier? Do you know how it is discussed and passed around or read aloud to others? Can you not imagine the effect of a letter from a soldier's commander? Form the habit of writing personal letters to the parents of your soldiers on proper occasion. It places a human touch on a relationship that is impersonal and detached.

CONCLUSION

Now that you as an actual leader have progressed through the study of leadership as an academic subject, have received some practical application of principles as a cadet, ROTC student, or officer candidate, and have performed the responsibility of an actual assignment in command, you may recognize some consoling truths. There are no quick rules of thumb or easily memorized axioms that will assure a junior leader of success. The superlative qualities that have been described are impossible for all leaders to have, and no leader has had all of them. The young leader will understand that diligence, patience, honor, integrity, devotion to a cause and to his or her soldiers, when combined with knowledge, are all included. After progressing for a time with your first responsibility in command you will have learned that it is results in the execution of command that count. You will develop acceptance of a further truth: *Army commanders must anticipate that someday they may lead troops in battle.* Set about the development of the qualities you must possess to meet this responsibility successfully. Then you will have adopted a sound course.

There are visible rewards for success in leadership. It may lead to promotion with increased pay, decorations, and the finest assignments. But the greatest reward is the trust and approval of your officers and soldiers, plus the invisible reward of satisfaction with being a leader who accomplishes the missions assigned. If you should aspire to become a Bradley, MacArthur, Eisenhower, Pershing, Lee, Grant, or Washington (and why not?) set your goal and proceed. The Army has vast opportunity for talent.

18

Staff Assignment

Any military organization has a commander who alone is responsible for all that the unit does or fails to do. All policies, basic decisions, and plans must be authorized by the commander before they are put into effect. All orders from a higher unit to a lower unit are given to the commander thereof and are issued by or for the commander of the larger unit. Each individual in the Army is accustomed to look to his or her immediate superior for orders and instructions. By this means, authority and responsibility are definitely fixed, and the channels of command are definitely established.

WHY A STAFF?

It should be apparent, however, that there are a myriad of details involved with the day-to-day operation of any organization. As the size of the organization increases, the number and variety of the details increase. The commander cannot devote personal attention to all of them.

Therefore, a staff is provided as an aid to command. It serves to relieve the commander of details by providing basic information and technical advice by which he or she may arrive at decisions; by developing the basic decision into adequate plans, translating plans into orders, and transmitting them to subordinate leaders; by ensuring compliance with these orders through constructive inspection and observation for the commander; by keeping the commander informed of everything he or she ought to know; by anticipating future needs and drafting tentative plans to meet them; by supplementing the commander's efforts to secure unity of action throughout the command; and by learning the commander's policies and working within them. In short, a properly functioning staff is an extension of the eyes, ears, and will of the commander.

Value of a Staff Assignment. An assignment to staff duties provides an opportunity for increased knowledge and capability for an officer of any grade. The staff officer learns the detailed organization and missions of each component of the command and how the commanding officer and the subordinate commanders solve the problems that confront them. The staff officer works with each staff section and gains a knowledge of their responsibilities and methods. It is splendid training for a future assignment to command.

STAFF ORGANIZATION

The organization of the staff of any military unit is prescribed in the Tables of Organization and is based upon the duties and responsibilities of the commander whom it serves. The battalion is the smallest unit that has a staff, although even in the company there are officers and noncommissioned officers who have duties that parallel those of staff officers. These include such duties as food service officer, supply officer, and motor officer, and the training NCO and information and education NCO. At the company level, such duties generally are assigned in addition to the primary duties of the company officers or noncommissioned officers.

Functional Areas. The staff assists the commander in the performance of four functional areas of responsibility, which are as follows: (1) personnel, (2) military intelligence, (3) operations and training, and (4) logistics. At the battalion level, the staff officers having general responsibility in these areas are designated the S1, S2, S3, and S4, respectively. At division level and higher, these staff officers are designated G1, G2, G3, and G4; while on joint and combined staffs, the designations J1, J2, J3, and J4 are used. In addition, on higher level staffs, additional numbers sometimes are used for staff officers having responsibility in specific areas of prime importance to the organization, for example, civil affairs or communications.

General Staff. These four functional areas comprise the areas of responsibility of the general staff. The size of the staff section provided in each case is determined by the workload and complexity of operations encountered. The general staff operates under the supervision of the *chief of staff,* who is the principal assistant to the commander. The chief of staff transmits the will of the commander to those who act in the commander's name, and is the principal coordinating agent to ensure efficient functioning of the staff and of all troops in the command. At battalion level, the *executive officer* fills the function of the chief of staff, while the company executive officer serves in a similar capacity.

Special Staff. Within the overall framework of the four functional areas, there are certain specific functions that warrant the attention of a specialist. These specific functions vary with the size and the mission of the organization, but may include such matters as engineering, transportation, communications, ordnance, and medical support. To fill these specific needs, a special staff is provided, consisting of such staff officers as the Engineer, the Transportation officer, the Signal officer, the Ordnance officer, or the Surgeon. These special staff officers operate under the direction of the general staff, reporting to such general staff officer as may be appropriate. For example, on matters pertaining to construction or maintenance of roads, cantonment areas, or similar facilities, the Engineer deals with the G4, while on matters pertaining to operations or training he or she deals with the G3. Similarly, the Engineer deals with the G2 on engineer technical intelligence matters.

Personal Staff. In addition to the *general staff* and the *special staff,* commanding generals are authorized a *personal staff.* This personal staff consists of authorized aides, or *aides-de-camp,* and other assistants. The whole purpose of the personal staff is to relieve the general from time-consuming personal matters so that he or she may devote full attention to matters of command, and discharge heavy responsibilities with efficiency and continuity. The duties of an aide to a general officer are discussed in the final ssction of this chapter.

FUNCTIONS OF A BATTALION STAFF

The staff of a battalion includes the executive officer, the S1, S2, S3, S4, and special staff officers. The commander may either follow the TOE and assign staff officers to duties consistent with AR 611-101, which details their job descriptions, or may "tailor" the staff in accordance with his or her mission and their numbers, experience, capabilities, and grades.

The commander may divide the staff's functions into administration and operations; and, to reduce the span of control while enhancing supervision, assign the executive officer to monitor administration and the S3 operations.

The Executive Officer. At battalion and brigade level, the executive officer may serve as the second-in-command and as the principal assistant to the commanding officer. He or she usually directs, coordinates, and supervises the activities of the staff sections. The EO is often appointed the materiel readiness officer. It is the best possible training toward becoming a battalion commander.

The S1 (Adjutant). The S1 is charged with staff responsibility for personnel management, matters pertaining to unit strength, morale, discipline, and miscellaneous administrative tasks. He or she is usually charged with correspondence of the executive officer and the commanding officer, and with the headquarters files requiring familiarity with AR 340-15, *Preparing Correspondence.*

The S2 (Military Intelligence). The S2 is responsible for the production and dissemination of combat intelligence and counterintelligence matters. He or she assists the commanding officer and other staff officers in security matters including safes, filing, clearances, intelligence training, and related duties. To fulfill the primary responsibility of producing combat intelligence, the S2 collects, collates, evaluates, and interprets information of the enemy, weather, and terrain, which may influence the accomplishment of the unit mission. Of equal importance is the duty of disseminating this information to the commanding officer, other staff officers, subordinate commanders, and adjacent units.

The S3 (Operations). The S3 has staff responsibility for planning the successive combat operations, organization, and training as directed by the commanding officer. In his or her field are operational directives, plans, orders, command post exercises (CPXs), field training exercises (FTXs), training aids, ammunition requirements, school allocations and quotas, and a host of related duties. The S3 prepares estimates and recommends to the commander actions or decisions for the accomplishment of the mission. It is a vital mission in which he or she works in close coordination with the executive officer and the commanding officer.

The S3 has staff responsibility for the unit readiness of the command. Especially in this function, the S3 works closely with the executive offficer, who is usually appointed the materiel readiness officer.

The S4 (Logistics). The S4 is the battalion logistics officer and has staff responsibility for the logistics services and facilities available to the battalion. These are supply, transportation, maintenance, logistics plans and records, and other matters in the field of logistical support. The S4 prepares logistical plans and appropriate

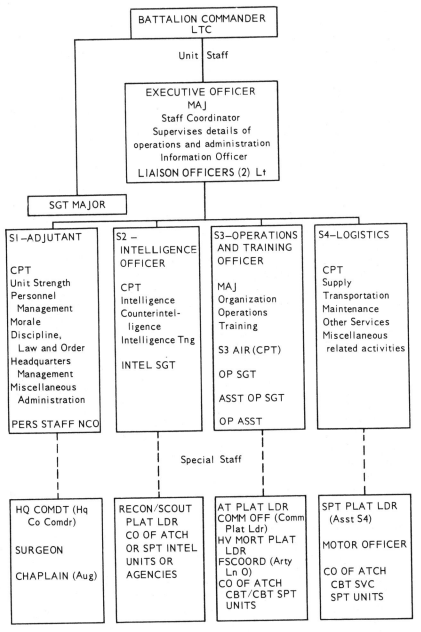

BATTALION COMMANDER
LTC

Unit | Staff

EXECUTIVE OFFICER
MAJ
Staff Coordinator
Supervises details of
operations and administration
Information Officer
LIAISON OFFICERS (2) Lt

SGT MAJOR

S1—ADJUTANT

CPT
Unit Strength
Personnel
 Management
Morale
Discipline,
 Law and Order
Headquarters
 Management
Miscellaneous
 Administration

PERS STAFF NCO

S2 —
INTELLIGENCE
OFFICER

CPT
Intelligence
Counterintel-
 ligence
Intelligence Tng

INTEL SGT

S3—OPERATIONS
AND TRAINING
OFFICER

MAJ
Organization
Operations
Training

S3 AIR (CPT)

OP SGT

ASST OP SGT

OP ASST

S4—LOGISTICS

CPT
Supply
Transportation
Maintenance
Other Services
Miscellaneous
 related activities

Special Staff

HQ COMDT (Hq
 Co Comdr)

SURGEON

CHAPLAIN (Aug)

RECON/SCOUT
PLAT LDR
CO OF ATCH
OR SPT INTEL
UNITS OR
AGENCIES

AT PLAT LDR
COMM OFF (Comm
 Plat Ldr)
HV MORT PLAT
 LDR
FSCOORD (Arty
 Ln O)
CO OF ATCH
CBT/CBT SPT
UNITS

SPT PLAT LDR
(Asst S4)

MOTOR OFFICER

CO OF ATCH
CBT SVC
SPT UNITS

— Unit Staff responsibility for staff supervision.

BATTALION STAFF ORGANIZATION.

portions of published plans and orders. During operations, he or she is responsible for the location and operation of the battalion trains. The S4 is responsible for local security measures within the trains' area and for coordination with higher units and adjacent units in this responsibility. In some battalions the S4 is also a commander of a service supporting unit.

The Special Staff. There are certain specific functions that warrant the assignment of a specialist. These special functions vary with the size, mission, and organization of a battalion or larger unit. The preceding chart of the battalion staff organization illustrates the staff, including the special staff, of an infantry battalion. Special staff activities are coordinated by some part of the unit staff. In some units, the members of the special staff command the related support unit, which increases their responsibilities.*

BASIC FUNCTIONS OF A STAFF OFFICER

The Army has standardized many of the basic staff techniques and procedures. The primary reference is Field Manual 101-5, *Staff Organization and Operations.* In addition, branch service schools have developed excellent texts; as a useful example, the *Operations and Training Handbook,* U.S. Army Infantry School, Fort Benning, Georgia. Effective staff procedures are essential in the effective performance of mission by the entire unit; a fine staff accomplishes completed staff action with coordination and timeliness.

Informing. Exchange of information is the first key of good staff procedures. It is the first step in assuring a common basis of understanding by staff officers and their commander in making estimates and decisions. No staff officer can operate effectively as a loner or in a vacuum. He or she must provide information to other staff officers, as well as receive information from them. This goal is attainable only by good working relationships within a staff, and with other staffs, with a talent for good human relationships leading to fine coordination and teamwork.

Estimating. An estimate of the situation is a procedure for the logical analysis of a problem by which one arrives at the workable choices of mission accomplishment and the selection of the one to be adopted. It is continuous, systematic, and as complete a process of reasoning as time permits. The accompanying list shows the definite steps in the process.

The sequence established by the standard estimate of the situation is applicable to all staff problems, not alone the classic one of a combat decision. The staff uses the estimate procedure to recommend a course of action, while the commander uses it to choose or decide what he or she will order.

Estimate of the Situation
1. MISSION (Problem)
2. THE SITUATION AND COURSES OF ACTION:
    a. Considerations affecting possible courses of action
    b. Opposing conditions
    c. Own courses of action
3. ANALYSIS OF OPPOSING COURSES OF ACTION
4. COMPARISON OF OWN COURSES OF ACTION
5. DECISION

---

*Because of their special technical skills, warrant officers often are assigned as special staff officers.

Recommending. Staff officers make recommendations upon their own initiative or when requested to do so. Such recommendations result from a careful estimate of the situation and, when offered, must be clearly presented, with neither equivocation nor ambiguity. If another staff agency is involved, which is usually the case, the recommendation must be coordinated with that agency. Should a failure to agree develop, the divergent view must be presented fairly and objectively. The staff officer is not settling a debate, but is presenting facts and views, with a recommendation, on which the commander will make a decision, which may be quite different than the one recommended.

Noteworthy Tradition. When the commander chooses a course of action different from, or opposite to the staff officer's recommendation, as happens in all headquarters, the staff officer applies his or her maximum talents to make certain the commander's decision is executed precisely. No pique, no bruised feelings, no silent resolution that "next time she will get what I think she wants." The tradition is discussed more fully in the section THE MILITARY TRADITIONS, chapter 3, *The Code of the Army Officer,* and especially in General Ridgway's directive to the Army staff. The staff is an arm or a tool of the commander to assist in the discharge of heavy responsibility involving many people, many problems, and many techniques. But the commander is the responsible official, and the one who decides. The staff officer shows an understanding of this essential principle of carrying out the commander's decision to his or her highest capability, never indicating that he or she had recommended a different course of action.

Preparing Plans and Orders. Once the commander has stated a decision, the staff prepares the detailed orders for the entire command, if the circumstances require written orders and if time permits their preparation. Routine matters coming under previously approved policy are handled by the staff without repeated visits to the commander; however, as to important matters or action that is unusual, the staff informs the commander at the first convenient opportunity. Orders involving missions for subordinate commanders, particularly tactical ones, are prepared with more consultation and approval by the commander.

Estimating the value of good plans and orders for achieving success in battle is hazardous at best; some authorities have stated they are 90 percent of the battle and implementation 10 percent. But it is certainly true that the commander must direct clearly *what* is to be done, *where* and *when* it is to be done, with a specific mission for each element involved, or the who factor, and in some instances a statement of the *why* is helpful. Good plans and good orders are clear and precise. The staff officer should have in mind the ancient truth that "any order that *can* be misunderstood, *will* be misunderstood."

The following both describes General Marshall and points out a major factor in his success as a commander: *"The order must be comprehensive, yet not involved. It must appear clear when read in poor light, in the mud and rain. That was Marshall's job, and he performed it 100 percent. The troops which maneuvered under his plans always won." George C. Marshall, Education of a General,* by Forrest Pogue, Viking Press, 1963.

PLAN FOR AN OPERATIONS ORDER

An accompanying illustration shows the plan format for an operations order, or the standard five-paragraph field order form. It is more than a mere form—it is a logical process of thought that should be used as a matter of course in the issue of simple instructions as well as detailed, written, operations orders. It is helpful for staff officers as well as commanders to memorize the sequence and develop skill in its use.

Supervision. The execution or implementation of plans and resultant orders must have both command and staff supervision. The beginning staff procedure calls for being informed, which involves seeing, visiting, and inspecting by direct contact. Desk or "mahogany-bound" staff officers are unlikely to serve the commander ably. Going out to see and check is the better way to keep informed. On the part of the staff officer it requires tact, for he or she is not the commander. If erroneous action is discovered, and the time factor requires, the staff officer may issue corrective orders on the spot but only in the name of the commanding officer: "The Commanding Officer directs . . ." In the usual case the staff officer will inform the commander at the earliest opportunity of his or her action. In inspections and reports to the commander, the staff officer is not a talebearer; most successful staff officers inform the subordinate commanders of their finding, discuss it with them, and inform them of the exact nature of the report to be made to the commander.

A staff visit, which is discussed above as a part of supervision or follow-up, has the essential purpose of coordination, teamwork, and mutual understanding between the commander and subordinate commanders, between staff divisions, and between the staff and subordinate commanders. Such visits may uncover misunderstandings and provide correction before becoming serious and requiring command action. The written word is not always clear, however carefully it is prepared, just as the oral word may also be misunderstood. Here is ever-present opportunity for the staff officer to serve the commander well, and help in an important manner the achievement of the mission.

LIMITATION OF STAFF AUTHORITY

A staff officer, as such, has no authority to command. He or she does not prescribe policies, basic decisions, or plans, for that responsibility rests with the commander.

When it becomes necessary for a staff officer to issue an order in the name of the commander, responsibility for such an order remains with the commander even though he or she may not have seen the order as actually written or heard it if given orally.

Staff officers who exercise supervision over any phase of operations must restrict their control to the sphere of the commander's announced decisions and orders. When circumstances arise that in their opinion may make advisable a deviation from established policy, even in the most minor degree, the situation should be presented to their commander for decision.

When a commander has given specific instructions to a staff officer, the actual issue of the necessary orders or instructions to members of the command are properly given in the name of the commander by the staff officer, thus: "The Commanding Officer directs" or "For the Commander." The orders may be given orally or over the signature of the staff officer.

Where a commander has decided upon a policy to be followed and has indicated that policy to a staff officer, all future questions that fall completely under that policy should be handled without further reference to the commander. Routine matters are handled according to written or uniformly observed SOP—Standing Operating Procedures.

Some commands and staffs have a formal policy file for nonroutine but special matters of concern to the commander. All experienced staff officers will establish

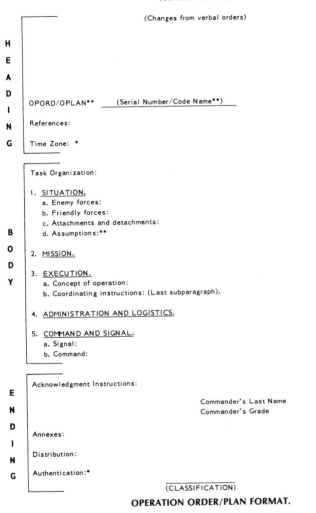

(CLASSIFICATION)

(Changes from verbal orders)

H
E
A
D
I
N
G

Copy No. _____
Issuing Headquarters
Location of CP (Coord)
Date/Time Group
Message Reference No.

OPORD/OPLAN**   (Serial Number/Code Name**)

References:

Time Zone: *

B
O
D
Y

Task Organization:

1. SITUATION.
   a. Enemy forces:
   b. Friendly forces:
   c. Attachments and detachments:
   d. Assumptions:**

2. MISSION.

3. EXECUTION.
   a. Concept of operation:
   b. Coordinating instructions: (Last subparagraph).

4. ADMINISTRATION AND LOGISTICS.

5. COMMAND AND SIGNAL.
   a. Signal:
   b. Command:

E
N
D
I
N
G

Acknowledgment Instructions:

Commander's Last Name
Commander's Grade

Annexes:

Distribution:

Authentication:*

(CLASSIFICATION)

OPERATION ORDER/PLAN FORMAT.

an informal personal policy file if a formal one does not exist. An established policy provides the limits within which the staff can function without continual reference to the commander.

A staff officer must never usurp the prerogatives of command. In the event of an unforeseen emergency when immediate action is imperative and the commander cannot be consulted, the staff officer should be prepared to state to the senior line officer with whom he or she is able to get in touch the action he or she believes the commander would desire. The decision then becomes the responsibility of the senior officer consulted, and is not the responsibility of the staff officer.

Relation of the Staff to the Commander. No two commanders operate exactly in the same way with respect to the details of this relationship. Some commanders announce broad policies and desire members of the staff to proceed with confidence in the execution of tasks with little consultation on the details; others will wish to give personal approval to at least the more important phases that are encountered. The staff must adjust itself quickly to the method of operation desired by the commander.

COMPLETED STAFF WORK

Completed staff work is Army doctrine. The staff officer who is skilled will think through each problem assigned for staff action and then will plan courses of action. The staff officer must determine the information needed and where to seek it and must list the individuals who have an interest in the problem, or knowledge of the problem, and plan to see them. He or she will determine all the angles and consider the varying viewpoints on important matters. "Leg work" is the requirement. A staff officer who neglects these essentials is unlikely to succeed.

The completed staff work doctrine means more work for the staff officer, but it results in more freedom for the commander to do the things and see the things that are essential to the discharge of his or her own responsibilities. It also spares the commander from half-baked ideas, immature oral guesses, or voluminous memoranda that he or she has no time to study.

The final test of completed staff work is this: *If you were the chief would you be willing to sign the paper you have prepared, and stake your professional reputation on its being right?* If not, take it back, and do it over, for it is not completed staff work.

There is a special dividend about being a skilled staff officer. The young staff officer of today may be assigned to command much sooner than he or she has anticipated. The requirements of a fast-moving Army, on the vast missions of this period in our history, find the "best-qualified" officers and lead them forward, as discussed in chapter 12, *Professional Development. The officer who becomes an excellent staff officer, thoroughly trained in staff responsibilities, limitations, and procedures, will find on becoming commander that he or she knows what to expect from a staff and how to handle one.* It is a major attribute to success in command.

A sometimes baffling situation confronts the staff officer as to which problems or communications should be presented to the commanding officer, and which ones should be handled by the staff without reference to the commander. The commander must be informed of matters of importance, surely, and must be spared from trivia. But where to draw the line? There is no single answer, or policy, because commanding officers differ in their wishes, just as staff officers differ. Indeed, the confidence of the commander in the individual members of the staff bears upon the problem and its solution.

Reproduced below is a memorandum for the staff, written many years ago, which was included in early editions of *The Army Officer's Guide.* The author was Major General Frank S. Cocheu, now deceased. It is far from universally applicable, of course. But it may point the way to the choice of a workable policy in the busy headquarters of today.

MEMORANDUM: *For the Staff.*

1. The following will be brought without delay to the attention of the Commanding General:

a. Subjects of importance which require prompt action and are not covered by existing policies and instructions.

b. Disapprovals from higher authority.

How To Get It	How To Do It
Assignment of a problem and a request for a solution in such a way that completed staff work is readily possible.	Study of a problem and presentation of its solution in such form that only approval or disapproval of the completed action is required.
1. Know the problem.	1. Work out all details completely.
2. Make one individual responsible to you for the solution.	2. Consult other staff officers.
3. State the problem to him clearly, precisely; explain reasons, background; limit the area to be studied.	3. Study, write, restudy, and rewrite.
4. Give the individual the advantage of your knowledge and experience in this problem.	4. Present a single, coordinated, proposed action. Do not equivocate.
5. Set a time limit; or request assignee to estimate completion date.	5. Do not present long memorandums or explanations. Correct solutions are usually recognizable.
6. Ensure that you are available for discussion as work progresses.	6. Advise the chief what to do. Do not ask him.
	If you were the chief, would you sign the paper you have prepared and thus stake your professional reputation on its being right?
Adequate guidance eliminates wasted effort and makes for completed staff work.	If not, take it back and work it over; it is not yet completed staff work.

COMPLETED STAFF WORK.

c. Errors, deficiencies or irregularities alleged by higher authority.

d. Communications that allege neglect or dereliction on the part of commissioned personnel.

e. Correspondence or proposed correspondence conveying even a suggestion of censure.

f. Appeals from subordinates from decisions made at this headquarters.

g. Subjects which affect the good name or reputation of an officer or organization.

h. Subjects involving financial or property irregularities.

i. Serious accidents involving personnel of the command.

2. The following will be presented to the Commanding General for final action:

a. Requests and recommendations to be made to higher authority.

b. Suggested disapprovals.

c. Communications that contain a suspicion of censure.

d. Communications that involve the good name of an officer or organization.

e. Reports of financial and property irregularities.

f. Letters to civil authorities in high positions.

g. Endorsements on efficiency reports.

h. Correspondence concerning war plans.

i. Communications of exceptional information.

3. A copy of these instructions will be kept exposed at all times upon the desk of each staff officer of this headquarters.

SELECTED STAFF PROCEDURES

The basic reference of staff officers in the understanding of command and staff relationships, responsibilities, functions, and procedures is Field Manual 101–5, *Staff Organization and Operations.* In addition, any well-organized headquarters has a staff manual or administrative procedures manual that contains the organization chart of the headquarters and details the responsibilities of each staff section.

Obtaining Background on a Staff Assignment. After studying the headquarters staff manual, the newly assigned staff officer should then become familiar with all important staff actions of his or her particular section during some reasonable past period, such as the past six months or the last training cycle. Staff sections of tactical headquarters generally are obliged to keep journals wherein such staff actions are recorded. Individual staff officers maintain files or correspondence, "stay-backs," on which or together with which is a "Memorandum for Record" that summarizes the events leading up to the particular action in question, with a statement of concurrences, or other information that might be useful for future reference. From these sources, the newcomer can quickly get oriented. He or she will learn that the major problems confronting the staff section are few, although the details and ramifications may be myriad. All of the problems quite likely have roots; and after they have been identified, the handling of details or new developments of an old problem will be less difficult.

The Staff Officer's Records. The commander relies upon staff officers for the maintenance of required and useful charts, files, and records as well as for the initiation of routine reports. This is an important responsibility for the staff. In the field there are required records that are prescribed in field manuals. In garrison there are other records and correspondence that must be available when needed. A staff officer should become completely familiar with the administrative requirements of his or her office, train the personnel charged with preparation of records or filing, and frequently check to assure that they are maintained as desired.

However, the staff officer should not become "chart happy," covering office walls with multitudinous useless status charts that are impressive to see but require major efforts by lower echelons to provide information and by staff assistants to prepare and maintain.

Mission Analysis and Staff Studies. Although the use of formalized procedures for mission analysis and preparation of written staff studies pertains more to the headquarters of major commands and the Department of the Army staff in Washington, the principles are generally applicable. In any case, the actual use of a staff study, and the analysis that leads to its preparation, depends upon the complexity of the problem and the time available for its consideration. It is a good principle that formal, written staff studies should be avoided, unless they are truly needed; but a staff officer at any level of organization may need to make such an analysis and write such a study.

The accompanying diagram, *The Sequence of Staff Actions,* provides the basis for mission analysis and the staff estimate. Noteworthy is the planning guidance, which is often supplied by the commander; this guidance will not suggest the answer, but may provide factors to consider, people to consult, the time to complete the study, or other matters the commander considers essential for staff understanding.

The staff study is a logical analysis that leads through a consideration of the specific problem, the facts and assumptions that bear upon the problem, information to set forth the facts, the reaching of conclusions, and the action the staff officer recommends. It should be both complete and brief. A way of describing a good staff study is the presentation of a problem so the commander can reach an independent decision, as well as exercising the option of accepting the recommendation submitted by the staff officer. The accompanying illustration, *a staff study format,* should be followed, whether the study is prepared in twelve months

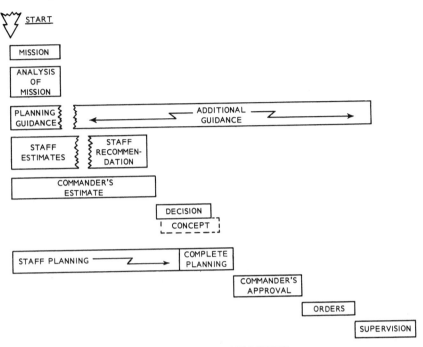

THE SEQUENCE OF STAFF ACTIONS.

or twelve hours, for it is time-tested and generally used. The condensed essential points should be presented on a single page, although some commanders will accept two pages. If detail is needed, attach annexes and appendices, as required, but keep the basic paper brief. Busy commanders depend upon their staffs to save their time, and one way to do it is to prepare clear, concise, brief staff studies— when a staff study is needed.

Relations with Higher Headquarters. It is important to the commander that good relations are enjoyed with higher headquarters. His or her own standing and capacity for getting results will be enhanced when a favorable situation is created, and harmed seriously when bad relations exist. Therefore, each staff officer must become personally acquainted with his or her "opposite number" on the next senior staff, for the same reasons that he or she must know opposite numbers in subordinate staffs. It is all a matter of acquaintance, understanding, and teamwork.

Relations Between the Staff and the Troops. The staff serves the troops as well as the commander. It has been said that the staff that serves the troops best serves its commander best. Good staff work requires the staff to know and appreciate fully the situation of the troops, their morale, their state of training, the state of their equipment and supply, and all other conditions affecting their efficiency.

As a rule when a staff officer visits troop units he or she first calls upon the commander. It is desirable that the staff officer state at once the purpose, if any in particular, that the visit is to accomplish. A cordial relationship between staff officers and subordinate troop commanders must be developed. It is desirable that, before leaving, the result of his or her observations be disclosed to the unit commander, and disclosed exactly in the same way to his or her commanding officer. Distrust is easily created and is difficult to dissipate. A mutual feeling of trust and confidence must be built up and confirmed by each recurring contact.

Coordination and Concurrences. Proper coordination among staff officers is absolutely essential. Without it, the commander easily could be placed in the position of issuing conflicting orders or directives.

During the course of preparation of any staff action, be sure to contact all other staff officers or staff sections who may have an interest in the problem or its solution. Obtain the views of other staff members as to the recommended solution, and take these views into account when completing your action. When your action is completed, but before presentation to your chief, take the completed package back to the interested sections to obtain their concurrence.

The purpose of this coordination is not to share responsibility with others—it is to ensure that your action has not compromised the position of other staff sections and that it is not in conflict with previous actions.

The concurrence of all interested staff sections is desirable before the completed action is submitted for the approval of the commander; however, it is not mandatory. It sometimes happens that different staff sections have conflicting viewpoints on the proper solution of a problem. In such a case, the views of the differing section should be so noted and considered in the action; however, if you are convinced that your solution is the correct one, stick to your guns. Just don't be bullheaded about it (and remember that you will have to continue working with the other section tomorrow and next week and next month). Usually the executive officer or the chief of staff will decide between conflicting points of view or recommendations. If he or she cannot, the commander must and will.

A Staff Study Format

                                                            HQ
                                                            PLACE
OFFICE SYMBOL   DATE
SUBJECT:

   1. *PROBLEM:* Concise mission statement of what is to be accomplished by the study and/or the problem.

   2. *ASSUMPTION(S):* Influencing factors which are assumed to be true. May be non-factual or incapable of being proved.

   3. *FACTS BEARING ON THE PROBLEM:* Essential facts considered in the analysis and in arriving at the conclusions.

   4. *DISCUSSION:* An analysis and evaluation of the facts as influenced by the assumptions and which present sufficient detail to support the conclusions.

   5. *CONCLUSION(S):* Statement of the findings and the implications of an analysis and evaluation.

   6. *ACTION RECOMMENDED:* Concise statement of what is to be done to solve the problem and who should do it.

                                                    SIGNATURE BLOCK
ATTACHMENTS: (Supporting detail on each of the above sections.)

CONCURRENCES/NONCONCURRENCES:

(SECTION/AGENCY) Concur_____ Nonconcur_____

(SECTION/AGENCY) Concur_____ Nonconcur_____

(Each officer involved shows C/NonC by inititals, followed by rank, name, position title and telephone number. The reason for a NonC must be stated here or on a separate page.)

CONSIDERATION OF NONCONCURRENCES:

(The author of the staff study states the results of the consideration of any NonC. He then signs or initials the NonC.)

Maintaining Perspective. It is very easy for an officer immersed in details at a desk to lose perspective. He or she may become desk-tied in viewpoint and fail to understand the impact that his or her recommendations, if approved, may have in the field. Some call it an occupational disease. It is a good reason for limitation of length of assignment. When it happens the value of a staff officer shrinks swiftly. Never put aside your own appreciation of the impact of official communications that reach the field.

It is a wise course to make field trips as opportunity arises. Go and see for yourself how the projects of your interest are working. Talk with the officers concerned. Urge them to state their views. See if you can work out better ways to accomplish the ends sought with a higher standard, in swifter time, at reduced cost. Get the feel of the field with all its enthusiasms and zeal, its hardships, and human frailties. Then go back to your desk with perspective renewed. You will do a better job.

AIDES TO GENERAL OFFICERS

General officers commanding large units and other general officers occupying positions designated specifically by the Department of the Army are authorized aides, or *aides-de-camp,* as a personal staff. (AR 614–16.) Duties of aides are not prescribed in training manuals but are such as the general officer may prescribe.

Number and Grades Authorized. Aides-de-camp are authorized, in the numbers and grades stated below. *Exceptions:* General officers assigned as Chiefs of MAAGs, JUSMAGs, and Military Missions are authorized one aide-de-camp per general officer, not to exceed the maximum grade appropriate for the rank of the general as stated in the table below.

General Officers	COL	LTC	MAJ	CPT	LT	Total
General of the Army.............. (or Chief of Staff, USA)	1	1	1	..	..	3
General	..	1	1	1	..	3
Lieutenant general..............	..	..	1	1	..	2
Major general	..	..	..	1	1	2
Brigadier general	..	..	..	..	1	1

When a general officer is authorized two or more aides, the senior in rank generally is designated unofficially as the senior aide and in this capacity coordinates the activities for which he or she may be charged. This may include the issue of instructions to the other aide or aides, the secretarial staff that serves the general, the orderlies, driver, and others. When a general officer uses two aides, one may be used to advantage as operations aide and one as administrative aide. Normally the maximum continuous tour of duty as an aide-de-camp will be two years, although there is no limitation on length of tour.

Duties of Aides. As stated earlier in this chapter, there is great need for a personal staff to free the general from time-consuming personal arrangements so that he or she may perform heavy responsibilities with efficiency and continuity. A good aide will see to it that the tools and facilities needed by the general are on hand when needed. Examples of duties that a general officer may wish an aide to perform are discussed below.

The establishment of a new command post may involve an aide. The aide will learn from the chief of staff the location of the area to be used by the general. Measures will be taken at once to move all equipment and personnel in the routine use or service of the general to the new site and resume operations.

While the general is in the office or at the command post, an aide often is assigned to keep the general's appointment schedule to facilitate the transaction of business. In the performance of this task the aide should consult the chief of staff and be guided always by his or her desires, for the aide is in no sense a link in the chain of command. It is likely that all generals will expect an aide to maintain a list of future appointments, including social engagements, and remind them in ample time so they may be kept. The general's spouse should be kept informed of the general's social engagements, especially those to which the spouse is invited, as well as those that will require the general's presence outside of office hours.

Many generals will wish their aides to assume charge of their personal and confidential files.

On change of station or other moves, the aide should take full charge of all arrangements as directed by the general so the general may work with full efficiency up to the time of departure and resume operations at once upon arrival.

Careful thought should be given by aides to arrangements for trips of whatever length or duration. The aide should make all arrangements for tickets, hotel reservations if needed upon arrival, movement of baggage, and all other matters. If appropriate, notification of expected time of arrival, security clearance (if required), and how many members in the general's party should be sent to the proper officials.

The aide should keep the record of expenses incurred that are reimbursable by submission of the necessary voucher after completion of the journey. Many general officers provide the aide with a personal fund from which to make expenditures for the general for minor items, keeping an informal record as they are paid.

Welcoming committees or individuals meeting or receiving a general officer for some official or unofficial occasion may assume expenses on behalf of the visiting general from their own resources. This is a courtesy, of course, but general officers wish to avoid accepting the payment of expenses that are covered by their official travel allowances, or that should be borne from their own funds. In such instances, the aide should ascertain the expenses and provide reimbursement with expression of appreciation for the thoughtfulness and the courtesy.

Aides are often used to transmit highly personal, important, or secret messages.

It is common practice for general officers to assign aides as assistants to staff officers, particularly in general staff sections of the headquarters. This is particularly the case when the general is to be absent and unaccompanied by aides, or during times of stress when *additional* staff assistants are needed in the staff section. Accordingly, a good aide will become schooled in the duties and techniques of each staff section to become a useful member of the group even if the assignment is temporary. While so assigned, the aide is responsible to the chief of section in the same manner as other officers.

Visiting dignitaries may be accompanied by an officer to serve them temporarily as aide. Senior officers may be detailed to serve in this capacity for high officials, such as very senior officials of a friendly foreign power.

On social occasions the aides may assist in preparing the invitation list, or they may make the invitations orally for their general. When this is the case they must be very careful to provide the date, hour, place, nature of the event, and other appropriate information. If spouses are to be present, the aides will save much time by including information about dress, and whether the general's spouse will wear formal or informal dress may as well be settled at the time the invitation is issued as later. The nature of the occasion must be made clear, too, and if it is to be a dinner, or cocktail gathering that does not include a dinner, the invitation should not be susceptible of misunderstanding. For a social event to be held at a club or hotel the aide may be charged with making all arrangements after being instructed by the general. At a formal reception the aide is often asked to introduce the guests; in this case the aide's position is near the head of the receiving line where he or she greets all guests, ascertains their names, and introduces them clearly to the individual heading the receiving line. This action and position may cause the aide some concern until familiar with the experience. The aide too is a guest. Certainly he or she must not behave like a butler or servant, nor for that matter, the host. Perhaps it is best described as the position of an elder son or daughter assisting parents in the pleasant task of entertaining friends.

For ceremonial occasions aides must familiarize themselves with the appropriate regulations and the exact arrangements insofar as they can be foreseen. Field Manual 22-5 and Army Regulations 600-25, with their most recent changes, will answer most questions.

Some aides prepare an SOP and a checklist for recurring activities such as trips by motor, air, rail, movement of the command post or headquarters, and other events.

A general officer is obliged to meet a very large number of people, military and civilian. The aides may render a most valuable service to their commander by maintaining a list of names of individuals with whom more than passing contact has been held or may be held. This file should contain, in addition to names, essential data about each individual such as position or business connection, former military status if any, address, telephone number, current activities of military interest, and a statement of occasions when the general has been in touch with the individual. Before any occasional visitor, military or civilian, is permitted to fill an appointment with the general, the aide should brief the general on the visitor including who he is and what he wants, if the latter is known. When the general is to attend any large gathering, it will be helpful for the aide to ascertain the more important personages who will be present and inform the general in advance.

Care must be exercised by aides to avoid transgressing upon the fields of other staff officers. In this connection, many general officers require that their secretary, chauffeurs, and orderlies work under personal control of the aides. Where a pilot is provided, the aide and the pilot must work closely together, the pilot generally receiving all information about proposed trips from the aide.

General officers will expect their aides to be models of military courtesy, tact, military appearance, and soldierly attitude and bearing. They will also wish them to be unobtrusive and quiet, as well as ladies or gentlemen. Aides are cautioned that they are not commanders or assistant commanders. It is an honored, responsible position. Most general officers choose their aides based on their fine records, experience in extended combat, and decorations for valor, as well as for their personality and appearance. An officer chosen as aide to an Army general has opportunity to acquire experience that will be extremely helpful as his or her responsibilities increase.

For lapel and other insignia worn by aides, see chapter 22, *Uniforms of the Army.*

19

New Duty Assignment

It is a fact of Army life that the officer experiences periodic reassignments to new responsibilities and new positions, as well as station changes within the United States and oversea commands. Do you like variety? A change from staff to command, to duty as student? Or instructor? If so, the Army is surely the life for you with its great breadth of duty and experience. The normal career includes as a matter of course a series of assignments, each building upon the present for something bigger and more challenging as the years arrive. With each new assignment there is opportunity to make a fresh start, to apply the lessons learned so as to do a better job, to avoid the errors of the past, and build better because of experience gained. Chapter 12, *Professional Development,* explains the scope and makes clear the reasons for these periodic changes. The wise officer will seek to make the most of each change of duty assignment to increase his or her knowledge and professional capacity.

The Commander's Responsibility and Opportunity. The commander or chief who receives a newly assigned officer has a special responsibility that may have a most important effect upon the future success of the newcomer. Each officer should be carefully counseled on the scope of his or her work, standing operating procedures, objectives to be attained, job expectations, and standards of performance expected. (DA Pam 600-3, *Commissioned Officer Professional Development and Utilization* and DA Pam 600-11, *Warrant Officer Professional Development.*)

In the building of a proud organization, in which individuals have arrived one by one or in small groups, the way in which each person is received by the commander, or chief, and new associates, is extremely important. Each person must be made to feel welcome on arrival. It is important that the commander makes certain the mission is understood. The commander will start each newcomer with a clean slate and with his or her trust. Most officers will live up to it.

Many years ago, at the outset of a mobilization, a skilled commanding general assembled several hundred of his newly arrived officers on a high hill overlooking the area of the camp. He caused them to face so that they could look out over the area and identify the places where they were assigned. He then addressed them: *"Gentlemen, as your commander I bid you welcome. There before you are the training areas in which we will work, and the men we must train. Ours is a grave responsibility. Some among us will succeed greatly, win promotions, decorations, and victories against our enemies. Perhaps a few will fail. We expect and hope that all will succeed and be able when it is all over to return to your homes with pride and satisfaction that you served your country well.*

"That is all. Return to your men."

MAKING THE BEST POSSIBLE FIRST IMPRESSION

Whenever you assume a new duty assignment it follows that you will work under new superior officers and have new associates and new subordinates. While it is likely that all will extend a true welcome, and take for granted that you are competent, it is of the highest importance that you put your best foot forward at the outset in order to obtain the initial good will and confidence of the official group that you join.

Let it be known at once that the assignment is welcomed; find things to comment upon favorably, avoiding all criticism; become acquainted promptly with associates, especially junior leaders; learn your responsibilities and discharge them fully from the start, seeking information and assistance as circumstances require. Solicit the support of your new organization. Try to stimulate a feeling of confidence and enthusiasm in the minds of associates as to your assignment.

Some Useful Don'ts. Strive to make a favorable first impression, of course. Use equal care to avoid those things that give a bad one.

Don't overtalk, especially of yourself. Your standing among new associates will depend wholly upon what you accomplish in the future, not your prideful past. While you are sizing up the new command and its members, as you must, your new associates are also sizing up their new officer. Some will find occasion for critical comment, given a chance. Just weigh those words!

Go slow, too, with changes that affect the life and likes of your personnel. More than likely they prefer things the way you find them. Later, when you have complete information, improvements you may make will be satisfying and enhance your own standing. But bide your time until surmises can be replaced with reasoned conclusions fortified by discussions and recommendations of subordinates. Make improvements, make changes for the good, mold the organization to your special judgments—but don't do it all at the start.

Never make a statement that could possibly be considered as a reflection upon your predecessor. As he or she has departed and cannot defend himself or herself, such acts are cowardly. More than likely the former commander has the respect and even the admiration of all or most of the troops, because that is the rewarding experience of most good officers; for you as the new commander to make harsh or belittling remarks about your predecessor is to injure greatly and perhaps permanently your own chances of gaining the trust and respect of these same individuals.

In a sense, the commander holds a lonely position. You must put your best foot forward and keep it there. You must set the example. Thoughtless statements, careless attention to appearance, little violations, weigh heavily when done by the commander whereas if done by others they might be forgotten. The higher the command, the more they weigh.

First Actions. Whatever the nature of the new assignment, there are certain first actions necessary to gain knowledge of the missions, responsibilities, and personnel. They are keys to getting off to a good start.

What Is the Mission? Seek information from the departing predecessor whenever this is possible. Go to your new chief and listen most carefully. Study the policy file, if one is available. Discuss the job to be done with other officers, noncommissioned officers, or civilians concerned with the work of the organization.

What Are the Current Training or Work Projects? You need to know at once what is being done to execute the missions, and this means the principal immediate projects, who is working on them, their status, and expected completion dates.

Who Are Your Officers and Soldiers? Meet them and talk candidly with them. Precede this discussion by study of each individual's personnel record. Determine their experience and special training. Establish as to key individuals the normal length of further service with the organization prior to reassignment or discharge. Provide an opportunity for each to state personal aspirations as to progress in the military service. Inquire about family problems.

What Reports are Required? Obtain a list of periodic reports required to be submitted, when they are due, and who is to prepare them.

Find Out Who Does What. To the extent necessary, have each key individual write out his or her specific duties and responsibilities.

Check on Handling of Classified Material. Find out quickly what classified material is held by the unit and learn the local regulations for its physical security. If there are indications of carelessness, correct them at once. Many officers have been reprimanded (or worse) for inattention to the security of classified documents and for overlooking the procedures for their handling.

ASSUMPTION OF A STAFF POSITION

Staff officers are selected for assignment by the commander whom they serve. Upon reporting for duty on a staff assignment you should report to the chief of your section, branch, or division, and then as directed to the executive officer or chief of staff.

All well-administered headquarters have staff manuals or Standing Operating Procedures (SOP), which set forth the organization of each staff section and its specific responsibilities. This manual should show you the specific duties of your own particular segment of the staff. Your first effort must be to become thoroughly familiar with this manual, for you have become a member of the staff team, and the purpose of the manual is to provide for teamwork. (See chapter 18, *Staff Assignment,* for helpful information about responsibilities and procedures.)

The next step should be to become acquainted with other members of the staff with special reference to those individuals of other staff sections with whom you will work. The chief or executive of the branch or division will provide this information. At the same time the acquaintance should be sought of the unit commanders and unit officers served by the staff. For example, as a new staff officer of a battalion, you should seek out and introduce yourself to the company commanders and company officers of the battalion. Each staff officer must work continually with officers having similar spheres of responsibility, in headquarters junior as well as senior to his or her own. Such individuals are referred to frequently as "opposite numbers." For example, the intelligence officer of a battalion will work regularly in coordination with the intelligence officers of other battalions and with one or several individuals of the intelligence staff of brigade or division headquarters. He or she must have close working liaison with intelligence officers of other units of the division. Personal acquaintance with commanders and staff officers with whom you work should be acquired as soon as practicable after assuming a staff position.

Each staff will have its own operating procedures and ways of getting things done. They will depend upon the desires of the commander, chief of staff, or executive officer. There may be special office forms and routines; prescribed ways of writing reports or staff studies; prescribed reports to be received and studied, and the like. In order to become a good member of the team these measures must be learned and followed.

A staff assignment is a splendid place to develop tact and diplomacy, the ability to coordinate, and the capacity to keep the work of the day within your own field running smoothly and harmoniously.

ASSUMPTION OF A COMMAND POSITION

The Opportunity. As an Army officer, you must anticipate that you may be assigned without warning to assume command of a unit larger than ordinarily associated with your grade.

Familiarity with problems of command of the next higher unit should be a part of individual training and planning. Be ready for such opportunities. In battle they are normal. Success of an engagement may depend upon the speed and efficiency with which lost leaders are replaced. Command duty is the highest honor that can be given an officer.

Assumption of Command in Battle. During operations against an enemy, replacement of fallen leaders must be accomplished at once. In the absence of prior instructions to the contrary, seniority of the officers assigned to the unit will determine the line of succession. But this procedure may itself lead to defeat. Circumstances will govern but there will be no time for inquiry or the niceties of position. If you are the officer who discovers the situation, assume prompt command and adjust as necessary as time permits. This will require you to notify at once your commander and leaders of subordinate and adjacent units of your assumption of command. Aggressiveness, promptness, and the need for control require the most available officer to take over the task of leadership. At once you must learn your predecessor's mission and, if available, his or her plan to meet it. Next, you must learn the position of your new units. Thereafter you must meet with positive action whatever situations may arise.

The leader who develops a knowledge of the officers and noncommissioned officers of adjacent units will find the information useful when suddenly becoming responsible for their command.

It should be clear that learning your own job is not enough. You must learn your captain's job and your major's job as well.

Assumption of Command Under Conditions Other Than in Battle. Whenever the commander is detached from command of an organization for any reason, the senior officer present for duty with it automatically assumes command, pending different orders from higher authority. If you are that officer who succeeds to any command or duty, you stand in regard to your duties in the same situation as your predecessor. Within the bounds of reason and common sense, you should avoid those actions that amount to permanent commitments.

Transfer of Command Responsibilities. An officer assuming command of an organization is required to take over the mission and all administrative, fiscal, logistical, training, and any other responsibilities of his or her predecessor. The changeover must be made so that the old commander is fully relieved and the successor fully informed. A period of three to five days (or three to five nights) is not unusual to complete the required steps, and it is to be remembered that the work of the organization must continue during the transfer period.

Transfer of the responsibilities of a company will include the following steps: The mission of the command; organization records including classified documents; property supplied the unit as shown by the Company Property Book; property in hands of organization members; official funds or allowances; the unit fund and property purchased from the fund; and a clear understanding of training or work in progress.

Suggestions to an Outgoing Commander. Careful preparation in advance of the transfer will be required. Make certain that subordinates have all their records posted correctly and up to date, that the number of actions pending is reduced to a minimum, and that property to be checked and funds to be transferred are all in correct order. Smooth transition of command requires the elimination of dangling, unfinished actions.

Transfer of property may be a time-consuming task. Supply personnel should make their own preliminary check. Are there missing articles? Broken or unserviceable articles? Take steps to clear the records at once. Never seek to conceal such matters or to deceive the incoming commander. Are there overages? They should be returned or picked up on property records. Never depart a unit with the property records not signed over to another officer.

The same principles apply to the unit fund. Pay the outstanding bills, and determine any further obligations. Check the property that has been purchased from the fund. If there are shortages, or items that are broken or unserviceable, take appropriate steps to clear the records or repair the articles. Be sure all is in balance, and all is clear.

The outgoing commander will wish to make a clean, complete severance. You must never try to cover up or deceive the incoming commander, as it will all be disclosed later. One inescapable test of your competence as a commander, and important because it will be the impression remembered, is the condition of your unit, disclosed upon your transfer from command.

Suggestions to the Incoming Commander. Simplify the problem by finding out at the start exactly what is to be done. The old and new commanders should make a joint inventory and check all of the matters involved. The transfer is often supervised by an officer designated by the appropriate higher commander. Still, the responsibility passes from the old commander to the new. Understand the requirements, and do it thoroughly.

The Unit Mission. Discuss with the commander being relieved, and with the next higher commander, the status and mission of the organization. Find out about the state of training, work or training in progress, and current problems. As soon as command has been assumed you will be expected to execute the new responsibility effectively.

Administrative Records. As the incoming commander, you must learn about the company files, personnel records, and organization records, where they are kept, by whom, and the extent of your responsibilities. If there are classified documents, you must inventory them and assure yourself that they are being correctly safeguarded.

Organization Property. All property in the organization (platoon, company, or battalion) is the responsibility of the commander; even though the Army system calls for records consolidation at battalion level with hand receipts to individual officers and noncommissioned officers. They are responsible, too, but the commander is in no way relieved. You must know what your soldiers are equipped with and its readiness for use. As soon as possible check all major items of equipment on a serial number basis. Have the battalion supply section assist you on nomenclature and proper maintenance. At the first Saturday inspection have all the troops display their individual clothing and equipment; with supply personnel in assistance; again, the check can be one against records and for completeness and readiness. Other property responsibilities are discussed in chapters 17 and 18, but the basic principle is simple; all are responsible that the property is available, always serviceable and ready for use.

A question that will arise is the disposition of overages. The supply system cannot function properly unless units requisition for items they need and unless they are able to eliminate shortages of their authorized equipment. "Pack-rat" policies by a few units can be ruinous. They store up secret surpluses, which may prevent another unit from obtaining supplies or equipment desperately needed. The best and the ordered action is to turn in overages to the battalion supply system as soon as they are found.

In general, if an article charged to the unit is there, see it, check it, and if reasonably serviceable check it off. Don't be picayunish, but do an accurate, swift, commonsense job with which you can live after your predecessor has departed.

Organization Funds. Wise use of the unit fund and its monthly income is a tool of vast importance to the commander. Maladministration of these funds invites failure. Start by assuming the responsibility correctly.

Check fully the cash assets on hand or on deposit, the accounts receivable, and the items of property purchased from the fund for the benefit of the organization. Check also the obligations and liabilities of the fund such as bills payable.

It is of the highest importance that the new commander assume responsibility for the unit fund in complete compliance with the Army regulations and the regulations of higher headquarters. Learn the local regulations about administering funds from an auditing officer or The Inspector General.

Know Your Personnel. As the commander of a small unit, you must become intimately acquainted with your troops. In the small unit, such as the platoon or company, if you are a wise commander you will have your soldiers appear before you, one by one, and seat them; you should have their individual records at hand during the interview, and go over the salient service, skills, and achievements.

Prepare a card or a page of a notebook for each individual on whom basic personal data can be prerecorded and on which you can make notes. Question each soldier about his or her duty assignment, hopes, specialization, promotion concerns, schools, and career thoughts. Try to obtain sincere recommendations about improving performance, enhancing morale, and other unit matters, but don't make it a complaint session. The spirit of the interview is to get to know the soldiers, letting them meet you, and showing them you care about them individually and personally.

Brigade and division commanders meet members of their large commands at group meetings, in a theater or outdoor assembly, with as many individual meetings with senior officers and noncommissioned officers as is feasible and as time permits. The more of their subordinates who are interviewed personally, or have personal contact with their senior commanders, the better for the command and its commander.

The important thing is to establish a personal, face-to-face contact with members of the organization at the start. Skillfully done it will work wonders in securing a favorable reaction from the new subordinates and give you as the new commander personal knowledge on which to build.

Development of Your Own Policies. Command of a unit is a very personal responsibility. The methods followed successfully by one commander may be entirely unsuited to another. With the passage of time, adjustment of these matters will be advisable. Such changes, however, should be made only after mature consideration. Infrequently, a new commander will unwisely set forth the opinion that the organization was at a very low ebb of efficiency when he or she assumed command. Such statements are usually accompanied by the further observation that since his or her own unusual powers were applied the very highest standards have been achieved. This approach to the assumption of command is a cowardly assault on the previous commander. The inevitable result is resentment by those members of the unit who may have worked for its progress. Study the methods in use, and when an opportunity for improvement is seen, do not hesitate to adopt it. Face each new assignment as a challenge to do better work and improve results.

Part Four • Regulations at a Glance

20
Pay and Allowances

Army personnel are assured that their services are appreciated by our government. There have been times in the past when military pay rates lagged far behind the pay scales in private industry, and indeed even far behind the pay scales of the federal civilian employees. Pay raises during the 1960s and 1970s brought military pay up to a level more comparable to that of civilian counterparts in the federal government and private industry. Inflation during the late 1970s coupled with "caps" on pay raises caused the military pay to fall behind again. Action taken during 1980 and 1981 restored comparability of military pay to that in the civilian sector, but successive "caps" on pay raises since then have again caused military pay to fall behind the civilian sector.

How Pay Is Established. Military pay rates are set in accordance with the provisions of the Federal Pay Comparability Act of 1970, which became law in January, 1971. This act, of far-reaching significance for all federal workers, provides that each year the federal civilian pay rates will be examined in relation to rates for comparable work in private industry. By 1 September of each year, the President will propose to the Congress adjusted pay rates based upon this comparison and, unless Congress disagrees, these new rates will become effective on 1 October.

While the comparability study applies strictly to federal civilian employees, by separate law the military pay rate is tied to the civilian rate. Thus, an increase in federal civilian pay automatically results in an equitable increase in military pay.

Military Pay. The accompanying table shows the monthly pay rates in effect on 1 January 1988.

PAY RATES IN EFFECT AS OF 1 JANUARY 1988

GRADE	under 2	over 2	over 3	over 4	over 6	over 8	over 10	over 12	over 14	over 16	over 18	over 20	over 22	over 26	Monthly without Dependents	BAQ with Dependents
COMMISSIONED OFFICERS																
0-10	5485.80	5679.00	5679.00	5679.00	5679.00	5896.50	5896.50	6041.70	6041.70	6041.70	6041.70	6041.70	6041.70	6041.70	$581.40	$715.20
0-9	4862.10	4989.30	5095.50	5095.50	5095.50	5225.10	5225.10	5442.60	5442.60	5896.50	5896.50	6041.70	6041.70	6041.70	581.40	715.20
0-8	4403.70	4535.40	4643.10	4643.10	4643.10	4989.30	4989.30	5225.10	5225.10	5442.60	5679.00	5896.50	6041.70	6041.70	581.40	715.20
0-7	3659.10	3907.80	3907.80	3907.80	3996.00	3996.00	4083.00	4083.00	4319.70	4535.40	4685.10	4989.30	5332.50	5332.50	581.40	715.20
0-6	2712.00	2979.90	3174.90	3174.90	3174.90	3174.90	3174.90	3174.90	3282.60	3390.60	3585.00	3693.60	3801.60	3822.60	533.70	648.60
0-5	2169.00	2547.00	2723.10	2723.10	2723.10	2723.10	2805.60	2956.20	3154.50	3154.50	3154.50	3196.50	3196.50	3196.50	503.70	597.60
0-4	1828.50	2226.60	2374.80	2374.80	2418.90	2525.70	2697.00	2849.70	2979.90	3110.40	3110.40	3196.50	3196.50	3196.50	461.70	546.30
0-3	1699.20	1899.60	2030.70	2247.00	2354.40	2439.00	2571.00	2697.90	2764.50	2764.50	2764.50	2764.50	2764.50	2764.50	373.80	455.40
0-2	1481.70	1618.20	1943.70	2009.10	2051.40	2051.40	2051.40	2051.40	2051.40	2051.40	2051.40	2051.40	2051.40	2051.40	301.20	390.60
0-1	1286.10	1339.20	1618.20	1618.20	1618.20	1618.20	1618.20	1618.20	1618.20	1618.20	1618.20	1618.20	1618.20	1618.20	258.30	350.10
COMMISSIONED OFFICERS WITH MORE THAN 4 YEARS ACTIVE DUTY AS ENLISTED OR WARRANT OFFICER																
0-3E	0	0	0	2247.00	2354.40	2439.00	2571.00	2697.90	2805.60	2805.60	2805.60	2805.60	2805.60	2805.60	373.80	455.40
0-2E	0	0	0	2009.10	2051.40	2116.20	2226.60	2311.50	2374.80	2374.80	2374.80	2374.80	2374.80	2374.80	301.20	390.60
0-1E	0	0	0	1618.20	1728.60	1792.20	1857.00	1921.80	2009.10	2009.10	2009.10	2009.10	2009.10	2009.10	258.30	350.10
WARRANT OFFICERS																
W-4	1731.00	1857.00	1857.00	1899.60	1986.00	2073.60	2160.60	2311.50	2418.90	2503.80	2571.00	2653.80	2742.60	2956.20	423.30	491.10
W-3	1573.20	1706.70	1706.70	1728.60	1748.70	1876.80	1986.00	2051.40	2116.20	2179.20	2247.00	2334.30	2418.90	2503.80	357.30	439.50
W-2	1377.90	1490.70	1490.70	1534.20	1618.20	1706.70	1771.50	1836.30	1899.60	1966.20	2030.70	2094.90	2179.20	2179.20	321.60	410.70
W-1	1148.10	1316.40	1316.40	1426.20	1490.70	1554.90	1618.20	1685.10	1748.70	1813.80	1876.80	1943.70	1943.70	1943.70	272.10	357.90

The monthly pay of 0-8, 0-9, and 0-10, is capped at $6041.70, which is the federal executive pay ceiling.
The monthly BAS for all officers is $114.90.

Service Creditable for Basic Pay. As seen in the table, pay increases in each grade with length of service. In computing the years of service for pay purposes, credit is given for all periods of active service in any Regular or Reserve component of any of the uniformed services. Credit may also be granted for service other than active duty. Officers are advised to consult the finance officer servicing their pay accounts with a statement of all their military service for consideration of credit that may be given under the laws.

Basic Allowance for Subsistence (BAS). The BAS is the same for all officers, regardless of grade. The amount is adjusted periodically as the base pay is adjusted. The BAS is not subject to income tax. The monthly rate in effect on 1 January 1988 is shown in the accompanying table.

Basic Allowance for Quarters (BAQ). The BAQ varies with the grade of the officer and is paid at a "With Dependents" or "Without Dependents" rate, depending upon the marital status and recognized dependents of the individual officer. The BAQ rates rise in accordance with increases in basic pay, but are adjusted periodically so that they reflect about 65 percent of the national median rental costs reported by members in each pay grade. The BAQ is not subject to income tax. The rates in effect on 1 January 1988 are shown in the accompanying table.

Variable Housing Allowance (VHA). In addition to the Basic Allowance for Quarters payable to members living in nongovernment housing, a Variable Housing Allowance is also paid to such members in high cost-of-living areas. The amount of the VHA is based on the member's rank, the type of regular quarters allowance being received, the average cost of housing in the area of assignment, and the national median housing costs of military members. The amounts vary based on annual local housing surveys. The combination of the BAQ and the VHA are supposed to cover about 80 percent of the housing costs of the officer living in nongovernment housing.

Definition of Dependent for Quarters Allowance. The law that authorizes the allowance for quarters for an officer with dependents provides that it includes at all times and in all places the lawful spouse and the legitimate unmarried children under twenty-one years of age. There are important additional provisions for other dependent family members, and for rulings in these instances the best course to follow is to consult the unit personnel officer or the finance officer.

OTHER PAY AND ALLOWANCES

In addition to basic pay and to allowances for subsistence and for quarters (for those officers not furnished government quarters), the following provisions for special pay or allowances are important.

Hazardous Duty Pay. Several types of duty assignment are classed as hazardous. Incentive pay is authorized for performance, under competent orders, of these types of duty: parachute duty, demolition duty, and experimental stress duty.

A member may receive hazardous duty pay for two types of such duty for the same period if qualified and required to perform multiple hazardous duties in order to carry out the mission of the unit. (An example would be to engage in regular and frequent parachute jumps and also to perform demolition duty when required to accomplish the mission of the unit.) The monthly rate of hazardous duty pay for all officers is $110.

Flight Pay. Flight pay for an officer serving as a crew member ranges from $125 to $400 per month based on the officer's years of service. Commissioned officers who have been in primary flying duties for specified periods when they attain the "gates" of twelve and eighteen years of service, are guaranteed continuation of flight pay, but at rates that decrease from $370 per month for over eighteen years of service to $250 per month for over twenty-five years of service. Warrant officers receive the same flight pay as commissioned officers during the first six years; thereafter, they receive flight pay at $400 per month so long as they are on flying duty.

Diving Pay. An officer on diving duty may receive diving pay ranging from $110 to $200 per month depending on the type of duties performed.

Hostile Fire Pay. Members performing duties within or near a designated hostile fire zone are entitled to a monthly payment of $110. Service not in a designated hostile fire zone, but where the member is in *imminent danger,* also entitles the member to a $110 monthly payment.

Special Pay for Doctors. The special pay for doctors is of several types. A doctor with less than two years' service, or who is serving as an intern, is eligible for special pay of $100 per month. The rate is $350 per month for more than two years of service. In addition, an annual payment of up to $10,000 is authorized based upon length of service, a bonus of from $2,000 to $5,000 is authorized for board-certified doctors, and an annual payment of up to $8,000 is authorized for doctors who are specialists in short-supply fields. The total special payments to doctors can be as much as $29,500 per year.

Special Pay to Dental Officers. Dental officers are entitled to special pay at the following rates:
$100 per month if they are interns or have completed less than three years of service.
$167 per month ($2,000 per year) if they have completed three but less than six years of service.
$333 per month ($4,000 per year) for six to ten years of service.
$500 per month ($6,000 per year) for ten to fourteen years of service.
$333 per month for fourteen to eighteen years of service.
$250 per month for over eighteen years of service.
In addition, dentists not on an internship or residency may receive additional special pay of from $6,000 to $10,000 in return for a written agreement to remain on active duty for one year. Board-certified dentists receive from $2,000 to $4,000 each year depending upon their years of service.

Special Pay to Veterinary Corps Officers and Optometry Officers. Veterinary corps officers and Optometry officers are entitled to special pay at the rate of $100 per month.

Continuation Pay, Scientific and Engineering Officers. Officers who have been certified as being technically qualified and who are detailed to scientific or engineering duties may be paid an amount equal to $3,000 times the years of obligated service, which shall not be less than one year or more than four years.

Foreign Language Proficiency Pay. A special payment of up to $100 per month is payable to officers who become proficient, or increase their proficiency, in foreign languages. Payment is at one of four rates, $25, $50, $75, or $100, depending upon the degree of difficulty of the language and the skill of the user. An individual with multiple language skills may be compensated for proficiency in more than one language, but the maximum authorized monthly payment is $100.

Family Separation Allowance. This allowance is payable only to service members with dependents. The Family Separation Allowance is of two types, both of which are payable to the same individual if he or she meets the qualifications for both listed below. Each type of allowance may be paid to a member who qualifies therefore in addition to any other allowance or per diem to which the member may be entitled.

1. One allowance, equal to the basic monthly allowance for quarters payable to a member in the same pay grade without dependents, is payable to a member with dependents who is on permanent duty in Alaska or anywhere else outside the continental United States, when:

a. Movement of dependents to the member's permanent station or a place nearby is not authorized at government expense, and the member's dependents are not residing at or near the station; and

b. No government quarters are available for assignment to the member.

2. The other type of Family Separation Allowance, equal to $60 *per month,* is payable (except in war time or national emergency declared by Congress) to a member with dependents who is authorized a basic quarters allowance, when:

a. Movement of dependents to the member's permanent station or a place nearby is not authorized at government expense and his or her dependents are not residing at or near the station; *and*

b. The member is on duty aboard ship away from the ship's home port continuously for more than thirty days; or

c. The member is on temporary duty away from his or her permanent station continuously for more than thirty days and the member's dependents do not reside at or near the temporary duty station.

Dislocation Allowance. Upon permanent change of station, when dependents are authorized to accompany the officer, a dislocation allowance is payable in the amount of one month's quarters allowance. If the officer is single, or if the dependents do not move, the allowance is payable if the officer is not assigned government quarters at the new station. There is a limitation of one such payment per year with two exceptions: Two allowances may be paid under some conditions when officers are ordered to service schools, or when approved by the Secretary of the Army.

Uniform Allowance, Reserve Officers. *Upon Initial Appointment.* (Armed Forces Reserve Act of 1952.) A newly appointed Reserve officer or officer of the Army of the United States without component is entitled to $200 as reimbursement for the purchase of required uniforms. This accrues upon first reporting for active duty for a period in excess of ninety days; upon completion as a member of a Reserve component of not less than fourteen days active duty or active duty for training; or completion of fourteen periods of not less than two hours each in the Ready Reserve where wearing of the uniform is required. In addition to the $200 initial allowance, a Reserve officer upon first reporting is also entitled to a $100 active duty allowance. Warrant officers are entitled to the $200 initial allowance when first appointed and to the additional $100 if they had not previously been on active duty.

Uniform Allowance, ROTC Vitalization Act of 1964. This act provides a uniform allowance of $300 for all ROTC graduates on their initial appointment, whether commissioned in the Regular Army or the Army Reserve. It is not an allowance in addition to that stated above; but it extends to individuals commissioned into the Regular Army from the ROTC the uniform allowance of $300.

The Four-year Allowance. A Reserve officer is entitled to an additional $50 upon completion of each four-year period of active status in a Reserve component, which must include at least twenty eight days of active duty or active duty for training.

The Allowance for Reentry upon Active Duty. A Reserve officer who has been on inactive duty for a period of two years, and is then recalled to active duty of more than ninety days duration, may qualify for $100 as reimbursement for additional uniforms and equipment required on such duty.

Station Allowances, Overseas. Station allowances to equalize the cost of living and housing are authorized for uniformed personnel stationed in a number of foreign countries. The allowances are planned to equalize the total of selected essential expenditures of the foreign station with those in the United States. It is to be noted that there must be an officially computed difference in the cost of living factors that are considered as to the United States and oversea stations, with the cost greater in the oversea station, for the allowance to be authorized. It is known as the *Cost of Living Allowance* or *COLA*. Consult the finance officer as to the allowance, if any, at a station of interest.

PAYMENTS AND HOW OBTAINED

A military pay voucher (DA Form 2349) is prepared by the unit personnel officer for each person entitled to pay. All items of entitlement or obligation are shown. The voucher is forwarded to the most convenient disbursing officer who makes the payment, furnishing a copy of the voucher to the payee, which shows in detail the total amount due and how the pay was computed. Payment is made monthly, normally on the last duty day. *Caution:* Check the copy each month to be certain pay is correctly computed.

Advance and Partial Pay. Prior to starting travel an officer may draw an advance of pay. The approval of the commanding officer is often required but is granted liberally. This is meant to assist the officer in purchasing transportation tickets or in paying automobile expenses. Should an officer need funds at another time, he or she may draw up to the amount accrued for that month as a partial payment of that month's salary. Partial payments are not encouraged as a routine need; however; no officer is expected to borrow money at an interest rate when that officer's own salary can provide for an emergency.

DEDUCTIONS FROM PAY

Income Tax. Military base pay is subject to federal and state income tax. As in the civilian community, an amount is withheld from the pay each month, based upon the number of exemptions claimed and the estimated total pay for the year. The amount withheld is itemized on the monthly pay voucher, DA Form 2349. About 1 February of each year, the finance officer furnishes a W2 Form showing total taxable pay and the total deducted for federal income tax and state income tax.

Quarters and subsistence allowances are not taxable; dislocation allowances and incentive pay are taxable.

Social Security Tax. The finance officer is required to deduct Social Security Tax (F.I.C.A.) from each pay account. See chapter 9, *Financial Planning.*

21

Travel
Allowances

This chapter provides information normally required by an officer performing travel under individual travel orders, moving family members on permanent change of station, and shipping household goods. Excluded are unusual situations and special cases of travel not generally encountered by the majority of individuals performing routine travel. (See AR 37-106 and Joint Travel Regulations.)

TRAVEL OF OFFICERS

Travel Status Defined. Officers are entitled to travel and transportation allowances as authorized in accordance with existing regulations, only while actually in travel status. They are in travel status while performing travel away from their permanent duty station, upon public business, pursuant to competent travel orders, including necessary delays en route incident to mode of travel and periods of necessary temporary duty or temporary additional duty. Travel status, whether travel is performed by land, air, or sea (except as a member of ship's complement), will commence with departure from permanent duty station or ship, and will include any of the conditions shown below:

Temporary Duty or Temporary Additional Duty. Travel in connection with necessary temporary duty or temporary additional duty, including time spent at a temporary duty station or a temporary additional duty station, without regard to whether duty is required to be performed while traveling, and without regard to the length of time away from the permanent duty station. Temporary Duty (TDY) assignments will normally be limited to periods not in excess of six months.

Permanent Change of Station (PCS). Travel from one permanent duty station to another permanent duty station.

Delay. Delay incident to mode of travel, such as necessary delay while awaiting further transportation after travel status has commenced.

To and from Hospital. Travel to or from a hospital for observation or treatment.

Travel by Air. Travel performed by military or commercial aircraft when proceeding from one duty station to another under orders of competent authority. Air travel includes one or more landings away from the starting point and the necessary delays incident to this mode of travel. Aircraft flights for crew training purposes come under this category.

Aerial Training Flights. Aerial flights for training purposes made in the absence of travel orders when it is necessary to remain away overnight.

Special Circumstances or Conditions. Special circumstances or conditions not heretofore defined that may be determined jointly in advance, contemporaneously or subsequently, by the Secretaries of the uniformed services to constitute a travel status.

Traveling with Troops. An officer is traveling with troops when he or she is physically traveling as a member of, or on duty with, any body of troops that is subsisted en route from a kitchen car, rolling kitchen, field range, ship's galley, or other comparable facilities for preparing complete cooked meals en route.

Members traveling with troops will not be paid mileage or reimbursed on a per diem basis for expenses incurred. Under no circumstances will members obtain meals on meal tickets, or meal receipts. Transportation, and sleeping accommodations, if available and required, will be furnished in kind.

Group Travel. Group travel is a movement of three or more members traveling under one group order from the same point of origin to the same destination when a member is designated in the order as being in charge of the group.

Standard of Accommodations. When a member is entitled to transportation in kind and uses government transportation requests, such member shall be furnished first-class accommodations, except when travel is by commercial aircraft. Then, tourist class accommodations normally are furnished.

Type of Carrier on Which to Travel. Within the continental United States the individual may elect to travel by any mode of transportation at personal expense, subject to reimbursement upon completing the journey.

Termination of Travel Status. Travel status will terminate upon return to the permanent duty station or upon reporting at a new permanent duty station ashore or afloat, except that travel status terminates when the member reaches the assigned port if the vessel to which he or she is reporting for duty is already in port.

Transportation in Kind. Transportation in kind includes travel by all modes of commercial transportation and military facilities, but does not include travel at personal expense. In all matters pertaining to transportation consult your transportation officer, *prior to commencing travel.*

Transportation Request. A transportation request (TR) is a requisition issued to a commercial carrier to furnish specified transportation services. The TR is issued by the transportation officer or other competent authority.

TRAVEL ORDERS

No reimbursement for travel is authorized unless orders by competent authority have been issued therefor. Reimbursement for travel is not authorized when the travel is performed in anticipation of or prior to receipt of orders.

Travel orders issued under unusual conditions that are not originated by competent authority must be approved by competent authority to allow reimbursement for travel expenses.

Types of Travel Orders. *Permanent Change of Station.* The term *permanent change of station,* unless otherwise qualified, means the transfer or assignment of a member of the uniformed services from one permanent station to another. This includes the change from home or from the place from which ordered to active duty, to first station upon appointment, or call to active duty, and from last duty station to home or to the place from which ordered to active duty upon separation from the service, placement upon the temporary disability retired list, release from active duty, or retirement.

Temporary Duty. The term *temporary duty* means duty at a location other than permanent station to which a member of the uniformed services is ordered to temporary duty under orders that provide for further assignment to a new permanent station or for return to the old permanent station.

Blanket or Repeated Travel. Blanket travel orders are issued to members who regularly and frequently make trips away from their permanent duty stations within certain geographical limits in performance of regular assigned duties. Travel must not be solely between place of duty and place of lodging.

REIMBURSEMENT FOR TRAVEL EXPENSES

Travel at Personal Expense. When authorized travel is performed by commercial transportation at personal expense, you will be reimbursed for the actual costs incurred. Be sure to retain receipts to be able to support your claim.

Travel by Privately Owned Vehicle (POV). For temporary duty travel actually performed by privately owned vehicle (POV) under orders authorizing such mode of transportation as more advantageous to the government, you will be paid a monetary allowance in lieu of transportation (MALT) at the rate of 20 cents, 20.5 cents, or 45 cents per mile depending upon the mode of travel (motorcycle, car, or privately owned aircraft, respectively), for the official distance in addition to authorized per diem. When the official travel by POV is for the convenience of the individual, the rate is 7 cents per mile.

Mileage. Mileage is an allowance applicable to permanent change of station under the following circumstances:

1. When travel is by privately owned conveyance.
2. When travel is by rail and available transportation requests were not used.
3. On relief from active duty.
4. On separation from the Service.
5. On transfer to the temporary disability retired list.
6. On retirement.

Mileage is computed by finance officers from a table of official distances. These distances govern, regardless of the actual route followed by the traveler.

Per Diem. Per diem allowances are designed to cover the costs of room rentals, meals, and miscellaneous expenses incident to performing official government travel. Rates are specified in the Joint Travel Regulations. For round trips of ten hours or less within one calendar day, no per diem is authorized.

The military uses a "lodgings plus per diem" method of reimbursement for travel expenses. Under this method, the actual costs of lodging, ranging from a minimum of $35 per day up to a specified maximum for each area, is payable to the traveler.

The maximum rate is now $103 per day for the New York City area. In addition to the costs for room rental, the traveler is entitled to a fixed reimbursement of either $25 per day or $33 per day, again depending on the area, to cover expenses of meals and miscellaneous items. On the day of departure and the day of return, the reimbursement for meals and miscellaneous expenses is calculated on a quarter-day basis. The day is divided into four quarters (0001–0600, 0601–1200, 1201–1800, and 1801–2400) and the entitlement is calculated based upon the number of quarters of the day the individual is in a travel status. Thus, starting travel at 0900 would entitle you to three-quarters of the daily rate, while starting at 1500 would entitle you to one-half the daily rate.

Trailer Allowance. Costs of transporting a mobile home during a permanent change of station move are reimbursable up to an amount equal to the estimated cost of transporting a member's authorized maximum of baggage and household effects via commercial movers. Mobile homeowners also are entitled to a dislocation allowance for quarters and in-transit mobile home storage of up to 180 days.

Reimbursable Expenses. In the past many officers have paid travel expenses for which reimbursement might have been received. On a long trip that loss can be material. The following are reimbursable:

Taxi Fares. Reimbursement is authorized for taxicab fares between places of abode or business and stations, wharves, airports, other carrier terminals, or local terminus of the mode of transportation used, between carrier terminals while en route when free transfer is not included in the price of the ticket or when necessitated by change in mode of travel, and from carrier terminals to lodgings and return in connection with unavoidable delays en route incident to the mode of travel. Itemization is required.

Allowed Tips. Tips incident to transportation, such as tips to baggage porters, red caps, and so on, are reimbursable, but are not to exceed customary local rates; tips for baggage handling at hotels are excluded; the number of pieces of baggage handled will be shown on the claim. Itemization is required.

Checking and Transfer of Baggage. Expenses incident to checking and transfer of baggage are reimbursable. The number of pieces of baggage checked will be shown on the claim. Itemization is required.

Excess Baggage. When excess baggage is authorized, actual costs for such excess baggage in addition to that carried free by the carrier are reimbursable. Receipt is required.

Registration Fees. Registration fees incident to attendance at meetings of technical, professional, scientific, or other nonfederal organizations are reimbursable when attendance is authorized or approved. Receipt is required. (See annual appropriation acts.)

Bachelor Officers' Quarters Fees. When government quarters are available and used, the cost of the lodging in the government quarters is reimbursable. A receipt from the billeting facility is required.

Government Auto. Cost of storage of government automobiles when necessary is reimbursable if government storage facilities are not available. Receipt is required.

Telephone, Telegraph, Cable, and Other Communication Services. Cost of official telephone, telegraph, cable, and similar communication services is reimbursable when incident to the duty performed or in connection with items of transportation. Such services, when solely in connection with reserving hotel room, and so on, are not considered official. Copies of messages sent are required for all mechanical transmissions unless the message is classified, in which case a full explanation and a receipt will suffice. Local and long distance telephone calls are allowable when itemized.

Stenographic Services. Charges for necessary stenographic services or rental of typewriters or similar machines in connection with the preparation of reports or official correspondence are reimbursable when authorized or approved by the headquarters directing the travel. This provision does not apply when stenographic services are performed by military personnel or government employees. Receipts are required.

Local Public Carrier Fares. Expenses incident to travel on streetcar, bus, or other usual means of local transportation are allowed. Itemization is required. Commercial or government (GSA) Rent-a-Car expenses are reimbursable; authorizations for such rentals are normally made in advance and indicated on travel orders.

Toll Fares. Ferry fares, and road, bridge, and tunnel tolls are reimbursable when travel is performed by government vehicle or by authorized hired conveyance; or when performed by privately owned conveyance within the surrounding area of a duty station.

Receipts. Receipts should be obtained for all reimbursable expenses greater than $15. Without a supporting receipt, your claim may be denied.

Advance Payment of Travel and Transportation Allowances. Travel and transportation allowances for an officer's travel are authorized to be paid in advance, except in connection with retirement and upon first entering active duty. See the post finance officer.

TRAVEL EXPENSES NOT PAYABLE BY THE GOVERNMENT

Travel expenses of the type listed in the examples below are not payable from government funds:

1. Expenses incurred during period of travel that are incident to other duties (such as traveling aboard a vessel in performance of temporary duty on such vessel).

2. Travel from leave to official station for duty. Individuals departing from their official duty station on leave do so at their own risk. If ordered to return from leave they must assume the expense involved.

3. Travel under permissive orders to travel in contrast to orders directing travel requires the individual to pay the costs.

4. Travel under orders but not on public business. Example: travel as a participant in an athletic contest. Such travel may be paid from unit or command welfare funds, which are generated through operation of exchanges and motion picture theaters.

5. Return from leave to duty abroad. Unless government transportation is available, such as space on a MAC flight, the individual on leave in the United States from an oversea command must defray his or her own return expenses.

6. Attendance at public ceremonies or demonstrations whose expenses are borne by the sponsoring agency.

TRAVEL OUTSIDE THE UNITED STATES

Travel expenses for travel outside the United States are furnished in advance or are reimbursable on essentially the same basis as temporary duty travel performed in the United States. That is to say, the traveler is entitled to the costs of transportation, per diem allowance, and costs of incidental necessary expenses.

Per diem rates for oversea travel also vary according to quarters and mess availability and charges for same. Consult your local finance officer for assistance prior to and after any oversea travel.

Certificates are required from the traveler and from the commanding officer or a designated representative of an installation at which a traveler performs temporary duty.

PASSPORTS

Passports issued by the Department of State are required for persons visiting foreign countries. Mexico and Canada do not normally require passports for entry from United States citizens. (AR 600-290.)

There are four classes of passports: Diplomatic (no-fee), Official (no-fee), Regular (no-fee), and Regular (tourist).

Diplomatic passports are issued to officers accredited to any embassy or legation of the United States abroad and to members of the household of such officers. Field grade officers and above assigned to military assistance program missions have been granted diplomatic passports.

Official passports are issued to officers proceeding abroad under orders in the discharge of their official duties. Family members accompanying or traveling to join bearers of official passports who are stationed abroad may apply for official passports.

Regular (no-fee) passports are issued to family members of a military member whose assignment does not warrant issuing the family members diplomatic or official passports.

Regular (tourist) passports are obtained and paid for by persons who are traveling abroad for personal reasons.

Each Army installation and activity in the United States, Guam, and Puerto Rico has a passport agent. Apply for passports to your station passport agent.

All service members traveling overseas on official business to a country requiring a passport and all command-sponsored family members will obtain separate no-fee passports. This is true regardless of destination or the age of the family member. There are special rules for alien family members, for which see your passport agent.

Each passport application must be accompanied by two identical, clear, front-view, full-face photographs measuring two by two inches. The photographs may be either in color or black and white. Group photographs are unacceptable. Each photograph must be signed in the presence of the passport agent. A parent may sign for a minor child, as "Richard Doe by Jane Doe (mother)." It is recommended that the nonmilitary parent sign the passport applications and the photographs for minor children.

Each passport application must be accompanied by documentary evidence of citizenship.

Visa. An endorsement made on a passport by the proper authorities (usually Embassy or Consular officials) of a country to be visited, showing that the passport has been examined and that the bearer may proceed to that country.

TRAVEL OF FAMILY MEMBERS

Basic Entitlement. Members of the uniformed services are entitled to transportation of family members upon a permanent change of station for travel performed from the old station to the new permanent station or between points otherwise authorized. As to officers there are some important exceptions as follows:

1. An officer assigned to a school or installation as a student, if the course of instruction is to be of less than twenty weeks' duration.

2. Separation from the service or relief from active duty under conditions other than honorable.

3. Call to active duty for training for less than one year.

4. Call to active duty for other than training duty for less than six months.

5. An officer who fails to receive revocation of permanent change of station orders because he or she took advantage of leave of absence and the notice of revocation was received at the officer's old permanent station sufficiently in advance of the time that would have been required to proceed under the original orders.

6. When the family member is a member of the uniformed service on active duty on the effective date of the orders.

7. For any portion of travel performed by a foreign registered vessel or airplane, if American registered vessels or airplanes are available by the usually traveled route.

8. Where the family members departed the old permanent station prior to the issuance of orders, and the voucher is not supported by a certificate of the commanding officer, or a designated representative, of the headquarters issuing the orders that the officer was advised prior to the issuance of change of station orders that such orders would be issued.

9. When dependency does not exist on the effective date of the order directing permanent change of station.

10. For family members receiving any other type of travel allowances from the government in their own right.

Reimbursement for Costs of Dependent Travel. An officer who transports lawful family members at personal expense, from a location where transportation requests are not available, may elect to be reimbursed for the actual cost of the transportation authorized in lieu of the monetary allowances stated below.

An officer who elects to transport family members at personal expense may obtain reimbursement. The amount is payable only after travel has been completed. The total entitlement is determined on the basis of $50 per day per diem plus 15 cents per mile for the service member; the mileage rate increases to 17 cents per mile if the member is accompanied by one dependent, to 19 cents per mile for two dependents, and to 20 cents per mile if more than two dependents travel with the member. In addition, a flat rate of $37.50 per day per diem is authorized for dependents twelve and over and $25.00 per day for dependents under twelve years of age.

It is also possible to obtain reimbursement for the movement of family members in two vehicles under certain specific circumstances. To obtain approval, the use of two cars must be deemed advantageous to the government and one of the following sets of circumstances must apply:

- If more family members are traveling together than can reasonably be accommodated, with luggage, in one vehicle.
- If a dependent requires special accommodations because of age or physical condition that makes a second vehicle necessary.
- If dependents are prevented from accompanying the service member for acceptable reasons, such as school, the sale of property, settlement of business affairs, disposal of household goods, or inadequate housing at the new station.
- If dependents move before the service member because of acceptable reasons such as enrollment in school.
- If dependents are involved in unaccompanied travel between authorized points, such as traveling to the new station while the service member is officially carried as TDY en route to the new assignment.

If movement of two cars is authorized, each car with a single driver is entitled to reimbursement of 15 cents per mile. Additional dependents increase the entitlement as noted earlier for movement by a single vehicle. For example, if the service member and two dependents move by two cars, one would be reimbursed at the rate of 15 cents per mile while the second car would be reimbursed at 17 cents per mile.

Travel of Family Members Beyond the Continental Limits of the United States. Upon the permanent change of station of an officer to a station outside the continental United States to include Alaska, Hawaii, and possessions of the United States, he or she becomes entitled to transportation of family members, when authorized, at government expense.

TRANSPORTATION OF HOUSEHOLD GOODS

Shipment of household goods consists of transportation, including packing, crating, drayage (at point of shipment and destination), temporary storage, uncrating, and unpacking at government expense. DA Pamphlet 55-2, *It's Your Move,* should be used as a basic reference by all officers preparing to move, and a copy should be in each officer's library of important official documents.

These services are performed or expenses paid for an officer ordered to active duty at a permanent station, or assigned to a new permanent station, or relieved from active duty, or retired. (See AR 55-71.)

Local transportation officers should be consulted in connection with such movements as soon as orders are received. They will provide the best possible guidance in preparing for the shipment of household property so that it will proceed smoothly for the family making the shipment. Follow their guidance carefully. Special attention should be given to the necessity for temporary storage and the allowable period for such storage up to ninety days. An additional ninety days may be authorized under exceptional circumstances.

Household Goods Shipped at Government Expense. The term *household goods* includes clothing, baggage, all other personal effects of a similar character, professional books, papers, and equipment, as well as the items normally required to equip a home with furniture, appliances, and the like.

There are items that are excluded from government shipment, and the recommendation is to consult the transportation officer. There are special requirements as to shipment of personal household property in a mobile home.

Authorized weight allowances are shown in the accompanying table.

Excess Costs. The transportation charges for unauthorized articles, excess weight, or excess mileage will be borne by the owner.

Insurance. A claim against the government for damage or loss incident to a shipment may be relied upon to obtain a fair and just settlement. However, personal property of high value should be covered by commercial insurance. Recommended is the coverage that can be obtained from the United Services Automobile Association, San Antonio, Texas, or from Armed Forces Insurance, Fort Leavenworth, Kansas. These two associations were established to serve the needs of officers and their families, and their rates probably are more favorable than you can obtain elsewhere. Consult your JAG Claims Officer if you have any questions.

Very Important Caution. All reliable moving companies are in business to provide good service. These companies are doing all that is possible to ensure speedy, efficient moves, with the avoidance of confusion and disappointment. Still, not all meet the standard. It is essential that Army officials be able to identify the superior companies, the average ones, and the poor ones. Keeping current on this information requires the cooperation of Army families.

Fill out with care and accuracy the *Customer Satisfaction Report.* Be accurate and be prompt. Be fair to the company, but be fair also to yourself, the Army, and Army families who will make future moves. This report indicates to the transportation officials and to the transfer firm just what kind of service you received.

A good way to start is to confer with the transportation officer well in advance of the move. Get his or her advice as to preparation. And learn precisely the service you are supposed to receive. In that way most misunderstandings are prevented. You are supposed to receive fine service. Do your full part to get it. Report on the proper form just what you did receive.

What You Should Do to Assist in the Move.

1. Contact your transportation officer as soon as possible after receipt of orders.

2. Advise the transportation officer that you have professional books and papers to be shipped in order that they may be packed and weighed separately from your household goods.

3. Have sufficient copies of your change of station orders (usually six to nine for each shipment).

4. If you will proceed to your new duty station prior to the time you will want your household goods shipped, leave or send your spouse or agent sufficient copies of your change of station orders. Be sure that you or your duly authorized agent is on hand at the time of packing, loading, unpacking, and unloading of your household goods and has been furnished instructions regarding the signing of the packer's inventory, the Statement of Accessorial Services Performed, the carrier's shipping documents, and the government bill of lading.

5. If you have silver, gold, or other valuables, it's a good idea to carry these items with you, or insure commercially as noted under *Insurance* in the earlier section.

6. Request storage at point of origin whenever you are in doubt as to the place you will want your goods shipped. Be sure to check the allowable time limits for storage to match your plans for leave, house hunting, and the like.

7. If your household goods are moving by van, be sure to obtain a copy of the carrier's inventory from the driver; also, you will be requested to sign a DD Form 619, Statement of Accessorial Services Performed. The certificate contains an itemized list of the units of packing performed at your residence. Be sure to check the certificate carefully, and never sign before it has been filled in.

Table of Weight Allowances (Pounds) on Change of Station

	Temporary Change	PCS Allowance
General & General of the Army	2,000	13,500
Lieutenant General.	1,500	13,500
Major General	1,000	13,500
Brigadier General	1,000	13,500
Colonel.	800	13,500
Lieutenant Colonel.	800	13,000
Major & Chief Warrant Officer (CW4)	800	12,000
Captain & Chief Warrant Officer (CW3).	600	11,000
First Lieutenant & Chief Warrant Officer (CW2)	600	10,000
Second Lieutenant & Warrant Officer (W1)	600	9,500

8. Notify your transportation officer immediately if your orders are cancelled or modified or if a change in the destination of the shipment is desired.

9. Appliances are serviced for transporting at government expense. The transportation officer makes arrangements for you with the packing or moving firm. Similarly, after delivery, the appliances are to be "de-serviced."

10. The refrigerator should be defrosted and well cleaned the day before the move, so that its interior will be dry at time of loading. The shelves and trays will be removed by the packers and placed in suitable containers for safe movement.

11. Obtain from your transportation officer the approximate date of arrival of your household goods at destination.

12. Be sure you or your agent are at home on the day of expected move and make arrangements for receipt of the property at destination.

13. Turn over all your household goods for the same destination at one time.

14. Clean china and cooking utensils before packers arrive.

15. Set aside and call to the attention of the movers extra-fragile items, such as chinaware and delicate glassware, and professional books that must be packed and weighed separately.

16. Keep nonperishable groceries and food supplies together in one area for proper packing.

17. Remove articles from drawers of the furniture intended for shipment. Let the packer determine which, if any, light, bulky articles may be shipped in the drawers.

18. Be sure to inventory your household goods with the van driver. Do not allow an entry of "marred and scratched" on the inventory form unless such entry is correct. This broad language may cover extensive damage. Insist upon accurate descriptions of the condition of the furniture, such as, "1-inch scratch, left leg," or "rubbed, right front corner."

19. Make arrangements to have telephone service and other utilities disconnected.

20. Dispose of opened but unused foods that might spill or spoil en route. They should never be stored or shipped.

21. Don't include plants, fresh fruits, or flowers in shipment, as this is prohibited in many states.

22. Separate and collect into one place all items that are not to be included in the shipment. Show the van operator the articles, if any, that have been set aside and are not to be included in the shipment.

Claims for Loss or Damage Incident to Shipment. Regardless of when your household goods are delivered, cause the carrier or local agent to unpack all boxes and to de-service all appliances. Carefully note all damaged and lost items on the carrier's forms; be as meticulous as the company was that packed you. Usually, the local agent will make immediate arrangements for repair or replacement. Once you have checked all your belongings including the operation of appliances, consult with your transportation officer, the claims officer, and the local agent. You may claim for the difference between what you believe fair and what the carrier or the insurance company will allow. (See AR 27-20). All have deduction tables for depreciation in values according to how old the item is, and all have time limits for presenting claims.

22

Uniforms
of the Army

This chapter contains essential information of special interest to officers about the Army's uniforms. Extracts and illustrations have been drawn from the following official publications: AR 670-1, *Wear and Appearance of Army Uniforms and Insignia;* CTA 50-900, *Clothing and Individual Equipment;* and AR 700-84, *Issue and Sale of Personal Clothing.*

GENERAL

There are three general categories of uniforms for both male and female Army officers—service uniforms, dress uniforms, and utility uniforms. Included in each category are uniforms of appropriate weight and material for cold weather and warm weather, for wear in an office environment, when participating in social activities, or while performing duty in the field. Each officer is required to possess some of them, while the purchase of others is optional. Certain of the utility uniforms are issued by the organization if their wear is to be required.

The service uniforms are further classified as class A and class B, while the utility uniforms are referred to as class C. The class A uniform for males consists of the Army green coat and trousers, a long- or short-sleeve Army green shade 415 shirt, a black four-in-hand necktie, and authorized accessories. The class B uniform for males is the same as the class A, except that the green coat is not worn and the necktie is optional when wearing the short-sleeve shirt. For females, the Army green classic coat and skirt, or slacks, an Army green shade 415 long- or short-sleeve shirt, and a black neck tab, with other authorized accessories, comprise the class A uniform. The same components minus the green coat comprise the class B uniform. The black neck tab is optional for wear with the short-sleeve shirt. Either the necktie or the neck tab, as appropriate, is always worn with the long-sleeve shirt. These service uniforms and the class C uniforms are described in greater detail later in this chapter.

Each uniform is comprised of prescribed components, and the regulations describe how the uniform is to be worn. There are a number of accessory items and several types of grade and branch insignia, with associated rules as to how and when they may, or must, be worn. Decorations, service medals, and badges are authorized for wear on some uniforms, in prescribed locations and order of precedence, but are not authorized to be worn on other uniforms. As an Army officer, you must learn the details regarding the proper wear of uniforms. The Army is a uniformed service where discipline is judged, in part, by the manner in which individuals wear their uniforms. Unless you first set the example, you cannot expect your soldiers to present a neat, well-groomed appearance, which is fundamental to building the pride and esprit of an effective military force.

This chapter contains general information regarding the wearing of uniforms and suggestions on how to select and care for uniforms, as well as discussion regarding personal appearance. It presents condensed descriptions and illustrations of the authorized uniforms with occasions for their wear. Insignia and ornamentation are discussed as they relate to proper wear on the uniform. Thoughtful study of this chapter and its companion, chapter 23, *Decorations, Service Medals, and Badges,* will enable you to dress appropriately for each occasion and to wear your uniform with the confidence and pride befitting an officer of the U.S. Army.

UNIFORM APPEARANCE AND FIT

Uniforms will be properly fitted, clean, serviceable, and pressed as necessary. Articles carried in pockets are not to protrude from the pockets; nor should they be so bulky as to cause the pockets to bulge. Uniforms must be worn buttoned, zippered, or snapped as appropriate; metallic devices must be kept in proper luster and free of scratches and corrosion; medals and ribbons must be clean and not frayed; shoes and boots must be clean and shined.

The proper fit of uniforms is prescribed in AR 700-84 and Technical Manual 10-227. Refer to the regulations for details. The general fitting guidelines are as follows:

Male Officers. The sleeves of long-sleeve shirts will extend to the center of the wrist bone; the sleeves of uniform coats and jackets will extend 1 inch below the bottom of the wrist bone; the sleeve of the black, all-weather coat will be 1/2 inch longer than the sleeve of the service coat. The bottom of the black all-weather coat will extend 1 1/2 inches below the mid-point of the knee (crease in the back of the knee).

Trousers are fitted and worn so that the bottom of the waistband is at the top of the hip bone, plus or minus 1/2 inch. The front crease should extend to the top of the instep, with the bottoms (no cuffs) finished on a diagonal so that the rear crease extends to a point about midway between the top of the heel and the top of a standard shoe. A slight break in the front crease is permissible (but not desirable—Author).

Female Officers. Sleeve length of shirts, coats, and the black all-weather coat is the same as prescribed for male officers, as is the length of the black coat. Slacks are fitted and worn so that the center of the waistband is at the natural waistline. The legs of slacks are finished as per the description for male trousers. Knee-length skirts and dresses will extend to a point not more than 1 inch above or more than 2 inches below the crease in the back of the knee.

The coat front will overlap to form a straight line from bottom of the lapel to the bottom of the coat. It will be fitted to produce a military effect, but it will have ease over the hips. It will not be buttoned so closely at the waist as to cause folds or wrinkles. The skirt will fit smoothly, so that it does not drape in folds under the coat. It will form a continuation of the lines of the coat and will not flare at the sides; nor will it be pegged.

Hats and Caps. Hats and caps are part of the uniform and are worn with the uniform except as follows: (1) headgear need not be worn in private vehicles or commercial conveyances; (2) headgear may be removed if it would interfere with the proper operation of a military vehicle; (3) headgear will not be worn indoors unless under arms in an official capacity or unless directed by the commander; and (4) females are not required to wear headgear with the mess and evening mess uniforms, or with the Army blue or white dress uniforms to an evening social event, or with the Army green maternity uniform when worn to an evening social event.

Personal Appearance. The best-fitted uniform is to no avail if it is worn by a soldier (or an officer) who does not have a military bearing. Stand or sit erect, chest out, stomach in; don't slouch. Look the world and your associates squarely in the eye. You are an honorable person in an honorable profession. Do your best to look the part. This includes long-term attention to physical fitness and such self-control as is necessary to meet the weight standards. Remember, it is much easier to put on a few pounds than it is to take them off.

All personnel are to maintain their fingernails clean and neatly trimmed, and of a length so as not to interfere with the performance of duty. Use of nail polish is discussed later.

Hair. There are many acceptable hair styles, so long as they are not extreme or faddish. If dyes, tints, or bleaches are used, the resulting color must look like natural human hair.

Males. The hair on the top of the head must be neatly groomed. The length and bulk of the hair will be such that it does not present a ragged, unkempt, or extreme appearance. The hair should present a tapered appearance when combed and not fall over the ears or eyebrows or touch the collar except for the closely cut hair at the back of the neck. In all cases, the bulk or length must not interfere with the normal wear of headgear or protective masks.

Sideburns must be neatly trimmed. The base will not be flared, nor will it extend below the lowest part of the exterior ear opening. The bottom will be a clean-shaven horizontal line.

The face is to be clean-shaven except that a moustache is permitted, provided it is kept neatly trimmed, tapered, and tidy. No portion of the moustache may cover the upper lip or extend sideways beyond the corners of the mouth, nor will it present a chopped-off appearance. Handlebar moustaches, goatees, and beards are expressly forbidden.

The wearing of a wig or hairpiece is forbidden except to cover natural baldness or physical disfiguration caused by an accident or medical procedure. When worn it will conform to haircut criteria stated above. As an exception to this policy, Army National Guard (ARNG) and U.S. Army Reserve (USAR) personnel may wear a wig or hairpiece conforming to the haircut criteria during unit training assemblies or when serving on active duty for training or full-time training duty for periods of thirty days or less. When ordered to active duty for periods greater than thirty days, ARNG and USAR personnel fall under the same rules as other active duty personnel.

Females. Hair will be neatly groomed. The length and bulk will not be excessive or present a ragged, unkempt, or extreme appearance. Hair will not fall over the eyebrows or extend below the bottom edge of the collar. The hair style must not interfere with the proper wearing of headgear or protective masks. Hairnets are not authorized unless required for health or safety reasons. Wigs may be worn so long as the hairpiece is a natural color and conforms to the criteria above. Hair-holding ornaments (barrettes, pins, clips), if used, must be transparent or similar in color to the hair, and must be inconspicuously placed. Beads or similar ornamental items are not authorized.

Females may wear cosmetics applied conservatively and in good taste. Exaggerated or faddish styles are not authorized. Lipstick and nail polish may be worn with all uniforms so long as the color is conservative and complements the uniform. Extreme shades such as purple, gold, blue, and white are not permitted.

Wearing of Jewelry and Eyeglasses. The wearing of a wrist watch, a wrist identification bracelet, and not more than two rings is authorized (a wedding set is considered one ring), provided the styles are conservative and in good taste, unless prohibited for health or safety reasons. No jewelry, watch chains, or pens and pencils will appear exposed on the uniform. Authorized exceptions are a conservative tie tack or tie clasp, which may be worn with the black four-in-hand necktie, and a pen or pencil, which may appear exposed on the hospital duty and flight uniforms. Fad devices, vogue medallions, personal talismans, or amulets are not authorized for wear with the uniform or on duty. The wear of religious articles and jewelry is authorized provided they are not visible or apparent.

Male soldiers are forbidden to wear earrings of any type when in uniform or when wearing civilian clothing on duty. Female soldiers may wear earrings with the service, dress, mess, and evening mess uniforms, but not with utility uniforms. Earrings may be of the clip-on, screw-on, or post type; they must be unadorned and spherical in shape; not more than 6mm (1/4 inch) in diameter; and of gold, silver, or white pearl. Earrings must be worn in matched pairs, not more than one earring per ear lobe.

Conservative prescription civilian eyeglasses are authorized for wear. Conservative prescription and nonprescription sunglasses are authorized except when in formation. Eyeglasses or sunglasses that are faddish or have lenses or frames with initials or other adornments are not authorized.

Identification Tags and Security Badges. Identification tags (dog tags) will be worn when engaged in field training, when traveling in aircraft, and when outside CONUS. Security badges will be worn in restricted areas for identification as prescribed by the commander in accordance with applicable regulations.

Personal Protective or Reflective Clothing. The wear of commercially designed protective headgear is authorized when riding a motorcycle, bicycle, or similar vehicle. Such headgear will be removed and authorized uniform headgear will be donned when travel is complete. Commanders may authorize the wear of protective/reflective outer garments with uniforms when safety considerations so dictate.

Wear of Civilian Clothing. Civilian clothing is authorized for wear when off duty unless the wear is prohibited by the installation commander in CONUS or by the MACOM commander overseas. Commanders down to unit level may restrict the wear of civilian clothes by those soldiers who have had their pass privileges revoked under the provisions of AR 630-5.

When on duty in civilian clothing, Army personnel will conform to the appearance standards stated previously unless specifically authorized by the commander for specific mission requirements.

SELECTION, PURCHASE, AND CARE OF UNIFORMS

All officers, commissioned and warrant, are responsible for procuring and maintaining uniforms appropriate to their assigned duties. The accompanying table lists the minimum quantities of uniforms normally prescribed by commanders. Officers are responsible for ensuring that their uniforms and insignia conform to the requirements of AR 670-1. In addition to the required uniforms, sufficient quantities of appropriate accessories, insignia, footwear, undergarments, headgear, and handgear are to be purchased and maintained. It is mandatory that all officers dress in accordance with their positions as officers of the U.S. Army and in accordance with the traditions and customs of the service.

OFFICER UNIFORM REQUIREMENTS

The major items of uniform clothing normally prescribed by commanders and the minimum quantitites that should be in the possession of each officer are as follows. Sufficient quantities of personal items necessary to ensure acceptable standards of personal hygiene and appearance will also be procured and maintained.

Item	Male	Female	Note
Coat, all-weather, Army, black	1	1	N/A
Uniform, Army green	1	N/A	1
Uniform, Army green classic	N/A	1	1
Uniform, Army blue dress	1	1	2,5
Uniform, Army green maternity	N/A	2	3
Uniform, utility	4	4	4
Coat, cold-weather, woodland pattern camouflage (field jacket)	1	1	N/A

Notes:
1. The Army green classic uniform replaced the green pantsuit and the Army green (female) uniforms on 1 October 1986.
2. The Army blue dress uniform is required for all officers on extended active duty for six months or more.
3. As required by AR 635-100 and chapter 17 of AR 670-1.
4. Officers will have four utility uniforms, two of which will be temperate camouflage uniforms and two of which will be hot-weather camouflage uniforms.
5. Additional quantities of Army blue dress uniforms required by officers for performance of official duties, such as when the mission includes band formations, reviews, parades, ceremonial events, and the like, are authorized as organizational issue.

The minimum quantities of uniforms shown in the table are just that. Depending upon one's assigned duties and the availability of laundry and dry-cleaning facilities, more than the minimum numbers of uniforms will be needed. The junior officer faces a dilemma of what to buy and how to dress well without becoming impoverished. The total expenditure for these uniform items is considerable. The initial uniform allowance provided to Reserve officers and to some newly appointed Regular Army officers helps to defray the initial cost, but it is unlikely to cover all expenditures. The wise officer will exercise care and judgment in selections to make certain that the articles bought will meet service standards and that they fit well, all to the end that he or she may wear the uniform with pride and credit to the service. To be an Army officer, you should strive not only to be a good officer but also to look like a good officer.

Where to Purchase Uniforms. Under an agreement with the U.S. Army Troop Support Agency, the Army and Air Force Exchange Service handles the retail sales of official uniform items. These are uniform items purchased by the Defense Personnel Support Center (DPSC) and are the same items as those issued to enlisted soldiers. They are stocked in the Army Military Clothing Sales Store (AMCSS). The AMCSS also stocks commercial and optional uniform items and accessories. The commercial items displayed along with the DPSC items afford an individual the opportunity to comparison-shop. You will realize the maximum economy in price by purchasing your uniforms at the AMCSS. Certainly junior officers, unless they are independently wealthy, will wish to make most of their purchases of required uniforms at the AMCSS.

Civilian Tailoring Companies. There are a number of quite large and reliable companies in the United States that specialize in uniforms for officers. There also are many small custom tailoring establishments well known as uniform specialists, and some of these tailors have been in this field for years with well established reputations. There is just one reason to choose a proven civilian source over the official outlets, and that is quality of individual tailoring. Officers who can afford the cost, career officers and senior officers especially, are justified in purchasing some of their uniforms from carefully chosen custom tailors. The added cost should pay for the belief that they look their military best.

Now, some words of caution. Let the buyer beware. It is a simple matter to sell for less any item that is manufactured of cheap components or by poor workmanship; a civilian outlet attempting to compete on a price basis should receive most careful examination before a purchase is made.

Summary. Officers of all components, all grades, and of short service or long, are obliged to meet high standards as to their uniforms. There is no variation in official requirements. Still, as a practical matter, the standard will be established at the top, by general officers and field officers of a command. A high standard will be expected of career officers. Whatever your grade or component, do your part. Be meticulous in procurement of uniforms that fit very well indeed and are maintained always in a clean, well-pressed condition, so that you may wear them with pride.

The Commanding Officer's Responsibility. The commanding officer is required to make periodic inspections of the uniforms with which members of his or her command, including officers, have equipped themselves. Inspection will include checking as to possession of the items required; that uniforms fit properly; that they are maintained in a neat and correct manner; and that only duly prescribed items of insignia and ornamentation are worn with the uniform.

Cautions in Purchasing Uniforms. There are cautions to be observed in buying uniforms. The first caution is to know what is required and what may soon change.

Various kinds of cloth are authorized for the various uniforms, with a choice of weights to meet varying climatic conditions. Uniforms may not be mixed, e.g., do not wear a serge coat with trousers or skirt of gabardine. Reserve officers on limited tours of active duty who wish sensible economy may choose the wool serge material, because these uniforms may be obtained through the AMCSS. At most stations in the United States, two uniform weights will be needed for the calendar year—the lightest weight serge for the summer months and a medium weight for the winter months. Career officers may prefer a wider choice.

If you do buy uniforms from other than official sources, check for the warranty labels certifying to the quality and meeting of Army standards. Uniforms and accessories bought at bargain stores may have been rejected by government purchasers.

Apply the same kind of reasoning to choice of material for the Army blue dress uniform and for the various mess and evening mess uniforms should you decide to purchase these optional garments. These are all-year uniforms. You should seek a fine appearance in these uniforms, but be mindful of comfort in summer as well as winter. As to the materials for the Army white uniforms, the options provide materials that are normally laundered and others that are normally dry-cleaned. At your station, what is the nature of the laundry and dry-cleaning service, and what of its costs?

There are numerous items of ornamentation that call for gold or gold-color materials. Here are the rules:

Wherever gold lace or gold bullion ornamentation are prescribed for wear with the uniforms, gold-color nylon or rayon or synthetic metallic gold may be substituted subject to the following limitations:

- If trouser and sleeve ornamentation is gold bullion, cap decoration and shoulder strap insignia must be bullion.
- If trouser and sleeve ornamentation is of synthetic material, cap ornamentation and shoulder strap material may be of either bullion or the synthetic material.
- Ornamentation on the visors (male) or hatbands (female) of all Army service caps will be of gold bullion, synthetic metallic gold yarn, or anodized aluminum in 24-karat gold color.

The Reserve officer on inactive duty status is required to provide himself or herself with service uniforms and insignia of the branch in which commissioned for use when ordered to active duty. A proper minimum for such officers is suggested as a complete Army green uniform (male) or Army green classic uniform (female) with extra trousers or skirts, and one or two extra shirts in winter, with the black all-weather coat. This minimum will permit the officer to report for duty and to perform duties in uniform until he or she can procure basic needs of the station and duty. The total cost of all the suggested items would approximate the initial allowance provided for the purchase of uniforms. The allowance is provided to permit newly appointed officers to procure the uniforms needed for their start without financial sacrifice.

Care of Uniforms. Good uniforms and appropriate accessories deserve the treatment that will assure maximum durability and appearance to the owner who has paid good money to obtain them. An old uniform of good quality that fits well and is clean, neat, and unfaded will look better than a new and costly one that is noticeably soiled or out of press. The care that should be given to uniforms and equipment need not be burdensome. But it must be done regularly and correctly. This discussion, which includes points of common experience, should be helpful.

A modest amount of regular care of your uniforms is necessary. Upon removing uniform garments, brush them, inspect for spots or soil, and promptly use effective cleaning solvents, not forgetting soap and water; place garments upon good wooden or plastic hangers, and hang them where they can air and dry. Trousers and slacks are best hung at full length. Such care will result in restoration of the press and removal of small wrinkles, and provide a uniform ready to wear when needed. It isn't necessary to have a uniform cleaned and pressed as frequently when these habits are followed.

Underarm sweating is destructive to uniforms, including shirts, causing rot as well as discoloration. For the sake of your uniforms, use a good antiperspirant, and for the sake of your associates, combine it with a good deodorant, not forgetting to apply soap and water regularly, as circumstances permit.

Have a number of regulation neckties or neck tabs. A soiled or badly wrinkled tie is as objectionable as gravy on a vest. Ties soil quickly and require dry cleaning. Replace them before they approach the point of unattractiveness.

Moths, and mildew from excess humidity, are the enemies of uniforms in storage. Be certain such uniforms are clean and well brushed at the time of storage. Place them in a tight container with an adequate supply of moth preventive. Some dry-cleaning establishments provide mothproofing service.

Care of Ribbons, Decorations, and Service Medals. Ribbons for decorations and service medals must always be worn fresh and bright. Never wear frayed or soiled ribbons. Never use ribbons covered with transparent plastic or impregnated with a substance to increase their life. Dry cleaning will not injure them. Keep the metallic parts clean; some of them require shining. Wear them with pride.

Care of Brass Items of Uniform. Items of solid brass, such as the belt buckle, must be brightly shined and free of scratches. The cloths impregnated with polish, as those sold at the exchanges, are very good for this purpose. Avoid touching a freshly shined article with the bare hands, as it will tarnish at once.

Uniform buttons may be cleaned with ammonia and water; do not clean them with brass polish. Permanently shined, gold-color, anodized aluminum buttons are authorized.

Care of Gold Braid. Gold braid or an authorized substitute, now a part of several uniforms, is found on such items as the cap, shoulder knots, insignia of grade of dress uniforms, sleeve ornamentation, and trouser stripes. Gold braid items are costly. Due to the cost, it is unlikely that any officer will choose gold braid these days. However, should you elect to purchase items with gold braid, with correct care you can keep them serviceable for a very long time. But incorrect handling can ruin them quickly. If cleaning is attempted at all, it should be done only by someone who has proven skill in doing it.

Tarnish is the enemy of gold braid. When not in use, these items should be stored where they will be dry, protected from light, and wrapped in tarnishproof paper. Such paper may be obtained from jewelers. Ordinary paper contains sulfur and will cause tarnish, as will rubber. Dry cleaning will not injure trouser stripes or sleeve decorations of gold.

Care of Shoes. The most important point in preserving and prolonging the useful life of good shoes is to place them on properly fitted shoe trees as soon as they are removed. They will then dry in the correct shape, without wrinkles, and be comfortable when worn again. Have several pair of shoes and rotate their use.

Clean shoes as required. Saddle soap works well. Castile or other mild soap is a good cleaning agent for leather. Applying coat upon coat of polish, without intermediate cleaning, merely piles polish on dirt. Leather that becomes dry and lifeless may be restored with leather dressings, or by a light application of neat's-foot oil on the flesh side. Use good polishes; the exchanges carry reliable brands.

Boots worn in field service must be strong, well fitted, comfortable, and treated to resist water penetration. The wise officer will keep one pair of such boots in top-notch condition ready for instant use.

Mighty few slovenly appearing individuals have ever become officers, or remained long as officers. But the Army has had its careless individuals. If you look like a good officer, it may aid you in gaining the reputation of being a fine officer. It's worth a try!

UNIFORMS FOR MALE OFFICERS

The names of the Army uniforms for male officers are:

Army green service uniform—Male
Army blue uniform—Male
Army white uniform—Male
Army blue mess and evening mess uniforms—Male
Army white mess and evening mess uniforms—Male

In addition, there are various utility uniforms authorized for both male and female officers. These are discussed later in this chapter. Another later section, *ACCESSORY ITEMS OF UNIFORMS*, provides details regarding the various accessory items worn with the uniforms.

ARMY GREEN SERVICE UNIFORM—MALE

The class A and class B Army green service uniforms are authorized for year-round wear by all male personnel. The class A green uniform consists of the Army green coat and trousers, an Army green shade 415 short- or long-sleeve shirt, and a black four-in-hand necktie. The class B green service uniform consists of the green trousers and either the short- or long-sleeve shirt. The black necktie is always worn with the long-sleeve shirt. The short-sleeve shirt has a convertible collar and may be worn with or without a tie. When worn without a tie and with the black cardigan or black pullover sweater (see the later section on uniform accessories), the shirt collar is worn outside the sweater. Note that either shirt is worn tucked into the trousers so that the shirt edge, the front fly opening of the trousers, and the outside (right) edge of the belt buckle form a straight line.

Occasions for Wear. The Army green service uniform, class A or class B, is the normal duty uniform, unless the nature of the duties requires one of the utility uniforms. Either the class A or class B versions may be worn by all male personnel when on duty, off duty, and during travel. These uniforms are acceptable for informal social functions after retreat unless other uniforms are prescribed by the host. When the uniform is not prescribed for formations or other occasions, the selection between class A and either of the class B versions is made based upon weather conditions, duties, and the formality of the occasion.

Authorized Materials. There are eight materials that may be chosen by officers for the uniform coat and trousers. Consistency is required; the coat and trousers must be of the same material. The materials are:

Wool serge, 12- or 15-ounce, Army green shade 44.
Wool elastique, 16-ounce, Army green shade 44.
Wool gabardine, 11-ounce, Army green shade 44.
Polyester/wool blended fabric, gabardine weave, 11-ounce, Army green shade 344.
Polyester/wool blended fabric, tropical weight, plain weave, Army green shade 344.
Polyester/wool blended fabric, double knit weave, 16-ounce, Army green shade 444.
Polyester textured woven serge, 6.5 ounce, Army green shade 434.
Polyester/wool serge, 11-ounce, Army green shade 344.
The wool serge and the polyester/wool tropical weave are the two materials

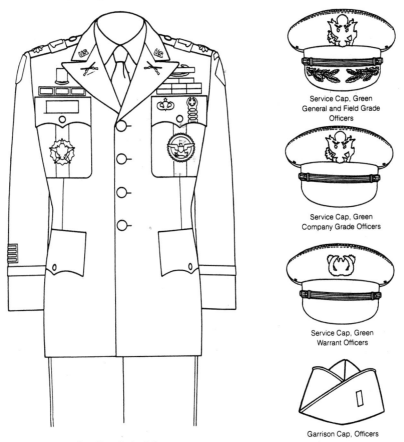

Army Green Service Uniform

Service Cap, Green
General and Field Grade
Officers

Service Cap, Green
Company Grade Officers

Service Cap, Green
Warrant Officers

Garrison Cap, Officers

furnished enlisted men and are two of the options available to officers. Except in regions of low temperatures for extended periods, garments made of the lighter or medium-weight fabrics may be worn comfortably during the major portion or all of the year.

Coat and Ornamentation. The coat is single-breasted, with peaked lapels, extending below the crotch, fitting easily over the chest and shoulders, with a slight drape effect in front and back. It is fitted slightly at the waist, conforming to the figure without tightness and with no pronounced flare. General officers wear a band of black mohair or mercerized cotton braid 1½ inches wide on each sleeve, the lower edge 3 inches up from the end of the sleeve. Other officers wear a ¾-inch braid of the same material on each sleeve in the same position.

Trousers and Ornamentation. The bottom of the front crease of the trousers should rest on the top of the shoes, and the bottom of the rear crease should be about 1 inch above the top of the heel. Both measurements are to be taken when wearing standard shoes. The trouser crease should hang straight, not twisted. A slight break in the front crease is permissible (but not desirable—Author).

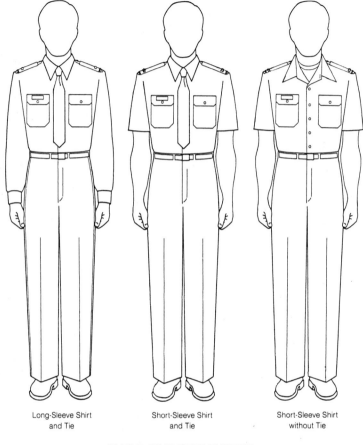

Long-Sleeve Shirt
and Tie

Short-Sleeve Shirt
and Tie

Short-Sleeve Shirt
without Tie

CLASS B ARMY GREEN UNIFORM.

Headgear. Two caps, plus berets, are authorized for wear with the class A and class B service uniforms, as follows:

Service Cap. This (the visored cap) is of adopted design as shown in the accompanying illustration. Officers are authorized at their option to wear the cap frame with removable cover. This cap is mandatory for wear with the class A uniform except when in travel status, when assigned to units authorized to wear organizational berets, or when assigned to air assault units. It is optional for wear with the class B uniform.

There is a prescribed "wear" position for the service cap. *Caution:* When you purchase a cap, to get a perfect fit, be careful that your hair is trimmed just as you wish it, and use care to get a cap that does fit perfectly; an Army cap a little too large or a little too small looks bad and is uncomfortable. Wear the cap straight on the head so that the braid band establishes a line around the head parallel to the ground. Such positioning of the cap automatically positions the leather visor correctly so that it does not interfere with vision or ride up on the forehead.

The visor of the service cap is of black leather or poromeric material in a leather finish. For general and field grade officers, the top of the visor is covered in black cloth with two arcs of oak leaves in groups of two, embroidered in gold bullion or synthetic metallic gold yarn, or of anodized aluminum in 24-karat gold color. For other officers, the top is plain black shell cordovan or shell cordovan finish leather. Officers' caps have chinstraps of natural or light brown pigskin or sheepskin.

Garrison Cap. This cap may be worn with the class B uniform and with the class A uniform while in travel status or while assigned to air assault units. Braid is secured to the top edge of the curtain of the cap; general officers wear cord edge braid of gold bullion or synthetic metallic gold yarn, while other commissioned officers wear cord edge braid of gold bullion or synthetic metallic gold yarn with black rayon or black polyester intertwined. Warrant officers wear cord edge braid of silver bullion, silver color rayon, or synthetic metallic silver yarn with black rayon or black polyester intertwined.

The garrison cap is worn so that the bottom of the front vertical crease of the cap is at the center of the forehead in a straight line with the nose and at a point between 1 and 1½ inches above eyebrow level. The cap is then tilted slightly to the right, but in no case will the side of the cap rest on top of the ear. The cap is placed on the head in such a manner that the front and rear vertical creases and the top edge of the crown form unbroken lines in silhouette. The crown will not be crushed or shaped so as to form peaks at the top front and top rear of the cap.

Berets. Organizational berets are authorized for wear with the class A and class B service uniforms by personnel assigned to Ranger units (black beret), Special Forces units (green beret), and Airborne units (maroon beret). Except for color, they are the same. All are organizational issue items. The beret is worn with the headband straight across the forehead, 1 inch above the eyebrows, with the top draped over the right ear and the stiffener positioned over the left eye. The adjusting ribbon is cut off and the knot concealed inside the edge binding at the back of the beret.

Ornamentation and Insignia. Officers wear the following ornamentation on the green service uniform.

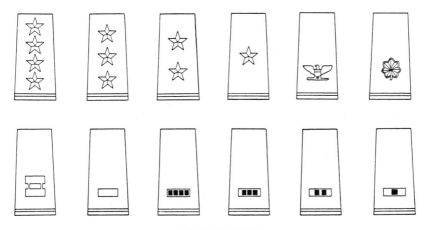

SHOULDER MARKS.
Marks for females are slightly smaller than those for males.

Class A:
Headgear insignia
U.S. insignia
Insignia of grade
Insignia of branch to which assigned or detailed
Decoration ribbons and service medal ribbons
Unit awards
U.S. badges (identification, marksmanship, combat, special skill; special skill
   and marksmanship tabs)
Foreign badges
Regimental affiliation crest
Distinctive unit insignia
Shoulder sleeve insignia (current assignment—left shoulder; former wartime
   unit—right shoulder)
Nameplate
Combat leader's identification tab
Distinctive items for infantry personnel
Branch of service scarves (when prescribed for ceremonies)
Overseas service bars
Brassards
Aiguillette; fouraggere/lanyard

Class B:
Headgear insignia
Insignia of grade (shoulder marks)
Decorations and awards (ribbons)
Nameplate
Distinctive unit insignia (only on black pullover sweater)

ARMY BLUE UNIFORM—MALE

The Army blue uniform is authorized for year-round wear by all male personnel. All officers are required to own the Army blue uniform for wear on appropriate occasions. Excepted are Reserve component officers in a Reserve status and officers on active duty for periods of 6 months or less, who may purchase the uniforms as an option.

Occasions for Wear. The Army blue uniform is worn for social functions of a general or official nature before or after retreat, on duty as prescribed by the local commander, and on other appropriate occasions as desired by the individual.

Composition. The Army blue uniform consists of a dark blue coat, dark or light blue trousers, and a long-sleeve white shirt with a turndown collar. Black oxford shoes are worn with this uniform. When worn with the black four-in-hand necktie, it is considered an informal uniform. When worn with a black bow tie, it constitutes a formal uniform corresponding to a civilian tuxedo.

Authorized Materials. There is a choice of barathea, 14-ounce; wool gabardine, 11- or 14.5-ounce; wool elastique, 16-ounce; or wool tropical, 10.5-ounce, each in dark blue, Army shade 150; or polyester/wool blend in twill weave, 9.5-ounce or polyester/wool blend in plain weave, 9.5-ounce, each in dark blue, Army shade 450. For general officers, both the coat and the trousers are of this material and shade. For other officers, the coat is of the material and shade noted above, but the trousers are light blue, Army shade 151 or 451, of the same material as the coat. The trousers may be high waisted, suitable for wear also with the Army blue mess uniform.

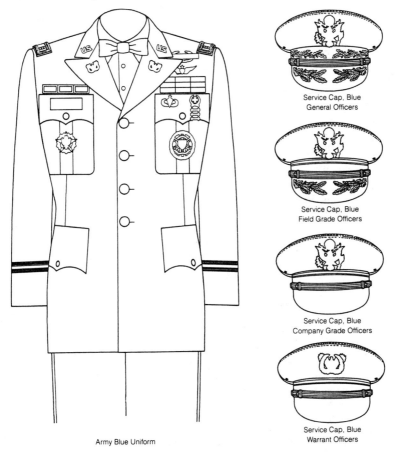

Service Cap, Blue
General Officers

Service Cap, Blue
Field Grade Officers

Service Cap, Blue
Company Grade Officers

Service Cap, Blue
Warrant Officers

Army Blue Uniform

Many people believe that the better-appearing Army blue uniforms are tailored from the heavier weights of cloth. However, since it is an all-year uniform, the lighter-weight fabrics provide the best year-round comfort. A well-fitted, carefully tailored uniform, clean and freshly pressed, will look well with any of the authorized weights of material. Advised: the light-weight fabrics, for reasons of economy and comfort.

Coat and Ornamentation. The Army blue coat is cut to the same general style as the green service coat. Ornamental gold braid is worn on the sleeves of the blue coat (bullion or one of the authorized substitutes). For general officers, a 1 1/2-inch gold braid is positioned with the bottom of the braid parallel to and 3 inches above the bottom of each sleeve. For all other officers, the braid consists of two 1/4-inch gold stripes positioned 1/4 inch apart over silk material of the first-named color of the officer's basic branch. The braid is positioned with the bottom parallel to and 3 inches above the bottom of each sleeve.

Trousers and Ornamentation. The trousers are cut and fitted as described for the green service trousers, except that they may be high waisted, suitable for wear with the blue mess uniform. Trouser ornamentation consists of gold braid stripes (of the same material as used on the coat sleeves) sewn over the outer seams of the trouser legs. General officers wear two 1/2-inch-wide stripes of gold braid, spaced 1/2 inch apart. All other officers wear a 1 1/2-inch stripe of gold braid.

Headgear. The Army blue service cap of standard design and specification is worn with the Army blue, Army blue mess, and Army blue evening mess uniforms. The cap material is either the same material and shade as the coat, or officers may wear a cap of fur felt, 9-ounce, dark blue, Army shade 250. Officers also have an option to wear the cap frame with removable cover of the same material as the coat.

The visor of the cap is of black leather or of poromeric material with a leather finish. For general and field grade officers, the top of the visor is of black cloth with two arcs of oak leaves in groups of two, embroidered in one of the authorized gold color materials. General officers have similar ornamentation on the cap band. For company grade officers and warrant officers, the top of the visor is of plain black shell cordovan finish leather.

Shoulder Straps. The insignia of grade for wear with the Army blue uniform are embroidered on shoulder straps, 1 5/8 inches wide by 4 inches long. The shoulder straps clip on to the shoulder of the blue coat near the edge of the shoulder seam. For general officers, the background of the shoulder straps is blue-black velvet. For all other officers, the background is a rayon grosgrain ribbon in the first-named color of the officer's basic branch. The strap has a 3/8-inch gold-color border surrounded on the inside and outside by a strand of gold jaceron. If the officer's basic branch has two colors, then the second branch color is used as a 1/8-inch inside border instead of the gold jaceron. Grade insignia on the strap will be rayon embroidery or bullion and jaceron. See the accompanying illustrations.

Ornamentation and Insignia. Officers wear only the following ornamentation and insignia with the Army blue uniform:
Headgear insignia
U.S. insignia
Insignia of grade (shoulder straps)
Insignia of branch to which assigned or detailed

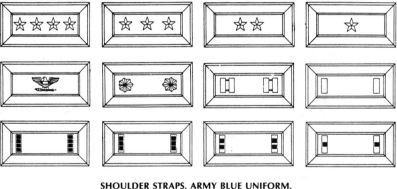

SHOULDER STRAPS, ARMY BLUE UNIFORM.
Size: Male—1 5/8 inches by 4 inches,
Female—1 5/8 inches by 3 1/2 inches

Authorized decoration ribbons and service medal ribbons—Full-size or minia-
   ture decorations and service medals may be worn after retreat
Badges (identification, marksmanship, combat special skill)—Dress miniature
   combat and special skill badges may be worn when miniature medals are
   worn
Regimental affiliation crest
Distinctive items for infantry personnel
Nameplate
Aiguillette (dress or service)
Fouraggere/lanyards
The manner of attaching and wearing insignia and other accouterments is discussed
later in this chapter.

ARMY WHITE UNIFORM—MALE

The Army white uniform is authorized for wear by all male personnel as an
optional dress uniform. It is normally worn from April to October except in clothing

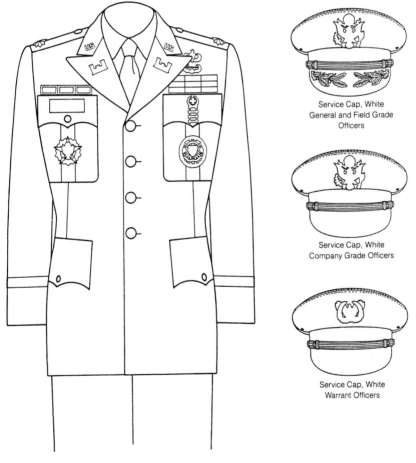

Service Cap, White
General and Field Grade
Officers

Service Cap, White
Company Grade Officers

Service Cap, White
Warrant Officers

Army White Uniform

zones I and II (I—warm or hot all year; II—warm or hot summers, mild winters; see CTA 50-900) where it may be worn year-round.

Occasions for Wear. The Army white uniform may be worn on duty in all areas when appropriate and authorized by the local commander, and off duty for social occasions.

Composition. The Army white uniform consists of the white coat and trousers, a long-sleeve white shirt with turndown collar and either barrel or French cuffs, either a black four-in-hand necktie or a black bow tie, and black oxfords. When worn with the black necktie, the uniform is informal. When worn with the black bow tie, it constitutes a dress uniform corresponding to the civilian summer tuxedo.

Authorized Materials. The authorized materials for the coat, trousers, and headgear are white cotton twill, 8.2-ounce; white polyester/wool blended fabric in tropical weave, 9-ounce; white polyester/viscose blended fabric in gabardine weave, 8-ounce; or white polyester, texturized woven serge, 6.5-ounce.

Coat and Ornamentation. The coat is cut along the same lines as the Army green service coat. All officers wear a band of white cotton or white mohair braid, 1/2 inch in width, on each sleeve, with the lower edge of the braid parallel to and 3 inches above the end of the sleeve.

Trousers and Ornamentation. The trousers are cut along the same lines as the green service trousers. There is no ornamentation on the trousers.

Headgear. The authorized headgear is a service cap of the same design and ornamentation as the service cap worn with the Army green uniform, but covered with the same material as the Army white coat and trousers.

Ornamentation and Insignia. As stated earlier for the Army blue uniform. Note, however, that regular insignia of grade is worn on the shoulder loops as with the green service uniform, not on the shoulder straps as with the Army blue uniform.

ARMY BLUE MESS AND EVENING MESS UNIFORMS—MALE

The Army blue mess and blue evening mess uniforms are authorized for year-round wear by all male personnel.

Occasions for Wear. The blue mess and blue evening mess uniforms may be worn at social functions of a general or official nature after retreat, and at private formal social functions after retreat. The blue mess uniform is for "black tie" functions and corresponds to the civilian tuxedo. The blue evening mess uniform is the most formal Army uniform and corresponds to the civilian "white tie and tails" tuxedo.

Composition. The Army blue jacket and dark or light blue high-waisted trousers comprise the basic uniform. Worn with a white, semiformal dress shirt, black bow tie, and a black cummerbund, it is the blue mess uniform. The blue evening mess uniform uses a white formal dress shirt, a white bow tie, and a white vest.

Authorized Materials. The authorized materials for the jacket are: wool barathea, 14-ounce; wool gabardine, 11- or 14.5-ounce; wool elastique, 15-ounce; or wool tropical, 9-ounce, all in dark blue, Army shade 150; or polyester and wool blended fabric in plain weave, 9.5-ounce; or polyester and wool blended gabardine, 9.5-ounce, each in dark blue, Army shade 450. The trousers for general officers will be of the same material and shade (dark blue) as the jacket. All other officers will wear trousers of the same material as the jacket, but the color will be light blue, Army shade 151 or 451.

Army Blue Mess Uniform
General Officers

Army Blue Evening
Mess Uniform
Other Officers

Jacket and Ornamentation. The jacket is cut on the lines of an evening dress coat; it descends to the point of the hips and is slightly curved to a peak in the front and in back. Two 25-ligne buttons, joined by a small gold or gold-color chain, may be worn in the upper button holes. Shoulder knots of gold bullion or substitute material are worn on the shoulders of the jacket by all officers.

Lapels. Lapels of the jacket will be of rayon, acetate, or other synthetic fabric in colors as follows: general officers, except chaplains—dark blue; chaplains—black; all other officers—first-named color of the officer's basic branch.

Sleeves. General officers wear a cuff of blue-black velvet, 4 inches in width, positioned 1/8 inch from the bottom of each sleeve, with a band of gold oak leaves in groups of two, about 1 inch in width, placed 1 inch below the upper edge of the cuff. Insignia of grade is centered on the outside of the sleeve 1 inch above the upper edge of the sleeve cuff. Whenever insignia of branch is worn, it is placed 1 inch above the top of the cuff and the insignia of grade is placed 1 inch above the insignia of branch. Insignia of grade and branch, if worn, are of embroidered silver bullion.

All other officers wear on each sleeve a band of two 1/4-inch gold stripes, placed 1/4 inch apart over a silk stripe of the first-named color of their basic branch, the bottom of the sleeve band to be 3 inches above and parallel to the bottom of the sleeve. A trefoil consisting of a knot of three loops of 1/4-inch gold braid, interlaced at points of crossing, is placed on the outside of the sleeves with the ends resting on the sleeve band. Insignia of grade, metal or embroidered, is worn vertically in the center of the space formed by the lower curves of the knot and the upper edge of the sleeve band. Previously authorized sleeve ornamentation may be worn for the life of the jacket, provided the number of trefoils reflects the correct grade.

Trousers and Ornamentation. The trousers are cut on the lines of civilian dress trousers with a high waist, without pleats, cuffs, or hip pockets. Ornamentation is gold stripes as described for the Army blue uniform trousers. Suspenders may be worn with these uniforms, but they may not be visible.

Headgear. The Army blue service cap is the authorized headgear with the blue mess and blue evening mess uniforms.

Accessories. Accessories worn with these uniforms are: a white, semiformal dress shirt, black bow tie, and black cummerbund with the mess uniform; a white, formal dress shirt, white bow tie, and white vest with the evening mess uniform. Officers also are authorized to wear a blue cape with these uniforms instead of the black all-weather coat. See the later section, *ACCESSORY ITEMS OF UNIFORMS,* for a description of these items.

Ornamentation and Insignia. Insignia of grade and branch are worn as described for the jacket ornamentation. The only other authorized items of ornamentation are:

> Regimental affiliation crest
> Miniature decorations and service medals
> Identification badges
> Dress miniature combat and special skill badges
> Dress aiguillette

See the later section for the manner of wear of these items.

ARMY WHITE MESS AND EVENING MESS UNIFORMS—MALE

The Army white mess and white evening mess uniforms are authorized for optional wear by all male personnel. These uniforms normally are worn from April to October except in clothing zones I and II (see CTA 50-900), where they may be worn year-round.

Occasions for Wear. The same as for the Army blue mess and blue evening mess uniforms.

Composition. The Army white jacket and black, high-waisted trousers comprise the basic uniform. Worn with a white semiformal dress shirt, black bow tie, and black cummerbund, it is the white mess uniform. The white evening mess uniform uses a white formal dress shirt with wing collar, a white vest, and a white bow tie.

Authorized Materials. The jacket and vest are of white cotton twill, 8.2-ounce; white polyester/wool blend in plain weave, 9-ounce; white polyester/wool blend in gabardine, 10.5-ounce; or white polyester texturized woven serge, 6.5-ounce. The trousers are black, commercial tuxedo design in a lightweight material.

Jacket and Ornamentation. The cut and fit of the jacket, the wearing of shoulder knots, and the use of an optional gold or gold-color chain joining the upper button holes are as described for the Army blue mess jacket.

General officers wear a white cuff of mohair or mercerized cotton braid, 4 inches in width, positioned ⅛ inch above the bottom of each sleeve. Insignia of grade is centered on the outside of the sleeves 1 inch above the upper edge of the cuffs. If insignia of branch is worn, it is centered on the outside of the sleeve 1 inch above the upper edge of the cuffs, and the insignia of grade is positioned 1 inch above the insignia of branch. The grade insignia is of embroidered white cloth or silver bullion.

All other officers wear a ½-inch band of white mohair or mercerized cotton braid with the lower edge 3 inches from the end of the sleeve, with a trefoil consisting of a knot of three loops of ¼-inch white soutache braid, interlaced at points of crossing, with the ends resting on the sleeve bands. Insignia of grade, metal or embroidery, is worn vertically in the center of the space formed by the lower curves of the knot and the upper edge of the sleeve band. Previously authorized sleeve ornamentation may be worn for the life of the jacket, but the number of trefoils must reflect the correct grade. Note that, except for general officers, no insignia of branch is worn on the white mess jacket.

Trouser Ornamentation. The commercial design, black tuxedo trousers have a black silk or satin braid sewn on the outside seam of each trouser leg, running from the bottom of the waistband to the bottom of the trouser leg.

Headgear. The Army white service cap is worn with these uniforms.

Accessories. The black cummerbund, white vest, bow ties, and the formal and semiformal dress shirts are the same ones worn with the Army blue mess and blue evening mess uniforms. They are described in a later section, *Accessory Items of Uniforms.*

Ornamentation and Insignia. The authorized grade insignia are as described above for the jacket ornamentation. Other authorized ornamentation is as prescribed for the Army blue mess and blue evening mess uniforms.

UNIFORMS FOR FEMALE OFFICERS

The names of the Army uniforms for female officers are:

Green classic service uniform—Female
Green maternity service uniform
Army blue uniform—Female

Army White Mess Uniform
General Officers

Army White Evening
Mess Uniform
Other Officers

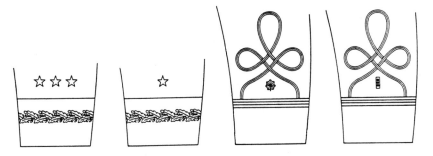

Sleeve Insignia, Blue Mess Jacket, Male and Female

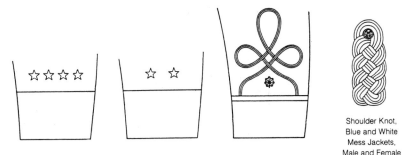

Shoulder Knot,
Blue and White
Mess Jackets,
Male and Female

Sleeve Insignia, White Mess Jacket,
Male and Female

Army white uniform—Female
Army blue mess and blue evening mess uniforms—Female
Army white mess, all-white mess, and evening white mess uniforms—Female
Army black mess and black evening mess uniforms—Female

In addition, there are various utility uniforms authorized for both female and male officers that are described later in this chapter. Another later section, *ACCESSORY ITEMS OF UNIFORMS,* provides details regarding the various accessory items worn or carried with the uniforms.

GREEN CLASSIC SERVICE UNIFORM—FEMALE

The class A and class B green classic service uniforms are authorized for year-round wear by all female personnel. The class A green classic uniform consists of the green classic coat and skirt or slacks, an Army green shade 415 short- or long-sleeve shirt, and a black neck tab. The class B green classic uniform consists of the green classic skirt or slacks and either the short-sleeve or long-sleeve green shirt. The black neck tab is always worn with the long-sleeve shirt. Its wear with the short-sleeve shirt is optional. When the short-sleeve shirt is worn without the neck tab, but with the black cardigan or black pullover sweater, the shirt collar is worn outside the sweater. The shirts may be worn either tucked into or left out of the skirt or slacks.

Occasions for Wear. The Army green classic service uniform, class A or class B, is the normal duty uniform unless the nature of the duties requires one of the utility

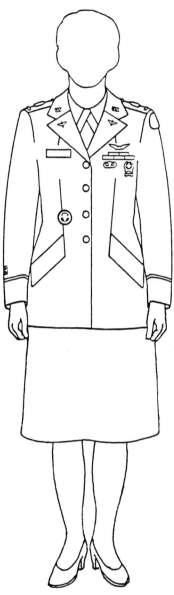

Army Green Classic
Uniform with Skirt

Army Green Classic
Uniform with Slacks

uniforms. Either the class A or the class B versions may be worn by all female personnel when on duty, off duty, or during travel. These uniforms are acceptable for informal social functions after retreat unless other uniforms are prescribed by the host. When the uniform is not prescribed for formations or other occasions, the selection between class A and any of the versions of the class B uniform is made based upon weather conditions, duties, and the formality of the occasion.

Authorized Materials. The coat, slacks, and skirt will be of the same material and shade. Two materials are authorized: polyester and wool (55/45) serge weave, 7-ounce, Army green shade 344; and polyester and textured woven serge (100 percent), 6.5-ounce, Army green shade 434.

Coat and Ornamentation. The green classic coat is a single-breasted, four-button, hip-length coat with two slanted flap front pockets, buttoned-down shoulder loops, notched collar, and side-body construction. General officers wear a 1 1/2-inch-wide band of black mohair, polyester, or mercerized cotton braid on each sleeve, with the lower edge parallel to and 3 inches above the end of the sleeve. For all other officers, the braid width is 1/2 inch, worn as above.

Slacks and Ornamentation. The slacks are straight-legged with slightly flared bottoms and a zipper-front closure. The newer version of the slacks has two side pockets, while the older version has no pockets; either may be worn. General officers wear on the outer seam of each slacks leg, two 1/2-inch-wide black mohair, polyester, or mercerized cotton braids, 1/2 inch apart. For all other officers, a single braid of the same material, 1 inch wide, is worn in the same locations. The front crease of the slacks should rest on the top of the shoe without a break. The back crease should extend to a point about 1 inch above the top of the heel of the shoe. A slight break in the front crease is permissible (but not desirable—Author).

Skirt. The skirt is knee-length, slightly flared, with a waistband and a zipper closure on the left side. It has no ornamentation.

Headgear. Three types of headgear are authorized for wear with the green classic uniform, as follows:

Service Hat. The green service hat is of fur felt or wool felt, 9-ounce, Army green shade 244. The hat has an oval crown and a detachable hatband. The hatband has three rows of stitching of matching thread at the top, and ornamentation as follows: General officers have two arcs of laurel leaves in groups of two, embroidered in gold or authorized substitute material; all other officers will have a 1/2-inch-wide band of gold braid placed on the bottom edge of the hatband.

The hat is worn straight on the head so that the hatband establishes a line around the head parallel to the floor, with the brim resting 1/2 inch to 1 inch above the eyebrows. No hair is to show on the forehead below the brim.

The service hat is mandatory for wear by officers with the class A uniform (if not wearing the black beret) except when in travel status, or when assigned to a unit authorized to wear an organizational beret, or to an air assault unit.

Garrison Cap. The garrison cap may be worn by officers with the class B uniform or when in travel status. It will replace the black beret. General officers wear a cord edge braid of gold bullion or synthetic metallic gold yarn on the garrison cap. Other commissioned officers wear a cord edge braid of the same material intertwined with black rayon or black polyester. Warrant officers wear a cord edge braid of silver bullion, synthetic metallic silver yarn, or silver rayon intertwined with black rayon or black polyester.

The garrison cap is worn with the front vertical crease centered on the forehead

ARMY GREEN CLASSIC UNIFORM, CLASS B VARIATIONS.

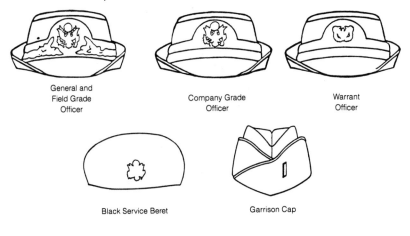

General and
Field Grade
Officer

Company Grade
Officer

Warrant
Officer

Black Service Beret

Garrison Cap

**SERVICE HATS, FEMALE
GREEN, BLUE, AND WHITE UNIFORMS (STYLE).**

and the bottom of the crease about 1 inch above the eyebrows. The top of the cap is open to cover the crown of the head and the back fits snugly to the head. No hair is to show on the forehead beneath the front bottom edge of the cap.

Black Beret. The black beret is being replaced by the garrison cap, but a phase-out date has not been established. The black beret (or the service hat) is mandatory for wear by officers with the class A uniform except when in a travel status, when assigned to an air assault unit, or when assigned to a unit authorized to wear an organizational beret.

The black beret is worn with the headgear insignia centered on the forehead. The beret is placed not forward of the forehead hairline and is worn so as to retain its original blocked contour.

Ornamentation and Insignia. The ornamentation and insignia authorized for wear on the green classic service uniform is the same as that itemized earlier for the Army green uniform for male officers, except that females do not wear the distinctive items for infantry personnel.

GREEN MATERNITY SERVICE UNIFORM

The green maternity service uniform is authorized for year-round wear as a service or dress uniform by pregnant personnel when prescribed by CTA 50-900, AR 700-84, and the commander.

Composition. The class A green maternity uniform consists of green maternity skirt or slacks, tunic, and the Army green shade 415 short- or long-sleeve shirt with a black neck tab. The class B uniform consists of the skirt or slacks and the long-sleeve or short-sleeve shirt. The black neck tab always is worn with the long-sleeve shirt. Its wear with the short-sleeve shirt is optional.

Occasions for Wear. The class A or class B green maternity uniform may be worn by all female personnel on or off duty or during travel. These uniforms are accept-

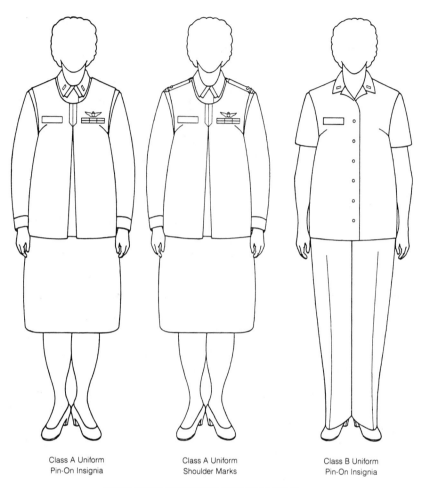

| Class A Uniform | Class A Uniform | Class B Uniform |
| Pin-On Insignia | Shoulder Marks | Pin-On Insignia |

ARMY GREEN MATERNITY SERVICE UNIFORM.

able for social functions of a formal or informal nature after retreat. Appropriate civilian maternity attire is also authorized in lieu of the uniform. Worn with the skirt, the class A uniform constitutes a dress uniform and is authorized for wear at social functions of a private or official nature either before or after retreat, and as designated by the host.

Authorized Material. The skirt, slacks, and tunic all are made of 100 percent texturized polyester, Army green shade 434. The skirt is three-gored, knee length, with an elastic waistband and a nylon knitted stretch front panel. The slacks are straight leg, with an elastic waistband and a nylon knitted stretch front panel. The tunic is hip length, sleeveless, with inverted pleat, waist adjustment tabs and a back centered side closure.

Ornamentation. There is no ornamentation on the tunic or skirt. The slacks have a 1-inch-wide braid of black mohair, mercerized cotton, or polyester sewn on the outside seam of the legs from the bottom of the waistband to the bottom of the legs.

Headgear. The service cap, garrison cap, and black beret are authorized (see the descriptions earlier). Headgear is not required when the maternity dress uniform is worn to evening social functions.

Ornamentation and Insignia. The following are authorized for wear on the class A green maternity uniform:

> Insignia of grade (pin-on or shoulder marks)
> Headgear insignia
> Distinctive unit insignia
> Regimental affiliation crest
> Decoration and service medal ribbons
> Unit awards
> U.S. badges (identification, marksmanship, and special skill)
> Nameplate
> Aiguillette, fouraggere/lanyard

Insignia and ornamentation on the class B uniform are:

> Insignia of grade
> Headgear insignia
> Decorations and awards
> Nameplate

ARMY BLUE UNIFORM—FEMALE

The Army blue uniform is authorized for year-round wear by all female personnel. All active duty female officers are required to own the uniform, unless the period of active duty is for six months or less.

Composition. The Army blue uniform consists of a blue coat and skirt with a white shirt and a black neck tab. Black pumps with sheer stockings are the authorized footwear. A black dress handbag of leather (on duty or off duty) or fabric (off duty only) is carried with this uniform.

Occasions for Wear. The blue uniform may be worn on duty as prescribed by the local commander, for social functions of a general or official nature before or after retreat, and on other appropriate occasions as desired by the individual.

Authorized Materials. The coat, skirt, and service hat will be of the same material. Authorized materials are: wool barathea, 12- or 14-ounce; wool gabardine, 11- or 14.5-ounce; wool elastique, 16-ounce; wool tropical, 10.5-ounce; and polyester/wool blend in gabardine, 10.5-ounce, all Army blue shade 150; or polyester/wool blend in tropical weight, 9.5-ounce, Army blue shade 450.

Coat and Ornamentation. The coat is single-breasted, hip length, with two slanted front pockets, long sleeve, and an easy-fitting open collar. It has four buttons. General officers wear on each sleeve a 1 1/2-inch-wide band of gold braid (or authorized substitute material) positioned parallel to and with the bottom of the braid 3 inches above the end of the sleeve. All other officers have a 3/4-inch braid consisting of two 1/4-inch gold braids spaced 1/4 inch apart over silk material of the first-named color of their basic branch. The bottom of the braid is parallel to and 3 inches above the bottom of the sleeve.

Skirt and Ornamentation. The skirt is an approved pattern, knee length, slightly flared with a waistband and a zipper closure on the left side. The skirt has no ornamentation.

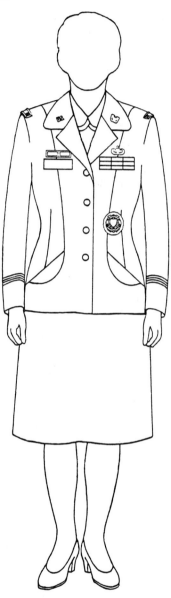

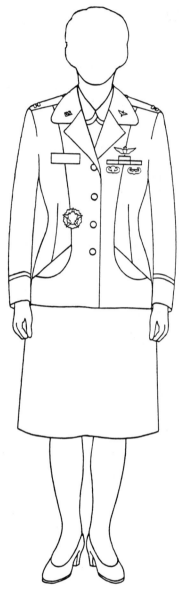

Army Blue Uniform   Army White Uniform

Headgear. The Army blue service hat is worn with this uniform. The hat is the same shape as the service hat for the green classic uniform and uses the detachable hatband with ornamentation as described earlier for the green service hat.

Shoulder Straps. Insignia of grade for the Army blue uniform are embroidered on shoulder straps as described earlier for the male Army blue uniform. Shoulder straps for female officers are identical to those for male officers except for size. The female shoulder strap is 3½ inches long, while the male shoulder strap is 4 inches long. Both are 1⅝ inches wide.

Ornamentation and Insignia. As described earlier for the Army blue uniform for male officers, except that distinctive items authorized for infantry personnel are not worn by female officers.

ARMY WHITE UNIFORM—FEMALE

The Army white uniform is authorized for optional wear by all female personnel. It normally is worn from April to October except in clothing zones I and II (I—warm or hot all year; II—warm or hot summers, mild winters; see CTA 50-900) where it may be worn year-round.

Composition. A white coat and skirt with a white shirt and attached black neck tab comprise the Army white uniform. A white leather handbag may be carried both on duty and off duty with this uniform. A white fabric handbag may be carried after duty hours. White pumps with sheer stockings are the authorized footwear.

Authorized Materials. The authorized uniform materials are: white cotton twill, 8.2-ounce; white polyester/rayon blended fabric in gabardine, 6- or 8-ounce; and white polyester texturized woven serge, 6.5-ounce. Coat, skirt, and hat are of the same material.

Coat and Ornamentation. The Army white coat is long sleeve, single-breasted, four-button, hip length, with two slanted front pockets. All officers wear a band of white mohair or white mercerized cotton braid, ½ inch wide, sewn on each sleeve parallel to and with the bottom edge 3 inches above the bottom of the sleeve.

Skirt and Ornamentation. The skirt is of an approved pattern, knee length, slightly flared, with a waistband and a zipper closure on the left side. It has no ornamentation.

Headgear. The white service hat is of the same shape as the green service hat. It is made of the same material as the coat and uses the detachable hatband ornamented as described for the green service hat.

Ornamentation and Insignia. Ornamentation and insignia worn on the white coat are the same as described for the male Army white uniform, except that distinctive items for infantry personnel are not worn by females.

ARMY BLUE MESS AND EVENING MESS UNIFORMS—FEMALE

The Army blue mess and blue evening mess uniforms are authorized for year-round wear by all female personnel.

Composition. The blue mess uniform consists of the Army blue jacket, a blue knee-length skirt, a white formal blouse with dress black neck tab, and a black

Army Blue Mess Uniform
General Officers

Army Blue Evening
Mess Uniform
Other Officers

cummerbund. The blue evening mess uniform substitutes a full-length skirt for the knee-length skirt. Black pumps with sheer stockings are worn with these uniforms, and a black fabric handbag (dress) is carried.

Occasions for Wear. The blue mess and blue evening mess uniforms are authorized for wear at social functions of a general or official nature after retreat, and at private formal social functions after retreat. The blue evening mess uniform is the most formal uniform worn by female personnel.

Authorized Materials. The authorized materials for the Army blue mess jacket and skirts are: wool barathea, 14-ounce; wool elastique, 15-ounce; wool gabardine, 11- or 14.5-ounce; or wool tropical, 9-ounce, each in Army blue shade 150; and polyester and wool blended fabric in gabardine, 9.5-ounce; or polyester and wool in tropical, 9.5-ounce, each in Army blue shade 450.

Jacket and Ornamentation. The Army blue mess jacket is cut on the lines of an evening dress coat, descending to the point of the hips, and slightly curved to a peak in the front and the back. It is fully lined, with an inside vertical pocket on the right side. The coat front has six gold-color 20-ligne buttons. Two 20-ligne gold-color buttons may be joined by a small gold or gold-color chain in the upper buttonholes. Shoulder knots of gold bullion (or authorized substitute) are worn on the shoulders of the jacket by all officers.

Lapels. Lapels of the jacket are of rayon, acetate, or other synthetic fabric in colors as follows: general officers, except chaplains—dark blue; all chaplains—black; all other officers—first-named color of the officer's basic branch.

Sleeves. General officers wear a cuff of blue-black velvet braid, 4 inches in width, positioned 1/8 inch from the bottom of each sleeve, with a band of oak leaves in groups of two, 1 inch in width, positioned with the top of the band 1 inch below the top of the cuff. Insignia of grade, of embroidered silver bullion, is centered on the outside of the sleeves, 1 inch above the upper edge of the cuff. If branch insignia is worn, it is centered on the outside of the sleeve, 1 inch above the top of the cuff, and the insignia of grade is positioned 1 inch above the branch insignia. Other officers wear on each sleeve a 3/4-inch braid consisting of two 1/4-inch stripes of two vellum gold (or authorized substitute) spaced 1/4 inch apart over a silk stripe of the first-named color of their basic branch. The braid is positioned so that it is parallel to, with the bottom 3 inches above, the end of the sleeve. On each sleeve is a trefoil consisting of a knot of three loops of 1/4-inch gold (or authorized substitute), interlaced at the points of crossing, with the ends resting on the sleeve band. Insignia of grade (metal or embroidered silver bullion) is worn vertically in the center of the space formed by the lower curves of the knot and the top of the sleeve band.

Skirts and Ornamentation. The blue mess skirt is knee length, while the blue evening mess skirt is full length. Both have a one-piece front with waist darts on each side, a four-piece back, a zipper closure on the left side, and a sewn-on waistband, which is closed with three hooks and eyes. Both skirts are fully lined. Neither has any special ornamentation.

Headgear. None.

Cape. Either the Army blue or the Army black cape is authorized for optional wear with the blue mess and blue evening mess uniforms. For a description of the capes and the other uniform accessories, see the later section, *Accessory Items of Uniforms.*

Ornamentation and Insignia. Ornamentation and insignia are the same as for the male blue mess and blue evening mess uniforms, except that females wear no headgear insignia.

ARMY WHITE MESS, ALL-WHITE MESS, AND EVENING WHITE MESS UNIFORMS—FEMALE

The Army white mess, all-white mess, and evening white mess uniforms are authorized for wear by all female personnel. These uniforms normally are worn from April to October, except in clothing zones I and II (CTA 50-900) where they may be worn year-round.

Occasions for Wear. These uniforms are worn to social functions of a general or official nature after retreat, and to private formal social functions after retreat.

Composition. The Army white mess uniform consists of the Army white jacket, a black knee-length skirt, the white formal blouse with dress black neck tab, and the black cummerbund. The all-white mess uniform is the same except that a white knee-length skirt is substituted for the black skirt, and a white cummerbund is substituted for the black cummerbund. The evening white mess uniform uses a full-length black skirt instead of the knee-length skirt; it is worn with the black cummerbund. Black pumps and sheer stockings are worn with—and a black fabric handbag may be carried with—the white mess and white evening mess uniforms. White pumps are worn with the all-white mess uniform, and a white fabric handbag may be carried. None of these uniforms has any headgear.

Authorized Materials. The white jacket and white skirt are made from either white polyester/rayon fabric in a gabardine weave, 6- or 8-ounce; or white texturized polyester serge, 6.5-ounce. The black skirts are made from wool tropical, 8.5-ounce, Army black shade 149; or polyester and wool blended fabric in tropical weave, 10-ounce, Army black shade 332.

Jacket and Ornamentation. Two versions of the jacket are authorized.

New Version. The jacket is cut along the natural waistline and is slightly curved to a peak in the front and the back. The jacket has a shawl collar and is fully lined, with an inside vertical pocket on the right side. Three 20-ligne gold-color buttons are on each side of the front opening. Two additional 20-ligne gold-color buttons with a short (about 1 1/2 inches) gold-color chain may be used to join the upper buttonholes. All officers wear shoulder knots of gold bullion or authorized substitute material. On the sleeves, general officers wear a cuff of white mohair or mercerized cotton braid, 4 inches in width, positioned 1/8 inch from the end of the sleeve. Insignia of grade, of embroidered white cloth or silver bullion, is centered on the outside of the sleeve, 1 inch above the cuff braid. If branch insignia is worn, it is centered on the outside of the sleeve, 1 inch above the top of the cuff braid, and the insignia of grade is positioned 1 inch above the branch insignia.

Other officers wear on each sleeve a band of white mohair or white mercerized cotton, 1/2 inch in width, with the bottom of the band parallel to and 3 inches above the bottom of the sleeve. On each sleeve is a trefoil, consisting of a knot of three loops of 1/4-inch white soutache braid, interlaced at points of crossing, with the ends resting on the sleeve band. Insignia of grade, pin-on metal or embroidered cloth, is worn vertically in the center of the space formed by the lower curves of the knot and the top of the sleeve band.

Old Version. The jacket is single breasted with a natural waist length and a shawl-type collar. There are three 20-ligne gold-color buttons on each side of the front. General officers wear gold (or authorized substitute material) shoulder knots, and sleeve ornamentation as described for the new version of the jacket. Other

Army White Evening
Mess Uniform
General Officers
(Old Version)

Army White Mess Uniform
Other Officers
(New Version)

officers wear shoulder boards denoting grade and on each sleeve a band of $\frac{1}{2}$-inch-wide white mohair or white mercerized cotton braid, with the bottom of the braid parallel to and 3 inches above the end of the sleeve. The old version of the white mess jacket may be worn until no longer serviceable.

Skirts and Ornamentation. Both the white mess skirt (black) and the all-white mess skirt (white) are knee length with a one-panel front and a four-panel back, of straight design, with a waistband and a zipper closure on the left side. The full-length black skirt for wear with the white evening mess uniform is of similar design but with an overlapped center back pleat. None of the skirts has any ornamentation.

Headgear. None.

Accessory Items. The black cummerbund, the white cummerbund, the formal blouse, and the Army blue or Army black capes (either of which may be worn with each of the uniforms) are described in the later section, *Accessory Items of Uniforms*. Black pumps with sheer stockings are worn with the white mess and white evening mess uniforms, while white pumps with sheer stockings are worn with the all-white mess uniform. The black dress fabric handbag is carried with the white mess and white evening mess uniforms, and the white dress fabric handbag is carried with the all-white mess uniform.

Ornamentation and Insignia. Ornamentation and insignia are the same as for the male white mess and white evening mess uniforms, except that there is no headgear insignia for females.

ARMY BLACK MESS AND EVENING MESS UNIFORMS

The Army black mess and black evening mess uniforms are authorized for year-round wear by all female officers. These uniforms are being replaced by the Army blue mess and blue evening mess uniforms, but no wear-out date has been established.

Occasions for Wear. The black mess and black evening mess uniforms are worn after retreat at social functions of a general or official nature and at private formal social functions.

Composition. The Army black mess uniform consists of a black jacket, a black knee-length skirt, a white formal blouse with dress black neck tab, and a black cummerbund. The black evening mess uniform is the same except that a full-length black skirt is worn instead of the knee-length skirt. Black fabric pumps and sheer stockings are worn with these uniforms, and a black fabric dress handbag is carried.

Authorized Materials. The authorized materials for the jacket and skirts are wool tropical, 8.5-ounce, Army black shade 149; and polyester and wool blended fabric, 10-ounce, Army black shade 332.

Jacket and Ornamentation. The jacket is single breasted, natural waist length, with a shawl-type collar. It has a two-piece front (each side) and a two-panel back. Three 20-ligne gold-color buttons are worn on each side of the front. General officers wear shoulder knots on each shoulder (see the earlier description for the Army blue mess jacket), while other officers wear shoulder boards denoting grade.

Sleeves. General officers wear a cuff of blue-black velvet, 4 inches in width, positioned $\frac{1}{8}$ inch from the lower edge of each sleeve. On each cuff braid, 1 inch below the upper edge, is a 1-inch band of embroidered oak leaves, in groups of two, of gold or authorized substitute material. Insignia is placed on the sleeve as described for the Army blue mess jacket. Other officers wear a band of black

Army Black Evening
Mess Uniform
General Officers

Army Black Mess Uniform
Other Officers

mohair or black mercerized cotton braid, $1/2$ inch in width, on each sleeve, positioned so that the bottom of the braid is parallel to and 3 inches from the bottom edge of the sleeve.

Skirts and Ornamentation. The Army black mess skirt and the black evening mess skirt are the black skirts described earlier that are worn with the Army white mess and the white evening mess uniforms. The skirts have no ornamentation.

Headgear. None.

Accessory Items. The black cummerbund, the white formal blouse with dress black neck tab, and the Army blue or Army black capes (either of which may be worn with these uniforms) are described in the later section, *ACCESSORY ITEMS OF UNIFORMS*.

Ornamentation and Insignia. Ornamentation and insignia are the same as for the Army blue mess and blue evening mess uniforms.

FIELD AND UTILITY UNIFORMS

Field and utility uniforms for both male and female personnel and various organization uniforms such as hospital duty uniforms and flight uniforms are all categorized as class C uniforms. In general, these uniforms are for duty wear only and are not to be worn off the military installation except in transit between the individual's quarters and the duty station. However, installation commanders in CONUS, the MACOM commanders overseas, and the state adjutants general for ARNG personnel may publish exceptions to this policy. These uniforms are not intended to be worn when other uniforms are more appropriate.

TEMPERATE AND HOT-WEATHER BATTLE DRESS UNIFORM

The battle dress uniforms (BDUs) are authorized for year-round on-duty wear by all personnel when prescribed by the commander.

Occasions for Wear. BDUs may only be worn on duty when prescribed by the commander. They are not for travel and may not be worn off the military installation except when in transit between the station and the individual's quarters, unless a special exception has been granted in writing by the authorized commander.

Composition. The BDUs consist of a coat and trousers, a visored cap, and a cold-weather coat (field jacket—Author), all in camouflage patterns. Both hot-weather and temperate coat-and-trouser combinations are available. The fabric of the hot-weather BDU is 100 percent ripstop cotton, while the fabric of the temperate BDU is 50/50 nylon and cotton twill. The same BDU cap is worn with both the hot-weather and the temperate BDUs.

Accessories. A black web belt with black, open-face buckle, combat boots, and brown undershirts are worn with the BDUs. Females may carry either the black service handbag or, at their option, a black, clutch-type handbag, only while in a garrison environment. An organizational beret may be worn in lieu of the BDU cap, and jungle boots may be worn in lieu of the combat boots when not in formation. The green scarf may be worn with the cold-weather coat.

Insignia and Accouterments. Only the following insignia and accouterments are worn with the BDUs:

> Badges (subdued), (combat and special skill, identification, and special skill and marksmanship tabs)
> Brassards
> Branch insignia

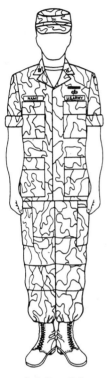

Cold Weather Cap
Camouflage

Cold Weather
Jacket
(Field Jacket)

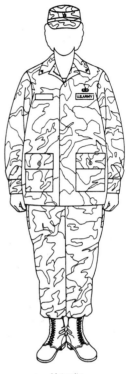

Battle Dress Uniform
Temperate and Hot Weather

Maternity
Work Uniform

    Grade insignia
    Headgear insignia
    Combat leader's identification tab
    Subdued shoulder sleeve insignia (current organization and former wartime
       service)
    Nametape and U.S. Army distinguishing tape

Foreign badges, distinctive unit insignia, and regimental affiliation crest are not worn on the BDUs.

Manner of Wear. The BDUs are not to be altered; they are designed to be loose fitting. The waist take-up tabs of the coat will be buttoned at all times. Trousers will be bloused or tucked into the boots. The sleeves may be rolled above the elbow, but not more than 3 inches above the elbow, and the camouflage pattern must remain exposed. The BDUs may be pressed but not starched.

    The BDU cap is worn straight on the head so that the cap band creates a straight line around the head parallel to the ground. No hair will be visible on the forehead under the cap. The cap will not be blocked. Officers wear nonsubdued insignia of grade on the cap while in a garrison environment and subdued insignia of grade in the field. The organizational beret may be substituted for the BDU cap if authorized.

MATERNITY WORK UNIFORM

    The maternity work uniform is authorized for year-round wear by pregnant female personnel when prescribed by the commander.

Occasions for Wear. The maternity work uniform is worn in lieu of the BDU and under the same restrictions for wear as the BDU.

Composition. The maternity work uniform consists of the BDU cap, the cold-weather coat, and the maternity coat and maternity trousers, both in a camouflage pattern. However, it is not to be referred to as a maternity BDU.

Accessories, Insignia, and Manner of Wear. The maternity work uniform is worn with the same accessories, the same insignia, and accouterments, and in the same manner as the BDU.

DESERT BATTLE DRESS UNIFORM

The desert battle dress uniform (DBDU) is authorized for year-round wear on duty by all personnel when issued as organizational clothing and prescribed by the commander.

Occasions for Wear. The DBDU is worn under the same guidelines and the same restrictions as the BDU.

Composition. The DBDU consists of a coat, trousers, and hat in a desert camouflage, daytime pattern; and a parka and trousers in a desert camouflage, nighttime pattern.

Accessories, Insignia, and Manner of Wear. The DBDU is worn with the same accessories, the same insignia and accouterments, and in the same manner as the BDU. The DBDU hat is worn so that no hair is visible on the forehead under the hat and with the chin strap pulled up under the chin. The parka is worn buttoned.

COLD-WEATHER UNIFORM

The OG 108 cold-weather uniform is authorized for year-round wear by all personnel when issued as organizational clothing and prescribed by the commander.

Occasions for Wear. The cold-weather uniform is worn under the same guidelines and with the same restrictions as the BDU. Components of this uniform may be worn with utility and other organizational uniforms as part of a cold-weather ensemble when issued and prescribed by the commander.

Composition. The basic uniform components are of wool serge, olive green shade 108. The uniform consists of a wool serge shirt (male and female versions), wool serge trousers, cold-weather wind-resistant cotton and nylon trousers, and either the cold-weather cap or the BDU cap.

Accessories. The black web belt with open face black buckle, combat boots, and a brown undershirt are worn with this uniform. Either the BDU field jacket or a cold-weather coat (parka) may be worn, as well as black leather gloves and the olive green scarf.

Insignia and Accouterments. Only the following insignia and accouterments may be worn with the cold-weather uniform:

    Badges (combat and special skill, subdued, pin-on only)
    Brassards
    Branch insignia (subdued, pin-on only)
    Grade insignia (subdued, pin-on only)
    Headgear insignia

Nametape and U.S. Army distinguishing tape (the nametape will not be worn on the parka)

Combat leader's identification tab (only on the field jacket)

Shoulder sleeve insignia will not be worn on the shirts, nor will pin-on collar insignia or nametapes and U.S. Army distinguishing tapes if the shirts are prescribed for wear only as undergarments. Foreign badges, distinctive unit insignia, regimental affiliation crest, and sew-on badges and insignia of grade will not be worn on this uniform.

Manner of Wear. The cold-weather uniform is designed to be loose fitting, and alterations are not authorized. When the shirt is worn as an outer garment, it will be tucked inside the trousers and a belt will be worn with the trousers. If the trousers are worn as an outer garment, they will be bloused. The shirt sleeves may not be rolled up. Females may, at their option, wear either the female or male version of the shirt. When the cold-weather cap is worn, it will be worn so that no hair is visible on the forehead. Ear flaps will either be fastened up or fastened under the chin. The BDU cap may be worn, or an organizational beret may be worn if authorized. The shirt collar is worn inside the field jacket and other authorized outer garments.

HOSPITAL DUTY UNIFORM—MALE

The male hospital duty uniform is authorized for year-round wear by all male officers in the Army Nurse Corps and the Army Medical Specialist Corps.

Occasions for Wear. The hospital duty uniform is worn on duty in medical care facilities as prescribed by the medical commander. It is not for travel and may not be worn off the military installation except when in transit between the station and the individual's quarters. Commanders may authorize exception to this policy when medical personnel are providing support to civilian activities such as parades and ceremonies.

Composition. There are three principal components of this uniform: a hip-length white smock with left breast pocket, front button closure, and straight-cut bottom; white trousers of standard design with two slash pockets in front, two patch pockets in back, and front zipper closure, with belt loops; and a white, knee-length, physician's smock with front button closure and upper and lower pockets. Officers wear white oxford shoes and white socks with this uniform. The black web belt with open face buckle is worn on the trousers. The garrison cap is the standard headgear.

Insignia and Accouterments. Nonsubdued branch and grade insignia, headgear insignia, and a nameplate are the only authorized items worn with this uniform.

Manner of Wear. Officers assigned to the Army Nurse Corps wear the short white smock and white trousers. Officers assigned to the medical, dental, veterinary, medical service, or medical specialty corps may wear the physicians' white smock over the service or utility uniforms while in the medical care facility or on duty as directed by the facility commander.

HOSPITAL DUTY AND MATERNITY UNIFORMS—FEMALE

The female hospital duty and hospital duty maternity uniforms are authorized for year-round wear by all female officers in the Army Nurse Corps and the Army Medical Specialist Corps.

Occasions for Wear. Same as for the male hospital duty uniform.

Composition. Uniform materials are white cotton or white polyester. There are two principal variants of the hospital duty uniform. One is a knee-length, short-sleeve white dress with front button closure, wing tip collars, and a belt. The second is a tunic and pants uniform; the tunic is an over-the-hip design with wing collars, short sleeves, and side pockets; the pants are straight legged. The physician's smock, as described previously, is part of the ensemble.

The maternity variants of the uniform consist of a white maternity dress, and white maternity slacks and tunic, both of any plain, unadorned, commercial design, with wing collars suitable for placement of insignia.

White oxfords and white stockings or socks will be worn with these uniforms by officers. The tunic is worn outside the pants. The garrison cap or the black beret are authorized headgear.

Insignia and Accouterments. Only nonsubdued grade and branch insignia, headgear insignia, and a nameplate are worn with this uniform.

FLIGHT UNIFORM

The flight uniform is authorized for year-round wear by all Army personnel in accordance with CTA 50-900, when prescribed by the commander.

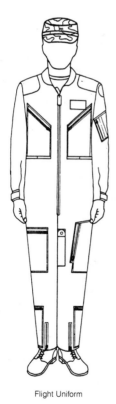

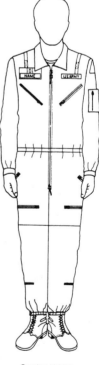

Nomex Jacket
(CVC Uniform)

(Flight Jacket
similar)

Flight Uniform

Combat Vehicle
Crewman's Uniform

Occasions for Wear. The flight uniform is worn on duty when flying, when on standby awaiting flight, or as directed by the commander. It is not worn for travel or off military installations except when in transit between the station and the individual's quarters.

Composition. The basic flight uniform is a one-piece flight suit (coveralls), unlined, with zipper front closure, hook and pile fastener tape adjustments for the waist and sleeves, and a zipper at the bottom of each leg. There are six patch pockets, two at the breast, two at the thigh, and two at the lower leg. all with zippered closures, plus a zippered utility pocket on the left sleeve and a knife pocket on the inside of the left thigh. Flight gloves and a fully lined flight jacket complete the ensemble. The BDU cap or an organizational beret are authorized headgear. The uniform is worn with combat boots, but unbloused.

Insignia and Accouterments. A 2-inch by 4-inch black leather nameplate is attached to a 2-inch by 4-inch Velcro attachment on the left breast. The nameplate has the appropriate crewmember's badge on the first line, full name (first, middle initial, last) on the second line, and abbreviated grade and the words *U.S. Army* on the third line. Subdued shoulder sleeve insignia is worn 1/2 inch below the shoulder seam. Officers wear subdued embroidered insignia of grade on each shoulder of the flight suit and the flight jacket. Local commanders may authorize the wear of solid baseball caps by aircraft and ground crewmembers as a safety and identification measure.

COMBAT VEHICLE CREWMAN UNIFORM

The combat vehicle crewman (CVC) uniform is authorized for year-round wear by combat vehicle crewmen when issued in accordance with CTA 50-900 and prescribed by the commander.

Occasions for Wear. The CVC uniform is worn on duty when prescribed by the commander. It is not worn for travel or off the military installation except when in transit between the station and the individual's quarters.

Composition. The basic uniform consists of a one-piece coverall and a cold-weather jacket. The coveralls have a zippered front closure, drop seat, extraction strap located at the upper back, and pockets located on the left sleeve, right-left chest, right-left front hips, right-left upper thigh, and right-left lower legs. All the pockets have zipper closures. The cold-weather jacket is single breasted with a zipper closure and an inside protective flap. The back has a yoke and retrieval strap opening. There are two slash pockets and a utility pocket on the left sleeve; the sleeves have elbow patches. The cuffs and waistband are rib knit. The uniform is worn with combat boots, but unbloused. The BDU cap is the standard headgear when the CVC helmet is not being worn. The jacket may be worn only with the CVC uniform.

Insignia and Accouterments. Only the following insignia are authorized for wear with the CVC uniform:

Grade insignia (subdued)
Headgear insignia
Nametape and U.S. Army distinguishing tape
Shoulder sleeve insignia (subdued, current organization)

The U.S. Army tape is worn approximately 1/2 inch up from the outside zipper seam on the left chest, horizontal to the ground. The nametape is worn on the right side in line with the U.S. Army tape. Subdued sew-on insignia of grade is worn centered and ¼ inch above the nametape. On the cold-weather jacket, the nametapes and U.S. Army tapes are positioned approximately 1½ inches above the top of the pocket flaps. Otherwise, positioning of insignia on the coveralls and the jacket is the same.

PHYSICAL TRAINING UNIFORM

The physical training uniform is authorized for year-round wear by all personnel when prescribed by the commander.

Occasions for Wear. The physical training uniform may be worn on duty and off duty, both on and off the military reservation, when actually engaged in physical training. It may be worn while in transit between the individual's quarters and the duty station.

Composition. The uniform consists of a reversible jersey, gym shoes, sweat pants, sweat shirt, and general-purpose trunks. It may be worn with a navy blue knit cap and with running shoes, gloves, long underwear, or other items appropriate to weather conditions when authorized by the commander.

Insignia. No insignia are worn on this uniform.

Manner of Wear. The physical training uniform is organizational issue. Commanders may allow physical training to be conducted in utility uniforms or individually purchased athletic clothes. Females cannot be required to wear the jersey or an undershirt as an outer garment. They may wear the sweat shirt, if issued, the utility shirt if a utility uniform is prescribed, or the corresponding outer garment when wear of individually purchased athletic clothing is authorized.

ACCESSORY ITEMS OF UNIFORMS

There are a number of articles that are used with all or a number of the uniforms. In addition, there are a number of optional items that may be worn or carried. These are described in this section. See AR 670-1 for detailed descriptions. Issue items may be purchased by officers through the military clothing sales store (MCSS) at the post exchange. The PX also carries many of the optional items, purchased from commercial sources.

Belt, Waist. Two web waist belts are available, one with a black tip, which is an enlisted clothing bag issue item, and one with a brass tip, for optional purchase. The black-tipped belt with an open face black buckle is worn with utility uniforms. Either the black-tip belt or the optional brass-tip belt is worn with a solid brass buckle on service and dress uniforms. The belt is worn with the tipped end passing through the buckle to the wearer's left. The belt fabric may not protrude beyond the edge of the brass buckle, and the tipped end of the belt will not protrude more than two inches beyond the end of the open face buckle.

Beret. Organizational berets are authorized for wear by personnel assigned to Ranger units (black beret), Special Forces units (green beret), and Airborne units (maroon beret). Except for color, all berets are the same. All are organizational issue items. The beret is worn with the headband straight across the forehead, 1 inch above the eyebrows, with the top draped over the right ear and the stiffener positioned over the left eye. The adjusting ribbon is cut off and the knot concealed inside the edge binding at the back of the beret. Berets may be worn only with service uniforms and utility uniforms. Personnel wearing berets may wear combat boots with the service uniform with the trousers or slacks bloused.

Boots. The black combat boots are issue items. A new style boot with a deep lug tread sole, a closed-loop lace system, and a padded collar is replacing the older style, but either style is authorized for wear. In addition, boots of commercial design with a plain or capped toe may be worn. Boots of patent leather or poromeric material are not authorized. The boots are diagonally laced with black laces, with the excess lace tucked into the boot top or under bloused trousers or slacks. Organizational boots (jungle boots, flyer boots, safety boots) prescribed and issued by the commander may be worn instead of the combat boot with field and utility uniforms.

Buttons. Buttons used on the service, dress, and mess uniforms are of prescribed design, gold-plated or gold-color anodized aluminum. Officers other than those of the Corps of Engineers wear the button bearing the U.S. Coat of Arms. Engineer officers wear the Essayons button. This is believed to have been designed by Col. Jonathan Williams, first Chief Engineer of the present Corps of Engineers, who was also the first Superintendent of the U.S. Military Academy. The first authoritative reference to the special design is contained in General Orders No. 7, AGO, 18 February 1840.

Blouse, Formal. The white formal blouse worn by females with the mess and evening mess uniforms is an optional purchase item. It is tuck-in style, made of polyester and cotton, with a front closure having seven removable, dome-shaped buttons. Three rows of vertical ruffles are on each side of the front opening.

Cap, Cold-Weather. The cold-weather cap is an optional purchase item. It is of Army green shade 344 fabric with a black synthetic fur visor and side flaps. An eyelet is provided in the center of the visor to attach headgear insignia. The cap is worn straight on the head with the headgear insignia centered and with no hair showing on the forehead. The side flaps either will be fastened up or fastened under the chin if worn down. The cap is authorized for wear only when wearing the black, all-weather coat with the service, dress, and mess uniforms. It may not be worn with the black windbreaker or the black pullover sweater.

Capes. *Male.* Officers may purchase a blue cape for wear with the Army blue dress, blue mess and blue evening mess uniforms. The cape extends to the mid-point of the knee. The capes are fully lined. The lining color for general officers is dark blue. For all other officers, the color of the lining is the first-named color of the officer's basic branch.

Female. Officers may purchase either a blue cape or a black cape for wear with any of the mess and evening mess uniforms. The blue cape is finger-tip length, with lining as described for the male cape. The black cape is knee-length with a white satin lining.

Chaplain's Apparel. Chaplain's scarves are organizational issue items. Black scarves for the Christian faith and black or white scarves for the Jewish faith have appropriate ecclesiastical markings embroidered on one end and the U.S. Coat of Arms embroidered on the other end. Chaplains are authorized to wear the military uniform, vestments, or other appropriate attire when conducting religious services.

Coat, All-Weather. The black all-weather coat is an issue item. The coat is worn by all personnel and may be worn with or without a zip-in liner with the service, dress, mess, and hospital duty uniforms. Only nonsubdued insignia is worn on the coat. Without insignia, the coat may be worn with civilian clothing.

| Black Cape Female | Blue Cape Female | Cardigan Sweater Female |

| Blue Cape Male | Windbreaker | Cardigan Sweater Male |

Cover, Cap. A transparent plastic rain cap cover with a visor protector is authorized for optional purchase and wear by male personnel when wearing the green, blue, or white service caps.

Cuff Links and Studs. Cuff links and studs are authorized for optional purchase and wear. Gold cuff links, round, plain face, and ½ to ¾ inches in diameter may be worn by male personnel with the Army blue and Army white uniforms, and with the Army blue mess and Army white mess uniforms. Studs for these mess uniforms also are gold-color, ¼ to ⅜ inches in diameter. For wear with the blue evening mess uniform, plain white (such as mother-of-pearl) cuff links and studs, with or without platinum rims, or white gold, will be worn.

Cummerbunds. Cummerbunds are authorized for optional purchase and wear. Each is of commercial design with four or five pleats running the entire length and is worn with the pleats facing down. Males wear a black cummerbund with a bow tie of the same material with the blue mess and white mess uniforms. Females wear a black cummerbund with all mess and evening mess uniforms, except that a white cummerbund is worn with the all-white mess uniform.

Gloves. Three types of gloves are authorized. Black leather shell gloves with inserts are issue items and are for wear with utility uniforms by all personnel. Black leather dress gloves, also an issue item, are for wear by all personnel with the class A service uniform, and when wearing the black all-weather coat or black wind-breaker. White dress gloves are authorized for optional purchase for wear with the dress, mess, and evening mess uniforms. When prescribed by the commander, military police may wear white gloves with the service uniforms.

Handbags. There are four types of handbags.

A black service handbag, of polyurethane or leather, is an issue item and may be carried with the service, utility, and Army dress uniforms.

A black, clutch-type handbag of leather, polyurethane, or vinyl, with zipper, snap, or envelope-type closure, is authorized for optional purchase. It may be carried with the green service uniform and the utility uniforms in a garrison environment. The handbag may have a wrist strap but not a shoulder strap. The leather version of this handbag is also authorized to be carried with the female Army blue uniform during and after duty hours.

A black dress handbag of fabric or leather is authorized for optional purchase. It is untrimmed, envelope or clutch style, of commercial design, with or without chain. The leather version may be carried with the Army blue uniform during and after duty hours. The fabric version may be carried with the blue and black mess and evening mess uniforms, and may be carried with the Army blue uniform after duty hours.

A white dress handbag of fabric or leather is authorized for optional purchase. It is untrimmed, of commercial design, envelope or clutch style, with or without chain. The leather handbag may be carried with the Army white uniform during and after duty hours. The fabric handbag may be carried with the all-white mess uniform and with the white dress uniform after duty hours.

Judge's Apparel. Judge's robes are organizational issue. They are of the type customarily worn in the U.S. Court of Military Appeal and are worn over the service uniform.

Neck Tabs. The black service neck tab for females is an issue item. It is always worn with the AG 415 long-sleeve shirt and may be worn with the short-sleeve AG 415 shirt. A black dress neck tab is an optional purchase item for wear with the formal white blouse with the mess and evening mess uniforms.

Neckties. The black four-in-hand necktie for males is an issue item. It is always worn with the green long-sleeve shirt and may be worn with the short-sleeve green shirt. A black bow tie is an optional purchase item for wear with the Army blue and white uniforms after retreat, and with the blue mess and white mess uniforms. A white bow tie may be purchased for wear with the blue evening mess and white evening mess uniforms.

Overshoes. Black overshoes of rubber or synthetic material, commercial design, are authorized for optional purchase and wear with oxford shoes by male person-nel when not in formation. They may be worn with the service, dress, and mess uniforms.

Scarves. A black scarf of commercial design, about 12 by 52 inches, of wool, silk, or rayon, may be purchased and worn by all personnel with the black all-weather coat and the windbreaker. When worn, the scarf will be folded in half lengthwise, and crossed left over right at the neck, with the ends tucked neatly into the neckline of the outer garment. An organizational issue green wool scarf may be worn with the field jacket. Manner of wearing is the same as for the black scarf.

Shirts. *Female.* A white, short-sleeve shirt with black neck tab is worn by female personnel with the Army blue dress and Army white dress uniforms.

Male. A white, long-sleeve shirt of standard design with turn-down collar and either barrel or French cuffs is worn by male personnel with the Army blue dress and Army white dress uniforms.

A white semiformal dress shirt with long sleeves, a soft bosom, French cuffs, and a standard turn-down collar is worn by males with the blue mess and white mess uniforms.

A white, formal dress shirt with long sleeves, a stiff bosom, French cuffs, and a wing-type collar is worn by male personnel with the evening mess uniforms.

Shoes. *Males.* Black oxfords of leather (issue item) or poromeric material without contrasting soles are worn with the service, dress, and mess uniforms. Patent leather is not authorized. A chukka boot or similar commercial design is also authorized. White oxfords are worn by Army Nurse Corps and Army Medical Specialist Corps officers with the hospital duty uniform.

Females. Black oxfords of leather (issue item) or poromeric material with at least three eyelets, closed toe and heel, and heels no higher than 2 inches are worn with the service uniforms. A jodhpur-type boot is also authorized when wearing slacks. Similar white oxfords are worn by officers with the hospital duty and hospital duty maternity uniforms.

Inclement weather boots of black leather, rubber, or synthetic material may be purchased for optional wear by females. These are over-the-foot boots of commercial design, not more than knee high, in a plain style with no trimming. They will have inconspicuously placed zipper or snap closures, and heels no higher than 3 inches. The boots may be worn during inclement weather with the service, dress, and mess uniforms, but must be exchanged for standard footwear when indoors.

Pumps, service, in black (issue item) and white (optional) will be of fine-grain calfskin, poromeric material, or patent leather, untrimmed, with closed toe and heel, and with heels from 1 to 3 inches high and soles not more than $1/2$ inch thick. The black service pumps are authorized for wear by all female personnel with the service and blue dress uniforms. White pumps are authorized for wear with the white dress uniform.

Pumps, dress, in black or white fabric, are of commercial design, untrimmed, with closed toe and heel, heel height from 1 to 3 inches and a sole not more than $1/2$ inch thick. The black dress pumps are worn with the blue and black mess and evening mess uniforms and may be worn with the Army blue uniform after duty hours. The white pumps are worn with the all-white mess uniform and with the Army white uniform after duty hours. *Caution:* Pumps and the handbag must be of the same material.

Socks. Black socks (issue item) are worn with the black oxford by males. White socks are purchased by officers for wear with the white oxford as part of the hospital duty uniform. Olive green, cushion-sole socks are worn by all personnel when wearing combat or organizational-issue boots. Females wear sheer or semi-sheer stockings without seams, and in flesh tones complementary to the wearer and the uniform with the service, dress, and mess uniforms. White stockings, sheer or semi-sheer, are worn with the white oxford with the hospital duty or maternity hospital duty uniforms. Black socks may be worn when wearing the slacks of the service uniform, and white socks may be worn with the white oxfords when wearing the hospital duty pantsuit.

Suspenders. Suspenders may be purchased and worn by males with the dress and mess uniforms, but they must not be visible.

Sweaters. A black cardigan sweater may be purchased and worn within the individual's immediate work area. The male version has five buttons; the female version has no buttons. If worn with the short-sleeve shirt without necktie or neck tab, the shirt collar will be worn outside the sweater. The sweater may also be worn as an outer garment with the hospital duty uniform within a medical facility. Sleeves may not be rolled or pushed up beyond the wrist. Males will wear their sweaters fully buttoned. The cardigan sweater is authorized for wear with civilian clothes.

A black, 100 percent wool, pullover sweater is authorized for optional purchase and wear by all personnel. It may be worn as an outer garment with the class B service uniforms. The collar of the short-sleeve shirt is worn outside the sweater if no tie or neck tab is worn. The sweater may be worn under the black coat and the black windbreaker, but it must not show below the windbreaker. Officers will wear shoulder marks indicating rank on the shoulders of the sweater. The nameplate will be worn centered on the patch. If distinctive unit insignia is also worn, the nameplate must be centered 1/2 inch above the bottom of the patch, with the distinctive unit insignia centered from left to right and from top to bottom above the nameplate. The sweater sleeves may not be rolled or pushed up beyond the wrist. Without insignia, the sweater may be worn with civilian clothes.

Umbrellas. Female personnel only may carry a black umbrella when wearing the service, dress, and mess uniforms. It may not be carried with field or utility uniforms. Males never carry an umbrella.

Undergarments. *Brassieres and panties* of commercial design, white or neutral, will be worn by females with all uniforms. *Slips* of commercial design, white or neutral, are worn by females with the service, dress, and mess skirts, and with the hospital duty dress.

Drawers, either briefs or boxer style, will be worn by male personnel with all uniforms. Brown, boxer-style drawers are the issue item. *Undershirts* of commercial design, white with short sleeves and a V-neck or crew neck (T-shirts) will be worn by male personnel with the service, dress, mess, and hospital duty uniforms.

A *brown undershirt* (issue item) is worn by all personnel with all field uniforms.

Vest. A white vest, single breasted, cut low with a rolling collar and pointed bottom and fastened with three detachable small white buttons is worn by male personnel with the blue evening mess and the white evening mess uniforms.

Windbreaker. A black windbreaker is authorized for optional purchase and wear by all personnel with the class B service and with the hospital duty uniforms. It is worn with nonsubdued grade insignia and must be worn zipped at least three-fourths of the way up. Without insignia, it may be worn with civilian clothing.

INSIGNIA

Insignia worn on the Army's uniforms identify the wearer as to status. Insignia denote grade, branch, organization, duty assignment, and prior Army service. Insignia are made of appropriate color metal or embroidery and are worn on prescribed uniforms, in precise locations.

The "U.S." Insignia. *Male* officers wear the "U.S." insignia on both collars of the Army green, Army white, and Army blue uniform coats. The insignia are positioned 5/8 inch above the cut of the lapel, with the centerline of the insignia bisecting the notch and parallel to the inside edge of the lapel.

Female officers wear the "U.S." insignia on both collars of the coat of the Army

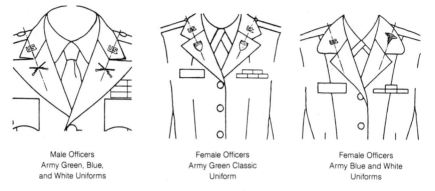

Male Officers
Army Green, Blue,
and White Uniforms

Female Officers
Army Green Classic
Uniform

Female Officers
Army Blue and White
Uniforms

PLACEMENT OF "U.S." AND BRANCH INSIGNIA.

green classic uniform. The insignia are centered on the collars, ⅝ inch up from the collar and lapel seam, with the centerline of the insignia parallel to the inside edge of the lapel. On the Army white and Army blue uniform coats, female officers wear a single "U.S." insignia on the right collar, 1 inch above the notch, with the insignia centerline parallel to the inside edge of the lapel.

See the accompanying illustrations.

Branch Insignia. *Male* officers, except for most general officers, wear branch insignia on each lapel of the Army green, Army white, and Army blue uniform coats. The insignia are positioned 1¼ inches below the "U.S." insignia and with the centerline of the branch insignia coinciding with the centerline of the "U.S." insignia. Officers affiliated with a regiment will wear regimental collar insignia instead of branch insignia. Regimental insignia is the branch insignia with numerals affixed indicating the number of the regiment.

Female officers wear branch insignia on each lapel of the Army green classic uniform coat. The branch insignia are positioned along the same centerlines as, and approximately 1¼ inches below, the "U.S." insignia. On the Army white and Army blue uniform coats, female officers wear a single insignia of branch on the left collar, 1 inch above the notch, with the centerline of the insignia parallel to the inside edge of the lapel. As with male officers, female officers affiliated with a regiment will wear the regimental insignia instead of branch insignia.

On the hospital duty uniform, both male and female officers wear the branch insignia on the left collar, centered between the inside edge and the outside edge, 1 inch from the lower edge of the collar, and with the centerline parallel to the the lower edge of the collar.

Except for chaplains, no branch insignia are worn on the AG 415 long- or short-sleeve green shirt. Chaplains wear branch insignia centered over the left pocket of the shirt.

On field and utility uniforms, all officers wear subdued insignia of branch centered on the left collar, 1 inch up from the lower edge of the collar, and with the centerline of the insignia parallel to the lower edge of the collar. Either pin-on metal or embroidered insignia on cloth backing may be worn, but both the branch insignia and the grade insignia must be of the same material. Only nonsubdued, pin-on insignia of grade and branch are worn on the hospital duty uniform.

General officers may, at their option, wear the insignia of the branch in which

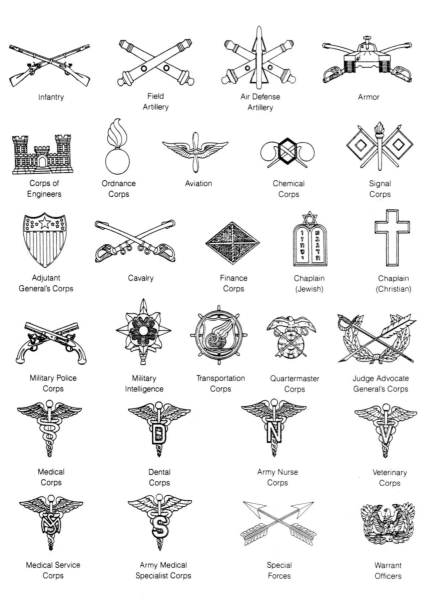

OFFICERS' INSIGNIA OF BRANCH.

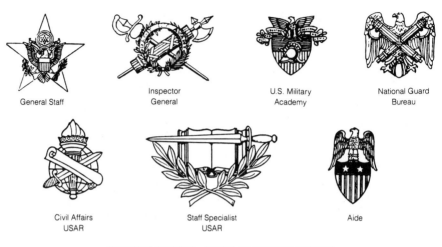

General Staff   Inspector   U.S. Military   National Guard
                     General   Academy   Bureau

Civil Affairs   Staff Specialist   Aide
USAR   USAR

OFFICERS' INSIGNIA—OTHER THAN BASIC BRANCH.

appointed or assigned to duty. All other commissioned officers wear the insignia of their basic branch or the insignia of the branch to which detailed. All warrant officers wear warrant officer insignia regardless of assignment.

General Staff Corps Insignia. The General Staff Corps insignia will be worn by those commissioned officers, other than general officers, whose assignments meet the following exact conditions:

1. Assigned to the offices of the Secretary of the Army, the Undersecretary of the Army, and the Assistant Secretary of the Army, who are authorized by the Secretary of the Army to wear this insignia during their tour of duty in these offices;

2. Detailed to duty on the Army General Staff;

3. Detailed to General Staff with troops (See AR 614-100);

4. As directed by the Chief of Staff;

5. Assigned to departmental or statutory tour Table of Distribution and Allowance (TDA) positions in the National Guard Bureau.

Inspector General Insignia. The Inspector General insignia will be worn by The Inspector General and by those officers detailed as inspectors general under AR 614-100.

Judge Advocate General Corps Insignia. Officers detailed to the JAGC but not yet admitted to practice law before a federal court or the highest court of a state will wear the insignia of their basic branch. They may wear the JAGC insignia after they are admitted to practice.

Aide Insignia. Officers detailed as aides to general officers and other high government officials will wear aide insignia appropriate to their position. See AR 670-1 for descriptions.

Other Insignia. Special insignia also is provided for wear by officers assigned to the National Guard Bureau, to Civil Affairs (USAR), and to the Staff Specialist Reserve. See AR 670-1 for authorization for wear.

Insignia of Grade. Officers wear pin-on, nonsubdued insignia of grade on the shoulders of the Army green (male), Army green classic (female), and Army white uniform coats, and on the black, all-weather coat and the windbreaker. Insignia is centered on the shoulder loops, 5/8 inch from the outside shoulder seam. On the hospital duty uniform, both male and female officers wear nonsubdued, pin-on

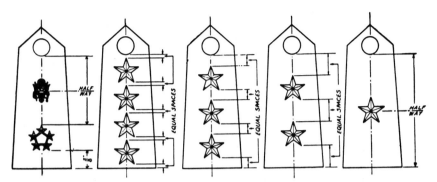

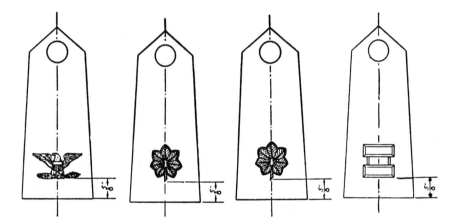

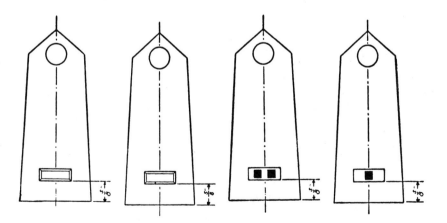

ATTACHMENT OF SHOULDER LOOP INSIGNIA.
Army Green and Army White Uniforms

grade insignia, centered on the right collar, 1 inch from the lower edge of the collar, with the centerline of the insignia parallel to the lower edge of the collar.

All officers wear shoulder straps with embroidered grade insignia on the coat of the Army blue uniform as described in the earlier sections describing these uniforms.

Insignia of grade on the mess and evening mess uniforms is discussed in the earlier sections describing these uniforms.

On the field and utility uniforms, all officers wear subdued insignia of grade, centered on the right collar, 1 inch up from the lower edge of the collar, and with the centerline of the insignia parallel to the lower edge of the collar. Subdued insignia of grade is worn on the shoulder straps of the cold weather coat (field jacket), centered on the straps, 5/8 inch from the outside shoulder seam. Either pin-on metal or embroidered insignia may be worn, but both grade insignia and branch insignia must be of the same material. *Caution:* Only pin-on insignia is authorized for wear on organizational clothing. Note, however, the exception to this policy as regards the flight uniform and the combat vehicle crewman uniform, where sew-on insignia is prescribed. See the earlier descriptions of these uniforms.

When the AG 415 short- or long-sleeve shirt is worn as an outer garment (class B uniforms), shoulder marks are worn on the shoulder loops. Shoulder marks also are worn on the black pullover sweater when it is worn as an outer garment. On the old style AG 415 maternity shirt, female officers wear insignia of grade on each collar, positioned as described for the hospital duty uniform. Officers may, at their option, purchase a modification kit to convert the old style maternity shirt to the new style shirt with shoulder straps, after which shoulder marks will be worn instead of the pin-on collar insignia.

Cautions Regarding Affixing Grade Insignia. Observe that there is an exact position for attaching each item of grade and other articles of insignia and ornamentation on the uniform. Here are some special ones easily overlooked.

A point of each of a general's stars points to the button of the shoulder loop, and is placed point upward on the garrison cap, helmet, helmet liner, and the sleeves of the mess uniform jackets. The beaks of each of a colonel's eagles are extended forward, never backward. The stem of the silver leaf and the oak leaf, of lieutenant colonel and major, are on the outside or on the bottom, as affixed to shoulder loop, garrison cap, or sleeves of the mess uniform jackets.

Combat Leader's Identification. The combat leader's identification is worn by leaders of Category I (organization TOE specifies category) Active Army, Army National Guard, and Army Reserve organizations, plus division and corps commanders, and commanders of Category II organizations, the majority of whose subordinate elements are Category I units. The specific leaders are: commanders, deputy commanders, platoon leaders, command sergeants major, first sergeants, platoon sergeants, section leaders, tank commanders, and rifle squad fire team leaders. This identification is a green cloth loop, 1 5/8 inches wide, worn in the middle of both shoulder straps of the Army green coats and the cold-weather coat (field jacket). It will cease to be worn when an individual entitled thereto is reassigned from a command position or from a combat unit that had provided authority for its wear.

Caution: Make certain of your right to wear this coveted device before you add it to your uniform.

Distinctive Unit Insignia. Subject to approval by the Institute of Heraldry, a distinctive unit insignia (DUI) is authorized for wear on the service uniforms by personnel designated in AR 670-1 as a means of promoting esprit de corps. When a DUI is authorized, it will be worn by all assigned members except general officers. The DUI is authorized only in metal, or metal and enamel. A complete set of DUI consists of three pieces, one for each shoulder strap and (for enlisted personnel) one for the garrison cap or organizational beret. Officers wear DUI centered on the shoulder strap of the Army green, or green classic, uniform coats, equal distance between the insignia of grade and the shoulder strap button, with the base of the insignia toward the outside shoulder seam. The DUI also is worn centered above the nameplate on the black pullover sweater.

Regimental Distinctive Unit Insignia. Each of the regiments of the Army has a regimental DUI. Personnel affiliated with the regiment are authorized to wear the regimental DUI. *Males* wear the regimental DUI centered and 1/8 inch above the right pocket flap of the Army green, white, and blue uniforms, or 1/2 inch above unit awards or foreign badges, if worn. On the mess jackets, the regimental DUI is worn centered on the right lapel, 1/2 inch below the notch, with the vertical axis of the crest perpendicular to the ground.

Females wear the regimental DUI centered and 1/2 inch above the nameplate (right side) or 1/2 inch above unit awards or foreign badges, on the Army green classic, white, and blue uniforms. On the blue, white, and black mess jackets, the regimental DUI is worn centered on the right side between the lapel and shoulder seam with the top of the crest aligned with the top row of miniature medals, and the vertical axis of the crest perpendicular to the ground. Females do not wear the regimental DUI on the lapels of the mess jackets.

Airborne Insignia. If authorized, officers wear the airborne insignia centered on the right curtain of the garrison cap, 1 inch from the front crease. The insignia consists of a white glider and parachute on a blue disk with a red border, about 2 1/4 inches in diameter. *Caution:* There are two versions of the insignia. Make certain the glider is facing forward when the insignia is sewn on the cap.

Airborne and Air Assault Background Trimming. Distinctive background trimming, oval-shaped, 1 3/8 inches high by 2 1/4 inches wide, is worn under the airborne or air assault badges. The trimming is subject to approval by the Institute of Heraldry when authorized by HQDA. When authorized, the trimming is worn by all assigned personnel who have been awarded the airborne or air assault badge. Only one background trimming will be worn.

Distinctive Items for Infantry Personnel. Officers and enlisted personnel of the Infantry who have been awarded the combat infantryman badge or the expert infantryman badge, or who have, as members of assigned infantry units, completed the basic unit phase of an Army training program, or the equivalent thereof, wear the Infantry shoulder cord of infantry blue. The cord is worn on the right shoulder of the Army green, white, and blue uniform coats. The blue cord passes under the arm, and the cord attaches to a 20-ligne button sewn on the shoulder seam 1/2 inch outside the collar edge.

Aiguillettes. Service and dress aiguillettes are provided to officers authorized to wear them (attaches and aides). Authorization for wear and manner of wear are as stated in AR 670-1.

Headgear Insignia. *Garrison Cap.* Officers wear nonsubdued insignia of grade on the garrison cap, centered on the left curtain, 1 inch from the front crease.

Male Service Cap and Cold Weather Cap. For male commissioned officers, the insignia is the Coat of Arms of the United States, 2 3/8 inches high, of gold-color

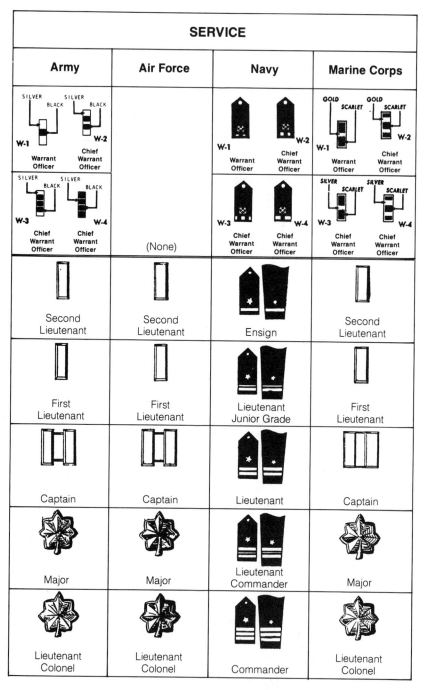

SERVICE			
Army	**Air Force**	**Navy**	**Marine Corps**
W-1 Warrant Officer / W-2 Chief Warrant Officer / W-3 Chief Warrant Officer / W-4 Chief Warrant Officer	(None)	W-1 Warrant Officer / W-2 Chief Warrant Officer / W-3 Chief Warrant Officer / W-4 Chief Warrant Officer	W-1 Warrant Officer / W-2 Chief Warrant Officer / W-3 Chief Warrant Officer / W-4 Chief Warrant Officer
Second Lieutenant	Second Lieutenant	Ensign	Second Lieutenant
First Lieutenant	First Lieutenant	Lieutenant Junior Grade	First Lieutenant
Captain	Captain	Lieutenant	Captain
Major	Major	Lieutenant Commander	Major
Lieutenant Colonel	Lieutenant Colonel	Commander	Lieutenant Colonel

GRADE INSIGNIA, OFFICERS.

Note: Grade insignia of 2d Lieutenant and Major are gold; of other officer grades in Army, Air Force, and Marine Corps, silver. Naval insignia are gold color. The Navy pin-on (collar) insignia are the same as for the other services except that the devices are smaller, and the enamel bands on the warrant officers' bars are Navy blue.

SERVICE			
Army	**Air Force**	**Navy**	**Marine Corps**
Colonel	Colonel	Captain	Colonel
Brigadier General	Brigadier General	Rear Admiral (Lower Half)	Brigadier General
Major General	Major General	Rear Admiral (Upper Half)	Major General
Lieutenant General	Lieutenant General	Vice Admiral	Lieutenant General
General	General	Admiral	General
General of the Army	General of the Air Force	Fleet Admiral	(None)

GRADE INSIGNIA, OFFICERS (Continued).

Note: All insignia above are silver color except Navy, which is gold.

ENLISTED

ENLISTED INSIGNIA OF GRADE.

Black
Pullover Sweater

Green and Green Classic,
Blue, and White Uniforms

Mess Jackets
Male

WEAR OF REGIMENTAL CREST.

metal. For warrant officers, the insignia is an eagle rising with wings displayed, standing on a bundle of two arrows, all enclosed by a wreath. The insignia is of gold-color metal, 1 1/2 inches high.

Female Service Hat, Cold Weather Cap, and Black Beret. For female commissioned officers, the insignia is the Coat of Arms of the United States, 1 5/8 inches high, of gold-color metal. Female warrant officers wear the same insignia as male warrant officers.

Organizational Beret. Officers wear nonsubdued insignia of grade centered on the organizational flash, which is sewn centered on the stiffener of the beret.

BDU Cap and DBDU Hat. All officers wear nonsubdued insignia of grade when in a garrison environment and subdued insignia when in a field environment. Chaplains wear branch insignia instead of grade insignia. Insignia is worn centered on the front of the headgear.

Helmet Liner and Helmet Camouflage Cover. All officers wear subdued insignia of grade on the front, approximately 2 1/2 inches up from the bottom rim.

Baseball-Style Cap. When wear of these caps is authorized by the commander, officers wear nonsubdued insignia of grade centered on the front of the cap.

Insignia, Distinguishing, "U.S. Army." This insignia is a woven tape, 1 inch wide and either 4 1/2 inches long or the width of the pocket, olive green in color, with the inscription "U.S. Army" in black, block letters 3/4 inch high, either printed (issue) or embroidered (optional purchase). This tape is worn on the BDU coats and BDU field jacket, and on organizational clothing when prescribed by the issuing commander. It is sewn on the uniform, immediately above and parallel to the top seam of the left breast pocket, or in a similar position on clothing with slanted or no pockets. On the Desert BDU, the approved background color of the tape is brown, although commanders may authorize wear of the olive green tape.

Nametapes and Nameplates. Nametapes are worn over the right breast pocket on the same uniforms and in the same manner as the U.S. Army distinguishing tape. The nametape and the U.S. Army distinguishing tape must be the same length and each must be either printed or embroidered.

Nameplates are of black laminated plastic, either gloss or nongloss, 1 inch by 3 inches by 1/16 inch thick, with a white border not to exceed 1/32 inch in width. Lettering is block type, indented, 3/8 inch high, and centered on the nameplate. Only the last name is used.

Male personnel wear the nameplate on the flap of the right breast pocket, centered between the button and the top of the pocket, on the Army green shirts;

on the coats of the Army green, white, and blue uniforms; and in a comparable position on the hospital duty uniform. The nameplate is worn centered on the patch of the black pullover sweater. If a DUI is also worn, the nameplate will be worn $1/2$ inch above the bottom of the patch with the DUI centered, left to right and top to bottom, above the nameplate.

Female personnel wear the nameplate between 1 and 2 inches above the top of the top button on the right side of the Army green classic uniform coat, centered from side to side. It is worn in a comparable position on the blue and white uniform coats, slightly above the top button, and on the green shirts, maternity tunic, and hospital duty uniform. On the black pullover sweater, the nameplate is worn as described for male personnel. The patch positioning may be adjusted to conform to individual figure differences.

Organization Shoulder Sleeve Insignia. Approved designs of shoulder sleeve insignia (SSI) are authorized for wear by personnel of units definitely assigned to an organization having Department of the Army authorization for its use. See AR 670-1.

Individuals entitled to the privilege may wear the SSI of their current unit on the left sleeve of the Army green coat and, in a subdued version, on the BDU coats, BDU field jacket, flight jacket, flight suit, and the combat vehicle crewman uniform. SSI is *not* worn on the black all-weather coat or windbreaker, on any dress uniform, or on organizational clothing, except for the flight suit and the combat vehicle crewman uniform.

In the same manner, but on the right sleeve, SSI of a former wartime organization may be worn by individuals entitled to do so. AR 670-1 sets the entitlements.

Overseas Service Bars. The male version of this device is a golden-lite-color rayon bar, $1\,5/16$ inches in length, $3/16$ inch in width, on an Army green background that forms a $3/32$-inch border around the bar. The female version is the same except the size is $1/8$ inch wide by $7/8$ inch long, with a $1/8$-inch border.

One overseas bar is authorized for each period of six months of active federal service as a member of the Army or another U.S. Service during periods of hostilities as designated in AR 670-1, when serving in hostile fire areas. Service of less than six months' duration, which otherwise meets the requirements, may be combined with additional service to determine the number of overseas bars authorized.

The overseas bar is worn centered on the outside bottom half of the right sleeve of the Army green and Army green classic uniforms, with the lower edge of the bar parallel to and $1/4$ inch above the braid. Additional bars are worn parallel to and above the first bar with a $1/16$-inch space between bars.

Colors of Branches. There are official colors of the branches of the Army. These colors appear as piping on uniform components, in facings, and elsewhere on the blue and blue mess uniforms. They are as follows:

Adjutant General's Corps—dark blue and scarlet
Air Defense Artillery—scarlet
Armor—yellow
Army Medical Department—maroon and white
Aviation—ultramarine blue and golden orange
Cavalry—yellow
Chaplains—black
Chemical Corps—cobalt blue and golden yellow
Civil Affairs, USAR—purple and white
Corps of Engineers—scarlet and white

Field Artillery—scarlet
Finance Corps—silver gray and golden yellow
Infantry—light blue
Inspector General—dark blue and light blue
Judge Advocate General's Corps—dark blue and white
Military Intelligence—oriental blue and silver gray
Military Police Corps—green and yellow
National Guard Bureau—dark blue
Ordnance Corps—crimson and yellow
Quartermaster Corps—buff
Signal Corps—orange and white
Staff Specialist, USAR—green
Transportation Corps—brick red and golden yellow
Warrant Officers—brown
Branch Immaterial—teal blue and white

Branch of Service Scarves. Branch of service, bib-type scarves may be worn, when issued and prescribed for wear by the local commander, with the service and utility uniforms for ceremonial occasions only. Colors are as indicated below:

Black—Chaplain
Bottle Green—Special Forces and Psychological Operations
Brick Red—Transportation
Buff—Supply, Quartermaster, Supply and Service, Supply and Transportation, and Support
Cobalt Blue—Chemical
Crimson—Ordnance and Maintenance
Dark Blue—National Guard Bureau, Judge Advocate General, Inspector General, and Adjutant General
Green—Military Police and Staff Specialist
Infantry Blue—Infantry
Maroon—Army Medical Specialist Corps, Army Nurse Corps, Dental Corps, Medical Corps, Medical Service Corps, and Veterinary Corps
Orange—Signal
Oriental Blue—Intelligence
Purple—Civil Affairs
Scarlet—Artillery; Engineers; and Permanent Professors, Registrar, and Civilian Instructors of the U.S. Military Academy
Silver Gray—Finance
Ultramarine Blue—Aviation
Yellow—Armor and Cavalry
Teal Blue—Branch Immaterial
Camouflage—As determined by local commander

WEAR OF THE UNIFORM BY PERSONNEL OTHER THAN MEMBERS OF THE ACTIVE ARMY

Individuals who possess a current military status other than as a member of the Active Army are restricted as to the occasions when they may wear the uniform. AR 670-1 presents detailed regulations under which the categories of personnel listed below may wear the uniform.

Army National Guard personnel
U.S. Army Reserve personnel
Retired personnel

Persons who have been awarded the Medal of Honor
Separated personnel who have served honorably during war

Occasions of Ceremony. Authority to wear the uniform on occasions of ceremony needs definition. It means an occasion essentially military in character at which the uniform is more appropriate than civilian clothing, e.g., military balls, military parades, military weddings, military funerals, memorial services, and meetings or functions of associations formed for military purposes, the membership of which is composed largely or entirely of honorably discharged veterans of the Armed Forces or of Reserve personnel. This authorization includes authority to wear the uniform while traveling to and from the ceremony, provided such travel can be completed on the day of the ceremony.

Army National Guard and U.S. Army Reserve Officers, Inactive Status. Officers of the National Guard and of the Army Reserve, while on inactive status, are authorized to wear the uniform during periods of military instruction. They may also wear it on occasions of ceremony, as stated above. Members of the Army National Guard may also wear the uniform in the performance of state service when so authorized by their respective state Adjutant General. Consult the commanding officer for authority to wear the uniform on other occasions.

Retired Personnel. The uniform of retired personnel that may be worn on occasions of ceremony as discussed above will be, at their option, either the uniform for persons of their grade and branch at the time of retirement, or the uniform of persons on the active list. However, the two uniforms will not be mixed. A U.S. Army Retired shoulder patch has been developed for wear by retired personnel with their uniform on occasions of ceremony. It may also be worn on civilian clothing.

Persons Who Have Been Awarded the Medal of Honor. Persons who have been awarded the Medal of Honor are authorized to wear the uniform any time except:

In connection with the promotion of any political or commercial interests or when engaged in civilian employment;

When participating in public speeches, interviews, picket lines, marches, rallies, or public demonstrations except as authorized by competent authority;

When wearing the uniform would bring discredit on the Army; and

When specifically prohibited by regulation.

23

Decorations, Service Medals, and Badges

Decorations awarded to members of the armed services are a symbol of acknowledgment by the government of our nation of a job well done. They consist of awards for heroism, the highest of which is the Medal of Honor, and awards for achievement, the highest of which is the Defense Distinguished Service Medal. Just as there is a variation in degree of heroism or achievement above and beyond the call of duty, so there is also a variation in the rank of the several awards given for these two purposes.

The granting of awards by governments stems at least as far back into history as the Roman era. It was during that period that Roman rulers took the laurel wreath unto themselves. The Greeks also crowned citizens who were outstanding in war, athletics, literature, and oratory with the laurel wreath and, therefore, it is natural that it forms a part of our nation's highest award for valor.

During the age of feudalism there grew up a system of rewards in the form of titles and prerogatives. Persons who performed valiant feats of arms or other great deeds were honored by induction into an order, such as the British "Most Noble Order of the Garter." Further deeds brought additional titles, lands, and pensions. The symbols for the Orders were medals, generally worn on neck ribbons, which were the forerunners of our present-day decorations.

Concurrently, as the use of armor increased and it became more difficult to recognize individuals on the battlefield, the knights, barons, earls, dukes, and other leaders began to have their personal family symbols painted on their shields, so that they could be easily recognized. Eventually, these paintings on the "arms" were extended to other personal items, including being sewn on the individual's coat or cape; hence the term *coat of arms*. The coats of arms could be considered the forerunners of today's shoulder patches, serving as a means of ready identification. However, they also were a pictorial history of the deeds of the family members. As the deeds increased in numbers, so did the production of coats of arms. The designs became more complex, and the whole field of heraldry and heraldic art developed.

The several subjects discussed in this chapter have been placed in the following sequence:

Decorations and Awards (a general overview)
U.S. Army and Department of Defense Decorations (illustrated in color)
U.S. Army and Department of Defense Unit Awards (illustrated in color)
Other U.S. Army Awards (illustrated in color)
U.S. Military Service Medals and Ribbons (illustrated in color)
U.S. Army Service and Training Ribbons (illustrated in color)
Non-U.S. Service Medals (illustrated in color)
U.S. Army Badges and Tabs (illustrated in color)
Appurtenances to Decorations and Service Medals (illustrated)
Foreign Decorations and Gifts
Certificates and Letters for Service
Order of Precedence of Decorations and Awards
Guide for Wearing Awards (illustrated)

DECORATIONS AND AWARDS

Purpose and Categories of Awards. The purpose of the awards program of the Army, with similar programs in the other services, is to provide tangible recognition for acts of valor, exceptional service or achievement, special skills or qualifications, and acts of heroism not involving actual combat. Medals constitute a principal form for such recognition, but other methods are provided and all are discussed in this chapter. Most awards are made to individuals. There are also unit awards and citations. Most awards may be given only to a member of the military service; a few may be awarded to either a member of the service or a civilian; and there are awards that may be granted to civilians only.

This chapter is based on official publications and is intended to be sufficiently comprehensive for the personal needs of the officer. For the administration of the program, or for official action regarding the program, reference should be made to the official publications, with their changes. The basic publication for the awards program is AR 672-5-1. Wearing of decorations, medals, and badges is discussed in AR 670-1. Other documents of reference are cited as they apply in the discussions in this chapter.

The broad categories of awards include the following:

Individual Awards—
Decorations for valor or achievement
Good Conduct Medal (for enlisted personnel only)
Service medals
Combat and special skill badges and tabs
Foreign individual awards
Certificates and letters

Unit Awards—
Unit decorations
Infantry and medical streamers
Campaign streamers, war service streamers, and campaign silver bands
Foreign unit decorations

Important Definitions. Definitions of words or terms that are in common use in recommending individuals for awards, or in making awards, must be understood. The following are important.

Above and Beyond the Call of Duty. This is exercise of a voluntary course of action the omission of which would not justly subject the individual to censure for failure in the performance of duty. It usually includes the acceptance of existing danger or extraordinary responsibilities with praiseworthy fortitude and exemplary courage. In its highest degree it involves the voluntary acceptance of additional danger and risk of life. (This definition is the most important.)

Active Federal Military Service. The term means all periods of active duty and excludes periods of active duty for training. Service as a cadet at the USMA is considered to be active duty. For the award of the Armed Forces Reserve Medal, active duty for training counts in determining eligibility.

Citation. A citation is a written, narrative statement of an act, deed, or meritorious performance of duty or service for which an award is made.

Combat Heroism. This covers an act or acts of heroism by an individual engaged in actual conflict with an armed enemy or in military operations that involve exposure to personal hazards due to direct enemy action or the imminence of such action.

Combat Zone. The region where fighting is going on; the forward area of the theater of operations where combat troops are actively engaged. It extends from the front line to the front of the communications zone.

Distinguished Himself (Herself) By. A person to have distinguished himself or herself must, by praiseworthy accomplishment, be set apart from other persons in the same or similar circumstances. Determination of this distinction requires careful consideration of exactly what is or was expected as the ordinary, routine, or customary behavior and accomplishment for individuals of like rank and experience for the circumstances involved.

Duty of Great Responsibility. Duty that, by virtue of the position held, carries the ultimate responsibility for the successful operation of a major command, activity, agency, installation, or project. The discharge of such duty must involve the acceptance and fulfillment of the obligation so as to greatly benefit the interests of the United States.

Duty of Responsibility. Duty that, by virtue of the position held, carries a high degree of the responsibility for the successful operation of a major command, activity, agency, installation, or project, or that requires the exercise of judgment and decision affecting plans, policies, operations, or the lives and well-being of others.

Heroism. Heroism is defined as specific acts of bravery or outstanding courage, or a closely related series of heroic acts performed within a short period of time.

In Connection with Military Operations against an Armed Enemy. This phrase covers all military operations including combat, support, and supply that have a direct bearing on the outcome of an engagement or engagements against armed opposition. To perform duty or to accomplish an act of achievement in connection with military operations against an armed enemy, the individual must have been subjected to either personal hazard as a result of direct enemy action, or the imminence of such action, or must have had the conditions under which his duty or accomplishment took place complicated by enemy action or the imminence of enemy action.

Key Individual. A person who is occupying a position that is indispensable to an organization, activity, or project.

Meritorious Achievement. An act that is well above the expected performance of duty. The act should be an exceptional accomplishment with a definite beginning and ending date. The length of time involved is not a primary consideration, but speed of accomplishment may be a factor in determining the value of an act.

Meritorious Service. Service that is distinguished by a succession of outstanding acts of achievement over a sustained period of time.

Officer. Except where stated otherwise, the word *officer* means commissioned or warrant officer. And *he, his, him,* includes *she* and *her* as appropriate.

Army Personal Decorations. A decoration is awarded in recognition of performance of duty involving heroism, or high achievement. There are degrees of heroism and of achievement, and for that reason there are awards to recognize these varying standards. All soldiers are expected to do their duty, and to accept the normal hazards of duty, for which there is no special individual award. Return for a moment to consider the definition of "above and beyond the call of duty." This definition is the key to understanding. In the field of combat heroism, the Medal of Honor is our highest award; other awards for heroism in descending scale are the Distinguished Service Cross, Silver Star, Distinguished Flying Cross, Bronze Star Medal, Air Medal, Joint Service Commendation Medal, and the Army Commendation Medal. In the area of achievement, the Defense Distinguished Service Medal is the highest award. Those which follow are the Distinguished Service Medal, Defense Superior Service Medal, Legion of Merit, Distinguished Flying Cross, Bronze Star Medal, Defense Meritorious Service Medal, Meritorious Service Medal, Air Medal, Joint Service Commendation Medal, Army Commendation Medal, Joint Service Achievement Medal, and the Army Achievement Medal. Some awards, it is to be noted, may be awarded both for heroism and for achievement. The Purple Heart, the oldest decoration in our service, is awarded only for wounds or death resulting from wounds. It is worn following the Bronze Star Medal.

The table following, from AR 672-5-1, lists the awards to Army individuals in the order of their precedence, and the order in which they are worn on the uniform.

Approval Authority for Decorations. The regulations are specific and detailed as to the approval authority for award of the various decorations. The criteria vary depending on whether the award is made during peacetime or wartime. Consult the regulations, AR 672-5-1, for details.

UNITED STATES ARMY AND DEPARTMENT OF DEFENSE DECORATIONS

Medal of Honor. The Medal of Honor, established by Act of Congress in 1862, is the highest and most rarely awarded decoration conferred by the United States. The deed for which the Medal of Honor is awarded must have been one of personal bravery or self-sacrifice so conspicuous as to clearly distinguish the individual for gallantry and intrepidity above his comrades and must have involved risk of life. Incontestable proof of the performance of the service is exacted, and each recommendation for the award of this decoration is considered on the standard of extraordinary merit.

Presentation of the Medal of Honor is made only by the President.

No special personal privileges or exemptions from military obligations accompany the award. Medal of Honor winners may receive free air transportation (MAC) on a space-available basis, however. Sons and daughters of winners of the Medal of Honor, otherwise qualified for admission to the United States Military Academy, are not subject to quota requirements.

Army personnel holding the Medal of Honor may apply to HQDA (DAPC-PDA), Alexandria, VA 22332, to have their names entered on the Medal of Honor Roll. Persons on the roll and otherwise eligible may, upon application, qualify for a special lifetime pension of $200 per month.

Distinguished Service Cross. Established by Act of Congress on 9 July 1918 and amended by act of 25 July 1963, this medal is awarded to a person who, while serving in any capacity with the Army, distinguishes himself or herself by extraordinary heroism not justifying the Medal of Honor while engaged in an action against an enemy of the United States, while engaged in military operations involving conflict with opposing foreign forces, or while serving with friendly foreign forces engaged in an armed conflict against an opposing armed force in which the United States is not a belligerent party.

Defense Distinguished Service Medal. Established by Executive Order 11545 of 9 July 1970, this medal is awarded by the Secretary of Defense to any military service officer who, while assigned to joint staffs and other joint activities of the Department of Defense, distinguishes himself or herself by exceptionally meritorious service while in a position of unique and great responsibility. It ranks between the Distinguished Service Cross and the Distinguished Service Medal in order of precedence. It will not be awarded to any individual for a period of service for which a Distinguished Service Medal or similar decoration is awarded.

Distinguished Service Medal. Established by Congress on 9 July 1918, this medal is awarded to any person who, while serving in any capacity with the Army, distinguishes himself or herself by exceptionally meritorious service to the government in a duty of great responsibility. For service not related to actual war the term *duty of great responsibility* applies to a narrower range of positions than in wartime and requires evidence of conspicuously significant achievement. Awards may be made to persons other than members of the Armed Forces of the United States for wartime service only, under exceptional circumstances, and with the approval of the President.

Silver Star. Established by Act of Congress 9 July 1918 and amended by act of 25 July 1963, the Silver Star is awarded to a person under the same circumstances as described above for the Distinguished Service Cross but where the gallantry is of a lesser degree but performed with marked distinction.

Defense Superior Service Medal. Established by Executive Order 11904 of 6 February 1976, this medal is awarded by the Secretary of Defense to any member of the Armed Forces of the United States who, while assigned to joint staffs and other joint activities of the Department of Defense, renders superior meritorious service while in a position of significant responsibility. It ranks between the Silver Star and the Legion of Merit in order of precedence. It will not be awarded to any individual for a period of service for which a Legion of Merit or similar decoration is awarded.

Legion of Merit. Established by Congress 20 July 1942, this medal is awarded to any member (usually key individuals) of the Armed Forces of the United States or of a friendly foreign nation who has distinguished himself or herself by exceptionally meritorious conduct in the performance of outstanding services. For service not related to war, the term *key individuals* applies to a narrower range than in wartime. Awards are made to U.S. nationals without reference to degree, and, for each award, the Legion of Merit (Legionnaire) is issued. The award may be made to foreigners, under conditions prescribed in AR 672-5-1, in one of four degrees—Chief Commander, Commander, Officer, or Legionnaire.

Distinguished Flying Cross. Established by Congress 2 July 1926, this medal is awarded to any member of the Armed Forces of the United States and of friendly foreign nations who, while serving in any capacity with the Army, distinguishes himself or herself by heroism or extraordinary achievement while participating in aerial flight.

Soldier's Medal. Established by Congress 2 July 1926, this medal is awarded to any person who, while serving with the Army, distinguishes himself or herself by

Decorations (In order of precedence)	Established By	Awarded for		Awarded to				
				United States Personnel			Foreign Personnel	
		Heroism	Achievement or Service	Military	Reserve Components	Civilian	Military	Civilian
Medal of Honor	Joint Resolution of Congress, 12 July 1862 (amended by acts 9 July 1918 and 25 July 1963)	Combat		War[1]				
Distinguished Service Cross	Act of Congress 9 July 1918 (amended by act of 25 July 1963)	Combat		War		War[2]	War	War[2]
Defense Distinguished Service Medal	Executive Order 11545 9 July 1970		War Peace	War Peace				
Distinguished Service Medal	Act of Congress 9 July 1918		War Peace	War Peace	Peace	War[2]	War[2]	War[2]
Silver Star	Act of Congress 9 July 1918 (amended by act of 25 July 1963)	Combat		War		War[2]	War	War[2]
Defense Superior Service Medal	Executive Order 11904, 6 February 1976		War Peace	War Peace	War Peace			
Legion of Merit	Act of Congress 20 July 1942		War Peace	War Peace	Peace		War Peace[3]	
Distinguished Flying Cross	Act of Congress 2 July 1926	Combat Noncombat	War Peace[4]	War Peace	Peace		War	
Soldier's Medal	Act of Congress 2 July 1926	Noncombat		War Peace	Peace		War Peace	
Bronze Star Medal	Executive Order 9419, 4 February 1944 (superseded by Executive Order 11046, 24 August 1962)	Combat[5]	War Peace	War Peace		War Peace	War Peace	War Peace[2]
Purple Heart	General George Washington, 7 August 1782, revived by War Department General Orders 3, 1932 as amended by Executive Order 11016, 25 April 1962, as further amended by Executive Order 12464, 23 February 1984; and Public Law 98-525, 19 October 1984	Wounds received in combat	War Peace[6]	War				
Defense Meritorious Service Medal	Executive Order 12019, 3 November 1977		Peace	Peace	Peace			
Meritorious Service Medal	Executive Order 11448, 16 January 1969 as amended by Executive Order 12312, 2 July 1981		Peace	Peace	Peace		Peace	

Decorations (In order of precedence)	Established By	Awarded for			Awarded to				
					United States Personnel			Foreign Personnel	
		Heroism	Achievement or Service		Military	Reserve Components	Civilian	Military	Civilian
Air Medal	Executive Order 9158, 11 May 1942 as amended by Executive Order 9242-A, 11 September 1942	Combat[5] Noncombat	War Peace[4]		War Peace	Peace	War	War	War
Joint Service Commendation Medal	DOD Directive 1348.14, 17 May 1967 as superseded by DOD Directive 1348.14, 7 February 1977	Combat[5] Noncombat	War Peace		War Peace				
Army Commendation Medal	War Department Circular 377, 18 December 1945 (amended in DA General Orders 10, 1960)	Combat[5] Noncombat	War Peace		War Peace[7]	Peace		War Peace[7]	
Joint Service Achievement Medal	DOD Directive 1348.28, 29 March 1984		Peace		Peace[7]				
Army Achievement Medal	The Secretary of the Army, 10 April 1981		Peace		Peace[7]	Peace		Peace[7]	

[1]The Medal of Honor is awarded only to United States military personnel.
[2]Not usually awarded to these personnel.
[3]Awarded to foreign military personnel in one of four degrees.
[4]Approval authority for peacetime award is HQDA.
[5]Awarded with Bronze V device for valor in combat.
[6]Awarded to military personnel wounded by terrorists or while members of a peacekeeping force.
[7]Not awarded to general officers.

heroism not involving actual conflict with an armed enemy. The same degree of heroism is required as for a Distinguished Flying Cross. The award is not made solely on the basis of having saved a life.

Bronze Star Medal. The Bronze Star Medal was established by Executive Order in 1944, which was superseded by Executive Order 11046, 24 August 1962. It is awarded to any person who, while serving in any capacity in or with the Army of the United States after 6 December 1941, distinguishes himself or herself by heroic or meritorious achievement or service, not involving participation in aerial flight, in connection with military operations against an armed enemy or while engaged in military operations involving conflict with an opposing armed force in which the United States is not a belligerent party.

Awards may be made for acts of heroism that are of lesser degree than required for award of the Silver Star.

Awards may be made for achievement or meritorious service that, while of lesser degree than that required for the award of the Legion of Merit, must nevertheless have been meritorious and accomplished with distinction.

Purple Heart. The Purple Heart, established by Gen. George Washington at Newburgh, N.Y., on 7 August 1782 and revived by the President as announced in War Department General Orders 3, 22 February 1932, as amended by Executive Order

11016, 25 April 1962, as further amended by Executive Order 12464, 23 February 1984, and Public Law 98-525, 19 October 1984, is awarded in the name of the President of the United States to any member of an armed force or any civilian national of the United States who, while serving under competent authority in any capacity with one of the United States armed services after 5 April 1917, has been wounded, killed, or has died or may die after being wounded:

1. In any action against an enemy of the United States;

2. In any action with an opposing armed force of a foreign country in which the Armed Forces of the United States are or have been engaged;

3. While serving with friendly foreign forces engaged in an armed conflict against an opposing armed force in which the United States is not a belligerent party;

4. As the result of an act of any such enemy or opposing armed force;

5. As the result of an act of any hostile foreign force;

6. After 23 March 1973, as a result of an international terrorist attack against the United States or a foreign nation friendly to the United States, recognized as such an attack by the Army, or jointly by the separate armed services concerned if persons from more than one service are wounded in the attack; or

7. After 23 March 1973, as a result of military operations while serving outside the territory of the United States as part of a peace-keeping force.

A Purple Heart is authorized for the first wound suffered under conditions indicated above, but for each subsequent award an oak-leaf cluster shall be awarded to be worn on the medal or ribbon.

A Purple Heart will be issued to the next of kin of each person entitled to a posthumous award. Issue will be made automatically by the Commanding General, Total Army Personnel Agency (TAPA) upon receiving a report of death indicating entitlement.

Defense Meritorious Service Medal. Established by Executive Order 12019, 3 November 1977. It is awarded in the name of the Secretary of Defense to any active duty member of the Armed Forces of the United States who distinguishes himself or herself by noncombat meritorious achievement or service while assigned, or on temporary duty for at least 60 days, to joint staffs and other joint activities of the Department of Defense. It ranks between the Bronze Star Medal and the Meritorious Service Medal. It will not be awarded to any individual for a period of service for which any similar decoration has been awarded.

Meritorious Service Medal. Established by Executive Order 11448, 16 January 1969, as amended by Executive Order 12312, 2 July 1981. It is awarded to a member of the Armed Forces of the United States or to any member of the armed forces of a friendly foreign nation who, after 16 January 1969, distinguishes himself or herself by outstanding meritorious achievement or service in a noncombat situation. It ranks between the Defense Meritorious Service Medal and the Joint Service Commendation Medal as a noncombat award.

Air Medal. Established by Executive Order 9158 on 11 May 1942, and amended by Executive Order 9242-A, 11 September 1982, this medal may be awarded to any person who, while serving in any capacity in or with the Army, distinguishes himself or herself by meritorious achievement while participating in aerial flight. The medal may be awarded for heroism in combat, for single acts of meritorious service involving superior airmanship, and for meritorious service involving sustained distinction in the performance of duties that require regular and frequent participation in aerial flight for a period of at least six months in combat.

Joint Service Commendation Medal. Department of Defense Directive 1348.14, 17 May 1967 (superseded by DOD directive 1348.14, 7 February 1977), established this medal. This decoration is awarded in the name of the Secretary of Defense and takes precedence with, but before the Army Commendation Medal. It is awarded to any active member of the Armed Forces who distinguishes himself or herself by meritorious achievement or service while serving with offices and agencies of the Secretary of Defense and the Joint Chiefs of Staff as described in AR 672-5-1. Awards may include the V device if the citation is approved for valor in a designated combat area.

Army Commendation Medal. The Army Commendation Medal, established by War Department Circular 377, 18 December 1945 and amended in Department of the Army General Orders 10, 1960, is awarded to any member of the Armed Forces of the United States who, while serving in any capacity with the Army after 6 December 1941, distinguishes himself or herself by heroism, meritorious achievement, or meritorious service. Award may also be made to a member of the armed forces of a friendly foreign nation for acts of heroism, extraordinary achievement, or meritorious service that has been of mutual benefit to a friendly foreign nation and the United States.

Awards may be made for acts of valor performed under circumstances described above that are of lesser degree than required for award of the Bronze Star Medal. These acts may involve aerial flight.

An award may be made for acts of noncombatant-related heroism that do not meet the requirements for an award of the Soldier's Medal.

The Army Commendation Medal is not awarded to general officers.

Joint Service Achievement Medal. Established by DOD Directive 1348.28, 29 March 1984, this medal may be awarded to any member of the U.S. Armed Forces below the grade of colonel (O-6) who distinguishes himself or herself by meritorious achievement or service while serving in specified joint activities after 3 August 1983.

Army Achievement Medal. Established by the Secretary of the Army on 10 April 1981, this medal is awarded to any member of the Armed Forces of the United States or to any member of the armed forces of a friendly foreign nation who, while serving in any capacity with the Army in a noncombat area on or after 1 August 1981, distinguishes himself or herself by meritorious service or achievement of a lesser degree than required for award of the Army Commendation Medal. This medal may not be awarded to general officers.

U.S. ARMY AND DEPARTMENT OF DEFENSE UNIT AWARDS

Unit awards are authorized in recognition of group heroism or meritorious service, usually during a war, as a means of promoting esprit de corps. They are of the following categories: unit decorations, Infantry and medical streamers, campaign streamers, war service streamers, and campaign silver bands. Only personnel who were assigned to the unit during the period for which the unit award is made are entitled to wear an emblem signifying receipt of the decoration. Streamers and silver bands accrue to the unit only and are displayed on the guidon or color.

United States Unit Decorations. United States unit decorations, in order of precedence shown below, have been established to recognize outstanding heroism or exceptionally meritorious conduct in the performance of outstanding services:

Presidential Unit Citation (Army and Air Force); Presidential Unit Citation (Navy); Joint Meritorious Unit Award; Valorous Unit Award (Army); Meritorious Unit Commendation (Army); Navy Unit Commendation; Air Force Outstanding Unit Award;

Coast Guard Unit Commendation; Army Superior Unit Award; Meritorious Unit Commendation (Navy); Navy "E" Ribbon; Air Force Organizational Excellence Award; and Coast Guard Meritorious Unit Commendation.

These awards may be worn permanently by those who served with the unit during the cited period. The Presidential Unit Citation (Army), the Valorous Unit Award, the Meritorious Unit Commendation, and the Army Superior Unit Award may be worn temporarily by those serving with the unit subsequent to the cited period. The Presidential Unit Citation (Air Force) is awarded under the same criteria as established for the Presidential Unit Citation (Army). The Air Force award was derived from the Army award and the two awards are equal in precedence.

Presidential Unit Citation. The Presidential Unit Citation is awarded to units of the Armed Forces of the United States and cobelligerent nations for extraordinary heroism in action against the armed enemy occurring on or after 7 December 1941. The unit must display such gallantry, determination, and esprit de corps in accomplishing its mission under extremely difficult and hazardous conditions as to set it apart from and above other units participating in the same campaign. The degree of heroism required is the same as that which would warrant award of a Distinguished Service Cross to an individual. Extended periods of combat duty or participation in a large number of operational missions, either ground or air, is not sufficient. Only on rare occasions will a unit larger than a battalion qualify for award of the decoration.

The Presidential Unit Emblem (Army) is a blue ribbon set in a gold-colored metal frame of laurel leaves. It is authorized for purchase and wear as a permanent part of the uniform by those individuals who served with the unit during the cited period. It may be worn temporarily by those persons serving in the unit subsequent to the cited period.

Joint Meritorious Unit Award. Awarded in the name of the Secretary of Defense to Joint Activities of the DOD for meritorious achievement or service, superior to that normally expected, during combat with an armed enemy of the United States, during a declared national emergency, or under extraordinary circumstances that involved the national interest.

Valorous Unit Award. Criteria are the same as those for the Presidential Unit Citation except that the degree of valor required is that which would merit award of the Silver Star to an individual. The initial eligibility date is 3 August 1963. The emblem is a scarlet ribbon with the Silver Star color design superimposed in the center, set in a gold-colored metal frame with laurel leaves.

Meritorious Unit Commendation. Awarded for at least six months of exceptionally meritorious conduct in support of military operations to service and support units of the Armed Forces of the United States and cobelligerent nations during the period 1 January 1944–15 September 1946, during the Korean War, and after 1 March 1961. The degree of achievement is that which would merit the award of the Legion of Merit to an individual. The emblem is a scarlet ribbon set in a gold-colored metal frame with laurel leaves.

Army Superior Unit Award. Awarded for outstanding meritorious performance of a difficult and challenging mission under extraordinary circumstances by a unit during peacetime. Peacetime is defined as any period during which wartime or combat awards are not authorized in the geographical area in which the mission was executed. The emblem is a scarlet ribbon with a vertical green stripe in the center on each side of which is a narrow yellow stripe, set in a gold-colored metal frame with laurel leaves.

Infantry Streamers. Infantry streamers are awarded to United States infantry units that have participated in combat or that have been designated as Expert Infantry units. When 65 percent or more of the TOE strength of an infantry unit, brigade, or smaller has been awarded the combat infantryman badge, the unit is awarded the *combat infantry streamer*. It consists of a white streamer with the words "Combat Infantry (Brigade) (Battalion) (Company)" embroidered in blue. The *expert infantry streamer* is awarded when 65 percent of the TOE strength has been awarded either the combat infantryman badge or the expert infantryman badge. It consists of a white streamer with the words "Expert Infantry (Brigade) (Battalion) (Company)" embroidered thereon.

Medical Streamers. The *combat medical streamer* is awarded when 65 percent of the TOE strength of a medical unit authorized a color, distinguishing flag, or guidon has been awarded the combat medical badge. It is a maroon streamer with a 1/16 inch white stripe on each edge and the words "Combat Medical Unit" embroidered in white. The *expert medical streamer* is awarded when 65 percent or more of the assigned strength of a medical unit authorized a color, distinguishing flag, or guidon has been awarded the combat medical badge or the expert medical badge.

Campaign Streamers and War Service Streamers. These streamers are awarded to organizations that have been authorized an organizational color or standard. Campaign streamers are awarded for active federal military service to recognize award of campaign participation credit. War service streamers are awarded to recognize active federal military service in a theater of operations under circumstances when a campaign streamer is not authorized for the same service.

Campaign Silver Bands. To recognize combat participation credits campaign silver bands are awarded for active federal military service to units authorized a guidon. They are awarded only if the company or comparable unit is not a table of organization component part of an organization that is authorized an organizational color or standard and that has been awarded a campaign streamer for the same service.

OTHER U.S. ARMY AWARDS

Good Conduct Medal (Army). This is a medal awarded only to enlisted personnel in recognition of exemplary behavior, efficiency, and fidelity under prescribed conditions as to time and ratings. A distinctive clasp is awarded for each successive period of three years' service that meets the requirements.

Army Reserve Components Achievement Medal. Established by DA General Orders 30, 1971, this medal may be awarded upon recommendation of the unit commander for four years of honest and faithful service on or after 3 March 1972. Service must have been consecutive, in the grade of colonel or below, and in accordance with the standards of conduct, courage, and duty required by law and customs of the service of an active duty member of the same grade. The reverse of this medal is struck in two designs for award to personnel whose service has been primarily in the Army Reserve or primarily in the National Guard.

UNITED STATES MILITARY SERVICE MEDALS AND RIBBONS

Service (campaign) medals denote the honorable performance of military duty within specified limiting dates in specified geographical areas. They may also denote military duty anywhere within specified time periods.

They are worn as described later in this chapter.

United States service medals are those awarded by the Army, Navy, and Air Force. Other service medals of the federal government or awarded by a state or other inferior jurisdiction are regarded as civilian service medals and are not worn on the uniform.

Service Medals Authorized Prior to Vietnam War. Service medals, appurtenances, and devices that pertain only to wars or campaigns prior to the War in Vietnam are not included since there are no, or few, officers still on active duty who might wear such items. See AR 672-5-1 for details on these awards.

National Defense Service Medal. This medal has been authorized for honorable active service for any period between 27 June 1950 and 27 July 1954 and between 1 January 1961 and 14 August 1974. A second award of this medal is designated by a service star. Persons on active duty for purposes other than extended active duty are not eligible for this award.

Antarctica Service Medal. The Antarctica Service Medal is awarded to persons serving with U.S. expeditions to the Antarctic from 1 January 1946 to a date to be determined by the Secretary of Defense.

Armed Forces Expeditionary Medal. This medal, established by Executive Order on 4 December 1961, is authorized for specified U.S. military operations, U.S. operations in direct support of the United Nations, and U.S. operations of assistance for friendly foreign nations. The second and subsequent awards are denoted by service stars. Generally thirty days, or the full period of the operation, in the following areas of operations are required:
Berlin—From 14 August 1961 to 1 June 1963.
Lebanon—From 1 July 1958 to 1 November 1958.
Quemoy and Matsu Islands—From 23 August 1958 to 1 June 1963.
Taiwan Straits—From 23 August 1958 to 1 January 1959.
Cuba—24 October 1962 to 1 June 1963.
Congo—From 14 July 1960 to 1 September 1962 and 23–27 November 1964.
Laos—From 19 April 1961 to 7 October 1962.
Vietnam—From 1 July 1958 to 3 July 1965 and 29–30 April 1975.
Dominican Republic—From 28 April 1965 to 21 September 1966.
Korea—From 1 October 1966 to 30 June 1974.
Cambodia—From 29 March 1973 to 15 August 1973 and 11–13 April 1975.
Mayaguez Operation—15 May 1975.
Thailand—29 March 1973 to 15 August 1973.
Grenada—From 23 October 1983 to 21 November 1983.
Lebanon—From 1 June 1983 to a date to be announced.
Libya—Operation Eldorado Canyon. From 12 April 1986 to 17 April 1986.

Vietnam Service Medal. The Vietnam Service Medal was established by Executive Order on 1 October 1965. It was awarded to servicemen serving in Vietnam or contiguous waters or air space from 3 July 1965 through 28 March 1973.

Individuals who served in Vietnam between 1 July 1958 and 3 July 1965 and are qualified to wear the Armed Forces Expeditionary Medal, discussed above, are qualified to receive the newer award in lieu of the Expeditionary Medal. No person may be awarded both medals for Vietnam service, however.

Humanitarian Service Medal. Established by Executive Order 11965 on 19 January 1977. It is awarded by the Secretary of Defense or by the Secretary of Transportation to members of the Coast Guard when that service is not operating as a military service in the Navy. It is awarded to members of the Armed Forces of the United States, including Reserve components, who meritoriously participate in a military act or operation of a humanitarian nature. Award of this medal does not preclude or conflict with other medals awarded on the basis of valor, achievement, or meritorious service. Only one medal for service may be awarded for participation in a given military act or operation, however. Meritorious participation in subsequent acts or operations are recognized by award of service stars.

Armed Forces Reserve Medal. Honorable and satisfactory service is required in one or more of the Reserve components of the Armed Forces for a period of ten years, not necessarily consecutive, provided such service was performed within a period of twelve consecutive years. Periods of service as a member of a Regular component are excluded from consideration. Required also is the earning of a minimum of fifty retirement points per year. (AR 135-180.) Individuals are advised to consult the unit instructor of their organization as to individual eligibility.

10-year Device. One 10-year device is authorized to be worn on the suspension and service ribbon to denote service for each ten-year period in addition to and under the same conditions as prescribed for the award of the medal. It is a bronze hour glass with a Roman numeral X superimposed thereon, $5/16$ inch in height.

U.S. ARMY SERVICE AND TRAINING RIBBONS

Army Service Ribbon. Established by the Secretary of the Army on 10 April 1981, the Army Service Ribbon is awarded to officers upon successful completion of their basic/orientation or higher level course, or upon completion of four months of honorable service. This ribbon is awarded only once.

Overseas Service Ribbon. Established by the Secretary of the Army on 10 April 1981, the Overseas Service Ribbon is awarded for completion of a creditable overseas tour that is not recognized by award of another service medal. Subsequent awards are designated by numerals.

Army Reserve Components Overseas Training Ribbon. Established by the Secretary of the Army on 11 July 1984, the ribbon is awarded to members of the U.S. Army Reserve components for successful completion of annual training or active duty for training for a period of not less than ten days on foreign soil. Numerals are used to denote second and subsequent awards.

NON-U.S. SERVICE MEDALS

United Nations Medal. Established by the United Nations Secretary-General, 30 July 1959, and DOD Instruction 1348.10, 11 March 1964. It is awarded for service of not less than six months with United Nations teams and forces that are in or have been in Lebanon, Palestine, India and Pakistan, and Hollandia.

Multinational Force and Observers Medal. Established by the Director General, Multinational Force and Observers, 24 March 1982, and accepted by DOD Memorandum of 28 July 1982. This medal may be awarded to personnel who have served with the international peacekeeping force, the MFO, in the Sinai Peninsula for a period of at least ninety days after 3 August 1981. Effective 15 March 1985, the periods of service must be for six months (170 days minimum). Subsequent awards are designated by numerals.

Republic of Vietnam Campaign Medal. Authorized for award to individuals by DOD Instruction 1348.17, 31 January 1974, for six months' service in Vietnam or in direct combat support of operations in Vietnam during the period 1 March 1961 to 28 March 1973; during this period, the recipient must have met the criteria established for the Vietnam Service Medal or the Armed Forces Expeditionary Medal (Vietnam). Lesser periods of service are acceptable if the individual was wounded, captured, or killed by hostile forces.

UNITED STATES ARMY BADGES AND TABS

Badges and tabs are appurtenances of the uniform. In the eyes of their wearers several badges have a significance equal to or greater than all but the highest decorations. There is no established precedence with badges as there is with decorations and service medals, or ribbons. The badges are of three types: combat and special skill badges, marksmanship badges and tabs, and identification badges. Badges are awarded in recognition of attaining a high standard of proficiency in certain military skills. Subdued combat and special skill badges and the Ranger and Special Forces tabs are authorized on field uniforms.

Combat and Special Skill Badges. These include the combat infantryman badges; expert infantryman badge; combat medical badges; expert field medical badge; Army astronaut badges; aviator, flight surgeon, and aircraft crewman badges; glider badge; parachutist badges; combat parachutist badges; pathfinder badge; air assault badge; Ranger tab; Special Forces tab; diver badges; driver and mechanic badge; explosive ordnance disposal badges; nuclear reactor operator badges; and the parachute rigger badge.

These badges are awarded to denote excellence in performance of duties under hazardous conditions and circumstances of extraordinary hardship as well as for special qualifications and successful completion of prescribed courses of training. (See AR 672-5-1 for details.)

Combat Infantryman Badges. Awarded to infantry personnel in the grade of colonel or below who, subsequent to 6 December 1941, satisfactorily perform duty while assigned or attached as a member of an infantry brigade, regiment, or smaller unit during any period such unit is engaged in active ground combat. Members of attached Ranger companies are also eligible as well as officers of other branches who command similar size infantry units under similar circumstances for thirty consecutive days.

These badges are authorized for otherwise qualified Army members for service in Vietnam subsequent to 1 March 1961, in Laos from 19 April 1961 to 6 October 1962, and in Korea subsequent to 4 January 1969.

Expert Infantryman Badge. Awarded to infantry personnel of the active Army, ARNG, and USAR who satisfactorily complete prescribed proficiency tests.

Combat Medical Badges. Awarded to members of the Army Medical Department, the Naval Medical Department, or the Air Force Medical Service in the grade of colonel (Navy captain) or below who have satisfactorily performed medical duties while assigned or attached to a medical detachment of an infantry unit meeting the requirements for the combat infantryman badge.

Expert Field Medical Badge. Awarded to Army Medical Service personnel who satisfactorily complete prescribed proficiency tests.

Stars for Combat Infantryman and Combat Medical Badges. The second and succeeding awards of the combat infantryman and the combat medical badges, made to recognize participation and qualification in additional wars, are indicated by the addition of stars to the basic badges.

Only one award of the combat infantryman badge is authorized for service in Vietnam, Laos, the Dominican Republic, Korea (subsequent to 27 July 1954), and Grenada regardless of whether an individual has served one or more tours in one or more of these areas.

Note that either, but not both, the combat infantryman badge or the combat medical badge may be awarded for the same period of service in Vietnam or Laos.

Army Astronaut Badges. An Army astronaut badge has been added to the authorized special skill badges. The requirements for award of this badge are not stated in the regulations, however.

These badges are awarded in three degrees—basic, senior, and master.

Army Aviation Badges. There are nine badges relating to army aviation—three each for Army aviators, flight surgeons, and aircraft crewmen—in the degrees of basic, senior, and master. The following publications will give information on these badges.

AR 672-5-1, *Military Awards.*

AR 600-105, *Aviation Service of Rated Army Officers.*

The master Army aviator badge, the senior Army aviator badge, and the Army aviator badge are awarded upon satisfactory completion of prescribed training and proficiency tests as outlined in AR 600-105.

The master flight surgeon badge, the senior flight surgeon badge, and the flight surgeon badge are awarded to Army Medical Corps officers who complete the training and other requirements prescribed by AR 600-105.

The master aircraft crewman badge, the senior aircraft crewman badge, and the aircraft crewman badge are authorized for award to enlisted personnel who meet the prescribed requirements. (AR 672-5-1.)

Glider Badge. No longer awarded, but still authorized for wear by individuals who were previously awarded the badge.

Parachutist Badges. To be awarded the master parachutist badge an individual must have participated in sixty-five jumps, twenty-five with combat equipment, four at night, and five mass tactical jumps; have graduated as jumpmaster or served as jumpmaster on one or more combat jumps or on thirty-three noncombat jumps; have been rated excellent in character and efficiency; and have served on jump status for not less than thirty-six months.

For the senior parachutist badge an individual must have been rated excellent in character and efficiency with participation in thirty jumps, including fifteen jumps made with combat equipment, two night jumps, and two mass tactical jumps; have graduated from a jumpmaster course or served as jumpmaster on one or more combat jumps or fifteen noncombat jumps; and have served on jump status for not less than twenty-four months.

The parachutist badge is awarded for satisfactory completion of the course given by the Airborne Department of the Infantry School, or while assigned or attached to an airborne unit, or for participation in at least one combat jump.

Combat Parachutist Badges. Participation in a combat parachute jump entitles the individual to wear a bronze star affixed to the parachutist badge.

Pathfinder Badge. Awarded upon successful completion of the Pathfinder course conducted at the Infantry School.

Air Assault Badge. Awarded to personnel who have satisfactorily completed either the Training and Doctrine Command (TRADOC) prescribed training course or the standard air assault course while assigned or attached to the 101st Air Assault Division since 1 April 1974.

Ranger Tab. Awarded to any person who successfully completes a Ranger course conducted by the Infantry School.

Special Forces Tab. Awarded to any person who successfully completes the Special Forces Qualification Course conducted by the Special Forces School of the Special Warfare Center. This tab also may be awarded for former wartime service. See the regulation (AR 672-5) for details.

Diver Badges. Awarded after satisfactory completion of prescribed proficiency tests (AR 611–75). Five badges are authorized for enlisted personnel. As this edition goes to press, authorization of a gold badge for officers is pending.

Driver and Mechanic Badge. Awarded only to enlisted personnel to denote a high degree of skill in the operation and maintenance of motor vehicles.

Explosive Ordnance Disposal Badges. There are three badges under this heading, any of which may be awarded to officers: master explosive ordnance disposal badge, senior explosive ordnance disposal badge, and explosive ordnance disposal badge. They are awarded to individuals assigned to duties involving the removal and disposition of explosive ammunition under hazardous conditions.

Nuclear Reactor Operator Badges. The shift supervisor badge, the operator first class badge, the operator second class badge, and the operator basic badge were awarded upon completing the Nuclear Power Plant Operators Course or equivalent training and after operating nuclear power plants for specific periods. The reactor commander badge (same as the shift supervisor badge) was authorized for award to officers. These badges are no longer awarded but are still authorized for wear by individuals to whom they were previously awarded.

Parachute Rigger Badge. Awarded to any individual who successfully completes the Parachute Rigger course conducted by the U.S. Army Quartermaster School and who holds a Parachute Rigger MOS or Skill Identifier.

Physical Fitness Training Badge. Established by the Secretary of the Army on 25 June 1966, this badge is awarded to soldiers who obtain a minimum score of 290 on the Army Physical Readiness Test (APRT) and who meet the weight control requirements of AR 600-9. Once awarded, the badge may be retained as long as the individual achieves a minimum passing score on subsequent APRTs and continues to meet the weight requirements. This badge is worn only on the left breast of the physical training uniform.

Marksmanship Badges and Tabs. These include basic marksmanship qualification badges, excellence in competition badges, distinguished designation badges, the United States distinguished international shooter badge, and the President's Hundred tab.

Only members of the Armed Forces of the United States and civilian citizens of the United States are eligible for these qualification badges. Qualification badges for marksmanship are of three types: basic qualification, excellence in competition, and distinguished designation. Basic qualification badges (including expert, sharpshooter, and marksman badges) are awarded to those individuals who attain the qualification score prescribed in the appropriate field manual for the weapon concerned. Excellence in competition badges are awarded to individuals in recognition of an eminent degree of achievement in firing the rifle or pistol. Distinguished designation badges are awarded to individuals in recognition of a preeminent degree of achievement in target practice firing with the military service rifle or pistol.

The distinguished international shooter badge is awarded to military or civilian personnel in recognition of an outstanding degree of achievement in international competition.

A President's Hundred Tab is awarded each person who qualifies among the top 100 contestants in the President's Match held annually at the National Rifle Matches.

Identification Badges. These include Presidential service identification badge; Vice-Presidential service identification badge; Secretary of Defense identification badge; Joint Chiefs of Staff identification badge; Army Staff identification badge; Guard, Tomb of the Unknown Soldier identification badge; Army ROTC Nurse Cadet Program identification badge; Drill Sergeant identification badge; U.S. Army Recruiter badge; the U.S. Army Reserve Recruiter badge; the U.S. Army National Guard Recruiter badge; and the Career Counselor badge.

Presidential Service Identification Badge. The Presidential Service Certificate and the Presidential Service badge were established by Executive Order 11174, 1 September 1964.

The Presidential Service certificate is awarded in the name of the President of the United States, as public evidence of deserved honor and distinction, to members of the armed forces who have been assigned to duty in the White House for at least one year subsequent to 20 January 1961. It is awarded to Army members by the Secretary of the Army upon recommendation of the Military Aide to the President.

The Presidential Service badge is issued to members of the armed forces who have been awarded the Presidential Service certificate. Once this badge is awarded, it may be worn as a permanent part of the uniform.

Vice-Presidential Service Identification Badge. The Vice-Presidential Service badge was established by Executive Order 11544, 8 July 1970. It may be awarded upon recommendation of the Military Assistant to the Vice President and may be worn as a permanent part of the uniform.

Secretary of Defense Identification Badge. Military personnel who have been assigned to duty and have served not less than one year after 13 January 1961 in the Office of the Secretary of Defense are eligible for this badge. Once awarded, it may be worn as a permanent part of the uniform. It also is authorized for temporary wear by personnel assigned to specified offices of the Secretary of Defense.

Joint Chiefs of Staff Identification Badge. May be awarded to military personnel who have been assigned to duty and who have served not less than one year after 16 January 1961 in a position of responsibility under the direct cognizance of the Joint Chiefs of Staff. Once awarded, the badge may be worn as a permanent part of the uniform.

Army Staff Identification Badge. This badge has been awarded by the Army since 1920 and is the oldest of the five types of identification badges now authorized for officers. It was instituted to give a permanent means of identification to those commissioned officers who had been selected for duty on the War Department General Staff, with recommendation for award based upon performance of duty. It has been continued under the present departmental organization.

The requirements for award of this badge include service of not less than one year between 1 August 1977 and 28 May 1985 as a commissioned officer, or between 22 August 1980 and 28 May 1985 as a warrant officer, while detailed to duty on the Army General Staff and assigned to permanent duty in a TDA position on the Army General Staff, to the Office of the Secretary of the Army, the National Guard Bureau, or the Office, Chief Army Reserve. Between 30 September 1979 and 28 May 1985 the badge could also be awarded to the Sergeant Major of the Army and to other senior staff NCOs (SGM E9) assigned to duty with the same staff units. Effective 28 May 1985, qualifying service must be on the Army General Staff or assigned to the Office of the Secretary of the Army. Once awarded, this badge may be worn as a permanent part of the uniform.

Guard, Tomb of the Unknown Soldier Identification Badge. (See AR 672-5-1.)
Army ROTC Nurse Cadet Program Identification Badge. (See AR 672-5-1.)
Drill Sergeant Identification Badge. (See AR 672-5-1.)
U.S. Army Recruiter Identification Badge. (See AR 672-5-1.)
Army National Guard Recruiter Identification Badge. (See AR 672-5-1.)
U.S. Army Reserve Recruiter Identification Badge. (See AR 672-5-1.)
Career Counselor Badge. (See AR 672-5-1.)

APPURTENANCES TO DECORATIONS AND SERVICE MEDALS

Appurtenances are authorized as indicated in the following paragraphs.

Oak-Leaf Cluster. A bronze (or silver) twig of four oak leaves with three acorns on the stem is issued in lieu of a decoration for the second or succeeding awards of United States military decorations (other than the Air Medal), the Army Reserve

Components Achievement Medal, and unit awards. A silver oak-leaf cluster may be worn in lieu of five bronze oak-leaf clusters for the same decoration. Oak-leaf clusters are worn with the stem of the oak leaves pointing down toward the wearer's right and are attached to the ribbons of the decorations to which they pertain.

Numerals. Arabic numerals $\frac{3}{16}$ inch in height are issued in lieu of a decoration for second and succeeding awards of the Air Medal, the Multinational Force and Observers Medal, the Overseas Service ribbon, and the Army Reserve Components Overseas Training ribbon. The numerals are centered on the ribbon of the medal and on the ribbon bar.

Letter V Device. A bronze block letter V is worn on the suspension and service ribbons of the Bronze Star Medal, the Air Medal, the Joint Service Commendation Medal, and the Army Commendation Medal to denote an award made for valor. Not more than one V will be worn. When worn with oak-leaf clusters or numerals on the same ribbon, the V is to the wearer's right.

Arrowhead Device. A bronze arrowhead device is awarded for wear on the appropriate service medal ribbon to signify that the wearer participated in a parachute jump, a glider landing, or an amphibious assault against enemy-held territory. The device is worn with the point upward. It is placed to the right of all service stars.

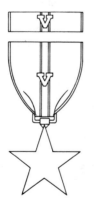

Bronze Star
with V Device

Air Medal with
Numerals 14

Service Ribbon
with V Device
and Oak Leaf
Cluster

Wearing
Arrowhead and
Service Stars on
Service Ribbon

Service Stars. Service stars, signifying participation in a combat campaign, are worn on service medal ribbons, point of star upward. A silver star is worn in lieu of five bronze stars. A bronze star is also worn on the Parachutist badges to denote participation in a combat parachute jump.

Miniatures. Miniature decorations and appurtenances are replicas of the corresponding decorations and appurtenances on the scale of one-half. Miniatures are not presented or sold by the Army but may be purchased from civilian dealers. There is no miniature of the Medal of Honor. Except for the Medal of Honor, only miniature decorations and service medals, dress miniature combat and special skill badges, and dress miniature versions of Ranger and Special Forces tabs may be worn on the mess and evening mess uniforms.

FOREIGN DECORATIONS AND GIFTS

The Constitution requires the consent of Congress for an individual holding a federal office or position of trust to accept a foreign decoration. Individuals may participate in ceremonies and receive the tender of a foreign award or gift, however. Foreign awards may be accepted and worn after receiving approval of Headquarters, DA (DAPC-DPA). The foreign award with accompanying documents will be retained by the individual until the individual is informed of the final DA action. Gifts of minimal value (retail value of less than $165) may be accepted and retained by the individual. The burden of proof as to the value is the responsibility of the individual accepting the gift, however. For gifts of more than minimal value, receipt of the gift will be immediately reported through command channels to HQDA (DAPC-DPA), and within 60 days the gift must be forwarded to the same address.

CERTIFICATES AND LETTERS FOR SERVICE

Several types of certificates may be awarded to individuals, as follows:

Certificates for Decorations. Each individual who has been awarded a decoration is entitled to a certificate on a standard Department of the Army form, bearing a reproduction of the decoration.

Certificate of Honorable Service. The certificate (DA Form 1563) is issued to the next of kin of those who die in line of duty while on active service in time of peace. In time of war an accolade with facsimile signature of the President has been used.

Certificate of Achievement. Commanding officers may issue such a certificate in recognition of faithful service, acts, or achievements. DA Form 2442, Certificate of Achievement, or a similar form of local design may be used.

Letters of Commendation and Appreciation. Acts or services that do not meet the criteria for decorations or the various certificates may be recognized by letters of commendation or appreciation. Such letters, typed on letterhead stationery, may be issued to military personnel and, as specified in AR 672-20, to civilians or civilian groups.

ORDER OF PRECEDENCE OF DECORATIONS AND AWARDS

There is a definite ranking among categories of decorations and awards, and within each category there is also an order of precedence. This section provides the rules. Consult it before you assemble authorized decorations and awards on your uniform to be sure you have them in the right sequence.

Categories of Medals. The listing below indicates the order of precedence by category when medals of two or more categories are worn simultaneously. The same order of precedence applies when service ribbons are worn in lieu of decorations and service medals.

United States military decorations
United States unit awards
United States nonmilitary decorations
Good Conduct Medal
Army Reserve Components Achievement Medal
United States service and training ribbons
United States Merchant Marine awards
Foreign military decorations
Foreign unit awards
Non-U.S. service awards

United States Military Decorations. The listing above gives the order of precedence of different categories of medals with the United States military decorations at the top, or most honored position. United States military decorations of the Army, Navy, Air Force, and Coast Guard are worn by Army personnel in the following order:

Medal of Honor (Army, Navy, Air Force)
Distinguished Service Cross
Navy Cross
Air Force Cross
Defense Distinguished Service Medal
Distinguished Service Medal (Army, Navy, Air Force, Coast Guard)
Silver Star
Defense Superior Service Medal
Legion of Merit
Distinguished Flying Cross
Soldier's Medal
Navy and Marine Corps Medal
Airman's Medal
Coast Guard Medal
Bronze Star Medal
Purple Heart
Defense Meritorious Service Medal
Meritorious Service Medal
Air Medal
Joint Service Commendation Medal
Army Commendation Medal
Navy Commendation Medal
Air Force Commendation Medal
Coast Guard Commendation Medal
Joint Service Achievement Medal
Army Achievement Medal
Navy Achievement Medal
Air Force Achievement Medal
Coast Guard Achievement Medal
Combat Action Ribbon

United States Unit Awards. These awards may be worn as a permanent part of the uniform by personnel who were assigned to the unit during any part of the period during which the unit earned the award. In addition, as regards the four

Army unit awards, personnel who were not present with the unit at the time the award was earned may wear the award temporarily while they are assigned to the unit at some later date. For elements of regiments organized under the New Manning System or the Combat Arms Regimental System, the emblem may be worn temporarily only by personnel assigned to the earning unit. The awards are worn in the following order:

Presidential Unit Citation (Army and Air Force)
Presidential Unit Citation (Navy)
Joint Meritorious Unit Award
Valorous Unit Award (Army)
Meritorious Unit Commendation (Army)
Navy Unit Commendation
Air Force Outstanding Unit Award
Coast Guard Unit Commendation
Army Superior Unit Award
Meritorious Unit Commendation (Navy)
Navy "E" Ribbon
Air Force Organizational Excellence Award
Coast Guard Meritorious Unit Commendation

United States Nonmilitary Decorations. These decorations may be worn on the uniform only with one or more military decorations or service medals. They are worn after the Combat Action Ribbon and before service medals. They are listed in order of precedence.

Presidential Medal of Freedom
Gold Lifesaving Medal
Medal for Merit
Silver Lifesaving Medal
National Security Medal
Medal of Freedom
Distinguished Civilian Service Medal
Outstanding Civilian Service Medal
Selective Service Distinguished, Exceptional, and Meritorious Service Medals
Civilian Service in Vietnam Medal

The Good Conduct Medal Worn with Other Decorations. The Good Conduct Medal takes precedence immediately after all authorized United States military and nonmilitary decorations. Good Conduct Medals from the other services follow the Army Good Conduct Medal.

Army Reserve Components Achievement Medal. The Army Reserve Components Achievement Medal takes precedence immediately following the Army Good Conduct Medal and/or the Good Conduct Medals of the other services.

Service Medals. United States service medals are worn following the military and nonmilitary decorations, the Good Conduct Medal, and the Army Reserve Components Achievement Medal, if worn. Service medals for actions or time periods prior to the Vietnam War are not included here. The order of precedence is as follows:

National Defense Service Medal
Antarctica Service Medal
Armed Forces Expeditionary Medal
Vietnam Service Medal

Humanitarian Service Medal
Armed Forces Reserve Medal
NCO Professional Development Ribbon
Army Service Ribbon
Overseas Service Ribbon
Army Reserve Components Overseas Training Ribbon

Service medals of the United States Navy, Air Force, Marine Corps, Coast Guard, and Merchant Marine may be worn on the uniform. Others issued by state and local governments, fraternal societies, United States Maritime Service, and professional groups and organizations are prohibited for wear on the uniform.

Foreign Decorations. The wearing of foreign decorations on the uniform is governed by both law and regulations. The reader is referred to AR 672-5-1 for a check of complete information as to authorized wearing of foreign decorations. Foreign decorations or unit awards will not be worn under any circumstances unless at least one U.S. decoration or service medal or ribbon is worn at the same time.

Non-U.S. Service Medals and Ribbons.

United Nations Medal
Multinational Force and Observers Medal
Republic of Vietnam Campaign Medal

Combat and Special Skill Badges. Combat and special skill badges are grouped into categories with an order of group precedence by category as follows:

Group 1   Combat Infantryman badges (3 awards) and Expert Infantryman badge.

Group 2   Combat Medical badges (3 awards) and Expert Field Medical badge.

Group 3   Army Astronaut badges (3 degrees), Army Aviator badges (3 degrees), Flight Surgeon badges (3 degrees), and Aircraft Crewman badges (3 degrees).

Group 4   Glider badge, Parachutist badges (3 degrees), Combat Parachutist badges, Pathfinder badge, and Air Assault badge. *Note:* For purposes of classification and wear policy, the Ranger and Special Forces metal tab replicas are considered Group 4 badges.

Group 5   Diver badges (5 badges), Driver and Mechanic badge (6 clasps), Explosive Ordnance Disposal badges (3 degrees), Nuclear Reactor Operator badges (4 badges), and Parachute Rigger badge.

Group 6   Physical Fitness Training badge.

Marksmanship Badges. Marksmanship badges authorized for wear on the Army uniform are worn in the following order of precedence:

U.S. Distinguished International Shooter badge
Distinguished Rifleman badge
Distinguished Pistol Shot badge
National Trophy Match badges
Interservice Competition badges
U.S. Army Excellence in Competition Rifleman badge
U.S. Army Excellence in Competition Pistol Shot badge
Marksmanship Qualification badges (Expert, Sharpshooter, and Marksman)

In addition, the President's Hundred tab is a marksmanship award, but it must compete with other tabs (see below) for wear on the uniform.

DECORATIONS, SERVICE MEDALS, AND BADGES

U.S. ARMY AND DEPARTMENT OF DEFENSE MILITARY DECORATIONS

Medal of Honor (Army)

**Distinguished Service
Cross (Army)**

**Defense Distinguished
Service Medal**

**Distinguished Service
Medal (Army)**

Silver Star

**Defense Superior
Service Medal**

Legion of Merit

**Distinguished Flying
Cross**

**Soldier's Medal
(Army)**

Bronze Star Medal

Purple Heart

**Defense
Meritorious Service
Medal**

**Meritorious Service
Medal**

Air Medal

Joint Service Commendation Medal

Army Commendation Medal

Joint Service Achievement Medal

Army Achievement Medal

OTHER U.S. ARMY AWARDS

**Good Conduct
Medal (Army)**

**Army Reserve Components
Achievement Medal**

PRE-VIETNAM U.S. MILITARY SERVICE MEDALS

**World War II
Victory Medal**

**Korean
Service Medal**

U.S. ARMY AND DEPARTMENT OF DEFENSE
UNIT AWARDS

**Presidential Unit
Citation (Army)**

**Valorous Unit
Award**

**Joint
Meritorious Unit
Award**

**Meritorious Unit
Commendation (Army)**

**Army
Superior Unit
Award**

U.S. MILITARY SERVICE MEDALS AND RIBBONS

**National Defense
Service Medal**

**Antarctica
Service Medal**

**Armed Forces
Expeditionary
Medal**

**Vietnam
Service Medal**

**Humanitarian
Service Medal**

**Armed Forces
Reserve Medal**

U.S. ARMY SERVICE AND TRAINING RIBBONS

**NCO
Professional Development
Ribbon**

**Army
Service Ribbon**

**Overseas
Service Ribbon
(Army)**

**Army Reserve Components
Overseas Training Ribbon**

NON-U.S. SERVICE MEDALS

**United Nations
Medal**

**Multinational Force
Observers Medal**

**Republic of Vietnam
Campaign Medal**

U.S. ARMY BADGES AND TABS

Combat and Special Skill Badges

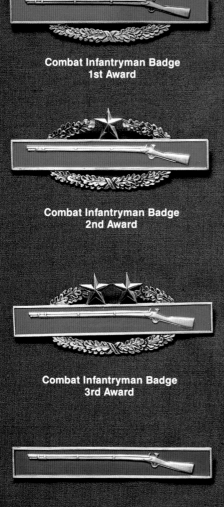

**Combat Infantryman Badge
1st Award**

**Combat Medical Badge
1st Award**

**Combat Infantryman Badge
2nd Award**

**Combat Medical Badge
2nd Award**

**Combat Infantryman Badge
3rd Award**

**Combat Medical Badge
3rd Award**

Expert Infantryman Badge

Expert Field Medical Badge

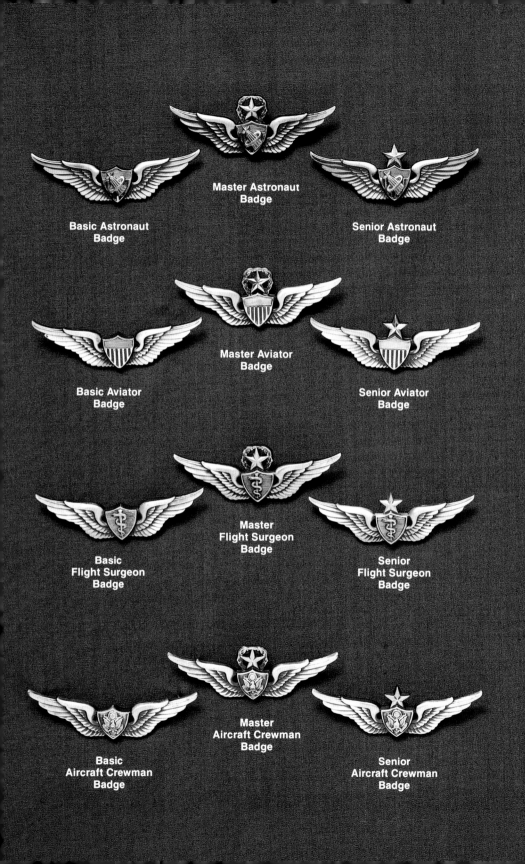

**Master Astronaut
Badge**

**Basic Astronaut
Badge**

**Senior Astronaut
Badge**

**Master Aviator
Badge**

**Basic Aviator
Badge**

**Senior Aviator
Badge**

**Master
Flight Surgeon
Badge**

**Basic
Flight Surgeon
Badge**

**Senior
Flight Surgeon
Badge**

**Master
Aircraft Crewman
Badge**

**Basic
Aircraft Crewman
Badge**

**Senior
Aircraft Crewman
Badge**

**Master Parachutist
Badge**

**Basic Parachutist
Badge**

**Senior Parachutist
Badge**

**Combat Parachutist
Badge (1 Jump)**

**Combat Parachutist
Badge (2 Jumps)**

**Combat Parachutist
Badge (3 Jumps)**

**Combat Parachutist
Badge (4 Jumps)**

**Combat Parachutist
Badge (5 Jumps)**

Air Assault Badge

Glider Badge

Pathfinder Badge

**Special Forces Tab
(Metal Replica)**

**Ranger Tab
(Metal Replica)**

**Salvage Diver
Badge**

**Second Class Diver
Badge**

**First Class Diver
Badge**

**Master Diver
Badge**

**Scuba Diver
Badge**

**Master Explosive
Ordnance Disposal Badge**

**Basic Explosive
Ordnance Disposal Badge**

**Senior Explosive
Ordnance Disposal Badge**

**Nuclear Reactor Operator
Badge (Basic)**

**Nuclear Reactor Operator
Badge (Second Class)**

**Nuclear Reactor Operator
Badge (First Class)**

**Nuclear Reactor Operator
Badge (Shift Supervisor)**

**Parachute Rigger
Badge**

**Driver and Mechanic
Badge**

Marksmanship Badges

Marksman

Sharpshooter

Expert

Identification Badges

Presidential Service

Vice-Presidential Service

Secretary of Defense

Joint Chiefs of Staff

Army Staff

Guard,
Tomb of the Unknown Soldier

Drill Sergeant

U.S. Army Recruiter
(Active Army)

U.S. Army Recruiter
(Army National Guard)

U.S. Army Recruiter
(U.S. Army Reserve)

Identification Badges. Authorized identification badges are worn in the following order of precedence:

Presidential Service Identification badge
Vice-Presidential Service Identification badge
Secretary of Defense Identification badge
Joint Chiefs of Staff Identification badge
Army Staff Identification badge
Guard, Tomb of the Unknown Soldier Identification badge
Army ROTC Nurse Cadet Program Identification badge
Drill Sergeant Identification badge
U.S. Army Recruiter Identification badges (Active Army, ARNG, and USAR)
Career Counselor badge

Special Skill Tabs. There is no order of precedence among the special skill tabs, but only one tab at a time may be worn on the uniform. The authorized tabs are:

President's Hundred tab
Ranger tab
Special Forces tab

Foreign Badges. No more than one foreign badge may be worn on the uniform at any one time and then only if at least one U.S. medal or service ribbon is worn simultaneously. Special permission must be obtained from HQDA to accept, retain, and wear a foreign badge. (See AR 672-5-1 for details.) The following foreign badges from Vietnam are authorized for wear:

Parachute badge
Ranger badge
Explosive Ordnance Disposal badge

GUIDE FOR WEARING AWARDS

When an officer wears decorations, service medals, badges, and other uniform accouterments, he or she must be certain to wear them correctly. This means wearing them on proper occasions, on the correct garments, and in prescribed order or arrangement. There is a prescribed place and position for each item authorized in relation to others which may be worn at the same time. Metallic portions must be clean and bright, ribbons clean. Wear them correctly—or don't wear them at all!

Military tailors assemble the ribbons of decorations and service medals in rows, when a wearer is entitled to several, and attach them to the garments in correct position. The wearer must indicate the order of arrangement and be certain of its accuracy upon completion. This is the simplest and best practice. They can also be assembled on pins for use on any appropriate garment.

Occasions for Wearing Decorations, Service Medals, or Their Ribbons. Commanding officers may prescribe the wearing of these items at parades, reviews, inspections, funerals, and on ceremonial and social occasions.

They may be worn at the option of the wearer on the service and dress uniforms on normal duty (when not prohibited) and when off duty. Also, miniature medals may be worn on formal civilian attire at formal social functions when it is inappropriate or unauthorized to wear the Army uniform.

Prohibited Wearing. The items are not worn on any uniform other than as authorized by AR 670-1 (as detailed in this chapter), by officers while suspended from either rank or command; by enlisted personnel while serving sentence of confinement; or when wearing civilian clothing. A lapel button in the form of a miniature service ribbon may be worn.

Penalty for Unauthorized Wearing. It is a violation of law to wear decorations other than those to which an individual is entitled, or to wear their ribbons or other decoration substitutes. Serious penalties may be invoked.

The preceding section lists the categories of awards and itemizes the relative order of precedence both among and within categories. This section describes when, how, and where the authorized awards may be worn on the uniforms. The rules are specific. If in doubt after studying these two sections, consult AR 670-1.

While the rules for wear may seem quite involved, no one individual needs to know all the rules pertaining to all the awards. Just be sure you understand the rules that pertain to the awards you are authorized to wear so that you may assemble them correctly and wear them on your uniform with confidence and pride.

The descriptions and the accompanying illustrations should answer most questions about the correct placement of decorations and awards. For all decorations and awards, the place of honor is on the wearer's right and at the top. The order of precedence then is from right to left and from top to bottom.

Wear of Service Ribbons. Decoration and service medal ribbons may be worn on the coat of the Army green or Army green classic service uniforms and on the Army blue and Army white uniform coats. The ribbons are worn in one or more

Ribbons – Male

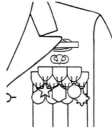

Full Size and Miniature Medals – Male

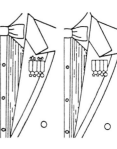

Miniature Medals on Mess Uniforms – Male

Ribbons – Female

Full Size and Miniature Medals – Female

Miniature Medals on Mess Uniforms – Female

WEAR OF RIBBONS AND MEDALS.

rows in order of precedence, with either no space or a ⅛-inch space between rows. No more than four ribbons may be worn in any row, but a second row is not started unless four or more ribbons are worn. The first two rows will contain the same number of ribbons (either three or four) before starting a third row. The third and succeeding rows will contain the same number or fewer ribbons than the first two rows. The top row will be centered on the row beneath or aligned to the left edge of the row underneath, whichever presents the best appearance.

Males wear the ribbons centered ⅛ inch above the left breast pocket in as many rows as necessary.

Females wear the ribbons on the left side with the bottom of the bottom row on the same horizontal line as the bottom of the nameplate. Placement may be adjusted to conform to individual figure differences.

Wear of Full-Size Decorations and Service Medals. Full-size decorations and service medals may be worn on the Army blue and Army white uniforms after retreat and by enlisted personnel on the Army green dress uniform when worn for social functions. The medals are worn in order of precedence, in one or more rows, with ⅛-inch spacing between rows. The second and subsequent rows will not contain more medals than the row below. The number of medals worn in a row depends on the size of the coat; they must not overlap within a row. Service and training ribbons are not worn with the full-size medals.

Males wear the first row of medals attached immediately above the seam of the left breast pocket.

Females wear the medals so that the bottom of the bottom row of pendants is on the same horizontal line as the bottom of the nameplate.

Wear of Miniature Decorations and Service Medals. Miniature medals are half-scale replicas of the full-size decorations and service medals. They are available for all medals except the Medal of Honor, which is worn only in full size. Except for the Medal of Honor, only miniature medals are authorized for wear on the various mess and evening mess uniform jackets. They may also be worn on the Army blue and Army white dress uniforms after retreat when these uniforms are worn as formal attire (bow ties). Only the dress miniature versions of the combat and special skill badges may be worn with miniature medals. Service and training ribbons are not worn in combination with the miniature medals. Miniatures may also be worn on the left lapel of formal civilian attire on occasions when wear of the uniform is inappropriate or unauthorized.

Miniature medals are mounted on holding bars in order of precedence from the wearer's right to left, in more than one row if necessary. They are worn side by side when there are four or fewer medals. They may be overlapped up to 50 percent when five, six, or seven medals are in the row. The overlap is equal for all medals with the right medal showing in full. When more than one row of medals is worn, the pendants on the lower row must be fully visible.

Males. On the Army blue and Army white dress uniforms, the medals are worn as described for the full-size medals. Up to three of the dress miniature combat and special skill badges from groups one through five may be worn above the medals in order of group precedence.

On the blue and white mess jackets, the medals are worn centered on the left lapel, about ½ inch below the notch. They do not extend beyond the edge of the lapel. Up to four of the dress miniature combat and special skill badges may be worn with the miniature medals on the mess jackets. They are worn in order of group precedence above the miniature medals. When two are worn, they are placed side by side immediately above the medals. When a third is worn, it is centered ¼ inch above the first two. If a fourth badge is worn, it is placed ¼ inch above the third badge.

Females. Miniature medals are centered on the left side of the uniform coats or the mess jackets, not on the lapels. The bottom of the bottom row of pendants is positioned approximately in line with the top edge of the top button on the Army blue and and Army white coats, and in a comparable position on the blue, white, and black mess jackets. Dress miniature combat and special skill badges are worn as described for the male uniforms.

Wear of U.S. and Foreign Unit Awards. Unit award emblems are worn in order of precedence, not more than three per row, with no space between emblems, and up to ⅛-inch space between rows. A permanent U.S. unit award has a gold-colored metal frame with laurel leaves, while a temporary award (authorized for wear only while assigned to the unit that earned the award) does not have the frame.

The framed awards are worn with the laurel leaves pointing upward. The unit award emblems may be worn with service ribbons or full size medals but are not worn with miniature medals. Foreign unit awards are worn after U.S. unit awards in order of date of receipt of the award. The foreign unit awards from the Vietnam War era, authorized only for permanent wear, are the Vietnam Presidential Unit Citation badge, the Republic of Vietnam Gallantry Cross Unit Citation badge, and the Republic of Vietnam Civil Actions Unit Citation badge.

Males wear the unit awards on the coats of the Army green, Army blue, and Army white uniforms. The awards are worn centered and with the bottom row ⅛ inch above the seam of the right breast pocket flap.

Females wear the unit awards on the coats of the Army green classic, Army blue, and Army white uniforms. The awards are centered on the right side with a ½-inch space between the bottom of the bottom row and the top of the nameplate.

Wear of Appurtenances. Appurtenances are devices affixed to service or suspension ribbons to denote additional awards or other distinguishing characteristics of the award.

Oak-Leaf Cluster. A bronze twig of four oak leaves with three acorns on each stem is worn to denote the second or succeeding awards of a decoration (other than the Air Medal) or a unit award. A silver oak-leaf cluster is worn in lieu of five bronze oak-leaf clusters. A silver cluster is worn to the right of any bronze clusters. The device is centered on the ribbon (or equally spaced if more than one device is worn) with the stem pointing down to the wearer's right.

V Device. The V device is a bronze, block letter V. It is worn on certain decorations to denote that the award was received for acts of heroism involving

Male   Female   ARRANGEMENT OF RIBBONS.

WEAR OF UNIT AWARDS.

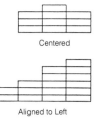

Centered

Aligned to Left

conflict with an armed enemy. When awarded, the V device is worn centered on the ribbon, or to the right of any oak-leaf clusters, on the service or suspension ribbons of the Bronze Star Medal, the Air Medal, the Joint Service Commendation Medal, and the Army Commendation Medal.

Numerals. Arabic numerals are worn on the ribbons of the Air Medal, the Overseas Training Ribbon, and the Reserve Components Overseas Training Ribbon to denote receipt of additional awards. For these awards, the ribbon constitutes the first award, and numerals starting with a 1 denote the second and subsequent awards. On the Multinational Force and Observers Ribbon the numeral 2 denotes the second award.

Service Stars. A bronze service star is worn on a service medal ribbon to denote participation in a campaign as specified in AR 672-5-1. A silver service star is worn in lieu of five bronze service stars. The service stars are worn to the left of an arrowhead device, if authorized. A bronze service star is also affixed to a parachutist badge to denote participation in a combat parachute jump.

Arrowhead. A bronze arrowhead is worn on service medal ribbons to denote participation in a combat parachute jump, a combat glider landing, or an amphibious assault landing. It is worn point upward, to the right of all service stars, only one per ribbon.

Ten-Year Device. A bronze Roman numeral X is worn on the ribbon of the Armed Forces Reserve Medal to denote ten years of satisfactory service as specified in AR 672-5-1. Additional devices may be worn for each ten-year period.

Wear of Marksmanship Badges and Tab. Not more than three marksmanship badges may be worn at one time, and only on the coats of the Army green or Army green classic, the Army blue, and the Army white uniforms. These badges are worn by males on the flap of the left breast pocket, under the service ribbons, and by females in a comparable position. There will be no more than three clasps per badge, and the total number of marksmanship badges and special skill badges will not exceed three. At least one marksmanship badge will normally be worn by all personnel except for those individuals who are exempted by regulation.

Males wear a single marksmanship or special skill badge centered on the left breast pocket flap, with the top of the badge 1/8 inch below the seam. When two such badges are worn, they are placed side by side about 1/8 inch below the seam with the special skill badge to the wearer's right and the badges equally spaced on the flap from right to left. Three such badges in any combination are worn in similar fashion except when one special skill and two marksmanship badges are worn. In this case the special skill badge may be worn centered on the pocket flap 1/8 inch below the seam, with the marksmanship badges centered between the button and the right or left side of the pocket flap, and with the bottom of the badge coinciding with the bottom of the flap.

Females wear marksmanship and special skill badges on the left side, approximately 1/4 inch below the bottom row of ribbons, but otherwise as prescribed for males.

The President's Hundred tab is worn 1/2 inch below the shoulder seam on the left sleeve of the Army green or Army green classic uniform coats. It competes in this position with the Ranger and Special Forces tabs. Only one of the three tabs may be worn at a time.

Wear of Combat and Special Skill Badges and Tabs. As stated in the earlier section, *Order of Precedence,* combat and special skill badges and tabs are categorized into six groups and an order of group precedence is established. The only badge in Group 6 is the Physical Fitness badge, which is worn only on the

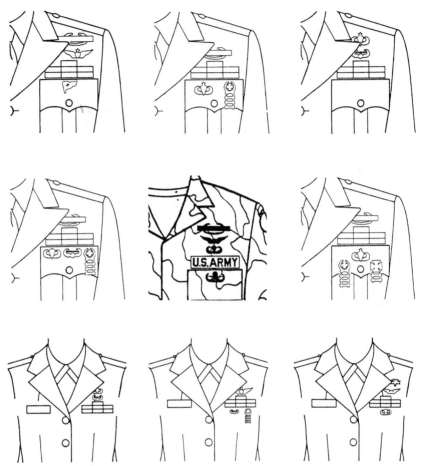

**WEAR POSITION FOR VARIOUS COMBINATIONS
OF COMBAT, SPECIAL SKILL, AND MARKSMANSHIP BADGES.**

physical training uniform. Of the remaining badges, a maximum of four may be worn at one time on the coats of the Army green or Army green classic, the Army blue, and the Army white uniforms. This total does not include the Ranger or Special Forces tabs, which may be worn on the left shoulder of the green uniform coat. Only one badge from groups 1, 2, 3, and 5 may be worn at a time. Two badges from group 4 may be worn if no badge from group 5 is worn.

Within a group, a combat badge takes precedence over a skill badge. For example, the combat infantryman badge would be worn instead of the expert infantryman badge if both are authorized. Up to three badges from groups one through three (one from each group) may be worn one above another, ½ inch apart, and with the bottom badge ¼ inch above the ribbons, or the pocket flap if no ribbons are worn. If no badges from groups 1 through 3 are worn, a total of two special skill badges from groups 4 and 5 (two from group 4 or one from group 4 and one from group 5) may be worn above the pocket or the ribbons as described for badges in groups 1 through 3. When badges from groups 1 through 3 are worn, badges from groups 4 and 5 are worn on the pocket flap or underneath the ribbons as described earlier under *Wear of Marksmanship Badges and Tab.*

Wear of full-size or miniature combat and special skill badges is authorized on the blue and white dress uniforms. In instances where the number of ribbons or medals worn causes the badges to be obscured by the lapel, the badges may be worn aligned with the left edge of the ribbons or medals.

On the Army blue and Army white dress uniforms, when wearing miniature medals, only dress miniature combat and special skill badges will be worn. A maximum of three of these badges from groups 1 through 5 may be worn one above another, above the medals. Special skill and marksmanship badges are not worn beneath the miniature medals.

On the mess uniform jackets, up to four dress miniature combat and special skill badges may be worn. Two medals are worn side by side, centered above the miniature medals. When three badges are worn, the third will be centered $1/4$ inch above the first two badges, and a fourth badge, if worn, will be centered $1/4$ inch above the third badge.

Subdued pin-on or embroidered sew-on combat and special skill badges may be worn on the BDU coats. Subdued pin-on badges may be worn on the cold-weather uniform shirt. When one badge is worn, it will be centered over the "U.S. Army" tape, with the bottom approximately $1/4$ inch above the tape. If two badges are worn, they are worn one above the other, centered over the "U.S. Army" tape with $1/2$ inch between badges. If three badges are worn, two are as described above, and the third is worn centered on the pocket flap or in a comparable position on uniforms without pockets. If four badges are worn, three are worn in a vertical line centered above the "U.S. Army" tape, and one is worn centered on the pocket flap or in a comparable position.

Ranger and Special Forces tabs are worn on the left shoulder of the green or green classic uniform coats, sewn $1/2$ inch below the shoulder seam. Only one of these tabs or the President's Hundred tab may be worn at a time. Full-size metal tab replicas of the Ranger and Special Forces tabs may be worn with ribbons or full-size medals on the Army blue and Army white dress uniforms. In this case, they are considered as group 4 badges and placement is as discussed earlier. Only one of the metal tab replicas may be worn at a time. Dress miniature versions of the Ranger and Special Forces tabs (metal replicas) may be worn with miniature medals. In this case, they are also considered and handled as group 4 badges. A subdued Ranger or Special Forces tab may be worn on the left shoulder of the BDU coats or the field jacket, sewn on $1/8$ inch below the shoulder seam.

Wear of Identification Badges. Identification badges are worn on the pockets or in comparable positions on the uniform coats. No more than two badges may be worn on one pocket or on one side of the coat at a time. When two badges are worn on one pocket or on one side of the coat, the order of precedence is from the wearer's right to left. The Presidential Service Identification badge, the Vice-Presidential Service Identification badge, the Army Staff Identification badge, and the Guard, Tomb of the Unknown Soldier Identification badge are worn on the right side of the uniform. The Secretary of Defense Identification badge and the Joint Chiefs of Staff Identification badge are worn on the left side of the uniform.

Males. On the green service and the blue and white dress uniforms, the ID badge is worn centered on the breast pocket, midway between the bottom of the flap and the bottom of the pocket. If two badges are worn, they are equally spaced from right

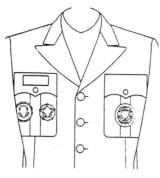

Green, Blue and,
White Uniforms—Male

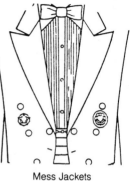

Mess Jackets
Male

Green Classic, Blue and,
White Uniforms—Female

Mess Jackets
Female

WEAR POSITION FOR INDENTIFICATION BADGES.

to left on the pocket. On the blue and white mess jackets, the ID badge is worn centered between the upper two buttons on the appropriate side of the jacket.

Females. On the green classic service uniform and the blue and white dress uniforms, the ID badge is worn at waist level and centered on either the right or left side. On the blue, white, and black mess jackets, the badge is worn centered between the lower two buttons on the appropriate side of the jacket.

Wear of Foreign Badges. Foreign badges, if authorized, may be worn only one at a time, and then only if worn in conjunction with at least one U.S. medal or service ribbon, and only on the green service and the blue and white dress uniform coats.

Males wear the foreign badge 1/8 inch above the seam of the right pocket flap or 1/4 inch above any unit awards.

Females wear the foreign badge 1/2 inch above the nameplate or 1/2 inch above any unit awards.

24

Authorized Absences

The Army recognizes that all personnel require periods of respite from routine duty and to permit personal attention to matters not related to the military service. The types of authorized absences from duty include leave, passes, and administrative absences. It is Army policy that all personnel be encouraged to utilize their authorized leave to the maximum extent possible. Frequent utilization of leave is beneficial to health and morale, which are essential to the maintenance of maximum efficiency. The judicious application of leave policies of the Army is an important command responsibility. (This chapter is based upon AR 630-5.)

DEFINITIONS AND TYPES OF LEAVE

Leave. Leave is authorized absence from place of duty, chargeable against the service member's leave account, for the purpose of providing the member a rest from the working environment or for other specific reasons.

Accrued Leave. Accrued leave is earned by active service performed. Leave accrues at the rate of two and a half calendar days for each month of active service and is credited to the member's leave account. In general, the service member must be in normal performance of duties to accumulate leave credits; absence without leave and other improper acts void leave credit accumulation.

Annual Leave. Annual leave, also called ordinary leave, is leave granted in execution of a command's leave program and chargeable to the member's leave account. It normally is granted at the request of a service member within the limits of accrued leave and/or that leave that may be advanced. Annual leave programs are established to provide maximum opportunity for all personnel to take leave.

Advanced Leave. This is leave granted a service member, with pay and allowances, prior to its accrual based on the reasonable expectation that the amount advanced will be earned prior to the member's separation. The maximum will not exceed thirty days or two and a half days for each month remaining in active service, whichever is lesser.

Excess Leave. Leave in excess of that which is accrued and that which may be advanced is designated as excess leave. It may be granted upon application of a service member under emergency or unusual circumstances. Excess leave when authorized will be without pay and allowances. Leave credits do not accrue to the member's leave account during periods covered by excess leave.

Leave En Route. Leave en route is leave granted upon request of the service member when traveling to a new station in connection with temporary duty and/or permanent change of station orders. It is charged to the member's leave account and is in addition to authorized travel time. Leave en route is authorized only by use of a leave request, DA Form 31.

Emergency Leave. Emergency leave is granted upon request of a service member when it is established that a family emergency exists requiring the member's presence. It normally is granted for a thirty-day period, is chargeable to the member's leave account, and is the basis for priority travel at government expense from, to, and between oversea areas, as specified in AR 630-5. Leave within the continental United States, even though prompted by emergency circumstances, is annual leave.

Convalescent Leave. Convalescent leave for the purpose of recuperation from wounds or illness is granted by the hospital commander or by the organization commander upon recommendation of the attending physician. It normally is granted for a period not to exceed thirty days and is not charged to the member's leave account. Personnel who have incurred illness or injury in line of duty while eligible to receive hostile fire pay (chapter 20, *Pay and Allowances*) are entitled to travel and transportation allowances for a round trip from place of hospitalization in the United States (including Hawaii and Alaska) to a selected place that is approved by the hospital commander. The return trip may be to the same or a different medical treatment facility.

Prenatal and Postpartum Leave. An individual who becomes pregnant while on active duty will continue to perform duty during the prenatal period until such time as duty is no longer considered feasible by the attending physician. The member is then placed in a sick-in-quarters status until admitted to the hospital due to complications or the onset of labor or until her medical condition permits her return to duty. When admitted to the hospital due to complications or the onset of labor, the member's status changes to sick-in-hospital. Both of the above periods are duty time. Following delivery, postpartum leave will be granted by the hospital commander, or by the unit commander upon recommendation of the attending physician, as necessary for the member's recuperation and convalescence. No fixed period of convalescent leave is prescribed. Such leave as is granted will terminate on the date the attending physician or the hospital commander determines that the member is medically fit to return to duty. Any leave taken in excess of the convalescent leave is chargeable as ordinary leave.

Rest and Recuperation Leave. Rest and recuperation (R&R) leave is granted in conjunction with R&R programs established in those areas designated for hostile fire pay, when military considerations preclude full execution of annual leave programs. One R&R leave is permitted each twelve-month period. Military transportation to and from R&R areas is provided on a space-required basis, with time spent in travel status considered duty time. The leave period in the R&R area is charged to the member's leave account.

Environmental and Morale Leave. Environmental and morale leave is granted in conjunction with an environmental and morale leave program established at oversea installations where adverse environmental conditions exist that offset the full benefit of annual leave programs. It differs from R&R leave in that military transportation is on a space-available rather than a space-required basis, and the entire period of absence, including travel time, is chargeable to the member's leave account.

Graduation Leave, USMA. This is leave granted at the time of graduation from the U.S. Military Academy and is not chargeable to accrued leave, or to leave to be accrued in the future. It is limited to thirty days except on a case-by-case basis when the graduate is awaiting start of a training course. It must be completed within three months of the date of graduation and may not be carried forward as a credit beyond the reporting date to the first permanent duty station, or to the POE for duty outside CONUS. The Superintendent, USMA, is the approving authority for graduation leave.

Leave Awaiting Orders. Leave that may be granted to a service member while awaiting orders pending final action on disability retirement proceedings. It is chargeable as ordinary leave to the maximum extent possible.

Special Rest and Recuperation (SR&R) Leave. A special rest and recuperation leave, not chargeable to the leave account, is authorized for enlisted personnel in certain specialties who voluntarily extend their overseas tours. See AR 630-5 for details.

LEAVE COMPUTATION AND LEAVE REQUEST

Computation. The day of departure on and the day of return from leave will not be counted as days of leave if the member is at his or her place of work and performs duty for more than one-half of the normal workday. Otherwise, these days will be charged to leave. If the day of departure is a nonduty day, that day will be charged to leave regardless of the hour of departure. If the day of return from leave is a nonduty day, that day will not be charged to leave regardless of the hour of return. Ordinary leave begins and ends on post at the duty location, or at the location from which the member normally commutes to work.

Requests for Leave. Leave may be granted only upon request by the individual concerned. DA Form 31 is used as request for leave and as the document authorizing leave. See illustration.

Extension of Leave. A request for extension of leave may be submitted by any convenient means. It must include specific reasons for requesting the extension, period of extension desired, and member's destination, reporting date, and last duty station. If the leave is in connection with a move to a new unit, your DA Form 31 will be annotated to show the appropriate installation and telephone number to contact for a leave extension, if necessary. If you are on leave from your assigned

REQUEST AND AUTHORITY FOR LEAVE
For use of this form, see AR 630-5; the proponent agency is US Army Military Personnel Center.
(See Instructions on Reverse)

PART - I

1. NAME (Last, First, Middle)	2. SOCIAL SECURITY NO.	3. PAY GRADE	4. DATE	5. CONTROL NO.

6. ORGANIZATION AND STATION	7. TYPE OF ABSENCE		8.	DATES
	a. ☐ ORDINARY LEAVE		a. FROM	b. TO
	b. ☐ OTHER (Specify)			

	9. NO. OF DAYS LEAVE	10. NO. OF DAYS ACCRUED LEAVE	11. NO. OF DAYS ADVANCED LEAVE	12. NO. OF DAYS EXCESS LEAVE

13. LEAVE ADDRESS (Include ZIP Code and Telephone No.)	14. SIGNATURE OF REQUESTOR	15. SUPERVISOR RECOMMENDATION
		☐ APPROVAL ☐ DISAPPROVAL
		SIGNATURE

16. NAME, TITLE, ORGANIZATION OF APPROVING AUTHORITY	17. SIGNATURE OF APPROVING AUTHORITY

18. DATE/TIME OF DEPARTURE	19. NAME/TITLE OF AUTHENTICATING AUTHORITY	20. SIGNATURE OF AUTHENTICATING AUTHORITY

21. EXTENSION (No. of days and date approved) APPROVING AUTHORITY

22. DATE/TIME OF RETURN	23. NAME/TITLE OF AUTHENTICATING AUTHORITY	24. SIGNATURE OF AUTHENTICATING AUTHORITY

PART - II

APPLICABLE TO AUTHORIZED TRAVEL ONLY

25. SO, LO, DA FORM 662 OR AUTHORITY FOR TRAVEL

26.	INSTRUCTIONS FOR SERVICING STATION/ORGANIZATION
	(APOE, APOD, TDY Station, Others)
	DATE/TIME STAMP WHEN SERVICE MEMBER ARRIVES/DEPARTS YOUR STATION/ORGANIZATION

a. ARRIVE STATION 1	b. DEPART STATION 1	c. ARRIVE STATION 2	d. DEPART STATION 2

e. ARRIVE STATION 3	f. DEPART STATION 3	g. ARRIVE STATION 4	h. DEPART STATION 4

27. DATE/TIME OF ARRIVAL	28. NAME OF GAINING/PARENT ORGANIZATION	29. SIGNATURE OF AUTHENTICATING AUTHORITY

30. REMARKS:

DA₁ FORM OCT 73 **31**

LEAVE REQUEST.

unit, to which you will return, the request for extension should be submitted to the original approving authority. For unusual cases, see AR 630-5.

Limitations on Cash Settlements and Leave Accruals. Personnel may accumulate up to sixty days of accrued leave. Accrued leave in excess of sixty days is lost at the end of the fiscal year. It is Army policy to have its members make full use of the leave time to which they are entitled. At the time of separation or retirement, unused leave up to sixty days will be compensated by a final payment.

Individual Record of Leave Accruals and Leaves Taken. Leave records are maintained by the unit clerk or the Personnel and Administration Center (PAC). Members are responsible for verfiying the accuracy of the leave balance. Check your monthly Leave and Earnings Statement.

Leave taken and leave credited will be accounted for on a fiscal year basis. When only a part of the fiscal year is considered, leave will be credited at the rate of two and a half days for each month of active service.

Leave of absence that commences in one and is completed in another fiscal year will be apportioned to the fiscal year in which each portion falls and charged accordingly.

PASSES

A pass, as differentiated from leave, is an authorized absence from post or place of duty for a relatively short time. A pass is a privilege when granted by a commander, but it is not a right to which one is entitled.

Regular. Regular passes may be granted to deserving individuals for those periods when they are not required to be physically present with their unit. Normally, regular passes are valid only during specified off-duty hours. Regular pass periods normally will not exceed seventy-two hours.

Special. Special passes may be of three-day (seventy-two-hour) or four-day (ninety-six-hour) duration. The three-day special pass period may include nonduty days, but it must include at least one duty day. The four-day special pass period must include at least two consecutive nonduty days. Special passes may be granted to deserving individuals on special occasions or in special circumstances as specified in AR 630-5.

Pass forms are not required by any military personnel.

Limitations. A pass will not be issued to an individual so that two or more passes are effective in succession, or used in series through reissue immediately after return to duty. They will not be granted in conjunction with leave. They will not be combined with a public holiday or with a nonduty weekend when the combined period of continuous absence will exceed seventy-two hours for the three-day pass or ninety-six hours for the four-day pass.

Such absences in compliance with all of the above are not chargeable against accrued leave.

When it is desired to extend a period of absence granted as a pass beyond seventy-two hours for a regular or three-day special pass or ninety-six hours for a four-day special pass, the portion in excess of the pass period is charged as leave.

OTHER ABSENCES

An individual may be away from post or place of duty without being considered as in a leave status or on pass.

Permissive TDY. Examples are activities of a semiofficial nature such as medical, ecclesiastical, professional, or scientific, or participation in competitive sports events such as those sponsored by the Army. These absences are without expense to the government. Commanders may grant permissive TDY of up to ten days for the purpose of house hunting in conjunction with a PCS move if government quarters are not immediately available or not required to be occupied at the new station. This period may be granted prior to departure from the old station, in conjunction with PCS travel and leave, or after arrival at the new station.

Proceed Time. Proceed time, not to exceed four days, may be granted for the purpose of allowing the military member on a PCS move to or from an "all others" overseas tour to accomplish necessary processing prior to departing the old duty station and after arrival at the new duty station. It is designed to provide the individual an adequate period of absence from duty to attend to the details of changing and arranging a residence, auto licensing, voting registration, taxes and similar personal matters. It is not intended as time to process on or off post, which is to be accomplished during normal working hours. Proceed time is duty time for record purposes and is granted consistent with the needs of the individual and military operational requirements. It may be taken in increments and may be granted prior to departure from the old station, between stations, or immediately following arrival at the new station. It is not to be used to augment, nor as a substitute for, permissive TDY for house hunting. It may not be granted as a substitute for leave or pass, or to personnel being reassigned at the same station, between two stations in CONUS, between two stations in an oversea command in proximity to one another, or incident to assignment to the member's first duty station, or separation, release from active duty, or retirement.

HOLIDAYS

Public holidays, established by law and listed below, will be observed except when military operations prevent. When such holidays fall on a Saturday, the preceding Friday will be considered a holiday, and when such holidays fall on Sunday, the succeeding Monday will be considered a holiday.

Holiday	Date Observed
New Year's Day	1 January
Martin Luther King's Birthday	3rd Monday in January
Washington's Birthday	3rd Monday in February
Memorial Day	Last Monday in May
Independence Day	4 July
Labor Day	1st Monday in September
Columbus Day	2nd Monday in October
Veterans Day	11 November
Thanksgiving Day	4th Thursday in November
Christmas Day	25 December

While not classified as public holidays, the following have special significance to the Army and are observed as directed by local commanders or the Department of Defense.

Army Birthday, 14 June
Armed Forces Day, third Saturday in May
Flag Day, 14 June

VISITING AREAS OUTSIDE THE UNITED STATES

Specific permission must be obtained by active duty personnel to visit foreign countries. Special permission is not needed to visit Puerto Rico, Virgin Islands, Guam, American Samoa, or the Northern Mariana Islands.

Reporting requirements, authorized clothing that may be worn, and documents that must be in the member's possession vary from country to country. Readers are advised to consult AR 630-5 and to initiate action to obtain permission for the visit well in advance of the intended leave date.

25

Rights,
Privileges,
and Restrictions

A citizen who enters the military service undergoes at once a change in legal status. He or she assumes additional hazards, obligations, and responsibilities. They are balanced by the grant of additional benefits. Think about it. The military service cannot be democratic in operation. It cannot be managed, led, or directed efficiently if the whim of each individual is to be honored. Members must go as directed to the station assigned and perform their duties as their orders require. Military efficiency requires the imposition of restrictions and, in return, there is the granting of rights and privileges. They pertain to military status during and after military service. Thus former members enjoy veterans benefits, while retired members enjoy benefits but are restricted from dealings that might impair the functioning of those still active. The laws bestowing rights, privileges, and restrictions must be in a reasonable balance in our republic.

This chapter seeks to illuminate this important subject, which is so widely misunderstood. The chapter is not all-inclusive, nor could it be. But it establishes sound principles for reasoning, and it provides a large number of examples of importance to Army officers. These examples should enable the reader to fit other benefits or requirements into the pattern established.

MILITARY STATUS

The sum of these factors constitutes a definite part of the military way of life. When a citizen assumes the office of an officer, or becomes a soldier, that individual must become informed on these matters and continue to keep his or her understanding current because laws, regulations, local orders, and customs change with the passage of time.

Justification for Benefits. There are strong reasons for the granting of military rights and privileges, which herein are called benefits. Those citizens who are members of the Army, Navy, Marines, or Air Force have the primary mission of protecting and preserving the Constitution, including our free institutions and way of life; the prosecution of wars with the incident hazard; and service to the federal government wherever duty is directed. They give up many freedoms of choice that the civilian takes for granted and that, if denied, would be considered unreasonable.

The development of an efficient military system depends upon the volunteers who are the Regulars. They are backed up by the several categories of Reserves, also volunteers, many of whom serve extended tours with the active Army. Volunteers will not be obtained in the numbers required or the quality necessary unless the conditions of their life and lot are acceptable. If unacceptable it must be presumed they would choose another vocation or avocation. Beset as we are by international strains and recurrent wars or conflicts short of war, our country needs as its first essential the armed force necessary to protect itself; and this armed force must be strong enough, brave enough, and proud enough to do its job. The expansion of the Army officer corps during emergencies must continue into the greater numbers a moral fiber that is tough and resilient.

A phase of this subject invariably overlooked by the critic of things military is that even in wartime officers of the Regular and Reserve components are volunteers. *As long as the nation has the need of the best military leadership of all grades and ages, it will be pleased to recognize this condition by granting appropriate benefits, first to attract them to service, and then to hold them.*

There is an inescapable difference between the individual in civilian employment and the member of the service. The civilian may quit or refuse a task with no greater penalty than loss of employment, being thereafter free to choose another job, even to be sustained on relief funds. But the wearer of the uniform can do so only at the peril of punishment by action of court-martial which, if refusal or cowardice before an enemy is involved, may result in a death penalty.

We may hope that the voices raised periodically against military benefits, always louder when danger is remote, will grow dim through a proper understanding.

Justification for Restrictions. There is a sufficient case also for the imposing of restrictions upon military people, especially officers, that are not borne by civilians.

The government must have a clearly defined power to deploy its forces and require individuals to perform specific missions, however unpleasant or hazardous such locations or duties may become.

The government must insist upon full service of its officers and thus is justified in defining and prohibiting improper outside activities of individuals.

Since procurement officers and others in the business end of government have many prerogatives incident to the letting of contracts, the government must require high standards of ethics as well as clearly codified methods of conducting these affairs.

In order to assure fair treatment for all and prevention of abuses in the exercise of federal power, limitations must be placed on authority, especially in the field of punishments, sentences of courts-martial, and the like.

Let no one rebel inwardly over these restrictions in principle. Whenever circumstances change so as to make them unnecessary they are removed.

RIGHTS

You cannot possibly have a broader basis for any government than that which includes all the people, with their rights in their hands, and with an equal power to maintain their rights. —William Lloyd Garrison.

Let us be sure in this military way of life of our meaning in this matter of rights. To do so, if followed by consideration of some examples, will identify many benefits in their true perspective. It will be seen that while there are many obligations of service there are not many actual rights.

Definition. The dictionary helps only a little. We must contrive our own definition. A right in the sense of this discussion is a benefit established for military people by federal law. Unless a benefit is established by law, in contrast to a department regulation that is subject to administrative change or withdrawal, it is something less than a right. Further, we should note that a right, having been established by federal law, can also be withdrawn or amended by subsequent federal law. It is a point to be considered when contemplating military service and subsequent retirement.

Acquisition of Military Rights. A citizen who has subscribed to the oath of office as an officer, or oath of enlistment if an enlisted person, becomes entitled at once to certain rights of military service; for example, the right to wear the uniform. Other rights accrue only by completing specified requirements; example, the right to retire after completing a stipulated period of service.

The Right to Wear the Uniform. Members of the military service have the right to wear the uniform of their service. That the department may require the wearing of the uniform off duty as well as on duty is beside the point. First of all, it is a right.

Members of the Reserve components on inactive status, retired personnel, and former members of the services who have been honorably separated have the right to wear the uniform only at stipulated times or circumstances and unless these conditions exist the right is denied. Chapter 22 describes these conditions fully.

The Right of Officers to Command. In the commission granted an officer by the President will be found these words: *"And I do strictly charge and require those officers and other personnel of lesser rank to render such obedience as is due an officer of this grade and position."* The commission itself may be regarded as the basic document that gives military officers the right to exercise command and to exact obedience to proper orders.

Army Regulation 600-20, as to the Army, establishes this right in further detail, along with definite restrictions on this right.

Warrant officers, when assigned duties as station, unit, or detachment commander, are vested with all powers usually exercised by commissioned officers except as indicated in AR 600-20. Commissioned warrant officers are vested with the same powers as other commissioned officers.

The Right to Draw Pay and Allowances. Pay scales for grade and length of service are established by law. See chapter 20, *Pay and Allowances,* and chapter 21, *Travel Allowances.*

The rights as to pay and allowances may be suspended, in part, by action of a court-martial or forfeited in part by absence without leave.

The Right to Receive Medical Attention. Members of the military service are entitled to receive appropriate medical or dental care for the treatment of their wounds, injuries, or disease. In fact, refusal to accept treatment ruled to be necessary may be punishable by courts-martial.

The Right to Individual Protection Afforded by the Uniform Code of Military Justice. All members of the military service are under the jurisdiction established by the Articles of the Uniform Code of Military Justice. Many persons regard the Manual for Courts-Martial, United States, which contains these articles, merely as the authorization of courts-martial and the implementation of their procedures as a means of maintaining discipline or awarding punishment for crime. This is a shallow view. Except for the punitive articles, Nos. 77 to 134, incl., UCMJ, they pertain in considerable measure to the protection of individual rights. Here are samples:

No person may be compelled to incriminate himself/herself before a military court.

No person shall without his/her consent be tried a second time for the same offense.

Cruel and unusual punishments of every kind are prohibited.

While the punishment for a crime or offense is left to the discretion of the court, it shall not exceed such limits as the President may from time to time prescribe.

The Right to Administer Oaths. Article 136 of the Uniform Code of Military Justice establishes the right of designated persons on active military duty to administer oaths. (See AR 600-11.)

The Soldiers' and Sailors' Relief Act. The Soldiers' and Sailors' Relief Act, passed in 1940 and still in effect, has for its purposes the relief of draftees, enlistees, and reservists on active duty of some of the pressure of heavy financial obligations they may have assumed in civil life. Of importance to officers on active duty, the act protects military personnel from double taxation in such cases as state income taxes, automobile licenses, and so on.

The Right to Obtain a Home Loan. The Federal Housing Authority (FHA) can guarantee to a mortgage company that an in-Service loan will be paid by an officer on active duty or the government will pay it. This home loan program applies principally to officers who do not have a Veterans Administration (VA) loan entitlement and who have two or more years on active duty. Those who have served in wars or conflicts (Korea, Vietnam), recognized by congressional act, may receive a home loan guaranteed by the VA. An officer is a good credit risk because of his or her high principles and stabilized income. See chapter 9, *Financial Planning.*

The Right of Equal Opportunity. It is a policy of the Army to conduct all of its activities in a manner that is free from racial discrimination and that provides equal opportunity and treatment of all uniformed members irrespective of their race, color, religion, or national origin. This applies to on-duty matters and off-duty situations including on-post housing, transportation, facilities, and schooling. AR 600-21 prescribes the regulations that carry out the principles of Title II of the Civil Rights Act, 1964. Strict compliance with these regulations is more than a matter of law, it is a matter of good leadership resulting in the willing service of each service member.

Redress of Wrong. Each of the armed services provides a procedure by which any member of the military service may seek redress of wrong. Each officer should become fully acquainted with this matter. An officer may have occasion to register an official objection, or complaint, with respect to personal treatment, although such occasions should be rare since most officers complete their entire service without finding it necessary to use this privilege. But he or she should certainly know that juniors also enjoy this right, and if the officer takes action that is grossly injurious to an individual, or so considered, he or she may be obliged to endure the process as the injuring party rather than the injured. (Article 138, Uniform Code of Military Justice).

The Right to File Claims for Losses Incident to Service. The Military Personnel Claims Act (AR 27-20) establishes the right of military personnel on active duty to file claims for losses to personal property incident to military service.

A claim for loss may be submitted for consideration and in proper cases will be approved for payment. Examples of claims that are covered are as follows:

1. Damage to property located at quarters or other authorized place from fire, flood, hurricane, or other serious occurrence;
2. Transportation losses (see chapter 21);
3. Marine or aircraft disaster;
4. Enemy action or public service;
5. Money held in trust for others, and personal funds, under some conditions; and
6. Motor vehicles lost when used in mandatory performance of military duty and during authorized shipment overseas.

Caution: In order to secure reimbursement for losses it is necessary to establish the facts, and immediately upon an occurrence that may justify a claim the interested individual should set about the task of collecting essential documents, statements of witnesses, or other matters that will be of assistance in supporting the claim.

The Right to Vote. Legislation enacted by the Congress in 1955 establishes the right of voting by members of the armed forces, and commanding officers are required to establish facilities for absentee voting for members of their commands. See AR 608-20.

The Right to Retire. After satisfying specific requirements of honorable service, or having endured physical disability beyond a fixed degree, officers of the armed forces have the right to retire.

The Right to Be Buried in a National Cemetery. The rights of a deceased service member to be buried in a national military cemetery are discussed in chapter 9, *Financial Planning.*

PRIVILEGES

In the discussion of rights of military people, it was argued that unless a benefit were established by federal law it was something less than a right. There are other benefits of importance. For the most part they are granted or authorized by departmental regulations. Some have been established through custom, and with respect to such privileges reference is made to chapter 7, *Customs of the Service.* Some important privileges are granted by civilian communities, churches, clubs, and fraternal organizations.

Now let us examine some examples. The list is illustrative only and could not be complete. But its analysis will enable the reader to identify others and classify them as genuine or assumed accordingly.

Post Exchange, Commissary, Theater, and Medical Privileges. Authorized patrons and their family members must qualify themselves as to eligibility for the receipt of certain benefits such as obtaining medical service by family members, patronage of post exchange or commissary, attendance at theaters of the Army and Air Force Exchange Service, and others. Possession and display of the correct personnel identification card is necessary.

The Privileges of Rank and Position. That "rank has its privileges" (RHIP) is a saying as old as armies. It is the deference extended in all walks of life to one's elders or seniors. In the Army it is no more or less pronounced, although it may be more codified, than among faculty members, or in a business establishment, a legislative body, or among doctors, lawyers, and ministers. Throughout chapter 6, *Military Courtesy,* and chapter 7, *Customs of the Service,* will be found numerous examples.

Leave of Absence. Under current laws and regulations military people become entitled to accumulate leave and to take it when their duties permit. This is merely the civilian vacation. See chapter 24, *Authorized Absences.* But people in uniform must apply for permission to take leave from their stations and duties regardless of its accumulation to their credit. Application may be denied. The training or tactical situation will govern the decision. If service members absent themselves without this permission they are subject to forfeiture of pay and to disciplinary action. Hence it is a privilege.

Political Activities and Election to Public Office. An officer who considers entering political activity of any kind whatever should study most carefully AR 600-20 in its latest change or issue. See also Article 88, Uniform Code of Military Justice.

Members of the Army while on active duty will not use their official authority or influence for the purpose of interfering with an election or affecting the course or outcome thereof. They are not permitted to participate in any way in political management or political campaigns. This includes the making of political speeches, activity at political conventions or on political committees, the publication of articles, or any other activity looking to the influencing of an election or the solicitation of votes for themselves or others.

Membership in Officers' Clubs. All officers assigned at a station have the privilege of membership in the officers' club (open mess). They must follow the rules of the club as to payment of dues, bills, and other matters, and unless they do so this privilege may be curtailed or denied.

The Privilege of Writing for Publication. The professional Army officer who has ideas or experience of great importance to the nation, or a high degree of interest to our citizens, should grasp the opportunity to write for service magazines or journals, magazines of general circulation, or books. It is the principal means of making known the point of view of the military professional; just as it is also the principal means for expanding sources of information and reference on military subjects. An active duty or a retired officer may with complete propriety write for publication. Official regulations are not especially restrictive. It is the only way we can continue to develop a military literature. There is ample precedent for it. Articles of military interest are sought by service journals. Stackpole Books, publisher of *The Army Officer's Guide,* has produced a large number of books written by military authors.

Nor need the field be restricted to military subjects. The entire field from history to almanacs is available.*

When will the military author write for publication? He or she will regard writing

---

*See also Sec. II, AR 360-5, which details Army policies and cautions members of the Army to "exercise good judgment."

as a hobby and devote such time to it as others will utilize for their hobbies such as gardening, woodworking, photography, golf, bridge, the movies, just sitting around, and so on. If time does not permit, an officer does not write. Certainly it must not interfere with the performance of duty.

Here is the departmental policy, as announced in AR 600-20: The policy of the Department of Defense is that military personnel who desire to engage in public writing for personal profit are on an exact parity with civilian professional writers so far as accessibility to classified current technical or operational military information is concerned. This policy covers military personnel on active duty, retired persons, and members of the Reserve components. Further, an officer may use his or her military title as author, as authorized specifically in AR 600-50.

Officers desiring to write on military subjects must obtain the approval of the Department of the Army prior to furnishing a manuscript to the publisher except for articles for service journals and official Army publications. Material prepared for service journals may be prepared as an official duty utilizing military facilities and clerical help. Manuscripts will be submitted for review and clearance as to security of safeguarded information at least fifteen days in advance of the proposed release. It is wise to allow even more time. The officer should work with the local information officer in processing the manuscript. There is no charge for this review.

Retired Officers and Military Writing. There is no requirement that retired Army personnel submit writings and public statements for official review. If material they prepare may violate security regulations, they may submit it for review to the Department of the Army, Washington, DC 20310. Retired officers who write on military subjects are advised to consult DA Pam 600-5.

Authorized Use of Military Titles after Retirement. Retired Army members not on active duty are permitted to use their military titles socially and in connection with commercial enterprises subject to precise restrictions. Retired officers who wish to use their military titles in connection with their employment or a commercial enterprise are advised to consult DA Pam 600-5. Of course, they must never be used in any manner that would bring discredit upon the Army.

See also chapter 6, *Military Courtesy,* under THE CORRECT USE OF TITLES.

Authors of material for publication may use their military titles while on either extended active duty or in inactive status. Clearance by the Department of Defense is required prior to publication. (AR 600-50.)

See the discussions under *Restrictions on Use of Military Titles,* below, wherein the authority to use military titles in connection with a commercial enterprise is prohibited for personnel on extended active duty.

Inventions and Incentive Awards. Active duty personnel may seek to supplement their income through inventions and suggestions. In the case of inventions, AR 27-60 prescribes the techniques of obtaining a patent while in service, and a pamphlet is available from the Commissioner of Patents, Washington, DC, pertaining to all citizens.

The Army Incentive Awards Program is detailed in AR 672-20. It provides for cash awards for adopted suggestions that result in tangible monetary savings. These can be ideas for improving procedures as well as inventions pertaining to materiel. This privilege is often overlooked by officers whose ideas and inventions are eagerly sought by the Army. Scientific achievements are also awarded, but most officers could take advantage of the idea category without any specialized or technical background.

RESTRICTIONS

There are many "Thou Shalt Nots" in the military life. They consist for the most part of restrictions or standards of conduct inapplicable to the civilian. Some are contained in federal laws. Others are in departmental regulations. A few are included only in observed customs. See also chapter 4, *The Officer Image*, and chapter 7, *Customs of the Service.*

They need not be regarded as onerous. They have come about through experience and necessity. In any event they are well balanced by the military benefits, which have been discussed. Since their violation would be regarded as a serious matter, at the worst resulting in trial by a court-martial, officers should know of them. The list here is not represented to be complete. There are certainly many more. For example, local commands often find it necessary to prescribe restrictive orders. But they serve as examples and establish a pattern.

Effect of Conduct Unbecoming an Officer and a Gentleman or Lady. The 133d Article, Uniform Code of Military Justice, reads as follows: *Any officer, cadet, or midshipman who is convicted of conduct unbecoming an officer and a gentleman shall be punished as a court-martial may direct.*

There are certain moral attributes that belong to the ideal officer and the gentleman or lady, a lack of which is indicated by acts of dishonesty or unfair dealing, of indecency or indecorum, or of lawlessness, injustice, or cruelty. Not everyone can be expected to meet ideal standards or to possess the attributes in the exact degree demanded by the standards of the time; but there is a limit of tolerance below which the individual standards in these respects of an officer or cadet cannot fall without his or her being morally unfit to be an officer or cadet or to be considered a gentleman or lady. This article contemplates such conduct by an officer or cadet that, taking all the circumstances into consideration, satisfactorily shows such moral unfitness.

This article includes acts made punishable by any other articles of the UCMJ, provided such acts amount to conduct unbecoming an officer and a gentleman or lady; thus, an officer who embezzles military property violates both this and the preceding article.

Instances of violation of this article are: knowingly making a false official statement; dishonorable neglect to pay debts; opening and reading another's letters without authority; giving a check on a bank where the officer knows or reasonably should know there are no funds to meet it, and without intending that there should be; using insulting or defamatory language to another officer in his or her presence, or about the officer to other military persons; being grossly drunk and conspicuously disorderly in a public place; public association with notorious prostitutes; failing without a good cause to support one's family.

Liability Regarding Classified Documents. By the very nature of their duties, officers are required to have possession of and to utilize secret, confidential, and other classified or specially restricted documents. Officers must be mindful of the restrictions placed upon such documents and the punitive action that may be taken against them for their improper handling or use.

AR 380-5, *Department of the Army Information Security Program,* is the principal source of instructions. The inclusion of classified military information in any article, speech, or discussion by a member of the Army of the United States is prohibited unless specifically authorized by the Department of the Army. Additional information may be found in AR 600-20.

The statute that governs the subject is quoted below.

"Whoever, being entrusted with or having lawful possession or control of any

document, writing code book, signal book, sketch, photograph, photographic negative, blueprint, plan, map, model, note, or information, relating to the national defense, through gross negligence permits the same to be removed from its proper place of custody or delivered to anyone in violation of his trust, or to be lost, stolen, abstracted, or destroyed, shall be punished by imprisonment for not more than ten years and may, in the discretion of the court, be fined not more than $10,000. (June 5, 1917, c. 30, Title I, Sec. 1; 40 Stat. 217. Act of March 28, 1940; Public No. 443, 76th Congress. 3d Session.)"

Keeping of Personal Diary Containing Classified Information Restricted. An officer who keeps a personal diary in which he or she records classified information is in violation of departmental orders.

Participation in Public Demonstrations. Participation by members of the Army in public demonstrations, not sanctioned by competent authority, including those pertaining to civil rights, is prohibited:

1. During the hours they are required to be present for duty.
2. When they are in uniform.
3. When they are on a military reservation.
4. When they are in a foreign country.
5. When their activities constitute a breach of law and order.
6. When violence is reasonably likely to result.

Clearly the principles are twofold: The demonstration is not to receive an official Army sanction nor is the Army to be discredited by the presence of a member. (See AR 600-20.)

Officers Subject to Fine by Action of Commanding Officer. Nonjudicial punishment is exercised by authority of Article 15, UCMJ, using The Manual for Courts-Martial, United States, as amended, paragraph 131b (1) (b) of which prescribes the authorized punishment upon officers, if imposed by a general officer or officer exercising general courts-martial jurisdiction, as forfeiture of half pay for two months, or detention of half pay for three months.

Restrictions of an Officer under Arrest. An officer in arrest (AR 633-30)—
Cannot exercise command of any kind.
Will restrict himself/herself as directed.
Will not bear arms.
Will not visit his/her commanding officer or other superior officer, unless directed to do so.
Will make requests of every nature in writing, unless otherwise directed.
Will, unless otherwise directed, fall in and follow in the rear of his/her organization at formations and on the march.

Effect of Disrespectful Language Concerning Certain Government Officials. The 88th Article, UCMJ, reads as follows: *Any officer who uses contemptuous words against the President, Vice President, Congress, Secretary of Defense, or a Secretary of a Department, a Governor or a legislature of any State, Territory, or other possession of the United States in which he is on duty or present shall be punished as a court-martial may direct.*

It is an act of wisdom to refrain from critical comments publicly expressed about former civilian officials. The officer must support with equal zeal leaders of either major political party when they are in positions of responsibility and power. Criticism of a former official may be interpreted as a statement with political intent.

Officers on active duty retain the right to vote, to express their opinions privately and informally on all political subjects and candidates, and, in certain cases, to become candidates for public office. See AR 600-20. Active participation in other political activities is strictly limited.

Restrictions on Use of Military Titles, Active Duty Personnel. Military titles may not be used in connection with a commercial enterprise by individuals on active duty. This applies specifically to Regular personnel of the active list, and Retired and Reserve component personnel on extended active duty. *Exception:* Authorship of material for publication is exempted from this provision, but such material is subject to review and clearance by the Department of Defense. See AR 600-50 and the preceding discussion, PRIVILEGES.

Restrictions on Outside Activities. Officers of the Army will not engage in nor permit their names to be connected with any activity, participation in which is incompatible with the status of an officer of the Army. (AR 600-20 and 600-50.)

Acting as Attorney or Agent. No member of the military establishment on the active list or on active duty, or a civilian employee of the Army or of the Department of the Army, whose official duties are concerned with patent activities, shall act as agent or attorney in connection with the inventions or patent rights of others, except when such action is a part of the official duties of the person so acting. (AR 27-60.)

Restrictions on Representing Clients. An officer previously assigned to military duty is disqualified for life after the time such service has ceased from representing in any manner or capacity any interest opposed to the United States with which he or she was directly connected during government service. There is also a two-year ban on representing anyone on a matter that was previously under the officer's official responsibility.

Acting as Consultant for Private Enterprise Prohibited. No member of the military establishment on the active list or on active duty, or a civilian employee of the Army or of the Department of the Army, shall act as a consultant for a private enterprise with regard to any matter in which the government is interested. (AR 600-50.)

Stoppages of Pay. The pay of officers may be withheld under section 1766 of the Revised Statutes on account of indebtedness to the United States.

Contributions or Presents to Superiors Prohibited. Military and civilian personnel of the Department of the Army will not solicit a contribution from other government employees, military or civilian, for a gift to an official superior; will not make a donation as a gift to an official superior; and will not accept a gift from other government personnel subordinate to themselves. However, voluntary gifts or contributions of nominal value are permitted on special occasions such as marriage, transfer, illness, or retirement, provided any gifts acquired with such contributions shall not exceed a nominal value.

Acceptance of Gratuities Prohibited. The acceptance of gratuities by either military or civilian personnel of the Department of the Army, or members of their families, from those who have or seek business with the Department of Defense or from those whose business interests are affected by Department functions is forbidden. Such acceptance, no matter how innocently tendered or received, may be a source of embarrassment to the Army, may affect the objective judgment of the personnel involved, and may impair the public confidence in the integrity of the government. With certain limited exceptions, DA personnel will not solicit, accept, or agree to accept any gratuity for themselves, members of their families, or others, either directly or indirectly from any source with business interests of the type noted above. The exceptions are detailed in AR 600-50. Officers are urged to study the regulation so as to be fully aware of both the details and the philosophy involved. In case of doubt, consult your superior or the legal assistance officer.

General Prohibition. All Department of the Army personnel, military and civilian, will avoid any action, whether or not specifically prohibited by the regulations, that might result in or reasonably be expected to create the appearance of:

Using public office for private gain.

Giving preferential treatment to any person or entity.

Impeding government efficiency or economy.

Losing independence or impartiality.

Making a government decision outside official channels.

Affecting adversely the confidence of the public in the integrity of the government.

Conferring Honorary Titles Prohibited. Conferring honorary titles of military rank upon civilians is prohibited. Honorary titles heretofore conferred will not be withdrawn. (AR 600-20.)

Effect of Refusal of Medical Treatment. An officer or enlisted person may be investigated by a board of medical officers and subsequently be separated from the Army or be brought to trial by court-martial for refusing to submit to a surgical or dental operation or to medical or dental treatment, at the hands of the military authorities, if it is designed to restore or increase his or her fitness for service.

Attempts to Influence Legislation Prohibited. Except as authorized by the Department of the Army, efforts by any person in the active military service of the United States or by any retired member of the Regular Army to procure or oppose or in any manner influence legislation affecting the Army or to procure personal favor through legislation except to procure the enactment of private relief legislation are forbidden. (AR 600-50.) However, any member of the Army may communicate directly with any member of Congress concerning any subject unless such communication is in violation of law or in violation of regulations necessary to the security of the United States.

Abuse of Privilege. A few people have the idea that authority is always right no matter how it may choose to exercise itself—a throwback, perhaps, to the ancient but discredited doctrine, "The King can do no wrong." The thought is a grave mistake. The possession of authority does not make the possessor any less the hired servant of the society in which his or her authority is exercised. The evil that has been practiced by the few and that has discredited many of the officer corps is abuse of privilege. It consists of taking advantage of position or rank to secure pleasures or facilities to which they are not entitled by law, regulation, or custom. It is "getting away with something."

Here is a simple way to determine whether an alleged benefit or privilege is genuine or spurious. Find the answer to these two questions. If it is affirmative for either you are quite secure in its enjoyment.

1. Is there authorization in any current Army or major command document?

2. Observe the five or ten best officers of experience known to you whom you observe frequently. They must have high standing as good officers among their fellows. Is the questioned privilege practiced by half or more of them?

Standards of Conduct, AR 600-50. The code of the Army and of Army officers is for a high standard of action and conduct in all matters, official and personal.

This applies with special emphasis upon avoiding all possible conflict between private interests and official duties (AR 600-50).

This regulation is very inclusive and very precise. Except when your activities are entirely official, or entirely personal—as in the routine investment of personal funds—you should be mindful of the possibility of conflict of interest. One need not jump behind trees in the matter, or live in fear of unintentional involvement. But in case of any slight doubt you should consult your commanding officer, or the legal assistance officer, for guidance.

26

Resignation and Elimination

The Army must have ways of removing from active duty, or terminating appointments within the corps of officers, those individuals who do not measure up to its standards of conduct or efficiency. This is protection of the essential interests of the government and of the Army. Since these matters are of grave importance to the individual officer, the laws and regulations require thorough examination by boards of officers following judicial processes, and the review of their recommended action. This is protection of the individual. This chapter is based for the most part upon AR 635-100, *Officer Personnel,* and AR 635-120, *Officer Resignations and Discharges.* However, they are not all-inclusive on this subject. Officers may be dismissed or reduced in grade by sentence of a general court-martial. Regular Army officers twice passed over for permanent promotion may be removed from the active list as discussed in chapter 27, *Retirement.* Officers may be separated from active duty for reasons of age or physical incapacity. During any period of reduction of military strength, such as is necessary to meet reduced budgetary authorization, separation of non-Regular officers may be made by routine administrative action.

Character and Integrity Standard Identical for All Officers. Officers must meet high standards of personal honor and integrity because otherwise they could not continue to be useful members of the corps of officers. In this respect all officers must meet identical standards, without regard to their grade, length of service, component, or other consideration. Failure to measure up will result in elimination by action of a board of officers or trial by court-martial.

An interesting and helpful discussion of the importance of integrity in establishing a favorable impression on others is contained in chapter 4, *The Officer Image.*

Standards for Performance of Duty. The situation as to standard of duty performance is quite different, for in this quality there is an acceptable variation. See chapter 14, *Evaluation Reports,* with special reference to the parts of the report form that compare the rated officer with others of the same grade, military schooling, and time in grade.

ELIMINATION AND THE CAREER PLANNING PROGRAM

This is not a pleasant subject to discuss or to include in *The Army Officer's Guide.* But elimination of officers after a period of service is a necessary part of personnel administration and should be understood by all. This is an appropriate place to emphasize the fair, carefully governed process used by the Army in applying this essential power.

The Army's concept of career planning and individual development of each officer continues to broaden, and its purposes continue to be more clearly defined. Just as promotion of those best qualified is a part of the planning process, so also is elimination of those officers who for adequate reasons have not attained or maintained the standard required.

Each officer deserves a fair chance to demonstrate individual capabilities. The Army system requires and ensures it. Special counseling and training must be given to newly commissioned officers and newly appointed warrant officers who encounter initial difficulties from inexperience. The officer who fails to achieve or maintain minimum standards must be identified promptly and positive action must be taken to improve his or her performance. If the officer fails to achieve reasonable standards of performance or conduct, elimination action must be taken. (See also the discussion of counseling, chapter 14, *Evaluation Reports.*)

FRIENDLY ADVICE TO OFFICERS ASKED TO "SHOW CAUSE"

The receipt of a letter about elimination action proposed under AR 635-100 will be a disconcerting experience. Thoughtless actions at this time may prejudice the outcome. The wise officer who wishes to salvage the most from the situation may be assisted by following these well-intended suggestions.

Upon receipt of the letter, keep your own counsel. Don't spout. Don't start hunting for a fight. Don't rush to the originator of the letter with recriminations and countercharges. If liquor is at the root of the trouble, as will be the case in some instances, don't choose this occasion to go off on a bender. Don't discuss the matter with associates. Study the letter most carefully. Study this chapter. Obtain official regulations cited in your letter of notification and study them. Continue to perform your duties and be sure to do them well.

If a selection board decides you should show cause for retention, a commanding officer with general court-martial (GCM) jurisdiction will notify you and give you five days to select an option to resign, request discharge, apply for retirement if eligible, or appear before a board of inquiry. Should the case originate in another manner, the commander with GCM jurisdiction will give you seven days to submit a statement in regard to the allegations and recommendation for elimination. You may secure counsel including civilian counsel at your own expense, or one will be provided you who is legally qualified. The commander upon forwarding your statement will offer you the same options as in the first case.

Assuming you take one day to settle down and to seek counsel, your perspective should have adjusted somewhat. Although the time limits seem short for reaction, you may be assured the administrative process will be careful, deliberate, judicial, and unhurried. You will have full opportunity to present your case, be represented by a counsel of your choice, and be protected under both law and regulation from such matters that could constitute self-incrimination and double jeopardy.

The next step is to consult others. Go first to your immediate commander even though he or she may in some way be responsible for the action. Regardless of your commander's position in your case, an expression of regret on your part along with a positive declaration that you had aspired to be a good officer will be beneficial. Your commander will grant you the time to prepare your case, and may offer assistance and provide advice. Your next step is to seek additional counsel from a more senior officer whom you consider capable and objective enough to give you impartial and wise advice.

The remaining days are spent in preparing your case with the accumulation of refutations, mitigating circumstances, and other supporting evidence to establish why you should remain on duty. An honest, but difficult, appraisal on your part along with counsel from others could be to elect one of the other options. If you elect to appear before the board, you should spend the intervening time in proving the desirability of your retention. Work with your counsel, accepting his or her advice and providing factual evidence based on candor and truth.

If the outcome is favorable, as will be the case in a fair percentage of hearings, start anew with determination to be a fine officer, casting out weaknesses that led to the action. The history of these hearings has many examples where officers retained in service have gone on to make exemplary records. If given the opportunity you will wish to do the same.

ELIMINATION PROCEDURES

Detailed procedures for elimination proceedings are spelled out in AR 635-100. Officers who may be concerned with such action are advised to consult this regulation, the provisions of which are summarized briefly in the following paragraphs.

Elimination Policy. Retention of officers substandard in performance of duty or conduct, deficient in character, or otherwise unsuited for military service cannot be justified in peace or war. There is no room for such individuals in any part of the Army. Elimination action, however, is not used in lieu of disciplinary action under the Uniform Code of Military Justice.

Elimination, Officers with More Than Three Years' Service. Elimination proceedings are judicial in nature with the officer concerned entitled to legal counsel. Elimination actions progress from the immediate commander through the commander exercising general courts-martial jurisdiction, through a Board of Inquiry, through a Board of Review, to the Secretary of the Army. At each point, in accordance with the procedures established by law and detailed in AR 635-100, a determination must be made that there is cause for elimination before the case progresses to the next step. At any point in the chain, a determination that there is not cause for elimination is enough to cause the case to be closed. The decision of the Secretary of the Army is final in those cases reaching that level.

Within five days of official notification to show cause for retention, the officer concerned must acknowledge receipt of the notification and state his or her election:

To tender a resignation; or

To request discharge (applicable only to Regular Army commissioned officers); or

To apply for retirement in lieu of elimination, if otherwise eligible for voluntary retirement; or

To appear before a Board of Inquiry to show cause for retention.

Elimination, Officers with Less Than Three Years' Service. In addition to the causes for elimination listed earlier, which are applicable to all officers, the following additional reasons are applicable to Regular Army commissioned officers and Regular Army warrant officers having less than three years' service in their present component and to all officers having less than three years' service in the AUS without component:

Failure by a Regular Army officer of a basic service school course.

Failure to be considered fully qualified for promotion to first lieutenant or to chief warrant officer, CW2.

The discovery of medical conditions or other conditions that, if they had been known at the time of appointment, would have precluded appointment.

The discovery of any other condition that evidences that the officer's retention in the Army would not be in the best interests of the United States.

Elimination Procedure. Processing of officers with less than three years' service will not normally include reference to a Board of Inquiry and a Board of Review. Cases are referred to a Selection Board that will recommend for retention or elimination of the officer. The Selection Board may, however, determine that the officer should be required to show cause for retention before a Board of Inquiry in the same manner as for the officer of longer service.

Special Action When a Student Officer of Less Than Three Years' Service Fails a Service School Course. Failure by a Regular Officer is handled as stated above.

An Army Reserve officer who fails a Branch Orientation or Branch Familiarization Course is subject to relief from active duty and discharge by the school commandant. Under like circumstances, a National Guard officer's name is forwarded to the Adjutant General for appropriate action.

Refusal of Regular Army Appointment. In accordance with the Defense Officer Personnel Management Act (DOPMA), commissioned officers who do not already hold Regular Army appointments are offered such appointments at the time they are selected for promotion to major. Failure to accept such an appointment will result in termination of the officer's active service.

Conclusion. There are several truths here worth noting. Action to separate an officer from his or her commission or warrant is a serious matter and is taken seriously by the Army. Such recommendations must never be submitted lightly; to do so will bring discredit upon the recommending officer. On the other hand, to fail to put them in when justified is to hold in the service an unfit officer, a serious weakness in itself. The elimination procedure should be understood as thorough, unhurried, and objective so as to eliminate hasty or ill-considered actions.

RESIGNATION

If mature consideration indicates a true preference for a different vocation, a person with but one life to live is entitled to make his or her own choices. An officer in good standing who decides to change to a different vocation must base the decision on facts. The tender of a resignation is a very serious act, for upon acceptance military status is terminated and, although it is possible to be reappointed, the time lost in terms of grade and rank cannot be recouped. Should reappointment be denied, the resignation is permanent.

It appears to be quite true that the resignation of a commission or warrant by an officer must be an act completely voluntary. However, there are several categories of resignation that are now provided, from that of an officer in highest standing who has completed all service obligations and merely wishes to terminate his or her military status, to the officer who resigns in the face of certain conviction by court-martial. Because of this broad situation, officers are advised to consult AR 635-120, with all changes, when they seek information as to any category of resignation.

The following information is supplied as first reference.

Service Requirements for Unqualified Resignation Eligibility. Although an officer may be in good standing in every way, his or her right to resign the commission or warrant as an "unqualified resignation" is subject to a number of requirements. During periods of emergency when Reserve component units have been called into active federal service, resignations are not accepted by the Secretary of the Army unless reasons considered to be in justification for the action are stated and accepted. During periods of emergency, Department of the Army may announce restrictions on the approval of applications for resignation for individuals who possess critical skills or who hold assignments in key positions. Officers contemplating voluntary resignation should see their unit personnel officer.

A Regular Army officer must meet the following requirements to be eligible for acceptance of unqualified resignation: (AR 601-100, and AR 635-120.)

Have served at least three years of active service, commissioned or warrant, subsequent to date of acceptance of appointment in the Regular Army, except individuals whose source of commission is the United States Military, Naval, or Air Force Academy, who have a service obligation of five years active duty.

Resignation in Lieu of Elimination. An officer who has been selected or recommended for elimination or removal from the active list under any provision of law may tender a resignation at any time prior to final action on the proceedings. (AR 635-120.) Such action saves time and paperwork for the Army, and may save embarrassment for the officer. The type of discharge to be furnished will be determined on the basis of facts and will be discretionary with the Secretary of the Army.

Resignation for the Good of the Service. A resignation for the good of the service generally involves a violation of honor or commission of offenses for which trial by court-martial would follow. When the nature of the offense is such that punishment more severe than dismissal would be warranted, such a resignation is denied so that trial may follow. There must be no element of coercion in a tender of such a resignation. However, an appointed counsel will advise the officer of the implications of such resignation. The officer should be allowed a reasonable time to decide on a course of action.

A resignation for the good of the service, if accepted by the Department of the Army, normally will be accepted as under other than honorable conditions, in which case the officer will be furnished a Discharge Certificate (Under Other Than Honorable Conditions). (DD Form 794A). If it is determined by the Department of the Army that the resignation should be accepted under honorable conditions, the officer will be furnished an Honorable Discharge Certificate (DD Form 256A), or a General Discharge Certificate (DD Form 257A), as appropriate. In addition to these types of certificates, a warrant officer may be awarded a Dishonorable Discharge Certificate (DD Form 260A) if such is deemed appropriate.

Benefits Cancelled by Discharge Other Than Honorable. Military service is rewarded by many benefits available to veterans upon separation from the service, always assuming that the separation is under honorable conditions. The list that follows comprises the important losses an officer would endure whose service is terminated under other than honorable conditions and for which Discharge Certificate DD Form 794A or Dishonorable Discharge Certificate DD Form 260A is supplied:

Severance, or readjustment pay

Compensation for unused leave credit

Transportation of dependents and household goods

Physical disability retirement benefits, or severance pay

In addition, it may be a bar from all rights, based upon the period of service from which separated, under laws administered by the Veterans Administration.

Resignation of Female Officers for Reason of Marriage, Pregnancy, or Parenthood. Female officers of the Army have broad options as to resignation in event of marriage, pregnancy, or parenthood, for which see chapters 6, 7, 8, AR 635-120.

Withdrawal of Resignation. An officer may request that his or her tender of resignation be withdrawn at any time prior to commencing travel pursuant to orders issued for the purpose of separation. Such requests are forwarded through channels with each endorsement recommending approval or disapproval.

Acceptance of Resignation. Until the acceptance of a resignation becomes effective, the officer tendering it continues to be an officer of the Army. The effective date of resignation is the date specified in the Department of the Army orders that announce the separation of the officer.

Resignation may be declined by the Department for a number of reasons: In time of war, when war is imminent, or in a period of emergency declared by the President; or when the officer is under investigation, under charges, awaiting result of trial, absent without leave, absent in hands of civil authorities, insane, or in default with respect to public property or funds.

SEPARATION, SEVERANCE, AND READJUSTMENT PAY

Several categories of special payments are authorized for officers who are involuntarily separated from active service.

Separation Pay. Regular and Reserve officers who are involuntarily separated (generally for failure of selection for promotion), with more than five but less than twenty years of commissioned service, are entitled to a lump sum separation payment equal to 10 percent of their annual base pay times their years of service, not to exceed $30,000. If the separation is for adverse reasons such as misconduct or substandard performance of duty, the separation payment may not exceed one-half the above.

Severance Pay. Regular officers who were on active duty prior to 14 December 1981 and who are involuntarily separated may elect to receive severance pay instead of separation pay, whichever is to their advantage. There are many variations under which severance pay is authorized, but in general it is computed on the basis of either (1) two months' base pay times years of service, not to exceed $15,000, or (2) one months' base pay times years of service, not to exceed twelve years.

Readjustment Pay. Reserve officers who were on active duty prior to 14 December 1981, and who are involuntarily released from active duty after serving at least five years of continuous active duty, may elect to receive readjustment pay instead of separation pay. It is calculated on the basis of two months' base pay times years of service, but may not exceed two years' base pay or $15,000, whichever is less.

Disability Severance Pay. An officer on active duty who is determined to be physically unfit for military service is entitled to disability severance pay when discharged, provided the disability: (1) was incurred or aggravated while entitled to base pay, (2) was incurred in line of duty, (3) is rated at less than 30 percent by the Veterans Administration, and (4) is, or may be permanent. It is computed by multiplying the monthly base pay of the highest grade in which the officer served satisfactorily by twice the number of years of service, but with a maximum of two years of basic pay. *Caution:* Retirement pay and VA compensation may be affected by acceptance of this disability severance pay. An individual concerned with this situation should take his or her complete military record to the appropriate agency for complete information and computation.

27
Retirement

The laws governing retirement from the armed forces are important to the government in order to maintain capably led armed forces, and they are important to the individual who elects to follow a military career. The purpose of retirement, voluntary and involuntary, is to assure that the Army has an officer corps of the highest caliber. To achieve this standard, officers are retired by statutory provisions involving physical limitations, age, time in grade, and by board action when performance of duty or conduct is below standard. The officer who serves well need not fear early retirement. The officer who desires a second career may retire with full and deserved honor (but at reduced pay) at twenty years, creating a promotion vacancy and stimulus for those who choose to serve to complete the full thirty-year career. Retirement laws that are fair and equitable, both to the government and to the individual officer, are essential to governmental military personnel administration.

This chapter will serve to orient the officer on this important subject; however, serious study of retirement should include the following references: AR 635-100, *Officer Personnel;* AR 635-40, *Physical Evaluation for Retention, Retirement, or Separation;* DA Pamphlet 600-5, *Handbook on Retirement Services;* and AR 608-25, *Retirement Services Program for Army Personnel and Their Families.*

STATUS OF RETIRED OFFICER

It is noteworthy that an officer who is retired retains status as an officer with many of its rights and privileges. He or she remains on the official roles of the Army and may be returned to active duty under applicable laws and departmental regulations. By tradition and law, retired Army personnel are considered to be in a real sense members of the Army. Therefore, close affinity does exist between the active Army and its retired personnel. The Retired List is not a roster of former officers; it is a designation of personnel, who by age, length of service, or disability should be regarded as having been transferred from one Army category to another.

Upon retirement from the Army, members are placed on one of the following retired lists: *U.S. Army Retired List,* for Regular Army commissioned officers, warrant officers, and enlisted personnel retired for any reason, who are granted retired pay. *Army of the United States Retired List,* for officers other than Regular Army officers, who are members and former members of the Reserve components, and personnel who served in the Army of the United States without component, who are granted retired pay, and retired warrant officers and enlisted personnel of the Regular Army who by reason of service in temporary commissioned grade are entitled to receive retired pay of the commissioned grade. *Temporary Disability Retired List,* for officers and enlisted personnel placed on the list in accordance with law for physical disability that may be of a permanent nature.

Use of Military Title after Retirement. See chapter 6, *Military Courtesy,* under THE CORRECT USE OF TITLES, and the cross references therein.

Retirement Services Offices. Retirement Services Offices have been established at Headquarters, Department of the Army, in Army areas throughout the United States, and in some oversea commands. These are the offices from which retired individuals may obtain guidance and assistance regarding their rights, benefits, and privileges. Retired members are invited to write or visit these units whenever assistance is needed in their personal affairs.

Correspondence directed to the Department of the Army should be addressed to The Adjutant General, ATTN: AGPO-AA, Department of the Army, Washington, DC 20315. DA Pam 600-5, *Handbook on Retirement Services,* provides information about Retirement Services Offices; it is issued to each retiring officer.

AFTER ARMY RETIREMENT—WHAT NEXT?

It is prudent for Army officers to anticipate the life they wish to lead after military retirement, and to plan with long-range foresight the vocation they may choose to follow as a second career. Under our current laws, officers who begin their Army careers at the normal ages of twenty-one to twenty-four will retire for length of service in their early fifties; or if they elect to retire after twenty years' service, in their early forties. Unless disability is a factor, many officers will wish to enter a new vocation. They may require additional income to meet family obligations, or to realize special desires. They may follow a new vocation to achieve results in a different field. All the reasons will be personal, but for everyone a thorough consideration of the possibilities, starting long before retirement, is a prudent course to adopt.*

COMPUTATION OF RETIRED PAY

Computation of retired pay used to be a relatively straightforward matter. It was set as a percentage of active duty pay and increased with increases in active duty pay. However, the Military Pay Act of 1963 established the principle that retired pay would be subject to cost-of-living adjustments without regard to active duty pay scales. Further changes to the law in 1980 and 1986 have complicated the calculation and have resulted in the military now operating on three distinct,

---

*For more information, consult *Transition from Military to Civilian Life,* a comprehensive guide to preretirement planning, published by Stackpole Books.

although related, retirement systems, depending upon when the retired member entered military service. Your understanding of how these laws affect you is essential to your long-range planning.

Service Prior to 8 September 1980. For members who entered the Army prior to 8 September 1980, retired pay is calculated on the basis of 2.5 percent × the years of service × the final basic pay to which entitled prior to retirement. Thus, a member with a final base pay of $3,000 per month ($36,000 per year) retiring after twenty years' service would receive retired pay of (2.5 percent × twenty) × $36,000 = 50 percent × $36,000 = $18,000 per year. The maximum retired pay of 75 percent of basic pay is reached at thirty years' service.

Members Entering after 8 September 1980 and Prior to 1 August 1986. For members who entered the Army on or after 8 September 1980, but before 1 August 1986, retired pay will be calculated using the same multiplier for years of service, but using the average of the three highest years of basic pay. Thus, if the member in the previous example had a final base pay of $3,000 per month, but had received this pay for only one year, with the previous two years being at the rate of $2,800 per month, the average base pay for the three-year period would be $34,400. Retired pay would then be calculated as 50 percent × $34,400 = $17,200 per year.

Members Entering after 1 August 1986. For members who enter the Army on or after 1 August 1986, the same high-three average pay will be used, and retirement still will be calculated on the basis of 2.5 percent for each year of service, but with a penalty of 1 percent applied for each year of service less than thirty years. Using the previous example, for retirement at twenty years' service, the multiplier becomes 40 percent instead of 50 percent, calculated as (2.5 percent × twenty) − (1 percent × ten). The retired pay based upon the high-three years of base pay thus would be 40 percent × $34,400 = $13,760 per year. At the member's age sixty-two, the penalty would be removed and the retired pay recalculated as 50 percent of the high-three average base pay. The law also provides that, for members who entered the Army prior to 1 August 1986, any cost-of-living (COLA) increase will be at a reduced rate based upon the increase in the Consumer Price Index minus 1 percent (CPI-1). At the member's age sixty-two, there will be a one-time adjustment to the full COLA level, after which any further adjustments will be at CPI-1 for life.

RETIREMENT: AFTER TWENTY OR AFTER THIRTY YEARS' SERVICE?

An officer may apply for retirement after completing twenty years of active service. Such retirements retain the right to retired pay and other benefits that are discussed in chapter 9, *Financial Planning.* The law and its current implementing policy are stated later in this chapter under the headings, VOLUNTARY RETIREMENT and *After Twenty Years' Service.*

This law was enacted by the Congress after thorough consideration. At the time of its enactment, vacancies in the higher grades of the Army had been so limited as to create a history of severe promotion stagnation. It was recognized that to provide attractive Army careers there must be sufficient vacancies to permit capable individuals to reach grades above lieutenant colonel at ages permitting adequate utilization by the government. Retirement of officers who wished to terminate their active service at twenty years permitted other officers who wished to remain to be promoted, and to hold the positions of high responsibility to which their grades pertained. The fact that many officers did choose to retire with less than thirty years' service has been of considerable concern to some members of Congress. The change to the law in 1986 regarding computation of retired pay was an obvious attempt to induce officers to serve longer careers to avoid the cost penalty of early retirement. However, there still is an opportunity for retirement between twenty and thirty years' service if desired.

While many officers wish to remain in active service until the date of compulsory retirement, it is not the case of all officers. Situations develop during long years of service, which could not possibly have been foreseen at appointment, that make it necessary or desirable for an officer to terminate a military career, often with great regret. Such reasons are usually very personal. They may be caused by a cruel health situation of a family member that precludes the change of station situation of the Army officer. They may result from financial requirements, coupled with opportunity to secure a higher income. The officer may contemplate his or her military record, conclude that it offers little chance of high success during the remaining years, and prefer to leave the Army to start an entirely new career. There are other personal reasons, all understandable, but not necessarily overriding those for not retiring.

The Wisdom in Thorough Analysis. The officer should approach this decision with care. There is need for thorough analysis of his or her present and future prospects in the Army, the forces suggesting retirement, and the civilian expectancy for employment and living. Retirement is extremely final. There have been tragic mistakes by some officers who found after retirement that their decision was unwise. Others have been highly successful and entered rewarding lives. It is because of these diverse developments that this discussion is included. It is not intended to advise officers to retire or not to retire, as they attain eligibility to choose. The purpose is to assist in understanding and evaluating.

The Change in Living Conditions. The officer who loves the service life, and his or her family who find it equally attractive, will undergo a serious adjustment if the tie is severed. Some of the customs and benefits officers and their families take for granted have very real values. These intangibles merit thought.

The Rewards of the Final Ten Years. During the final ten years of service, your assignments will be among those of heaviest responsibility and the greatest interest. You will have the opportunity for selection to high position. You will receive some of the benefits of seniority such as assignment of more desirable quarters. The officer with an outstanding record who terminates active service forfeits prospects of great value and of high rewards.

Consider the Pay Shrinkage. The need for prudent analysis is illustrated by comparing the retirement pay of a lieutenant colonel with twenty years' service who might have retired as a colonel with thirty years' service. Other examples may be computed from the pay tables.

In the case at hand, however, the colonel's monthly retired pay will be nearly twice that of the lieutenant colonel, the lieutenant colonel's retired pay being computed at only 50 percent of basic active duty pay, but the colonel's based on 75 percent. This disparity increases to a factor of nearly three using the retirement rules for officers entering the service after 1 August 1986.

In candor, there is another side to this coin. Let us look at it. Fewer than half the lieutenant colonels can attain the grade of colonel under present law, because of the lack of vacancies. A similar situation obtains for warrant officers contemplating promotion from CW3 to CW4. Lieutenant colonels may anticipate retirement upon completing twenty-eight years' service. Suppose a commissioned officer approaching the end of his or her twentieth year contemplates the future, and estimates chances of reaching the grade of colonel as low, an estimate perhaps gained by consulting the career manager at OPMD, in Washington. Now the concern involves the difference in retired pay computed at 50 percent (twenty years' service) vs. 70 percent (twenty-eight years' service), both computations based on the pay of a lieutenant colonel. Comparable numbers for an officer who entered the Army on or after 1 August 1986 would be 40 percent (twenty years' service) and 68 percent (twenty-eight years' service).

This comparison discloses a different (and difficult) situation. The officer who wishes to make the most of remaining employable years may find these facts to be convincing reasons for twenty-year retirement to start a new career. He or she may have financial obligations that cannot be satisfied by the prospective retired income in the grade of lieutenant colonel. This discussion states the factual comparison. It is neither to advocate retirement at the earliest opportunity, nor to remain on active duty without regard to the probabilities. The decision is wholly personal and should be based on personal preferences, financial considerations, opportunities in another vocation, and the many likes and dislikes of the individuals concerned.

Consider the Reduction in Security. As discussed in chapter 9, *Financial Planning,* important benefits provided active duty personnel are terminated or curtailed upon retirement. These are subjects to be identified and evaluated. They must be faced by officers who retire after thirty years' service, too; but the officer retiring at an earlier year accepts them at a younger age.

In Your Own Case What About Civilian Employment? It is certainly true that many officers of long service who have resigned or retired have obtained civilian employment with above average earnings, and a large number hold positions of the highest importance in civilian fields. We may be proud of our fellow officers who have won such outstanding recognition. One might assume it to be a group expectancy but it isn't universal and no certainty exists in changing times and in nongovernmental, highly competitive, and variable occupations. It is an individual matter entirely, worth most careful examination before forwarding the retirement application.

What was your education as to beckoning civilian employment? What has been your service training and experience fitting you for specific civilian employment? Or, have you planned to undertake training to fit you for a profession or employment?

Do you have a definite, responsible offer from a company or a responsible person who has such a decision in his or her power?

Summary. Early retirement may be wise for some officers, heartbreakingly unwise for others. Decision as to this problem should be reached only on an evaluation such as you have been trained to make in military service: Get all the facts, analyze them carefully, then decide which is best for you and for your family.

RETIREMENT—AN OVERVIEW

It is true that the beginning of military retirement calls for a major readjustment in the lives of most officers and their families. There is a real need for the career officer to gain a clear understanding of his or her own postretirement situation and the probable wishes of family members as they can be foreseen. A reasonable degree of planning for the period of retirement is advisable, and it should start long before retirement is requested or ordered.

Medical Service for Retired Individuals and Their Family Members. Retired personnel and their dependents are authorized to receive medical care and hospitalization at facilities of the uniformed services, when available, and at civilian facilities, if military facilities are unavailable. See chapter 9, *Financial Planning.*

Use of Post and Station Facilities. Retired members, their dependents, and unremarried widowed spouses are authorized the use of various facilities on military installations when facilities are available. Proper identification is required. This privilege includes authority to use and patronize the following: (DA Pamphlet 600-5.)

Commissaries
Post exchanges
Clothing sales stores
Laundry and dry cleaning plants
Military theatres
Army recreation service facilities
Officers' clubs (upon application to and approval of the club concerned)

As interservice custom, retired members are usually welcomed into club and other facilities of the sister services.

Travel to Home. At any time within one year after retirement, an officer is entitled to be moved, at government expense, to any authorized location in the world where he or she intends to establish a bona fide home. For details, consult a post transportation officer.

RETIREMENT FOR PHYSICAL DISABILITY

The first stage in any proceeding for separation for physical reasons is a finding by the Service that the person, by reason of a disability, is not qualified to perform his or her duties. If a person is kept on duty, there are, of course, no separation proceedings.

But if a finding is made that the person *cannot* be retained in service, the proceedings enter a second stage. If the disability was due to intentional misconduct or willful neglect or incurred during unauthorized absence, the government gives the member nothing, merely separates him or her.

Third, if the disability was not due to misconduct or neglect, the next question is: Is the disability 30 percent or more under the Veterans Administration standard rating? (Loss of an eye or loss of use of a limb, and chronic, severe, high blood pressure are disabilities of 30 percent or more; loss of one or two fingers or one or two toes, loss of hearing in one ear, or defects or scars that do not seriously interfere with functions, are not.)

If the disability is less than 30 percent, no retirement is given (except for some persons of long service). Instead, the person is given *severance pay,* which is two months' basic active duty pay for each year of active service, to a maximum of two full years' active pay. Half or more of a year counts as a full year.

Officers with less than eight years' service whose disability is not the proximate result of the performance of active duty are entitled only to severance pay.

VOLUNTARY RETIREMENT

Voluntary retirement includes all types of retirement that the officer initiates by his or her own application. Approval of an officer's voluntary retirement may be mandatory, or discretionary, dependent upon specific provisions of the law under which retirement is sought.

After Twenty Years' Service. A commissioned officer of the Army who has at least twenty years of active federal service, at least ten years of which have been as a commissioned officer, may upon personal application and in the discretion of the Secretary of the Army, be retired.

After Thirty Years' Service. An officer of the Army who has at least thirty years of service may upon his or her own application and in the discretion of the President be retired. After forty years of service an officer shall be retired upon personal request without need of approval.

Policy on Acceptance of Retirement Applications. When an officer has completed all service obligations prescribed in AR 635-100, his or her retirement application normally is approved. During periods of emergency, Department of the Army may announce restrictions on the approval of retirement applications. Individuals who possess critical skills or hold assignments in key positions may be denied retirement (or resignation). Officers should consult their unit personnel officer for information that may influence their action.

MANDATORY RETIREMENT

Mandatory retirements are those retirements required by law and must be effected regardless of the desire of the individual or of the preferences of the Department of the Army. Computation of service is based on AR 635-100.

Retirement for Age. Unless retired or separated at an earlier date, each commissioned officer whose regular grade is below major general, other than a professor or the Registrar of the USMA, shall be retired on becoming sixty years of age. Unless retired or separated earlier, each commissioned officer whose regular grade is major general, and whose retirement for length of service has been deferred, shall be retired at age sixty, or if not deferred, will be retired at age sixty-two.

Retirement for Length of Service. Unless retired or separated at an earlier date, officers shall be retired for length of service as follows:

Major Generals. Each officer in the grade of major general shall be retired on the fifth anniversary of the date of appointment in that grade or on the thirtieth day after completion of thirty-five years of service, whichever is later.

Brigadier Generals. Each officer in the grade of brigadier general, other than a professor of the USMA, shall be retired on the fifth anniversary of the date of his or her appointment in that grade or on the thirtieth day after completion of thirty years service, whichever is later.

Colonels. Each officer in the grade of colonel shall be retired on the fifth anniversary of the date of his or her appointment in that grade or on the thirtieth day after completion of thirty years of service, whichever is later. Also, upon the determination of the Secretary of the Army that there are too many colonels on the active list, the Secretary may convene a board of five general officers to recommend officers for early retirement.

Lieutenant Colonels. Each officer in the grade of lieutenant colonel shall be retired on the thirtieth day after completion of twenty-eight years of service. In each of the above cases, retirement takes place on the first day of the month following the month in which service requirements are met. If the officer is on a recommended list for promotion to the next higher grade, the officer will be retained and will fall under the criteria for the next grade when promoted.

Selective Retirement. In accordance with the Defense Officer Personnel Management Act (DOPMA), lieutenant colonels and colonels may be selected for early retirement by board action, where rapid reduction of the numbers of officers in these grades is necessary.

Deferred Officers Not Recommended for Promotion—Majors, Captains, and First Lieutenants. Under the provisions of the Defense Officer Personnel Management Act (DOPMA), officers in the grades of first lieutenant, captain, and major who twice fail to be selected for promotion will be involuntarily separated from the Army. However, DOPMA also contains provisions that allow the Secretary of the Army to selectively continue in grade certain of the captains and majors to fill Army specialty needs. In such cases, captains may be continued in grade to a maximum of twenty years' service, and majors may be continued in grade to a maximum of twenty-four years' service.

Exceptions. The retirement laws are generally applicable to both male and female officers. However, there are exceptions for officers of the Army Nurse Corps and the Army Medical Specialist Corps.

The Secretary of the Army may defer the retirement of a lieutenant colonel in either of the corps named above until the last day of the month in which the officer completes thirty years and thirty days of service as computed officially.

Removal from Active List. If an officer is removed from the active list of the Regular Army under the provisions of Title 10, USC, Chapter 359, and, if on the date of removal he or she is eligible for voluntary retirement under any provision of law then in effect, then the officer shall be retired in the grade and with the retired pay to which entitled had the retirement been upon his or her own application.

RETIRED GRADE, RANK, AND STATUS

Retired Grade. In accordance with the provisions of DOPMA, officers promoted to lieutenant colonel and above after 15 September 1981 must serve in the new grade for at least three years to be eligible to retire in that grade. Unless specifically exempted by the President, officers who elect to retire prior to completion of three years' service in grade will be retired at the next lower grade in which they have served for a minimum of six months.

Physical Disability. An officer of the Regular Army retired for physical disability incurred while serving under a temporary appointment in a higher grade shall have the rank and receive retired pay computed as otherwise provided by law for officers of such higher grade.

It is noteworthy that a retired officer continues his or her status as an officer of the Army, subject to return to active duty under provisions of our laws. In time of war or emergency many officers are recalled, although few (if any) are restored to active duty without their consent.

The laws are quite favorable as to the protection afforded officers recalled from retirement in the event of incurring physical disability, or additional physical disability. Officers on the Retired List who have return to active service under consideration are urged to inform themselves as to the specific basis their own return would include.

Retired Status. A Regular Army officer placed on the retired list is still an officer of the United States (31 Ct. Cl. 35).

Certificate of Retirement. Each member of the Army, upon retirement, will be furnished a Certificate of Retirement (DD Form 363-A) by The Adjutant General.

RETIREMENT OF NATIONAL GUARD AND RESERVE OFFICERS

Retirement for Physical Disability. The laws governing retirement for physical disability apply equally to all officers on active duty whether of the Regular Army or the Reserve components. This principle was first established by enactment of the Act of 3 April 1939 and is affirmed in the Career Compensation Act of 1949 and codified in Title 10, USC, Chapter 61.

Retirement for Age and Length of Service. National Guard and Reserve officers may become eligible for retirement based upon age and length of service in accordance with the provisions of Title 10, USC, Section 1331. They must meet the following criteria to be eligible:

Have attained age sixty.

Have completed a minimum of twenty years of qualifying service.

Have served at least the last eight years of qualifying service as a member of a Reserve component. The last eight years of qualifying service need not be the last eight years of military service, nor do they have to be continuous.

If a member of a Reserve component or the Army of the United States without component prior to 16 August 1945, must have performed active service during some portion of the periods 8 September 1940 to 1 January 1947, 26 June 1950 to 28 July 1953, 13 August 1961 to 31 May 1963, or 4 August 1964 to 28 March 1973. The active service must have been other than for training.

In addition, to qualify for receipt of retired pay under the provisions of Title 10, USC, the officer:

Must not be entitled to retired pay from the armed forces under any other provision of law.

Must not have elected to receive disability severance pay (see chapter 26, *Resignation and Elimination*) in lieu of retired pay at age sixty.

Must not fall within the purview of the Hiss Act, i.e., must not have been convicted of a national security-type offense, or must not have refused to testify before a duly constituted judicial or congressional proceeding on a matter related to the national security.

There are many forms and categories of qualifying service. Officers are advised to consult AR 135-180 and their personnel officer for information as to the creditability of their own service.

THE RETIRED OFFICERS ASSOCIATION

The Retired Officers Association has for its purpose the aid of retired personnel in every proper and legitimate manner. Included are the presentation of subjects important to retired officers before the appropriate members of Congress. It provides assistance in securing employment and offers many other helpful services. It is located at 201 North Washington Street, Alexandria, VA 22314.

UNITED STATES ARMY WARRANT OFFICER ASSOCIATION

The United States Army Warrant Officer Association is a professional association of Army warrant officers of all components, both active and retired, dedicated to recommending programs for the improvement of the Army and the Warrant Officer Corps, and to disseminating professional information to warrant officers in the field. Services include a bi-monthly newspaper to members, liaison with the Department of the Army, Department of Defense, Veterans Administration, and Congress. Membership is open to any Army warrant officer who holds or has held a warrant issued by the Secretary of the Army. The address of the association is P.O. Box 2040, Reston, VA 22090.

NATIONAL ASSOCIATION OF UNIFORMED SERVICES

The National Association of Uniformed Services (NAUS) has for its purpose the promotion of legislation that will uphold the security of the nation, sustain morale of the armed forces, and provide equitable consideration for all members of the uniformed services—active and retired. NAUS is nonprofit and nonsocial. Membership is open to all servicemen and women, active and retired. It is located at 5535 Hempstead Way, P.O. Box 1406, Springfield, VA 22151. Telephone (703) 750-1342.

28

Organization and Missions

Landpower is the decisive arm of American military force because it changes history. The 168 campaign streamers on the Army colors are ample testimony that landpower, in conjunction with sea power and air power, has served this nation well throughout history—a strength that must continue into the future. Although landpower's traditions are firmly rooted in our past, its relevance today is greater because the threats to our national security are more dangerous. . . . American and allied soldiers of previous generations made an investment to ensure the peace we enjoy. The greatest legacy our Army can leave to the generations that follow is that same opportunity to be free. Only by vigilant commitment of confident and professional soldiers motivated by peace, dedicated to freedom, and skilled in their craft can such a legacy be guaranteed. Freedom can and must endure. Americans can and must be free. Landpower can and must play a key role in assuring peace.—General John A. Wickham, Jr., Chief of Staff, U.S. Army, October 1984 for the *Army Greenbook,* October 1984.

This statement by the Army's Chief of Staff expressed his views as to the importance of landpower and the continuing need of our nation for skilled, dedicated, professional soldiers who are motivated by peace but who are prepared to fight if necessary to preserve our freedom.

The Army must be ready to fight today, with the weapons and equipment on hand today, anywhere in the world as directed by our nation's civil leaders. The mission continues to provide for the security of the nation, and of our people, and to accomplish its assigned tasks in upholding the commitments made by our government. Prevention of war is the primary goal. But if war—or combat short of war—cannot be prevented, the mission of the Army and its sister services is to end the conflict as quickly as possible under conditions accept-

LESSON RELEARNED
Reproduced by permission of the Allentown (Pa.) *Morning Call*.

able to our government. *The Army must be ready to fight at once with the personnel and with the equipment we have ready for immediate deployment.*

At the same time that we are fighting with personnel and equipment on hand, we also rush into an era with new developments as to weapons and other equipment, with the need for personnel especially trained in their effective employment. There is a certainty that versatile and powerful weapons will be developed to become available for employment where needed. *Just as the Army must be ready and able to fight effectively and promptly, wherever ordered, with personnel and weapons available, it must also prepare itself to fight the battles of the future, with the weapons it will then have on hand. Members of the armed forces expect that weapons and equipment provided for their use will be the very best our national capabilities can develop and produce.*

This chapter is provided as a source of authentic, interesting, current information about the Army. It includes discussions of the following subjects:

Objective of the Army
Army Change and Progress
Organization—Headquarters, Department of the Army
Major Army Field Commands

OBJECTIVE OF THE ARMY

The objective, or purpose of the Army should be understood clearly by all members of the Army, and by each of our nation's citizens. It is firmly established in Title 10, USC, as follows:

It is the intent of Congress to provide an Army that is capable, in conjunction with the other armed forces, of—

(1) preserving the peace and security and providing for the defense of the United States, the Territories, Commonwealths, and possessions and any areas occupied by the United States;

(2) supporting the national policies;

(3) implementing the national objectives; and

(4) overcoming any nations responsible for aggressive acts that imperil the peace and security of the United States.

In general, the Army, within the Department of the Army, includes land combat and service forces and such aviation and water transport as may be organic therein. It shall be organized, trained, and equipped primarily for prompt and sustained combat incident to operations on land. It is responsible for the preparation of land forces necessary for the effective prosecution of war except as otherwise assigned and, in accordance with integrated joint mobilization plans, for the expansion of the peacetime components of the Army to meet the needs of war.

ARMY CHANGE AND PROGRESS

While the objectives or missions of the Army remain unchanged through the years, the Army itself undergoes continuing change in order to be able to best meet these objectives. The Army is trained and equipped to wage many forms of war: general, limited, nuclear, conventional, counterinsurgent. It must be ready to meet a crisis with whatever the situation requires and as our government directs. The Army is doing this job, as directed by the civil leaders of our government, around the world. There is a flexibility of organization and equipment to provide a measured and effective response to any form of aggression.

To attain and retain this flexibility requires that the Army be in a continual state of change, adapting its thinking and organization to new doctrine and equipment as they are developed. Failure to make these adjustments would result in a loss of the capability and flexibility so necessary to meet the exacting tasks assigned.

The strength of the active Army is established by our nation's leaders to meet the estimated need for Army forces in support of national goals. Current policy is to maintain an active Army of about three-quarters of a million soldiers organized into divisions, separate brigades and regiments, and support units as necessary to provide adequate defense for our Nation and to back up and give support to our foreign policy decisions.

These active forces are backed up by the U.S. Army Reserve and Army National Guard forces who stand ready, as directed, to augment the active Army forces should the world situation so demand. Together, these three elements—the Active Army, the U.S. Army Reserve, and the Army National Guard—constitute the Total Force on which our nation depends.

The divisions, separate brigades, and smaller supporting units of the Army's Total Force are using the best weapons and equipment our country has to offer, which are very good indeed. Even better weapons and equipment are under development. As newer weapons, equipment, and doctrine become available, the Army will change as necessary to make the best use of what is furnished, always with the view of performing in a superb manner the tasks assigned to it by the civil leaders of our government.

It takes trained and determined personnel to do these vital jobs. This is a fact to be remembered always by our civil leaders, by industrial and educational leaders, members of vocations who mold public opinions, and our citizens generally. Understanding of the requirements to provide for our nation's security, or to keep its solemn commitments, is enhanced when a person thinks of the soldier behind the rifle who aims it and fires it, or the crew of a tank or helicopter who operate and guide, aim, and fire. The emphasis must remain upon equipping the soldier, not merely manning the equipment. Army power means power applied by soldiers in person, at close range, as the nation's mission demands. The heart of the Army is the officer and the soldier. The soldier's training, pride in service, confidence in the excellence of equipment, and conviction as to the worthiness of the national cause, are all matters that must concern our government, our leaders, and our citizens.

ORGANIZATION—HEADQUARTERS, DEPARTMENT OF THE ARMY

The Headquarters, Department of the Army, in the Pentagon, Washington, D.C., is the place of final decision as to Army affairs, and it is the nerve center for control of execution of the military missions pertaining to the Army. It is an organizational component of the Department of Defense. Located together are the command and control elements of the Department of Defense, and the Departments of Army, Navy, and Air Force, so they may work together in easy teamwork, and operate together in jointly planned and executed combined operations. (AR 10-5).

As a result of legislation passed in 1986, the Goldwater-Nicols Department of Defense Reorganization Act, a major restructuring of the Department of the Army staff and the staff of the Secretary of the Army was implemented in 1987. The resultant organization at the highest levels of the Army will result in more immediate control of Army activities by the Secretary of the Army; it is part of a larger effort to enhance the role of the Joint Chiefs of Staff and the Secretary of Defense. The revised organizations for the Secretary of the Army and the Army Staff are shown on the accompanying charts.

The Secretary of the Army. The Secretary of the Army, a civilian, is the head of the Army and has primary responsibility for all affairs of the Army establishment. The position illustrates the application of civilian control under our Constitution. The Secretary is assisted by other civilian officials as follows:

The Undersecretary of the Army. This official acts as deputy to the Secretary and is the Secretary's principal assistant. The Undersecretary also is the Army's acquisition executive and, in that capacity, reports directly to the Undersecretary of Defense for Acquisition. A Deputy Undersecretary is provided to handle Operations Research matters.

The Assistant Secretaries of the Army (A/SA). There are five Assistant Secretaries of the Army for: Civil Works; Manpower and Reserve Affairs; Research, Development and Acquisition; Installations and Logistics; and Financial Management. The Director of Information Systems, C⁴ (Command, Control, Communications, and Computers) also is on the staff of the Secretary, reporting at the Assistant Secretary level.

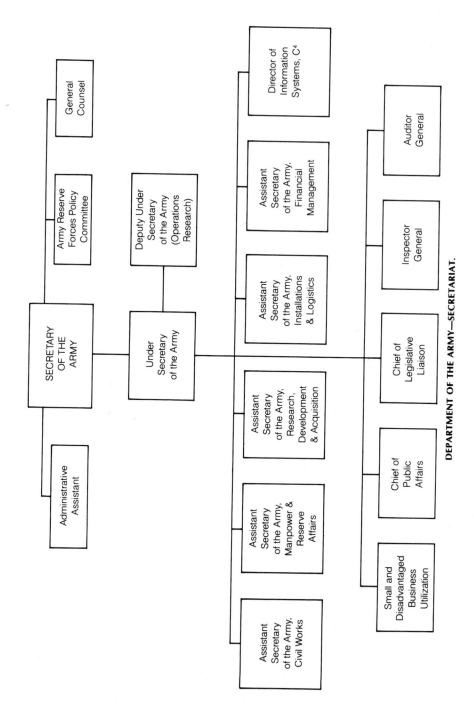

DEPARTMENT OF THE ARMY—SECRETARIAT.

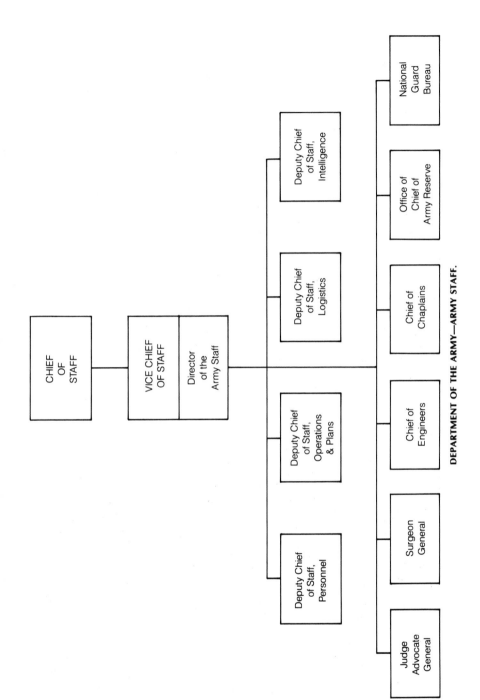

DEPARTMENT OF THE ARMY—ARMY STAFF.

Other Assistants to the Secretary. The following are also responsible directly to the Secretary: Administrative Assistant, General Counsel, Army Reserve Forces Policy Committee, Office of Small and Disadvantaged Business Utilization, Chief of Public Affairs, Chief of Legislative Liaison, The Inspector General, and The Auditor General.

In this staff restructuring, responsibility was transferred from the Chief of Staff to the Secretary of the Army in the areas of acquisition, auditing, comptroller activities, information management, inspector general functions, and research and development.

The Army Staff. The Secretary of the Army is assisted by the Army Staff, which is the professional military staff at the Headquarters, Department of the Army. It consists of the Chief of Staff, the Army General Staff, the Special Staff, and the Personal Staff.

The Chief of Staff. The Chief of Staff is the highest military assistant or advisor to the Secretary of the Army. He or she occupies the pinnacle position within the Army. He or she is a member of the Joint Chiefs of Staff. As Army Chief of Staff, his or her responsibility is to the Secretary of the Army and includes the worldwide Army mission as well as its administration, training, and supply.

Office of the Chief of Staff. The Office of the Chief of Staff includes the Vice Chief of Staff, Director of the Army Staff, and other staff members as may be required.

The Army General Staff. The Chief of Staff is assisted by other staff officers, each heading a general staff agency charged with a particular function. These functions pertain to the people, planning,   logistics, and intelligence aspects of the Army. The general staff officers are: the Deputy Chief of Staff for Operations and Plans (DCSOPS), the Deputy Chief of Staff for Personnel (DCSPER), the Deputy Chief of Staff for Logistics (DCSLOG), and the Deputy Chief of Staff for Intelligence (DCSI).

The Special Staff. The Chief of Staff also is assisted by staff officers heading special staff agencies, each of which is charged with exercising responsibility for specialized activities.

The Special Staff consists of the following officers: Chief of Engineers; Surgeon General; Chief, National Guard Bureau; and the Chief, Army Reserve.

The Personal Staff. The Personal Staff assists the Chief of Staff in specifically designated areas. It consists of the aides to the Chief, other individual staff officers whose advice and assistance he or she desires to receive directly, and those staff agencies whose functions and activities he or she desires to coordinate and administer directly.

The Personal Staff officers include the Chief of Chaplains and the Judge Advocate General.

The heads of the following Staff agencies command personnel, facilities, and organizations in addition to their staff duties. These are separate and distinct functions: the Chief of Engineers, the Surgeon General, and the Judge Advocate General.

MAJOR ARMY FIELD COMMANDS

The missions of the Army are carried out through nine major Army field commands, whose missions are described below.

U.S. Army Forces Command (FORSCOM). U.S. Army Forces Command with headquarters at Fort McPherson, Georgia, is responsible for the operations and readiness of all Active Army and Army Reserve units in every state except Hawaii, as well as in the Commonwealth of Puerto Rico and the Virgin Islands of the United

THE ARMY FLAG.

The Army Flag is made up of the national colors with a yellow fringe. It is of standard size. The flag of white silk bears an embroidered blue replica of the offical seal of the War Office over a broad scarlet scroll on which "United States Army" is inscribed in white letters. Beneath the scroll are the numerals "1775" denoting the year of the Army's founding by action of the Continental Congress on 14 June 1775. The flag was unfurled officially on 14 June 1956.

States. If ordered to active federal service during full mobilization, Army National Guard units of those forty-nine states and territories would also become part of FORSCOM, bringing the total strength of the command to 800,000 soldiers, more than two-thirds of the U.S. Army's total ground combat forces. The Commanding General of FORSCOM also serves for planning purposes as Commander-in-Chief, U.S. Army Forces, Atlantic. In July 1987, FORSCOM was designated a joint-service specified command, assuming missions previously assigned to the U.S. Readiness Command, which was deactivated to form the new U.S. Special Operations Command.

Third Army. Third U.S. Army serves as the Army component headquarters for the U.S. Central Command. The mission of Third Army is to plan, exercise, and deploy Army forces in response to contingencies threatening vital U.S. interests in Southwest Asia. The Deputy Commanding General of FORSCOM also serves as the Commanding General of Third Army.

Continental Armies. Five of FORSCOM's armies are designated continental armies or CONUSAs. The CONUSAs are regional commands, and within their respective areas the commanding generals supervise Army National Guard training and command Army Reserve units. Upon mobilization, the CONUSAs interface with the Federal Emergency Management Agency for the land defense of the continental United States and will command all Army forces in their areas.

National Training Center. The National Training Center (NTC) at Fort Irwin, California, opened formally in July 1981. It capitalizes on the unique combinations of maneuver space, highly proficient opposing forces on an instrumented battle-field, live fire, and standard evaluation. Maneuver battalions from the Active Army and the Reserve forces are obtaining realistic training at the NTC.

U.S. Army Training and Doctrine Command (TRADOC). With headquarters at historic Fort Monroe, Virginia, the Training and Doctrine Command (TRADOC) is responsible for determining how the Total Army will train and fight and how it will be organized and equipped. In fulfilling these responsibilities, TRADOC manages all institutional training for officers from the basic officer courses through the Command and General Staff College, and for enlisted personnel from basic training through the Sergeants Major Academy.

TRADOC commands the Army's service schools and manages officer procure-ment through the Reserve Officer Training Corps (ROTC) and the Officer Candi-date School (OCS). Doctrinal and materiel requirements are developed by the service schools and are coordinated through three integrating centers—the Com-bined Arms Center at Fort Leavenworth, Kansas; the Soldier Support Center at Fort Benjamin Harrison, Indiana; and the Logistics Center at Fort Lee, Virginia, all under the command of TRADOC. Additionally, TRADOC supports Total Army training by developing, producing, and distributing training support materials to command-ers in the field. In accomplishing these missions, TRADOC conducts extensive coordination with AMC, FORSCOM, our sister services of the Navy, Air Force, and Marine Corps, and representatives of allied armies. TRADOC also operates a worldwide network of liaison officers to maintain effective communication with Army operational forces as well as those of our sister services and our allies.

Installations. Major installation commanders have designated geographical areas of responsibility within which they are responsible for budgeting, funding, and logistical support of Army, Army Reserve, and ROTC elements, as well as special functions such as public affairs and disaster control. The installation com-mander may be responsive to FORSCOM or TRADOC, or both, in carrying out assigned functions, depending upon the activities and units assigned within his or her area.

U.S. Army Materiel Command (AMC). The U.S. Army Materiel Command, with headquarters in Alexandria, Virginia., directs the development, test and evaluation, procurement, distribution, maintenance, and disposal of nearly all Army equip-ment. It deals with the Army's hardware. AMC controls various research and development and material readiness subordinate commands.

The subordinate elements of AMC are the Armament, Munitions and Chemical Command at Rock Island, Illinois; the Aviation Systems Command at St. Louis, Missouri; the Belvoir R&D Center at Fort Belvoir, Virginia; the Chemical R&D Center at Aberdeen Proving Ground, Maryland; the Communications-Electronics Command at Fort Monmouth, New Jersey; the Depot System Command at Cham-bersburg, Pennsylvania; the Laboratory Command at Adelphi, Maryland; the Mis-sile Command at Redstone Arsenal, Alabama; the Tank-Automotive Command at Warren, Michigan; the Test and Evaluation Command at Aberdeen Proving Ground, Maryland; the Troop Support Command at St. Louis, Missouri; AMC-Europe at Seckenheim, Germany; the Foreign Science and Technology Center at Charlottesville, Virginia; the Logistics Management Center at Fort Lee, Virginia; the Security Affairs Command at Alexandria, Virginia; and the White Sands Missile Range in New Mexico.

U.S. Army Intelligence and Security Command (INSCOM). The U.S. Army Intelligence and Security Command, with headquarters at Arlington Hall Station,

FIVE CONTINENTAL
UNITED STATES ARMY AREAS

Virginia, near Washington, D.C., has worldwide responsibilities for intelligence collection and production, counterintelligence and security.

U.S. Army Information Systems Command. The U.S. Army Information Systems Command with headquarters at Fort Huachuca, Arizona, manages the Army's portion of the worldwide Defense Communications System (DCS), including the planning, engineering, installation, and operation of the Army's portion of this system. It also provides engineering, installation, and technical support services, as required, for assigned Army communications; and for Army air traffic control facilities.

U.S. Army Criminal Investigation Command. The U.S. Army Criminal Investigation Command has its headquarters in Falls Church, Virginia, near Washington, D.C. It exercises centralized command and control of Army criminal investigative activities worldwide.

U.S. Army Military District of Washington (MDW). The Military District of Washington commands Army units, activities, and installations and is responsible for designated Army functions in the metropolitan area of Washington, D.C. Its headquarters is located at Fort Leslie J. McNair in Washington. D.C.

U.S. Army Health Services Command. The U.S. Army Health Services Command, with headquarters at Fort Sam Houston, Texas, is the Army's single manager for health care delivery and supportive services within CONUS and in Alaska and Hawaii, including command of the Army hospital system. It supervises all medical training for the Army.

U.S. Army Corps of Engineers (USACE). The U.S. Army Corps of Engineers, with headquarters in Washington, D.C., manages Army real property; manages and executes engineering, construction, and real estate programs for the Army and the Air Force; and manages and executes the civil works program for the Army.

ARMY COMPONENTS OF UNIFIED COMMANDS

The Army furnishes components of unified joint service commands operating under the operational direction of the Secretary of Defense through the Joint Chiefs of Staff. The Secretary of the Army is responsible for administrative and logistical support of these component commands and elements.

There are now four Army components of unified commands:

U.S. Army, Europe. The U.S. Army, Europe, with headquarters in Heidelberg, Germany, is the Army component of the unified U.S. European Command.

Eighth U.S. Army. The Eighth U.S. Army is the Army component of the unified U.S. Forces, Korea.

U.S. Army, Pacific. The U.S. Army, Pacific, with headquarters at Fort Shafter, Hawaii, is the Army component of the unified U.S. Pacific Command.

Military Traffic Management Command (MTMC). The Military Traffic Management Command, with headquarters in Washington, D.C., executes the Army's function as Single Manager for the Department of Defense of all military traffic management, land transportation, and common-user ocean terminal service within CONUS, and for worldwide movement and storage of household goods for the Department of Defense. It is the Army component of the unified U.S. Transportation Command (TRANSCOM).

Other unified commands, such as the U.S. Space Command, the Special Operations Command, and the U.S. Southern Command have Army elements that receive their administrative and logistical support from the U.S. Forces Command (FORSCOM).

ORGANIZATION BY COMPONENT

The Army of the United States consists of the Regular Army, the Army National Guard, and the Army Reserve. The terms of service differ as to each of the three components, but the purposes for which each is formed and maintained are identical: the security of the United States, its Constitution, its government and people, and its commitments with allies.

The Regular Army. Members of the Regular Army, both officer and enlisted members, are on active, full-time military duty, as volunteers. It is the permanent, professional force. The station and duty of members is as directed by military authority. In war or peace, in good times or bad, the Regular Army must be ready to undertake whatever mission is directed by proper governmental authority. Members of the Regular Army are the "United States Army."

The Reserve Components. The Reserve components are the Army National Guard of the United States and the Army Reserve. Members of these components may be on inactive military status, at their homes or locations of their own choice, while receiving military instruction at times of minimum interference with their civilian vocations. They may be called into active federal military service in time of war or other national emergency, when so determined by the President in accordance with law. That is to say, a member of the Reserve forces may be inactive and perform part-time military service, or may be active and be as fully engaged in military affairs as a member of the Regular service, with the same hazards and the same rewards.

The Active Army. That part of the Army of the United States that is on full-time service is called the Active Army. It includes under all conditions the United States Army (the Regular Army) as our full-time professional force, plus those individuals or complete units drawn from the Army National Guard or Army Reserve to serve on a full-time basis to meet conditions of war or overall strength requirements determined by the President and the Congress. Specified units of the Reserve components are designated to round out or augment active Army units in an emergency.

The Army National Guard (ARNG). The Army National Guard traces its lineage back to 1636 when three militia units, the North, South, and East Regiments, were formed in the colony of Massachusetts. Since that time, National Guard units have been mobilized for national defense nearly two dozen times, including major participation in every war except Vietnam. For that conflict, a decision was made not to mobilize the ARNG, although a number of smaller units were called into federal service.

Since 1945, the ARNG has had a dual status. During peacetime, it is a state force under the control of the respective state governors, and is designed to preserve peace, order, and public safety in the state during emergencies. In wartime or a declared national emergency, the ARNG can be mobilized (called into federal service) by the President. In this latter role, the ARNG constitutes a major portion of the total force available to the Army of the United States.

The ARNG has a total all-volunteer strength of more than 450,000. It thus represents about 30 percent of the total Army strength. It is organized into six infantry divisions, two armored divisions, one mechanized infantry division, one light infantry division, nineteen separate brigades (nine infantry, six mechanized infantry, three armor, one light infantry), and four armored cavalry regiments, in addition to two special forces groups, twenty field artillery brigades, and a number of separate battalions. Nearly half of the Army's combat units are in the ARNG.

A baccalaureate degree is now required for initial appointment as a commissioned officer in the Army National Guard, and for promotion to major. Lieutenants must complete an officer basic course at one of the active Army's service schools, in residence, to qualify for promotion to captain. Completion of the advanced course is required for promotion to major.

U.S. Army Reserve (USAR). In contrast to the ARNG, the U.S. Army Reserve traces its beginnings back only to the early years of this century. The National Defense Act of 1916 authorized an Officers Reserve Corps and an Enlisted Reserve Corps, and created the Reserve Officers Training Corps (ROTC). More than 160,-000 Reservists served on active duty during World War I.

After that war, a Reserve force of thirty-three divisions was planned, but lack of funds and support prevented the planning from becoming reality. Training funds were scarce, and there were only limited funds available to pay for paid drill periods. The result was that only small cadre groups were assigned to only some of the divisions. However, many officers coming out of the ROTC program were commissioned into the Reserves during the period. As World War II got underway, many of these officers were called into active service, so that by the summer of 1941, about 90 percent of the active duty company grade officers were Reservists who had been called to active duty. Almost the entire Reserve mobilization for World War II was in the form of individual replacements rather than Reserve units. The Reserve units that were mobilized were staffed largely with personnel who had not been members of the units before the war.

About 200,000 Reserve personnel were mobilized to serve during the Korean

War, many as individual replacements, but there also were a number of Reserve units with their personnel that were mobilized.

Problems encountered with the Korean War mobilization led to a major restructuring of the Reserve forces. The U.S. Army Reserve was established in 1952, replacing the previous Officers Reserve Corps and Enlisted Reserve Corps that had been created by the Act of 1916. During the late 1950s and the 1960s, the Reserves became increasingly oriented toward combat support and combat service support missions, as contrasted to actual combat maneuver units.

The USAR today consists of about 280,000 individuals in the Selected Reserve and nearly 300,000 in the Individual Ready Reserve. Officers in the USAR include some who have terminated their active service, but who desire to remain in the USAR or who have a remaining service obligation. Input is received each year from among the graduates of the ROTC program. In addition, there are provisions for direct commissioning into the USAR. Completion of an officer basic course is required to qualify for promotion to first lieutenant or captain, and completion of an advanced course is required for promotion to major.

The Total Force. At about the time the draft ended in 1973, the Army adopted a Total Force concept that pared the strength of the active duty forces to the minimum estimated to be required to maintain the peace (currently about 780,-000), and relied upon well-trained, well-equipped Reserve forces that could be mobilized on short notice to augment the active duty forces. Under this Total Force policy, the ARNG now provides nearly 50 percent of the total combat units available in emergencies to the Army of the United States. The USAR units provide much of the combat support and combat service support strength that would be required to support operations of a mobilized Army of the United States, as well as a pool of individual replacements who are already trained and who could be called into service as fillers in active Army units to help bring them up to full strength.

To assure that the Reserve forces are trained and ready for mobilization if necessary, much emphasis is being placed on training. Under the Roundout program, nine of the twelve active Army divisions are manned at less than full strength, with identified units of the Reserve forces designated to augment, or round out, the active forces in the event of an emergency. Through the Capstone program, these designated round out units receive supervision, training assistance, and guidance from the active Army units they would join in an emergency. The roundout units train for this role, and some of their training is conducted with the active Army unit to which they would be assigned. ARNG and USAR personnel are participating in the various Army exercises, including overseas training duty, so they may become familiar with the local environment to which they likely would be assigned.

In sum, the Active Army, the Army National Guard, and the U.S. Army Reserve each play a vital role in the planning for the defense of U.S. interests around the world. The complementary missions of these three components of the Total Force provide assurance that the Army of the United States can successfully conduct such operations as may be assigned by our national authorities.

ORGANIZATION BY BRANCH

Officers of the Army are appointed into a basic or special branch, wear the branch insignia as a part of their uniforms, and are known, for example, as Infantry officers, Engineer officers, Quartermaster officers, and so on. Officers may be temporarily detailed to another branch, such as to the Inspector General or to

General Staff, but unless there is a transfer of branch, each officer will remain assigned to the branch in which appointed throughout his or her career. An introductory description of the branches appears in chapter 29, *Branches of the Army,* and each branch is described in detail in chapters 30 through 33.

ORGANIZATION BY UNITS

There follows a short discussion of Army units, from the smallest to the largest. The system and the terminology are fairly uniform throughout the different arms and services, and once identified, the various terms fit readily into the total pattern.

Tables of Organization and Equipment (TOE), issued by the Department of the Army, establish as to each category of Army unit its title, the number and grades of its officers and enlisted personnel, its organic equipment, and its interior organization. Using the TOE as the base document, units organized under Modified Tables of Organization and Equipment (MTOE) are tailored to the unit's requirements as determined by the major Army command (MACOM). Tables of Distribution and Allowances (TDA) prescribe the organization and equipment for special purpose temporary units. A newly assigned officer should study his or her unit's TOE or TDA as soon as possible.

Units of Separate Arms and Services. The *rifle fire team* is the smallest tactical unit under a noncommissioned officer as leader. It is a team that can be controlled by one person, generally by use of voice.

The *squad* is the smallest and basic military unit. The number of soldiers assigned to a squad varies but may be visualized as from eight to eleven persons.

The *platoon* consists of the platoon leader, an officer in the grade of lieutenant, and two or more squads.

The *company* has been the appropriate command for a captain. It includes its headquarters and two or more platoons, and can function for short periods as a separate command. In the artillery, the term *battery* is used instead of company, and the term *section* corresponds to the squad. In cavalry units, the term *troop* is used instead of company.

Battalion. Traditionally, the battalion has included its commander, his or her staff and headquarters elements, with two, three, or four companies (infantry, armor), batteries (field artillery, air defense artillery), or troops (cavalry). The cavalry unit corresponding to the battalion is designated squadron. In the Army of Excellence (AOE) divisions there are a fixed number of combat battalions (infantry, airborne infantry, mechanized, tank, aviation), the number and type of battalions depending on the type of division and its mission. Also in the division are battalions of artillery, engineers, signal, cavalry, and those in the support command providing maintenance, supply, and medical support.

Divisional Brigades. In the AOE divisions there are four brigade headquarters (infantry, armor, or aviation), each capable of controlling from two to five combat battalions. The necessary combat support and administrative elements are furnished the brigade by the division.

Division. Except for the Armored Cavalry Regiment and separate maneuver brigades, the division is the smallest unit of the combined arms and services. There are currently six types of combat divisions: armored, mechanized, light infantry, motorized, airborne, and air assault. The division is the appropriate command of a major general. Strengths of the divisions range from about 10,000 for the light infantry division to about 16,500 for the larger armor and mechanized divisions. Other divisions fall within these personnel ranges.

Each type of division has command and control, combat, combat support, and combat service support elements. The command and control element includes division headquarters and four brigade headquarters. The combat element includes varying proportions of combat battalions of the different types (armor, infantry, mechanized, air assault, airborne infantry, and aviation) to make up the division (armored, six tank and four mechanized battalions; mechanized, five mechanized and five tank battalions; light infantry, nine light infantry battalions; airborne, nine airborne infantry battalions; air assault, nine air assault infantry battalions; motorized, seven combined arms and two light attack battalions). The mix of units can be further tailored to accomplish a specific task. The armored and mechanized divisions combine fast maneuver with tremendous firepower. The light infantry division is designed for rapid deployment to any contingency. It can be employed against light enemy forces in all terrain and can be used on restrictive terrain where it can take maximum advantage of the terrain against enemy heavy forces. The airborne division is for vertical envelopment by airborne assault, using parachutes and Air Force troop carrier and assault landing aircraft. The air assault division with its helicopters demonstrated in Vietnam its ability to deliver firepower quickly anywhere. Combat support and combat service support elements are included in each division.

The Army last reorganized in the mid-1960s as a result of the ROAD study. In structuring for the Vietnam conflict, with its infantry-airmobile emphasis, the Army had, in fact, missed a modernization cycle. In 1976, the Army began a restructuring study to develop the optimum size, mix and organization of Army divisions for the 1980–1985 timeframe. The effort was designated Division 86—the modernized heavy division of the future. In 1983 the Army leadership determined that the total personnel and equipment required to fill the Division 86 structure greatly exceeded total Army authorizations. Additionally, Division 86 units (divisions) were too large and unwieldy, they were difficult to deploy to contingency areas, and they were geared primarily to a NATO/European type environment, thus precluding their deployment to support contingencies and war plans in other, more likely, low- to mid-intensity conflicts. In late 1983, the Army initiated the Army of Excellence Study (AOE) to pare down the size of the existing divisions to make them more deployable and maneuverable, and to provide a force of light infantry divisions readily deployable and capable of being used in a range of terrain and conflicts. The objective of the Army of Excellence was to develop the most effective organization for the Army's divisions by developing advanced battlefield concepts and harnessing the combat power of the new generation of weapons and systems to enter the force in the mid-1980s to the mid-1990s.

Army Corps. An army corps consists of its headquarters, two or more divisions, and such other organizations as its mission may require. The additional units may consist, for example, of artillery, aviation, engineer units, medical units, and others.

Field Army. If a numbered field army is required, it will be an organization consisting of a TDA headquarters, two or more army corps, and other organizations of all kinds needed for sustained field operations.

Theater Army. The Army component of a U.S. unified command in a theater of operations. An echelon above the corps organization, it provides combat support and combat service support to U.S. Army combat and combat support forces in the theater. It must be tailored for each theater.

Separate Brigades and Groups. It is necessary to discuss separate brigades and groups as a special case. Separate brigades may include separate combat brigades, field artillery, engineers, special forces, and air defense artillery. Combat brigades include the heavy separate armored brigade, the heavy separate infantry brigade (mechanized), and the separate infantry brigades (light), a combination of light/motorized infantry. There also are numbered groups of two or more battalions and in some cases four or more companies or batteries. These are tactical assignments for such units as field artillery, engineers, special forces, and air defense artillery. Such organizations are constituted from units that are not organic to divisions.

Regiments. There are two meanings for the term *regiment*. In the tactical sense, there are several armored cavalry regiments, which consist of three cavalry reconnaissance squadrons. The term is more closely associated, however, with the historical and heraldric meaning.

The Army has established a new Army Regimental System aimed at creating a climate of stability and continuity in line units whose combat arms–qualified members will be affiliated with their regiments throughout their careers. It is expected that training, readiness, family life, and the sense of belonging and commitment will be enhanced by the new system. The new regiments will link like groups of U.S.-based and overseas-based battalions and provide a framework within which soldiers, and eventually units, can rotate. When the new regimental system is fully operational, soldiers affiliated with a regiment will know where they will be stationed in the U.S. and where they will serve overseas. Nonregimental duty will be served, insofar as practicable, near their home base.

There will be a total of sixty-four regiments of combat arms: twenty-six infantry, twenty field artillery, twelve armor and six air defense artillery. The regimental system is used only for manning and assignments. The tactical organization still is by brigades and divisions. Each regiment will have an adjutant to handle assignments and honorary regimental colonels. These are distinguished, senior, retired officers having an association with the regiment who look after regimental traditions. In addition to the combat arms regiments, the various combat support and combat service support branches are being brought under the regimental system.

Soldiers affiliated with a regiment wear distinctive unit insignia. (See chapter 22, *Uniforms of the Army*).

SPECIAL OPERATIONS

The 1st Special Operations Command (Provisional) (SOCOM) was established at Fort Bragg, North Carolina, on 1 October 1982 to take command of all Army special operations forces. These include the John F. Kennedy Special Warfare Center, which controls the 5th and 7th Special Forces Groups, located at Fort Bragg; the 10th Special Forces Group, located at Fort Devens, Massachusetts; the 75th Infantry Regiment (Ranger); the 4th Psychological Operations Group, located at Fort Bragg; and the 96th Civil Affairs Battalion, also at Fort Bragg.

The establishment of SOCOM has enabled the Army to standardize a great deal of the training of all special operations forces, as well as giving those forces an enhanced planning capability and better R&D capability for the small volumes of special equipment used by such forces.

On 16 April 1987, the Department of Defense activated the U.S. Special Operations Command as a unified command reporting to the Joint Chiefs of Staff. Initial staffing of the new command was obtained by dissolving the older, unified, U.S. Readiness Command, whose previous missions were distributed to other commands. The Special Operations Command is headquartered at MacDill Air Force Base in Florida. It controls Rangers and Special Forces personnel from the Army, Air Force special operations forces, and Navy SEALs. The 1st Special Operations

Command of the Army and the John F. Kennedy Special Warfare Center and School are the Army components of the U.S. Special Operations Command.

Special Forces. The mission of Army Special Forces is to train personnel and to form units for the conduct of counterinsurgency operations, psychological operations, and unconventional warfare; and for employment as directed by constitutional authority in cold, limited, or general war. Members of these forces are selected individuals who must be airborne-qualified before beginning the training. With rare exceptions, and then only for officers, all Special Forces personnel are volunteers. The officer volunteer must have at least two years' service remaining at the time of entering Special Forces. Training includes amphibious, swamp, jungle, and arctic environments; training time ranges from twenty-four weeks to as much as fifty-eight weeks, according to the specialty in which trained. Members are authorized to wear the distinctive green beret.

The Army initiated psychological warfare training in 1950 when it established the Psychological Warfare Division, Army General School at Fort Riley, Kansas. In 1952, it was transferred to Fort Bragg, North Carolina, and given the name of the Psychological Warfare Center. At the same time, the 10th Special Forces Group (Airborne) was activated at Fort Bragg. While closely allied in interests, the Center was a training organization, while the 10th Special Forces Group (Airborne) was an operational force of the Army. Today, the Psychological Warfare Center has become the U.S. Army Institute of Military Assistance, while the 10th Special Forces Group (Airborne) has become the John F. Kennedy Special Warfare Center, in recognition of the interest of then President Kennedy in such activities.

The Special Forces performed perilous and highly creditable work in southeast Asia during the conflict in Vietnam. Many members voluntarily served consecutive or repetitive tours to aid the beleaguered natives of that region.

In the summer of 1987, the Army approved plans to establish Special Forces as a separate career branch of the Army. It is a non-accession branch. Company grade officers may transfer to Special Forces only after they have completed the advanced course for their entry branch and have successfully completed the nineteen-week Special Forces qualification course at Fort Bragg. After transfer to Special Forces, officers will follow the career plan for Special Forces officers, including the assignment of a functional area designation during their seventh year of service.

The Army plans for the new branch to have a total of about 1,500 commissioned officers, 200 warrant officers, and 3,200 enlisted personnel, making it one of the Army's smallest branches. Only males may volunteer for transfer to the branch. The new branch will not include Rangers, psychological operations, civil affairs, or aviation special operations officers. See also SPECIAL FORCES in chapter 30, *Combat Arms.*

Rangers. The 75th Infantry Regiment (Ranger) was formally activated at Fort Benning, Georgia, on 1 July 1984, although the first of its three battalions came into being a decade earlier. The 1st Battalion, 75th Infantry (Ranger) is located at Hunter Army Airfield, Georgia; the 2nd Battalion, 75th Infantry (Ranger) is located at Fort Lewis, Washington; and the 3rd Battalion, 75th Infantry (Ranger) is located at Fort Benning, Georgia.

The Ranger name goes back to an irregular force used during the 18th century in the French and Indian War. During World War II, inspired by the British Commandos, the first Army Ranger battalions were formed, and they trained in Northern Ireland during 1942. Except for one battalion used in the Pacific area (Merrill's Marauders), the Rangers saw service only in Europe during that war. During the Korean and Vietnam conflicts, Ranger units were assigned to division and corps headquarters. These were primarily long-range reconnaissance companies and were used extensively for patrolling behind enemy lines.

The new Rangers do not have the long-range reconnaissance mission. Rather, their basic mission is to conduct raids, participate in recovery operations for both equipment and people, and interdiction.

All personnel assigned to Ranger units must be volunteers and must be airborne-qualified. All key leaders, including all officers, must also be Ranger-qualified. Rangers are authorized to wear the distinctive black beret.

ASSOCIATION OF THE UNITED STATES ARMY

Members of the Association of the United States Army believe that a strong Army, well led, of high morale, and provided with an adequate supply of weapons and equipment as good as or better than can be thrown against it, is essential to protect the United States during these times of danger. The association's membership includes officers and soldiers of the Regular and Reserve components of the Army; leaders of government; leaders in industry, science, and education; and interested civilians generally. The essential characteristic of members is belief in our Army, its mission, and its capability of providing the necessary security for our nation and our people. Their convictions are sound. The organization is necessary. It corresponds to the Navy League and the United States Air Force Association.

A monthly magazine, *ARMY,* is essential reading for the active Army officer of Regular or Reserve component. Army officers and others interested in the Army should be members of the Association. Headquarters of the Association is at 2425 Wilson Blvd., Arlington, VA 22201.

29

Branches of the Army

The classification of military personnel according to "branch of service," symbolized by means of distinctive devices of metal and enamel worn on the uniform, represents no recent development in military history or even a tradition that is peculiar to the U.S. Army. The existence of at least two separate species of fighting men—mounted (cavalry) as well as unmounted (infantry)—can reasonably be assumed to trace back to the domestication of the horse. The Old Testament recounts (I Chronicles 18) an ancient battle where "David slew of the Syrians seven thousand men which fought in chariots, and forty thousand footmen." Further refining this rudimentary division of labor, Alexander the Great (356–323 B.C.), whose invincible field armies conquered much of Asia, was obliged to create a massive combat service support corps to maintain supply lines extending from his kingdom in Macedon to northern India. And the famous Roman legions are known to have been organized into light and heavy infantry, cavalry, and siege trains; this third category contained ordnance, quartermaster, and transportation elements, together with Caesar's celebrated corps of engineers, whose durable roads, aqueducts, and fortifications can still be found in parts of Europe.

The branch of service concept persists, in the civilian life as well as in the Army, because it has repeatedly been proved to provide a highly workable management device for any large organization with a variety of missions and a considerable technological capability. Thus every modern corporation is structured along functional lines, with a separate department and specially trained personnel for each major activity, such as production, sales, advertising, research and development, accounting, and so on. The same is true of other large enterprises—governmental agencies, schools and colleges, and professional societies. The Army's branch system resembles those developed for civilian institutions in that it is designed to ensure the most efficient and economical deployment of skilled manpower and, at the same time, to assist the individual in realizing full potential.

In actual practice, however, there are subtle differences between the branches of the Army and those of most civilian endeavors. The most conspicuous of these is the strong tradition that a person commissioned in any arm or service should be an officer first, and only then a specialist. In the past, this unwritten rule was observed quite literally, to the effect that the basic function of every officer (other than those with specified graduate degrees, such as chaplains and medical officers) was to command troops. In an era of ever-increasing reliance upon technology and specialization, this ideal has lost much of its previous relevance. However, the Army's professional development program (see chapter 12) assures that each officer will be branch qualified initially; many officers may also develop expertise and serve alternating assignments in a particular functional area such as R&D or Procurement. Today, however, the "officer-first" tradition is interpreted as meaning that an officer, irrespective of branch or assignment, is above all things a leader, rather than a super-technician; and that in the exercise of professional duties he or she is still required to exhibit the qualities of honor, integrity, and responsibility. The warrant officer, of course, is expected to be a super-technician and normally can expect to remain in and become most proficient in his or her primary MOS.

There are indicators of the importance the Army attaches to professionalism among its officer corps. Perhaps the most important of these is the fact that officers tend to remain within the arm or service in which they were originally commissioned. However, the Officer Personnel Management System (OPMS) provides that officers may now follow a sequential track development that allows, and in some cases may require, branch transfer with subsequent assignments in the new branch or alternating between the new branch and the officer's functional area. The branch of service with which an enlisted soldier is identified varies with the unit of assignment; that is, the enlisted soldier will normally wear Infantry insignia while serving with an infantry brigade, Transportation Corps insignia when assigned to a transportation company, and so on. On the other hand, an officer's branch of service will remain the branch in which the officer was commissioned, or to which the officer transferred, regardless of the particular assignment.

Finally, the sense of professional esprit kindled by association with a particular branch of service is sustained by the relative stability of the branches themselves. With the gradual evolution of the Army's mission and its techniques for achieving that mission, the need for a given branch sometimes disappears; World War II saw the last days of both the historic cavalry and the somewhat youthful Coast Artillery Corps. Similarly, new challenges occasionally produce new branches such as Civil Affairs (USAR) and Air Defense Artillery, both created since World War II, and more recently the Aviation and Special Forces branches. By and large, however, the arms and services have responded to new weapons and new requirements, and not a few of them existing today may be traced back to the very beginnings of the U. S. Army.

The operative principle governing one's initial appointment in a given arm or service is "convenience of the government"; that is, the manpower needs of the Army at a particular time. This immutable fact is not always understood by newly commissioned officers, who feel they could serve more effectively in a branch other than that to which they have been appointed. More than one ROTC student majoring in business administration, for example, has been disappointed to be commissioned a second lieutenant of Infantry after having expressed a preference for the Finance Corps, the Quartermaster Corps, or the Adjutant General's Corps. In such a situation, the likelihood is that, perhaps because of casualties or a shortage of replacements, Infantry units throughout the Army are understrength, while the technical services have achieved or surpassed their authorized manning levels; under these circumstances, the infantry assignment is inevitable. However, the sequential track career pattern now authorized enables the officer to transfer to the branch of choice after initial assignments in the Infantry or other combat arm.

One of the fringe benefits of permanent affiliation with a particular branch of the service is the feeling of camaraderie that develops among its members, particularly seasoned officers with a multitude of assignments behind them. This family spirit, the almost inevitable result of common interests and shared experiences, is pleasant in itself, and for younger officers has the additional advantage of providing a dependable, first hand source of professional counsel and supervision. On a more formal, but scarcely less valuable, basis, the junior officer has always at his or her disposal the services of the career branch chief, who maintains individual files and a guidance facility in the Officer Personnel Management Directorate of the Total Army Personnel Agency (TAPA). Officers are authorized and encouraged to communicate directly with this service and to make arrangements, from time to time, for personal visits to the branch chief for such purposes as examining evaluation reports, reviewing their professional progress, and obtaining timely and informed advice on future schooling, assignments, and the like. Few private corporations offer so helpful and comprehensive a system of career management for their personnel, but much of the responsibility for exploiting this unique service is left to the initiative of the individual officer. (See chapter 12.)

At this time, there is a total of 24 branches of the Army authorized for active service. They are:

Infantry	Finance Corps
Air Defense Artillery	Quartermaster
Field Artillery	Ordnance
Armor	Transportation
Aviation	Chaplain Corps
Special Forces	Judge Advocate General's Corps
Corps of Engineers	Medical Corps
Signal Corps	Dental Corps
Military Police Corps	Veterinary Corps
Chemical Corps	Medical Service Corps
Military Intelligence	Army Nurse Corps
Adjutant General's Corps	Army Medical Specialist Corps

The Army has a number of ways of classifying these branches (e.g., arms and services, basic and special), but perhaps the most convenient and readily understood categories would be combat, combat support, and combat service support. Combat arms are those directly involved in the conduct of actual fighting; these are Infantry, Air Defense Artillery, Field Artillery, Armor, Aviation, Special Forces and Corps of Engineers. Combat support arms are those that provide operational assistance to the combat arms, including engagement in combat when necessary, but who have additional responsibilities in providing logistical and administrative support to the Army as a whole; these include the Signal Corps, Military Police Corps, Chemical Corps, and Military Intelligence. Finally, the combat service support branches are those whose chief mission is to provide logistical and administrative support and whose personnel are not usually directly engaged in combat operations; these are the remaining thirteen branches. In addition, there are two branches that exist only in the Reserve components: the Staff Specialist (Corps) and Civil Affairs. In the event of mobilization of the USAR, the former would be absorbed by existing branches, while the latter would probably retain branch integrity. Finally, there exist a small number of officers who wear distinctive insignia, such as Inspector General or General Staff insignia, while temporarily detailed to duties apart from the established branches.

Each of the active duty branches of the Army is explained in the next four chapters, with a brief history of each, a general discussion of its purpose and functions, and an outline of the various kinds of duty assignments one might expect to receive if assigned to that branch. All the duties that could conceivably be assigned to an officer of a given branch cannot, of course, be described in detail. Certain types of assignments are appropriate to all branches and, moreover, junior officers are usually called upon to perform duties unrelated to branch when "additional duty" assignments are made. (See Appendix.) The typical jobs referenced within each branch description have been chosen to represent types of assignments that are peculiar to that branch only or would be more likely assigned to officers of that branch than any other. Chapter 12, *Professional Development,* provides information on usual educational assignments. Chapter 10, *Army Posts and Stations,* specifically indicates the major activities of each installation, and for most branches will serve as a guide to the places personnel of a particular branch might be assigned. Because of the extensive treatment of both subjects in these chapters, the branch material following does not attempt to cover them in detail. Rather, it has been written specifically to present the young junior officer with an objective image of the Army's branch organization, and especially to aid the ROTC and USMA cadet in finding and requesting that branch assignment that will most fully utilize his or her talents and training in a way that will best serve both the individual's and the Army's needs.

BRANCH COLORS AND INSIGNIA

Contrary to beliefs held by many officers through the years, branch insignia and colors are basically in existence only for the purpose of identification. Selection of insignia in most cases was completely arbitrary although the evolution of logical symbolism can be found in every design. The choice and assignment of a branch color or colors is purely for providing immediate recognition when worn as a significant part of the uniform. According to the Institute of Heraldry, U.S. Army, there is no basis for widespread assumption that a particular branch color has a specific symbolism (i.e., blue was not chosen to indicate courage; red, bravery; and so on). That fact, however, should not make the designation and use of branch colors any less influential in the development of esprit de corps, nor discourage inclusion and reference to the branch color in traditional ceremonies and morale-building activities.

Although illustrative and descriptive detail on branch insignia appears in Chapter 22, each of the branch descriptions includes a short historical narrative of the insignia to help set the image of that branch.

30
Combat Arms

AIR DEFENSE ARTILLERY

Air Defense Artillery (ADA), a combat arms branch of the Army, performs multiple missions for the combined arms commander by providing air defense coverage on the air-land battlefield. ADA ensures our forces' freedom of maneuver, protects the command and control centers that manage the battle, protects logistical centers, and depletes enemy resources by destroying enemy aircraft. Branch officers lead and train soldiers and employ air defense weapons in support of combat operations against enemy aircraft and missile attacks in accordance with AirLand Battle doctrine.

ADA encompasses positions dealing with the employment of air defense gun and missile units, directing technical operations and targeting techniques used by the various weapon systems, and evaluating tactical situations and system capabilities to direct the engagement of hostile aircraft and missiles according to proper doctrine. Besides possessing required leadership skills, an ADA officer must have extensive tactical and technical expertise to handle the highly specialized air defense weapon systems in a combined arms environment.

Today, ADA is in the midst of an ambitious modernization program. The branch is in the process of fielding an entirely new family of air defense weapons known as the Forward Area Air Defense System (FAADS). This is a sophisticated ADA system with five major components designed to operate autonomously or collectively in the forward area of the battlefield. Pedestal Mounted Stingers will be deployed in the brigade rear and in the division and corps areas. A new non-line-of-sight (NLOS) system will be employed near the forward line of troops where it can be masked from enemy view, yet still defeat enemy helicopters that are themselves behind masking terrain. The fiber-optic guided missile (FOG-M) is the leading candidate for this system. A line-of-sight forward element (LOS-F) will be used in the close combat zone of both heavy and light divisions and will probably be a gun-missile hybrid. Other combined arms units form another component of FAADS, including contributions from guns on tanks, Bradley Fighting Vehicles, and even air-to-air missiles on helicopters. Finally, the whole system is tied together with a new command, control, and intelligence network (C^2I). Each of the FAADS components is at a different stage of development, with final fielding of all elements expected to continue into the early 1990s.

Guided missiles, in the sense that they can be controlled and guided to specific targets, are a recent phenomenon in warfare, although military use of self-propelled projectiles dates back at least to the thirteenth century in China. British use of rockets during the War of 1812 is immortalized in our own National Anthem. Experimentation with rockets by U.S. forces is known to have occurred in 1846–1848 during the war with Mexico and then was abandoned for lack of efficiency compared to the rifled cannon in use at the time.

Serious military thought about missiles as weapons lay dormant until the German ''buzz'' bomb attacks on Britain caused a new look at this possibility. By the end of World War II the United States had developed a missile comparable to the German V–1, but the missile development program became, for a time, a victim of postwar reductions in priorities. The idea for the first U.S. air defense artillery missile, the Nike Ajax, was conceived in the fall of 1944 at Fort Bliss, Texas. This evolved further into the sophisticated and successful Nike Hercules and Hawk missile systems. The Nike Hercules has recently been replaced by the impressive Patriot system. With its multicapable, phased-array radar and long-range, high-altitude missile, the Patriot is the most formidable air defense system in the world today.

Officers assigned to Air Defense Artillery are members of one of the oldest and most demanding combat arms of the Army. Indeed, the ability to lead troops having control of such highly technical equipment requires a unique leadership ability. The U.S. Army Air Defense Artillery School at Fort Bliss, Texas, which plays an important role in developing this leadership, traces its lineage directly to the Coast Artillery School, which was organized at Fort Monroe, Virginia, in April 1824. This school, the oldest service school in the Army, laid the foundation for the present system of military education in the Army. On 18 May 1858, the name was changed to the Artillery School, which was eventually split into the Field Artillery and the Coast Artillery Schools on 1 August 1907. The Coast Artillery School had responsibility for antiaircraft artillery, which was developed during and after World War I. By 1940, antiaircraft artillery subjects predominated the courses at the Coast Artillery School, and in March 1942, the antiaircraft responsibility was transferred to the newly established Antiaircraft Artillery School at Camp Davis, North Carolina. In October 1944, the school was moved to Fort Bliss, Texas, its

Design of the Air Defense Artillery insignia was first approved in 1957 for the then single Artillery branch. The crossed field guns indicate branch ties to the Field Artillery, the superimposed missile symbolizing modern developments. This insignia became the identification of ADA when it was authorized as a separate branch in 1968.

present home. On 1 July 1957, after several name changes, the school was officially designated the U.S. Army Air Defense School. In 1983 the school was redesignated the U.S. Army Air Defense Artillery School.

Officers commissioned in ADA start their career with attendance at the ADA Officer Basic Course at the Air Defense Artillery School. During this ten-week course, they are prepared for their first duty assignment, and become familiar with the family of air defense weapons and their tactical employment. Based on assignment, graduates of the course immediately attend a particular weapon system course which follows the ten-week basic course.

After this basic schooling, new officers are normally assigned as platoon leaders in a Hawk, Patriot, or Chaparral/Vulcan battery, or as Redeye/Stinger section/platoon leaders. The officers' responsibilities will include the operational training and tactical employment of their platoon, maintenance of equipment, and the welfare and morale of their soldiers.

Officers assigned to platoons in Hawk or Patriot units will have the responsibility of initiating and controlling the engagement sequence, which includes launching missiles to destroy hostile aircraft. In Chaparral/Vulcan units, the platoons will often operate independently from parent batteries to provide area air defense support for infantry and armor elements. As Redeye/Stinger section leaders, their teams will be deployed to protect elements of the maneuver battalions and supporting field artillery.

Through this training and experience, the ADA officer normally qualifies for positions of increasing responsibility as an Air Defense Artillery Unit Commander, Command and Control Officer, or Staff Officer in the various Air Defense organizations deployed around the world. These positions provide for both new challenges and professional development opportunities in a branch with a vital mission for preserving peace.

Troop unit duty might be with any one of the currently authorized TOE organizations: Hawk, Chaparral/Vulcan, Patriot, or Redeye/Stinger, deployed overseas and throughout CONUS.

The next phase of formal training occurs between the third and fifth year of commissioned service and is known as the ADA Officer Advanced Course, a twenty-week training course conducted at the Air Defense Artillery School. The advanced course prepares officers to command at the battery level and to serve as battalion and brigade-level staff officers. Also included in the advanced course is instruction in the tactical employment of ADA batteries and other elements of the combined arms team.

A quick-reacting air defense, provided by a family of complementary weapon systems, is essential for success on the modern air-land battlefield. This requirement is justified by the ever-increasing destructive power of today's modern aircraft and the nuclear weapons threat. ADA provides numerous deterrent weapons in support of land warfare operations and in the defense of CONUS. Research into ballistic missile defense technology for the defense of CONUS is an additional ADA responsibility. The burden of these numerous, vital, and diverse responsibilities rests with the dedicated and capable officers of the Air Defense Artillery.

ADA continues to be one of the major combat arms of the Army, and its proper utilization could make the difference on the modern air-land battlefield. Ever prepared and vigilant, the branch has earned its motto of "First to Fire" in warfare around the world. As technology continues to advance, ADA will require dedicated officers who possess the leadership, tactical, and technical skills that will enable them to meet successfully the many diverse challenges within the branch and the Army in the future.

Approved in 1950, the current Armor insignia blends the past and present. Its base is formed by the traditional crossed sabers adopted for the Cavalry in 1851, on which a front view of the M26 tank is superimposed. It symbolizes Armor's heritage in the first "mounted" troops and today's role as a mechanized force.

ARMOR

The responsibility for the development and conduct of mobile warfare, originally the province of the horse cavalry, rests with the U.S. Army's Armor Branch. Although modern technology has produced weaponry and transportation systems that are far more efficient than the horse, the incomparable spirit of the old cavalry and the impetuous character of its leaders are instantly recognizable in its modern counterpart. The impulse to devastating attack that has governed the tactics of mounted warfare from antiquity continues to dominate the doctrines and combat operations of Armor Branch. Its three subcomponents of Armored Cavalry, Air Cavalry, and Armor provide the Army with its most powerful reconnaissance and striking forces, all of which are trained to maneuver and fight under the most stringent of conditions.

The concept of combative systems augmented by armor protection and increased mobility is not a new one. Military leaders of man's most ancient cultures constantly sought means through which to increase the individual's destructive force on the battlefield while rendering him impervious to harm.

The introduction of the horse to combat brought an entirely new dimension to warfare, as conflicts could now be fought swiftly—and won even by numerically inferior forces who used their agile mounts to maximum advantage. Imperial Egypt and Assyria—as well as Asia's Huns and Mongols—all achieved their greatest conquests through the concentrated application of cavalry, and all exploited its psychological impact to the fullest.

The distinguished history of the U.S. Cavalry dates from the Revolutionary War. One outstanding cavalry unit of that war was the Light Horse of the City of Philadelphia, a troop organized in 1774 and still active today in the Pennsylvania Army National Guard. It served as General Washington's personal escort through the bitter days of Trenton and Princeton, displaying, in Washington's words, "a Spirit of Bravery which will ever do Honor to them and will ever be gratefully remembered by me." Although the Army maintained no Regular cavalry units for the better part of the next fifty years, volunteer units existed in all of the states. Mounted Kentucky militia played a crucial role in General Anthony Wayne's victory at Fallen Timbers in 1794, driving the Indian warriors from their covered positions to the open prairie.

Union cavalry was employed largely as an escort and security element in the early part of the Civil War, and hence was of no strategic and only limited tactical value. However, Union cavalry commanders, impressed by the accomplishments of massed Confederate cavalry under Generals Turner, Ashby, Stuart, and Forrest, were employing their forces much more efficiently by the end of the war. Grant's use of Grierson's cavalry during the Vicksburg campaign was instrumental to Union success in the West.

From 1868 until the turn of the century, those cavalry units retained on an active status were sent to the western frontier to meet the growing threat of the Plains Indians. Conventional infantry proved to be ineffective against the mounted raiding parties of the Sioux and the Comanches, and ten cavalry regiments dispersed among fifty-five posts throughout the West finally brought peace to the new territories. In every major ground action until World War I—from Col. Theodore Roosevelt's Rough Riders in Cuba (who, however, fought on foot during the entire war) to Gen. Adna Chaffee's Sixth Cavalry, the first force to take the Forbidden City during China's Boxer Rebellion—the U.S. Cavalry led the way. General Pershing's pursuit of the Mexican bandit, Pancho Villa, in 1916 was the last major action of the horse cavalry. From that point on, cavalry was to undergo an all-too-gradual mechanization that was to lead to its present incorporation into Armor Branch's combined arms team.

World War I heralded the birth of the team's second component, the tank. First developed by the British Royal Navy, and disguised for intelligence purposes as "tanks for water in Russia" or "tanks for water in Mesopotamia," tanks saw their first engagement in September of 1916, when they participated in the Battle of the Somme. The American Tank Corps, initially a part of the Infantry Branch, fought its first battle in 1918, using French tanks due to the nonavailability of American-built machines. During the Meuse-Argonne attack General Pershing offered "anything in the A.E.F." for 500 additional tanks, but they were simply not available. By the end of the war, tanks had been employed by the British, French, Germans, and Americans in over ninety engagements.

Although the value of tanks in modern warfare had proved substantial, few major military leaders were prepared to recognize this. The U.S. Army—together with the principal European armies—believed that tanks should be relegated to an infantry-support role. Consequently, through the National Defense Act of 1920, the Tank Corps was assigned to the Chief of Infantry. The first Tank School was organized at Fort Meade, Maryland, but the program was subsequently moved to Fort Benning, Georgia, and renamed the Tank Section of the Infantry School. During this same period the Chief of Cavalry was authorized to develop mechanized weapons, and Fort Knox, Kentucky, was designated as the new home of the mechanized cavalry.

The spectacular successes of German armor in the early days of World War II helped speed the creation of a United States armor-based military branch. A War Department order of 10 July 1940 created the Armored Force, and the U.S. Army Armor School was instituted a few days later. Although there had been little involvement in tank-to-tank fighting in the early stages of the war, the North African campaign soon changed the concept of armored warfare. In those tremendous expanses of open terrain, tanks—often as many as 500 on each side—clashed in massive engagements. In Europe, General George S. Patton, Jr. commanded the armored elements of his Third Army so aggressively that they sometimes advanced more than 100 miles in one day, outdistancing their own lines of supply. Supplementing the sixteen American Armored divisions deployed to Europe were several Armored Cavalry units employed in the classic reconnaissance-security role.

When the Korean conflict erupted in June of 1950, North Korean-manned Soviet T-34 tanks accompanied the Communists in their southward drive. The U.S. Army, which had not originally considered the terrain in that part of the world "tankable," fought without them until mid-July, when the first American tanks reached the peninsula. By August there were over 500 tanks in action within the Pusan Perimeter, outnumbering the enemy's by over five to one. For the remainder of the war, tank units of battalion size and smaller participated in most combat actions.

After the Korean truce the Army launched a serious investigation relating to the possibilities of the rotary wing aircraft for use in combat operations. The first Sky Cavalry unit, equipped with unarmed helicopters for reconnaissance purposes only, underwent testing during exercise Sagebrush in 1955. Shortly after the Sagebrush exercise the Continental Army Command directed the Army Aviation School to establish a project entitled Armed Helicopter Mobile Task Force. In 1958 the Armor School was first charged with the responsibility of preparing the doctrine for tactical employment of Air Cavalry. By 1962 three Air Cavalry troops had been organized, one at Fort Knox, Kentucky, one at Fort Carson, Colorado, and another at Fort Hood, Texas. Also in 1962 the Defense Department directed General Hamilton Howze to establish an Air Mobility Requirements Review Board. The Howze Board established the requirement for organizing the Air Assault Division and the Air Cavalry Squadron.

In 1965 the First Cavalry Division (Airmobile) was deployed to South Vietnam. Its Air Cavalry squadron proved so successful that additional Air Cavalry units were organized and deployed to Vietnam. The earliest helicopter gunships were the UH-1 Hueys—originally designed as troop carriers. A later arrival was the AH-1G HueyCobra—the first aircraft in the Army inventory designed specifically as a weapons platform. Although the terrain in South Vietnam initially was considered unsuitable for armored vehicles, as had been the case earlier in Korea, the Air Cavalry soon was complemented on the ground by the employment, between 1965 and 1973, of three medium tank battalions and seventeen Armored Cavalry squadrons and separate troops. These units utilized the M48A2 and M48A3 tanks, the M551 General Sheridan Armored Reconnaissance/Airborne Assault Vehicle, and the versatile M113 Armored Personnel Carrier. These three dimensions of Armor, working in conjunction with both mechanized and dismounted Infantry forces, achieved substantial combat success in the counterinsurgency environment of the Republic of Vietnam. Near the end of U.S. troop participation in Vietnam, armored units, both ground and air, comprised over 54 percent of the total combat maneuver forces and were the last units to redeploy to the United States. Air Cavalry, particularly when teamed with ground units of Armor and Armored Cavalry, proved its worth as one of the Army's most versatile combat weapons systems.

Contemporary Armor and Cavalry tactics incorporate cohesive and aggressive emphasis upon mobility, firepower, and shock action to overcome an enemy force. The combined arms team concept includes tanks, armored and air cavalry, mechanized infantry/artillery/engineers, and Army aviation, all supported by a flexible and swift communications network and a highly mobile and responsive combat service support system. While the tank continues to be the principal armor-defeating weapon in the combined arms team, it is primarily intended for general application against the entire enemy force. Armor is continually evolving to meet worldwide challenges and potential threats. With the inception of the Aviation Branch in 1983, the Armor Branch transferred proponency of scout and attack helicopters to the Aviation Center.

Armor officers have educational patterns and career programs similar to those found in other branches. The Armor School at Fort Knox offers the Armor Officer Basic and Advanced Courses, as well as specialized instructional programs for noncommissioned officers and senior-grade commissioned officers. Notable among the special courses for officers is the Junior Officers' Maintenance Course. In the eight weeks of the Junior Officers' Maintenance Course, students receive meticulous instruction on maintenance management, supervision and inspection of vehicular maintenance and repair procedures, and the complex material requirements of Armor/Calvalry field operations.

Upon completion of the Advanced Course, Armor officers will usually gain experience as company/troop commanders. Then they could expect assignments in battalions, brigades, or divisions as staff officers. Armor officers are also in demand as planners, directors, and special staff officers at major Army headquarters, on joint staffs, at the Department of the Army, and in research and development projects related to combined arms concepts.

Armor is rich in tradition and exciting in potential. Officers who apply and are selected for assignment to Armor Branch are assured of an unusually dynamic and rewarding career.

AVIATION

The Aviation Branch,* one of the newest of the combat arms branches of the Army, has origins traced to the acceptance of "U.S. Army Aeroplane Number One" from the Wright brothers on 30 July 1909. Subsequent Army Aviation organizations included the Signal Corps Aviation Section, Air Service, and Army Air Corps. However, the Aviation Branch came into being as a combat arm of the Army on 12 April 1983. Its primary mission is to find, fix, and destroy any enemy through fire and maneuver, and to provide combat support and combat service support in coordinated operations as an integrated member of the Combined Arms Team. The principal aviation organization for the future is the aviation brigade (AB). In addition to the aviation units at corps and higher echelons, almost every Army division will have an aviation brigade as one of its maneuver brigades. Essentially all of the aviation resources of the divisions will be located in these highly mobile and flexible maneuver brigades, which are tailored to fight as members of the combined arms team. Making optimal use of new aviation systems, these brigades will provide tactical flexibility to division commanders. Combat aviation is well suited to conduct attack, air assault, reconnaissance, intelligence, and logistical operations. The AB can also assume control of ground assets if missions so require.

On 12 April 1983, the Secretary of the Army approved the establishment of the Army Aviation Branch. Implementation of the new branch began on 6 June 1983, the forty-first anniversary of organic Army aviation.

Army Aviation, as distinguished from the Army Air Corps, had its beginning during World War II. On 6 June 1942, the War Department approved the establishment of organic Army aviation as an adjunct to the Field Artillery. The Department of Air Training was established at Fort Sill, Oklahoma, and the first class of aviators began training at the new school on 1 August 1942. The mainstays of organic Army aviation during World War II were the L-4B Piper Cub, the L-2 Taylorcraft, the L-3 Aeronca, and the Stinson L-5.

The first exposure of Army aviators to combat in World War II was during the

Approved in 1983, the Aviation insignia symbolizes Army Aviation from the beginning. It consists of a silver propeller superimposed on gold wings.

*The information regarding the Aviation Branch is based primarily on material originally prepared by Dr. Herbert P. LePore, Command Historian at the U.S. Army Aviation Center, Fort Rucker.

North African campaign. On 9 November 1942, three L-4 spotter aircraft took off from the deck of the aircraft carrier USS *Ranger* off the coast of North Africa. Ironically, these small aircraft had to evade the antiaircraft fire of their own ships and later, over land, the fire from American units ashore. It was an inauspicious beginning.

The spotter planes were used in all theaters of operation during World War II, including Europe, the Pacific, India, and China. These little aircraft, sometimes called Grasshoppers and Puddle Jumpers, did yeoman service in all theaters. Their fire direction missions for the field artillery, and sometimes for naval gunfire, wreaked havoc on thousands of enemy soldiers, disrupted communications and supply lines, and in general made life miserable for the enemy. In addition, they served as liaison aircraft, flew medical evacuation missions, made supply drops to beleaguered units, and flew staff personnel and commanders throughout the war zones.

After World War II, the National Security Act of 1947 separated what had been the Army Air Corps from the Army and established it as the U.S. Air Force, a coequal service with the Army and the Navy. What had been the organic Army aviation remained with the Army. Specific tactical missions were delineated for the new U.S. Air Force and for the remaining aviation resources organic to the Army. As a result of this act and developments in equipment, Army aviation underwent significant reorganization and transition during the postwar period. One of the most significant events to occur during this period was in 1945, when Captain Robert J. Ely became the first Army aviator to pilot a helicopter, a Sikorsky R-4. In 1947 the Army bought the Bell Model 47 helicopter, designating it the H-13. As part of its new mission, the Air Force began providing primary helicopter training to Army pilots at San Marcos, Texas. The first class for Army pilots began on 1 September 1947.

With the beginning of the Korean War on 25 June 1950, the mission of Army aviation took a new direction. Several new airplanes were procured for service in Korea, the most versatile of which proved to be the Cessna L-19 Bird Dog. Like its renowned predecessor, the L-4, the L-19 provided numerous support missions for American and United Nations forces in Korea, such as reconnaissance, supply drops, transportation, and medical evacuation.

The Korean War was the first war in which the helicopter was utilized on a regular basis and in which it played an important role, particularly in the area of medical evacuation. On 3 August 1950, Army and Air Force medical and aviation personnel tested the use of helicopter evacuation in a school yard in Taegu, Korea. The Army was so impressed with the results it requested that it be allowed to undertake medical evacuation of wounded personnel from the battle area. Allowed to do so, the Army assembled its H-13s and flew its first medical evacuation mission on 3 January 1951. Between then and the cessation of fighting on 27 July 1953, Army helicopter pilots evacuated 21,212 wounded personnel. By the end of the war, the Army also had put two transportation helicopter companies into the field in Korea, the 6th and the 13th, each with twenty-one H-19 Sikorsky 12-place helicopters. These H-19s were used to transport soldiers and supplies and were involved in medical evacuation and prisoner repatriation. The Korean War proved the worth of the helicopter. An ever-expanding role for the helicopter in military operations would follow.

The Army Aviation School relocated from Fort Sill, Oklahoma, to Camp Rucker, Alabama, in September 1954. Camp Rucker had served as a training post for four Army divisions during World War II and was redesignated Fort Rucker on 13

October 1955. The Aviation School was at Fort Rucker less than two years when it assumed responsibility for all Army aviation training in April 1956.

From the late 1950s on, the Army greatly expanded its aircraft inventory. In the fixed wing area, the Army obtained the CV-2 Caribou, the OV-1 Mohawk, the U-21 Ute, and the C-12 Huron. In the rotary wing aircraft category, the Army procured the UH-1 Iroquois (Huey), which later became the most famous helicopter used in Vietnam. The Army also obtained the CH-47 Chinook transport helicopter of Vietnam fame, and the world's first attack helicopter, the AH-1 Cobra.

In 1962, the Secretary of Defense directed that an in-depth study be made of the tactical mobility of the Army ground forces, particularly with regard to the potential for air mobility. Gen. Hamilton H. Howze, who earlier had been the first Director of Army Aviation, was tasked to establish a board at Fort Bragg, North Carolina, to study airmobility capabilities for the Army. The Howze Board, as it became known, conducted numerous tests and studies. The Board concluded that Army aircraft could provide the airmobile assets necessary to enhance the combat effectiveness of ground forces. Recommendations of the Howze Board resulted in the forming of the 11th Air Assault Division at Fort Benning, Georgia, to undergo tests; on 1 July 1965, it became the 1st Cavalry Division (Airmobile).

President Lyndon B. Johnson ordered the deployment of the first of several divisions with their organic aviation assets to South Vietnam in August of 1965. The division was the 1st Cavalry Division (Airmobile). By late 1965 and early 1966, the 1st Cavalry Division was engaged in bitter fighting in areas such as the Ia Drang Valley and throughout the II Corps Tactical Zone. A second airmobile division, the 101st Airborne Division, was fully deployed to South Vietnam in 1967 to fight alongside the six other American divisions and several brigades already in country. Noteworthy is the establishment of the Army's 1st Aviation Brigade, which was activated in Vietnam on 25 May 1966. It used assets of a provisional aviation unit that had been organized in March of that year. The Aviation Brigade eventually became one of the largest commands in Vietnam, having over 4,000 aircraft under its control at the peak of the fighting. Along with division organic aviation assets, the Brigade conducted missions as varied as tactical combat assaults, direct fire support, aerial reconnaissance and surveillance, medical evacuation, troop lifts, and evacuation and relocation of Vietnamese civilians in support of the Rural Development Program. The brigade left Vietnam in March of 1973 and was sent to Fort Rucker as a training component.

"Uncommon valor was a common virtue" for Army aviation personnel in Vietnam. Seven Army aviators received the Congressional Medal of Honor, two of them posthumously, for their acts of heroism. Every day, the commissioned and warrant officer pilots and the enlisted crewmen flew countless missions in all kinds of weather and under all types of tactical situations. Many times, Army aviators flew into areas from which they received withering ground fire, yet they still fulfilled their missions, or attempted to do so. Army helicopter pilots took great pride in their flying skills, their aircraft and flight crews, and above all in their sense of fealty to the ground forces whom they supported.

In the 1970s and 1980s, Army aviation underwent further changes in doctrine, weaponry, and mission. The Army aviation community used the 1970s as a period to develop new tactics, such as nap-of-the-earth and adverse weather flying. Doctrine developed during the 1970s emphasized the use of helicopters in a European combat scenario, and included high density combat and deep penetration capabilities. At Fort Rucker during this period, combat development became the byword of Army aviation. Infantry and aviation were to be integrated into viable, fast-acting brigades, capable of being sent anywhere to fight. Today, as state-of-the-art aircraft, advanced technology, and highly qualified personnel come on board, Aviation Branch offers one of the most challenging and exciting careers in the Army.

Newly commissioned aviation officers first attend the Aviation Officer Basic Course at Fort Rucker, Alabama. This course is forty-five weeks long and is conducted in three phases. The first phase of nine weeks emphasizes physical training, field training, and combined arms operations. The second phase of thirty-four weeks is the Initial Entry Rotary Wing Course. The final phase is two weeks in length and prepares the new lieutenant for an operational unit assignment. Assignments are governed by Army requirement, and graduates of the Basic Course may attend additional courses in specialty aircraft.

After completing the Aviation Officer Basic Course, commissioned officers are normally assigned as section leader/platoon leader in one of the variety of different type units. Some of the aircraft found in these units are the AH-1, UH-60, UH-1, OH-58, CH-47, and a variety of fixed-wing aircraft. Assignments also will be available in the near future in new advanced helicopers such as the Apache (AH-64) and the AHIP (OH-58D).

Between the third and eighth years of service, Aviation commissioned officers attend the Aviation Officer Advanced Course. This twenty-week course prepares Aviation captains for command and other leadership positions, and provides a sound training background in combined arms tactics. Following graduation, the Aviation officer will continue to build experience through assignments to staff positions at different levels and command at company/troop level.

All Aviation officers receive continuing aviation education. As they rotate between assignments, their aviation skills are upgraded to whatever system the new assignment will require. For example, it is currently required that Aviation commanders at brigade and lower levels be instructor-pilot qualified in the aircraft most common to their command. This usually requires a temporary assignment to Fort Rucker for qualification courses prior to assuming command.

Because of the high-tech nature of aviation, there are numerous opportunities for Aviation officers to pursue graduate study at leading universities. Along with management, logistics, and research and development disciplines, highly technical graduate work in engineering sciences, aeronautical testing, and aviation safety are strongly encouraged.

CORPS OF ENGINEERS

This branch, one of the most widely diversified in responsibility, has a history of developments and activities that have benefited the nation as a whole. Engineer officers such as Lewis and Clark have figured prominently in the history of the expansion and development of the nation from the Atlantic states to the Pacific Ocean and beyond. The Corps activities encompass, today, both military engineering and civil works, and all related planning, organization, training, operation, supply, and maintenance.

As an integral part of the U.S. Army, the Corps of Engineers traces its beginning to 16 June 1775, when the Continental Congress provided for a Chief Engineer with two assistants "at The Grand Army." On 3 July 1775, General Washington appointed Richard Gridley to this post, and one of his first efforts was to lay out the defenses of Breed's Hill. He later directed the fortifications that forced the British to evacuate Boston in March, 1776. Further development came in 1778, when the Congress authorized three companies of sappers (British slang for construction workers in an engineering unit) and miners (engineering troops). These first three companies of engineers built the siege works and fortifications that brought a final

The triple-turreted castle identifying members of the Corps of Engineers was adopted in 1840 and symbolizes two major functions: construction and fortifications.

victory for the colonies at Yorktown. In 1779, Congress formally established the first Commandant of the Corps of Engineers. In 1783, the Corps was dissolved along with most of the Army but reestablished in 1802, when Congress provided for the present Corps and "constituted" it a military academy at West Point, New York. Thus, in the beginning and for nearly sixty-four years, the U.S. Military Academy was almost exclusively an engineering school.

Combat engineers—engineer units that accompany the forward elements of the Army in the field to assist the advance of combat arms and, when necessary, fight as infantrymen—became a reality in 1846 with service during the Mexican War. Some of the combat engineers in that conflict who were later to distinguish themselves were (then) Captain Robert E. Lee and Lieutenants George B. McClellan and P.G.T. Beauregard. Military engineering became more complex during the Civil War, with the successful building of the first pontoon bridge being only one of an extensive list of engineering achievements.

The first World War was a conflict full of accomplishments for the Corps of Engineers. The Corps acquired and developed many of the military functions that it has today: construction of ports, docks, roads, bridges, transportation facilities, camps, hospitals, and depots; and responsibility for mapmaking, camouflage, mine warfare, obstacle emplacement and reduction, and terrain analysis.

Engineer battalions became organic to all types of divisions by the time World War II was on the horizon, and in 1941 the construction, maintenance, and repair of all Army facilities, as well as acquisition and disposal of all real estate were added to the responsibilities assigned to the Corps. Among the many notable accomplishments during the war were the Alcan Highway, Burma Road, and the Manhattan Project—the development of the atomic bomb. Some have said that the Pacific Island operations in general were an engineer's war.

In the United States, the Corps of Engineers has undertaken all navigational and harbor improvements since the first Rivers and Harbors Bill, passed by Congress in 1824. Many public structures, such as the Washington Monument, the Library of Congress, the Pentagon, and the St. Lawrence Seaway project have been built by the Corps. One foreign achievement known to all was the construction of the Panama Canal. In the more recent past, the construction support of our highly successful space program, such as NASA Headquarters in Houston and the J. F. Kennedy Space Center launching facilities at Cape Canaveral, was accomplished by the Corps. Support has not been limited to this planet. Prior to the consolidation of the mapping, charting, and geodesy functions of all the services in a single DOD agency—the Defense Mapping Agency—in 1972, the U.S. Army Topographic Command, which had responsibility for the Corps' geodesy and mapping mission, had begun mapping the moon. This imaginative and aggressive thinking is also being applied on earth as the Corps works hand-in-glove with the Environmental Protection Agency to prevent further pollution of our streams and waterways and to restore them to their former purity and beauty. The increased amount of leisure time now available to all strata of American society has only heightened the importance of the Corps' role in providing for recreational facilities, major factors in the decision to construct inland lakes and waterways.

Engineer officers are responsible for training and leading troops in combat, mapmaking, and construction operations essential to the Army in the field. They direct the operation and maintenance of Army facilities worldwide. They also develop and manage the Army's extensive Military Construction and Civil Works Programs.

Engineers participate in combat operations as members of the combined arms team. They assault fortifications as well as construct them; they breach mine fields as well as emplace them; they reduce obstacles as well as create them; they provide topographic and terrain analysis support; and they participate in assault river crossings and amphibious operations in addition to other combat engineering tasks.

Officers serve as engineer staff officers at all levels, coordinating, planning, and providing staff supervision of engineer operations, to include support of the Air Force.

The home of the Corps of Engineers and the U.S. Army Engineer School is Fort Belvoir, Virginia. It serves as the center of Army Engineer activities, including combat and training developments, training and doctrine, and proponency and evaluation of engineer equipment. Most engineer officers begin their careers there and return periodically to become qualified to handle one or more of the many assignments open to engineer officers. (In the summer of 1989, the Engineer School will relocate to Fort Leonard Wood, Missouri, the location where most enlisted engineer training is now conducted.) Such assignments for which they are trained at the Engineer School include: conduct of combat engineer operations; supervising the design, construction, and contract administration of military construction and government civil works projects; developing, producing, and reproducing maps; surveying and mapping projects; bridge classification and construction; terrain studies; and natural resource and environmental studies. Engineer officers are also trained to process and exploit captured engineer equipment; test and evaluate all military engineering hardware and software; and plan, construct, repair, and rehabilitate posts, camps, stations, airfields, structures, ports, harbors, roads, inland waterways, railways, pipelines, and utility plants and systems. These, and a myriad of related responsibilities involving real estate are reflected in extensive and diversified engineer units and duty positions.

Types of engineer organizations to which an officer will likely be assigned include the various combat engineer units attached or organic to infantry or armored elements; medium girder bridge companies; float bridge companies; mobile assault bridge companies; port construction companies; engineer equipment companies; topographic companies; terrain analysis detachments; and utilities maintenance units.

In addition to the diversified unit commander positions, Engineer officer assignments include special jobs such as division engineer, district engineer, facilities engineer, topographic engineer, project engineer, staff engineer, and civil engineer.

Branch schooling includes basic, advanced, and special courses. Many Engineer officers have the opportunity to return to graduate school to participate in such highly sophisticated fields of study as civil engineering, nuclear engineering, geodetic science, engineer administration, and operations research/systems analysis.

Officers selected for the Corps of Engineers can look forward to professional opportunities limited only by their own abilities and ambitions.

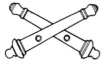

Field Artillery officers have been identified by the insignia of crossed field guns since 1834 and, although the design went through several variations with the establishment of the Coast Artillery and the advent of missiles, the current design is basically that of the original.

FIELD ARTILLERY

The idea of artillery as a facet of warfare is as old as the written word. The Bible mentions the use of ingenious machines, comparable to artillery, on the walls of Jerusalem over 2,700 years ago. Archimedes, with his oversized slingshot capable of hurling a 300-pound stone 300 yards, terrorized the Roman Legions of Marcellus at the siege of Syracuse in 211 B.C. Caesar's ballista, a huge crossbow apparatus, supported his landing on the shores of Britain.

The first use of rockets as a weapon of war was recorded in 1232, when they were used by the Chinese against the Tartars. The first rocket was an arrow with a propelling device tied to it. The development of artillery as we know it, however, began in a serious way during the Hundred Years' War in the fourteenth century. Cannon were used extensively during sieges; but the cannon of that age had no carriage; they were placed on the ground and elevated only by building dirt piles under the muzzle. By the year 1600, the gun had developed firepower unsurpassed by the weapons of the mid-nineteenth century. One tremendous weapon of the 1600s was the Mons Meg of Edinburgh Castle, which threw a nineteen-and-one-half-inch iron ball 1,400 yards or a stone ball twice that far.

Gustavus Adolphus, the great Swedish warrior-king of the seventeenth century, is credited with putting artillery in its rightful place on the battlefield. He limited his artillery to weapons no heavier than twelve-pound cannon; he increased the rapidity of the fire by combining the powder charge and projectile into a single cartridge; he frequently assembled guns into strong batteries that could neutralize enemy fire with concentrated firepower. His cavalry neutralized immovable enemy guns. Thus he developed the three primary facets of victory: firepower, mass, and mobility; and his plan of the use of artillery remains valid today.

Artillery has been "American" since *before* the Revolution. The Ancient and Honorable Artillery Company of Boston (founded in 1637) served with the British Royal Artillery at the fall of the French bastion, Louisberg, during the French and Indian Wars, in 1745.

During the Revolutionary War, the colonies' artillery, under the command of Alexander Hamilton, performed magnificently at the Battle of Trenton, and the skill of American gunners forced the British into siege trenches at Yorktown.

Throughout the early years of the country, artillerymen were considered the Army's elite. Their pay was above the rate for infantrymen and even the cavalry. In 1784, when all of the Army was abolished except for a single detachment of eighty men to guard government stores, those men were artillerymen. Thus the Artillery is the only part of the Army that has been in continuous service since the Revolution. In 1824, the Artillery School was established at Fort Monroe, Virginia, beginning the comprehensive system of service schools that is important today.

The many uses and value of artillery through the nineteenth-century military campaigns, including the Civil War, are far too comprehensive to detail here.

It wasn't until 1907 that two separate artillery corps were established. The Field Artillery and the Coast Artillery were organized with specific missions obvious from the names, and during World War I the Coast Artillery was given the additional job of developing railroad-mounted and antiaircraft artillery pieces.

Development of bigger and better guns and vastly improved Field Artillery tactics and techniques for using them was rapid with the onset of World War II. By the end of the war, artillery firepower had grown beyond all dimensions previously known to man. During this war, new weapons were developed that were to revolutionize our concept of war—nuclear weapons, guided missiles, and radar.

The modern Field Artillery officer is trained to know all of the artillery weapons, fire direction operations, and target acquisition systems and how to employ them in support of combined arms operations. This training includes the study and practices of both non-nuclear and nuclear ammunition. Once commissioned, the Field Artillery officer is trained to be a technical expert as well as troop leader and attends basic and advanced courses at the Field Artillery School, Fort Sill, Oklahoma, at appropriate career points. After completion of the Officer Basic Course, the Field Artillery officer is normally assigned to a battalion-size organization where the officer performs various duties that allow for professional development and growth.

Some of the units in the Field Artillery to which most officers will be assigned early in their tours of duty include the 155mm towed or self-propelled battery; 105mm towed battery; 8-inch self-propelled battery; Multiple Launch Rocket System (MLRS) battery; Pershing and Lance missile units; warhead support units; Target Acquisition and Remotely Piloted Vehicle (RPV) batteries; and, of course, the applicable headquarters and service batteries of these weapons units.

Although the number and type of Field Artillery units and organizations are among the most extensive in the TOE structure, the actual areas of concentration required for Field Artillery officers are few, which indicates the interchangeability expected of those assigned to this branch. These areas of concentration are basic to the branch: cannon field artillery officer, light missile/rocket officer, heavy missile officer, and target acquisition survey officer.

Further evidence of the versatility of the Field Artillery Officer is contained in the official job descriptions. The Field Artillery Unit Commander, for instance, is also qualified to serve as an Artillery Aerial Observer, Forward Observer, and Fire Support Officer. As commander, the officer is trained to control and direct the tactical employment of either a cannon, rocket, or missile unit in combat. This includes related combat necessities such as intelligence evaluation, situation estimates, and battle-plan formulation. The officer is called upon to advise higher commanders, staffs, and supported units on the capabilities of artillery. In combat or otherwise, the Field Artillery unit commander is solely responsible for the unit's administration, training, supply, transportation, communications, organizational maintenance, and security.

In order for the Field Artillery officer to accomplish these duties, training at the Field Artillery School centers on developing the qualifications needed. In the Basic Course, the newly commissioned lieutenants are provided with knowledge of the field artillery systems, with skills and in-depth knowledge in the areas of observed fire, fire direction, and management of individual training that prepares them to become fire support team (FIST) chiefs, to serve as cannon battery executive officers, and to manage maintenance and training at the battery level. This training qualifies the officer to be a cannon field artillery officer. Depending upon the officer's initial assignment, training may continue in either the Lance Officer Course or the Pershing Officer Course to qualify the individual as a light missile/rocket officer, heavy missile officer, or target acquisition officer.

The Advanced Course develops the knowledge and skills required to perform as a battery commander, fire support officer, or battalion fire direction officer. This course includes maneuver force, target acquisition, survey, and counterfire training. Also included are the Field Artillery gunnery problems, to include fire direction, observed fire, and firing battery operations. Leadership, training management, maintenance and supply procedures, and communications/electronics complete the Advanced Course. The Advanced Course now incorporates the Nuclear and Chemical Target Analysis Course into its instruction, preparing each officer to perform the duties of a nuclear/chemical target analyst.

Each Field Artillery officer is expected to have this basic knowledge. To qualify for some assignments, however, some special training is required. For instance, the nuclear weapons officer must be able to meet stringent security tests and know all of the complicated details of storage, transportation, logistical management, staff procedures, policies, directives, and procedures for interservice cooperation, and of course, the special tactical applications.

As with each of the other combat arms, the Field Artillery officer is trained to be a diverse individual, capable of providing accurate, effective and responsive fire support when required. Once branch qualified, the Field Artillery officer may be assigned to a functional area such as personnel management or research and development, where the officer's experience and individual talents may be used to assure the success of missions not necessarily related to Field Artillery.

The Field Artillery provides every officer the opportunity to lead and develop soldiers, as well as work with the latest in technology. These things make the Field Artillery officer amply suited for high-level command and staff assignments.

1875 was the year a design of crossed muskets was authorized for wear by Infantry officers. Several subsequent changes reflecting newer models ended in 1924 when the present design, based on the first type of musket used by U.S. Army troops, was approved.

INFANTRY

The Infantry is the oldest of the combat arms. From the dawn of time, wars have been predominantly fought by men on foot. Long before men domesticated the horse, or invented any kind of boat, the Infantry was represented in the intertribal wars of prehistory.

At first, infantry battles were really hand-to-hand encounters of pairs of warriors, or simple mob actions. Rude tactical plans were sometimes carried out, but more often than not, tactical plans miscarried due to the lack of discipline and cohesiveness of the Armies of prehistory.

The Greeks overcame this problem with one of the great military innovations of all times—discipline. Under the Greek system, infantrymen were drawn up in a solid block of men, sixteen ranks deep. Armed with spears nearly twenty feet long, trained to a high degree of physical fitness, and held in their ranks by discipline, the Greek infantrymen were almost invincible. They changed the course of history when they formed their *Phalanx* on the Plain of Marathon and defeated the Medes and Persians who threatened to overwhelm the entire civilized world.

The Greek *Phalanx* dominated warfare for centuries, until the Romans developed a superior organization. The Roman Legion combined the discipline of the *Phalanx* with a flexible battle formation called the *Maniple*. Maniples were small handfuls of men who fought under the leadership of junior officers. Because of their small size, maniples could be easily maneuvered over rough ground. The Roman armies were trained so that the individual members of the maniples worked as a team, and the maniples in turn worked together to bring about victory. One advantage that the maniple had was that it placed a premium on the intelligence and initiative of the junior leader. Since Roman times, four factors have characterized all successful infantry: discipline, teamwork, initiative, and resourceful junior leadership.

In the years after the fall of the Roman Empire, the Roman infantry organization fell out of use, and for almost a thousand years, the wars of Europe were fought by knights on horseback. Infantry was represented on the medieval battlefield by footmen and pages who cared for the knights' horses and equipment.

Near the end of the Middle Ages, the Swiss mountaineers rediscovered the military organizations of the Greeks and Romans. Armed with pikes reminiscent of the spears of the *Phalanx* and drawn up into squares called hedgehogs, the Swiss were able to stop the charge of the armored knights. At about the same time, the English bowmen were demonstrating the havoc they could wreak on cavalry with their yard-long arrows; with the adoption of gunpowder and firearms, the infantry fully regained its former role as the first and foremost combat arm—a role that it retains to this day.

The Infantry is the basic ground-gaining arm of the Army. Its mission is "to close with the enemy by fire and maneuver in order to destroy or capture him, or to repel his attack by fire, close combat, or counterattack."

Modern infantry is much more complex than the infantry of the Greeks, Romans, or Swiss. Today's infantryman can move by land, sea, or air. The modern infantryman may fight on foot, or go into action by parachute, helicopter, armored personnel carrier, assault boat, or the Bradley fighting vehicle. The Infantry can operate at night, or under any climatic conditions, and can overcome natural and man-made obstacles that would stop other forces.

The Infantry has been variously described as "the Queen of Battle" and "the ultimate weapon." Both of these descriptions are fully justified in terms of the role of the Infantry in warfare. The foot soldier has picked up some less elegant titles. "Doughboy" is a nickname that dates back to the Mexican War, and refers to the mixture of flour and water that the Infantry ate as their first meal in forty-eight hours after storming Molino del Rey. "Dog Soldier" is a nickname the Infantry picked up fighting Indians on the plains. The Indians likened the Infantry to the most respected and feared of the war societies of the Plains tribes, the Cheyenne Dog Soldiers.

The oldest Infantry regiment still on active duty is the Third Infantry, "The Old Guard," authorized by Act of Congress on 3 June 1784. The First Infantry was authorized on 3 March 1791, and the Second Infantry on 12 April 1808. Many other units have been authorized since then, and many reorganizations have been made, but the purpose of the Infantry remains the same.

Perhaps two keywords in describing an Infantry officer's role are *diversity* and *accomplishment.* The satisfaction and personal development the officer experiences from the leadership of soldiers and the management of challenging staff assignments prove invaluable both within the military and in later civilian pursuits. Normally, all Infantry officers have the opportunity to lead a platoon during their initial tour of duty. A few command companies during the same period.

The involvement of Infantry officers with personnel of their commands is total. It will tax the depth of their backgrounds and develop them in all areas. They serve as instructors, counselors, and focal points bearing total responsibility for their assigned personnel. The soldier's problems become their problems, the soldier's needs their needs. To be successful, they must know their soldiers.

Duty as an Infantry platoon leader or a company commander is an opportunity to lead and practice leadership in a demanding, complex job. It is the management of priorities among collective as well as individual training and provides the young Infantry lieutenant the opportunity to make tough decisions, accept responsibilities, hone leadership skills, and develop proficiency in the most demanding tactical and technical techniques associated with the Infantry branch in both combat and peacetime roles. During the first two years of service, Infantry lieutenants can expect to experience at least one staff assignment. Generally these staff assignments are at the troop level in positions such as assistant adjutant, supply officer, or motor officer in battalion or brigade-size units.

A second major area in which Infantry officers can expect to serve in staff roles is the Army's special commands where training, administration, and management are the principal functions of the organization. For example, Infantry lieutenants presently serve at Fort Benning at the training center. Duty positions include company training officer and instructor. Newly commissioned Infantry officers receive training in basic military techniques in order to enable them to serve competently and confidently in any initial assignments they might face. Infantry officers must first receive a solid background at the small unit level. It is desirable that young Infantry officers serve in both light infantry and mechanized infantry assignments early in their careers to develop broad-based tactical knowledge for later field grade development. Later in their careers, they may be eligible for additional schooling opportunities, both military and civilian.

The first assignment for newly commissioned Infantry officers is attendance at the Infantry Officers Basic Course (IOBC) at Fort Benning, Georgia. The course is sixteen weeks in duration and is composed of approximately one-third classroom work and two-thirds field practical exercises. It is designed to prepare each newly commissioned Infantry officer to train and lead an Infantry platoon and to appreciate fully his role in the organization and functioning of the Infantry rifle company. The officers study techniques of tactics, leadership, management, and administration that each must know to be effective. The course of instruction, presented in a learning environment enhanced by a thoroughly professional and experienced faculty, is constantly revised to present only the most current concepts in an interesting as well as informative manner.

In order to enhance an officer's background between major schooling periods some temporary duty (TDY) courses of instruction are offered. The Ranger Course was established in order to provide training in the techniques of small-unit leadership. Emphasis is placed on tactical realism, patrolling, and exposure to various terrain and climatic environments while further developing individual leadership qualities such as prompt obedience, self-discipline, self-confidence, resourcefulness, and determination. The Airborne Course is a three-week program designed to qualify volunteers in military parachuting. The course is divided into three phases (ground week, tower week, and jump week), during which an individual progresses from physical conditioning and mastery of parachute landing falls, to control of an opened parachute, and the proper exiting from an aircraft. The Bradley Commander's Course is designed to train leaders on the employment and operations of the most advanced Infantry fighting vehicle in the world.

The Advanced Course is normally given to Infantry officers between their third and fifth years of commissioned service. It prepares officers to command companies and to serve on battalion and brigade staffs. Successful completion of the course is essential for the career officer and is required before an officer can proceed into specialization or into postgraduate civil schooling programs. All officers will also attend the Combined Arms and Services Staff School between their seventh and ninth years of commissioned service. This school prepares the officer for brigade, division, and installation staff assignments. During the eighth through fifteenth years of service, the officer progresses through the intermediate stage of professional development, gaining proficiency in branch duties or developing expertise in a particular functional area. During this period the officer may be selected for higher-level civilian and military schooling. Each officer is engaged in command and staff duties designed to develop a broad understanding of the overall role of the Army.

An Infantry officer's chances of pursuing graduate study at leading universities are good. Selection is made by Infantry Branch. Present policy in selecting officers for the graduate program is that an officer is not selected until after completion of the Infantry Officer Advanced Course. Factors bearing on selection include an officer's undergraduate record, the degree of competitiveness as reflected by the officer's evaluation reports, and whether the officer has had a good branch background in terms of proficiency in positions held.

Also during the ninth through thirteenth years, an officer may be considered for attendance at the Command and General Staff College located at Fort Leavenworth, Kansas. The nine-month course is designed to provide an officer with an understanding of the procedures and tactics involved in the higher level command and staff positions. Specially selected officers will attend one of the other service staff colleges with an equivalent program of instruction, in lieu of the Command and General Staff College.

The advanced portion of an officer's career pattern, consisting of performing high-level staff and command duties, ranging from the command of an Infantry battalion and brigade to the management of a critical Department of the Army staff agency, is reached at some time between the officer's sixteenth and twenty-third years of service. Outstanding officers may qualify for senior service schooling to enable them to perform at the highest Army levels.

SPECIAL FORCES

The newest of the Army's branches, Special Forces, came into being 19 June 1987. The decision to make Special Forces a branch was based on an analysis of the current and future threat, the integration of Special Forces into the Army's current warfighting doctrine and force structure, and the various missions of Special Forces.

Special Forces missions—deep reconnaissance, strike, foreign internal defense, and unconventional warfare—are an important part of the Army's AirLand Battle Doctrine. Mobile training teams of Special Forces soldiers travel to various countries as teachers. In fact, more than one-third of the security assistance teams sent from the U.S. to other countries come from Special Forces units, which make up only 1 percent of the Army. Special Forces assignments are worldwide, and expansion of Special Forces has created a number of openings in the units, offering

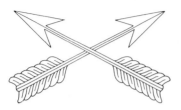

Approved in 1987, the crossed arrows of the Special Forces insignia were worn by Indian Scouts during the late 1800s, and during World War II by officers of the First Special Service Force.

officers and enlisted soldiers more opportunities for responsibility and advancement.

Special Forces currently has four active duty groups: the 5th and 7th, headquartered at Fort Bragg, North Carolina; the 10th, headquartered at Fort Devens, Massachusetts; and the 1st, headquartered at Fort Lewis, Washington. There are two Army Reserve groups: the 11th, headquartered at Fort Meade, Maryland, and the 12th, headquartered at Arlington Heights, Illinois; and two Army National Guard groups: the 19th, headquartered at Salt Lake City, Utah, and the 20th, headquartered at Birmingham, Alabama.

The 1st Special Operations Command was created in October 1982 to unify all Army special operations units under one command. Included in the 1st SOCOM units are all Special Forces as well as the 75th Infantry Regiment (Ranger), headquartered at Fort Benning, Georgia; the 4th Psychological Operations Group, headquartered at Fort Bragg; the 96th Civil Affairs Battalion, also at Fort Bragg; and the 160th Aviation Group at Fort Campbell, Kentucky.

The JFK Special Warfare Center and School, established in July 1983, conducts training for Special Forces, psychological operations, and civil affairs personnel; and for foreign area officers; as well as training for survival, evasion, resistance, and escape. The Center is also responsible for Special Forces doctrine and research and development of new Special Forces equipment and force modernization. As the proponent for the Special Forces Branch, it directs personnel policy development.

On 16 April 1987 the Department of Defense activated the U.S. Special Operations Command as a unified command reporting to the Joint Chiefs of Staff. The USSOCOM is headquartered at MacDill Air Force Base, Florida. It has operational command of Army Rangers and Special Forces, Air Force special operations forces, the Naval Special Warfare Command, and the Naval Special Warfare Center. Army components of the unified command are the 1st SOCOM and the JFK Special Warfare Center and School.

Special Forces are directly descended from the World War II Office of Strategic Services (OSS) and 1st Special Service Force. Though separate units, each was formed to handle unconventional warfare. The 1st Special Service Force (the Devil's Brigade) was originally trained for sabotage missions in Nazi-occupied Norway. OSS operational groups, OSS Detachment 101, and Jedburgh teams parachuted behind enemy lines to organize resistance fighters—Detachment 101 in Burma, and the operational groups and Jedburghs in France. Late in the war the Devil's Brigade was deactivated; shortly after the war the OSS also was dissolved, and the mission and capability of unconventional warfare were lost.

It was not until 20 June 1952 that a new military unit, the 10th Special Forces

Group, was formed at Fort Bragg to meet the need for a force able to wage guerrilla warfare in the event of a Russian invasion of western Europe. The new unit was placed under the command of Col. Aaron Bank, a former Jedburgh team member. Bank's new group trained in jungle and underwater operations, demolitions, airborne techniques, and foreign weapons.

The new Special Forces group continued to grow. In November 1953 some of its soldiers went to Bad Tolz, West Germany, retaining the name of 10th Group. Those remaining at Fort Bragg became the 77th Special Forces Group. In June of 1957 a cadre from the 77th moved to Okinawa to form the 1st SF Group. In June 1960 the 1st Special Forces was formed under the Combat Arms Regimental System to be the parent regiment of all Special Forces groups. The 77th Group was also renamed the 7th Group.

By 1960 Special Forces soldiers from the 1st and 7th Groups were serving temporary duty as advisors in South Vietnam where government troops were fighting communist guerrillas. In September 1961 the 5th SF Group was formed, with its orientation toward the Republic of Vietnam.

The next month, the Army authorized the wear of the green beret for Special Forces soldiers. The beret, unofficial headgear for years, was worn officially for the first time during President John F. Kennedy's visit to Fort Bragg on 12 October 1961. Kennedy said the beret would remain "a mark of distinction in the trying times ahead."

Those times were not far away; soon the new 5th Group was sending increasing numbers of mobile training teams to South Vietnam, and in October 1964, 5th Group headquarters moved to Nha Trang. Special Forces missions in Vietnam included training South Vietnamese in counterinsurgency and strike operations and conducting civic action programs. They also trained various mountain tribes, collectively called Montagnards, to fight Viet Cong and North Vietnamese forces in South Vietnam's central highlands.

During the same period, Special Forces units sent a number of MTTs (mobile training teams) to various Latin American countries, Laos, and Liberia. To meet the demands of the growing number of missions, Special Forces expanded with the formation of the 3rd, 6th, and 8th SF Groups.

Toward the close of the Vietnam War troop reductions began. The 3rd SF Group was deactivated in December 1969, the 6th in March 1971, the 8th in June 1972, and the 1st in June 1974. With cutbacks reaching nearly 70 percent, even the strength of the remaining SF units was reduced considerably.

Increasing awareness of the need for Special Forces in the early 1980s resulted in a revitalization and expansion of the branch. The 1st Special Forces Group was reactivated in 1984.

The Special Forces detachment officer is the leader of the team who must direct and employ the other Special Forces experts. He is trained in the principles, strategies, and tactics of unconventional warfare, foreign internal defense, strike operations, and strategic reconnaissance, as well as other special operations activities such as psychological operations and civil affairs. He must meet the same physical training standards as the enlisted members of his team and be thoroughly familiar with their skills.

The Special Forces Detachment Officer Qualification Course lasts 23 weeks. Special Forces training is divided into three phases: Phase I, which covers basic skills such as survival, land navigation, and patrolling techniques; Phase II, which teaches specific advanced skills; and Phase III, which organizes the students into operational detachments for a test of their skills in a simulated guerrilla warfare mission.

Beyond their basic qualifications, Special Forces officers may need additional training once they are assigned to an operational Special Forces group. This training may include language training for a particular geographic area; training for operations in arctic, jungle, and amphibious operations; and advanced skills such as military freefall parachuting and underwater operations.

Special Forces is a non-accession branch. Officers are eligible to request Special Forces training between their fourth and seventh years of commissioned service and after completion of their accession-branch basic and advanced courses.

Special Forces officers will be branch qualified once they finish their accession-branch advanced course, the Special Forces Detachment Officer Qualification Course, and twelve to eighteen months of successful command of an operational A-detachment.

Combat arms officers with Special Forces as a functional area are currently being given the opportunity to branch transfer to Special Forces. A board must first certify that these officers are administratively, medically, and physically qualified to branch transfer. They will then be given another functional area based on their qualifications and the needs of the Army.

Officers with the additional skill identifier 5G will be required to submit a branch transfer request. Officers who have a functional area of Special Forces and have not completed the qualification course must submit a request for Special Forces training in accordance with AR 614-162.

Promotion opportunities are comparable to those of other combat arms branches, according to the Army's Officer Personnel Management Directorate. Command opportunities for Special Forces captains and majors are the best in the Army, and command opportunities for lieutenant colonels are comparable to those of Infantry lieutenant colonels.

31

Combat Support Branches

 First adopted in 1917, the Chemical Corps insignia alludes to the chemistry-related functions of the branch.

CHEMICAL CORPS

As a combat support branch, the Chemical Corps provides the Army with expertise concerning all aspects of nuclear, biological, and chemical (NBC) warfare. Typical areas of responsibility for the Chemical Officer include Army NBC doctrine and equipment, nuclear and chemical weapons employment, NBC warfare threat capabilities, smoke operations, flame field expedient methods, and decontamination procedures. Approximately 80 percent of the positions within the branch are oriented toward these types of responsibilities.

The Chemical Corps also has a wide variety of research, development, and logistical functions relating to NBC systems and combat development. These responsibilities, which make up the remaining 20 percent of available positions, involve the management of weapon systems and defensive equipment, including their conception, development, and employment. Some disciplines often utilized in these areas are chemical engineering, nuclear engineering, chemistry, physics, and operations research analyst.

Chemical officers, to be effective, must grasp how their expertise can best support the Combined Arms effort. As a result, the majority of newly commissioned lieutenants in the Chemical Corps will begin their careers as the assistant operations/chemical officer in a combat arms battalion or as a platoon leader in a chemical unit. Because of the unique nature of the branch, these assignments offer many diverse and challenging experiences in direct support of front-line combat units. Specifically aimed at providing the lieutenant with basic tactical experience, these positions serve as preparation for higher level command and staff or service school instructor jobs.

There is one common misconception about the Chemical Corps that unnecessarily discourages many future officers from even considering the branch. Specifically, being a Chemical officer *does not* require an academic background in the basic sciences or engineering. Although the branch is technically oriented, specific assignment to jobs requiring these disciplines is a matter of choice. If an officer desires such an assignment, he/she may apply for the branch Advance Civil Schooling program to obtain a graduate degree in a required discipline at the Army's expense.

Modern gas warfare began in 1915 at Ypres, Belgium, two years before the United States entered World War I. During the war, a Gas Service was established overseas to coordinate all uses of gas as an offensive weapon by the American Expeditionary Force. As a result, the Chemical Warfare Service (CWS) was established in 1918 as an integral part of the temporary wartime army and became a permanent part of the Regular Army in 1920. CWS units distinguished themselves in battle during both world wars by providing a variety of combat and combat support functions, such as the Chemical Mortar Battalions, which gave close-in fire support (smoke, flame, high explosive) to the Infantry from their 4.2-inch heavy mortars.

After World War II, the Chemical Corps (renamed from the CWS) assumed responsibility for two additional missions—nuclear and biological defense. Particularly during the 1950s and early 1960s, advances in NBC warfare necessitated the further development of highly skilled officers trained in the complexities of this responsibility.

The changing political climate and declining interest in NBC warfare during the late 1960s and early 1970s resulted in a move to disestablish the Chemical Corps as a branch of the Army. In July 1976, this movement was dramatically reversed by the Secretary of the Army as a result of a heightened awareness of the Soviet Union's capability to wage NBC warfare on a massive and deadly scale. With its reestablishment, the Chemical Corps was given the mission of improving NBC readiness throughout the Army to meet the Soviet threat.

Since that time, significant changes have been made to expand the role of the Chemical Corps as reflected in its redesignation from a service support to a combat support branch. As a part of this revitalization effort, the size of the Corps has quadrupled since 1976. Smoke, decontamination, and reconnaissance chemical units are assigned as Divisional and Corps assets to improve the Army's ability to operate in an NBC environment. Additionally, in 1986, the Chemical Corps was organized under the U.S. Army Regimental System.

MILITARY INTELLIGENCE

Military intelligence has a history that dates back to the beginning of human conflict. It has been evident that foreknowledge of the capabilities and probable courses of action of an enemy, or a potential enemy, is of great value to a government and its military commanders in making sound decisions for the conduct of state affairs and military operations.

Military Intelligence is a basic branch and a combat support arm of the Army. Its officers are primarily concerned with the intelligence aspects of the Army's mission. This field of activity encompasses intelligence, counterintelligence, cryp-

A symbolic sun, patterned after that of the mythical Helios, god of the sun, who could see and hear everything, provides the base for the Military Intelligence design. The sun's rays indicate the worldwide mission of the branch; the superimposed rose revives the ancient symbol of secrecy; and the partially concealed dagger reminds of the aggressiveness, protection, and element of physical danger inherent to branch operations.

tologic and signals intelligence, electronic warfare, operations security, order of battle, interrogation, aerial surveillance, imagery interpretation and all related planning, organization, training and operations. Intelligence officers are assigned to both branch material and branch immaterial positions within all Army, joint, and combined commands and staffs.

The United States up to and including World War I found its Army ill-prepared in all fields of military intelligence, due to the lack of a consistent policy of planning and coordination in this field.

From a very small information division under The Adjutant General, the Military Intelligence Division (MID) appeared in 1918 under the General Staff of the War Department. The Corps of Intelligence Police (CIP) was formed in 1917 as the counter-intelligence agency of the Army. Following the end of World War I, these intelligence agencies were reduced drastically during the cutbacks and reductions of the 1920s.

It was not until World War II then, that military intelligence, due to excellent staff planning and coordination, began to take on the broad range and professional nature that characterizes this field today.

The Military Intelligence Service was organized in this early period of the war and began to gather specialists in intelligence and intelligence-related areas. Among these were linguists, language and area studies students, professional investigators, geographers, economic and technological experts, world travelers, and editors. Counterintelligence training was reconstituted in February 1941, and the official designation of the organization became Counter Intelligence Corps in 1942.

The Signal Security Agency was created in 1943 under the Chief Signal Officer and assumed the responsibilities and performed the functions formerly carried on by the Signal Intelligence Service.

In September 1945, the U.S. Army Security Agency (USASA) was created and placed under the direction of the Assistant Chief of Staff, G2, Intelligence, Department of the Army. It was redesignated as a major field command of the Department of the Army in 1964.

In June 1962, the Military Intelligence Branch, composed of ASA, Intelligence Corps, and strategic and combat intelligence officers, was formalized to meet the growing requirements for control and career guidance of the increasing numbers of officers in the intelligence field. It was designated as Army Intelligence and Security Branch.

In July 1967, the Army Intelligence and Security Branch was redesignated the

Military Intelligence Branch, and its mission was changed from combat service support to combat support.

In 1971, the United States Army Intelligence Center and School, The Home of Military Intelligence, was established at Fort Huachuca, Arizona.

On 1 July 1987, the Military Intelligence Corps was activated as a regiment under the U.S. Army Regimental System.

The primary function of Military Intelligence officers is the collection, analysis, production, and dissemination of intelligence. To accomplish this function, it is essential that they possess comprehensive knowledge of military strategy and tactics.

Military Intelligence officers are highly qualified through education, training, and experience for the following:

Commanding intelligence organizations or elements thereof that provide intelligence capabilities and support to major commanders;

Serving as intelligence staff officers at all levels, tactical and strategic, providing advice and assistance to commanders and their staffs;

Developing signals and electronic intelligence; providing signals and electronic security;

Performing specialized duties in the electronic warfare field;

Developing and managing programs for safeguarding defense information;

Developing order of battle information;

Interrogating prisoners of war, defectors, and other personnel as appropriate;

Providing information on all ground sensor systems and aerial surveillance and reconnaissance sensors and platforms; preparing aerial reconnaissance plans; employing Army aerial surveillance assets; coordinating requests for USAF tactical aerial reconnaissance; participating in aerial surveillance missions; and analyzing photographic and electronically produced images;

Managing the Army personnel security program;

Managing the Army industrial security program;

Managing the Army censorship program, except for press censorship;

Providing intelligence-related linguistic support to all levels of command;

Developing organizational and operational concepts; participating in the design, research, development, and testing of intelligence material and equipment; development of intelligence doctrine;

Serving as Defense and Army representatives with military attache offices in all nations of the world;

Serving as commandant, staff and faculty members of service schools primarily engaged in presenting intelligence instruction and as faculty members at other schools conducting related instruction;

Participating in special career and educational programs; and

Performing tasks associated with the career planning, development, management and assignment of Military Intelligence officers.

All newly commissioned Military Intelligence officers attend the Military Intelligence Officer Basic Course conducted at the U.S. Army Intelligence Center and School. These officers receive training in common Army skills and in all-source intelligence. The all-source intelligence training covers the entire spectrum of intelligence and accents the application to the tactical environment. Upon graduation from this course, most officers will go to tactical assignments. Between the third and sixth years of active federal commissioned service, Military Intelligence officers will attend the Military Intelligence Officer Advanced Course. During attendance at this course, they will receive specialized training in an area of concentration within Military Intelligence. Military Intelligence officers have continued opportunity for additional schooling throughout their careers. In addition to military schooling, there are also civilian educational programs available for advanced degrees. Selected officers can receive specialized training to broaden their knowledge and perspective and increase their value to the Army.

Under the newly established Branch Detail program, participating lieutenants are first selected for their career branch, i.e., Military Intelligence, Signal, Ordnance, Quartermaster or Transportation Corps. They currently are detailed to Infantry, Armor, Field Artillery, Air Defense Artillery, or Chemical Corps for their initial training and assignment. This program is designed to replace the previous Force Alignment Plan III, as it allows the officer to know at the start of his/her career the final career branch. Officers who desire Military Intelligence, and are participating in the Branch Detail Program, should request Military Intelligence as their first choice for a control branch.

The crossed pistols insignia of the Military Police Corps was officially adopted in 1922. The model for the insignia was the 1806 Harper's Ferry pistol—the first official U.S. Army handgun.

MILITARY POLICE CORPS

The Military Police Corps is a basic branch of the Army. It is both an arm and a service whose personnel perform combat, combat support, and combat service support missions. Military police (MPs) contribute to battlefield success by conducting combat operations against threat forces in the rear areas, combat support by expediting the forward movement of critical combat resources, and combat service support by evacuating enemy prisoners of war from the battle areas. Additionally, military police provide security in war and peace to critical Army facilities and resources, such as command posts and special ammunition. Military police also support the Army in peacetime by providing varied law enforcement services that ensure a secure environment for the Army community. Military police units provide support on a flexible mission basis, keyed to the commander's priorities, ranging from the aggressive execution of combat operations against rear area threat forces to the application of law enforcement measures in peacetime crisis situations.

Military police activity dates back as far as the Norman conquest of England. In those days, the provost marshal was personally appointed by the king to maintain the peace, safeguard royal interests, and handle disciplinary matters. By the time of King Henry VIII, the provost marshal's assignments were carried out by provost companies, and by 1611 a provost marshal was serving in the colony of Virginia under a Martial Code drawn up by the deputy governor.

A provost marshal was appointed to General Washington's Army of the United Colonies in January 1776, and two years later Congress passed a resolution establishing a "Provost Corps, to be . . . mounted on horseback and armed and accoutered as Light Dragoons." At the same time, General Washington directed the Corps to apprehend "deserters, marauders, drunkards, rioters and stragglers" and to perform other military police duties.

Between the American Revolution and the Civil War, there were no fixed Military Police units in the Army. Instead, temporary duty personnel performed military police functions. The Civil War witnessed the establishment of the position of Provost Marshal General of the United States. That official's prime responsibility was to enforce the North's draft laws. To assist him in that endeavor, Congress in 1863 created the Invalid Corps. Besides aiding in the enforcement of conscription, the members of this organization also served as Home Guards, prisoner of war escorts, railroad security guards, and garrison troops. In addition, each field army had its own provost marshal. He commanded details of provost guards drawn from the individual army's regiments. Their functions were to maintain march discipline, to combat desertion, and to return stragglers to their parent commands. All these positions and units disappeared following the end of the war.

It was not until World War I that the Office of Provost Marshal General was recreated. Once again its primary function was to enforce the draft system. It was also during that conflict that the Army took a first tentative step toward the creation of a permanent Military Police Corps. A month before the Armistice, the War Department approved the creation of such an organization. However, this proved to be a premature development. Except for a handful of active and reserve companies, the corps was disbanded following the conclusion of the war.

Finally, on 26 September 1941, the Secretary of War approved the creation of the Military Police Corps, and it became a branch of the Army. During World War II, it grew to include 200,000 enlisted men and 9,250 officers. Among other duties, they protected war plants and supplies, escorted and guarded prisoners of war, controlled traffic, and combated enemy infiltrators. During the Korean War, military police were responsible for controlling large numbers of refugees in addition to their normal police functions. It was here that the helicopter was first used by military police for battlefield circulation control and area security.

The Military Police Corps won widespread praise for its performance of duty during operations in the Republic of Vietnam. In 1965, the 18th Military Police Brigade was activated at Fort Bragg, North Carolina. It deployed to Vietnam, becoming operational there on 26 September 1966, the first of its kind to be deployed in combat. Brigade missions were expanded to include port and harbor security, and infantry-type tactical operations. During the Tet Offensive of 1968, military police distinguished themselves in the defense of the U.S. Embassy and other critical installations in Saigon, while keeping vital roads and waterways open throughout the Republic of Vietnam. The activities of the Military Police Corps in its combat support role led to the designation of the Corps as an arm as well as a service on 14 October 1968. This designation reflects formal recognition by the Department of the Army of the combat role which the Military Police Corps has always performed. This combat role was further reinforced by the Military Police in Grenada in 1983.

Today, military police personnel and units perform a wide range of combat, combat support, and combat service support operations. To accomplish battlefield support functions, Military Police Corps officers must possess a comprehensive knowledge of combat operations and tactics. Specifically, MP officers must be qualified through education, training, and experience to plan and execute military police combat, combat support, and combat service support operations. These include battlefield circulation control, area security, rear area operations, enemy prisoner of war and civilian internee operations, and law and order operations. In the garrison environment, military police are responsible for law enforcement, physical security, criminal investigations, and the confinement and correctional treatment of U.S. military prisoners. The fundamental objective for the Military Police Corps in garrison-related functions is to protect and assist fellow soldiers and their families.

A career in the Military Police Corps is one of wide variety, many different assignments, and educational opportunities. While most officers in the Corps are commissioned through the ROTC program, opportunities are also available for OCS graduates to request this branch. In addition, during each year since 1968, graduates from the U.S. Military Academy have been commissioned in the Corps. The Military Police Corps continually provides opportunities for additional education for its officers. From the beginning, when they receive their first comprehensive training in military police operations, until shortly before they retire, officers of the Military Police Corps receive formal professional training at progressively advancing levels. At the Military Police School at Fort McClellan, new officers are taught the principles and techniques of small unit leadership; tactical operations; management; and military police operations. Emphasis is placed on developing platoon leaders who are equally at home in both the tactical and garrison environments. Subsequent military schooling will include the MP Officer Advanced Course at Fort McClellan, the Combined Arms and Services Staff School at Fort Leavenworth, and, in all likelihood, other functional specialty courses as the opportunities arise. Then, as their careers progress, MP officers may be selected for attendance at the U.S. Army Command and General Staff College and senior service schools. In past years, military police officers have taken part in graduate study programs in the fields of education, personnel management, area studies, comptrollership, organizational behavior, operations research, ADP systems, criminology, correctional administration, and police science and administration.

The Military Police Corps' combination of battlefield and peacetime functions provides its officers with real opportunities, not only to achieve a unique blend of skills, but also to serve in a variety of challenging assignments. Since the Military Police Corps serves the entire Army, an officer may be assigned to almost any type of organization stationed wherever our troops are throughout the world. The initial assignment of a junior officer will probably be to an MP company or battalion, but may also be to a specific functional law enforcement position on any Army installation. Later, an officer could be selected for company command, for duty as a staff MP officer, or as a member of the staff and faculty at the U.S. Army Military Police School, an ROTC element or the U.S. Military Academy. Other possible assignments include duty as a correctional treatment officer, physical security officer, as a Reserve component advisor, as a member of the Department of the Army Staff, with the U.S. Army Criminal Investigation Command, or any other of a variety of branch related and branch immaterial positions. Officers naturally take on more and more responsibility in their assignments as they progress in rank and experience.

The latest and most exciting chapter in the history of the MP Corps is even now taking shape. A greatly expanded role on the battlefield has brought with it significant increases in firepower and combat effectiveness. At the same time, the motto "Of the Troops and for the Troops" is taking on renewed meaning for military police serving Army communities throughout the world. The pace is fast and the esprit is high as the Military Police Corps continues to welcome all professional challenges that the future may hold.

SIGNAL CORPS

In the entire history of the U.S. Army since the invention of semaphore, it would be difficult to find a commander who would not agree with the statement "the secret of command lies in the secret of communications." Signalling was, of course, the first effective means of fast communication between elements in the field, hence the name of this branch . . . although a much more apt and descriptive term for today's activities is "information systems management."

Within the classification of combat, combat support, and combat service support, the Signal Corps is a combat support branch with an overall mission involving the resources and activities employed in the acquisition, organization, develop-

The present design of crossed flags and torch was adopted in 1884 although enlisted men of the acting signal corps had worn crossed flags since 1868. The insignia represents the signalling system, invented by the first signal officer, which used flags during the day and torches at night.

ment, processing, transmission, use, integration, retention, retrieval, and management of information. This includes automation, communications, visual information, records management, and publications/printing.

Historically, the Signal Corps traces its beginning from 21 June 1860 when Maj. Albert J. Myer, who had developed the signalling system we know as semaphore as a result of his work with the deaf, was appointed Signal Officer of the Army. As a branch it was officially established in March 1863.

Subsequently, Signal officers and enlisted men were deeply involved in every aspect of the nation's growth and explorations. The use of the telegraph became a tactical necessity during the Civil War. Later, signalmen played important roles in developing the national weather service, linking the West to the East as the country expanded, exploring the Arctic, and opening Alaska to the Gold Rush. Thousands of miles of telegraph wire were installed and maintained during this period.

War with Spain in 1898 found only 8 officers and 52 enlisted men assigned to the Corps. Authorizations were received quickly to expand this group to a total of 138 officers and 1,115 enlisted men. It was during this conflict that the combat photographer became an integral part of the Corps.

Ballooning became a Signal responsibility in 1885; this led to the development and control of aviation by the Corps during World War I. The Corps had been busily engaged in the development of military aircraft since the successful flight of the Wright brothers, and an aviation section had been authorized in 1914. By 1918 there were 16,000 officers and 147,000 enlisted men engaged in air operations, and in May of that year they became the branch known as the Air Corps.

During the same period, many innovations in sound-producing communications systems were developed, and the first permanent Signal Corps post and training center was activated at Fort Monmouth, New Jersey. Among the new kinds of equipment designed by Corps personnel were vacuum-tube radios and detection gear to indicate approaching aircraft. In the field, the Signal Corps provided the required meteorological service for artillery and aviation, and photography operations were expanded to include motion pictures.

World War II saw the next major contribution of communications and sound to military operations. Radio had been perfected to then unbelievable levels of performance, and the development of radar, sonar, and radio-controlled weapons systems was only the beginning of technological advances undreamed of only a few years before.

Today, the responsibilities of the Signal Corps are more varied than ever. Establishing, maintaining, operating, and refining networks of information systems for tactical operations; operating the Army portion of the global strategic information network; training Signal specialists, officer and enlisted; carrying out research and development projects; handling the logistics of storage, distribution, and repair of communications-electronics materiel; staffing the Army photographic and pictorial services; developing highly specialized electronic equipment for use in the space satellite program; and being responsible for the Army's Information Mission Area offer unsurpassed technological opportunities for junior officers.

The complexities of today's Army require a flexible Signal Corps organization. In addition to TOE Signal organizations, Signal personnel are employed in practically every organizational structure throughout the Army. Major roles for Signal Corps personnel are found within the U.S. Army Information Systems Command, Army Material Command, Training and Doctrine Command, U.S. Forces Command, Department of the Army, and the Department of Defense agencies.

The U.S. Army Information Systems Command with its headquarters located at Fort Huachuca, Arizona, is the Army's Signal organization charged with the global mission of operating and maintaining assigned information systems at echelons above corps, supporting theater/tactical, strategic, and sustaining base operations. The command also is responsible for planning, developing, engineering, acquiring, and installing information systems; developing and implementing information systems; and advising, assisting, and providing tactical support. USAISC provides the interconnection of theater armies with activities of the Department of Defense, whether locally or over intercontinental distances.

A corps Signal Brigade is the Signal organization expressly formed to provide the planning, engineering, installation, supervision, and control of the command and area automation and communications systems within the corps area. Each corps Signal Brigade is structured to meet the needs of the corps it supports. The brigade assigns its various organic Signal battalions to plan, engineer, install, operate, and maintain the integrated network of command communications systems, and acts as the integrator of information systems serving the corps headquarters down to each division and separate combat brigade. Each division has its own organic Signal battalion. In addition, at each combat brigade within the division, there is a Signal Corps officer who serves as the combat brigade Signal officer, and every maneuver battalion assigned to the combat brigade—whether an infantry battalion, armored battalion, or a mechanized battalion—also has its own Signal officer, who is in charge of organic communications. This Signal officer is responsible not only for communications, but for total information systems integration on the battlefield at all levels.

A career in the Signal Corps offers a wide range of training and assignment possibilities, punctuated at appropriate intervals with education opportunities paralleling Branch Career programs.

The Army's training facility for the Signal Corps is the U.S. Army Signal Center and Fort Gordon. The school at Fort Gordon, Georgia, provides military education and practical training for officers to prepare them for positions concerned with Signal activities in theater/tactical, strategic, and sustaining base operations.

Fort Gordon is also the home of the Signal Corps Regiment, being designated as such on 1 June 1986. All Signal soldiers are affiliated with the regiment; however, at the same time, those that typically serve in combat arms regiments may elect to associate with the combat arms regiment in which they serve.

The majority of all Signal officers are commissioned as communications-electronics operations officers. During the first eight years, the officer attends the basic and advanced courses, with in-between assignments designed to provide opportunities for the development of leadership skills. After completing the Signal Officer Basic Course at Fort Gordon, a most challenging career lies ahead. The graduate of the Signal Officer Basic Course may receive additional training in either division and corps, or echelons above corps, information systems depending upon the pending assignment. After promotion to captain, the officer may receive training in one of the remaining Signal Corps areas of concentration. They are communications-electronics automation; communications-electronics engineering; information systems and networking; and communications-electronics materiel management. Professional development opportunities include Training with Industry and graduate-level education programs.

From about the eighth through the fifteenth year of service, the officer continues developing expertise in branch duties, but may concentrate his or her efforts in a functional area such as systems automation, research and development, procurement, and so on. From this point, the Signal Corps officer concentrates on enhancing professional qualifications, developing higher level management capability and increased managerial capacity for handling the most complex information systems activities of the Army and Department of Defense.

In summary, the Signal Corps provides the expertise and facilities that support information systems activities at every level in the Army. It continually researches, develops, and improves the equipment required to provide that support. The Corps trains its officers and enlisted personnel as professionals, equipped with the most sophisticated equipment available. The Signal Corps provides the media for command and control of all Army elements.

32

Service Support Branches

ADJUTANT GENERAL'S CORPS

Historically, the adjutant always has occupied a strong position on the commander's staff. This dates from the Roman legions, the word *adjutant* being derived from the Latin verb *adjutare,* meaning to assist or help. The French, recognized as great military organizers during the sixteenth and seventeenth centuries, first used the term *adjutant general,* meaning "aid to general."

The original function and the continuing mission of The Adjutant General (AG) has been to assist the commander. The entire staff structure as we know it today developed from this beginning. By the time of the English Civil War the British had adopted the title for officers who, in the modern American Army, would be adjutants general, chiefs of staff, and executive officers.

On 16 June 1775, the Continental Congress passed a resolution creating the Continental Army. The following day, it named Horatio Gates as Adjutant General. General Gates thus became the first officer after George Washington to be named to the Continental Army. In line with English precedent, the new Adjutant General assumed responsibility for a wide range of functions, all designed to unburden his commander. These functions included security, intelligence, and coordination, as well as purely administrative and clerical tasks for the commander—even to keeping correct time so watches could be kept synchronized in all units of the Army.

Horatio Gates first established the tradition of Adjutants General being soldier-administrators ably assisting the commander in battle. Recognizing Horatio Gates for his strategic victory over British Lt. Gen. John Burgoyne at the Battle of Saratoga on 17 October 1777, the

Continental Congress voted Horatio Gates the thanks of the nation and awarded him a Congressional Gold Medal.

The Adjutant General's Corps continues to foster this tradition of excellence by inducting deserving individuals into the Order of Horatio Gates and awarding them an officially struck U.S. Mint replica of the original Horatio Gates Gold Medal. Up until the time when the modern Army staff structure was formed in 1903, Adjutants General served as the commanders' chief of staff. During the War of 1812, Adjutants General continued to be the only officers invested with the authority to speak for the commander. Many of these officers proved to be soldiers of great character, judgment, and experience. The Adjutant General for Maj. Gen. Henry Dearborn, Col. Winfield Scott, is credited with the battlefield victory at Fort George, having assumed command of Dearborn's troops when the general was too ill to command. Two other War of 1812 Adjutants General heros are Brig. Gen. Pendleton Gaines and Maj. Gen. Alexander Macomb, both recipients of Congressional Gold Medals. The Adjutant General in 1813, Brig. Gen. Zebulon Pike, the famous explorer, was killed in battle by an exploding British ammunition bunker while leading the victorious American attack on York, Canada.

The War of 1812 once again proved the need for Adjutants General to be both capable administrators and exceptional leaders of the highest calling. By 1838 the Army almost exclusively appointed West Point graduates to Adjutant General positions up until the early 1900s. The first two West Pointers appointed as Adjutants General, Samuel Cooper and Lorenzo Thomas, both served as The Adjutant General during the Civil War. The Adjutant General of the Union Army, Colonel Cooper, resigned his commission in 1861 to become The Adjutant General in the Confederate Army. Brigadier General Thomas replaced Cooper as The Adjutant General in the Union Army, serving for eight years in this position. Throughout the Civil War Adjutant General officers commanded volunteer units, served in provost marshall and inspector general positions, and held key staff positions in the War Department.

In 1872 the Adjutant General's Department took over the work of the Bureau of Refugees, Freedmen, and Abandoned Lands, providing food, clothing, housing, and schooling for both refugees and recently freed slaves. In 1881 the Army tasked the Adjutant General's Department with setting up and running the post school system. Within one year Adjutant General officers established 147 schools, enrolling 975 soldiers and 1,100 children.

From 1886 to 1903 Adjutant General officers ran the Division of Military Information, training all Army attaches, issuing maps, preparing militia mobilization plans, and collecting items for display in the Army Museum of Military Relics. During the Spanish American War six Adjutant General officers served as the commanding general in volunteer units, while many other Adjutants General served in key staff positions within the War Department and with the Army in the field. President William McKinley consulted with The Adjutant General, Henry C. Corbin, on a daily basis on all matters involving the war. Rewarding his vital wartime service to the president, Major General Corbin was promoted to lieutenant general and given command of the newly formed Division of the Philippines.

In 1915 Congress vested the control and administration of the U.S. Disciplinary Barracks in The Adjutant General. The National Defense Act of 1916 added procurements, assignments, promotions, transfers, retirements, and discharge responsibilities to the Adjutant General's Department.

When America sent the American Expeditionary Force into World War I, Col. Benjamin Alvord set sail for France as the Adjutant General to Gen. John J. Pershing. Colonel Alvord established the role of Adjutant General officers in modern warfare by developing the critical wartime procedures of strength accounting, replacement operations, and casualty reporting. World War I clearly showed the need for a dedicated corps of Adjutant General officers serving at all levels, from Army headquarters to the divisions in the field.

During World War II the Army recognized the need for having a large corps of highly trained soldier-specialists to run and maintain a modern army on the battlefield. The Adjutant General's School was founded on 14 June 1941 at Arlington Cantonment, Virginia, to produce the corps of officers and enlisted soldiers we call the Adjutant General's Corps today. The diversity and sophistication of Adjutant General duties during the war led to the creation of the Adjutant General's Department Troops and Organizations in 1944. For the first time Adjutant General soldiers began wearing the department insignia superimposed on metal disks attached to their shirt collars and blue, red, and gold braids in their overseas caps.

Following World War II the Adjutant General's Department completed the massive administrative challenge of properly documenting the wartime service of over six million Army veterans. On 20 July 1950, against the backdrop of the Korean War and the expanding political and military role of the United States, the Adjutant General's Department was redesignated the Adjutant General's Corps and made a basic branch of the Army. This change signaled the rising prominence of the Adjutant General's Corps within the Army and the diversity and sophistication of Adjutant General missions. The Korean and Vietnam conflicts continued to show the need of having Adjutant General officers at all levels within the Army. On the modern AirLand battlefield, AG responsibilities continue to grow as the Army reexamines the vital role of personnel support in war.

The 1960s brought some sweeping changes to The Adjutant General's Office (TAGO). The responsibility for data processing came to TAGO with the Army Data Services and Administrative Systems Command in 1962. In that same year, certain functions relating to military personnel management were transferred from TAGO to a newly created Office of Personnel Operations (OPO). Concurrent with this change, The Institute of Heraldry was created, and administrative responsibility for the Standby and Retired Reserves was assigned to TAGO. Responsibility for Ready Reserve Mobilization was transferred to TAGO in 1965. This involved consolidation of almost 500,000 personnel records in a center at St. Louis, Missouri. The center later became the Reserve Components Personnel and Administration Center (RCPAC).

While OPO was formed in 1962, it did not represent total Army personnel consolidation under a single manager. A decade later, in 1972, the Military Personnel Center (MILPERCEN) was established in Alexandria, Virginia. All active Army personnel matters came under the cognizance of MILPERCEN, including activities concerned with separations, personnel records, promotions, and awards, which previously had been the responsibility of TAGO.

The Adjutant General Center (TAGCEN) was formed in 1973 to meet the de-

The shield identifying officers of the Adjutant General's Corps was first approved in 1872. However, it was not until 1924 that the colors of red, white (now silver), and blue were authorized. Differing slightly from, but nevertheless based on the shield portion of the Coat of Arms of the United States, it symbolizes the support of this branch to the Army and nation.

mands for initiative and response in the fields of administrative management and personal environmental support. It operates under the command of The Adjutant General to fulfill some of the Adjutant General's many responsibilities.

On 1 December 1984, a reorganization established the U.S. Army Community and Family Support Center as a field operating agency of the Deputy Chief of Staff for Personnel (DCSPER). The new organization is composed largely of elements previously assigned to TAGCEN, but it also includes other community life and administration functions previously performed by MILPERCEN and ODCSPER. The center is a HQDA organization responsible for developing policies and operating systems and programs for community and family assistance, morale, welfare, and recreation activities, and nonappropriated fund management. The center is co-located with MILPERCEN in Alexandria, Virginia.

In 1985, the Information Mission Area was created under the staff supervision of the Assistant Chief of Staff for Information Management (ACSIM), and there was a desire to clean up lines of authority between the Army Reserve Personnel and Administration Center (RCPAC) and the Army Reserve Personnel Center (AR-PERCEN). On 1 October 1985, records management, office automation, publications, and library functions were moved from TAG to ACSIM, and RCPAC was disestablished, with most functions moving to ARPERCEN under the control of the Office of the Chief of the Army Reserve. Concurrently, planning began to designate The Adjutant General as Director of a Personnel Service Support Directorate (PSSD) within the Military Personnel Center. This Directorate was formed on 1 June 1986 to focus on soldier sustainment and transition issues by drawing together functions formerly placed elsewhere in MILPERCEN, Office of the Deputy Chief of Staff for Personnel, the Community and Family Support Center, and the U.S. Army Recruiting Command. The Adjutant General ceased to be an Army Staff officer, but the title was retained by the Director, PSSD, because of its historical significance and the linkage to the Adjutant General Corps, whose officers and soldiers perform the personnel sustainment and separation roles for the Army.

The Personnel Service Support Directorate provides the following services:

Transition Management. Provides an integrated approach to retention of soldiers in the Total Army. Develops programs to enhance retention on active duty and, for those who choose to leave the active force, assignment to troop program units of the Guard and Reserve. A full pilot test of the Transition Management process began at Fort Bragg on 1 June 1987, scheduled to run for nine months. Transition Management integrates the processes of Total Army retention, career planning, soldier education, and job assistance; and operates the officer retirement system, enlisted transitions and appeals, and physical disability processing.

Soldier Education. Performs policy and operator roles for soldier education. The largest projects include: keeping sign-up rate for the GI Bill at the 80 percent and above level; initiation of the Green Tab Packet, which assists soldiers in getting enrolled in the college of their choice; Green to Gold program, which places promising soldiers in ROTC; and initiation of ties with various educational associations and consortiums to enhance recruiting and place retiring soldiers in teaching positions.

Central Personnel Security Clearance Facility. Located at Fort Meade, Maryland, the CCF ajudicates the award and withdrawal of all Army security clearances.

The Institute of Heraldry. Located at Cameron Station, Virginia, TIOH provides heraldic services to the Army and, on a reimbursable basis, to other services and governmental agencies. TIOH designs, procures, and provides quality control for unit crests, flags, shoulder-sleeve insignia, plaques, belt buckles, and other assorted accouterments.

Casualty and Memorial Affairs Operations Center. Receives and processes all

Army casualty reports; coordinates notification of next-of-kin; provides for casualty assistance and burial. Operates the Central Identification Laboratory in Hawaii, which performs anthropological and odontological identification of remains of U.S. servicemen from the Vietnam War, the Korean War, and World War II. Operates the West Coast Port of Entry Mortuary at Oakland, California, which processes the remains of U.S. service members and their family members who die in the Pacific Basin. Provides liaison with POW/MIA families. Operates the Army memorial affairs program.

Enlisted Records and Evaluation Center. Located at Fort Benjamin Harrison, Indiana, the center maintains the official personnel records of all active Army enlisted soldiers. Operates enlisted promotion and selection boards, processes enlisted evaluation reports, and runs the deserter information point. EREC is now serving as the test bed for the Army's Optical Digital Imagery project. This promising new technology may greatly enhance records use, storage, and retrieval.

Military Personnel Operations. Linked with the Army of Excellence Task Force at Fort McPherson, Georgia, this office is the ombudsman for field personnel support organizations. Underway is a major project to group personnel work done in the field into twenty-two major work categories and to provide a new series of regulations that detail the work to be performed down to the task and step level. Additionally, product managers are being assigned to each of the twenty-two work categories to provide the functional vision on how we should better automate this work in the future. Included in this effort is "fixing the PAC" to provide better service to soldiers.

Military Awards Branch. Provides policy and operational control over the U.S. Army awards and decorations program. Processes foreign awards and U.S. awards recommended to foreign military personnel.

Installation Support Division. Responsible for Army ID card policy; performs as the Army representative to the DOD, DEERS, and RAPIDS policy group; handles paternity and soldier indebtedness cases; responsible for the Army Voting Program, Census, and proffers to the Army.

Educational Incentives Office. Handles casework associated with the student loan repayment enlisted option, GI Bill, VEAP, and other enlistment incentive programs.

In addition to his functions as Director, PSSD, The Adjutant General concurrently serves as the Commanding General of the Physical Disability Agency, the Executive Director of the Military Postal Service Agency (a joint service organization that performs postal policy and operational missions for the Department of Defense), and Director of the Armed Forces Courier Service (a triservice organization that transports highly classified documents and equipment for the military services and other federal agencies).

Officer assignments within the Corps are as varied as in any other service support branch. Professional development of the Adjutant General's Corps officer parallels that of other branches in offering both the basic and advanced courses along with many special courses at the Adjutant General's School, Fort Benjamin Harrison, Indiana. The expected area of concentration for AGC officers is Personnel and Administrative Systems Management. All AGC officers are expected to have a thorough knowledge of the duties and activities of an Adjutant or Adjutant General. Examples of other military jobs typically assigned to AGC officers are postal officer, administrative officer, personnel officer, personnel management officer, manpower control officer, recruiting and induction officer, archivist, military historian, morale support officer, army band officer, publications officer, public education officer, public affairs officer, automatic data processing officer, and director of personnel and community activities.

Through more than two centuries of service Adjutant General officers have been providing vital support to the Army in war and peace. Our future promises many new concepts in personnel service support requiring a dedicated and knowledgeable corps of imaginative officers to take charge and lead the way. Our pride in the past is only surpassed by our optimism for the future. The next decade and beyond promises to bring forth many new concepts in all of the areas of Adjutant General's Corps responsibility, all of which will require a contingent of knowledgeable, imaginative, and dedicated officers—as much as, if not more than, any other technical service in the U.S. Army.

CHAPLAIN CORPS

Clergy serving in the U.S. Army are called chaplains. The English word *chaplain* derives from a legend: It is said that St. Martin of Tours divided his military cloak, giving a large piece to a beggar, and wearing the rest as a cape. This *capella* became a religious article and was taken on military campaigns for its supernatural value, just as the Ark of Covenant was carried by the Israelites. The place where the relic was safeguarded was known as the chapel, a term still used to designate houses of worship on military installations. The bearer of the religious article was the *capellanus,* or chaplain.

As a member of the clergy, the military chaplain is a representative of a particular religious faith. The primary mission of a chaplain is to perform ministry by conducting religious services and by providing a complete program of religious education for the American soldier, the dependent family, and authorized civilians. Chaplains conduct sacraments, rites, and ordinances consistent with their endorsing faith group. Counseling is one of the primary religious functions of the Army chaplain. Chaplains counsel on religious and quasi-religious subjects in chapels, hospitals, and quarters, and in combat, training, and recreational areas.

Chaplains are distributed throughout the Army by assignment to units or installations in an approximate ratio of one chaplain per 700 soldiers.

The chaplain is also a staff officer and serves on the personal staff of the commander. In this capacity, the chaplain advises the commander on matters of religion, morals, and morale as affected by religion. The chaplain maintains liaison with civilian religious groups and welfare agencies to facilitate cooperative programs. The chaplain has responsibility for participating in civic action projects and for advising the commander on matters of religion in the culture of the local inhabitants in oversea areas of operations.

In combat, the chaplain performs the functions of religious ministry, including

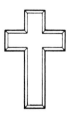

Christian

Jewish

The Chaplain Corps is authorized two distinctive insignia, the Cross and Tablets. The Cross is a symbol of Christianity and is worn by all Christian Chaplains, with no distinction between Protestant and Catholic. The Cross was approved as an insignia in 1898. Jewish chaplains wear the insignia symbolizing the Tablets of Moses, which have numerals representing the Ten Commandments inscribed on them. Above the Tablets of Moses is the six-pointed Star of David. The Jewish insignia was approved in 1918.

the spiritual care of the wounded and dying as well as for prisoners of war. The Army Forward Thrust program assigns chaplains to maneuver battalions, as far forward as possible. When captured and imprisoned, special status is accorded under the Geneva Convention, which permits the chaplain to continue ministry among fellow prisoners of war.

Army chaplains receive their training at the U.S. Army Chaplain Center and School, Fort Monmouth, New Jersey. Early in the career pattern, there is a nine-week basic course; sometime between the fifth and seventh year of service, there is a twenty-one week advanced course.

In addition to specialized military schooling, the Army chaplain is considered for special civil schooling in one or more disciplines, including religious education, clinical pastoral education, drug and alcohol abuse, and preaching. Other continuing education programs, some available from the Chaplain Center and School, supplement these educational opportunities.

The Army chaplain is responsible for providing religious coverage to all members of the unit of assignment and to a designated area of responsibility. Religious coverage is provided as permitted by the chaplain's endorsing faith group, and by other military or civilian clergy according to the religious needs of the command and/or area.

The organized chaplaincy in the American Army was established prior to the Declaration of Independence. The Second Continental Congress created the position of chaplain on 29 July 1775 on the recommendation of Gen. George Washington. Since that time, Army chaplains have served in all areas of the world, from the battlefields of the Civil War to the Bataan Death March and in the jungles of South Vietnam. Since the founding of the Corps, over 270 chaplains have died as a result of hostilities.

In recognizing the professional character of the chaplains, the Department of the Army provides chaplains with enlisted assistants. These enlisted volunteers, known as chaplain assistants, provide administrative support, perform as vehicle drivers, and guard the chaplain's life in combat. (Chaplains are defined as noncombatants by the Geneva Convention of 1949.) The enlisted assistant is a very important link between chaplains and service personnel in the religious program within the U.S. Army. Together, the chaplain and the assistant comprise the Unit Ministry Team.

To qualify for commissioning as an Army chaplain, the clergy person (male or female) must have satisfactorily completed college and theological or equivalent graduate training acceptable to the Department of the Army. The chaplain must be endorsed by a particular faith/denomination for ministry to Army personnel. A direct commission as an Army officer is the usual procedure for appointment of a chaplain. Theological students may be commissioned as chaplain candidates and begin training before graduation and ordination.

FINANCE CORPS

There has not been an army in history that was not influenced in one way or another by its pay, whether loot and plunder or legal tender. As the transition from occasional pillage to regular payment progressed, the need for a service to administer pay and account for monies, with a corps of officers to supervise, became inevitable.

The Finance Corps was born amid the tumult of the Revolutionary War. In June 1775, one year before the Declaration of Independence, the Second Continental Congress created the office of Paymaster General to manage and disburse the wages of General Washington's army. Even though the war ended and the army

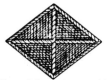

The diamond insignia worn by members of the Finance Corps is not without historical significance. Prior to the minting of coins, goldsmiths utilized the orle (diamond) as a mark of identification and to stamp the weight on gold bullion used in trade. Originally chosen by General Washington for his Paymaster General, it was approved by the Secretary of War in 1896 to be the insignia of the Pay Department, and later the Finance Corps. The Finance diamond represents the four basic functions of the Finance Corps (accounting, disbursing, administration and auditing) with the inner lines representing the coordination between the pay and procurement agencies of the Army.

disbanded, the Paymaster General's office continued in order to service the small force that remained on active duty. In 1816, with increasing financial demands, the Paymaster General's office gave way to the separate, enlarged, and renamed Pay Department. The Pay Department remained active through three wars until 1912 when, in a major reorganization, it was merged with the Quartermaster Department. This quickly proved to be impractical, and in 1920 Congressional action made the Finance Department a separate branch of the War Department. The office of the Chief of Finance remained a separate entity until World War II, when it was integrated with the office of the Fiscal Director, Army Service Forces, and given additional duties such as the sale of War Bonds and promotion of the National Service Life Insurance Program. After the war, the office of the Fiscal Director was dissolved and the Finance Department again became an independent Army Staff Agency.

The Army Organizational Act of 1950 changed the Finance Department to the Finance Corps with no changes in its primary mission. There were changes, however. Since 1949, with the designation of the position of Comptroller of the Army and the placement of comptrollers at every level of command, the Finance Corps has taken on wider responsibilities in budgeting and financial planning.

Today's Finance Corps has advanced immeasurably over the first Paymaster General's office, both in size and in quality of service and support to our Army and our soldiers. Since 1950, the Corps has felt the impact of automation in the form of a centralized automated pay system for active and retired military payrolls with worldwide, real-time inquiry capability, automated accounting and budget systems, and automated financial systems for travel, commercial accounts, civilian pay, reserve Army pay, and disbursing functions. This extensive automation leads to more efficient peacetime and wartime operations. It allows more time for the Finance officer to plan and implement more efficient functional methods and to train Finance soldiers to improve their tactical and technical competency. In this era of constant evolution, the Finance Corps has been characterized by progressive accomplishments aimed at providing better service and support.

On 7 May 1987, the Finance Corps was activated into the U.S. Army Regimental System under the whole branch concept for combat service support organizations. This historic ceremony marked the beginning of a new era in the proud lineage of the Finance Corps, one of the U.S. Army's oldest branches. Regimental affiliation provides the opportunity to further emphasize the history, customs, and traditions of the Corps, and it improves unit esprit through a sense of belonging.

The official home of the Finance Corps is the Army Finance School at the Soldier Support Center, Fort Benjamin Harrison, Indiana. It is part of the U.S. Army Soldier Support Institute. The Finance School was founded in 1920 to standardize and develop instruction for all members of the Finance Corps and Civil Service personnel. Today the school annually trains several thousand individuals, ranging from soldiers just beginning their new careers in Finance to colonels in the command phase of their Finance career, in subjects ranging from disbursing to resource management functions.

Newly commissioned active duty officers can expect to attend the Finance Officer Basic Course for sixteen weeks with their Army Reserve and National Guard counterparts shortly after entrance on active duty. Upon completion, some officers will receive additional training such as Military Accounting or attend other schools such as Airborne School. The Finance Officer Advanced Course is attended by career officers normally between their fifth and eighth year of service. This course is taught using the small group instruction method to better develop leadership skills needed by the company grade officer. In both the basic and the advanced course, tactical training is balanced with technical training to enhance an officer's performance in both peacetime and wartime missions. Because of the demands of the AirLand battlefield, physical fitness is an integral part of the Finance officer's curriculum. The Finance officer courses end with a command post and a field training exercise to test the student's knowledge, understanding, and application of Finance doctrine and tactical skills.

Finance Corps lieutenants perform the same leadership roles as other Army officers. They are expected to lead, train, and motivate the soldiers within their units; to maintain a high level of physical fitness, discipline, and morale; and to develop proficiency in survival skills. A new Finance officer is challenged to use limited time to conduct effective training for combat, since a majority of the finance unit's garrison time must be used to perform the unit's service support role.

A likely first-duty position for a Finance lieutenant is as a cash control officer or a disbursing officer. In these positions, the officer is appointed as an agent of the U.S. Treasury and is responsible for large sums of cash, negotiable instruments, expensive equipment, and supervision of civilian employees and finance soldiers. Another possibility is as chief of a military pay section, maintaining the military pay accounts for personnel in the area serviced by the section. Modern computer technology links finance offices around the world to the U.S. Army Finance and Accounting Center at Fort Benjamin Harrison, Indiana. The officer is responsible for the smooth flow of transactions through the section to ensure timely and accurate payment of all soldiers served by the section. The young officer also could be assigned as the chief or an assistant chief of a Pay and Examination Branch, with broader responsibilities to include civilian pay, travel, and commercial accounts, as well as military pay.

A Finance Corps lieutenant can also serve as a plans officer on a Finance staff at unit, corps, or theater level, with duties including the development of comprehensive training and contingency plans for subordinate finance units, coordinating and conducting inspections of these units, arranging logistical support, and other staff-related planning and programming. Assignment also is possible to nontactical finance units or Major Command staffs where the officer will work with or supervise a predominantly civilian work force.

The Finance Corps doctrine has changed significantly in recent years to reflect the organizational structure needed to provide battlefield support. Finance units have both a combat service support role and a combat role. Finance officers of all grades now serve in command positions in these new finance organizations at theater, corps, and unit levels, as well as in the more traditional finance roles.

Although the Finance Corps is the Army's smallest branch, there are opportunities for assignment worldwide. If you become a member of the Finance Corps, you could receive one of these challenging assignments to begin your Army career.

The Army's legal arm traces its insignia to the year 1890. The crossed pen and sword symbolize the recording of testimony and the military character of the branch. The wreath is the traditional symbol for achievement.

JUDGE ADVOCATE GENERAL'S CORPS
(The World's Largest Law Firm)

The legal affairs—military and civil—of the Army and the personnel in it are entrusted to this special group of officers, all of whom are graduates of accredited law schools, members of their state's bar, and commissioned in the Judge Advocate General's Corps. This Corps traces its beginning from July 1775, when William Tudor—a leading Boston lawyer—became the first Judge Advocate of the Army. A year later the designation of Judge Advocate General and the rank of lieutenant colonel were prescribed for this office.

Until 1802 other individuals were designated as Judge Advocate of the Army, but after that date and until the Corps was officially established, the term *Judge Advocate* was used rather freely in designating officers whose primary function was the prosecution of courts-martial and advising military commanders on matters pertaining to military justice and enforcing discipline in the Army.

By an act of Congress in 1849, the office of Judge Advocate of the Army was established on a permanent basis, but a corps of officers was not authorized until 1862. In 1864, the Judge Advocate was granted the rank and pay of a brigadier general and the Bureau of Military Justice was created as a forerunner of the Office of The Judge Advocate General. A merger of the Bureau and the corps of Judge Advocates in the field took place in 1884 and resulted in the creation of the Judge Advocate General's Department, by which it was known until 1948, when "Corps" was substituted for "Department."

Military law grew in scope and intensity from the time of the Civil War so that today the Judge Advocate General's Corps performs many duties and services not envisioned by those who created it. From The Judge Advocate General, who acts as legal advisor to the Secretary of the Army and all other agencies within Headquarters, Department of the Army, to a legal officer in a small installation, the day-to-day situations are more diversified than in most general civilian law practices. Today's Judge Advocate is skilled in the law of nations, the environment, labor relations, and contracts as much as in the traditional law of the Army and its criminal justice system. He or she also advises the commander on installation problems, personnel administration, patent and tax law, and a variety of claims by and against the government.

A primary responsibility of the Judge Advocate General's Corps is the complete administration of the Uniform Code of Military Justice in the Army. In order to fulfill its ever-increasing military justice responsibility, the strength of the Corps has been greatly increased in the past few years to provide competent legal advice and counsel for the accused in areas where previously no such right was guaranteed. Moreover, constant refinements in the Uniform Code and the implementing regulations foster an atmosphere of professionalism, free from the command restraints and influence of the past. For example, the Judge Advocates who act as military judges in courts-martial are organized in a separate command, the U.S. Army Legal Services Agency, and are assigned and rated in that channel.

Other services to and protections for the individual soldier have been introduced by recent regulations. Like the military judge, the military defense counsel has been placed in a separate organization, the U.S. Army Trial Defense Service; counsel is provided to the soldier in the many administrative and nonjudicial proceedings that can affect his or her career; and Judge Advocates are now authorized, in some jurisdictions, to take an active role in assisting soldiers with personal legal problems under the Expanded Legal Assistance Program.

The Judge Advocate General's School, located on the grounds of the University of Virginia at Charlottesville adjacent to the prestigious University of Virginia Law School, is where all new Judge Advocate officers receive initial orientation into the Army, and where other members of the Corps return for advanced and specialized courses. The Judge Advocate General's School is the Home of the Army Lawyer; its students include other uniformed Judge Advocates and civilian U.S. government attorneys from many agencies, and some legal officers from the armed forces of friendly foreign nations. The School's program of Continuing Legal Education supplements and hones the general skills of the practicing attorney with graduate-level instruction in more than twenty fields of law necessary to fulfill the Corps' complex mission. In addition to the basic and graduate courses, the school offers short courses to military judges, contracting officers, commanders, counsel, international law specialists, and others concerned with Army administration.

The Corps is a special branch, and its services are required throughout every level of command. Therefore the opportunities for assignment anywhere the U.S. Army has troops are plentiful and diversified. Early in his or her career, a Judge Advocate is likely to be involved in legal assistance, claims, or courts-martial. They are basic missions of the Corps, provide valuable trial experience, and are essentials to the development of the well-rounded legal officer. Experienced Judge Advocates can look forward to challenging assignments at levels within the Army's structure where policy and decisions of general importance are made.

The "shell and flame" insignia of the Ordnance Corps is patterned after a similar design used by British troops. It became official in 1832. Considered the oldest of branch insignia, it represents the early explosive devices and properly symbolizes that particular branch function today.

ORDNANCE

"Service to the line, on the line, on time" is the motto of the Ordnance Corps. The Ordnance mission is to develop, produce, acquire and support weapon systems, ammunition, missiles, and ground mobility materiel during peace and war in order to provide combat power for the U.S. Army.

The explosive growth of science and technology in the years since World War II has contributed significantly to the development of military materiel. The major developments of World War II—nuclear weapons, missiles, and electronics—have been exploited, refined, and applied in a variety of ways. As the pace and complexity of technological advancements have grown, the interaction between military materiel and operations has become increasingly important and has also had a significant impact on the manner of accomplishing the support mission. Ordnance officers can be found worldwide, performing the enormous task of maintaining ordnance-type equipment used by both our armed forces and those of our allies.

Ordnance officers may pursue a career in four challenging areas of concentration (AOC): Tank/Automotive Materiel Management (conventional tank and ground mobility equipment); Missile Materiel Management (guided missiles and free flight rockets); Munitions Materiel Management (nuclear and conventional); and Explosive Ordnance Disposal.

Tank/Automotive Materiel Management officers are responsible for the supply of repair parts and maintenance of artillery, armor, and infantry weapon systems; small arms weapons of all calibers; fire control equipment for weapon systems; track and wheel vehicles; engineer and power generation equipment; and quartermaster, chemical, and materiel handling equipment; as well as metalworking, fabrication, canvas repair, welding, and equipment recovery. Maintenance functions include inspection, test, service, repair, overhaul, and reclamation. The role of every officer in Tank/Automotive Materiel Management is efficiently and effectively to ensure that the maximum number of weapon systems are operational, ready, and available to combat commanders. Management of the Army's maintenance, in concert with actual maintenance operations in support units, is becoming an increasingly sophisticated challenge. Officers serving in this AOC can expect to serve in organizations located throughout the Army's structure. Tank/Automotive Materiel Management officers find that the demands of their duty positions will require a comprehensive knowledge of maintenance management, logistics, production control, and quality assurance as it applies to multiple commodity areas.

Officers assigned to Missile Materiel Management are responsible for the development, fielding, supply of repair parts, maintenance, and final disposition of air defense, land combat, and ballistics-weapons systems to include associated guidance, launching, handling, and test equipment. Officers serving in this AOC can expect to serve in organizations located throughout the Army's structure. Missile Materiel Management officers find that the demands of their duties require them to be competent managers skilled in logistics, production control, supply, and quality assurance techniques. The technical sophistication of the missile systems, their tactical importance, and the high dollar cost of fielding and maintaining these systems require officers with the highest scientific and managerial skills.

Munitions Materiel Management officers are trained for assignments around the world involving conventional, chemical, and nuclear munitions and warheads. Support functions include supply, maintenance, surveillance, inspection, stock control, and security, as well as maintenance of associated testing and handling equipment. The overall and increasing technical sophistication of various munitions in the Army's inventory and the use of robotics in the ammunition field will require officers serving in this AOC to develop expertise in several engineering technologies and management techniques. The munitions system is unique in that virtually the entire ammunition industry in the United States is owned and managed by the Army. Many opportunities are available for Ordnance officers to participate at all levels in managing this multibillion-dollar industry.

Explosive Ordnance Disposal (EOD) officers provide a unique and critical service to the Army. EOD officers are responsible for identifying, locating, and rendering safe handling, removal, salvage, and disposal of U.S. and foreign unexploded conventional, chemical, and nuclear munitions. Officers serving in this AOC can expect to serve in EOD units throughout the world and to serve on major command staffs as advisors on EOD matters. EOD officers advise and assist law enforcement agencies in the removal and disarming of explosive devices, provide support and protection to the President of the United States and other high-ranking American officials, and support intelligence activities through analysis of foreign munitions.

The organization of ordnance support today still follows the concept and philosophy upon which it was founded—direct support to the combat arms. The Ordnance Corps had its beginning with an Act of the Continental Congress on 27 May 1775, which established a committee to study and plan for the supply of weapons and other war materiel to the Continental Army. Soon after the act was passed, General Washington appointed Ezekiel Cheever to be the Commissary General of Artillery Stores. Cheever functioned in essence as a civilian Ordnance Chief, with Maj. Gen. Henry Knox, Chief of Artillery, in charge of all military components. From this beginning up to the present, the Ordnance Corps has changed as the Army changed. Early in the Revolutionary War, design of weapons was not considered an Ordnance function, primarily because U.S. Army weapons were either purchased abroad or captured from the enemy. Individual weapons were usually the property of the individual soldier. However, in 1777 the first arsenal for the manufacture of weapons was established at Springfield, Massachusetts. During the same year a storage facility was set up at Carlisle, Pennsylvania.

In 1801, Eli Whitney demonstrated a primitive method of mass-producing weapons, a process that revolutionized the manufacture of weapons. It was quickly adopted by our military armories, leading to formal authorization of the Ordnance Department on 14 May 1812. The first formally designated chief was Col. Decius Wadsworth. Full-scale mass production was not possible, however, until the eve of the Civil War.

Ordnance personnel received their baptism of fire in the War of 1812. When the British approached the Washington Arsenal, the installation was evacuated. Departing ordnance storage personnel dumped the remaining stores of powder in a nearby well. A British detachment investigating the premises lowered a lantern into the well. The resulting explosion killed several officers and about thirty enlisted men.

After the War of 1812, the Chief of Ordnance was responsible for contracting for arms and ammunition, for supervising the government armories and storage depots, and for recruiting and training artificers to be attached to regiments, corps, and garrisons. By 1816, five federal arsenals were in operation. These were Springfield and Harper's Ferry, making small arms; Watervliet, producing artillery equipment and ammunition; Watertown, producing small arms ammunition and gun carriages; and Frankford, making ammunition. Two others, Rock Island and Picatinny, were added before or during the Civil War. Early in the Civil War, Harper's Ferry was destroyed.

As a result of the large-scale, widely dispersed operations during the Civil War, ordnance concepts and activities were greatly improved.

The war with Spain brought new and difficult problems to the Ordnance Department. Procurement methods had to be revamped and methods of supply expanded to meet the requirements of our first overseas conflict. Most war supplies had been stored at established arsenals and depots; in most cases they were delivered directly to military units in field locations. When forces were being prepared for shipment by sea, a large depot was set up in Tampa, Florida, to complete the equipping of units moving through the port. This port depot and those field depots set up in Cuba were the beginning of Ordnance field service. From this experience came the realization that this job, now called logistics, must be performed by separate agencies so that combat troops could concentrate on fighting. World Wars I and II and the Korean Conflict did not change the mission of the Ordnance Department, renamed the Ordnance Corps in 1950, but the amounts of items procured, distributed, and maintained stagger the imagination.

During this period, small arms procurement mounted into the millions, rounds of ammunition into the billions, and other items produced increased proportionally. The Ordnance Department assumed proponency for wheeled vehicles after 1942. Ordnance field service was expanded along with the training of personnel and development of techniques in order to be responsive to the needs of the fighting forces.

The Atomic Age began an entirely new era of weapons and weapons systems and the continuing improvement of more conventional equipment. To meet these changes and the more complex requirements of a modern army, and to plan for the future, a new agency was created. The Army Materiel Command was given the responsibility for procurement and distribution of materiel that had formerly been divided among the various technical services. The Ordnance Corps, which in the past had been represented in organizational structures by name and was somewhat restricted in areas of employment, now furnished Ordnance-trained personnel to staff all logistic elements of the Army. Since 1983, the reconstituted Office, Chief of Ordnance, has reassumed responsibility for the career management of Ordnance personnel, working with the assignment officers of the Ordnance Branch of the Officer Personnel Management Directorate.

In the field of research and development, Ordnance Corps personnel have always had a major role. During the greater part of its history this role was restricted in research but had almost complete freedom in development. From its beginning in 1814 until the late 1930s, the Ordnance Corps was given requirements by the various chiefs of branch for equipment that would perform as each chief of branch desired. From these requirements, Ordnance engineers would produce the needed item. In 1942 the Ordnance Board was organized. The board was to be the research and development arm of the Chief of Ordnance, with a mission to design equipment, develop training procedures, study improvements in operational techniques, and develop TOEs for Ordnance units.

The test and evaluation mission of the Ordnance Corps had no established facility during its early history. At the turn of the century its first designated proving ground was established at Sandy Hook, New Jersey. Sandy Hook served its purpose until the beginning of World War I, at which time it became apparent that it was no longer suitable. Located on the seacoast, it was vulnerable to attack and sabotage; in addition, it had no direct rail connections. Despite the urgency, it took nearly two years before negotiations were completed for the purchase of a 35,000-acre tract along the Chesapeake Bay near Aberdeen, Maryland. Sandy Hook was eventually phased out and all its Ordnance activities transferred to the new location at Aberdeen. At first, Aberdeen Proving Ground was utilized for testing field artillery weapons, trench mortars, antiaircraft guns, ammunition, and railway artillery. Observation towers, small arms ranges, a hard surface area for testing bombs, and other facilities were added later. On 10 November 1918, Dr. Robert H. Goddard, the Father of American Rocketry, successfully demonstrated test rockets of his own design at Aberdeen.

From the beginning, the Ordnance Corps trained its personnel on an informal basis. Then, in 1902, the Ordnance School of Application was established at Sandy Hook. This school was replaced by the Ordnance School of Technology, activated at Watertown Arsenal in 1906. Later, in 1917, there were twelve supply schools established in various universities throughout the country. All of these schools, plus several others, graduated over 50,000 personnel, both commissioned and enlisted, during World War I. In 1936, all Ordnance training was centralized at Aberdeen Proving Ground. As a result, the Ordnance field school for enlisted men was moved from Raritan Arsenal in July 1940 and combined with the officer school to form the Ordnance School. This consolidated school for a time handled most of the school training for the Corps. In January 1942, the Bomb Disposal School was activated at Aberdeen and remained active until 1955. In October 1956, Bomb Disposal/EOD training was transferred to the Naval School at Indianhead, Maryland.

In July 1973, the U.S. Army Chemical School was merged with the Ordnance School, giving that school the added mission of providing the defense establishment with trained NBC specialists and continuously updated doctrine in the chemical field. However, the Chemical Corps was reestablished as a basic branch of the Army in 1976, and in 1979 the Chemical School was moved to Fort McClellan, Alabama, under the control of the Chemical Corps.

After rockets, missiles, and ammunition became almost an entity of their own, a second ordnance-oriented school, designated the U.S. Army Missile and Munitions Center and School, was established at Redstone Arsenal, Alabama. Until October of 1981, specialty proponency responsibility for the Ordnance Corps was divided between the Ordnance Center and School at Aberdeen Proving Ground and the Missile and Munitions Center and School at Redstone Arsenal. This led to a perceived split of decision-making authority for the Corps by two separate and autonomous training bases. This separation was resolved on 1 March 1983 when the MMCS was designated the Ordnance Missile and Munitions Center and School and was placed under the supervision of the Commanding General of the Ordnance Center and School, who thereby became the single voice of the Corps. The U.S. Army Ordnance Center and School and the U.S. Army Ordnance Missile and Munitions Center and School remain as the principal training centers for Ordnance personnel.

On 1 November 1983, the Office, Chief of Ordnance (OCO) was established to assist the Commanding General of the Ordnance Center and School in overseeing the operations and management of his two separate schools and focusing on Ordnance-related matters worldwide. The Commanding General of the Ordnance Center and School formally became the Chief of Ordnance on 28 October 1985, when the Ordnance Corps became the Army's first combat service support branch to be recognized under the U.S. Army Regimental System. This office concentrates, in a collective sense, on personnel management, materiel systems integration, training, doctrine, and force structure issues that cross organizational lines and/or have a broad impact on the Ordnance Corps. The OCO further assists the Chief by developing Ordnance Corps policy, providing for the welfare of the Corps, and publishing *The Ordnance Professional Bulletin.*

In addition to these Army training establishments, use is made of civilian universities and technical training establishments for selected officers and enlisted personnel.

The Ordnance officer of today's Army is a materiel-oriented manager. He or she functions and operates in an atmosphere of electronics, mobility, and high-technology weaponry—rifles, machine guns, artillery, trucks, tanks, rockets, missiles, and nuclear and conventional fire power. The Ordnance officer must have a basic qualification in military organization, operations, and tactics in addition to technical and managerial expertise to function in a variety of duties.

In staff positions, Ordnance officers provide advice and assistance to all commanders and other staff officers at all levels on ordnance matters. They are also assigned to instruct and train military and civilian personnel in maintenance, repair parts, ammunition, missile, and general logistical support doctrine and procedures.

In assignments to planning staffs, the Ordnance officer helps to develop concepts, doctrines, policies, and procedures for furnishing ammunition and maintenance support to the Army.

Performing integrated commodity (life cycle) management of ground vehicles, missile systems, weapons systems and ammunition; duties related to EOD; formulating plans, programs, and policies for industrial mobilization; and providing technical supervision and inspection for designated commodities are some of the fascinating assignments awaiting those who qualify, choose, and are selected for the Ordnance Corps.

Because of its widely diversified field mission, numerous TOE units are authorized Ordnance officers. From the Ammunition, Missile, and Maintenance Companies, Nuclear Weapons Support Detachments and EOD Detachments, to the Depots, Arsenals, and Ordnance Plants, assignments are varied and diversified. Ordnance jobs for company grade officers include platoon leader, missile maintenance officer, technical supply officer, production control officer, ammunition stock control officer, EOD officer, EOD detachment commander, company commander, Service school instructor, maintenance test officer, product/procurement manager, research officer, and range officer.

Further schooling at both the Ordnance Center and School, and at the Ordnance Missile and Munitions Center and School, as well as at selected civilian institutions is usually in the future of many career officers in the grade of captain and above. After appropriate field experience with battalion- and higher-level field organizations, and/or logistics staffs, selection for top-level Army schools is possible.

Changes in weaponry and the need to maintain weapons in fighting condition will be a primary activity so long as armies exist. Therefore, the young officer selecting Ordnance will quickly encounter exciting challenges and responsibilities in the Ordnance arena. Initial assignments are usually as maintenance or missile/munitions platoon leaders. Such assignments involve management of supply and maintenance personnel and maintenance of sophisticated Army equipment, such as the new M-1 Abrams tank or high technology missile systems.

The current range of Ordnance career possibilities is extensive. With weapon systems and equipment ranging from conventional to laser (computer and space age technology), the Ordnance Corps of today and the future presents a tremendous opportunity for those who qualify.

QUARTERMASTER

Advanced data processing equipment, sophisticated communications networks, and modern transportation techniques are the tools of the Quartermaster Corps officers in performing their logistical support missions around the world.

It's a far cry from the beginnings of the Corps in 1775, when the first Quartermaster General was appointed to provide some items of camp equipment and the transportation for the Army. Having virtually no money and no authority and

One of the more complex branch insignias is that of the Quartermaster Corps. A key, symbolic of storekeeping, is crossed with a sword indicating "military" and superimposed on a wagon wheel, pertaining to the delivery of supplies. The stars and spokes of the wheel represent the original 13 colonies and the origin of the Corps during the American Revolution. The eagle is used as a national symbol.

dependent upon the several states for supplies, it seems incredible that the early Quartermaster Department could accomplish its mission. Yet the Quartermaster played an important role in the successful defense of liberty made by the young nation. The most effective early Quartermaster General was Maj. Gen. Nathaniel Greene. He established the Army's first depot system, which in those days was used to supply forage for Army animals.

Military supply was largely under civilian control in the post–Revolutionary War period. At the outbreak of the war with England in 1812, Congress appointed a brigadier general to supply the Army. In 1814, quartermaster sergeants first appeared and were assigned to each of the three regiments of riflemen.

From 1818 to 1860, the Quartermaster General was Brig. Gen. Thomas S. Jesup, a remarkably able administrator. During his tenure the Quartermaster Department made great strides, emerging as the integrated, permanent supply agency of the Army. In this period the Department took over the procurement and distribution of clothing and other items of supply.

The Civil War brought the development of an effective depot system, and railroads were used extensively in establishing supply lines. The supply system and procedures developed during this period formed the basis for supply doctrine until World War I. In 1862, the Department assumed responsibility for the burial of the war dead and the maintenance of national cemeteries.

Congress, in 1912, consolidated the former subsistence, pay, and Quartermaster departments to create the Quartermaster Corps with its own officers and troops. The First World War showed the increasing importance of supply. The United States participated long enough to give the Quartermaster Corps its first set of huge figures: nearly four billion pounds of food valued at 727 million dollars, a billion dollars spent for clothing, and 3,606,000 tons of supplies.

To fill an increasing need for specialists in Army supply problems, the Quartermaster School was begun in a small way in 1910 at the Philadelphia Quartermaster Depot. The school remained in Philadelphia, except for a short period at Camp Johnston, Florida, in World War I, until it moved to Fort Lee in 1941. The school continues today to train the officers and enlisted specialists assigned to the Army's sophisticated logistical system.

During World War II, the Quartermaster Corps sent more and a greater variety of supplies to more men in more places in the world than any other Quartermaster activity had done in the history of the world. Also, the Quartermaster soldier often worked in the combat zone, and if the need arose, he took his turn fighting. It was during this conflict that transportation and construction were transferred to the Transportation Corps and the Corps of Engineers, respectively. With the loss of these two original functions, the Quartermaster Corps concentrated entirely on its supply and service missions.

The Corps pioneered in the field of air supply of ground troops, using both free fall and parachute delivery extensively in Korea as a regular means of supply for the first time in military history.

When the Department of the Army was reorganized in 1961–1962, the Office of the Quartermaster General was abolished and its functions and responsibilities reassigned to the Department of the Army staff agencies and commands established under the functional concept. The Quartermaster Corps, however, remained as one of the Army's important technical branches, and Quartermaster personnel are still performing the logistical functions within the new functional framework. The Commandant of the Quartermaster School is now the Branch Chief and principal Quartermaster adviser, and the school is the Home of the Quartermaster Corps.

Officers assigned to the Quartermaster Corps, while they function as members of a team within the current complex of logistical concepts, are still identified with the basics of supply—supply management, procurement, cataloging, inventory, management, storage, distribution, salvage, disposal, and the supervision of troop testing of all material except medical and cryptological items. A host of supply activities and service support responsibilities include graves registration, laundries, field bakeries, issue points at reception centers, food service, mess management, commissary management, petroleum and water distribution, and petroleum product testing.

Quartermaster officers are part of numerous TD (Table of Distribution) organizations to provide staff advice and counsel on supply and service operations. Within the TOE authorizations, officers can expect assignments to units such as the supply and transportation battalion, combat support battalion, supply and service company, petroleum operating and supply companies, airdrop equipment support company, airdrop equipment repair and supply company, field service company, and supply depot company.

Among the jobs offered by this branch are petroleum management officer, subsistence supply officer, food service officer, commissary management officer, supply and service management officer, materiel management officer, depot operations/storage officer, aerial delivery and material officer, and field services officer, all of which provide unusual career opportunities for the individual with a supply-related background and interests.

Formal schooling, including the basic and advanced Quartermaster officer courses at Fort Lee, is in the future of all Quartermaster officers. Each junior officer may expect training and early duty assignment in one of the supply fields of petroleum management, subsistence management, or materiel/services management. During career development, many special educational opportunities at the Quartermaster School and selected civilian institutions are open to Quartermaster officers. Officers also compete equally with officers from other branches for selection to attend top-level Army schools such as the Command and General Staff College, the Army War College, and the Industrial College of the Armed Forces.

Today's highly mobile Army requires professionalism in all stages of combat service support. Whether it's computing requirements for missile repair parts or operating a petroleum pipeline to keep the helicopters in the air, the Quartermaster officer provides the technical knowledge to get the job done right, and now. For the dedicated officer, the Quartermaster Corps offers unlimited opportunities for personal and professional development.

TRANSPORTATION CORPS

Firepower and mobility are the two fundamental, inseparable capabilities that ensure success in tactical operations, and the basic ingredient of mobility is trans-

Transportation by rail (represented by a flanged, winged wheel on a rail), air (represented by wings on the wheel), land (symbolized by the shield used as standard U.S. highway markers), and water (indicated by the ship's steering wheel) make up the Transportation Corps insignia. The current design was approved in 1942 and is based on a similar one in use since 1919.

portation—equipment to do the job in the best, fastest way, and people who know how to use it properly. That's the Transportation Corps (TC).

The Transportation Corps grew out of the increased necessity for centralized control and operations as a result of the Army's expansion during the mobilization and war years of 1940–1942. Prior to that, transportation responsibilities were split between Quartermasters and Engineers. The establishment of the Transportation Corps came at a critical time. The problems of moving millions of men and uncountable tons of supplies to virtually every corner of the world had no precedent in the history of man. Fledgling officers, many drafted from civilian counterpart jobs, became the nucleus of the new branch and admirably accomplished many of the most successful transport operations ever recorded. Every type of carrier was used. Ships of all sizes and description (the Army still has a navy of its own), aircraft, railroads, trucks, busses, military vehicles—everything that could be used was put to work to get the job done. Volumes have been published on the statistics and accomplishments of the Transportation Corps during World War II, which cannot even be capsuled here. Suffice to say that the Corps earned a place in the heart of every fighting man who reached for ammunition and found it or who walked into a rest area and discovered a full-course hot meal waiting. At the same time, it earned a permanent place in the technical support elements of an ever-mobile Army. On 31 July 1986, the Transportation Regiment was officially activated as a part of the U.S. Army Regimental System. It is named the Transportation Corps, and its home is at Fort Eustis, Virginia.

The majority of Transportation Corps officers are engaged in activities within four major commands and overseas in Europe and Asia. Those assigned to the development and improvement of tactical vehicles work under the Army Materiel Command (AMC). Transportation specialists concerned with the plans, doctrine, training, and methods of getting people and equipment to far places for specific combat missions labor within the Training and Doctrine Command (TRADOC). And those Transportation Corps officers providing the day-to-day support to Army units maintaining their readiness status while standing prepared for deployment anywhere in the world as may be necessary are working for the Forces Command (FORSCOM). Other Transportation Corps officers are working operating military ocean terminals in the United States and overseas as part of the Military Traffic Management Command (MTMC).

The tremendous expansion of Army Aviation in response to the Army's need for improved tactical and logistical mobility on the modern battlefield absorbed much of TC's interest and activity. Transportation Corps personnel were indeed prominent among the pilots, copilots, and flight crews who flew and maintained the Army's aircraft. Approximately one-fourth of the commissioned officers within the Transportation Corps were qualified aviators. However, in 1983 when Aviation was established as a separate branch, most of these personnel transfered from the Transportation Corps to the Aviation branch. The mission of aviation logistics also was transferred to the new branch. Training for this mission is conducted by the Aviation Logistics School, located at Fort Eustis.

TC officers are trained and involved in every conceivable transportation operation. As the Transportation officer of a post, camp, or station, he or she may control the use and movement of all kinds of modes, from helicopters and fixed-wing aircraft to operating the intrapost bus schedule. The organizational structure of the Army includes highway transport, such as light truck, medium truck, heavy truck, and motor transport units, terminal service, medium boat, light amphibian, floating craft support maintenance, logistic support vessel, landing craft utility, and medium- and heavy-lift helicopter companies, as well as service teams for watercraft and aircraft—all of which provide the Transportation Corps officer with a huge diversity of assignment and professional possibilities. In addition, railway equipment, train operating, and maintenance-of-way units are found in the Reserve Forces. In March 1987, Reserve component resident rail training was conducted at Fort Eustis, Virginia, with the arrival of two diesel electric locomotives.

Fort Eustis, Virginia, located near historic Williamsburg, Jamestown, and Yorktown, is the home of the U.S. Army Transportation School and center of TC activities. While attending the basic, advance, or specialty training courses here, the Transportation Corps officer is well grounded in the fundamentals of doctrine and operations. He or she sees the full range of Transportation Corps responsibilities from the systems operating within the continental United States—air, rail, highway, and inland waterways—to the many foreign ports and airheads used to funnel supplies and equipment to Army troops wherever they may be; learns where and how military, civilian, and host nation transportation fits into overall logistical planning for the fighting force; reviews the need for research and development; and may, at some time after completion of the advance branch course, be selected for graduate training at a college or university in a special field such as industrial management, transportation engineering, or management. College graduates with degrees majoring in these areas, as well as marine operations and marine engineering, are prime prospects for the Transportation Corps.

Of course, there are a wide variety of staff positions at all levels of the Army organization and the Department of Defense open to TC officers, and selection for attendance at a top-level Army or Armed Forces Staff College is a real possibility.

The Transportation Corps future looks to the increased use of robotics and missions in space for officers and enlisted personnel with specialties in cargo handling and documentation. The Transportation Corps will provide the leadership and the means to enable the Army to move into space.

33

The Army Medical Department

Of particular significance to the capability of all of the other arms and services to perform assigned missions are the six Corps of the Army Medical Department. Under various names, the medical services have been a part of the military establishment since appointment of the first Director General and Chief Physician, on 27 July 1775. Mankind has benefited ever since through the discoveries and techniques of military medical personnel working to assure improved treatment of casualties, or fitness for duty through preventive medicine. The Army Medical Department continues, as ever, to provide for every soldier and the soldier's family, medical care of the highest standards of the profession.

The basic insignia for the Corps of the Army Medical Department is the caduceus, a two-serpent adaption of the Staff of Aesculapius—one serpent each signifying preventive and corrective medicine—gold in color except for the Medical Service Corps, which is silver. The caduceus alone serves as the insignia for the Medical Corps. Each other Corps is identified by a letter or letters superimposed on the caduceus . . . "D" for Dental Corps, "N" for Nurse Corps, "V" for Veterinary, "MS" for Medical Service Corps and "S" for Medical Specialists Corps.

Army medical facilities and units are located throughout the world. Almost every permanent Army post has a modern hospital of recent construction, its size depending upon the assigned mission and the population served. These permanent hospitals are staffed and equipped in accordance with their approved Table of Distribution and Allowances (TDA). This authorization document provides considerable flexibility for adjusting personnel and equipment authorizations to meet changes in workload.

533

The Army Medical Department also includes a large variety of "field" (i.e., mobile) medical units. These units are established on the basis of approved Tables of Organization and Equipment (TOE). Currently there are in excess of fifty different types of these units. Some of these, such as the Division Medical Battalion, are organic to an Infantry, Airborne, or Armor division. Other medical units that are usually under a medical group, brigade, or medical command, also furnish direct support to combat troops and include the Combat Support Hospital, Field Hospital, Mobile Army Surgical Hospital, Evacuation Hospital, and General Hospital. Also within the field medical unit inventory are the Medical Depot, Preventive Medicine Teams, Medical Laboratory, and the Convalescent Center. Currently, the Convalescent Center is not operational in the active Army, but it is included in the Reserve forces and is in contingency plans for quick mobilization should the requirement arise. Reserve component personnel and units provide well over one-half of the total post-mobilization health care delivery capability.

The Army reorganization of 1973 established the U.S. Army Health Services Command with headquarters at Fort Sam Houston, Texas. This command acts as a single manager for health care delivery and supportive services within the United States, Panama, Alaska and Hawaii and supervises all medical training for the Army. The command's Medical Centers, thirty-one Army community hospitals, dental and veterinary clinics, and area dental laboratories provide comprehensive health care to service members, retired personnel, and their families. In addition, the Commander, Health Services Command, manages three military installations at Walter Reed Army Medical Center, Fitzsimons Army Medical Center, and Fort Detrick, Maryland. Health Services Command provides medical training from basic courses for enlisted persons and officers, through advanced technical and military education programs leading to advanced degrees at the Academy of Health Sciences, U.S. Army, Fort Sam Houston, Texas.

The Surgeon General, a lieutenant general, is a Medical Corps officer who is nominated by the President and confirmed by the Congress. As such, the Surgeon General serves as advisor directly to the Chief of Staff on all matters affecting the health of the Army. Each of the Chiefs of the other five Corps (Dental, Veterinary, Medical Service, Nurse, and Medical Specialist) and a Special Assistant for Medical Corps affairs are consultants to The Surgeon General; each has certain staff responsibilities for activities of the Corps he or she heads. The six Corps of the Medical Department have many things in common; these commonalities have been included only in the material that follows about the Medical Corps and not in each of the individual Corps descriptions.

First used as a cloth insignia in 1851, the caduceus in its present form was approved in 1902. Except for the Medical Corps, the caduceus worn by officers of the other Medical Department branches is superimposed with a letter or letters indicative of the specific Corps. Rooted in mythology, the caduceus has historically been the emblem of physicians, symbolizing knowledge, wisdom, promptness, and skill.

THE MEDICAL CORPS

After Gen. George Washington had been appointed as Commander-in-Chief of the Continental Army by the Continental Congress, he requested medical support for his troops, and on 27 July 1775 a Hospital Department was authorized; the forerunner of the original Army Medical Department.

From the end of the Revolutionary War until 1818, when the title of Surgeon General was authorized, the Chief of the Medical Department had little control over those physicians on duty with Army units, since they took their orders from the officers who commanded the units.

The Army Medical Department has kept pace with the times. When the early settlers were moving into the West, Army doctors went with them to dress their wounds and to deliver their babies. The very first Medal of Honor was awarded to First Lieutenant Assistant Surgeon Bernard J. D. Irwin for an act of heroism during an attack against Cochise and his Apache band of Chiricahua, on 14 February 1861, in the area that later became the state of Arizona. The Medal of Honor was not authorized until 3 March 1863, and the award to Dr. Irwin was not made until 21 January 1894. Another pioneer medical officer, Dr. Leonard Wood, also received the Medal of Honor for service in the Indian campaigns in the Southwest. He later became the only physician ever to serve as Chief of Staff of the Army.

The busts of two Army physicians are included in New York University's Hall of Fame—Dr. Walter Reed, for conquering yellow fever, and Dr. William Crawford Gorgas, for using Reed's discovery to improve health conditions in Panama to make the building of that canal possible. As an added honor, the very first Distinguished Service Medal ever issued went to Dr. Gorgas when he retired as Surgeon General of the Army in 1918.

One of the Army's finest contributions to medical knowledge began in 1836, when Dr. Joseph Lovell started collecting medical books for the Surgeon General's Library. After the Civil War, Dr. John Shaw Billings was appointed Librarian, and before he retired in 1895, the collection had expanded to several thousand volumes, and he was publishing the *Index Medicus* to make it possible for a physician to find a reference to everything ever published on any given medical subject. In 1956, the Library was turned over to the Department of Health, Education, and Welfare (now the Department of Health and Human Services) to become the National Library of Medicine. It is the most complete collection of medical literature in the world.

During the Civil War, Dr. William A. Hammond started a collection of morbid specimens for pathologic study. This was the beginning of the Army Medical Museum, which expanded to the Armed Forces Institute of Pathology, one of the foremost diagnostic, teaching, and research institutions in this country.

The Medical Corps has contributed to civilian health and medicine in many other ways: Army doctors established the first American school of medicine; they published the first American textbooks on surgery, psychiatry, and bacteriology, and the first pharmacopoeia (encyclopedia of drugs and their uses); introduced smallpox vaccination in this country; started the first systematic weather reporting; published the first summary on vital statistics; began the chlorination of water, and developed numerous vaccines against diseases of man and animals.

Today the Army maintains some of the finest medical treatment facilities in existence. Medical Centers, like Walter Reed Army Medical Center in Washington, D.C., are accredited teaching institutions where internship and residency training are given, and medical and dental research are of world renown.

With centralized control vested in The Surgeon General, the Medical Department initiated many far-reaching projects that affected the medical profession in general, and brought prestige and status to the Medical Corps. Military physicians held such titles as Surgeon, Assistant Surgeon, or Medical Inspector, and were not given military rank until 1847, when military rank was assigned to members of the Medical Corps then on active duty. An Act of Congress in 1908 established the Medical Corps Reserve, the first such Army Reserve group in this country, and the forerunner of the Officers Reserve Corps in 1916.

The all-physician Medical Corps is responsible for setting the physical standards for all individuals entering military service; maintaining their health while in service; and processing them for discharge or retirement. The clinical care of dependents and retired personnel gives the Army doctor a well-rounded practice, but essentially military medicine is aimed at the care of troops, whose average age at induction is eighteen. Hence prevention of disease and injury is as important as rehabilitation. The control of the environment is becoming increasingly vital in the Army's relations with its civilian neighbors.

Since 1969, the Special Assistant to The Surgeon General for Medical Corps Affairs has served as the equivalent of the Chief of the Medical Corps. This position is currently authorized in the grade of brigadier general and entitled Chief, Medical Corps Affairs. He shares responsibility for the professional guidance, assignment, education, training, and career development of Medical Corps officers with the Commander, U.S. Army Medical Department Personnel Support Agency. In addition, the Chief, Medical Corps Affairs is currently responsible for all Professional Services, including professional standards, preventive medicine, patient administration, and professional policies and practices for the delivery of health care in the Army.

Beginning in 1971, a program was established to train enlisted personnel to be physician assistants. Graduates of this two-year program are appointed as warrant officers. They serve in combat units and in troop health clinics under the supervision of a physician.

DENTAL CORPS

All specialties of dentistry are represented in the Army Dental Corps. The mission of the Corps is one of providing all levels of dental care necessary to preserve the oral health of the Army in support of its fighting strength.

The Chief of the Dental Corps, who is also designated as the Assistant Surgeon General for Dental Services, holds the grade of major general. He or she serves as the principal advisor to The Surgeon General and Chief of Staff of the Army on all matters concerning the Dental Corps and dental services, establishes professional standards and policies for dental practice, and initiates and reviews recommendations relating to dental doctrine and organizations.

Prior to 3 March 1911, when it was established as a branch, dental support of the military was performed by civilians under contract. The first Dental Corps consisted of sixty dental surgeons. In 1916, along with most of the Medical Department, the Dental Corps was reorganized, expanded, and became fully established as a needed and valuable contributor to the health and welfare of the entire Army. Since 1978, dental personnel have been organized into Dental Activities (DENTACs) and Area Dental Laboratories (ADLs), which are commanded by Dental Corps officers. The U.S. Army Institute of Dental Research, which has provided significant contributions to health care delivery, conducts research and assists in the development of materials and techniques related to combat dentistry.

Officers are appointed to the Dental Corps upon graduation from an accredited school of dentistry and after being awarded either a degree of Doctor of Dental

Surgery (DDS) or Doctor of Dental Medicine (DMD). During his or her Army career, a dental officer can expect a variety of assignments throughout the world. Early in their career, officers are normally assigned to dental clinics in direct patient care. Opportunities for advanced education and accredited residency training in a dental specialty are offered, on a competitive basis, usually after four to five years of active service. Other positions that may be available later in one's career are clinician, residency mentor or director, dental researcher, clinic chief, dental staff officer, or dental activity commander.

THE VETERINARY CORPS

Veterinarians have been associated with the nation's military services since the mid-1800s when veterinary surgeons were authorized for each cavalry regiment. The Veterinary Corps was made a part of the Medical Department on 3 June 1916, to centralize control of the veterinary personnel caring for the Army's animals and inspecting food supplies.

With the evolution of the mechanized cavalry and technological changes in food processing, the Veterinary Corps officer assumed new roles. By virtue of education and training, the veterinarian is eminently prepared to function not only in animal medicine, but in matters of public health and comparative medicine as an integral member of the military community health team. His or her professional services encompass food hygiene, veterinary public health and preventive medicine, and veterinary medical care of military animals. The veterinarians' services are vital to the management and care of the extensive laboratory animal resources and to military research and development. The Corps' primary mission is to protect and preserve the health of people in the armed forces.

The Chief of the Veterinary Corps, who is also designated as the Assistant Surgeon General for Veterinary Services, holds the grade of brigadier general. He or she participates in assignment and career planning of Veterinary Corps officers.

All members of the Corps are veterinarians who have graduated from an accredited college of veterinary medicine after being awarded either a Doctor of Veterinary Medicine (DVM) or Veterinary Medical Doctor (VMD) degree. Many positions in the Army now require postgraduate specialized training, and the Veterinary Corps takes this into account in matching talents and interest in career planning. Veterinary officers are assigned wherever food hygiene and nutritional quality control, preventive medicine, animal medicine, or research are conducted. Veterinary Corps specialties include veterinary services, laboratory animal medicine, veterinary pathology, veterinary microbiology, and veterinary comparative medicine.

In 1980, the Air Force Veterinary Service was disestablished and the Army Veterinary Corps became the executive agent for Department of Defense Veterinary Services. In 1981, a program was established to train enlisted personnel to be veterinary food inspection technicians. Graduates are appointed as warrant officers. They assist the Army Veterinary Corps in the greatly expanded mission of providing veterinary services support throughout the Department of Defense.

MEDICAL SERVICE CORPS

There are two distinct purposes for the existence of this Corps. One is to provide scientists and specialists in the specialties allied to medicine, and the other is to provide officers technically qualified to make the Medical Department self-sustaining in the areas of administration, supply, environmental sciences, mobilization preparedness, readiness training, and engineering activities. The Medical Service

Corps is the one Corps within the Medical Department that relies heavily on the ROTC as a source of officers.

The Chief of the Corps, who has the grade of brigadier general, serves as an advisor and consultant to The Surgeon General and participates in the assignment and career planning for MSC officers and Medical Department warrant officers. Within the allied sciences, pharmacists, optometrists, biochemists, physiologists, podiatrists, audiologists, and many other specialists are commissioned to support the full range of health care services available to all members of the Army, their dependents, and other beneficiaries.

As it is now constituted, the Medical Service Corps was established in 1947 to replace the Medical Administrative Corps, Sanitary Corps, and Pharmacy Corps. It is presently organized into four sections: Pharmacy, Supply, and Administration (PS&A); Medical Allied Sciences; Sanitary Engineering; and Optometry. The four sections are further divided into twenty distinct career fields or areas of specialization. The PS&A section includes positions related to personnel management, financial management, pharmacy operations, supply management, and patient administration. MSC officers are also assigned to units equipped for medical evacuation by helicopter. The specialties included in the Sanitary Engineering section are: environmental engineering, environmental science, medical entomology, and nuclear medical science. Except for the PS&A section, where changes do occur, officers commissioned in the Medical Service Corps usually remain within their specialty for their entire career. The specialties that are included in the Medical Allied Sciences section are: audiology, medical laboratory sciences (physiology, microbiology, biochemistry, immunology, parasitology, and related laboratory sciences), psychology, social work, optometry, and podiatry.

Along with those in other Medical Department Corps, officers commissioned in the Medical Service Corps can expect to attend an orientation course at the Academy of Health Sciences, U.S. Army, located at Fort Sam Houston, Texas. Upon completion of this course they are assigned to a medical facility or activity or other Army unit requiring their particular skill.

At higher levels of operation, MSC officers are assigned to duties as comptroller, plans and operations officer, personnel manager, materiel officer, in research and development, as Deputy Commander for Administration in medical centers and community hospitals or medical units, and as key staff advisors in major headquarters, Department of the Army, and Department of Defense.

A Medical Service Corps officer may perform as a faculty member at the Academy of Health Sciences, U.S. Army, or serve in various capabilities with Army Reserve or Army National Guard medical units. The Medical Service Corps provides an excellent opportunity for the ROTC cadet. Those who have been awarded at least a bachelor's degree with a major in accounting, business administration, chemistry, education, health care administration, management engineering, personnel administration, or statistics are eligible for direct appointment to the PS&A section; and those receiving special degrees in the allied sciences of optometry, environmental engineering, entomology, environmental sciences, health physics, or other health-care related disciplines are, of course, also encouraged to apply for appointment in the Medical Service Corps.

THE ARMY NURSE CORPS

The Army Nurse Corps, established in 1901 as a result of the devoted efforts of civilian contract nurses employed by the Army to care for the sick and wounded during the Spanish-American War, is the oldest Military Nurse Corps in the United States and the first women's component of the U.S. Armed Forces. Since 1955 both women and men have been eligible for commissions in the Army Nurse Corps. Currently an all commissioned-officer corps, its mission is to provide the best possible nursing care to the American soldier and his or her family.

The Chief of the Corps, who is a brigadier general, serves as an advisor and consultant to The Surgeon General on staff policies, procedures, activities, and other matters pertaining to nursing, nursing personnel, and the Army Nurse Corps.

Army nurses serve in seven clinical specialties—community health, psychiatric-mental health, pediatrics, obstetrics, operating room, anesthesia, and medical-surgical nursing—and three functional areas—education, administration, and research—and in nurse staff positions in the major Army commands, the Office of The Surgeon General, and TOE units.

Army Medical Department short courses and civilian education programs prepare the Army nurse for practice in traditional as well as the expanded nursing roles such as nurse midwifery, nurse practitioner, and nurse specialist. In 1977, the Army Nurse Corps received accreditation as an approval body for Continuing Health Education from the American Nurses Association. In November 1979, the Army Nurse Corps published DA Pam 40-5, *Army Medical Department Standards of Nursing Practice.*

In 1976, the first ROTC graduates entered the Army Nurse Corps. In the summer of 1981, the Army Nurse Corps and the U.S. Army Training and Doctrine Command (TRADOC) began a joint effort to increase nursing student participation in ROTC. To this end, fifty scholarships were dedicated specifically for nursing students. As an additional incentive, a hospital-based, preceptorship-type summer camp was offered as an alternative to the regular ROTC summer camp. Response was highly enthusiastic and as a result, it will be offered as an approved option for the ROTC nursing cadet.

THE ARMY MEDICAL SPECIALIST CORPS

The Army Medical Specialist Corps, formulated by the enactment of Public Law 36 on 16 April 1947, is composed of three unique medical specialties—dietitians, occupational therapists, and physical therapists. Although one of the younger corps of the Army Medical Department, the individual specialties of the Army Medical Specialist Corps have been contributing far longer; as early as the Spanish-American War, dietitians were serving as civilian practitioners, and all three specialties played a large role in the rehabilitation of World War I and II casualties.

The minimum educational qualification is a bachelor's degree within the particular specialty and the appropriate professional licensures, certification, or registration. However, the Army does provide specialty post-baccalaureate training for those qualified accessions who must complete a dietetic internship or occupational therapy affiliation to become eligible for registration or certification. Additionally, a master of physical therapy degree program, affiliated with Baylor University, is conducted to provide basic, entry-level professional education. In addition to the provision of specialty training of qualified individuals or the direct accession of fully qualified practitioners, ROTC graduates, when professionally qualified, are also eligible for commission within the Army Medical Specialist Corps.

The Chief, Army Medical Specialist Corps holds the rank of colonel and serves as an advisor and consultant to The Surgeon General on all matters pertaining to the Corps. By statute, there are three Assistant Chiefs who serve as consultants in their professional specialty areas and make recommendations on career management and professional development within their specialty.

In October 1981, the Army Medical Specialist Corps implemented clinical specialization paralleling current practice in civilian health care programs to enhance the provision of patient care, to support graduate medical education, and to increase career opportunities and job satisfaction.

Army Medical Specialist Corps officers play a vitally important role not only in the comprehensive treatment and rehabilitation of patients but also in the promotion of health and prevention of injury.

Since 1955, both men and women have been eligible for commission in the Army Medical Specialist Corps and are assigned to all Army Medical Centers and Army Community Hospitals in the United States and the major oversea commands; to the Academy of Health Sciences, teaching both officers and enlisted personnel; to data processing agencies; research units; the Office of The Surgeon General; and to major command headquarters.

Appendix—Additional Duty Guide

The additional duty is the Army's way of assigning mission, administrative, housekeeping, and personnel-related responsibilities outside of primary military occupations. This appendix brings together the practical and detailed counsel necessary to get started right and to develop a program to meet the needs of a particular assignment. It doesn't, of course, tell exactly how to do any particular job, but rather it is a guide to the things that will get the job started and much easier.

A few of the mission-related duties like motor officer, food service officer, supply officer, training officer, and so on, require more time and effort than others. Many additional duties are assigned at battalion or higher level. Some duties at company level are assigned to noncommissioned officers.

The twenty-one jobs described herein were selected as comprising the hard core of a seemingly unlimited number of additional duties. They are typical of those additional duties to be found, with minor variations, at almost every organizational level. What is said about each of them focuses somewhat on small unit operations and shares experience about the most practical ways of carrying out the instructions, the intent, and the programs or procedures prescribed in the related host of official directives.

Readers will find here a valuable auxiliary guide giving an introduction, references, and new emphasis to many areas and details often overlooked. This information can speed the acquaintance with new additional duties and will serve as a long-term reference for young officers. It will also serve as a concise and handy reference for commanders at all levels.

Early in any additional duty assignment you should get acquainted with the officially published material about that particular job. Unit reference libraries should have a copy of the most often used references. But how do you know they are complete and up to date? DA Pam 310-1 tells the story. The references listed for each of the additional duties described in this Appendix were extracted from this pamphlet.

DA Pam 310-1, *Consolidated Index of Army Publications and Blank Forms*, is published only in microfiche form. It is updated quarterly. This pamphlet contains a complete listing of all of the Army's administrative publications (regulations, circulars, pamphlets, and so on); blank forms; doctrinal, training, and organization publications; supply catalogs and manuals; technical manuals and bulletins; lubrication orders; and modification work orders. In short, DA Pam 310-1 provides an index of all the information available as to what has to be done in the Army as well as the information available on how to do it. About the only information not listed for which you may have a need are the movies and training aids available to help you with your training classes. This additional information is provided in DA Pam 108-1, *Index of Army Motion Pictures and Related Audio-Visual Aids.*

Sometimes reference copies of publications are kept in more than one library. The appropriate ones may be in the training office, maintenance shop, supply room, mess hall, or elsewhere. Be sure to check this possibility before deciding a publication isn't available.

If the unit library doesn't have the needed references, don't hesitate to order them; DA Pam 310-1 should be your guide.

The material in this chapter originally was prepared by Theodore J. Crackel and published in book form as *The Army Additional Duty Guide.* It has been updated as necessary and the format has been changed for inclusion in *The Army Officer's Guide,* but it retains the flavor of the author and is incorporated here with his permission. The additional duties discussed, in order of their appearance, are:

> Ammunition Officer
> Army Emergency Relief Officer
> Claims Officer
> Class A Agent (Pay) Officer
> Courts-Martial Member
> Food Service Officer
> Income Tax Officer
> Line-of-Duty (LOD) Investigating Officer
> Motor Officer/Maintenance Officer
> NBC Officer
> Postal Officer
> Range Safety Officer
> Records Management Officer
> Reenlistment Officer
> Safety Officer
> Savings Officer
> Supply Officer
> Training Officer
> Unit Fund, Custodian/Recorder
> Unit Fund Council, President/Member
> Voting Officer

AMMUNITION OFFICER

Like most jobs, the effort and time that duty as ammunition officer takes depends on the type of unit to which one is assigned. Combat service support units may have little more than small arms ammunition, which may be stored in the arms room. A combat unit, on the other hand, may have a quantity and variety that at first makes the job seem almost impossible. Regardless of the type of unit, the ammo officer's responsibilities (and problems) will fall in three areas; storage, maintenance, and accounting.

No matter where or what type the ammo is, it needs protection. Proper storage will eliminate most ammo troubles.

First of all, be sure any storage area is well policed of flammable materials of any kind. Pile ammo in neat stacks, separated by type, caliber, and lot number. Within the limitations imposed by the size of the storage area, locate the stacks far enough apart so that if one blows, others won't immediately go up, too. In any case, keep the ammo off the ground. Have wooden strips laid between the tiers of cases to keep air circulating around the boxes to help keep them dry. Cover the stacks with a tarp or waterproof cover, but be sure to let the air circulate freely. Otherwise moisture will be trapped and eventually cause damage. If there is no covering material available, stack the boxes in such a way that water will drain off.

Repair and restencil damaged boxes immediately. (Unidentifiable ammo is automatically classified Grade 3 and is not fired.)

White phosphorus (WP or PWP) rounds need special attention. Segregate them to a clear area, and store them with projectiles nose-up (except 3.5-inch rockets, which should be stored nose-down). The white phosphorous filler can soften or melt in hot weather and could dislocate within the projectile if not properly stored. Segregate rockets of all types and point them all one way—either nose-down or toward a revetment or barricade.

When storing ammo in vehicles, check the TM and SOPs for proper storage locations and procedures. Be sure that the primers of large-caliber rounds are properly protected both in handling and in storage. Break the seal on small arms ammo boxes only when absolutely necessary. Once the seal has been broken, however, remember to inspect and clean it periodically.

In many units a portion of the basic ammo load is carried in trucks or trailers that belong to the ammo section of the support platoon. Local SOP establishes the degree of responsibility that you as the ammo officer will have for these vehicles, but from a practical—and tactical—point of view, you'll be very interested since you depend on them to get needed ammo forward.

Check preventive maintenance (PM) on the truck. Even if ammo has been well cared for, it won't be of any use if the truck carrying it breaks down. This may take tact on your part since vehicle maintenance is usually someone else's responsibility.

Here are some hints to help keep this vehicle-loaded ammo in good shape:

—Place it on wooden floor racks and ensure that all drain plugs in the bed of the vehicle are open.

—Distribute the weight evenly over the entire bed of the vehicle.

—Brace the load to prevent shifting during movement.

—Place ridgepoles under the tarpaulin to prevent water pockets.

—Raise the tarpaulin periodically to air the load.

If part of the basic load must be stacked off the vehicle, stack it by vehicle load so that it won't have to be sorted when it's needed.

Ammunition stored in bunkers or other inside areas should also be on dunnage with stripping between layers. As usual, stack it by lot number with its nomenclature markings facing outward and readable. To allow for circulation, stack it at least six inches from walls and eighteen inches from the ceiling.

There are special problems with ammo stored in tanks, APCs, and other combat vehicles. Keeping it dry is one. Open the ramp or hatches whenever possible and keep the air circulating. If ammo does get wet, wipe it off or, if possible, lay it out and let the air dry it. Any ammo that's unpacked will need a lot of care. Take care of the dirt on small arms ammo by wiping it off with a clean rag. Tank and artillery ammo is a wholly different problem, but it, too, has to be cleaned and, if it's painted, touched up frequently. Like most things, there's a right and wrong way to go about this. The vehicle or weapon TM will give the lowdown of that particular ammo and will outline any special problems.

Here are some general cleaning tips. Cartridges are usually either uncoated brass or steel with a varnish coat. Projectiles are generally either covered with enamel or a laquer paint.

Brass Cartridges. Use a clean rag to wipe off the dirt, and use copper wool (not steel) to clean off corrosion. When it's clean, wipe it off with a rag dampened with solvent and let it dry.

Coated Cartridge Cases. Use steel wool to get the paint and foreign matter off corroded or rusty spots on cartridges and projectiles. Don't use steel wool on the rotating bands or fuses—for these USE ONLY COPPER WOOL. Clean the coated cartridge with solvent. *Caution:* Don't soak the cartridge in solvent. Unless one does a thorough job, it will have to be done over again in a short time. Finally, touch up the spots that are bare of varnish with the special epoxy varnish authorized for the job. (Never use any other type.) If the unit doesn't have or can't get this varnish, turn the ammo in to someone who can. It's important that all of the exposed surface get proper protection from the atmosphere.

Projectiles. Clean corroded spots with steel wool, except the fuses. After that, use thinner to wipe it down. Again be sure that it's wiped thoroughly. Touch up bare spots with the correct enamel to match the area concerned. Don't get the paint on too thick, especially over the bourrelet. If stenciled markings are painted over, they should be restored immediately.

While the ammo is being cleaned, you will have an excellent opportunity to inspect and inventory it and to check it for dents, bulges, or scratches. If a round seems badly damaged, turn it in to the ammunition support facility and let the experts make the final decision as to whether it is safe to fire or not. Not all dented or scratched rounds are bad. If dents and scratches are the only problems and if the rounds will seat properly in weapons, they are OK to fire. Try to wobble the projectile to see if it is loose. Check the eyebolt lifting plugs of separate-loading projectiles to see that they are not cracked. While inspecting small arms ammo look for short rounds (where the bullet has been pushed back into the case), loose bullets or long rounds, dents, burrs, and cracks in cases, and corrosion or dirt on the cartridge. On finding a bad round, turn it in. If you feel that you need technical assistance in matters of serviceability, routine maintenance, or supply, you should contact your ammunition support unit for a liaison or technical assistance team.

There are two aspects of ammunition supply—training and combat. Combat resupply is requested from the S4 in accordance with the unit SOP and is moved forward on battalion ammunition trucks. Generally, the smaller unit ammunition officer isn't involved at all. With training ammunition, however, it's a different story. Then the ammo officer will be responsible for requesting it. Requests for issue and turn-in of ammunition are made on a DA Form 581. Common-type ammunition allowances for training, including qualification/familiarization, are contained in TA 23-100-6. Special one-time allowances and allowances for special training or schools are contained in other publications of the TA 23-100 series. Regardless of the allowances, however, don't allow surplus ammunition to accumulate.

Requirements should be realistically determined, and requisitions should be only for that needed—not necessarily for the total quantities authorized. After training is finished, turn in the excess ammunition and the spent cartridge cases. Inspect small arms brass thoroughly to ensure that no live rounds are included. Check with the S4 or the ammunition supply point for the turn-in procedure.

You must work closely with the training officer to be sure that you have adequate ammunition for scheduled training. In addition, you can assist others by procuring special training ammunition or demolitions for instructional use.

Ammunition malfunctions (except NBC) are reported in accordance with AR 75-1. You must make sure that both you and your personnel are familiar with the information in this regulation. Accidents or incidents involving NBC ammunition are reported in accordance with AR 395-40.

Record and file inventories and inspection reports. Use the ammunition inspection and lot number report (DA Form 3127 or 3128). The reports are prepared as prescribed by local instructions.

Safety is always a concern around ammunition. All types merit special attention and careful handling. The FM and TM for each weapon will spell out precautions. Conduct training in the safe handling and maintenance of ammunition often enough to instruct new personnel in the unit and to refresh the old hands.

The storage and maintenance of special munitions is spelled out in appropriate TMs and local regulations or SOPs. Study these carefully.

REFERENCES
AR 350-4 *Qualification and Familiarization with Weapons and Weapon Systems*
AR 385-63 *Policies and Procedures for Firing Ammunition for Training, Target Practice and Combat*
AR 385-64 *Ammunition and Explosives Safety Standards*
AR 710-2 *Supply Policy below the Wholesale Level*
FM 9-6 *Ammunition Services in the Theater of Operations*
TM 9-1370-200 *Military Pyrotechnics*
TM 9-1901-1 *Ammunition for Aircraft Guns*
TM 9-1300-206 *Ammunition and Explosive Standards*
TM 9-1300-250 *Ammunition Maintenance*
TM 9-1300-200 *Ammunition, General*

ARMY EMERGENCY RELIEF OFFICER

Army Emergency Relief (AER), a private nonprofit organization, came into being in 1942 to provide assistance to members of the rapidly expanding Army and their dependents who were faced with financial problems with which they were unable to cope and for which no appropriated funds were available. The Army Relief Society (ARS), now assimilated into AER, was established in 1900 to assist needy widows and orphans of Regular Army personnel. One of the big jobs of AER officer is to see to it that all members of the command and their dependents know that they may receive financial assistance when emergencies arise that are beyond their ability to handle.

Generally AER officers are appointed only at installations with AER sections, which are Army-wide.

As AER officer you must familiarize yourself with the policies and procedures governing emergency financial assistance contained in appropriate regulations. You should confer with local American Red Cross representatives to understand the operating relationships of these two organizations.

As the AER officer you are responsible for receiving, safeguarding, disbursing, and accounting for all of the funds. You also prepare and maintain the required financial records and reports. You interview applicants for assistance, make necessary investigations, furnish counsel, and help them as necessary in accordance with AR 930-4. You may also make loan collections, although these are usually accomplished through AER allotments. AR 930-4 contains the details of section operation including financial, accounting, and reporting requirements.

All members of the Army, active and retired, and their dependents, including spouses and orphans of deceased Army members, are eligible to receive emergency financial assistance from AER. Assistance is generally extended in the form of a loan (without interest) since Army people usually want and are able to repay. Repayment (by AER allotment) is usually in monthly installments so as not to cause hardship. Occasionally, a combination of a loan and grant or an outright grant may be the best solution. Assistance to dependents of deceased personnel is almost invariably a grant. AER also provides educational assistance, on a limited basis as a secondary mission, for dependent children of Army members pursuing undergraduate studies.

Government funds are not appropriated to provide emergency financial assistance to military personnel and their dependents. AER therefore relies on voluntary contributions from members of the Army family, repayments of loans, and income from investments to finance current operations. AER makes no appeal for funds outside the Army. Unsolicited gifts and legacies are accepted.

The Army conducts an annual fund campaign for AER to raise funds to sustain AER's capability to meet the emergency financial needs of Army members and their dependents.

Campaign material is furnished by National Headquarters, AER. As an overall guide a dollar goal is established by installation, but neither units nor individuals should be assigned a dollar quota (see AR 600-29).

AER is organized to be an important and effective instrument of morale and exists only to help the Army take care of its own. The governing policies are intentionally broad to allow flexible utilization of AER by local commanders and the chain of command. As the AER officer you will be most effective if you are aware of the view and policies of your commander and if you keep him or her regularly informed of the type and amount of assistance being rendered.

REFERENCES
AR 600-29 *Fund Raising within Department of the Army*
AR 930-4 *Army Emergency Relief: Authorization, Organization, Operations and Procedures*
DA Pam 608-2 *Your Personal Affairs*

CLAIMS OFFICER

The duties of a claims officer are primarily investigative. The gathering and accurate reporting of basic facts surrounding an incident are prerequisite to and most necessary steps toward claims settlement. Investigations fall into two categories: those to determine the facts in a situation where a claim has been made, and those that report facts about any incident that *may later* give rise to a claim. The latter is usually referred to as a "potential claim" investigation.

Claims also are divided into two categories: small claims, those that may be settled for $750 or less, and large—more substantial—claims. Officers investigating small claims should remember:

—That the amount of investigative effort is less in smaller claims.

—That evidence about small claims may be gathered by telephone or personal interview, from incident reports and other hearsay reports. Written statements of witnesses, estimates of repairs, and so on are not required.

—To use DA Form 1668 (Small Claim Certificate) for recording their investigations with brief summaries of the evidence attached.

—To be objective and fair during all phases of investigation, protecting the rights of both the claimant and the government.

—That evidence must establish that the amount claimed or agreed to is reasonable, that the claimant is the proper person, and that the government is liable for the damage or injury.

The objective in handling any claim is to gather all possible evidence in the shortest practicable time, and to stress facts and events that help to answer when, where, who, what, and how. In the full investigation required for large claims, this evidence should include statements of all available witnesses, accident reports including those in civilian police files, photographs, maps, sketches, and so on. The investigator should visit the scene of the incident and make a physical inspection of any damage. If the claim involves injury, determine with the help of the claims judge advocate whether a medical examination is required, and if so, make the necessary arrangements. AR 27-20 provides some detailed guidance on investigations of specific incidents and the evidence required for dealing with any claim.

In completing the large-claim investigation, use DA Form 1208 (Report of Claims Officer) for the report. Make specific judgments about what the evidence says and recommendations as to the extent of the liability and the amount of compensation. Submit the report to the appointing authority, who comments if he or she desires and forwards it to the appropriate approving or settlement authority.

As the claims officer you should assist persons who indicate a desire to file a claim. They should be given general instructions concerning the procedure to follow, necessary forms, and assistance in completing them. You may also assist them in assembling evidence; however, you may not disclose information that may be made the basis of a claim or any evidence that you may have collected unless you have the permission of the claims judge advocate. Your opinions and recommendations will not be disclosed to a claimant. In addition, you may not represent them in any way and must not accept any gratuity for your assistance. These claims should be presented to the commanding officer of the unit involved, or to the nearest Army post or other military establishment convenient to the claimant. Evidence to substantiate the claim should also be submitted with the claim.

One special situation worthy of mention is maneuver damage resulting from field exercises. In this instance anything that can be done on the spot for both the government and claimant in the way of collecting evidence and advising the claimant how to proceed will save much work later. Most such on-the-spot investigations come under the "potential claims" possibility, but they should be accomplished as fully as possible while all individuals and property involved are available. Reports are marked "potential claim" and submitted like regular claims.

Apart from more routine investigation and report preparation, you may find it helpful to have an idea how compensation is determined. In cases of property damage that can be economically repaired, the allowable compensation is the actual or estimated cost of restoring it to the same condition it was in immediately before the damage. Allowances may be made for the depreciation or appreciation after repairs. When property is destroyed or cannot be repaired economically, the measure of the damage is the value of the property immediately before the incident less any salvage value. Lost property is compensated for on the basis of value immediately before the loss.

In claims involving personal injury and death, allowable compensation may include reasonable medical, hospital, or burial expenses actually incurred; future medical expenses, loss of earnings and services, diminution of earning capacity, pain and suffering, physical disfigurement, and any other factor that local law recognizes as injury or damage for compensation purposes. No allowances are made in any claim for attorney fees, court costs, bail, interest, travel, inconvenience, or any other miscellaneous expense incurred in connection with submission of a claim.

REFERENCES
AR 27-20 *Claims*
AR 27-40 *Litigation*
DA Pam 27-162 *Claims*
FM 105-5 *Maneuver Control*

CLASS A AGENT (PAY) OFFICER

Though most of the Army's payrolls have been automated it may still, under some circumstances, be necessary for an agent (or an accountable disbursing officer) either to pay troops, exchange foreign currency for military payment certificates (MPC) or U.S. currency, or make payments for specified purchases or rentals. Appointing orders specify what payments the agent may make.

If you are appointed class A agent, you are personally responsible for the funds entrusted to you and for the vouchers that account for that money. At your request, the unit commander should provide adequate armed guards to protect these funds and vouchers. If you have to keep funds overnight they should be secured in an adequate safe. Field safes and combination-lock file cabinets are not normally considered adequate. If these are all that are available, an armed guard should be kept posted. In addition, provision should be made for frequent checks of the secured area by a CQ or duty officer.

Here are a list of things which you should *NOT* do while a class A agent:
—Insure entrusted funds.
—Use funds except as stated in the appointing orders.
—Gamble while entrusted with funds—even with only personal money.
—Loan, use, or deposit in any bank any portion of the funds, except as specifically instructed by the finance officer.
—Mix the funds with personal monies or attempt to balance the funds by adding to or deducting from them.
—Entrust the funds or paid vouchers to any other person for any purpose, even for the purpose of returning them to the Finance office. Unless otherwise directed, you must return the funds or vouchers personally to the finance officer. (Other possible means could be through a class B agent, by courier, or by registered mail.)

Generally, class A agent duties will involve only the payment of troops. Here is a typical sequence of pay-day actions that such an agent might take:
—After receiving your orders, watch the daily bulletin or other local medium of notification for the time and place to pick up the funds and vouchers.
—Arrange for transportation (POVs should be avoided), guards, and a suitable place for payment (such as a dayroom or dining room).
—On the day of cash pick-up, inspect vehicle condition in advance. (It is also a good idea to vary the route and timing of trips periodically.)
—Upon arrival at the Finance office, you will need a copy of your appointing orders and your Armed Forces identification.

—Before you leave the office, you should verify the cash count given you. The currency is generally $1, $5, $10, and $20 bills, packed in bundles of $100. This eases the task of counting, but you should count the bills in each bundle to ensure they contain the proper amount. You will receive a change list showing the number and denomination of bills making up the payroll. For example, it may show that you should have 280 $20 bills, 120 $10 bills, 100 $5 bills, and 203 $1 bills. You should check your count of various denominations against this list. *This is the time for you to bring any discrepancy to the attention of the disbursing officer, not later.*

—Before departure, you must sign a receipt for payroll money received. You then proceed directly to the unit or activity to be paid.

—Before starting to pay, it is best to break the payroll down into individual payments. Errors are easiest to correct while you still have the money and vouchers. You should have the exact number and denomination of bills necessary to make up all of the different payments. So that everything will come out right, each payment is made up with the largest denomination of bills possible. (For example, if the amount is $237, use eleven $20 bills, and one $10 bill, one $5 bill, and two $1 bills.) Each individual payment can be placed in a plain mailing envelope or paper-clipped to the payee's copy of the voucher.

Your pay team should be made up of two or three individuals. You *will personally pass the money* to the person being paid. A responsible NCO should assist by obtaining signatures on the original (white) vouchers. You may have a clerk pass to the payee a copy of his or her voucher after payment has been made.

—The pay table should be set up in an area where troops cannot congregate. Payments should begin promptly at the designated time.

—At the proper time, a team NCO should call the name of the first individual to be paid.

—The payee moves to the table, salutes, and signs the receipt for payment. As pay agent, you do not return the salute. The payee's signature, as part of the pay process, is checked with his or her identification card and the name on the voucher.

—If the signature is correct, the voucher is passed to you for payment. You then count out the payment and ask the payee to verify the amount. If a correction has been made by the Finance office to the amount-paid entry on the voucher (lined out and a new amount entered) the payee is required to initial the corrected amount when signing his or her name or receiving the cash.

—After verifying the amount paid, the payee receives his or her copy of the pay voucher.

—This procedure is repeated until all persons present are paid. Soldiers not present for the regular pay call may be paid as soon as possible thereafter. Hospitalized personnel on the payroll should be paid next if you can reasonably travel to their location. When considering the reasonableness of traveling to pay a soldier away from home station, you should keep in mind the hardship that not being paid on time may cause the payee. The mere fact that you must arrange special transportation or stay overnight does not in itself make the travel unreasonable. The payroll shouldn't include persons AWOL or in confinement, but if it does, they will *not* be paid, but rather their pay is returned with other funds remaining and paid vouchers upon completion of the unit payment.

—Regulations allow the class A agent twenty-four hours after payment for the return of paid vouchers and cash; however, you should return the funds as soon as possible.

—When returned, a clerk will verify the vouchers and furnish a receipt for both the return of funds and the paid vouchers.

—The amount indicated on the receipt should agree with the amount of cash returned.

—You deliver the vouchers and receipt to the cashier and turn in all cash not paid to individuals. After verification, the receipt will be signed by the finance officer and a copy returned to you. You are then properly relieved of responsibility for the funds that were entrusted to you. Such receipts, of course, should be retained at least a year in case any question should arise.

When you are paying troops that you don't know on sight, or when you pay commercial vendors, your biggest problem is establishing positive identification. In the case of paying troops, the problem is fairly simple. Since the vouchers are prepared from official records, the name on the voucher should correspond exactly to the name of the individual's Armed Forces identification card. The signature obtained must also match the signature on the identification card.

Occasionally a payee will sign his or her name in an incorrect form, i.e., not the "payroll" signature. If the signature is not in the same form as the name shown on the voucher, the incorrect signature must be lined out and the payee required to sign it again so that it does agree with the voucher.

If for some reason the payee can't sign his or her name (i.e., a man with a broken arm), the payee may authorize some other individual to sign for him or her and that signature will be regarded the same as if signed by the payee. This signing, however, must be certified to by two witnesses and the certificate attached to the voucher. The mark (X) of an individual unable to write must be witnessed by a disinterested person whose signature and address are placed adjacent to the mark (X).

Receipts for payment to commercial firms must be signed by a duly authorized officer or agent of the company. The receipt must be signed with the company name, followed by the autograph signature of the officer or agent together with his or her title. In addition to ensuring positive identification of the company representative, you must assure yourself that the representative is authorized by the company to receive payment.

More detailed information on this subject is to be found in paragraph 6-41c, AR 37-103.

REFERENCES

AR 37-103 *Finance and Accounting for Installations—Disbursing Operations*
AR 37-104-3 *Military Pay and Allowances Procedures, Joint Uniform Military Pay System (JUMPS)*
AR 37-106 *Finance and Accounting for Installations—Travel and Transportation Allowances*

COURTS-MARTIAL MEMBER

The member of a military court is essentially a member of a jury. The president of the court is, in the same context, the foreman. Member duties, as prescribed in the Manual for Courts-Martial, 1984, are like those of a juror in that each member will hear the evidence and arrive at his or her own determination of the guilt or innocence of the accused. In addition, if the accused is found guilty, courts-martial members determine the penalty. Each member, regardless of rank or position, has an equal voice and vote with the other members in deliberating and determining a decision on all questions indicated by the specifications and charges.

Most courts-martial are assigned a military judge who gives the members all of their instructions. In the absence of a military judge, the president of a special courts-martial instructs the members of the court generally on their duties. The instructions are important and worth repeating here.

> As court members, it is your duty to hear the evidence and determine the guilt or innocence of this accused and if you find him guilty, to adjudge an appropriate sentence. Under the law, the accused is presumed to be innocent of the offense. The government has the burden of proving the accused's guilt beyond a reasonable doubt. The fact that charges have been preferred against this accused and referred to this court for trial does not permit any inference of guilt. You must make your determination of the guilt or innocence of the accused based solely upon the evidence presented here in court and the instructions which I will give you. Since you cannot properly make that determination until you've heard all the evidence and received instructions, it's of vital importance that you retain an open mind until all of the evidence has been presented and the instructions have been given.
>
> You must impartially hear the evidence, the instructions on the law, and only when you are in your closed session deliberations may you properly make a determination as to the guilt or innocence of an accused. Furthermore, with regard to sentencing, if it should become necessary, you may not have any preconceived idea or formula as to either the type or amount of punishment which should be imposed if the accused were to be convicted of this offense. You must first hear the evidence in extenuation and mitigation, as well as that in aggravation, if any; the law with regard to sentencing; and only when you are in your closed session deliberations may you properly make a determination as to an appropriate sentence after considering all of the alternative punishments of which I will later advise you.
>
> It is the duty of the trial counsel to represent the government in the prosecution of this case, and it is the duty of the defense counsel to represent the accused.
>
> Counsel are given an opportunity to put questions to any witnesses that are called. When counsel have finished, if you feel there are substantial questions that should be asked, you are given an opportunity to do so. The way we handle that is to write out the question, indicate at the top the witness to whom you'd like to have the question put, and sign at the bottom. This method gives counsel for both sides, the accused, and myself, an opportunity to review the question before it is asked, since your questions, like the questions of counsel, are subject to objection. Do not allow any other member of the panel to see your question. Whether or not your question is asked, it will be attached to the record as an appellate exhibit. There are a couple of things you need to keep in mind with regard to questioning. First, you cannot attempt by your questions to help either the government or the defense. Second, counsel have interviewed the witnesses and know more about the case than we do. Very often they do not ask what may appear to us to be an obvious question because they are aware this particular witness has no knowledge on that subject.
>
> During any recess or adjournment, you may not discuss the case with anyone nor may you discuss the case among yourselves. You must not listen to or read any account of the trial or consult any source written or otherwise, as to matters involved in this case. You must hold your discussion of the case until you are all together in your closed session deliberations so that all of the panel members have the benefit of your discussion. If anyone attempts to discuss the case in your presence during any recess or adjournment, you must immediately tell them to stop and report the occurrence to me at the next session.

For any one of several reasons, an individual may be ineligible to sit as a member of a courts-martial in certain cases. Whatever the reasons, they are usually referred to as "grounds for challenge." A number of grounds for challenge are listed in RCM 912(f), MCM, 1984. If you don't believe that you should sit on the court in a particular case, you should bring this to the attention of the convening authority before the court is formally opened. Usually, you will thereupon be relieved. If the grounds for challenge first come to your attention at the trial, the trial counsel will ask that you relate to them the "ultimate" ground for the challenge. You must thereupon be careful not to relate facts that, if heard by other members, might also prejudice or disqualify them.

Unlawful influence on any court member's decisions by a senior officer should never become a problem; however, members should bear in mind that neither the commanding officer, convening authority, or senior member of the court may unlawfully attempt to influence their independent judgment. This doesn't mean that members should ignore the opinion of their seniors in court deliberations, but rather that they should not let position or rank sway their own judgment.

In order to reduce the influence that ranking members of the court might have, discussion and oral voting (when required) usually begins with the junior in rank. Votes by members of a general or special courts-martial on the findings and on the sentence, and by members of a special courts-martial without a military judge upon questions of challenge, are by secret written ballot. The junior member of the court usually collects and counts the ballots. This count is checked and announced by the court president.

A court has no power to punish its members. Nevertheless, members are expected to conduct themselves in a dignified and attentive manner and misconduct as a member of a court may be a military offense. No member should ever become a champion of either the prosecution or the defense. Such partisan behavior would cast substantial doubt upon the fairness of a trial. You must be particularly careful in your contact with counsel or other members of the court when the court is not in session. You may, however, without referring to any case pending or then being tried, carry on a normal official and social relationship with other prospective or appointed members of the court. It is proper to ask such administrative questions as the scheduled date for the court to meet, location of the trial, physical arrangements for the trial, and other matters that have no bearing on the issues of a case.

Generally, there is no objection to making notes during the trial, and these can also be taken into closed session so long as they are purely for the court member's individual use.

The guiding principle to follow at all times is that you should perform your duties without being subjected to any out-of-court influence, direct, indirect, or covert. The legal rights of an accused demand no less.

You should be well acquainted with the Manual for Courts-Martial, 1984. Reading it will allow a good orientation for court duty, even without having had the experience of participating in a trial. A prospective but inexperienced court appointee may also take advantage of opportunities to watch actual trials, particularly those conducted by general courts-martial. When appointed to serve on a court you should resolve to do your best, as conscientiously as you can.

REFERENCES
AR 27-10 *Military Justice*
AR 350-212 *Military Justice*
DA Pam 27-7 *Guide for Summary Court-Martial*
DA Pam 27-10 *Military Justice Handbook: The Counsel and the Defense Counsel*
DA Pam 27-173 *Trial Procedure*
DA Pam 27-174 *Jurisdiction of Court-Martial*

FOOD SERVICE OFFICER

There is little doubt that the quality of Army food, both in its preparation and serving, contributes to morale. It is one of the main—and could be the chief—motivating factors contributing to overall unit performance. Because of this, the food service officer's job is one that must be taken seriously, not only from the point of view of unit effectiveness, but personally because of the challenges it presents to your leadership abilities. The days of jokes about Army chow and mess halls are past. In today's Army, food is prepared by professionally trained sergeants and cooks who take great pride in their work and accomplishments.

When you are assigned as a food service officer, you are the commander's direct representative in the dining facility. You are also the direct supervisor of the food service sergeant. His or her attitude will make a big difference in how hard or how easy your additional duty will be as food service officer. The size of the dining facility for which you are responsible will determine the size of your job. A dining facility for just your company may feed only 100–200 meals per day or even less. A large, consolidated facility may feed up to 7,500 meals per day. It is also possible that you will be a company dining facility officer but that your company eats in a consolidated facility that is the responsibility of another unit. In this case, you may have to do some coordination with the food service officer who actually runs the facility, but you will not be directly responsible for feeding until your unit goes to the field with its own field kitchen.

When you are appointed as a food service officer, one of your first tasks is to set up a meeting with your food service sergeant. You need to assure him or her, without question, that you will be fulfilling your duties, but at the same time recognizing the food service sergeant's professional authority to handle the day-to-day details. Before talking with the food service sergeant for the first time, you should familiarize yourself with AR 30-1, *The Army Food Service Program*. This will detail your responsibilities, which are considerable, and give you a feel for how a dining facility operates. The food service sergeant should then be able to give you a complete rundown on:

a. Dining Facility Administration:
   1. Current regulations and SOPs
   2. Scheduling for cooks
   3. Reports
   4. Sanitation
   5. Security
b. Training:
   1. OJT for MOS 94B cooks
   2. Cross-training programs
   3. Training for field operations
c. Food Preparation, Cooking, and Serving:
   1. Menu planning
   2. Production worksheets
   3. Standard operating procedures
d. Accounting:
   1. Requesting rations
   2. Inventories
   3. Headcount data and cash control
   4. Required records needing your signature

As part of this meeting you also need to let the food service sergeant know how you intend to operate. For example:

a. You will be checking food preparation, serving, and sanitation periodically. Also, you will be paying particular attention to the production worksheet.

b. You take seriously your responsibility to sign certain reports.

c. You want the food service sergeant to discuss with you problems he or she is having and improvements he or she wants to make.

d. You are available at any time, day or night.

How successful you are as a food service officer depends on how well you follow through with the stage you have set. Let's face it, the dining facility sergeant may wish to see as little of you as possible. It is only natural since the sergeant views the dining facility as his or her domain. This is what makes leadership interesting and challenging.

How you conduct inspections of the dining facility will set your chances for success or failure. Remember that daily activities must go on in the dining facility even during your inspections. Make allowances for this, but do not let it be an excuse for a poor operation. Arrange your schedule around the dining facility schedule. A good checklist for your inspections is contained in FM 10-23-1, *The Commander's Guide to Food Service Operations.* You can also get a checklist from your headquarters or installation food advisor.

The food advisor is a good person for you to get to know. Not only is he or she an experienced food service warrant officer, but the advisor is familiar with many facilities and can help you compare your facility with the others on your post. The food advisor is also your primary source for training about your responsibility as a food service officer.

AR 30-1 is the primary regulation you will use as a food service officer. It contains information on your specific responsibilities and the responsibilities of those above and below you in the dining facility chain of command. Among other responsibilities detailed in AR 30-1, you must:

a. Make a monthly review of requisitioning procedures in your dining facility.

b. Review receiving procedures twice each month on an unannounced basis.

c. Update the commander at least quarterly on actions needed to improve security in your dining facility.

d. Track the accountability of at least four high-dollar food items each month and report the results.

e. Conduct a monthly formal review of production schedules.

f. Make a review of the disposition of leftovers each week.

g. Compute the dining facility inventory each month.

When your unit goes to the field, food service becomes even more important because the soldier looks forward to mealtime even more in the field than in garrison. It is also harder for you to carry out your responsibilities as dining facility officer, because you are working harder than usual at your regular job when your unit is in the field. About the only way to ensure good dining facility performance in the field is to have excellent performance in garrison and let it carry over into the field because of good work habits. You are working with different equipment in the field: field ranges and immersion heaters, water trailers, and ice chests. Training needs to be done on this equipment in garrison, and it needs to be well maintained before it is brought to the field.

Remember, as the food service officer, you represent the unit commander in the dining facility. He or she expects the best-quality food for the troops. The responsibility has been entrusted to you to ensure that happens. It is a job that will test your leadership skills but also offers lots of personal reward every time a soldier gets a good meal. Your dining facility sergeant and his or her cooks have a strong professional pride in what they do. Use this to your benefit.

REFERENCES
AR 30-1, *Army Food Service Program*
AR 30-7, *Operational Rations*
FM 10-23, *Army Food Service Operations*
FM 10-23-1, *The Commander's Guide to Food Service Operations*
FM 10-26, *The Army Food Advisor*
TB MED 530, *Occupational and Environmental Health Food Service Sanitation*

A complete list of dining facility reference materials is contained in AR 30-1 or FM 10-23-1. Make sure you use them.

OTHER SOURCES FOR HELP
Army doctrine for dining facility operations and the appropriate regulations are prepared by:

> Commander
> U.S. Army Troop Support Agency
> ATTN: Troop Food Service Division
> Fort Lee, VA 23801–6020

Field manuals and all Army food service training are the responsibility of the:

> Commandant
> U.S. Army Quartermaster School
> ATTN: Subsistence and Food Service Department
> Fort Lee, VA 23801–5041

INCOME TAX OFFICER

This additional duty assignment is made so that members of a command will have the opportunity to get counsel and answers to questions about income tax. As the income tax officer, you are not expected to be a full-fledged tax expert, but you are expected to know how the law applies to soldiers. The staff judge advocate, if available, is the place to send persons for assistance in complicated situations, and that office may even offer some periodic formal training for all tax officers. Unit income tax officers should be sure to take advantage of it.

The questions that income tax officers are most often asked deal with filling out returns and claiming legitimate deductions. In addition to the instructions received with each tax form, it behooves the income tax officer to get a copy of *Your Federal Income Tax*. It's revised each year to reflect changes and interpretations of the laws and provides easy-to-understand examples of how they are applied in specific cases. Many items of interest to the military person are indexed under Armed Forces. The nearest IRS office should be able to supply a copy. Another excellent source of tax information is *Federal Income Tax Information for Armed Forces Personnel*. This Department of the Navy pamphlet (NAVSO P-1983) is published annually and is available through normal publication supply channels.

These annual references are a good bet for helping the income tax officer stay up-to-date. However, here are some general guides:

—Military personnel should always include their permanent home address on their return to help establish that they are in the Armed Forces.

—Military personnel have an automatic extension when in a combat zone. They must file within 180 days after leaving the area or after being discharged from a hospital outside CONUS. This rule applies to a joint return but not to the taxpayer's spouse if filing separately. If a soldier decides to take advantage of the extension, he or she indicates COMBAT ZONE on the return when it is finally filed. If his or her spouse files their joint return while the military member is still in a combat zone, the spouse also marks the form COMBAT ZONE. (It is then unnecessary for the military member to sign the return.)

—Military personnel who are prisoners of war or who have been detained in a foreign country against their will have ninety days after release to file a tax return.

—All military on duty outside the United States and Puerto Rico are allowed until June 15 to file. However, anyone using the extension must pay interest on the amount of tax from the due date and explain the reason for the delay.

Here's a guide to some of the taxable and nontaxable pay and allowances.

Taxable income is:

Basic pay
Reserve training basic pay
Dislocation allowance
Lump sum payments such as separation pay

Nontaxable income is:

Forfeited pay (but not fines)
Mobile home-moving allowances (actual expense)
Subsistence, or the value of subsistence
Uniform allowances
Quarters allowances or the value of quarters furnished
Housing and cost-of-living allowances received to defray the cost of quarters and subsistence at a permanent duty station outside the United States
Payments made to beneficiaries of soldiers who died in active service
Pay received by enlisted personnel or warrant officers for any month or part served in combat zone. For officers, the first $500 of such monthly compensation is nontaxable.
That part of a dependency allotment contributed by the government
Sick pay is nontaxable when one is in the hospital or not duty-assigned for thirty days or longer.

Reservists not on active duty may deduct the cost and maintenance of uniforms over and above allowances received and, if Reserve drills are in location away from the Reservist's *place of business,* he or she may deduct the cost of the round-trip transportation.

A quick trial set of calculations will usually indicate that service personnel should take the standard deduction. Exceptions might be those buying a house or other property, or with substantial loans who pay a significant amount of interest.

Military personnel are also required to file state income tax returns. Since the requirements vary from state to state, it may be necessary to advise the individuals to contact their states for copies of any material available.

REFERENCES
DA Pam 608-2 *Your Personal Affairs*
Your Federal Income Tax (Internal Revenue Service Pub 17)
Instructions for Preparing Your Federal Income Tax Return (IRS)
If Your Return Is Examined (IRS Document No 5202)
Federal Income Tax Information for Armed Forces Personnel (NAVSO P-1983), published annually by Department of the Navy

LINE-OF-DUTY (LOD) INVESTIGATING OFFICER

"Line-of-Duty" and "misconduct determinations" are phrases descriptive of the findings made to determine whether an individual's disease or injury was incurred while the person was conducting himself or herself properly *in his or her role as a member of the Army.* Those assigned to investigate and make these determinations must do so carefully, since they will have a great effect upon the concerned individuals and their dependents. Investigations are made primarily to provide data for the administration of federal statutes affecting the rights, benefits, and obligations of members of the Armed Forces.

Under specific circumstances, a finding could cause a person to be separated from the Service without entitlement to severance pay. In the case of death, these investigations could lead to findings that would make some person's dependents ineligible for many or all normal benefits. On the other hand, an LOD investigating officer could confirm that those concerned are indeed entitled to all benefits under the law. The importance of conducting a thorough and impartial investigation in accordance with the requirements of applicable regulations cannot be overemphasized.

The job of the line-of-duty investigating officer is generally to investigate, record, evaluate, make findings, and report these findings. The details of how to accomplish this are found in AR 600-33 (Line of Duty Investigations) and AR 15-6 (Boards, Commissions, Committees; Procedure for Investigating Officers and Board of Officers in Conducting Investigations). Here is a brief rundown of what you, as the LOD investigating officer, should be doing and some guidelines you may follow.

The Investigation. You must notify the individual concerned of the impending investigation. If practicable, he or she should be permitted to be present at the examination of witnesses if the investigation is to be continued beyond the examination of documentary evidence. If not present, the individual will be permitted to respond to adverse allegations.

You should visit the scene of the incident as early as possible. You should record all the relevant evidence such as statements of witnesses, photographs, diagrams, letters, results of laboratory tests, observations and reports of local officials, extracts of local laws and regulations, descriptions, weather reports, the date and exact time of the incident, and so on. This documentation should reflect every fact and circumstance that you will consider in making your findings and report. Before the testimony of witnesses is taken, they must be advised of their rights under Article 31 of the Uniform Code of Military Justice, or the Fifth Amendment to the Constitution.

The subject of the line-of-duty investigation is permitted to submit evidence or statements, sworn or unsworn. Before his or her statement is taken, the subject must be advised of legal rights under Article 31, Uniform Code of Military Justice, and of the purpose of the investigation. If a statement from the individual is not obtained, you must state the reason in your report.

After you have acquired the evidence, you must *evaluate* it and *determine,* in your judgment, the *exact circumstances* under which the injury, disease, or death occurred. You make a summary of your findings in the "Remarks" section of the report of investigation. Findings as to line of duty and misconduct must be arrived at by the investigating officer in all actions except death, in which case Headquarters, Department of the Army makes the final determination.

In every formal investigation, the purpose is to find out whether there is evidence of intentional misconduct or willful negligence that is substantial and of a greater weight than supports any different conclusion so as to rebut the presumption of "in line of duty." To arrive at such decisions, several basic rules can be applied to various situations. The specific rules of misconduct are:

Rule 1. Injury or disease proximately caused by the intentional misconduct or willful negligence is not in line of duty. It is due to misconduct. This is a general rule and must be considered in every case in which misconduct or willful negligence appears to be involved.

Rule 2. Mere violation of military regulations, orders, or instructions, or of civil or criminal laws, if there is no further sign of misconduct, is no more than simple negligence. Simple negligence is not misconduct.

Rule 3. Injury or disease that results in incapacitation because of the abuse of alcohol and other drugs is not in line of duty. It is due to misconduct.

Rule 4. Injury or disease that results in incapacitation because of the abuse of intoxicating liquor is not in line of duty. It is due to misconduct.

Rule 5. Injury incurred while knowingly resisting a lawful arrest, or while attempting to escape from a guard or other lawful custody, is incurred not in line of duty. It is due to misconduct.

Rule 6. Injury incurred while tampering with, attempting to ignite, or otherwise handling an explosive, firearm, or highly flammable liquid in disregard of its dangerous qualities is incurred not in line of duty. It is due to misconduct. This rule does not apply when a member is required by assigned duties or authorized by appropriate authority to handle the explosive, firearm, or liquid, and reasonable precautions have been taken.

Rule 7. Injury caused by wrongful aggression, or voluntarily taking part in a fight or like encounter, in which one is equally at fault in starting or continuing the fight, is not in line of duty. It is due to misconduct. The rule does not apply when a person is the victim of an unprovoked assault and he sustains injuries in an attempt to defend himself.

Rule 8. Injury caused by driving a vehicle when in an unfit condition, and the member knew or should have known about it, is not in line of duty. It is due to misconduct. A member involved in an automobile accident caused by his having fallen asleep while driving is not guilty of willful negligence solely because he fell asleep.

Rule 9. Injury because of erratic or reckless conduct, or other deliberate conduct without regard for personal safety or the safety of others, is not in the line of duty. It is due to misconduct.

Rule 10. A wound or other injury deliberately self-inflicted by a member who is mentally sound is not in line of duty. It is due to misconduct.

Rule 11. Intentional misconduct or willful negligence of another person is charged to a member if the latter has control over and is thus responsible for the former's conduct, or if the misconduct or neglect shows enough planned action to establish a joint enterprise.

Rule 12. The line of duty and misconduct status of a member injured or incurring disease while taking part in outside activities, such as business ventures, hobbies, contests, or professional or amateur athletic activities, is determinable as any other case under the applicable rules and facts presented in the case. To determine whether an injury is due to willful negligence, the nature of the outside activity should be considered with the training and experience of the member.

After you have completed your investigations and evaluation and have arrived at your findings, you are ready to complete the report. These reports are submitted on Report of Investigation—Line of Duty and Misconduct Status (DD Form 261). You must be sure that all of your conclusions are based solely on the evidence reflected in and attached to your report, and that the source of all the evidence is properly reflected. Then the finished report is forwarded to the appointing authority.

REFERENCES

AR 15-6 *Procedure for Investigating Officers and Boards of Officers Conducting Investigations*

AR 600-10 *The Army Casualty System*

AR 600-33 *Line of Duty Investigations*

AR 635-40 *Physical Evaluation for Retention, Retirement, or Separation*

MOTOR OFFICER/MAINTENANCE OFFICER

As the new Motor Officer your first questions are usually about the type and quantity of equipment you'll be responsible for. This will vary from a few wheeled vehicles to more than a hundred, and from wheeled vehicles alone to a variety of wheel and track vehicles such as those found in a tank or mech-infantry company.

One of the keys to success of the maintenance mission is the motor sergeant, who most likely was selected for technical knowledge, mechanical ability, and, most important, aptitude for organization and supervision. He or she is responsible to you for the implementation of your policies and the enforcement of SOP and regulations governing the operation of the maintenance section. It's important that you work through and with him or her.

If you just joined the unit, you should get acquainted with the maintenance area right away and make some mental notes about the general conditions of the shop and the appearance of the mechanics.

—Is the shop adequately lighted?

—Are safety precautions such as fire regulations followed?

—Is the shop floor free of grease, oil and dirt?

—Are blocks used under jacked-up vehicles and are the wheels chocked?

—Are vehicles that are not being worked on removed from the shop?

—Do mechanics seem adequately supervised?

—Are mechanics using the TMs to perform or check their maintenance properly?

—Are mechanics using the equipment inspection and maintenance worksheet (DA Form 2404) in their work?

—Are mechanics or supervisors making proper entries in the equipment record folder and historical records?

The answers to these basic questions will help you get the feel for the adequacy of your maintenance organization. If the answers are YES to all of these questions, then indications are that the organization is a real gem! If, on the other hand, you've had to answer NO to one or more questions, then you need to take a closer, more critical look at the operation.

Next, you should study the unit maintenance SOP. You should find out what the policy has been and not be in too big a hurry to change things. Check higher headquarters maintenance SOP and directives to see what can be expected in the way of support and what is required to receive it. Usually when unit workload exceeds the capabilities of a section, help can be obtained from battalion maintenance. (The same is often true of direct support maintenance assistance to separate companies.) One shouldn't ask for help unless it's needed, but when it is, neither foolish pride nor independence should be allowed to get in the way of ensuring that a unit's vehicles are ready to move.

Repair parts supply support is normally handled by the battalion maintenance shop. The repair parts stocked locally are determined by consolidated authorized organizational stockage lists (AOSL), organizational maintenance technical manuals and parts manuals on individual items of equipment, and documented demand experience of the unit. A list of the repair parts to be stocked locally is known as the prescribed load list (PLL). Necessary parts or assemblies other than those stocked will be ordered by the battalion parts section from the direct support maintenance unit servicing it. Arrange to follow the paperwork on some repair parts supply actions to see how the system works. You will probably find that you spend a lot of time checking on parts that have been ordered and not received. *Proper follow-up is necessary.* After designated periods (dependent on the priority of parts requests) the parts clerk should initiate tracers to check the status of requisitions. You should be sure that he or she does and that you are informed of the answers received. DA Pam 700-2 contains a detailed discussion of the repair parts supply system.

When you become a maintenance officer, you usually must sign for some or all of the tools, equipment, and vehicles assigned to your section. Here, as everywhere else, there should be a complete joint inventory with the old hand-receipt holder or property book officer. Don't sign for anything that can't be seen or found. Somewhere, sometime, there has to be an accounting, so don't get stuck with the responsibility (and pecuniary liability) for something that was never there.

One of the big bugaboos in an automotive maintenance account are the tool sets. The new maintenance officer cannot be expected to know what is in these sets or even what all of the items look like. *PS Magazine,* however, has come to the rescue and published complete lists of the tools with drawings to assist in their identification. Get these issues or reprints of them:

—Automotive Mechanics Tool Kit, Issue 156
—No. 1 Common, Issue 160
—No. 2 Common, Issue 176

Some separate units responsible for their own semiannual PM service may also get a No. 1 Supplemental Set. If that is the case, see PS Issue 172.

Reprints of these *PS Magazine* articles are often available in text or in the form of supplementary material for service schools. All of these tool sets are also described in applicable supply publications.

In addition to these "common" tool sets, Tool Kit, Special Set A, consists of special tools peculiar to each different vehicle and not included in the organizational maintenance or general mechanic's tools. These special sets are described in the organizational maintenance parts manual (−20P) for the applicable vehicle.

Basic Issue Items (BII) that should accompany each vehicle are described and listed in the back of the applicable operator's technical manual (−10).

In touring the maintenance area, you undoubtedly will see a variety of miscellaneous equipment such as generators, portable heating units, air compressors, and so on . Most of these require special operator training and licensing. You should find out who is responsible for the operation and operator's maintenance of this equipment. One soldier and an alternate should be appointed by the motor sergeant to operate each item. It's also a good idea to know who supports you with organizational and higher maintenance for this equipment. Operator manuals or instructions and applicable equipment record forms should be available for inspection and daily use. Certain safety requirements apply particularly to these pieces; for example, gasoline must not be stored in these items when they're kept in the shop.

Not all maintenance jobs can be accomplished at the organizational maintenance level. To find out exactly what one can and cannot do, see the maintenance allocation chart in Appendix II of each −20 manual.

It's easy to see how important publications are to the maintenance effort. There's no substitute for the proper manuals. You should have the −10, −12, −20, and −20P (Parts Manual) for each item of equipment in your unit. Check DA Pam 310-1 for the latest changes to technical manuals, supply manuals, and lubrication orders.

Today's Army requires more and more reliable information to plan replacement and procurement of the equipment needed to keep its operational readiness at the highest possible level. Data that provides DA with information about equipment age, reliability, and potential is recorded in the Army equipment record forms. DA Pam 738-750 is the guide and authority to this system. It contains a list of the necessary reportable equipment forms and instructions for completing and maintaining them.

Training organizational-maintenance personnel is always a problem. In the average unit, the ideal solution is to requisition school-trained replacements, or to utilize available schools by sending the unit's own untrained replacements. The only disadvantage to the latter course is shortened retainability, but it does offer the advantage that you can personally select your maintenance people. The least acceptable, but probably most often used method is supervised on-the-job training (SOJT). The most can be accomplished in SOJT by pairing off the new individual with a knowledgeable "old hand." This apprenticeship arrangement can be doubly rewarding since the senior individual gets an opportunity to develop leadership abilities. Personal interest on the part of both the motor officer and the motor sergeant is necessary to the success of the SOJT program. Individuals work harder and better when they know their supervisors are interested in *and* appreciate their efforts. The lack of formal training can be offset somewhat by local instruction.

If, after observing the operation for a while, you are not satisfied with the performance of your maintenance section, you should get together with the motor sergeant and work out a new arrangement. Support units may find that a job-by-job assignment of mechanics is best, while in a tactical unit, one mechanic may be assigned the responsibility for providing a single platoon with organizational-maintenance support. This will allow the mechanic to become intimately familiar with the equipment he or she is responsible for. These are but two of many possible solutions. Adopt the one that's best for the unit.

Being a motor officer is one job that requires some time—time to learn what it's all about, time to learn the mechanic's capabilities, time to supervise. The commander depends directly on the motor officer and maintenance section to provide vehicles and equipment for training or combat. If you learn your job well, train your people, and apply your knowledge and experience, you'll provide timely and efficient support.

A word about command maintenance inspections. These inspections are scheduled to check on the status of vehicles and equipment. These are usually scheduled and announced in advance so extra effort can be exerted to have everything in the best possible shape. They are designed to help motor officers tighten up on their maintenance procedures. Properly viewed, they are a valuable aid in the maintenance effort.

REFERENCES
AR 710-2 *Material Management for Using Units, Support Units and Installations*
AR 750-1 *Army Material Maintenance Concepts and Policies*
TM 9-243 *Use and Care of Handtools and Measuring Tools*
TM 9-8000 *Principles of Automotive Vehicles*
FM 21-300 *Driver Selection and Training (Wheeled Vehicles)*

FM 21-301 *Driver Selection, Training, and Supervision, Tracked Vehicles*
FM 21-305 *Manual for the Wheeled Vehicle Driver*
FM 21-306 *Manual for the Tracked Combat Vehicle Driver*
DA Pam 738-750 *The Army Maintenance Management System*
PS Magazine—All Issues

NBC OFFICER

As an additional duty this assignment presents a critical challenge. It is the NBC officer's responsibility to become proficient in ways to survive, exist, and function after a nuclear, biological, or chemical attack—and train the officer's unit to do the same.

First, it should be relatively easy for both the NBC officer and NCO to receive training at one of the Army's NBC schools. Find out from the unit training section what's available and apply right away. NBC training is a recurring subject, and repeated classroom hours are a drudgery for instructor and instructed alike. Practical hands-on training is without a doubt the best way, but it takes more planning, more material, and more instructors. Nevertheless, it's well worth the effort. The NBC officer must *plan ahead.* Plan for the time you'll need to prepare the instruction, get the supplies and training aids, and rehearse with assistant instructors. There are a number of training aids available for making training more realistic. TA 20-2 lists training equipment available for NBC training; training ammunition and miscellaneous ammunition and explosives are listed in TA 23-100 and TA 23-101; chemical supply data is given in FM 3-8; allowances of Chemical Corps expendable supplies is in TA 3-104; allowances of protective clothing are included in TA 50-901, TA 50-902, and TA 50-914. Each of these references can be used to advantage in planning the course. Appendix II of FM 21-48 discusses these training materials and practical ways to procure, fabricate, and use them.

Proficiency tests and exercises are among the most effective training vehicles. FM 21-48 will give you valuable help in setting them up. Integrate NBC training whenever possible with unit tactical training. After all, the object is to train the unit to continue its mission in an NBC environment. The necessity of continuing the mission applies to all units, combat and support. Appendix III, FM 21-48 gives examples of this integrated training. Through experience and knowledge, you can devise other training situations to meet your unit needs.

You should seek professional advice and assistance from the staff chemical officer at brigade, division, or other higher headquarters. He or she will advise in planning unit exercises and can give technical assistance when necessary.

One of the most vital aspects of NBC defense is the accurate and timely reporting of enemy attacks. You will have to use your imagination and experience to devise effective training mediums in this area—it has to be done. Merely writing the data on a slip of paper and handing it to a soldier to be put into the proper format and transmitted doesn't really accomplish much.

Once you have devised an effective training aid or system, you shouldn't keep it a secret. If you have set up a training course and trained assistant instructors to operate it, you can use it to train 500 people almost as easily as 50 or 100. You should expect to share your facilities with other units in the area. It's a two-way street and can be advantageous to all. Many units find it profitable (even necessary) to pool people and talents for NBC training.

The NBC officer's unit is required to have both survey and monitoring teams whose members are specially trained. You will have to set up these teams and train them. You will have to learn about area damage control. In rear areas this is directed primarily toward minimizing the impairment of combat service support after mass destruction or mass casualty attack. In forward areas this is directed toward minimizing interference with tactical operations and loss of combat power. The mission and organization of the particular unit determines to a large degree the mission of these teams, but in any case their make-up and procedures should be covered in the unit SOP. Since these teams are sent into hazard areas to assist individuals and units who have been subjected to an NBC attack, they need additional training on first aid, evacuation, and decontamination techniques. Special effort here could pay large dividends.

In addition to Department of the Army NBC literature, almost every level of command publishes regulations, directives, pamphlets, or SOPs on the subject. These should be studied for pertinent information about local problems and special requirements.

Remember that, as the NBC officer, your effort should be aimed at keeping your unit operationally effective within an NBC environment. Also remember that although soldiers can learn the principles of NBC from lectures, films, and demonstrations, they can learn best by direct, first-hand experience with toxic and simulated agents.

REFERENCES

AR 220-58 *Organization and Training for Chemical, Biological, and Radiological Defense*
AR 385-32 *Protective Clothing and Equipment*
FM 3-10 *Employment of Chemical Agents*
FM 3-12 *Operational Aspects of Radiological Defense*
FM 21-40 *NBC (Nuclear, Biological and Chemical) Defense*
FM 21-48 *Planning and Coordinating Chemical, Biological, Radiological (CBR) and Nuclear Defense Training*
FM 101-40 *Armed Forces Doctrine for Chemical Warfare and Biological Weapons Defense*
TM 3-216 *Technical Aspects of Biological Defense*
TM 3-220 *Chemical, Biological, and Radiological (CBR) Decontamination*
TM 3-221 *Field CBR Collective Protection*
TM 3-240 *Field Behavior of Chemical, Biological, and Radiological Agents*
TM 3-6665-225-12 *Maintenance Manual: Alarm Chemical Agent, Automatic . . .*
TM 3-6665-254-12 *Detector Kit Chemical Agent ABC-M18A2*
TM 8-285 *Treatment of Chemical Agent Casualties*
TM 10-277 *Chemical, Toxicological and Missile Fuel Handlers Protective Clothing*
TM 11-6665-213-12 *Radiac Meter IM-174/PD*
TM 11-6665-214-10 *Radiac Meters IM-93/UD, IM-93A/UD, and IM-147/PD*
TC 3-1 *How to Conduct NBC Defense Training*

POSTAL OFFICER

The postal officer has responsibility for the overall operation of unit mail service including active supervision of the mail clerk and daily checks and inspections of the mail room.

The mail room should be a separate and secure room, utilized for no other purpose. If registered or certified mail is handled, have a field safe or as a minimum, a locked container that can be physically secured to prevent its removal. Secure official registered or official certified mail that is held overnight in accordance with AR 380-5.

Only one mail clerk may have the keys or combinations to the mail room and locked containers. The unit postal officer has the second key (there must be only two) or the only other copy of combinations. This second set of keys and/or combinations should be sealed in separate envelopes (PS Form 3977) marked to identify the contents, and signed across the flap (the postal officer and clerk) to protect against tampering. The envelopes should be kept in a safe place such as a company safe.

Mail clerks are appointed on DD Form 285 (appointment of unit mail clerk or mail orderly). Enough copies should be made to allow distribution to the individual, the unit file, the serving APO or post office, and the battalion or consolidated mail room, if one is used. The forms must be validated by the serving postal facility.

Mailboxes or receptacles for outgoing mail must be strong enough to make deposited mail reasonably safe and must be physically secured to prevent removal.

Establish hours for collection and distribution of mail, based on the schedule of the serving postal unit. Record mail collection hours on a USPS Label 55 and post on all mail receptacles. Ensure that mail is picked up promptly as posted. Incoming mail must be delivered personally to addressees and *not,* for example, left on bunks or footlockers. Hold mail for soldiers temporarily absent or en route for later delivery. Forward or return to the sender immediately mail for personnel no longer with your unit.

The mail room must maintain a unit directory of all personnel (other than dependents) who receive mail through the unit. Individuals joining or departing prepare a DA Form 3955, which is used in making or updating the directory. These forms are maintained in alphabetical order in one file, regardless of grade or status. Upon departure, locator cards are retained as prescribed in DOD 4525.6-m, Vol. II.

Undeliverable mail can be a problem. This is the type of mail that tends to pile up since it takes extra time to process. You should watch for this in your checks and inspections. DOD 4525.6-m, Vol. II discusses the procedures and proper endorsements for returning undeliverable mail. A copy of this regulation and applicable changes must be kept in each mail room.

You should check daily that all registered, numbered insured, and certified mail is properly accounted for. You should verify the registers each day and retain them on file. Subordinate units, such as companies serviced by a battalion mail room, give a receipt for this; the original of this receipt remains at the battalion mail room. The duplicate is your record and you can use it to check accountability and delivery of these pieces. Each addressee signs the duplicate upon delivery of his or her mail. If a piece is undeliverable, the mail clerk should make a notation of the DD Form 434 showing the reason. PS Form 3801, "Standing Delivery Order," PS Form 3849A, "Delivery Notice or Receipt," or PS Form 3849B, "Delivery Reminder or Receipt," may be used. All of the undeliverable mail is returned to the source from which it was received. A chain of receipts must be maintained on all accountable mail.

Here are things to watch out for—first, the obstruction of correspondence and the theft or receipt of stolen mail (18 U.S.C. 1701, 1702, 1708); second, mailing obscene or indecent matter (18 U.S.C. 1461); and third, removal of postage stamps from mail (18 U.S.C. 1720).

The unit postal officer should report promptly any known or suspected postal offenses, including the loss, theft, destruction, or other mistreatment of mail to the installation postal officer, the postal officer at the serving APO, or the local military investigative agency. Unit mail clerks suspected of mistreatment of mail should not be relieved of postal duties while under suspicion or investigation.

Free mailing privileges have been granted military personnel serving in specifically designated combat areas. Personal letters, postcards, and tape-recorded correspondence qualify for this service when they have the complete return address in upper left corner and the word *free* handwritten in the upper right corner. Envelopes should be no larger than 5 inches x 11½ inches and should not be endorsed "Air Mail."

Even in areas or times when the free mailing privilege is not in force, any member of the Armed Forces may send letters without a stamp. Postage is collected from the addressee. This service is extended to handle emergency correspondence when stamps are not available, and shouldn't be overused. The envelope is marked "Soldier's Mail" and signed by the unit commander.

Mail service is particularly important in the field as a morale factor, so unit postal officers should try to ensure that everyone receives his or her mail as quickly as possible, especially those individuals in units that are cross-attached. Make arrangements also for proper handling of mail for dependents overseas who remain at "home station" during field exercises.

There are times in the field, usually around payday, when the troops need money orders, stamps, and other postal items. The unit postal officer authorizes the mail clerk to purchase them for these individuals, using unit mail clerk's receipt for funds and purchase record (DD Form 1118), which the mail clerk and the purchaser complete in duplicate. The original is kept by the unit and the duplicate given to the purchaser. The purchaser acknowledges receipt of the item by signing the original. The original copies are retained in the unit files.

Courses of instruction for postal clerks are generally given periodically by the serving postal facility. Every unit postal officer should take advantage of this training to refresh abilities of mail clerks and to train necessary replacements.

REFERENCES
AR 340-3 *Official Mail*
AR 340-5 *Correspondence and Mail Management*
DOD 4525.6-m, Vol. II

RANGE SAFETY OFFICER

The designation of range safety officer conveys a special responsibility and obligation to see that conditions and procedures that are normally safe do not become unsafe, resulting in injury to personnel and damage to equipment. Specific safety requirements for each different weapon and category of ammunition are spelled out in the applicable technical and training publications. Before going to the range, the safety officer should become familiar with these requirements. The range safety officer works for the range officer-in-charge (OIC), who has overall responsibility for the conduct of firing. The latter should be contacted for instructions or considerations about:

—Maintenance and policing of range.

—Selection of competent and qualified range safety personnel assistants.

—Preparation of necessary maps.

—Posting range guards, barriers, and signals.

—Prescribing the wearing of steel helmets under certain conditions.

—Stationing of ambulances, emergency-type medical vehicles, and medical personnel.

—Arrangement for alternate means of medical evacuation, such as by air, and the applicable notification procedures, frequencies, signals, and so on.

—Measures to protect down-range personnel.

—Taking suitable precautions to prevent unauthorized trespass or presence on ranges.

—Any other duty or activities to ensure safe operation of the ranges.

As the range safety officer, you should contact your safety team as soon as its members are designated and brief them on what their job will be. It is important that they understand what is expected of them. The specific safety requirements that apply to the weapons and ammunition that will be on the range should be reviewed with them. Remember, however, that while you can delegate part of your authority in regard to safety, you cannot likewise delegate your responsibilities.

One of your first duties at the range is to conduct a safety orientation for all personnel. You should do this prior to the opening of the range. You should also supervise the safe handling of ammunition. Both before and during firing, all ammunition and explosives or hazardous components must be handled and assembled in the manner prescribed by applicable safety regulations and appropriate technical manuals and field manuals.

—Place all ammunition at firing sites out of range of any weapon back-blast, and store it so as to minimize the possibility of ignition, explosion, or detonation.

—Issue ammunition to troops only on the "ready" or firing line.

—Cover all ammunition to protect it from the elements and against direct rays of the sun. Provide enough air circulation around the ammunition to maintain uniform temperature.

—Transport and store boosters, rockets, fuses, detonators, chemical munitions, and so on separate from other ammunition and as specifically prescribed.

—Fuse ammunition only on the firing line and only as needed.

—Do not allow any round of ammunition, including practice and blank ammunition, to be *forced* into the chamber of any type weapon.

See that weapons are handled safely. Be personally aware of all of the special requirements of each weapon, such as the danger areas behind weapons such as rockets and recoilless rifles.

Are necessary warning signals and signs in place? Display range and danger flags and, when necessary, warning signs or flashing red lights at appropriate points. Proper warning devices are available from the office responsible for range maintenance and supervision.

Restrict all firing to designated firing points. No person should leave the firing line or remove material from it without permission from the range safety officer or the officer in charge of the range.

Individuals assigned as range safety officers will supervise the handling of misfires, hangfires, and cookoffs. It's important that all personnel understand the nature of these malfunctions as well as their proper preventive and corrective procedures.

You must make the final determination *before firing* that settings placed on weapons and ammunition will impact the rounds within safety limits. This includes settings on fire-control equipment, fuse setting, and correct ammunition and charge. After firing, you require all weapons to be clear and safe before they are removed from the firing line.

You position yourself where you can exercise maximum supervision over the safe conduct of firing. You should have no other assigned duties on the range while acting as range safety officer. Your job is to minimize the possibility of accidents.

At the same time, you keep your assistants organized so that you can accomplish your mission without unduly interfering with the smooth progress of training.

REFERENCES
AR 75-15 *Responsibilities and Procedures for Explosive Ordnance Disposal*
AR 385-26 *Use of Explosives and Pyrotechnics in Public Demonstrations, Exhibitions and Celebrations*
AR 385-62 *Regulations for Firing Guided Missiles and Heavy Rockets for Training, Target Practice, and Combat*
AR 385-63 *Policies and Procedures for Firing Ammunition for Training, Target Practice, and Combat*
AR 385-64 *Ammunition and Explosives Safety Standards*
AR 385-65 *Identification of Inert Ammunition and Ammunition Components*
FM 5-25 *Explosives and Demolitions*
TM 9-1300-200 *Ammunition, General*
TM 9-1300-206 *Ammunition and Explosives Standards*
TM 9-1300-250 *Ammunition Maintenance*

RECORDS MANAGEMENT OFFICER

One of the things inspectors dig into first is a unit's records. A large part of what goes on in every unit is reflected in its files of actions, transactions, and training. A job as records management officer involves inspecting and supervising unit record-keeping to ensure compliance with regulations and established procedures. In most units files are everywhere—the orderly room, supply room, training office, maintenance shops, mess hall. The records management officer must find them.

The Army has established a functional files system, a method for keeping records and reference material, and a guide to its disposition when no longer needed. Since your role as unit records management officer is mostly advisory, you need to know the system thoroughly. You should study the references listed below. Unit files, wherever they are, are the direct responsibility of those who maintain them. Nevertheless, as records management officer, you have the responsibility to correct any misuse of the system. This takes a real diplomat and leader.

The records management officer's job is one of constant inspection, which should concentrate in two areas—proper *categorization* and proper *labeling*.

Many papers are difficult to classify for filing. However, there is always one major subject that serves as a basis for filing. For most units these major subjects—or functions—are spelled out in AR 340-2.

Because of the nature of the particular unit, there may be a need for special files not described in AR 340-2, but provided for in AR 340-18. For example, an engineer unit may have a need for mapping and geodetic files. Special files are authorized, as needed, below division level.

As you dig into the mechanics of the system you'll see why labeling of file folders is important. The label tells what is in the folder, how long it will be kept in the active file, and what to do with it at the end of the active period.

You have an indirect responsibility for all the files maintained by your unit. It's your job to help those with direct responsibility by detecting errors and helping correct them. Therefore, the more you know about the system, the better you can manage the attendant records.

REFERENCES
AR 340-1 *Records Management Program*
AR 340-2 *Maintenance and Disposition of Records in TOE and Certain Other Units of the Army*
AR 340-18 *Functional Files Update*

REENLISTMENT OFFICER

Officers with this primary duty are found in all major commands and in other commands or installations where the enlisted strength exceeds 5,000. Installations and organizations not authorized to have career-counseling personnel on a primary-duty basis appoint an officer and a noncommissioned officer to carry out the reenlistment functions on an additional duty basis. The reenlistment officer's job, hence, is to aid the commander in the reenlistment effort, and to provide guidance and assistance to NCO career counselors.

It is a cardinal rule that every reenlistment officer keep his or her commander informed on all matters pertaining to the reenlistment program. This includes changes in the qualifications or procedures used in processing applicants for reenlistment. These are outlined in AR 601–210.

As the reenlistment officer, you should be alert for changes in this and other pertinent documents by maintaining contact with reenlistment and personnel sections of higher headquarters. You should keep up to date on the availability and requirements for reenlistment options and other specialized career options.

The reenlistment officer should make sure that orientations are conducted for newly assigned officers and enlisted personnel in grades E-5 and above, informing them of the policies, procedures, responsibilities, and objectives of the reenlistment program. The program needs to be a continuing thing, but in the long run its effectiveness is a reflection of the prevalent attitude of the unit.

There are two films for use as a part of the orientation of new officers and NCOs. The first, *The Company We Keep,* offers suggestions and presents a philosophy for effective reenlistment programs. The second, *The One That Got Away* (MF 12-9323), may be shown to officers and NCOs at the discretion of the commander. If used, it should precede *The Company We Keep.* These films are available through the Audio-Visual Communication Center serving the unit.

New commanders want to be apprised of their responsibilities in relation to the reenlistment program. They are:

—Counseling and interviewing eligible individuals (see AR 601-210) eight to ten months prior to the expiration of term of service (ETS) and forwarding the name and mailing address of each individual recommended for reenlistment to the career counselor who includes him or her in a direct-mail reenlistment campaign. This campaign consists of five reenlistment information folders, mailed one per month by DA.

—Requiring all personnel completing their first tour (or with four years or less for pay purposes at ETS) to attend a showing of the film *Something to Build On* approximately four months before ETS.

—Informing recommended individuals of the reenlistment opportunities that will be available to them at the time of separation or within three months thereafter.

—Reenlisting individuals desiring unbroken service the day following the date of discharge, even when that day is a nonduty day.

—Establishing procedures to bar untrainable or unsuitable individuals from reenlisting (see para 8c, AR 635-200).

The *Reenlistment Handbook for Unit Commanders* is a guide designed to give support and information needed to formulate and conduct an effective unit reenlistment program. You should be sure that your unit commander has one, and you should get one for yourself. Occasionally a person is encountered who is felt to be exceptionally worthy of retention in the active Army, but who for some reason is not qualified for reenlistment. (The reason could be lost time, over-age, conviction of a minor offense, medical, or other.) In this case, you may request a waiver of reenlistment disqualification in accordance with AR 601-210. Waivers are also possible for personnel who want to attend an Army Service school, but who do not meet the minimum prerequisites for the desired course. These waiver requests are submitted as directed in paragraph 4-26, AR 600-200.

If the unit has room for a separate reenlistment office, it will do the most good if it is located where it is conspicuous enough to draw attention, yet private enough to allow an informal, friendly atmosphere for interviews. In any case each unit should have an effective display of reenlistment literature. In the unit area this should be a self-service display stocked with current reenlistment information.

You ought to use originality in the conduct of reenlistment ceremonies. The national flag should always be in the immediate vicinity, but this doesn't mean that reenlistments need to take place in an office. You can use the PIO facilities available to publicize enlistments and give your program a boost.

There is one important clerical area in the field of reenlistment—the reenlistment data card (DA Form 1315). It is designed as an aid to the reenlistment program. The form is initially completed at the Army Reception Station and forwarded with the individual's 201 file. If not, the unit personnel officer prepares one. When a person is transferred or reassigned prior to ETS, the losing unit commander makes an appropriate entry in the enlistment status section of the form. Review of the facts on the card will help prepare the officer for the interview. From it one can learn: age, dependency status, level of civilian education, civilian occupation, GT score, the top scores in the individual's qualifications battery, and whether the soldier is qualified for a reenlistment option. Prior interviews and viewing of a reenlistment film are recorded on the DA Form 1315. Stereotype remarks, e.g., "will not reenlist," "does not like Army," are *not* to be used. Chances are that you or someone else will have to interview the individual again, and some pertinent information from the record about the previous interviews will help jog thinking or serve as a guide to the new interviewer.

The reenlistment officer is required to maintain sufficient statistics to indicate the reenlistment efforts of each company-size unit. Local regulations usually spell out the nature and form of the required statistics.

In talking to a soldier about reenlistment it's not surprising to hear gripes about KP, guard, bed-check, or the billets. You should remember, however, that you are not reenlisting the soldier for a career of these things. What the Army wants are skilled technicians and leaders. You may point to these in your unit as an example that any young soldier should strive to emulate. You must try to make reenlistment the "in" thing to do, and gear your program to the individual.

In terms of broad objectives, the most important goal of any reenlistment effort is to select and retain those qualified soldiers who have shown the potential for greater service to themselves and the Army. You assist in evaluating the capabilities and attitudes of every person in the command. You must remember that the soldiers you reenlist will serve as trained replacements under you or some other commander. So you should never shortchange anyone for the sake of good-looking reenlistment statistics.

REFERENCES
*AR 600-200 *Enlisted Personnel Management System*
AR 601-208 *Recruiting/Reenlistment Publicity Program*
AR 601-210 *Regular Army Enlistment Program*
*AR 601-280 *Army Reenlistment Program*
*AR 635-200 *Enlisted Personnel*

*Incorporated in Enlisted Ranks Personnel Update

SAFETY OFFICER

Briefly, the safety officer's job is to develop a sustained safety education and accident-prevention program. Normally much of this effort is necessarily directed toward creating an interest in safety on the part of all personnel in the command.

Here are some guidelines for the newly appointed safety officer:

—Become familiar with the Army and subordinate command safety regulations (385-series), DA Pam 385-1 (Unit Safety Management), and local SOPs.

—Hold periodic briefings to keep supervisors, platoon leaders, and NCOs alert to safety requirements and programs.

—Promote original campaigns to keep individuals constantly aware of their responsibilities for accident-prevention, both on and off the job.

—Be sure that directives, policies, plans, and procedures on safety are realistic in terms of primary unit mission.

—Review accident statistics or reports to identify trouble areas and apply practical corrective measures.

—Investigate and report each accident accurately and promptly, irrespective of its severity, degree of injury, or damage cost.

—Organize a unit safety council to make recommendations and suggestions to improve the accident-prevention program.

—Conduct safety inspections, recommend action to remove or control hazards, and determine the need for safety training. Inspections help identify unsafe conditions or persons *before* accidents occur. This fact should be used to advantage.

Design safety programs to reduce or eliminate accidents, in essence to reduce hazards and to develop safe behavior among unit personnel. DA Pam 385-1 (Unit Safety Management) is an excellent guide and reference for planning a unit safety program. Here is a simple program checklist based on the requirements of AR 385-10, AR 385-40, and AR 385-55. This can be modified to meet any specific unit situation.

—Do SOPs include provisions for safe practices and procedures?

—Does the commander personally review the accident experience of the command periodically?

—Does the commander include safety as a topic in staff meetings?

—Has the safety officer been appointed on orders?

—Does the command receive and display safety publications, posters, and material?

—Does the safety officer conduct training and prepare safety material for presentation by others?

—Does he or she conduct safety inspections and surveys?

—Are summaries of accident data periodically assembled and reviewed?

—Are reports, records, and other accident information safeguarded as prescribed by current regulations (AR 385-40)?

—Do all unit SOPs contain clear and concise instructions on reporting of accidents?

—Are accident investigations thorough and timely?

—Are all accident reports being reviewed carefully for completeness and accuracy?

—Is remedial training for drivers involved in traffic violations required?

—Is disciplinary action initiated where traffic violations are the primary cause of an accident?

—Are the safe-driving rules for winter driving brought to the attention of the entire command?

—Is private-motor-vehicle accident-prevention emphasized?

—Does the command participate in local safe-driving campaigns?

—Are off-duty pass or leave personnel required to comply with directives regarding safe operation of private motor vehicles?

—Does the command have an adequate safety awards program?

—Is the program effective in stimulating interest in the reduction of accidental injury and/or property damage?

—Are individual safety awards being used and presented properly?

The best accident is one that has just been prevented. The time-proven methods that help keep accidents to a minimum are the "Three E's of Safety": Engineering, Education, and Enforcement. *Engineering* is identifying and locating hazards, eliminating hazards, compensating for those that cannot be removed, and avoiding the creation of hazards in new designs or operations.

Education and training have three aspects: the development of positive safety attitudes; the knowledge necessary for safe performance; and the skill level necessary for safe performance.

Engineering and education can prevent most accidents; however, there are some people who just won't be careful. For them, strict *enforcement* of safety practices, backed by prompt corrective action, is necessary. Punishment should not be for having an accident, but rather for violation of an order or procedure in effect to prevent such an accident.

Keep in mind the objectives of the program: to reduce hazards and develop safe behavior. Engineering and inspections help achieve the former, while education and enforcement contribute to the latter.

Safety inspections will generally be of the "continuing" type, conducted to discover accident-causing conditions or procedures throughout a unit area. As a part of this program, the safety officer should invite periodic inspections of specific areas by specialized teams. The installation safety director can help arrange these. Every unit safety inspection should cover all the activities of the unit in as much detail as possible.

Accident records and reports from previous inspections will indicate areas that may need particular attention. For each such inspection a check list should be used and a record of deficiencies kept. Appendix G, DA Pam 385-1, contains a suggested safety inspection list. Additional safety criteria and information may be obtained from publications (ARs, TMs, FMs, TBs, *PS Magazine*) appropriate to the unit and equipment.

The safety officer should serve as recorder for the safety council (not as its chairman). The recorder prepares a detailed agenda before each council meeting, including enough detail to show the extent of problems to be discussed and the need for doing something about them. The ideas and suggestions that come out of the meeting are also recorded. They can be used as a basis for developing safety promotion campaigns. To add emphasis, council members should be selected by the unit commander. The deciding factors when selecting individuals should be their interest in safety problems and leadership ability. Here are some items that could be considered by the council:

—Accident experience and trends.

—Accident reports, including cause-analysis and corrective action.

—Review of new equipment or procedures to determine any potential hazards and appropriate corrective action or SOP changes.

—Safety programs and recommended solutions.

—Evaluation of safety suggestions.

—Implementation of Army safety policy regulations and programs.

—Planning and implementation of safety contests, demonstrations, and orientation of personnel.

The safety officer, by virtue of his or her interest in safety and the experience gained, will normally be the best qualified person to act as accident investigator. A detailed discussion of accident investigation, reporting, and analysis is contained in DA Pam 385-1. This material should be studied in depth before attempting to investigate an accident.

Remember that one major purpose of accident investigation is to provide information that will be useful in preventing further similar occurrences. It is essential that the investigator go beyond the superficial causes and determine the WHY of the accident, seeking reasons, not alibis.

A good safety officer will take advantage of the safety management extension courses and subcourses presented by the U.S. Army Safety Center. Information on these and other nonresident courses can be obtained by writing:

> Commander
> US Army Safety Center
> ATTN: PESC–TM
> Fort Rucker, AL 36362–5363

In planning unit safety programs, remember that in the end, safety is a result of each individual's interest. Once this is developed sufficiently, accident statistics will begin to improve.

REFERENCES

AR 95-1 *Army Aviation—General Provisions*
AR 340-18 *Functional Files Update*
AR 385-10 *Army Safety Program*
AR 385-15 *Water Safety*
AR 385-30 *Safety Code Color Marking and Signs*
AR 385-40 *Accident Reporting and Records*
AR 385-55 *Prevention of Motor Vehicle Accidents*
AR 385-95 *Army Aviation Accident Prevention*
AR 600-55 *Motor Vehicle Driver—Selection, Testing, and Licensing*
DA Pam 108-1 *Index of Army Motion Pictures and Related Audio-Visual Aids*
DA Pam 385-1 *Unit Safety Management*
DA Pam 385-2 *You're Headed Home Stateside*
DA Pam 385-3 *Protective Clothing and Equipment*
DA Pam 385-4 *Army Safety Program*
DA Pam 385-5 *Fundamentals of Safety in Army Sports and Recreation*
FM 105-5 *Maneuver Control*
TM 5-682 *Facilities Engineering: Electrical Facilities Safety*

SAVINGS OFFICER

The savings officer is primarily a "General Sales and Promotion Manager," whose objective is to plan and conduct a continuous educational program that will encourage regular and systematic savings. He or she is responsible for the Savings Bond Program. The whole idea is to encourage voluntary savings. It is accomplished through the payroll savings plan for the purchase of savings bonds.

Savings bonds have been sold continuously by the Treasury since 1935. The payroll savings plan, initiated in 1941, has proved to be an easy and safe way for the average soldier to accumulate capital. The decision to participate in the program is entirely up to the individual. Savings officers must never use coercion, reprisals, or threats of reprisal to induce personnel to enroll in the program. Instead, the case for bonds should be presented on its own merits, together with information on how to enroll in the payroll savings plan—nothing more. The Army is very explicit that *this is all the savings officer can do.* How to best go about doing this much is the problem.

Each year the Army conducts a savings bond campaign during the month of May. The savings officer should arrange for a person-to-person canvass to explain the advantages of the savings program and to solicit participants. This covers explaining the benefits to both the government and to the individual. If the soldier is already buying bonds, increasing his or her present deduction can be suggested. During the canvass, each soldier should be provided with a SF 1192 form (Authorization for Purchase and Request for Change, United States Series EE Savings Bonds). The completed forms are sent to the finance section serving the unit. The savings officer may follow up periodically, but cannot harass or coerce. A good time to follow up any prospect—even those already taking a bond—is at the time of a pay raise or promotion when a payroll deduction would be most painless.

The Assistant Comptroller of the Army for Finance and Accounting, ACOA (F&A), furnishes material and guidance for the annual savings bond campaign. Locally reproducible material for canvassers is suggested and illustrated in Appendix B of AR 608-15.

In view of the many benefits, the savings officer should try to make the presentation of the program continuous and dynamic. Explain the program, sell its merits and advantages, make enrollment as easy and painless as possible—and *that is all.* Nothing else is required; nothing else is expected; nothing else is wanted; nothing else is allowed!

REFERENCES
AR 37-104-3 *Military Pay and Allowances Procedures, Joint Uniform Military Pay System (JUMPS)*
AR 608-15 *Army Savings Program*
DA Pam 608-2 *Your Personal Affairs*

SUPPLY OFFICER

Duties of the unit supply officer will vary from unit to unit. It may simply require responsibility for the operation of a small unit supply room that does little more than dispense expendable items and provide storage for the unit equipment. On the other hand, it may involve a large supply operation complete with requisitioning and accounting responsibilities.

In most company-size units a supply sergeant (under the supply officer's supervision) runs the supply room. As a new supply officer, your first move should be to meet the supply sergeant and visit the supply room. There you should determine what property the unit is authorized. There should be an up-to-date file of TOEs, MTOEs, FMs, SCs, TMs and so on, that apply to the supply activities of the unit.

Organizational property such as weapons, vehicles, and other items are included in modification tables of organization and equipment (MTOE's). Other items, such as helmets, canteens, and ponchos are authorized by CTA 50-900. Additionally, field and garrison furnishings and equipment authorizations, such as tentage, day-room equipment, and office furniture are authorized by CTA 50-909. (This equipment can be accounted for as organization or installation property. The latter does not normally accompany a unit to the field or on a change of station.)

Personal clothing is authorized by AR 700-84. This clothing is repaired and replaced with the cash maintenance allowance paid monthly to each enlisted soldier. AR 700-84 also outlines certain conditions for gratuitous issue and repair of personal clothing and describes the handling and disposition of clothing upon discharge or absence of the owner.

Recreation Service property, such as athletic, welfare, and recreation supplies, has no basic publication. Its expendability is established by the Army Master Data File (AMDF).

All nonexpendable unit property, except components of sets, kits, or outfits (SKO), is listed on hand receipts in the unit supply files. These files are a logical next step in the new supply officer's introduction to the supply room. (Nonexpendable and durable components of major end items must be recorded on hand receipt annexes. Nonexpendable and durable components of sets, kits, and outfits (SKO) must be recorded on component hand receipts.)

In accordance with ARs 340-2 and 340-18, unit supply files are established for supply control within the organization and are not records of accountability. Every unit has them. They should include as a minimum the following:

Hospital and Absence Without Leave File. Personal clothing of individuals in each of these categories is inventoried and a record of the inventory kept in this file.

Gratuitous Issue File. This file contains documents initiated in connection with gratuitous issue or repair of personal clothing.

Work Order File. This file contains work order requests for the repair of unit property. Responsibility for the items submitted for repair is temporarily transferred to the repairing agency. These work requests and job orders assist in supply control.

Laundry Files. These assist in the control and supervision of individual and organizational clothing sent to the post laundry. Most posts offer three laundry services: (1) Monthly payroll deduction rates, (2) Cash-per-bundle rates, and (3) Piece rates. The monthly payroll deduction rate plan has a maximum bundle limitation and a piece authorization though the fixed rate is charged whether or not the maximum authorization is used. The deduction is made by means of a roster. The per-bundle rates are collected when the laundry is turned in. The cash and signed voucher (DA Form 3136) accompany the bundles. Individual piece rate is handled as determined by the officials responsible for the local laundry service (DA Form 2741).

Two accountability records may at the discretion of the property book officer be maintained in the unit supply files. They are: the Organizational Clothing and Equipment Record (DA Forms 3645 and 3645-1), which record individual draw and turn-in of CTA 50-900 property; and personal clothing records, which are initially prepared upon entry into the service and forwarded to each new unit. Posting is accomplished by the supply sergeant (for example, as when uniform authorizations change).

You are now ready to take a critical look around. Is the supply room secure? Are "No Smoking" signs posted (AR 700-15) and are fire extinguishers present, filled, clean, and in operating order? Are the last inspections of the fire fighting equipment entered on the inspection tags in accordance with local fire regulations? The general appearance and organization of the supply room is a clue to the quality of supply management one can expect to find.

Next check the storage of equipment. Metal tools should be clean, free of rust, and oiled. Cutting edges should be protected. Wooden handles should be free of paint and treated with linseed oil (handles fitted to hammers, axes, and other like tools should be wedged to ensure secure mounting). Blankets and wool items should be clean and adequately mothproofed. Mattresses should be stored off the floor in mattress covers. They should be stored flat, no more than three high, and shouldn't have anything piled on top of them. Excess supplies, salvage, and unserviceable items should be turned in promptly. Don't be afraid to dig around in the bottoms of bins to locate excess salvage items. Every supply room has them and they should be gotten back into the system—someone else may need them.

Canvas items should be dried and cleaned before storage. Canvas should always be stored off the floor on dry, clean dunnage. This allows air to circulate freely around it. Poles and stakes should never be rolled with tents for storage. Tents should be pitched periodically and inspected. They should be clean and dry before storing. They should be tagged when stored with nomenclature, National Stock Number (NSN), date of storage, and date last aired. Canvas repair kits (authorized at company/detachment size unit) can be used to repair small holes and rips and to replace missing grommets.

Equipment that uses flammable fuels is stored in accordance with fire regulations. A mop string partially inserted into the fuel tank will act as a wick and ensure that tanks are dry and safe.

Sometimes material for unit projects is unavailable through normal supply channels. On occasion it can be found in the salvage yard of the supply installation serving the unit. As a rule the items can be issued as long as the items are not used for their originally intended purposes. See AR 755-2 for details.

Supply control in most unit supply rooms is a pretty simple thing. Items that are lost, damaged, or no longer needed are reported or turned in to the commander/property book officer. The loss, damage, or destruction without fault or neglect is reported to the commander/property book officer. For damaged property, he or she prepares a letter explaining the circumstances and forwards it to the next higher commander for concurrence, with a request for relief of accountability. If granted, the items are removed from the hand receipts and property book.

When fault or neglect are involved and pecuniary liability for the loss is admitted, collection is made in cash on a cash collection voucher (DD Form 1131) listing the property and value and including the statement "Used in lieu of a report of survey, AR 735-11," or is made in the form of payroll deductions by issuing a statement of charges (DD Form 362.) Receipted copies of either act as relief from responsibility. When pecuniary liability for the loss, damage, or destruction of property is not admitted, a report of survey (DA Form 4697) must be initiated by the hand receipt holder, accountable officer, or the person most knowledgeable.

Nonexpendable components of a set, kit, or outfit (SKO), such as hand tools, which are worn out through fair wear and tear, are turned in and replacement requested. The chain of accountability is maintained by using a turn-in tag (shoe tag) DA Form 2402. The lower portion of the tag is a receipt for the item and is later exchanged for the new replacement item.

Study in detail the discussion of accountability and supply procedures contained in AR 735-11.

Check the qualifications of supply personnel next. Even if they are experts in garrison supply procedures (which is rare) there is a lot that can be done to ensure adequate support in the field. For example, the supply section usually operates in rear areas, making daily trips between its unit and supply base. Map reading is an often neglected but necessary subject. The same is true of NBC training, vehicle maintenance, and all other basic military skills. The supply section is often overlooked or allowed to miss unit training on these subjects. Guard against this. The training (or lack of it) that the supply section receives could someday be the deciding factor in some critical combat decision. Chances are that most local supply personnel could use some training so you may be able to arrange larger classes and assistance in presenting them.

Responsibilities for supply and property are serious. Laxness in this area can be expensive in a personal way, not to mention its impact on the unit mission. It's wise for a new supply officer immediately to become very familiar with the regulations, orders, instructions, and SOPs that apply to supply and property accountability.

REFERENCES
FM 10-14 *Unit Supply Operations*
FM 10-14-1 *Commander's Handbook on Property Accountability at Unit Level*
FM 10-14-2 *Guide for the Battalion S4*
FM 10-14-3 *Surveying Officer's Guide*
FM 21-15 *Care and Use of Individual Clothing and Equipment*
FM 700-80 *Logistics*
AR 40-5 *Health and Environment (Field Sanitation)*
AR 638-1 *Disposition of Personal Effects of Deceased and Missing Personnel*
AR 700-15 *Preservation Packaging and Packing and Marking of Items of Supply*

UNIT SUPPLY UPDATE
AR 190-11 *Physical Security of Arms, Ammunition and Explosives*
AR 700-84 *Issue and Sale of Personal Clothing*
AR 710-2 *Supply Policy below the Wholesale Level*
DA Pam 710-2-1 *Using Unit Supply System Manual Procedures*
DA Pam 710-2-2 *Supply Support Activity Supply System Manual Procedures*
AR 735-5 *Property Accounting*
AR 735-11 *Accounting for Lost, Damaged, and Destroyed Property*

TRAINING OFFICER

Your duties as a training officer can vary considerably from unit to unit. In one, you might have a fairly free hand in planning and conducting your unit's training. In another, training may be directed almost completely from above. In either case, your responsibilities are considerable.

In all units, depending on what portion of the Army training program (ATP) is being conducted, certain training is mandatory. Whether your unit is undergoing individual or unit training, you should study FM 21-6 to get a good overall picture of training as the Army conducts it. For most combat-ready units, the Army subject schedules that pertain to the particular unit contain a detailed plan and program of training. You should be sure you have an applicable copy and have studied the requirements outlined in it. There are also training notes, sequence charts, and lesson outlines included that will help you. Next you should check the training directive of higher headquarters for a definition of training policies and particular requirements or objectives to be accomplished.

One of the first steps for you to take is to find out who actually plans the day-to-day training. You may be expected to do it, it may be done by the commander or by the training NCO, or it may be directed by higher headquarters. In any case, you will want to know how far ahead it is necessary to plan. This will depend to a great extent upon the availability of training areas, facilities, and training aids. It takes a certain amount of time to procure training aids, but this shouldn't be much of a problem. Training areas, however, are another matter. Unless you are at a most unusual post, they must be requested far ahead at periodic range conferences. These conferences are usually held semiannually or quarterly, with more frequent updating sessions. Planning should therefore be done far enough ahead to register unit requirements at the "3" shop before these main meetings. If all the needed facilities are not available at first, they may become available at the interim meetings. This, however, requires that you remain flexible and alert to short-notice opportunities. Major activities such as armor-unit tank gunnery programs may be scheduled by Division. Other activities such as brigade or battalion field exercises will be scheduled by those headquarters. You must fit your unit training into the schedule to complement the plans of higher headquarters. For example, you should have platoon and company tactical training before a battalion field exercise rather than after it.

Combat service support units have special problems when it comes to field training. The supported units don't just vanish when the servicing unit needs field training. A solution is to send one element of the supporting company to the field at a time to operate during field exercises of the maneuver units that depend on its service. Even this may not work for all organizations. You have to apply your imagination. Regardless of the organization, there is never enough time, facilities, or money to do all the training desirable. You will have to plan ahead and in detail, using knowledge, experience, and ingenuity to get the job done right.

Time is an important element in training. Obviously time must be included in the unit's schedule for training, but it is not so obvious in the planning phase that sufficient time be made available to instructors to study, prepare, and rehearse their classes. No class should be given without a rehearsal, preferably several. Someone should critique each lesson sufficiently in advance to allow time for instructors to rewrite or revise weak or unsatisfactory parts. The time required is well spent.

Stick to the essentials in training. When writing or reviewing a lesson, always ask "What does the soldier NEED to know to accomplish the mission?" Be sure that soldiers get all they need to know and that they learn it. Don't waste training time—the instructors' or the students'—on unnecessary or irrelevant information.

As much training as possible should be "hands-on" practical work. Even simple tasks are learned best when done rather than described. Next best is a demonstration with actual equipment. For example, camouflage training, basic to every unit, is sometimes difficult to accomplish since there are few places that allow the tree cutting necessary to do a really effective job. Here is where a demonstration of one vehicle or position properly camouflaged can do the trick. At the position, a soldier can see what's expected and by moving to an enemy viewpoint, both proper and improper examples can be illustrated. Night-light discipline is another example. One can talk about it for hours, but a simple nighttime demonstration of a few typical sources of light is quite easy and effective. Don't forget to include a demonstration of how to solve the problems brought up in discussion, in this case how to shield necessary light.

For specialized training and training beyond the scope of unit capabilities there are Service schools in almost all theaters. DA Pam 351-4 with its current changes lists these schools. School quotas are requested through battalion or post S-3 (G-3) office.

Training paperwork generally falls in two areas, training schedules and individual training records. Both are important. Local training directives usually spell out the requirements and the form of both.

Training schedules must be timely, i.e., they must be prepared early enough to allow the instructors reaction time to prepare their classes, to schedule classrooms or training facilities, and to obtain necessary training materials.

Individual training records, when properly maintained, are important to the unit program. See that they are kept up-to-date. In addition to revealing how much each soldier is progressing toward fulfilling the training requirements, they also tell which classes need to be rescheduled, or alternatively which individuals need to be sent to another unit's class for make-up work. Here is an area where close cooperation and coordination between training officers can pay dividends. One make-up class could suffice for an entire battalion (or more). If training is staggered among units, some soldiers that need make-up work may often be sent to another unit giving the same instruction as a part of their regular program. To do this, you have to stay on top of your own requirements and the training being conducted by other units around you. You should be prepared to offer the same help to other units that you may want for your own.

The standards of training your unit will largely reflect the attitude, interest, and ingenuity that you bring to your job. You should seek help and ideas from your subordinates as well as your superiors. There is always more than one solution to a problem, and you must always be prepared to pick or recommend the best.

REFERENCES

AR 350-1 *Army Training*
AR 350-4 *Qualification and Familiarization with Weapons and Weapon-Systems*
AR 350-30 *Code of Conduct*
AR 350-225 *Survival, Evasion, and Escape Training*
AR 351-1 *Individual Military Education and Training*
AR 351-20 *Army Correspondence Course Program*
AR 385-26 *Use of Explosives and Pyrotechnics in Public Demonstrations, Exhibitions, and Celebrations*
CTA 20-2 *Equipment for Training Purposes*
DA Pam 108-1 *Index of Army Motion Pictures and Related Audio-Visual Aids*
DA Pam 310-12 *Index and Description of Army Training Devices*
DA Pam 351-4 *U.S. Army Formal Schools Catalog*
FM 21-6 *How to Prepare and Conduct Military Training*
FM 21-75 *Combat Skills of the Soldier*

UNIT FUND, CUSTODIAN/RECORDER

Each unit commander appoints himself or herself (or another person in grade E-6 or above) as unit fund custodian; the custodian shall also be the recorder for the unit fund council (Para 3-23, AR 215-1).

The recorder is responsible for making and distributing the agenda prior to a scheduled meeting. (In small units this is a very informal—even word-of-mouth—process.) During the meeting, the proceedings of the council must be recorded showing:

—Members present and absent.
—Actions taken.
—A copy of the new financial statement of the fund.

The minutes are signed by the president and the recorder. Excerpts from the minutes or a copy of the minutes are made available for the council and members of the unit. Generally this is done by posting a copy on the unit bulletin board.

The custodian is responsible to the council for fund administration and will:

—Receive, safeguard, disburse, and account for funds and property in accordance with AR 215-1 and AR 215-5 and other applicable regulations, policies, and procedures prescribed by the council or local directive.

—Be financially liable for losses of funds and property when dishonesty, fraud, or culpable negligence on his or her part is established.

—Ensure that the accounting system conforms with AR 215-5 and local regulations.

—Prepare periodic financial statements and reports, and attest to their accuracy.

—Serve as the fund purchasing and contracting officer in accordance with DA Pam 215-4.

When "equitable benefits accrue to the military personnel of the unit as a whole," the unit fund is authorized to purchase or contract for:

—Supplies, equipment, or services that contribute to the entertainment, recreation, comfort, or education of the personnel of the unit, and enhancement of the unit mess. (The purchase of alcoholic beverages with an alcoholic content greater than 3.2 percent by weight is prohibited. See chapter 4, AR 215-2.)

—Supplies, materials, or services required for the maintenance of unit fund property and for emergency maintenance of government-owned welfare and recreational property issued to the organization.

—Labor-saving devices and articles that are not available through military supply services. If considering something of this nature, it is a good idea to get a Certificate of Nonavailability from the supply agency or section serving the unit.

—Authorized distinctive insignia or uniform trimmings for use, without reimbursement, by all eligible personnel of the unit.

—Unit histories and related materials for presentation to all members of the unit, and to new members as they join the unit.

—Awards of property, cash, or the equivalent, as individual prizes for proficiency in military pursuits, such as Soldier-of-the-Month, and for recreational and educational contests conducted by the fund in which all members of the unit have equal opportunity to participate. Individual awards are not to exceed $25.

Become completely familiar with the accounting and audit requirements and procedures outlined in AR 215-5 and local regulations. It's important to keep the accounting work of the fund up to date day-by-day. If a fund is behind, or if it has been poorly handled, the new custodian will be wise to contact the adjutant or other members of the command who have had experience with such funds, and get the fund records straightened out as soon as possible.

REFERENCES
AR 215-1 *The Administration of Morale, Welfare and Recreation Activities and Nonappropriated Fund Instrumentalities*
AR 215-2 *Alcoholic Beverages*
AR 215-5 *Nonappropriated Funds Accounting Policy and Reporting Procedures*

UNIT FUND COUNCIL, PRESIDENT/MEMBER

Unit fund councils are composed of at least one commissioned officer or warrant officer and two enlisted members of any pay grade. The number of members should be limited, but must include at least these three individuals. At company level, the commissioned officer is usually the unit commander. At higher headquarters, the commissioned officer is the unit commander or one of his or her staff. The enlisted representatives are members of the unit. The council president and members of the council are designated by the unit commander.

The council must meet at least once each quarter (more frequently when necessary) at the call of its president.

Every council member has a duty to:

—Ascertain and ensure that the fund is being properly administered and safeguarded as provided in AR 215-1, AR 215-5, and local regulations.

—Determine that all income has been received in full, properly recorded in the book of accounts, and accurately reflected in the financial statements.

—Approve the amounts and purposes of all expenditures of the fund. Such approvals may be of a general nature, such as total expenditures authorized for running a contest, fund administration, or recurring type program expenses, or they may be of a specific nature (such as expenditures for a particular purchase of supplies, equipment, or awards).

—Review the fund financial statements and other fund records as required to ensure that all expenditures are made in accordance with approved council actions and within the purpose for which the fund was established.

—Assure the accountability of all fund-owned property and the conduct of physical inventories of such property, and recommend disposition of that which is surplus to requirements.

—Assure that audits are scheduled and conducted as prescribed, and review reports of audits and inspections and take appropriate action thereon.

—After the council has examined monthly accounts, found them correct, and approved the expenditures, both the recorder/custodian and the president sign the Cash, Property and Reconciliation Report (CPRR). See AR 215-5, chapter 9.

REFERENCES

AR 215-1 *The Administration of Morale, Welfare and Recreation Activities and Nonappropriated Fund Instrumentalist*
AR 215-5 *Nonappropriated Funds Accounting Policy and Reporting Procedures*

VOTING OFFICER

The voting officer's job is to provide general voting information and to assist in the procedures of registering and requesting absentee ballots. He or she must also provide election information about respective states to include election date, officials to be elected, and constitutional amendments and other proposals to be voted on.

DA Pam 360-503 is published each federal election year to help voting officers. It contains current election dates and summaries of the voting laws of all states, District of Columbia, and territories. Supplements are issued periodically throughout the year. Other informational aids, such as posters, are made available well in advance of general election dates.

While much of the information given in this pamphlet is applicable to any absentee voter, it is particularly directed to members of the Armed Forces and Merchant Marine and their spouses and dependents, citizens temporarily residing outside the United States, and overseas civilians who may or may not intend to return to the United States.

As specified in the Federal Voting Assistance Act, these persons are:

—Members of the Armed Forces while in active service, and their spouses and dependents.

—Members of the Merchant Marine of the United States, and their spouses and dependents.

—Citizens of the United States temporarily residing outside the territorial limits of the United States and District of Columbia, and their spouses and dependents when residing with or accompanying them. As specified in the Overseas Citizens Voting Rights Act, these persons are:

> Citizens of the United States who are outside the United States and may not now qualify as a resident of a state, but who were last domiciled in such state immediately prior to departure from the United States and are not registered to vote and are not voting in another state.

The Federal Voting Assistance Act sets up both mandatory and recommended procedures for absentee voting by specified categories of people as guidance for the states. But, each state makes its own voting laws. It's important, therefore, that voting officers consult the summaries of the state laws in question, as given in DA Pam 360-503, before attempting to counsel persons on how to apply for registration or absentee ballot.

A special application form is printed and distributed for persons covered under the Acts, called the Post Card Registration and Absentee Ballot Request (Standard Form 76, revised 1981), commonly referred to as the FPCA.

The Department of Defense has directed the services to issue Federal Post Card Applications directly to all eligible personnel for general elections taking place at two-year intervals (see AR 608-20).

The FPCA is used to apply for an absentee ballot and registration if the state or territory so authorizes. Standards of acceptance and procedures vary from state to state. Filling out an FPCA and sending it to the proper officials of a person's home state does not always entitle that person to absentee registration or voting privileges. In some states it does; in others, the FPCA serves as a request for the state's own forms, which must be filled out and returned before final action is taken on the request.

In a few states, one FPCA serves for all elections in that calendar year. But one FPCA may never be used for more than one person. For instance, a spouse who is authorized by a state to use the FPCA must submit a separate form with his or her own signature.

In addition to abiding by the state's individual requirements for using the FPCA, voting officers should advise their personnel to follow these general rules:

—Print by hand or use a typewriter to fill in the form.

—Be sure all requested information is supplied, and be sure that it is written clearly and legibly.

—Show the name of the applicant twice—once printed or typed and once in the applicant's own handwriting. Anyone may fill out the card, but only the person who is to receive the ballot may write his or her name on line 15 (signature of person requesting ballot), unless the state specifies otherwise.

—Street and number, rural route, or place of residence are called for on the FPCA. It is also essential that an applicant include the name of his or her home county. This helps state officials speed action on the application when the form is not sent directly to the home county.

—Military addresses, particularly in abbreviated forms, are often confusing to civilians. The addresses should be clearly printed or typed so that no letter or number will be misread.

—Applicant's legal voting residence must be in a place where he or she actually lived—not just a residence of record. But no more than one such address may be given. If the applicant has had more than one such address in a state, give only the legal residence address.

—If required, members of the Armed Forces should have the FPCA certified by a commissioned officer unless the state specifies that a noncommissioned or warrant officer's attestation will also be accepted. Civilians not attached to the military should have the FPCA certified by a notary public or other person authorized to make attestations.

—Before addressing the FPCA, check the state's mailing instructions. In some cases, the card is to be addressed to the Secretary of State (who then sends it to the proper local official); in other cases it is to be addressed to a local official, such as the county clerk or auditor, or to an election board.

—Mail the FPCA as early as the state permits. No postage is required if mailed within the U.S. postal system or the APO/FPO system.

If the Federal Post Card Applications are not available, use a letter as an application for a state absentee ballot or registration. Provide the same information as the FPCA and mail in the same way you would the FPCA.

The state, city, county (township) in which a person lived before entering the military usually is considered a legal residence for voting purposes unless he or she establishes residence elsewhere.

All states will permit persons in the Armed Forces to acquire a new voting residence within their jurisdictions. When this is accomplished, voting rights in the old state of residence are lost.

Persons desiring to acquire a new voting residence must meet the new state's legal requirements. They must have lived within the state for the required length of time and presently must intend to make the new state their permanent home.

Time spent in military or federal service counts in meeting the total residence requirements. Where there is any question pertaining to voting residence, seek an answer through the legal affairs officer.

Many states permit registration by absentee process, and some will register a qualified voter when they accept a voted absentee ballot. In others, a voter must be registered before applying for a ballot. Procedures vary from state to state and must be understood and followed exactly on a state-by-state basis.

Application for registration should always be made as early as the state permits, especially in cases where registration must be completed before applications may be made for absentee ballot.

In some states, registration is permanent. Where such permanent registration laws are in effect, a person is not required to reregister for each election so long as certain requirements are met. In general, the requirements are that the applicant vote regularly and does not legally change his or her name or move away from the area (such as precinct or district), where registered.

Most states permit minors to apply for registration if they will be of legal voting age by the date of the election.

When a ballot is received from a state, the envelope containing the ballot should not be opened until instructions on the envelope have been read. This is important because some states require that the envelope be opened in the presence of a commissioned officer, notary public, or other authorized person. If there are no instructions on the outside of the envelope, it may be opened as any other mail.

States usually include full instructions inside the ballot envelope with the ballot form as a guide for persons voting by absentee process. Voting officers should help personnel follow these instructions, or advise them whenever no instructions have been sent by the state.

Polls or straw votes are prohibited in relation to elections or voting choices. In addition, no commissioned, warrant, or noncommissioned officer may attempt in any way to influence any person's choice of candidate. The actual marking of the ballot—the voting—must be done secretly. It's required by law.

Where possible, the voting officer should provide a place where ballots may be marked in secret. A fabricated voting booth, however crude, will not only meet the requirement but offers an opportunity to publicize the voting effort.

Voting officers who need more information should not contact state or local officials, but should write:

> The Adjutant General
> ATTN: DAAG-DPS
> Department of the Army
> Alexandria, VA 22331

REFERENCES
AR 608-20 *Voting by Personnel of the Armed Forces of the United States*
DA Pam 360-503 *Voting Assistance Guide* (Published each federal election year)
DA Cir 608-( ) Implements voting program at each general election
Television Tape number 46107 DA

Selected Acronyms

AAFES	Army and Air Force Exchange Service
ACDUTRA	Active Duty for Training
ACS	Army Community Service
ACSIM	Assistant Chief of Staff for Information Management
ADA	Air Defense Artillery
ADL	Area Dental Laboratories
AER	Army Emergency Relief
AERB	Army Education Requirements Board
AFN	Armed Forces Network
AFS	Active Federal Service
AFSC	Armed Forces Staff College
AG	Adjutant General or Army Green
AGC	Adjutant General's Corps
AIDS	Acquired Immune Deficiency Syndrome
ALO	Authorized Level of Organization
AMC	U.S. Army Materiel Command
AMCSS	Army Military Clothing Sales Store
AME	Average Monthly Earnings
AMP	Advanced Management Program
ANG	Air National Guard
AOC	Area of Concentration
AOE	Army of Excellence
AOSL	Authorized Organizational Stockage Lists
APC	Armored Personnel Carrier
APO	Army Post Office
APRT	Army Physical Readiness Test
AR	Army Regulation
ARAP	Army Research Associates Program
ARNG	Army National Guard

ARPERCEN	Army Reserve Personnel Center
AUS	Army of the U.S. (Total Active Army Force)
AWC	Army War College
AWL	Administrative Weight Limitation
AWOL	Absent Without Leave
BAQ	Basic Allowance for Quarters
BAS	Basic Allowance for Subsistence
BDFA	Basic Daily Food Allowance
BDU	Battle Dress Uniform
BOQ	Bachelor Officer Quarters
CAS³	Combined Arms and Services Staff School
CCF	Central Personnel Security Clearance Facility
CFS	Community, Family, and Soldier Support Command, Korea
CGSC	Command and General Staff College
CHAMPUS	Civilian Health and Medical Program of the Uniformed Services
C²I	Command, Control, and Intelligence Network
CIB	Combat Infantryman Badge
CID	Criminal Investigation Division
CIP	Corps of Intelligence Police
COLA	Cost-of-Living Allowance
CONUS	Continental United States
CONUSA	Continental U.S. Army
CPI	Consumer Price Index
CPO	Chief Petty Officer
CPX	Command Post Exercise
CQ	Charge of Quarters
CSA	Chief of Staff, Army
CTA	Common Table of Allowance
CVC	Combat Vehicle Crewman
CWS	Chemical Warfare Service
DA	Department of the Army
DBDU	Desert Battle Dress Uniform
DCS	Defense Communications System
DCSI	Deputy Chief of Staff for Intelligence
DCSLOG	Deputy Chief of Staff for Logistics
DCSOPS	Deputy Chief of Staff for Operations and Plans
DCSPER	Deputy Chief of Staff for Personnel
DDS	Doctor of Dental Surgery
DEERS	Defense Enrollment Eligibility Reporting System
DENTAC	Dental Activities
DIC	Dependency and Indemnity Compensation
DMD	Doctor of Dental Medicine
DOD	Department of Defense
DODDS	Department of Defense Dependent Schools
DOPMA	Defense Officer Personnel Management Act
DPSC	Defense Personnel Support Center
DUI	Distinctive Unit Insignia
DVM	Doctor of Veterinary Medicine
DVQ	Distinguished Visitor Quarters

EOD	Explosive Ordnance Disposal
ETS	Expiration of Term of Service

FAADS	Forward Area Air Defense System
FAO	Finance and Accounting Office
FHA	Federal Housing Authority
FIST	Fire Support Team
FOG-M	Fiber-Optic Guided Missile
FORSCOM	U.S. Army Forces Command
FPCA	Federal Post Card Application (Post Card Registration and Absentee Ballot Request)
FPO	Fleet Post Office
FTX	Field Training Exercise

GCM	General Court Martial
GED	General Educational Development
GSA	Government Services Administration

HHC	Headquarters and Headquarters Company
HHG	Household Goods
HQ	Headquarters
HQDA	Headquarters, Department of the Army
HRO	Housing Referral Office, Germany

IADC	Inter-American Defense College
ICAF	Industrial College of the Armed Forces
ID	Identification
INSCOM	U.S. Army Intelligence and Security Command
IOBC	Infantry Officers Basic Course
IRS	Internal Revenue Service

JAG	Judge Advocate General
JFTR	Joint Federal Travel Regulations
JUSMAG	Joint U.S. Military Advisory Group

KATUSA	Korean Augmentation to the U.S. Army
KCLFF	Kitchen Company Level Field Feeding

LOS-F	Line-of-Sight Forward Element

MAC	Military Airlift Command
MACOM	Major Army Command
MALT	Monetary Allowance in Lieu of Transportation
MCM	Manual for Courts-Martial
MDW	U.S. Army Military District of Washington
MECH	Mechanized
MFO	Multinational Force and Observers
MI	Military Intelligence
MIA	Missing in Action
MID	Military Intelligence Division
MILPERCEN	Military Personnel Center
MOS	Military Occupational Specialty

MP	Military Police
MPC	Military Payment Certificates
MS or MSC	Medical Service Corps
MSA	Morale Support Activity
MSTS	Military Sea Transport Service
MTL	U.S. Army Materials Technology Laboratory
MTMC	Military Traffic Management Command
MTOE	Modified Tables of Organization and Equipment

NASA	National Aeronautics and Space Administration
NATO	North Atlantic Treaty Organization
NAUS	National Association of Uniformed Services
NBC	Nuclear, Biological, and Chemical
NCO	Noncommissioned Officer
NDU	National Defense University
NG	National Guard
NLOS	Non-Line-of-Sight
NSSG	NATO/SHAPE Support Group
NTC	National Training Center
NWC	National War College

OCO	Office, Chief of Ordnance
OCONUS	Outside the Continental United States
OCS	Officer Candidate School
OER	Officer Evaluation Report
OHA	Overseas Housing Allowance
OIC	Officer-in-Charge
OJT	On-the-Job Training
OMPF	Official Military Personnel File
OOD	Officer-of-the-Deck
OPMD	Officer Personnel Management Directorate
OPMS	Officer Personnel Management System
ORB	Officer Record Brief
OSS	Office of Strategic Services
OTRA	Other than Regular Army

PAC	Personnel and Administration Center
PCS	Permanent Change of Station
PIO	Public Information Office
PLL	Prescribed Load List
PM	Preventive Maintenance
POE	Port of Embarkation
POV	Privately Owned Vehicle
POW	Prisoner of War
PRIMUS	Primary Medical Care for the Uniformed Services
PROV	Provisional
PS&A	Pharmacy, Supply, and Administration
PSSD	Personnel Service Support Directorate
PWP	White Phosphorus
PX	Post Exchange

| QM | Quartermaster |
| QMC | Quartermaster Corps |

RA	Regular Army
RASL	Reserve Active Status List
RC	Reserve Component
RCPAC	Army Reserve Personnel and Administration Center
R&D	Research and Development
REINF	Reinforced
RHIP	Rank Has Its Privileges
ROK	Republic of Korea
RON	Remain Over-Night
ROPMA	Reserve Officer Personnel Management Act
ROTC	Reserve Officers Training Corps
RPV	Remotely Piloted Vehicle
R&R	Rest and Recuperation
SBP	Survivor Benefit Plan
SGLI	Servicemen's Group Life Insurance
SHAPE	Supreme Headquarters, Allied Powers Europe
SKO	Set, Kit, or Outfit
SOCOM	Special Operations Command
SOJT	Supervised On-the-Job Training
SOP	Standing Operating Procedure
SSC	Senior Service College
SSI	Shoulder Sleeve Insignia
TAACOM	Theater Army Area Command
TAG	The Adjutant General
TAGCEN	The Adjutant General Center
TAGO	The Adjutant General's Office
TAPA	Total Army Personnel Agency
TC	Transportation Corps
TCS	Total Commissioned Service
TD	Table of Distribution
TDA	Tables of Distribution and Allowance
TDY	Temporary Duty
TIG	Time in Grade
TIOH	The Institute of Heraldry
TLA	Temporary Lodging Allowance
TM	Technical Manual
TOE	Tables of Organization and Equipment
TRADOC	U.S. Army Training and Doctrine Command
TRANSCOM	U.S. Transportation Command
TWOS	Total Warrant Officer System
UCMJ	Uniform Code of Military Justice
USACE	U.S. Army Corps of Engineers
USAF	U.S. Air Force
USAISC	U.S. Army Information Systems Command
USAR	U.S. Army Reserve
USAREC	U.S. Army Recruiting Command
USAREUR	U.S. Army, Europe
USARJ	U.S. Army, Japan
USARPAC	U.S. Army, Pacific
USASA	U.S. Army Security Agency

USMA	U.S. Military Academy
USO	United Service Organization
USSOCOM	U.S. Special Operations Command
VA	Veterans Administration
VEAP	Veterans Educational Assistance Act of 1984
VGLI	Veterans' Group Life Insurance
VHA	Variable Housing Allowance
VIP	Very Important Person
VMD	Veterinary Medical Doctor
VOQ	Visiting Officer Quarters
WO	Warrant Officer
WOEC	Warrant Officer Entry Course
WOS	Warrant Officer Service
WOSC	Warrant Officer Senior Course
WP	White Phosphorus

Index

(*NOTE:* Italicized numbers refer to material in charts, tables, or illustrations)

Some other fine military books from Stackpole
Your Military Publisher for Over 50 Years

The Servicemember's Legal Guide
Everything you and your family need to know about the law.
by LTC Jonathan P. Tomes, USA

Armed Forces Guide to Personal Financial Planning
Strategies for Managing Your Budget, Savings, Insurance, Taxes, and Investments.
by LTC Hobart B. Pillsbury, Jr. and LTC Robert H. Baldwin, Jr.

Guide to Effective Military Writing
A handbook for getting things written quickly, correctly, and easily.
by William A. McIntosh

Transition from Military to Civilian Life
How to plan a bright future now for you and your family.
by James D. Canfield and Merle Dethlefsen

The Guide to Military Installations
A comprehensive guide to the location, facilities, housing, climate, and customs of all Army, Navy, Air Force, and Marine installations in the U.S. and overseas.
by Dan Cragg

Combat Leader's Field Guide: 10th Edition
Information for the combat leader in a handy, pocket-sized volume.

Reflections on the Wall
The Vietnam Veterans Memorial.
Photographs by the Smithsonian Institution's Office of Printing and Photographic Services; Introduction and narration by Edward Clinton Ezell

The NCO Guide: 2nd Edition
Provides the noncommissioned officer of the eighties with guidelines for every official and social situation.
by Sgt. Maj. Dan Cragg, USA (Ret.)

Parent's Guide to the 5 U.S. Service Academies
A firsthand personal account of what you can expect along the way.
by Helen Powers

The Enlisted Soldier's Guide: 1st Edition
Latest information on Army trends and changing regulations—designed with the first-termer in mind.
by Sgt. Maj. Dennis D. Perez, U.S. Army (Ret.)

Roots of Strategy (Book 2)
3 military classics in one volume.
by Ardant du Picq, Carl von Clausewitz, and Antoine Henri Jomini

Home Cooking with Military Families
Easy-to-prepare recipes from U.S. service families around the world.
by Mary Jane Ryan, Executive Editor, FAMILY magazine

Available at your local bookstore, or for complete ordering information, write:
Stackpole Books
Cameron and Kelker Streets
Harrisburg, PA 17105
For fast service credit card users may call 1-800-READ-NOW
In Pennsylvania, call 717-234-5041